Lecture Notes in Artificial Intelligence 11927

Subseries of Lecture Notes in Computer Science

Series Editors

Randy Goebel
University of Alberta, Edmonton, Canada
Yuzuru Tanaka
Hokkaido University, Sapporo, Japan
Wolfgang Wahlster
DFKI and Saarland University, Saarbrücken, Germany

Founding Editor

Jörg Siekmann
DFKI and Saarland University, Saarbrücken, Germany

More information about this series at http://www.springer.com/series/1244

Max Bramer · Miltos Petridis (Eds.)

Artificial Intelligence XXXVI

39th SGAI International Conference
on Artificial Intelligence, AI 2019
Cambridge, UK, December 17–19, 2019
Proceedings

 Springer

Editors
Max Bramer
University of Portsmouth
Portsmouth, UK

Miltos Petridis
Middlesex University
London, UK

ISSN 0302-9743   ISSN 1611-3349 (electronic)
Lecture Notes in Artificial Intelligence
ISBN 978-3-030-34884-7   ISBN 978-3-030-34885-4 (eBook)
https://doi.org/10.1007/978-3-030-34885-4

LNCS Sublibrary: SL7 – Artificial Intelligence

This Springer imprint is published by the registered company Springer Nature Switzerland AG
The registered company address is: Gewerbestrasse 11, 6330 Cham, Switzerland

Preface

This volume, entitled *Artificial Intelligence XXXVI*, comprises the refereed papers presented at AI-2019, the 39th SGAI International Conference on Innovative Techniques and Applications of Artificial Intelligence, held in Cambridge in December 2019 in both the technical and the application streams. The conference was organised by SGAI, the British Computer Society Specialist Group on Artificial Intelligence.

The technical papers included present new and innovative developments in the field, divided into sections on 'Machine Learning, Knowledge Discovery and Data Mining' and 'Agents, Knowledge Acquisition and Ontologies.' This year's Donald Michie Memorial Award for the best refereed technical paper was won by a paper entitled "CascadeML: An Automatic Neural Network Architecture Evolution and Training Algorithm for Multi-label Classification" by A. Pakrashi and B. Mac Namee (Insight Centre for Data Analytics, University College Dublin, Dublin, Ireland).

The application papers included present innovative applications of AI techniques in a number of subject domains. This year, the papers are divided into sections on 'Medical Applications', 'Applications of Evolutionary Algorithms', 'Machine Learning for Time Series Data', 'Applications of Machine Learning', and 'Knowledge Acquisition'. This year's Rob Milne Memorial Award for the best refereed application paper was won by a paper entitled "Evolving prediction models with Genetic Algorithm to Forecast Vehicle Volume in a Service Station" by Himadri Sikhar Khargharia and Siddhartha Shakya (EBTIC, Khalifa University, Abu Dhabi, UAE), Russell Ainslie and Gilbert Owusu (British Telecom, UK).

The volume also includes the text of short papers in both streams presented as posters at the conference.

On behalf of the conference Organizing Committee we would like to thank all those who contributed to the organization of this year's program, in particular the Program Committee members, the executive Program Committees and our administrators Mandy Bauer and Bryony Bramer.

September 2019

Max Bramer
Miltos Petridis

Organization

AI-2019 Conference Committee

Conference Chair

Max Bramer   University of Portsmouth, UK

Technical Program Chair

Max Bramer   University of Portsmouth, UK

Application Program Chair

Miltos Petridis   Middlesex University, UK

Deputy Application Program Chair

Jixin Ma   University of Greenwich, UK

Workshop Organizer

Adrian Hopgood   University of Portsmouth, UK

Treasurer

Rosemary Gilligan   .

AI Open Mic and Panel Session Organizer

Andrew Lea   Amplify Life, UK

Publicity Organizer

Frederic Stahl   DFKI - German Research Center for Artificial
                              Intelligence, Germany and University of Reading,
                              UK

FAIRS 2019

Giovanna Martinez   University of Nottingham, UK

UK CBR Organizer

Miltos Petridis   Middlesex University, UK

Cambridge Walking Tour Organizer

Nadia Abouayoub   .

Conference Administrator

Mandy Bauer   BCS

Paper Administrator

Bryony Bramer   .

Technical Executive Program Committee

Max Bramer (Chair)	University of Portsmouth, UK
Frans Coenen	The University of Liverpool, UK
Adrian Hopgood	University of Portsmouth, UK
John Kingston	University of Brighton, UK
Jixin Ma	University of Greenwich, UK

Application Executive Program Committee

Miltos Petridis (Chair)	Middlesex University, UK
Nadia Abouayoub	.
Richard Ellis	RKE Consulting, UK
Rosemary Gilligan	.
Stelios Kapetanakis	University of Brighton, UK
Andrew Lea	Amplify Life, UK

Technical Program Committee

Per-Arne Andersen	University of Agder, Norway
Farshad Badie	Aalborg University, Denmark
Raed Sabri Hameed Batbooti	Southern Technical University/Basra Engineering Technical College, Iraq
Mirko Boettcher	University of Magdeburg, Germany
Soufiane Boulehouache	University of 20 Août 1955-Skikda, Algeria
Max Bramer	University of Portsmouth, UK
Krysia Broda	Imperial College, University of London, UK
Ken Brown	University College Cork, Ireland
Marcos Bueno	Radboud University Nijmegen, The Netherlands
Nikolay Burlutskiy	ContextVision AB, Sweden
Darren Chitty	Aston University, UK
Frans Coenen	The University of Liverpool, UK
Bertrand Cuissart	Université de Caen, France
Ireneusz Czarnowski	Gdynia Maritime University, Poland
Nicolas Durand	Aix-Marseille University, France
Frank Eichinger	DATEV eG, Nuremberg, Germany
Mohamed Gaber	Robert Gordon University, Aberdeen, UK
Adriana Giret	Universitat Politècnica de València, Spain
Peter Hampton	Ulster University, UK

Adrian Hopgood	University of Portsmouth, UK
Zina Ibrahim	Kings College, London, UK
Joanna Jedrzejowicz	University of Gdansk, Poland
Stelios Kapetanakis	University of Brighton, UK
Navneet Kesher	Facebook, Seattle WA, USA
John Kingston	University of Brighton, UK
Konstantinos Kotis	University of the Aegean, Greece
Ivan Koychev	University of Sofia, Bulgaria
Nicole Lee	University of Hong Kong, Hong Kong, China
Anne Liret	British Telecom, France
Fernando Lopes	LNEG-National Research Institute, Portugal
Jixin Ma	University of Greenwich, UK
Kyle Martin	Robert Gordon University, Aberdeen, UK
Stewart Massie	Robert Gordon University, Aberdeen, UK
Silja Meyer-Nieberg	Universität der Bundeswehr München, Germany
Roberto Micalizio	Università di Torino, Italy
Daniel Neagu	University of Bradford, UK
Joanna Isabelle Olszewska	University of West of Scotland, UK
Daniel O'Leary	University of Southern California, USA
Filipo Perotto	Normandy University, France
Danny Poon	BT, UK
Fernando Saenz-Perez	Universidad Complutense de Madrid, Spain
Miguel A. Salido	Universitat Politècnica de València, Spain
Sadiq Sani	BT, UK
Rainer Schmidt	University Medicine of Rostock, Germany
Frederic Stahl	DFKI - German Research Center for Artificial Intelligence, Germany, and University of Reading, UK
Andy Starkey	BT, UK
Simon Thompson	BT Innovate, UK
Jon Timmis	University of Sunderland, UK
M. R. C. van Dongen	University College Cork, Ireland
Martin Wheatman	Yagadi Ltd., UK

Application Program Committee

Nadia Abouayoub	BCS-SGAI
Tony Allen	Nottingham Trent University, UK
Ines Arana	Robert Gordon University, Aberdeen, UK
Mercedes Arguello Casteleiro	The University of Manchester, UK
Vasileios Argyriou	Kingston University, UK
Juan Carlos Augusto	Middlesex University, UK
Ken Brown	University College Cork, Ireland
Nikolay Burlutskiy	ContextVision AB, Sweden
Xiaochun Cheng	Middlesex University, UK

Contents

Machine Learning for Time Series Data

Applications of Machine Learning

Technical Papers

CascadeML: An Automatic Neural Network Architecture Evolution and Training Algorithm for Multi-label Classification (Best Technical Paper)

Arjun Pakrashi[✉] and Brian Mac Namee

Insight Centre for Data Analytics, University College Dublin, Dublin, Ireland
arjun.pakrashi@ucdconnect.ie, brian.macnamee@ucd.ie

Abstract. In multi-label classification a datapoint can be labelled with more than one class at the same time. A common but trivial approach to multi-label classification is to train individual binary classifiers per label, but the performance can be improved by considering associations between the labels, and algorithms like classifier chains and RAKEL do this effectively. Like most machine learning algorithms, however, these approaches require accurate hyperparameter tuning, a computationally expensive optimisation problem. Tuning is important to train a good multi-label classifier model. There is a scarcity in the literature of effective multi-label classification approaches that do not require extensive hyperparameter tuning. This paper addresses this scarcity by proposing CascadeML, a multi-label classification approach based on cascade neural network that takes label associations into account and requires minimal hyperparameter tuning. The performance of the CasecadeML approach is evaluated using 10 multi-label datasets and compared with other leading multi-label classification algorithms. Results show that CascadeML performs comparatively with the leading approaches but without a need for hyperparameter tuning.

Keywords: Machine learning · Multi-label classification · Cascade neural networks

1 Introduction

In *multi-label classification* problems a datapoint can be assigned to more than one class, or *label*, simultaneously [11]. For example, an image can be classified as containing multiple different objects, or music can be labelled with more than one genre. This contrasts with *multi-class classification* problems in which objects can only belong to a single class. Multi-label classification algorithms either break the multi-label problem down into smaller multi-class classification

This research was supported by Science Foundation Ireland (SFI) under Grant Number SFI/12/RC/2289_P2.

M. Bramer and M. Petridis (Eds.): SGAI-AI 2019, LNAI 11927, pp. 3–17, 2019.
https://doi.org/10.1007/978-3-030-34885-4_1

problems—for example *classifier chains* [22]—and are known as *problem transformation* methods; or modify multi-class algorithms to directly train on multilabel datasets—for example *BackPropagation in Multi-Label Learning* (BPMLL) [36]—and are known as *algorithm adaptation* methods. The most effective multi-label classification approaches, however, require careful tuning of hyperparameters and/or model architectures.

There has been a recent resurgence of research interest in machine learning methods that can automatically select optimal algorithms, features, model architectures, and hyperparameters for specific tasks—often referred to as *automatic machine learning* or *AutoML* [7]. Although there have been some recent efforts, [24,25,32], very little attention has been paid in this research to approaches specifically designed for multi-label classification problems.

Cascade2 [20] is a multi-class neural network training approach that learns model parameters and model architecture at the same time. In Cascade2, which is based on the cascade correlation neural network approach [6], training starts with a simple perceptron network, which is grown incrementally by adding a new cascaded unit with skip-level connections as long as performance on a validation dataset improves. Weights in each new cascaded unit are trained independently of the overall network which greatly reduces the processing burden of this approach. Casecade2, however, is a multi-class classification algorithm.

This paper proposes *CascadeML*, a new algorithm for training multi-label classification models, that is inspired by the Cascade2 algorithm and BPMLL. CasecadeML extends both of these approaches to create an algorithm that trains effective multi-label classification models without a requirement for extensive hyperparameter tuning. In a series of evaluation experiments the CasecadeML approach has been shown to perform very well without the extensive hyperparameter tuning required by state-of-the-art multi-label classification methods. To the best of authors' knowledge this is the first automatic neural network architecture selection and training approach for multi-label classification methods.

The remainder of this paper is structured as follows. Section 2 discusses existing related work including the BPMLL algorithm and the Cascade2 algorithm. The CascadeML method is described in Sect. 3. The design of an experiment to evaluate the performance of the CascadeML algorithm, and benchmark its performance against state-of-the-art methods is described in Sect. 4. Section 5 presents and discusses the results of this experiment. Finally, Sect. 6 discusses future research directions and concludes the paper.

2   Related Work

There are a small number of neural-network specific approaches to multi-label classification. These will be described in the next section. Following this, the Cascade2 algorithm, a multi-class classification approach, is described in detail as this is the inspiration for CascadeML.

2.1   Neural Networks for Multi-label Classification and BPMLL

The first neural-network based multi-label algorithm, *BackPropagation in Multi-Label Learning* (BPMLL), was proposed by Zhang et al. in 2006 [36]. It is a single hidden layer, fully connected feed-forward architecture, which uses the back-propagation of error algorithm to optimise a variation of the ranking loss function [37] that takes pairwise label associations into account. This loss function can be defined as follows:

$$E = \sum_{i=1}^{n} \frac{1}{|\boldsymbol{y}_i||\bar{\boldsymbol{y}}_i|} \sum_{(k,l)\in(\boldsymbol{y}_i \times \bar{\boldsymbol{y}}_i)} exp(-(c_i^{(k)} - c_i^{(l)})) \tag{1}$$

Here $\boldsymbol{y}_i$ indicates the set of labels assigned to $\boldsymbol{x}_i$ and $\bar{\boldsymbol{y}}_i$ indicates the set of labels not assigned. The network uses the *tanh* activation function and a bipolar encoding of the target variables: $y_i^{(l)} = +1$ if the label l is relevant to $\boldsymbol{x}_i$, and -1 if irrelevant. Here $c_i^{(k)}$ and $c_i^{(l)}$ are the outputs of the kth and l^{th} output units representing the corresponding label predictions for the datapoint $\boldsymbol{x}_i$.

The intuition behind this loss function is that for a pair of labels (k, l), where k is relevant to the datapoint $\boldsymbol{x}_i$ and l is not, if the prediction score for k is positive and the prediction score for l is negative then $exp(-(c_i^{(k)} - c_i^{(l)}))$ has the minimum penalty. An incorrect prediction score order results in higher penalty. Therefore, minimising Eq. (1) would result in pairs of labels being predicted correctly. For BPMLL, like any neural network algorithm, the number of hidden units has to be determined, which is a hyperparameter to be tuned.

There have been a small number of other neural network approaches specifically designed for multi-label classification. In [9] modifications to the BPMLL loss function were proposed. This modified version learns the network as in BPMLL, and also learns the values using which the predicted scores are thresholded to get label assignments. *Multi-label-based radial basis function networks* (ML-RBF) [35] is a multi-label extension of the RBF network that optimises the sum-of-squares function. *Multi-class multi-label perceptron* (MMP) [5] trains perceptrons for each label but in a way that the applicable labels are ranked higher than the incorrect labels, thus considering associations between labels. An improvement of MMP, *multi-label pairwise perceptron* (MLPP), was proposed in [15]. This approach trains perceptrons for each pair of labels. Nam, et al. [16] demonstrate the efficiency and effectiveness of cross-entropy for multi-label classification, improving the work of BPMLL by using several recent developments such as ReLU activation units, dropout and the use of the adaptive gradient descent algorithm AdaGrad [8].

Some work involving deep neural networks on computer vision and image recognition uses multi-label datasets as a part of the training pipeline [3,33,38, 39]. Similarly, [31] extends convolutional neural networks to predict multi-label images. In [21] the feature space of multi-label classification was modified using deep belief networks such that the labels become less dependent, after which well-known multi-label algorithms were applied in the modified space.

2.2   The Cascade2 Algorithm

In cascade correlation neural networks [6] training starts with a simple perceptron network, which is grown incrementally by adding new cascaded unit with
skip-level connections at a time, as long as performance on a validation dataset
improves. Since the proposal of the original cascade correlation algorithm [6], various improvements that follow a similar overall process to the original method
have been proposed [1,10,19,30]. Cascade2 [20] is the most well known of these.

For a multi-class classification problem with d inputs and q classes, the architecture of a cascade network trained using Cascade2 will have $d + 1$ inputs
(including a bias term) and q outputs (one for each class). Each of the network's
L hidden layers, l_i, will have only one unit, which receives incoming weights
from all of the $d + 1$ inputs as well as from all the hidden units in the previous
layers. The output of each hidden layer l_i is connected to the q output units of
the network. A layer with such a connection scheme is called a *cascade layer*.

Figure 1h shows an example of a simple cascade neural network with three
inputs, two output classes, and three hidden cascade layers (l_1, l_2, and l_3). All
connections flow from left to right and we can categorise the weights along the
connections in a cascade network into four types:

- **Input to output layer weights** connecting the $d+1$ inputs to the q outputs,
  forming a perceptron network.
- **Input to hidden layer weights** connecting the $d+1$ inputs to the L hidden
  cascade layers.
- **Hidden to hidden layer weights** connecting the output of all the previous
  hidden cascade layers $l_1, l_2, \ldots, l_{i-1}$, to the hidden cascade layer l_i.
- **Hidden to output layer weights** connecting the outputs of the cascade
  layers $l_1, l_2, \ldots, l_L$ to the q output units.

The cascade network is grown dynamically, one layer at a time and the four different types of weights are each trained in slightly different ways (explained in detail
below). Once training is complete, a straight-forward feedforward algorithm that
propagates values through the cascade layers is used to make predictions.

Cascade2 training starts with a simple perceptron network with $d + 1$ inputs
and q outputs. This network is referred to as the *main network*. The main network is grown as training proceeds by iteratively adding hidden cascade layers
to it. This is achieved by iteratively repeating two phases, *Phase I* and *Phase
II*, each of which trains different parts of the cascade network.

In Phase I, the input to output layer weights and hidden to output layer
weights of the main network are trained, while all other weights (input to hidden
layer and hidden to hidden layer) are frozen. The target values used in this
phase to calculate the loss of the network are the target classes from the original
dataset. The mean squared error (MSE) between the output of the main network
and the ground truth is minimised using gradient descent.

Phase II trains and adds a new cascade layer l_i, consisting of a single unit, at
the ith iteration of training. The inputs to the newly added layer are the $d + 1$
input dimensions, and the outputs from the previous hidden layers, $l_1, \ldots, l_{i-1}$,

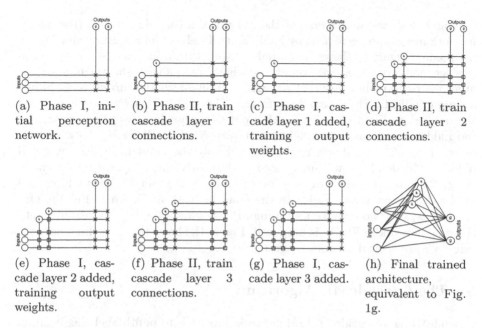

Fig. 1. An example of the Cascade2 algorithm. Nodes in the network are represented using circles. A weight between nodes in two layers exists, where horizontal and vertical lines intersect. Crosses indicate a weight that is trainable at a specific phase in the training process, while squares indicate a weight that is frozen at a specific phase. g is the activation function used at the output layer. (h) shows a more typical network diagram of the final network trained.

in the main network. At this phase only the weights involving the new hidden layer are trained. These are the input to hidden layer weights for l_i; hidden to hidden layer weights on connections of the output of previous hidden cascade layers, $l_1, \ldots, l_{i-1}$, to the current hidden layer, l_i; and the weights connecting the new hidden layer, l_i, to the output layer. All other weights in the main network are frozen. In this phase the target values used in training are not the original target values, but rather the error between the MSE of the main network constructed up to the previous iteration $i - 1$, and the output of the new layer l_i.

Once the weights associated with the new hidden layer have been trained the layer and these weights are added to the main network. The weights connecting the new hidden layer, l_i, to the output layer are negated when these are added to the main network. This is so that the contribution of the output of the newly added layer will minimise the error of the main network [17]—recall that the newly added layer was trained to predict the main network error.

When Phase II is complete, the algorithm returns to Phase I and continues iterating between the two phases until a maximum depth is reached, or a learning error threshold is not exceeded. Training always ends with Phase I.

Figure 1 shows an example of the growth of a cascade network (the neural network diagram scheme used by Fahlman and Lebiere [6] is used) trained using Casecade2. Figure 1a shows the initial network with 3 inputs and 2 outputs. In this schematic the intersections of the straight lines indicate the weights. A cross at an intersection indicates that a weight is trainable at the current phase, while a square indicates that a weight is frozen. The algorithm starts in Phase I and the network in Fig. 1a is trained. All input to output layer weights, are trained (no hidden to output layer weights exist yet). Next, in Phase II, a new cascade layer, l_1, is added as shown in Fig. 1b, and only the input to hidden layer and hidden to hidden layer weights related to the newly added layer, l_1, are trained. Next, the process goes back to Phase I and trains input to output layer and hidden to output layer weights in the main network as shown in Fig. 1c. This process iterates two more times through Phase I and II in Figs. 1d, e and f until the final network in Fig. 1g is produced. Figure 1h shows this same final network using a more typical network diagram.

3   The CascadeML Algorithm

CascadeML is a cascaded neural network approach to multi-label classification inspired by Cascade2 [20]. The main objective of this method is to find good multi-label classifier models that take advantage of label associations, while minimising the model selection and training time by omitting hyperparameter tuning and architecture tuning.

CascadeML uses a similar training process to that described in Sect. 2.2. CascadeML starts with a perception network with $d + 1$ inputs (including the bias unit) and q output units, one for each label. In Phase I, only the hidden to output layer and input to output layer weights are trained, as in Cascade2. Although CascadeML uses the BPMLL loss function in this stage as shown in Eq. (1), which allows CascadeML to consider label associations.

In Phase II CascadeML differs from Cascade2 in the following way. First, instead of adding hidden cascade layers with a single unit at each iteration, hidden cascade layers with multiple units are added. This gives rise to a hyperparameter selection problem as the number of units in each hidden layer needs to be determined. To overcome this, at each iteration of CascadeML, a *candidate pool* of many candidate hidden cascade layers is trained, that could be added to the main network. Each of the candidate hidden cascade layers is initialised with randomly selected initial weight values, a randomly selected activation function, and a randomly selected number of units. Each of the candidate hidden cascade layers is trained independently in parallel (minimising MSE as explained in Sect. 2.2). Once they have all been trained the best candidate hidden cascade layer from the candidate pool is selected (based on calculated loss on a validation dataset) and added to the main network.

To diversify the network architectures explored by CascadeML, the algorithm can include candidate hidden cascade layers that are *sibling* layers to the deepest hidden cascade layer already in the main network [1], as well as *successor* cascade

Table 1. Multi-label datasets

Dataset	Instances	Inputs	Labels	Labelsets	Cardinality	MeanIR
flags	194	26	7	24	3.392	2.255
yeast	2417	103	14	77	4.237	7.197
scene	2407	294	6	3	1.074	1.254
emotions	593	72	6	4	1.869	1.478
medical	978	1449	45	33	1.245	89.501
enron	1702	1001	53	573	3.378	73.953
birds	322	260	20	55	1.503	13.004
genbase	662	1186	27	10	1.252	37.315
cal500	502	68	174	502	26.044	20.578
llog	1460	1004	75	189	1.180	39.267

layers. This allows wide models as well as deep models to be explored. This is done by adding both successor and sibling layers to the candidate pool.

The candidate hidden cascade layers in the candidate pool can each be trained independently in isolation from the main network, because when training the candidate hidden cascade layer, l_i, the inputs to the layer, the targets and the weights of the main network are all fixed. Therefore, the hidden cascade layer, l_i, can be considered a subnetwork, trained in isolation and then added to the main network. When the best candidate hidden cascade layer is selected from the candidate pool, it is added to the main network by copying the input to hidden layer, weights to the main network, negating the hidden to output layer weights and connecting them to the main network as in Cascade2. The main network increases in depth or the deepest layer grows in breadth depending on whether a successor or a sibling candidate layer was selected.

For both Phase I and Phase II, an adaptive first order gradient descent algorithm iRProp- [12], a variant of RProp [12,23], is used. iRProp- is an adaptive algorithm which uses an adaptive learning rate and the sign of the partial derivative of the error function for each weight adjustment. This method mainly helps to accelerate learning in the flat regions of error space and near local minima. L2 regularisation [8] was used in both phases of CascadeML.

4   Experiment Design

To evaluate the effectiveness of CascadeML, an experiment was performed on ten well-known multi-label benchmark datasets. These are described in Table 1, where *Instances*, *Inputs* and *Labels* are the number of datapoints, the dimension of the datapoint and the number of labels respectively; *Labelsets* indicates the number of unique label combinations present; *Cardinality* measures the average number of labels assigned to each datapoint; and *MeanIR* [2] indicates the imbalance ratio of the labels.

The performance of models trained using CascadeML was compared with five other state-of-the-art multi-label classification algorithms: BPMLL, *classifier chains* [22] (CC), *RAkEL* [29], HOMER [27], and MLkNN [34]. These algorithms were selected to cover different types of multi-label classification techniques. BPMLL is a well-known multi-label specific neural network algorithm; Classifier chains, RAkEL and HOMER are ensemble methods that have been shown to achieve state-of-the-art performance [14,18]; and MLkNN is a nearest-neighbour based algorithm adaptation method. The implementations of these existing algorithms are from the MULAN library [28] and implemented in Java. CascadeML was implemented in Python[1].

To compare the performances of the methods, label-based macro-averaged F-Score [37] was used. This is preferred over Hamming loss [37], used in several previous studies (e.g. [4,26,34]), as when used with highly imbalanced multi-label datasets Hamming loss tends to allow the performance on the majority labels to overwhelm performance on the minority labels. Label-based macro-averaged F-Score does not suffer from this problem. For every dataset performance is evaluated using a 2 times 5-fold cross validation experiment. The mean label-based macro-averaged F-Score from these experiments are reported. The results presented are based on the best performing hyperparameter combinations found through tuning.

Although there is no hyperparameter tuning required for CascadeML, it does require some configuration. In the experiments described here, at each iteration, the candidate pool contained two candidates for each combination of layer type—*successor* or *sibling*—and activation unit type—*linear*, *sigmoid*, or *tanh*. This made for 12 candidate hidden cascade layers at each iteration. The number of hidden units in each candidate layer was randomly selected as a fraction of the number of input dimensions, d, following a uniform distribution in $(0, 1]$.

For the output layer of the main network the activation function used was *tanh* as the cost function requires bipolar encoding of the labels. During Phase II of training the outputs of the candidate layers in the pool use a linear activation function, as explained in Sect. 3. L2 regularisation was used in all training phases with regularisation value of 10^{-5}. In Phase I and Phase II training early stopping is used where training stops if the average loss (based on a validation dataset) calculated over a window of the last 20 training epochs increases from one iteration to the next. For both Phase I and Phase II iRProp- is initialised as recommended in [12]. The maximum number of iterations allowed for iRProp- in both phases was 2,000. To set an upper bound on network growth in CascadeML two stopping criteria were used: (1) a new cascade layer (sibling or successor) was added only if did not lead to an increase in the validation loss of the entire network, and (2) only 20 iterations are allowed.

For the other algorithms used in the experiment grid search hyperparameter tuning using 2 time 5-folds cross validation was performed. For classifier chains, RAkEL and HOMER, support vector machines [13] with a radial basis kernel (SVM-RBF) were used as the base classifier. In these cases 12 combinations of

---

[1] A version of CascadeML is available at: https://github.com/phoxis/CascadeML.

Table 2. Results of experiments. Rows indicate the datasets, columns indicate algorithms. Values in cells are mean label-based macro-averaged F-Scores and the standard deviations followed by relative ranks in parenthesis.

	CascadeML	RAkEL	CC	BPMLL	HOMER	MLkNN
flags	0.6723±0.06 (1)	0.6505±0.04 (2)	0.6405±0.06 (4)	0.5948±0.03 (6)	0.6479±0.04 (3)	0.6009±0.07 (5)
yeast	0.4624±0.01 (1)	0.4367±0.02 (4)	0.4510±0.01 (2)	0.4357±0.01 (5)	0.4478±0.02 (3)	0.3772±0.01 (6)
scene	0.7606±0.01 (5)	0.8017±0.01 (2)	0.8040±0.01 (1)	0.7777±0.01 (4)	0.8001±0.02 (3)	0.7424±0.02 (6)
emotions	0.6671±0.02 (2)	0.6281±0.02 (4)	0.6242±0.01 (5)	0.6899±0.02 (1)	0.6212±0.02 (6)	0.6294±0.03 (3)
medical	0.6758±0.02 (3)	0.6966±0.03 (1)	0.6924±0.04 (2)	0.5582±0.08 (5)	0.6108±0.05 (4)	0.5398±0.05 (6)
enron	0.2852±0.02 (3)	0.2882±0.04 (2)	0.2890±0.03 (1)	0.2806±0.02 (5)	0.2812±0.03 (4)	0.1771±0.03 (6)
birds	0.4812±0.03 (1)	0.1812±0.06 (4)	0.1582±0.06 (5)	0.3426±0.06 (2)	0.1551±0.05 (6)	0.2256±0.09 (3)
genbase	0.9403±0.02 (3)	0.9432±0.05 (2)	0.9440±0.04 (1)	0.8149±0.12 (6)	0.9394±0.05 (4)	0.8502±0.05 (5)
cal500	0.2263±0.01 (2)	0.1790±0.01 (5)	0.1849±0.01 (4)	0.2367±0.02 (1)	0.1988±0.02 (3)	0.1007±0.01 (6)
llog	0.2264±0.03 (6)	0.2998±0.05 (1)	0.2916±0.03 (3)	0.2953±0.06 (2)	0.2561±0.03 (5)	0.2630±0.05 (4)
Avg. rank	2.7	2.7	2.8	3.7	4.1	5.0

the regularisation parameter, C, and the kernel spread, σ, were included the hyperparameter grid. For RAkEL the subset size hyperparameter (ranging from 2 to 6) was also included, and for HOMER the cluster size hyperparameter (ranging from 2 to 6) was also included. For BPMLL the only hyperparameter in the grid search was the number of units in the hidden layer. Sizes of 20%, 40%, 60%, 80% and 100% of the number of inputs for each dataset were explored, as recommended by Zhang et al. [36]. In this case the L2 regularisation coefficient was set to 10^{-5} and a maximum of 10000 iterations were allowed, based on [18].

5 Results

The results of the experiments are shown in Table 2, where the columns indicate the algorithms and the rows indicate the datasets. Each cell of the table shows the label-based macro-averaged F-Score (higher values are better) followed by the standard deviation over the cross validation folds. The values in the parenthesis indicate the relative ranking (lower values are better) of the algorithm with respect to the corresponding dataset. The last row of Table 2 indicates the average rank of each algorithm.

Table 2 shows that CascadeML (avg. rank 2.7) performed better than BPMLL (avg. rank 3.7), HOMER (avg. rank 4.1), MLkNN (avg. rank 5.0) and CC (avg. rank 2.8). RAkEL had the same overall average rank as CascadeML. Although RAkEL and CC had similar average ranks to CascadeML, this was only achieved after extensive hyperparameter tuning which CascadeML did not require. Completing the CC and RAkEL benchmarks took multiple weeks (with multiple folds run in parallel) due to the hyperparameter tuning involved, whereas running the equivalent benchmark for CascadeML took less than a week.

Table 3. Summary trained CascadeML network sizes for all datasets.

	Cascade Depth	Scaled Hidden Node Count
flags	8.30 ± 2.87	0.47 ± 0.15
yeast	3.80 ± 0.79	1.16 ± 0.22
scene	5.10 ± 1.85	0.89 ± 0.28
emotions	5.00 ± 2.58	1.04 ± 0.32
medical	6.80 ± 3.16	0.80 ± 0.20
enron	3.60 ± 0.70	1.16 ± 0.21
birds	7.60 ± 1.58	0.64 ± 0.14
genbase	8.40 ± 3.24	1.04 ± 0.49
cal500	6.40 ± 2.84	1.34 ± 0.60
llog	8.10 ± 3.45	0.67 ± 0.20

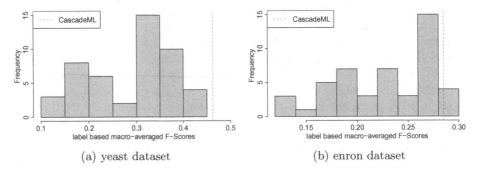

(a) yeast dataset   (b) enron dataset

Fig. 2. Histogram of label-based macro-averaged F-Scores achieved from all hyperparameter combinations of subset size for RAkEL and C, σ for the underlying SVM-RBFs. The vertical dotted lines indicate the performance of CascadeML.

To illustrate the importance of performing hyperparameter tuning, Fig. 2 shows the distribution of the label-based macro-averaged F-Scores for different combinations of hyperparamters explored for the RAkEL algorithm (label subset size, and C and σ values for the underlying SVM-RBFs) for the yeast and enron datasets. The F-Score values in these distributions vary significantly. For the yeast dataset, CascadeML performed the best, and for the enron dataset only 2.1% of the hyperparameter combinations explored led to better performance than CascadeML. In general the distributions skew towards models with relatively poorer performance. CascadeML attained similar high values of performance in both cases (0.4624 for the yeast dataset and 0.2852 for the enron dataset) without any need for hyperparameter tuning.

The incremental training process used in CascadeML is visible in Fig. 4d which shows the training cost for the scene dataset for one fold. The vertical dotted line indicates the addition of a new hidden cascade layer to the main network. After each addition the cost increases but then sharply decreases at first

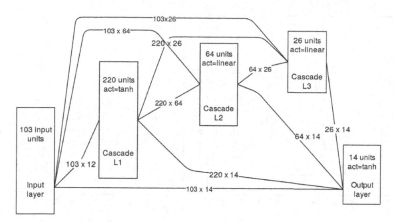

Fig. 3. An example network generated by a run of CascadeML on the yeast dataset. The rectangles represent layers and the lines connecting the layers indicate full connection (the text on each line indicates the number of weights involved in that connection).

then continues decreasing steadily. The nature of the incremental growth and training, in combination with the fast convergence allowed by iRProp- with L2 regularisation, helped the CasecadeML network to generalise as well as converge fast. Figure 3 shows a network learned by the CascadeML on the yeast dataset. For this specific execution, three cascaded layers were selected with L1 having 220 units and a *tanh* activation, L2 having 64 units and a *linear* activation, and L3 having 26 units and a *linear* activation.

The CascadeML algorithm can learn different network architectures for different datsets, and different training runs with the same datasets. Table 3 summarises the sizes of the networks learned using CasecadeML for each dataset across each fold of the final evaluation run, where *Cascade Depth* indicates the depth a cascade network, and *Scaled Hidden Node Count* indicates the total number of hidden nodes in a network divided by the number of inputs. Figures 4a and b show visualisations of these values. Note that although the standard deviations of the performances in Table 2 are small, the cascade depth and scaled hidden node count values have high standard deviations. Figure 4c shows a scatterplot of the depths and the scaled hidden nodes values over all datasets and folds. This indicates that the learned networks were either deep with fewer nodes per layer, or shallow but with more nodes per layer, therefore having a similar network capacity and hence the F-Score performance over the folds were similar, although the architecture learned were very different.

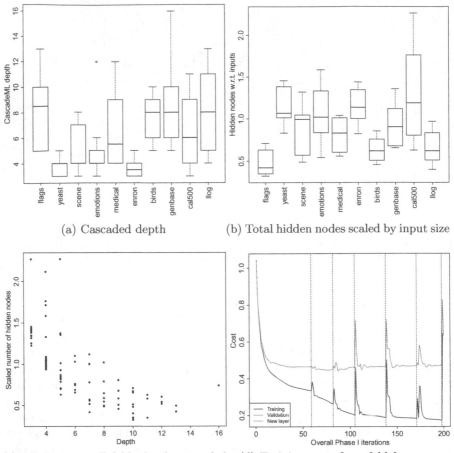

(a) Cascaded depth   (b) Total hidden nodes scaled by input size

(c) All datasets, all folds depth vs. scaled   (d) Training costs for a fold for scene
number of hidden nodes

Fig. 4. CascadeML trained network properties.

6   Conclusions and Future Work

The work introduces a neural network algorithm, CascadeML, for multi-label classification based on the cascade architecture, which grows the architecture as it trains and takes label associations into account. The method omits the requirement of hyperparameter tuning as it automatically determines the architecture, and uses an adaptive first order gradient descent algorithm, iRProp-.

In an evaluation experiment CascadeML was shown to perform competitively to state-of-the-art multi-label classification algorithms, where all the other multi-label algorithms required expensive hyperparameter tuning. CascadeML performed better on an average than classifier chains, HOMER with RBF-SVM,

BPMLL and MLkNN. RAkEL had the same overall average rank compared to CascadeML, but it did not require the extensive hyperparameter tuning.

CascadeML is the first automatic neural network algorithm with a competitive performance to hyperparameter tuned state-of-the-art multi-label classification methods. CascadeML can also be improved. A limitation of the BPMLL loss function used in CascadeML is that, because it uses pairwise comparisons, it does not scale well as the number of labels increases [16]. Therefore, it would be interesting to investigate alternative loss functions that can still take account of label associations without the need for expensive pairwise comparisons. Also, it would be interesting to examine the patterns in which layers grow during CascadeML so as different mechanisms for adding new layers could be introduced.

References

1. Baluja, S., Fahlman, S.: Reducing network depth in the cascade-correlation learning architecture. Technical report CMU-CS-94-209, Carnegie Mellon University, Pittsburgh, PA, October 1994
2. Charte, F., Rivera, A., del Jesus, M.J., Herrera, F.: Concurrence among Imbalanced labels and its influence on multilabel resampling algorithms. In: Polycarpou, M., de Carvalho, A.C.P.L.F., Pan, J.-S., Woźniak, M., Quintian, H., Corchado, E. (eds.) HAIS 2014. LNCS (LNAI), vol. 8480, pp. 110–121. Springer, Cham (2014). https://doi.org/10.1007/978-3-319-07617-1_10
3. Chen, Z., Chi, Z., Fu, H., Feng, D.: Multi-instance multi-label image classification: a neural approach. Neurocomputing **99**, 298–306 (2013)
4. Cheng, W., Hullermeier, E.: Combining instance-based learning and logistic regression for multilabel classification. Mach. Learn. **76**(2–3), 211–225 (2009)
5. Crammer, K., Singer, Y.: A family of additive online algorithms for category ranking. J. Mach. Learn. Res. **3**, 1025–1058 (2003)
6. Fahlman, S.E., Lebiere, C.: The cascade-correlation learning architecture. In: Touretzky, D.S. (ed.) Advances in Neural Information Processing Systems 2, pp. 524–532. Morgan-Kaufmann (1990)
7. Feurer, M., Klein, A., Eggensperger, K., Springenberg, J., Blum, M., Hutter, F.: Efficient and robust automated machine learning. In: Advances in Neural Information Processing Systems 28, pp. 2962–2970 (2015)
8. Goodfellow, I., Bengio, Y., Courville, A.: Deep Learning. MIT Press, Cambridge (2016)
9. Grodzicki, R., Mańdziuk, J., Wang, L.: Improved multilabel classification with neural networks. In: Rudolph, G., Jansen, T., Beume, N., Lucas, S., Poloni, C. (eds.) PPSN 2008. LNCS, vol. 5199, pp. 409–416. Springer, Heidelberg (2008). https://doi.org/10.1007/978-3-540-87700-4_41
10. Hansen, L.K., Pedersen, M.W.: Controlled growth of cascade correlation nets. In: Marinaro, M., Morasso, P.G. (eds.) ICANN 1994, pp. 797–800. Springer, London (1994). https://doi.org/10.1007/978-1-4471-2097-1_189
11. Herrera, F., Charte, F., Rivera, A.J., del Jesús, M.J.: Multilabel Classification - Problem Analysis, Metrics and Techniques. Springer, Cham (2016). https://doi.org/10.1007/978-3-319-41111-8
12. Igel, C., Hüsken, M.: Improving the Rprop learning algorithm. In: Proceedings of the Second International ICSC Symposium on Neural Computation (NC 2000), vol. 2000, pp. 115–121. Citeseer (2000)

13. Kelleher, J.D., Mac Namee, B., D'Arcy, A.: Fundamentals of Machine Learning for Predictive Data Analytics: Algorithms, Worked Examples, and Case Studies. The MIT Press, Cambridge (2015)
14. Madjarov, G., Kocev, D., Gjorgjevikj, D., Džeroski, S.: An extensive experimental comparison of methods for multi-label learning. Pattern Recogn. **45**(9), 3084–3104 (2012)
15. Mencia, E.L., Furnkranz, J.: Pairwise learning of multilabel classifications with perceptrons. In: 2008 IEEE International Joint Conference on Neural Networks (IEEE World Congress on Computational Intelligence), pp. 2899–2906, June 2008
16. Nam, J., Kim, J., Loza Mencía, E., Gurevych, I., Fürnkranz, J.: Large-scale multi-label text classification — revisiting neural networks. In: Calders, T., Esposito, F., Hüllermeier, E., Meo, R. (eds.) ECML PKDD 2014. LNCS (LNAI), vol. 8725, pp. 437–452. Springer, Heidelberg (2014). https://doi.org/10.1007/978-3-662-44851-9_28
17. Nissen, S.: Large scale reinforcement learning using q-sarsa (λ) and cascading neural networks. Unpublished masters thesis, Department of Computer Science, University of Copenhagen, København, Denmark (2007)
18. Pakrashi, A., Greene, D., Mac Namee, B.: Benchmarking multi-label classification algorithms. In: 24th Irish Conference on Artificial Intelligence and Cognitive Science (AICS 2016). CEUR Workshop Proceedings (2016)
19. Phatak, D.S., Koren, I.: Connectivity and performance tradeoffs in the cascade correlation learning architecture. IEEE Trans. Neural Netw. **5**(6), 930–935 (1994)
20. Prechelt, L.: Investigation of the cascor family of learning algorithms. Neural Netw. **10**(5), 885–896 (1997)
21. Read, J., Pérez-Cruz, F.: Deep learning for multi-label classification. CoRR abs/1502.05988 (2015)
22. Read, J., Pfahringer, B., Holmes, G., Frank, E.: Classifier chains for multi-label classification. Mach. Learn. **85**(3), 333–359 (2011)
23. Rojas, R.: Neural Networks: A Systematic Introduction. Springer, Heidelberg (1996). https://doi.org/10.1007/978-3-642-61068-4
24. de Sá, A.G.C., Freitas, A.A., Pappa, G.L.: Automated selection and configuration of multi-label classification algorithms with grammar-based genetic programming. In: Auger, A., Fonseca, C.M., Lourenço, N., Machado, P., Paquete, L., Whitley, D. (eds.) PPSN 2018. LNCS, vol. 11102, pp. 308–320. Springer, Cham (2018). https://doi.org/10.1007/978-3-319-99259-4_25
25. de Sá, A.G.C., Pappa, G.L., Freitas, A.A.: Towards a method for automatically selecting and configuring multi-label classification algorithms. In: GECCO (2017)
26. Spyromitros, E., Tsoumakas, G., Vlahavas, I.: An empirical study of lazy multilabel classification algorithms. In: Darzentas, J., Vouros, G.A., Vosinakis, S., Arnellos, A. (eds.) SETN 2008. LNCS (LNAI), vol. 5138, pp. 401–406. Springer, Heidelberg (2008). https://doi.org/10.1007/978-3-540-87881-0_40
27. Tsoumakas, G., Katakis, I., Vlahavas, I.: Effective and efficient multilabel classification in domains with large number of labels. In: Proceedings of ECML/PKDD 2008 Workshop on Mining Multidimensional Data (MMD 2008), vol. 21, pp. 53–59. sn (2008)
28. Tsoumakas, G., Spyromitros-Xioufis, E., Vilcek, J., Vlahavas, I.: Mulan: a Java library for multi-label learning. J. Mach. Learn. Res. **12**, 2411–2414 (2011)
29. Tsoumakas, G., Vlahavas, I.P.: Random k-labelsets: an ensemble method for multilabel classification. In: ECML (2007)
30. Waugh, S., Adams, A.: Connection strategies in cascade-correlation. In: The Fifth Australian Conference on Neural Networks, pp. 1–4 (1994)

31. Wei, Y., et al.: CNN: single-label to multi-label. CoRR abs/1406.5726 (2014)
32. Wever, M., Mohr, F., Hüllermeier, E.: Automated multi-label classification based on ML-Plan. CoRR abs/1811.04060 (2018)
33. Yu, Q., Wang, J., Zhang, S., Gong, Y., Zhao, J.: Combining local and global hypotheses in deep neural network for multi-label image classification. Neurocomputing **235**, 38–45 (2017)
34. Zhang, M.L., Zhou, Z.H.: ML-kNN: a lazy learning approach to multi-label learning. Pattern Recogn. **40**, 2038–2048 (2007)
35. Zhang, M.L.: ML-RBF: RBF neural networks for multi-label learning. Neural Process. Lett. **29**(2), 61–74 (2009)
36. Zhang, M.L., Zhou, Z.H.: Multilabel neural networks with applications to functional genomics and text categorization. IEEE Trans. Knowl. Data Eng. **18**(10), 1338–1351 (2006)
37. Zhang, M.L., Zhou, Z.H.: A review on multi-label learning algorithms. IEEE Trans. Knowl. Data Eng. **26**(8), 1819–1837 (2014)
38. Zhu, J., Liao, S., Lei, Z., Li, S.Z.: Multi-label convolutional neural network based pedestrian attribute classification. Image Vis. Comput. **58**, 224–229 (2017)
39. Zhuang, N., Yan, Y., Chen, S., Wang, H., Shen, C.: Multi-label learning based deep transfer neural network for facial attribute classification. Pattern Recogn. **80**, 225–240 (2018)

Machine Learning, Knowledge Discovery and Data Mining

Purity Filtering: An Instance Selection Method for Support Vector Machines

David Morán-Pomés[1] and Lluís A. Belanche-Muñoz[2(✉)]

[1] School of Informatics, Technical University of Catalonia, Barcelona, Spain
`david.moran@est.fib.upc.edu`
[2] Computer Science Department, Technical University of Catalonia, Barcelona, Spain
`belanche@cs.upc.edu`

Abstract. Support Vector Machines can achieve levels of accuracy comparable to those achieved by Artificial Neural Networks, but they are also slower to train. In this paper a new algorithm, called Purity Filtering, is presented, designed to filter training data for binary classification SVMs, in order to choose an approximation of the data subset that is more relevant to the training process.

The proposed algorithm is parametrized so to allow a regulation of both spatial and temporal complexity, adapting to the needs and possibilities of each execution environment. A user-specified parameter, the purity, is used to indirectly regulate the number of filtered data, even though the algorithm has also been adapted to let the user directly specify the number of filtered data. Using this algorithm with real datasets, reductions up to 75% of training data (using only 25% of the data samples to train) were achieved with no major loss on the quality of classification.

Keywords: Support Vector Machines · Data reduction · Classification

1 Introduction

Within the Machine Learning world, lots of learning techniques and methodologies [3] [1] have been developed over time, like Decision Trees, Artificial Neural Networks and kernel methods. Within kernel methods, Support Vector Machines (SVM) have experimented a remarkable increase in popularity [5]. SVMs were originally designed to solve binary classification problems, in which they show excellent generalization results [6]. The SVM is one but a member of the kernel methods family [16], which implies that there is a part of the method which can be tuned with a kernel function. This function is also a direct regulator of model complexity, because it directly influences the data representation in feature space.

Typically, an SVM has a cost parameter C which controls the complexity of the model. This cost parameter has values in the range $(0, +\infty)$, and its choice affects directly the quality of the obtained model. Most kernels have own internal parameters, which must be configured too (γ or σ^2 for the RBF kernel) and have a large impact in the final model. Despite the great number of advantages that this technique presents, a main drawback is found in its high computational cost. The trivial resolution of the optimization problem has temporal cost $O(n^3)$ and spatial cost $O(n^2)$, being n the training

© Springer Nature Switzerland AG 2019
M. Bramer and M. Petridis (Eds.): SGAI-AI 2019, LNAI 11927, pp. 21–35, 2019.
https://doi.org/10.1007/978-3-030-34885-4_2

set size [15]. The observed (empirical) training time depends on various factors, such as data complexity (separability, noise level...) and the values of certain parameters of the model (a low value of cost C reduces significantly the SVM training time) [2].

In this paper we develop a new algorithm, called Purity Filtering, designed to filter the training data of a soft-margin SVM in order to choose the subset of the data that is more relevant to the training phase. The proposed algorithm has a set of parameters that allows to regulate spatial and temporal complexity, thereby adapting its execution to the needs and possibilities of each environment. A user-specified parameter, the *purity* of the filtered data, is used to indirectly regulate the number of filtered data, even though the algorithm has also been adapted to let the user directly specify the number of filtered data. By using this algorithm with real datasets, reductions up to 75% of training data (using only 25% of the data samples to train) were achieved with no major loss on the quality of the classification. Results are very promising, and suggest that further study of the behavior of this algorithm when used with other datasets will be very interesting.

2   Relevant Previous Work

For the problem of reducing the training time of an SVM, there are (some more or less) satisfactory solutions, which can be classified into two categories:

- Solutions that modify how **SVM** internally work in order to make it learn faster;
- Solutions that modify **data** so as to make a standard SVM learn faster.

Solutions belonging to the first category usually aim to accelerate training without any loss in the accuracy of the classifier (usually, they try to get exactly the same model as the obtained by the QP solver), whereas those belonging to the second category aim to reduce the input data set, so as to achieve the maximum possible data reduction with the minimum accuracy loss.

Within the first category, the most remarkable techniques are **Chunking** [4] and, more importantly, **Sequential Minimal Optimization** (SMO) [14], which is one of the most prevalent methods to train SVMs. This last method achieves temporal cost $O(n^2)$ and spatial cost $O(n)$, and is practically the only of these techniques that has been standardized and included into the vast majority of programming language libraries. These two techniques perform a more efficient training of the SVM, but its optimized model is exactly the same as the QP solution, since solutions for the SVM optimization problem are unique independently of the solver used.

Within the second group, there are not many alternatives available. First ideas were based in **Reduced Sets** [18] [10], generally obtained by means of lineal combinations of the original data and pre-image computations. The main idea of these methods is to obtain a new training set that represents as good as possible the original dataset, but with fewer instances.

Nowadays, main research is focused towards identifying data which is "relevant" for the SVM training, and only using this data in the SVM training. An interesting technique is **Opposite Maps** [9]. This technique identifies data as relevant if they are the closest to a set of representatives of the opposite class, selected using any kind of clustering algorithm. Another recent idea is **Risk Zone** (RZ) [12] and its extension,

Generalized Risk Zone (GRZ) [13]. The former determines, for two classes, the set of points that have a higher risk of being classified incorrectly. This is performed using distances computed with respect to a representative of the opposite class. GRZ, on the other side, treats all points belonging to the same data class as a probability distribution, not like a single representative. Then, closeness of a point to the other class is computed by means of the Cauchy-Schwartz divergence [7] between probability distributions. Hence, the obtained result is much more flexible and precise than RZ, specially for complex data distributions. Technically, Opposite Maps and both variants of the Risk Zone can be considered instance selection methods, since they aim at choosing a subset of the data in order to accelerate the training time of the SVM.

Another promising technique used in accelerating the training of SVMs is called **instance selection** [11]. This technique, classically applied to k-nn classifiers, allows to reduce the training time of the SVM by reducing the number of data samples in such a way that the behaviour of the obtained model is similar to that of the model trained with all the data samples..

Assume the input data is a set $X = \{x_1, x_2, ..., x_n\}$. Let's also define $Acc_{test}(X)$ as the accuracy of the model trained with dataset X in a test dataset. Therefore, instance selection methods aim to choose a subset $S \subseteq X$ such that $Acc_{test}(S) \approx Acc_{test}(X)$.

The complexity of the models depend on the number of support vectors. Since we usually hold $|S|$ much more lower than $|X|$, complexity of the new model tends to be lower than the original one. This may lead to achieving $Acc_{test}(S) \geq Acc_{test}(X)$ if the original model is overfitting the data, but this is not the usual case. What we will usually find is $Acc_{test}(S) < Acc_{test}(X)$, and we want it to get this gap as low as possible. When dealing with large-scale datasets we also want to obtain a much more smaller subset of the data in order to make the resolution of the process much faster. Therefore, we can formalise the problem as minimising, at the same time, $Acc_{test}(X) - Acc_{test}(S)$ and $|S|$. Usually, it is not possible to achieve both to a higher extent, so we usually try to simply minimise $|S|$ subject to keeping $Acc_{test}(X) - Acc_{test}(S)$ *reasonably low*.

There is an additional constraint to take into consideration while trying to compute this subset of the data. It is important to recall that the main objective of this method is to make the training *faster*. This means that this methods should be very fast, or even having negligible execution time compared with the training of the SVM. In fact, the sum of the algorithm time (to select S) and the SVM training time (using subset S only) should never exceed the training time with the whole dataset X.

The instance selection problem can be analysed specifically for the SVM case. Let's suppose we use a training set X to train a SVM, and we obtain a set of support Vectors $S \subseteq X$. Since only support vectors $x_i \in S$ have $\alpha_i > 0$, any other $x_k \in X$ holding $x_k \notin S$ will have $\alpha_k = 0$. Now, since the SVM optimization problem has been solved with a certain optimal value (say, L_D^*), we can see that:

$$L_D^* = \sum_{i=1}^{n} \alpha_i - \frac{1}{2} \sum_{i=1}^{n} \sum_{j=1}^{n} \alpha_i t_i \langle \varphi(x_i), \varphi(x_j) \rangle t_j \alpha_j$$

But, since $\alpha_k = 0$, it also holds that:

$$L_D^* = \sum_{\substack{i=1 \\ i \neq k}}^{n} \alpha_i - \frac{1}{2} \sum_{\substack{i=1 \\ i \neq k}}^{n} \sum_{\substack{j=1 \\ j \neq k}}^{n} \alpha_i t_i \langle \varphi(x_i), \varphi(x_j) \rangle t_j \alpha_j$$

Therefore, the objective value of the SVM optimization problem is not modified (and therefore, is still optimal) if we remove a data point which is not a support vector. Formally, we can say that a model trained with dataset X is exactly the same as the model trained with dataset $X - \{x_k\}$ if x_k is **not** a support vector. If we apply this reasoning recurrently for each x_k that is not a support vector, we can conclude that a model trained with dataset X is exactly the same as the model trained only with the support vectors of the first one.

Since the solution of a SVM optimization problem is **sparse**, it will hold $S \subseteq X$ and $Acc_{test}(S) = Acc_{test}(X)$. This equality will hold for any S' such that $S \subseteq S' \subseteq X$. Therefore, we can conclude that training as SVM with the support vectors as training data will lead to the same exact model as training it with the whole dataset. Therefore, performing an instance selection method and selecting only the support vector will achieve the same exact testing accuracy as the model trained with all data samples.

3   Purity Filtering

As proven in the previous section, performing an instance selection method and selecting the set $S \subseteq X$ of support vectors guarantees to achieve exactly the same level of performance as a training with the whole dataset X. For simplicity, let us define $X^+ = \{x_i \in X | t_i = +1\}$ and $X^- = \{x_i \in X | t_i = -1\}$. That is, $X^+ \cup X^- = X$ and $X^+ \cap X^- = \emptyset$. The basic idea of the **Purity Filtering** method proposed here is precisely to filter all data points that are not support vectors. The method consists on the following steps:

A. Choose a subset of data $R \subseteq X$.
B. Estimate the separating hyperplane direction using R.
C. Estimate the upper and lower values of the margin.
D. Decide the set S of support vectors using the estimated margins.

3.1   Data Reduction

The **data reduction** phase of the algorithm consist on choosing a subset of data $R \subseteq X$ in order to perform an efficient estimation of the hyperplane direction. The size of the subset $m = |R|$ can be fixed by the user to adjust the tradeoff between the algorithmic complexity and the quality of the solution. In order to choose this subset R, two main ways have been considered: Individual choice and Clustering choice.

The former consists basically in deciding individually if each data point should be added to the subset R or not. For instance, choosing m individuals at random or picking each individual with fixed probability $p(pick)$ or non-fixed probability $p(pick|x_i)$ are examples of individual choice. The latter consists on performing a clustering over the dataset, and analyse the different clusters. Then, a representative of each cluster is chosen as a member of R. This representative can be chosen in many different ways, but usually the medoid of the cluster is chosen. The closest point to the centroid of the cluster can also be chosen too, and it is faster to compute than the medoid for big clusters (in the case of low number of clusters). Notice that this last option is independent of the clustering algorithm chosen. For instance, clustering algorithms like k-means, k-medoids, spectral clustering, kernel k-means, kernel k-medoids... can be chosen to perform this reduction. It is also usually useful to perform data reduction for both classes separately. This way, the obtained representatives tend to follow the same distribution as its original class. Also, there is more control on the number of samples on each class, potentially helping in the case of unbalanced datasets.

3.2 Hyperplane Estimation

Once we have decided the subset $R \subseteq X$, we need to estimate the separating hyperplane, defined by vector w and bias w_0. Since we are only after the **orientation** of this hyperplane, the bias term does not need to be estimated. Also, since we work in feature space, we will instead estimate α vector such that $w = \sum_{i=1}^{n} \alpha_i \varphi(x_i)$. In order to estimate the α vector, two main ways have been considered: SVM optimization and Kernel FDA [8].

The main benefit of using SVM optimization on R to estimate the separating hyperplane is that we are computing this hyperplane using the same method we are trying to estimate. This has the theoretical advantage that, if R is similar to the support vector set, the optimisation result will be very similar to the original hyperplane. Notice that the solution of the SVM over R is again **sparse**. This means than vector α will finally have size even lower than $|R|$, which will lead to faster execution time in the following steps.

The main drawback of using SVM optimization is that hyperparemeter C should be tuned properly. This drawback can be avoided by trying several values of the C parameter, and validating its accuracy with validation set $X - R$. Since only $R \subseteq X$ is used in this training, the rest of the data can be used to validate this approximation.

If we use the KFDA approach, there is no need on hyperparameter tuning. This leads to a somewhat faster training, but without the sparsity on the solution. Its principal drawback might be the fact that we are estimating SVM solution with KFDA algorithm, although there are some studies [17] that state that KFDA and SVM are closely related.

3.3 Margin Estimation

In order to perform margin estimation, we need to specify a parametrization that allows the user to have a direct control over the number of selected data samples. Since the selection is directly based on the margin estimation, these margins are the ones that should be parametrized. Let us first consider a certain hyperplane of the form: $\pi : \langle w, \varphi(x) \rangle + w_0 = 0$. We now define the **positive purity** of that hyperplane as the rate of positive points that are over it. Formally:

$$P_{\pi}^{+} = \frac{|\{x_i \in X^+ | \langle w, \varphi(x) \rangle + w_0 \geq 0\}|}{|\{x_i \in X | \langle w, \varphi(x) \rangle + w_0 \geq 0\}|}$$

We can analogously define the **negative purity** of that hyperplane:

$$P_\pi^- = \frac{|\{x_i \in X^- | \langle w, \varphi(x) \rangle + w_0 \leq 0\}|}{|\{x_i \in X | \langle w, \varphi(x) \rangle + w_0 \leq 0\}|}$$

Note there are an infinite number of parallel hyperplanes with exactly the same purity. For instance, all parallel hyperplanes between two consecutive points in its orthogonal direction will always have the same purity. The only case in which a hyperplane changes its purity is when it contains a data sample. The hyperplane with direction w that contains x_i fulfills: $\langle w, \varphi(x_i) \rangle + w_0 = 0$. In this case, we can compute the bias term as: $w_0 = -\langle w, \varphi(x_i) \rangle$. Now, we can define the **separating hyperplane** associated to x_i:

$$\pi_i : \langle w, \varphi(x) \rangle - \langle w, \varphi(x_i) \rangle = 0$$

We can define the **purity** of a point x_i as the purity of its associated hyperplane:

$$P_i^+ = \frac{|\{x_j \in X^+ | \langle w, \varphi(x_i) \rangle \geq \langle w, \varphi(x_j) \rangle\}|}{|\{x_j \in X | \langle w, \varphi(x_i) \rangle \geq \langle w, \varphi(x_j) \rangle\}|}$$

$$P_i^- = \frac{|\{x_j \in X^- | \langle w, \varphi(x_i) \rangle \leq \langle w, \varphi(x_j) \rangle\}|}{|\{x_j \in X | \langle w, \varphi(x_j) \rangle \leq \langle w, \varphi(x_j) \rangle\}|}$$

If the data is lineally separable, each hyperplane π that separates the data has $P_\pi^+ = P_\pi^- = 1$. In that case, optimum margins will be those parallel to π that are as separated as possible, keeping $P_\pi^+ = 1$ and $P_\pi^- = 1$. In the more general case, we can allow the margins to have purity lower than 1. Formally, the margins will be chosen so as to optimize the following problems:

$$i_{max} = \operatorname*{argmin}_i \{\langle w, \varphi(x_i) \rangle\} \qquad \text{Subject to: } P_i^+ \geq p$$

$$i_{min} = \operatorname*{argmax}_i \{\langle w, \varphi(x_i) \rangle\} \qquad \text{Subject to: } P_i^- \geq p$$

Where $0 \leq p \leq 1$ is a user-specified parameter called **purity**. The purity parameter allows to control the width of the margin, since higher purity values tend to result in wider margins, and hence more data selected. This way, the positive margin will be chosen to be as low as possible, while keeping its positive purity high enough. The negative margin is therefore chosen to be as high as possible, while keeping its negative purity high enough. The obtained hyperplanes are called **margin hyperplanes**.

In order to solve this problem, one has to take into account that the whole process can be efficiently kernelized. First, we define $z_i = \langle w, \varphi(x_i) \rangle = \sum_{j=1}^n \alpha_j k(x_j, x_i)$ as the projection of data $\varphi(x_i)$ in the direction of w. Then, we define the set Z as the one containing all z_i, $Z^+ = \{z_i \in Z | t_i = +1\}$ and $Z^- = \{z_i \in Z | t_i = -1\}$. Purities are computed:

$$P_i^+ = \frac{|\{z \in Z^+ | z \geq z_i\}|}{|\{z \in Z | z \geq z_i\}|} \qquad \text{and} \qquad P_i^- = \frac{|\{z \in Z^- | z \leq z_i\}|}{|\{z \in Z | z \leq z_i\}|}$$

The optimization problems turn into:

$$i_{max} = \operatorname*{argmin}_{i}\{z_i\} \qquad \text{Subject to: } P_i^+ \geq p$$

$$i_{min} = \operatorname*{argmax}_{i}\{z_i\} \qquad \text{Subject to: } P_i^- \geq p$$

Both optimization problems can be solved in linear time if the elements of Z are sorted, computing the purity of each data point incrementally. Since we are usually sorting finite-precision real numbers, a linear algorithm like *radix sort* can be used.

3.4 Data Selection

Once we have computed the margin hyperplanes, we need to select which data instances are more likely to be support vectors. If the margin hyperplanes were exactly the same as the SVM margins we are trying to emulate, we would only need to take all positive points **under** the positive margin and all negative points **above** the negative margin.

Since we have no guarantee to have perfectly estimated the SVM margins, it is somehow unsure to just take all these points carelessly. In order to make a more robust choice, only points **between both margins** are taken. This way, control over the number of samples is easier, and noisy points are omitted from the final result.

Input: Data set $X = \{x_1, ..., x_n\}$ and labels $t = \{t_1, ..., t_n\}$
Parameters : Purity $0 \leq p \leq 1$
Output: A subset $S \subseteq X$ of the data
Let $R \subseteq X$ be the **data reduction**;
Let α be the **hyperplane estimation** using R;
Let $z_i := \sum_{j=1}^{n} \alpha_j k(x_j, x_i)$ the **projection** of all data samples against α ;
Let $\tilde{t}$ be the set of labels t sorted in ascending order according to z_i;
Let $n_-^{\downarrow} := |X^-|, n_+^{\uparrow} := |X^+|, n_-^{\uparrow} := 0, n_+^{\downarrow} := 0$;
for $i = 1...n$ **do**

    if $\tilde{t}_i = -1$ **then**

        $n_-^{\downarrow} := n_-^{\downarrow} + 1$;

        $P_i^- := \frac{n_-^{\downarrow}}{n_-^{\downarrow} + n_+^{\uparrow}}$; $P_i^+ := \frac{n_+^{\uparrow}}{n_-^{\downarrow} + n_+^{\uparrow}}$;

        $n_-^{\uparrow} := n_-^{\uparrow} - 1$;

    else

        $n_+^{\downarrow} := n_+^{\downarrow} + 1$;

        $P_i^- := \frac{n_-^{\downarrow}}{n_-^{\downarrow} + n_+^{\downarrow}}$; $P_i^+ := \frac{n_+^{\uparrow}}{n_-^{\downarrow} + n_+^{\downarrow}}$;

        $n_+^{\uparrow} := n_+^{\uparrow} - 1$;

$i_{max} := \operatorname{argmin}_i \{P_i^- \geq p\}$; $i_{min} := \operatorname{argmax}_i \{P_i^+ \geq p\}$;
$S := \{x_i \in X | z_{i_{min}} \leq z_i \leq z_{i_{max}}\}$;
return S;

Algorithm 1. Purity Filtering algorithm

The number of selected data samples depends on the width of the margin, and therefore can be adjusted by controlling purity parameter p. Let S_p be the set of selected data samples by applying the previous procedure. If the user wants to fix the number of data points (say, k), one has to solve $f(p) = |S_p| = k$. Since all purities P_i^+ and P_i^- have been computed, deciding S_p can be done in linear time. Therefore, some simple root-finding algorithm like the bisection method can be applied to find the value of p that returns the desired number of data samples.

3.5   Theoretical Analysis

The purity parameter regulates the width of the margin. Since the relationship of this parameter with the margin depends on the distribution of the data, sometimes the output is very sensible to the value of p, but in any case the number of selected data samples will be (in general) inversely proportional to the specified purity.

The purity value can also be considered as an indicator of the "risk" of not selecting support vectors. If the method returns very few data samples using a high purity value, is is very unlikely that the non-selected data samples were support vectors. On the other side, if we set a low purity value to select that few data samples, we will probably be skipping some support vectors.

It is also interesting to talk about the margin hyperplanes and the separating hyperplane. In this method, the separating hyperplane is never used, even though it could be estimated by taking the average of the two margin hyperplanes or directly taking the hyperplane estimation on the second step of the algorithm. Not directly using this separating hyperplane leads to more flexibility on the choice of the data samples, and makes the method more robust to some noise in the estimation of the separating hyperplane.

In any case, the bias term of the separating hyperplane is not required, since only its direction is important and the margin hyperplanes are computed based on purity p and not on that bias term.

Now, let's talk about the influence of the purity parameter p on the margin hyperplanes found. Let's assume we found a separating hyperplane which direction is $w = \sum_{i=1}^{n} \alpha_i \varphi(x_i)$. Then, projections against this direction can be computed as $z_i = \sum_{j=1}^{n} \alpha_j k(x_j, x_i)$. We can also define the sets $Z^+ = \{z_i \in Z | t_i = +1\}$ and $Z^- = \{z_i \in Z | t_i = -1\}$. Therefore, purity values can be computed as follows:

$$P_i^+ = \frac{|\{z \in Z^+ | z \geq z_i\}|}{|\{z \in Z^+ | z \geq z_i\}| + |\{z \in Z^- | z \geq z_i\}|}$$

$$P_i^- = \frac{|\{z \in Z^- | z \leq z_i\}|}{|\{z \in Z^+ | z \leq z_i\}| + |\{z \in Z^- | z \leq z_i\}|}$$

Since projected points z_i follow some probability distribution, we can compute the expected values of the purity:

$$E[P_i^+] = \frac{p(z \in Z^+, z \geq z_i)}{p(z \in Z^+, z \geq z_i) + p(z \in Z^-, z \geq z_i)}$$

$$E[P_i^-] = \frac{p(z \in Z^-, z \leq z_i)}{p(z \in Z^+, z \leq z_i) + p(z \in Z^-, z \leq z_i)}$$

Since we are deciding i_{max} and i_{min} in terms of the purity parameter p, we can expect that $E[P^+_{i_{max}}] = E[P^+_{i_{min}}] = p$. If we apply these expressions to the previous equations, and turning joint probabilities into conditional probabilities, we obtain:

$$\frac{p(z \in Z^+ | z \geq z_{i_{max}})}{p(z \in Z^- | z \geq z_{i_{max}})} = \frac{p}{1-p} \quad \text{and} \quad \frac{p(z \in Z^- | z \leq z_{i_{min}})}{p(z \in Z^+ | z \leq z_{i_{min}})} = \frac{p}{1-p}.$$

Therefore, value $\frac{p}{1-p}$ can be interpreted in two ways:

- With respect to the data samples **above** the upper margin, it corresponds to the odds that a data point is positive against it being negative.
- With respect to the data samples **below** the lower margin, it corresponds to the odds that a data point is negative against it being positive.

Hence, increasing the value of p has the effect of increasing the ratio of positive data above the upper margin and the ratio of negative data under the lower margin. The following reasoning will be proved for the negative margin, but can easily be repllicated for the positive one. The previous conditional probability can be rewritten as:

$$\frac{p(z \leq z_{i_{min}} | z \in Z^-) \cdot p(z \in Z^-)}{p(z \leq z_{i_{min}} | z \in Z^+) \cdot p(z \in Z^+)} = \frac{p}{1-p}$$

We can consider $p(z \in Z^+) = \frac{|X^+|}{n}$ and $p(z \in Z^-) = \frac{|X^+|}{n}$. Now, let's assume normality of the projections for a given class and similar variances. Then variables can be standardized such that we have $Z^+ \sim N(\mu_+, 1)$ and $Z^+ \sim N(\mu_-, 1)$ with $\mu_+ + \mu_- = 0$ and $\mu_- < 0 < \mu_+$. If we also assume $z_{i_{min}} < \mu_- < \mu_+$, we have:

$$p(z \leq z_{i_{min}} | z \in Z^+) \approx A \cdot \exp(-B(z_{i_{min}} - \mu_+)^2)$$

$$p(z \leq z_{i_{min}} | z \in Z^-) \approx A \cdot \exp(-B(z_{i_{min}} - \mu_-)^2)$$

For certain positive values of A, B [20]. If we apply it to the previous expression, we can obtain:

$$z_{i_{min}} = -\frac{\ln \frac{p}{1-p} - \ln \frac{|Z^-|}{|Z^+|}}{4B\mu_+}$$

Here, several concepts can be identified. In fact, $\ln \frac{p}{1-p}$ are the logs of the odds of a data point being negative against it being positive. Also, $\ln \frac{|Z^-|}{|Z^+|}$ are the logs of the odds of a data sample being negative against it being positive. Since $B > 0$ and $\mu_+ > 0$, we can conclude that the lower margin gets more negative when the purity parameter gets higher, taking into consideration the ratio of the two classes. Indeed, for both distributions, we have:

$$z_{i_{min}} \propto \ln \frac{1-p}{p} \quad \text{and} \quad z_{i_{max}} \propto \ln \frac{p}{1-p}$$

Since $z_{i_{max}} - z_{i_{min}} \propto \ln \frac{p}{1-p}$ is monotonously increasing in the range $0 < p < 1$, we can state that the margin width increases when the purity value gets higher. Since we select $S = \{x_i \in X | z_{i_{min}} \leq z_i \leq z_{i_{max}}\}$, increasing $z_{i_{max}} - z_{i_{min}}$ can only increase the number of selected data samples. Hence, the number of selected data samples also increases with p. Finally, as for the purity parameter p, the following can be concluded:

– The value of p has a direct effect in terms of conditional probabilities of the non-selected data samples: It forces the margin to decrease to guarantee that the proportions of data outside the margin are respected.
– The width of the margin increases with the value of p, since $z_{i_{max}} - z_{i_{min}} \propto \ln \frac{p}{1-p}$ (which is a monotonously increasing function in p in the range $0 < p < 1$).
– The value number of selected data samples also increases with the value of p: When this value gets higher, so becomes the width of the obtained margin, and it is more likely that new data samples fall within the margins.

The choice of the purity as a parameter for the method is justified by all these reasons, since it has direct interpretation either in terms of probabilities, geometrical margins and number of selected data samples.

As for the temporal and spatial cost of this algorithm, some things have to be taken into account. First, there are some parts of the algorithm that can be done in different ways, such as **data reduction** and **hyperplane estimation**. Let's define this costs as T_{red} and T_{est}, respectively. Then, it can be clearly seen that the temporal cost of the purity filtering algorithm is $O(n \cdot m + T_{red} + T_{test})$. For instance, if k-*means* and *SVM* are used as **data reduction** and **hyperplane estimation** techniques, the final cost becomes $O(n \cdot m + m^2)$.

It is easy to see that the problem is **linear in the number of data samples** and **quadratic in the number of reduced data samples**. If the number of reduced data samples is low enough compared to the number of data samples, the method can even become linear. The spatial cost of the algorithm is $O(n)$, without taking into account the **data reduction** and **hyperplane estimation** techniques, which may require additional space. In the worst-case scenario, the whole kernel matrix of the reduced data will be needed, and therefore $O(m^2)$ space will be required.

4   Experimentation and Discussion

We evaluate the performance of the proposed method on two problems: A synthetic 2D problem in which it is easy to see how different selection methods work, and a binarized version of the *covertype* dataset [19]. Our aim is to analyze the capability of the proposed method in a situation where it *should* work well, and also in real-life large-scale dataset. It is important to achieve both low training time and good generalization performance.[1] In both problems, the following methods are tested and compared: the proposed method (Purity Filtering), Random selection, Cluster selection, Opposite Maps and the Generalized Risk Zone. All results are measured against the model obtained by direct training of a SVM on the whole dataset.

4.1   Synthetic Data

A synthetic dataset has been designed so as to make instance selection methods needed to best illustrate their functioning. This dataset is composed of 200,000 2D data points, divided into two classes, called 'A' and 'B'. Each of this classes has a squared mass of

---

[1] All the experiments were done in an Intel Core i7 2.8 GHz machine with 16 GB memory.

points containing 99% of the data samples of that class. The separation of both classes has the shape of a tanh and contains only 1% of the data samples. The dataset is almost perfectly separable, but there are almost no points in the region of separation (Fig. 1).

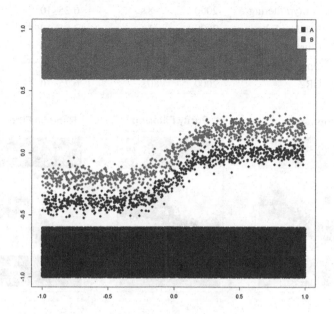

Fig. 1. Synthetic data used in the experiments.

As for the parameters of the methods, all of them (if possible) were configured to return exactly 2000 data samples, which is exactly 1% of the total number of data points. Therefore, purity was not required to be set explicitly. As for the size of the data selection, k-means selection was used with only 100 data samples per class, which is 0.1% of the total amount of data available. The kernel was set to be a gaussian kernel with $\gamma = 2^{-4}$ and the cost parameter for the SVM classifier was set to be $C = 2^8$. When the SVM is trained with these parameters using the whole dataset, the number of obtained support vectors was **453**.

The results of the different methods can be seen in Table 1. It can be seen that the trivial methods (Random Filtering and Cluster Filtering) perform much worse than the more advanced instance selection methods (Purity Filtering, Opposite Maps and GRZ), which achieve the same level of performance than the full-size SVM. It is important to notice than Opposite Maps does not allow to control the size of the selected size, so it may not be as useful as Purity Filtering on some other datasets. Moreover, the GRZ is not a valid candidate as a instance selection method for accelerating the training of an SVM, since its training time is much larger than the full-size SVM training.

Table 1. Results on synthetic data.

Method	Selected size	Training time	Error rate
Full-Size	200000	25 s	$6.25 \cdot 10^{-4}$
Purity Filtering	2000	8 s	$6.25 \cdot 10^{-4}$
Random Filtering	2000	1 s	$13.85 \cdot 10^{-4}$
Cluster Filtering	2000	8 s	$12.70 \cdot 10^{-4}$
Opposite Maps	1982	2 s	$6.25 \cdot 10^{-4}$
GRZ	2000	80 s	$6.25 \cdot 10^{-4}$

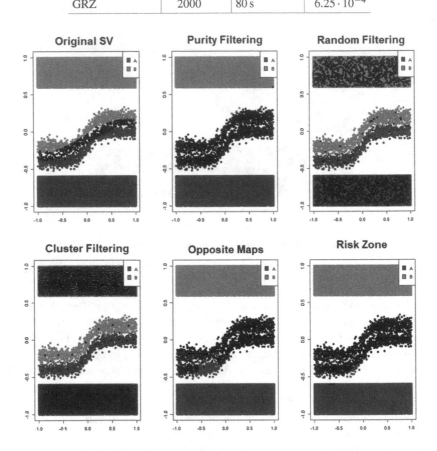

Fig. 2. Selected instances for each instance selection method.

It is also interesting to visualize the set of selected points of each method, and compare it with the support vectors the full-size SVM extracts. This can be seen in Fig. 2, which contains all the selected data samples of the previous executions. Here, it can be seen that random filtering and cluster filtering fail at picking data from the separation region, and that the rest of the methods succeed at it.

4.2 Covertype Dataset

The covertype dataset [19], available at the UCI Machine Learning Repository, is used to test the different methods in the same they were tested in the previous section. The dataset originally contains 581012 instances divided in 6 classes. In order to perform binary classification, only classes 1 and 2 are kept, resulting in a 495141 instance dataset. This dataset is randomly split into a train and a test dataset, with the first one holding 400000 instances and the second one holding 95141 instances. As for the parameters of the methods, all of them (if possible) were configured to return exactly 100,000 examples, 25% of the total. Due to the time requirements and the huge amount of data, random selection was used with 50000 data samples per class, which is again 25% of the total. The kernel was set to be a gaussian kernel with $\gamma = 1$ and the cost parameter for the SVM classifier was also set to be $C = 1$.

Table 2. Results on the covertype dataset.

Method	Selected size	Training time	Error Rate (%)
Full-Size	400000	>12 h	N/A
Purity Filtering	100000	1 h 38 min	12.95
Random Filtering	100000	35 min	14.46
Cluster Filtering	100000	45 min	14.23
Opposite Maps	N/A	>12 h	N/A
GRZ	N/A	>12 h	N/A

The results of the different methods can be seen in Table 2. Notice that in the case of **Opposite Maps** and **GRZ**, as well as for the **full-size SVM**, execution was halted after 12 h of continuous running. It does not seem reasonable than the processing of a dataset lasts for more than 12 h, specially when there are techniques that solve this problem good enough using less than 2 h.

In this table, it can be seen that only the fastest methods achieve reasonable training times. It is important to notice that we don't know how good are the results obtained in comparison with the full-size SVM, since it was not feasible to solve the whole problem.

5 Conclusions

One of the main advantages of the proposed method is that it has been specifically designed from the beginning to work with SVMs. This supposes an advantage against other techniques that are more generic (like the GRZ), since purity filtering is based on some theoretical justifications from the same SVM formulation. Besides, the method approximates the separating hyperplane with another SVM (or KFDA, which is highly related) which is an advantage over methods like Opposite Maps which, even though they have been specifically designed for SVMs, they do not use any kind of similarity or approximation of it.

Another advantage of the method is the huge level of control the user has in all the stages of the algorithm: All of them are parametrized with one or more parameters. Some of those parameters are used to modify explicitly the obtained solution (like the cost of the SVM in the hyperplane estimation), some of them are used to control the number of selected samples (like the purity parameter) and some of them are used to control the spatial and temporal complexity of the method (like the size of the reduction). All of these parameters have a clear interpretation and can be tuned or estimated by the user. The main disadvantage of the proposed method is that it is not impossible to find cases in which the application of the method is rendered useless: this would be the case when the selected number of samples is low and there is not enough data to train the SVM properly.

In the performed experiments, it worked well with both synthetic and real data. In both cases, it performed as well as the rest of the instance selection methods tested, and in some cases even better. If the number of selected samples is big enough, it is able to obtain the same separating hyperplane that would be obtained with the training using all the available data samples.

When working on a real dataset with large number of data samples, the more robust instance selection methods start to show prohibitive training times. In these cases, only the most simple algorithms can be used, which leads to poor testing results. Purity Filtering, on the other side, can be configured to keep reasonable training times, as well as being able to achieve better results than the simplest instance selection techniques.

References

1. Alpaydin, E.: Introduction to Machine Learning. MIT Press, Cambridge (2009)
2. Amami, R., Ayed, D.B., Ellouze, N.: Practical selection of SVM supervised parameters with different feature representations for vowel recognition. arXiv preprint arXiv:1507.06020 (2015)
3. Bishop, C.M.: Pattern Recognition and Machine Learning. Springer, New York (2006)
4. Boser, B.E., Guyon, I.M., Vapnik, V.N.: A training algorithm for optimal margin classifiers. In: Proceedings of the Fifth Annual Workshop on Computational Learning Theory, pp. 144–152. ACM (1992)
5. Campbell, C., Ying, Y.: Learning with support vector machines. Synth. Lect. Artif. Intell. Mach. Learn. 5(1), 1–95 (2011)
6. Cortes, C., Vapnik, V.: Support-vector networks. Mach. Learn. 20(3), 273–297 (1995)
7. Jenssen, R., Principe, J.C., Erdogmus, D., Eltoft, T.: The Cauchy-Schwarz divergence and Parzen windowing: connections to graph theory and mercer kernels. J. Frankl. Inst. 343(6), 614–629 (2006)
8. Mika, S., Ratsch, G., Weston, J., Scholkopf, B., Mullers, K.R.: Fisher discriminant analysis with kernels. In: Neural Networks for Signal Processing IX: Proceedings of the 1999 IEEE Signal Processing Society Workshop (Cat. no. 98th8468), pp. 41–48. IEEE (1999)
9. Neto, A.R., Barreto, G.A.: Opposite maps: vector quantization algorithms for building reduced-set SVM and LSSVM classifiers. Neural Process. Lett. 37(1), 3–19 (2013)
10. Nguyen, D., Ho, T.: An efficient method for simplifying support vector machines. In: Proceedings of the 22nd International Conference on Machine Learning, pp. 617–624. ACM (2005)

11. Olvera-López, J.A., Carrasco-Ochoa, J.A., Martínez-Trinidad, J.F., Kittler, J.: A review of instance selection methods. Artif. Intell. Rev. **34**(2), 133–143 (2010)
12. Pedreira, C.E.: Learning vector quantization with training data selection. IEEE Trans. Pattern Anal. Mach. Intell. **28**(1), 157–162 (2005)
13. Peres, R.T., Pedreira, C.E.: Generalized risk zone: selecting observations for classification. IEEE Trans. Pattern Anal. Mach. Intell. **31**(7), 1331–1337 (2008)
14. Platt, J.: Sequential minimal optimization: a fast algorithm for training support vector machines. Technical report, Microsoft (1998)
15. Schölkopf, B., Smola, A.J., Williamson, R.C., Bartlett, P.L.: New support vector algorithms. Neural Comput. **12**(5), 1207–1245 (2000)
16. Scholkopf, B., Smola, A.J.: Learning with Kernels: Support Vector Machines, Regularization, Optimization, and Beyond. MIT Press, Cambridge (2001)
17. Shashua, A.: On the relationship between the support vector machine for classification and sparsified Fisher's linear discriminant. Neural Process. Lett. **9**(2), 129–139 (1999)
18. Tang, B., Mazzoni, D.: Multiclass reduced-set support vector machines. In: Proceedings of the 23rd International Conference on Machine Learning, pp. 921–928. ACM (2006)
19. UCI: UCI ML repository: covertype data set. archive.ics.uci.edu/ml/datasets/covertype. Accessed 10 Sept 2019
20. Yerukala, R., Boiroju, N.K.: Approximations to standard normal distribution function. Int. J. Sci. Eng. Res. **6**(4), 515–518 (2015)

Towards Model-Based Reinforcement Learning for Industry-Near Environments

Per-Arne Andersen$^{(\boxtimes)}$ (ID), Morten Goodwin (ID), and Ole-Christoffer Granmo (ID)

Department of ICT, University of Agder, Grimstad, Norway
{per.andersen,morten.goodwin,ole.granmo}@uia.no

Abstract. Deep reinforcement learning has over the past few years shown great potential in learning near-optimal control in complex simulated environments with little visible information. Rainbow (Q-Learning) and PPO (Policy Optimisation) have shown outstanding performance in a variety of tasks, including Atari 2600, MuJoCo, and Roboschool test suite. Although these algorithms are fundamentally different, both suffer from high variance, low sample efficiency, and hyperparameter sensitivity that, in practice, make these algorithms a no-go for critical operations in the industry.

On the other hand, model-based reinforcement learning focuses on learning the transition dynamics between states in an environment. If the environment dynamics are adequately learned, a model-based approach is perhaps the most sample efficient method for learning agents to act in an environment optimally. The traits of model-based reinforcement are ideal for real-world environments where sampling is slow and in mission-critical operations. In the warehouse industry, there is an increasing motivation to minimise time and to maximise production. In many of these environments, the literature suggests that the autonomous agents in these environments act suboptimally using handcrafted policies for a significant portion of the state-space.

In this paper, we present The Dreaming Variational Autoencoder v2 (DVAE-2), a model-based reinforcement learning algorithm that increases sample efficiency, hence enable algorithms with low sample efficiency function better in real-world environments. We introduce the Deep Warehouse environment for industry-near testing of autonomous agents in logistic warehouses. We illustrate that the DVAE-2 algorithm improves the sample efficiency for the Deep Warehouse compared to model-free methods.

Keywords: Deep reinforcement learning · Model-based reinforcement learning · Reinforcement learning · Neural networks · Variational autoencoder · Markov decision processes · Exploration · Artificial intelligence

1 Introduction

The goal of reinforcement learning is to maximise some notion of feedback through interaction with an environment [23]. The environment can be known,

© Springer Nature Switzerland AG 2019
M. Bramer and M. Petridis (Eds.): SGAI-AI 2019, LNAI 11927, pp. 36–49, 2019.
https://doi.org/10.1007/978-3-030-34885-4_3

which makes this learning process trivial, or have hidden state information, which typically increases the complexity of learning significantly. In model-free reinforcement learning, actions are sampled from some policy that is optimised indirectly through direct policy search (Policy gradients), a state-value function (Q-learning), or a combination of these (Actor-Critic). There are many recent contributions to these algorithms that increase sample efficiency [8], reduce variance [10], and increase training stability [21].

It is challenging to deploy model-free methods in real-world environments because the current state-of-the-art algorithms require exhaustive sampling before learning an optimal policy. In contrast, model-based reinforcement learning has significantly better sample efficiency, which makes them an appealing approach to learn from real-world data [17]. The goal of a model-based algorithm is to learn a predictive model of the real-world environment that is used to learn how to act optimally. The downside of model-based reinforcement learning is that the predictive model may become inaccurate for longer time-horizons, or collapse entirely, which makes them unreliable for learning optimal policies.

We propose a model-based reinforcement learning approach for industry-near systems where a predictive model is learned without direct interaction with the environment. We use an Automated Storage and Retrieval Systems (ASRS) to benchmark our proposed algorithm. Because the training is isolated from the physical environment, the algorithm guarantees safety during training. If the predictive model is sufficiently trained, a model-free algorithm, such as DQN [19] can be trained off-line. Training can be done in large-scale distributed settings, which unquestionably reduces the training time. If the model-free algorithm is trained sufficiently, it will be able to replace a sub-optimal expert-system in the real-world environment with minimal effort.

The paper is organised as follows. Section 2 discusses the current state of the art in model-based reinforcement learning, and familiarise the reader of recent work in ASRS systems. Section 3 briefly outlines relevant background literature on reinforcement learning. Section 4 introduces the DVAE-2 algorithm and details the architecture thoroughly. Section 5 proposes the Deep Warehouse, a novel high-performance environment for industry-near testing of reinforcement learning algorithms. Section 6 presents our results using DVAE-2 in various environments, including complex environments such as Deep Warehouse, Deep RTS and Deep Line Wars. Finally, Sect. 7 concludes our work and outlines a roadmap for our future work.

2   Literature Review

Reinforcement Learning is a maturing field in artificial intelligence, where a significant portion of the research is concerned with model-free approaches in virtual environments. Reinforcement learning methods in large-scale industry-near environments are virtually absent from the literature. The reason for this could be that (1) model-free methods do not give the sample efficiency required and that (2) there is little evidence that model-based approaches achieve reliable performance. In this section, we briefly discuss the previous work in ASRS systems and present promising recent work in model-based reinforcement learning.

2.1 Automated Storage and Retrieval Systems (ASRS)

There is to our knowledge no published work where reinforcement learning schemes are used to control taxi-agents in ASRS environments. The literature is focused on heuristic-based approaches, such as tree-search and long-established pathfinding algorithms. In [20], a extensive survey of the advancements in ASRS systems, categorise an ASRS system into five components; System Configuration, Storage Assignment, Batching, Sequencing, and Dwell-point. We adopt these categories in search of a reinforcement learning approach for ASRS systems.

2.2 Model-Based Reinforcement Learning

The goal of model-based reinforcement learning is to learn a predictive model of the transitions between states in an environment. If the predictive model is stable, with low variance and improves monotonically during training, it is, to some degree, possible to learn model-free agents to act optimally in environments that have never been observed directly.

Perhaps the most sophisticated algorithm in model-based reinforcement learning is the Model-based policy optimisation (MBPO) algorithm, proposed by Janner et al. [16] The authors empirically show that MBPO performs significantly better in continuous control tasks compared to previous methods. MBPO proves to be monotonically improving given that the following bounds hold:

$$\eta[\pi] \geq \hat{\eta}[\pi] - C$$

where $\eta[\pi]$ denotes the returns in the real environment under a policy whereas $\hat{\eta}[\pi]$ denotes the returns in the predicted model under policy π. Furthermore, the authors show that as long as they can improve by at least C, the performance will increase monotonically [16].

Gregor et al. proposed a scheme to train expressive generative models to learn belief-states of complex 3D environments with little prior knowledge. Their method was effective in predicting multiple steps into the future (overshooting) and significantly improves sample efficiency. In the experiments, the authors illustrated model-free policy training in several environments, including Deep-Mind Lab. However, the authors found it difficult to use their predictive model in model-free agents directly [11].

The Neural Differential Information Gain Optimisation (NDIGO) algorithm by Azar et al. is a self-supervised exploration model that learns a world model representation from noisy data. The primary features of NDIGO are robustness to noise due to their method to cancel out negative loss and giving positive learning more value. The authors show in their maze environment that the model successfully converges towards an optimal world model even when introducing noise. The author claims that the algorithm outperforms previous state-of-the-art, being the Recurrent World Model from [4].

The Dreaming Variational Autoencoder (DVAE) is an end-to-end solution for prediction the probable future state $p(\hat{s}_{t+1}|s_t, a_t$. The authors showed that the algorithm successfully predicted next state in non-continuous environments and could with some error predict future states in continuous state-space environments such as the Deep Line Wars environment. In the experiments, the authors used DQN, PPO, and TRPO using an artificial buffer to feed states to the algorithms. In all cases, the DVAE algorithm was able to create buffers that were accurate enough to learn a near-optimal policy [3].

The algorithm VMAV-C is a combination of VAE and attention-based value function (AVF), and mixture density network recurrent neural network (MDN-RNN) from [12]. This modification to the original World Models algorithm improved performance in the Cart Pole environment. They used the on-policy algorithm PPO to learn the optimal policy from the latent representation of the state-space [18].

Deep Planning Network (PlaNet) is a model-based agent that interpret the pixels of a state to learn a predictive model of an environment. The environment dynamics are stored into latent-space, where the agent sample actions based on the learned representation. The proposed algorithm showed significantly better sample efficiency compared to model-free algorithms such as A3C [14].

In *Recurrent World Models Facilitate Policy Evolution*, a novel architecture for training RL algorithms using variational autoencoders. This paper showed that agents could successfully learn the environment dynamics and use this as an exploration technique requiring no interaction with the target domain. The architecture is mainly three components; vision, controller, and model, the vision model is a variational autoencoder that outputs a latent-space variable of an observation. The latent-space variable is processed in the model and is fed into the controller for action decisions. Their algorithms show state-of-the-art performance in self-supervised generative modelling for reinforcement learning agents [12].

Chua et al. proposed *Probabilistic Ensembles with Trajectory Sampling* (PETS). The algorithm uses an ensemble of bootstrap neural networks to learn a dynamics model of the environment over future states. The algorithm then uses this model to predict the best action for future states. The authors show that the algorithm significantly lowers sampling requirements for environments such as half-cheetah compared to SAC and PPO. [9]

DARLA is an architecture for modelling the environment using β-VAE [15]. The trained model was used to learn the optimal policy of the environment using algorithms such as DQN [19], A3C, and Episodic Control [5]. DARLA is to the best of our knowledge, the first algorithm to introduce learning without access to the ground-truth environment during training.

3   Background

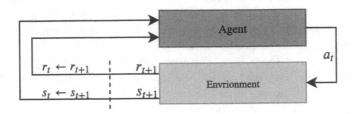

Fig. 1. The agent-environment interaction in a Markov decision process [23]

Markov decision processes (MDP's) are a mathematical framework commonly used to define reinforcement learning problems, as illustrated in Fig. 1. In an MDP, we consider the tuple $(\mathcal{S}, \mathcal{A}, r, \mathcal{P}, \mathcal{P}_0, \gamma)^1$ where $\mathcal{S}$ is the state space, $\mathcal{A}$ is the action space available to the agent, $r : \mathcal{S} \times \mathcal{A} \to \mathbb{R}$ is the expected immediate reward function, P is the transition function which defines the probability $\mathcal{P}(s', s, a) = Pr(s'|s, a)$ and $\mathcal{P}_0$ is the probability for the initial state s_0.

The goal of a reinforcement learning agent is to encourage good behaviour and to discourage bad behaviour. Optimal behaviour is achieved when the agent finds a composition of parameters that maximise its performance, thus finds the optimal policyπ^*. Consider

$$\pi^* = \arg\max_{\pi \in \Pi} J(\pi), \tag{1}$$

where $J(\pi)$ is the objective function for maximising the expected discounted reward defined as

$$J(\pi) = \mathbb{E}_{s_0, a_0, s_1, \ldots} \left[\sum_{t=0}^{\infty} \gamma^t r(s_t, a_t) \mid \pi, s_0 \sim \mathcal{P}_0 \right], \tag{2}$$

where $\gamma \in (0, 1)$ is the discounting factor of future rewards. If $\gamma = 1$, all future state rewards are accounted for equally, while $\gamma = 0$, we are only concerned about the current state.

4   Learning Policies Using Predictive Models

The Dreaming Variational Autoencoder v2 (DVAE-2) is an architecture for learning a predictive model of arbitrary environments. We improve the first version of the DVAE in notable ways [3] for better performance in real-world environments. A common problem in model-based reinforcement learning is a requirement of millions of samples to generalise well across sparse data. We aim to approve sample efficiency from the original DVAE and if possible, surpass the performance of model-free methods.

---

[1] $\mathcal{S}$ and $\mathcal{A}$ is defined for discrete or continuous spaces. $r : \mathcal{S} \times \mathcal{A} \to \mathbb{R}$ where r is commonly referred to as $\mathcal{R}(s, s')$ in the literature.

4.1   Motivation and Environment Safety

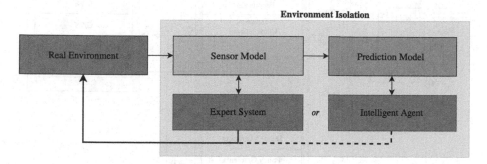

Fig. 2. The proposed model isolates the intelligent agent from the mission-critical sensor model. The real environment projects onto a sensor model that the expert system uses to control taxis in a real environment. The predictive model observes the behaviour of the sensor model and the actions performed by the expert system. The predictive model is trained using error gradients, where the loss is the distance between the sensor model and the predictive model. When the error becomes sufficiently low, an intelligent agent can be trained using only data from the predictive model. Assuming that the intelligent agent converges to some performance threshold, it can be deployed as a drop-in replacement to the expert system.

Figure 2 shows an abstract overview of DVAE-2 training in an environment. In real-world, industry-near environments, there is little room for interruptions. In model-free reinforcement learning, the agent interacts with the environment to learn its policy. Because this is not possible in many real-world environments, the DVAE-2 algorithm only observes during training. During training, the DVAE-2 algorithm learns how the transition function behaves and learns an estimated state-value function V that represent the value of being in that current state.

4.2   The Dreaming Variational Autoencoder V2

The original DVAE architecture had severe challenges with modelling of continuous state-spaces [3], and many algorithms were added to the model to improve performance across various environments including autoencoders, LSTMs, and fine-tuned variations of these. The DVAE-2 extends this with a split into three individual components; forming the **V**iew, **R**eason and **C**ontrol (VRC) model. The VRC model embeds all improvements into a single model and learns which algorithms to use under certain conditions in an environment

Figure 3 shows an overview of the proposed VRC. (1) A state s_t is observed. During training, this observation stems from the real-environment while at inference time, from the predictive model. The observation is encoded in the **view** component (e.g. via AE or GAN) and outputs an embedding z at time t w.r.t policy π. (2) The **reason** component learns the time dynamics between state

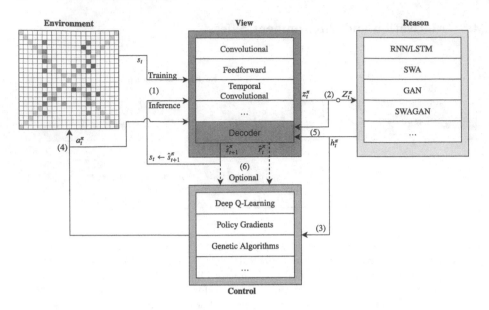

Fig. 3. The component-based DVAE-2 architecture.

sequences. Encoded states are accumulated into a buffer $Z_t^\pi = \{z_{t-n} \dots z_t\}^\pi$ and are then used to predict the hidden-state h_t^π w.r.t the encoded state sequence. The reason component typically consists of a model with RNN-like structure that generalises well on sequence data. (3) The hidden state is then used to evaluate an action using policy π, and (4) is sent to the environment and the view for the next iteration. (5) The decoder, prepares the hidden-state h_t^π and encoded state z_t^π, producing the succeeding state $\hat{s}_{t+1}^\pi$. The prediction is then used in the next iteration as current state s_t, which leads back to (1). As an optional mechanism, the controller can use the output from the decoder, instead of the hidden state information. This is beneficial when working with model-free algorithms such as deep q-networks [19].

4.3   Model Selection

During technique selection in the components, we perform the following evaluation. An observation s_t is sent to the view component of DVAE-2. All of the view techniques are initially assumed to be uniformly qualified to encode and predict future states. For each iteration, the computed error is summarised as a score, and during inference, the technique with the lowest score is used[2]. We use the same method for determining the best reasoning algorithm in a specific environment.

---

[2] In this setting, the lowest score is the technique with least accumulated error.

4.4   Implementation

The implementation of the DVAE-2 algorithm with dynamic component selection enabled several significant improvements to over the previous DVAE model [3]. Notably, the k-step model rollout from [16] is implemented to stabilise training. We found that using shorter model-rollouts provided better control policies, but at the cost of higher sample efficiency. Also, by embedding time into the encoded state improved the model stability and prediction capabilities [13]. The DVAE-2 algorithm is defined as follows[3].

Algorithm 1. DVAE-2: Minimal Implementation

1: Initialize policy $\pi_\theta(s_t|a_t)$, predictive model $p_\psi(\hat{s}_{t+1}, \hat{r}, h_t|s_t, a_t^\pi)$
2: Let $Z = \{z_{t-n}^\pi \ldots z_t^\pi\}$, a vector of encoded states
3: Initialize encoder $ENC(z_t^\pi|s_t, a_t^\pi)$, temporal reasoner $TR(h_t^\pi|Z)$
4: **for** N epochs **do**
5:     $\mathcal{D}_{env} \leftarrow$ Collect samples from p_{env} under predefined policy π
6:     Train model p_ψ on data batch $\mathcal{D}_{env}$ via MLE

7: **for** M epochs **do**
8:     Sample initial state $s_0 \sim U(0,1)$ from $\mathcal{D}_{env}$
9:     Construct $\{\mathcal{D}_{p_\psi}|t < k, TR(h_t^{\pi_\theta}|ENC(z_t|s_t, a_t)^{\pi_\theta}), s_t = s_0\}$
10:    Update policy π_θ using pairs of $(\hat{s}_t, a_t, \hat{r}_t, \hat{s}_{t+1})^{\pi_\theta}$

Algorithm 1 works as follows. (Line 1) We initialise the control policy and the predictive model (DVAE-2) parameters. (Line 2) The Z variable denotes a finite set of sequential view model (ENC) predictions that are used to capture time dependency between states in the reason model (TR). (Line 5) We collect samples from the real environment p_{env} under a predefined policy, such as an expert system, see Fig. 2. (Line 6) The predictive model p_ψ is then trained using the collected data $\mathcal{D}_{env}$ via maximum likelihood estimation. In our case, we use mean squared error to measure the error distance $MSE(p_\psi \| p_{env})$. When the DVAE-2 algorithm has trained sufficiently, the model-free algorithm will train for M epochs (Line 7) using the predictive model p_ψ instead of p_{env}. (Line 8) First, we sample the initial state s_0 uniformly from the real dataset $\mathcal{D}_{env}$. (Line 9) We then construct a prediction dataset $\mathcal{D}_{p_\psi}$ and predict future states using the control policy (i.e. sampling from the predictive model). (Line 10) The parameterised control policy is then optimised using $(\hat{s}_t, a_t, \hat{r}_t, \hat{s}_{t+1})^{\pi_\theta}$ pairs during rollouts.

5   The Deep Warehouse Environment

Training algorithms in real-world environments is known to have severe safety challenges during training and suffers from low sampling speeds [6]. It is therefore

---

[3] We use the mean squared error (MSE) loss in our implementation.

practical to create a simulation of the real environment so that researches can quickly test algorithm variations with quick feedback on its performance.

This section presents the Deep Warehouse[4] environment for discrete and continuous action and state spaces. The environment has a wide range of configurations for time and agent behaviour, giving it tolerable performance in simulating proprietary automated storage and retrieval systems.

5.1 Motivation

In the context of warehousing, an Automated Storage and Retrieval System (ASRS) is a composition of computer programs working together to maximise the incoming and outgoing throughput of goods. There are many benefits of using an ASRS system, including high scalability, increased efficiency, reduced operating expenses, and operation safety. We consider a cube-based ASRS environment where each cell is stacked with item containers. On the surface of the cube, taxi-agents are collecting and delivering goods to delivery points placed throughout the surface. The taxi-agents are controlled by a computer program that reads sensory data from the taxi and determines the next action.

Although these systems are far better than manual labour warehousing, there is still significant improvement potential in current state-of-the-art. Most ASRS systems are manually crafted expert systems, which due to the high complexity of the multi-agent ASRS systems only performs sub-optimally [20].

5.2 Implementation

Figure 4 illustrates the state-space in the deep warehouse environment. In a simple cube-based ASRS configuration, the environment consists of (B) passive and (C) active delivery-points, (D) pickup-points, and (F) taxis. Also, the simulator can model other configurations, including advanced cube and shelf-based automated storage and retrieval systems. In the deep warehouse environment, the goal is to store and retrieve goods from one location to another where each cell represents several layers of containers that a taxi can pick up. A taxi (F) receives feedback based on the time used on the task it performs. A taxi can move using a discrete or continuous controller. In discrete mode, the agent can increase and decrease thrust, and move in either direction, including the diagonals. For the continuous mode, all of these actions are floating point numbers between (off) 0 and (on) 1, giving a significantly harder action-space to learn. The simulator also features continuous mode for the state-space, where actions are performed asynchronously to the game loop. It is possible to create custom support modules for mechanisms such as task scheduling, agent controllers and fitness scoring.

---

[4] The deep warehouse environment is open-source and freely available at https://github.com/cair/deep-warehouse.

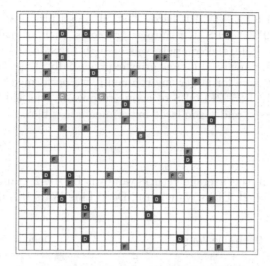

Fig. 4. Illustration of the graphical interface in the deep-warehouse environment using cube-based ASRS configuration.

A significant benefit of the deep warehouse is that it can accurately model real warehouse environments at high speed. The deep warehouse environment runs 1000 times faster on a single high-end processor core compared to real-world systems measured from the speed improvement by counting how many operations a taxi can do per second. The simulator can be distributed across many processing units to increase the performance further. In our benchmarks, the simulator was able to collect 1 million samples per second during the training of deep learning models using high-performance computing (HPC).

6 Experimental Results

In this section, we present our preliminary results of applied model-based reinforcement learning using DVAE-2. We aim to answer the following questions. **(1)** Does the DVAE-2 algorithm improve sample efficiency compared to model-free methods? **(2)** How well do DVAE-2 perform versus model-free methods in the deep warehouse environment? **(3)** Which of DVAE-2 VRC components is preferred by the model?

6.1 The Importance of Compute

According to AI pioneer Richard S. Sutton "The biggest lesson that can be read from 70 years of AI research is that general methods that leverage computation are ultimately the most effective, and by a large margin." [22]. It is therefore not surprising that computation is still the most decisive factor when training a large model, also for predictive models. DVAE-2 was initially trained using two NVIDIA 2080 RTX TI GPU cards that, if tuned properly, can operate at approximately 26.9 TFLOPS. For simpler problems, such as grid-warehouses of size 5 × 5 and CartPole, the compute was enough to train the model in 5 min, but for larger environments, this time grew exponentially. To somewhat mitigate the computational issue for larger environments, we performed the experiments with approximately 1.25 PFLOPS of compute power. This led to significantly faster training speeds, and made large experiments feasible[5].

6.2 Results

Figure 5 shows that the average return value of DVAE-2 training four tasks, including Deep RTS [2], Deep Warehouse, Deep Line Wars [1] and CartPole [7].

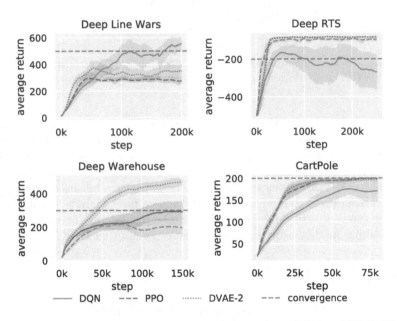

Fig. 5. We compare DVAE-2 using two baseline algorithms, DQN and PPO. The solid curve illustrates the mean of 12 trials and shaded regions is the standard deviation between all trials. The x-axis shows the number of episodes performed and the y-axis shows the average return.

Deep Warehouse: The environment for industry-near testing of autonomous agents is a contribution in this paper. The DVAE-2 algorithm outperforms both PPO and DQN in terms of sampling and performance during 150000 game steps. The score function is a counter of how many tasks the agent has performed during the episode. If the agent manages to collect and retrieve 300 packages,

---

[5] We recognise large experiments to consist of environments where the agents require significant sampling to converge.

the agent has sufficient performance to beat many handcrafted algorithms in ASRS systems. The environment is multi-agent, and in this experiment, we used a 30×30 grid with 20 taxis running the same policy.

Deep RTS is a flexible real-time strategy game (RTS) engine with multiple environments for unit control and resource management. In this experiment, we used the resource harvester environment where the goal is to harvest 500 wood resources before the time limit is up. The score is measured from -500 to 0, where 0 is the best score. For every wood harvested, the score increase with 1. We consider the task mastered if the agent has less than -200 score at the terminal state. DVAE-2 outperform the baseline algorithms in terms of sample efficiency but falls behind PPO in terms of score performance [2].

Deep Line Wars: Surprisingly, the DQN policy outperforms the DVAE-2 and PPO policy in 11×11 discrete action-space environment. Because we used PPO as the policy for DVAE-2, we still see a marginal improvement over the same algorithm in a model-free setting yielding better performance and better sample efficiency. We found that DQN quickly learned the correct Q-values due to the small environment size. In future experiments, we would like to include larger map sizes that would increase the state-space significantly, hence making Q-values more challenging to learn [1].

CartPole: As a simple baseline environment, we use CartPole from the OpenAI Gym environment suite [7]. The goal of this environment is to balance a pole on a moving cart using a discrete action-space of 2 actions. We found that DVAE-2 and PPO had similar performance, but DVAE-2 had marginally better sample efficiency after 25000 steps.

In terms of VRC, the algorithm tended to choose Convolutional + LSTM and Temporal Convolution and GAN for continuous control tasks (see Fig. 1). It should be noted that PPO and DVAE-2 are presented with the same hyperparameters, and are therefore directly comparable. We used PPO as our policy for DVAE-2, and we see that DVAE-2 is more sample efficient and performs equally good or better than model-free PPO in all tested scenarios.

7   Conclusion and Future Work

In this paper, we present DVAE-2, a novel model-based reinforcement learning algorithm for improved sample efficiency in environments where sampling is not available. We also present the deep warehouse environment for training reinforcement learning agents in industry-near ASRS systems. This section concludes our work and defines future work for the DVAE-2.

Although the deep warehouse does not behave identical to a real-world system, it is adequate to determine the training time and performance. DVAE-2 is presented as a VRC model for training reinforcement learning algorithms with a learned model of the environment. The method is tested in the Deep warehouse several continuous game environments. Our algorithm reduces training time and depends less on data sampled from the real environment compared to model-free methods.

We find that a carefully tuned policy gradient algorithms can converge to near-optimal behaviour in simulated environments. Model-free algorithms are significantly harder to train in terms of sample efficiency and stability, but perform better if there is unlimited sampling available from the environment.

Our work shows promising results for reinforcement learning agents in ASRS. There are, however, open research questions that are essential for safe deployment in real-world systems. We wish to pursue the following questions to achieve safety deployment in real-world environments. **(1)** How do we ensure that the agent acts within defined safety boundaries? **(2)** How would the agent act if parts of the state-space changes to unseen data (i.e. a fire occurs, or a collision between agents.) **(3)** Can agents with a non-stationary policy function well in a multi-agent setting?

References

1. Andersen, P.-A., Goodwin, M., Granmo, O.-C.: Towards a deep reinforcement learning approach for tower line wars. In: Bramer, M., Petridis, M. (eds.) SGAI 2017. LNCS (LNAI), vol. 10630, pp. 101–114. Springer, Cham (2017). https://doi.org/10.1007/978-3-319-71078-5_8
2. Andersen, P.A., Goodwin, M., Granmo, O.C.: Deep RTS: a game environment for deep reinforcement learning in real-time strategy games. In: Proceedings of the IEEE International Conference on Computational Intelligence and Games, August 2018. http://arxiv.org/abs/1808.05032
3. Andersen, P.-A., Goodwin, M., Granmo, O.-C.: The dreaming variational autoencoder for reinforcement learning environments. In: Bramer, M., Petridis, M. (eds.) SGAI 2018. LNCS (LNAI), vol. 11311, pp. 143–155. Springer, Cham (2018). https://doi.org/10.1007/978-3-030-04191-5_11
4. Azar, M.G., Piot, B., Pires, B.A., Grill, J.B., Altché, F., Munos, R.: World Discovery Models. arxiv preprint arXiv:1902.07685, February 2019. http://arxiv.org/abs/1902.07685
5. Blundell, C., et al.: Model-Free Episodic Control. arxiv preprint arXiv:1606.04460, June 2016. http://arxiv.org/abs/1606.04460
6. Botvinick, M., Ritter, S., Wang, J.X., Kurth-Nelson, Z., Blundell, C., Hassabis, D.: Reinforcement learning, fast and slow. Trends Cogn. Sci. **23**(5), 408–422 (2019). https://doi.org/10.1016/j.tics.2019.02.006. http://www.ncbi.nlm.nih.gov/pubmed/31003893
7. Brockman, G., et al.: OpenAI Gym. arxiv preprint arXiv:1606.01540, June 2016. http://arxiv.org/abs/1606.01540
8. Buckman, J., Hafner, D., Tucker, G., Brevdo, E., Lee, H.: Sample-efficient reinforcement learning with stochastic ensemble value expansion. In: Advances in Neural Information Processing Systems, vol. 32, pp. 8224–8234, July 2018. http://arxiv.org/abs/1807.01675
9. Chua, K., Calandra, R., McAllister, R., Levine, S.: Deep reinforcement learning in a handful of trials using probabilistic dynamics models. In: Advances in Neural Information Processing Systems, vol. 31, May 2018. http://arxiv.org/abs/1805.12114
10. Greensmith, E., Bartlett, P.L., Baxter, J.: Variance reduction techniques for gradient estimates in reinforcement learning. J. Mach. Learn. Res. **5**, 1471–1530 (2004)

11. Gregor, K., Rezende, D.J., Besse, F., Wu, Y., Merzic, H., van den Oord, A.: Shaping Belief States with Generative Environment Models for RL. arxiv preprint arXiv:1906.09237, June 2019. http://arxiv.org/abs/1906.09237

12. Ha, D., Schmidhuber, J.: Recurrent world models facilitate policy evolution. In: Advances in Neural Information Processing Systems, vol. 31, September 2018. http://arxiv.org/abs/1809.01999

13. Ha, D., Schmidhuber, J.: World Models. arxiv preprint arXiv:1803.10122, March 2018. https://doi.org/10.5281/zenodo.1207631, https://arxiv.org/abs/1803.10122

14. Hafner, D., et al.: Learning latent dynamics for planning from pixels. In: Proceedings of the 36th International Conference on Machine Learning, November 2018. http://arxiv.org/abs/1811.04551

15. Higgins, I., et al.: Beta-VAE: learning basic visual concepts with a constrained variational framework. In: International Conference on Learning Representations, November 2016. https://openreview.net/forum?id=Sy2fzU9gl

16. Janner, M., Fu, J., Zhang, M., Levine, S.: When to Trust Your Model: Model-Based Policy Optimization. arXiv preprint arXiv:1906.08253, June 2019. http://arxiv.org/abs/1906.08253

17. Kaelbling, L.P., Littman, M.L., Moore, A.W.: Reinforcement learning: a survey. J. Artif. Intell. Res. (1996). https://doi.org/10.1.1.68.466, http://arxiv.org/abs/cs/9605103

18. Liang, X., Wang, Q., Feng, Y., Liu, Z., Huang, J.: VMAV-C: A Deep Attention-based Reinforcement Learning Algorithm for Model-based Control. arxiv preprint arXiv:1812.09968, December 2018. http://arxiv.org/abs/1812.09968

19. Mnih, V., et al.: Playing Atari with deep reinforcement learning. In: Neural Information Processing Systems, December 2013. http://arxiv.org/abs/1312.5602

20. Roodbergen, K.J., Vis, I.F.A.: A survey of literature on automated storage and retrieval systems. Eur. J. Oper. Res. (2009). https://doi.org/10.1016/j.ejor.2008.01.038

21. Schulman, J., Wolski, F., Dhariwal, P., Radford, A., Klimov, O.: Proximal Policy Optimization Algorithms. arxiv preprint arXiv:1707.06347, July 2017. http://arxiv.org/abs/1707.06347

22. Sutton, R.S.: The Bitter Lesson (2019). http://www.incompleteideas.net/IncIdeas/BitterLesson.html

23. Sutton, R.S., Barto, A.G.: Reinforcement Learning: An Introduction. MIT Press, Cambridge (2018)

Stepwise Evolutionary Learning Using Deep Learned Guidance Functions

Colin G. Johnson[1,2]([✉]) [ID]

[1] School of Computing, University of Kent, Canterbury, Kent, UK
C.G.Johnson@kent.ac.uk
[2] IASH, University of Edinburgh, Edinburgh, UK
Colin.Johnson@ed.ac.uk

Abstract. This paper explores how Learned Guidance Functions (LGFs)—a pre-training method used to smooth search landscapes—can be used as a fitness function for evolutionary algorithms. A new form of LGF is introduced, based on deep neural network learning, and it is shown how this can be used as a fitness function. This is applied to a test problem: unscrambling the Rubik's Cube. Comparisons are made with a previous LGF approach based on random forests, and with a baseline approach based on traditional error-based fitness.

1 Introduction

The aim of this paper is to present a new kind of fitness function in evolutionary algorithms. Instead of the fitness being defined directly from an error function, a pre-training process is used to learn a fitness function from a set of solved examples of the problem class. This new kind of fitness is based on *Learned Guidance Functions*. These smooth out the fitness landscape by taking a set of solved examples for a problem, and learning a new fitness function based on the distance taken to move between state in the solved examples and the solved state. This function can then be applied to previously unseen examples.

The fitness function is one of the key components of evolutionary algorithms. Typically, a fitness function is either a domain-specific *loss function*, measuring how far a particular population member is from being a solution, or a ranking function that allows the comparison of two population members, returning the fittest. This is one of the powerful aspects of evolutionary algorithms—we can specify a problem by giving a single, simple function that allows us to choose between population members.

There are problems with such an approach. Most obviously, such functions typically have many local minima. Typically, this is seen as an intrinsic part of the problem, to be solved by the search process. A large amount of the evolutionary computation literature is dedicated to operators and other techniques that allow the search to escape local minima and ensure a balanced exploration of the search space. The focus of this work is typically on improvements to the search process. However, another strand of work is focused on transformations to the

M. Bramer and M. Petridis (Eds.): SGAI-AI 2019, LNAI 11927, pp. 50–62, 2019.
https://doi.org/10.1007/978-3-030-34885-4_4

fitness function itself. This has a long history in the evolutionary computation, typifed by work on *fitness scaling* [11,12,17,30]. The principle aim of fitness scaling prevent premature convergence of the search algorithm, by composing a scaling function with the fitness function that doesn't change the ranking of points in the search space but ensures a more even distribution of the fitness values allocated to those points.

A more recent version of this transformation approach is exemplified by geometric semantic genetic programming (GSGP) [21] which attempts to reconfigure the problem so that a much simpler search process such as hillclimbing can be used. The "intelligence" in these approaches is in this initial phase of reconfiguring the problem. However, these approaches have sometimes traded off this simplicity of search against another kind of complexity; for example, in basic GSGP, this tradeoff is against the size of the solution, though more recent implementations have used a caching strategy to make implementation more efficient [29]. This idea of reconfiguring the fitness function prior to the main evolutionary algorithms being run is one source of inspiration for the work in this paper; this has been explored elsewhere in evolutionary computation in work showing how a good choice of genotype-phenotype mapping can be used to create a smoother landscape [4].

Another form of smoothing the search landscape is in the form of *pattern databases* [6]. These consist of patterns in the search space such that the patterns have the same cost of solution—typically, these represent symmetries of the underlying problem. If a solution of a particular cost is known for one problem that matches the pattern, then any other solution matching the pattern will have at most that cost to solve because all of the moves to the solution can be similarly transformed. This has a similar idea of transforming the search space to the above work, but it is different because the pattern databases are produced based on domain knowledge. Some work has used learning methods to generalise from pattern databases—for example, by using neural networks to learn how pattern databases can be combined [20].

Another important source of inspiration is the view that traditional fitness functions take a very narrow view of the problem; whilst a traditional fitness function is a good guide as to which elements of the population to choose for the next generation, it is a very simple representation of the complexity of a problem. Instead, it is argued, rather than a fitness function that returns a single number or a ranking, we should be using more complex *fitness drivers* that give us more information about the population member, allowing a more directed application of operators [15,16]. However, such fitness drivers can require more domain-specific knowledge than a traditional fitness function. One of the aims of this paper is to give a generic method by which more information about problems can be incorporated into the evolutionary search, in this case by pre-training.

A more fundamental problem for evolutionary algorithms is that for some problems, defining the fitness function is difficult, because each problem has a different goal state. Call these *non-oracular problems*. As an example, consider the protein-folding problem in bioinformatics [7]. Biological proteins consist of a sequence of amino acids, which then fold into a three-dimensional shape, which is (with a few exceptions such as prions) entirely dependent on the sequence. To define this as a traditional evolutionary search is problematic, because we do not have access to a measure of how far a particular configuration is from the solution—indeed, if we did know what configuration we were searching for, we would have solved the problem! Therefore, evolutionary computing approaches to these types of problems have focused on learning parameters in, or functional forms of, a domain-specific model [31].

Another potential advantage to pre-training for simplifying the fitness landscape is that more extensive computational effort can be expended during an early training phase, and then when evolution is applied to a specific problem, the evolutionary algorithm can run in fewer generations because more domain-specific information has been encoded into the fitness function. This may be of importance in some application where running a traditional evolutionary algorithm might be infeasible because of the need for a large population and many generations to escape local minima, whereas a smaller population and fewer generations might be needed for the simpler function.

2   Deep Learned Guidance Functions

Fitness functions in evolutionary learning are provided as part of the problem definition. Typically, these are then used directly—individuals are evaluated using the fitness function, and operators in the search are used to avoid problems in the fitness landscape such as local minima. However, an alternative approach has been applied in both evolutionary learning [28] and reinforcement learning [8], where the fitness function is *shaped* so that it more directly represents routes through the fitness landscape from an arbitrary point to the desired target.

A form of this called *Learned Guidance Functions* (LGFs) was introduced by Johnson [14]. The input to this is a search space and set of existing solution trajectories for the problem. For example, in the protein folding problem these would be sequences of points in the space of three-dimensional structures, going from a sequence to a completely folded structure. For an image denoising problem, this would be a sequence of images from a clean image to a very noisy one. These are an example of *True Distance Heuristics* [26], but with a particular layered structure and the use of a predictive function to give the heuristic value rather than a look-up table.

These solution trajectories can be obtained in a number of ways. For some problems, we will have access to a set of already-solved examples. For others, we can construct artificial examples by starting from a solved state and carrying out a number of moves from that solved state to generate trajectories in reverse (a similar approach has been called *Autodidactic Iteration* in [19]).

These trajectories can then be used to create a training set for a supervised learning problem. Each trajectory will consist of a number of states in the search space of the problem, each of which is paired with a number that is the number of steps away from the target that it took to get to that state. These pairs then become the training set: so, the task for the supervised learning problem is to build a model that takes an arbitrary state of the system and assigns a number predicting how many steps it will take to get to the target state. The LGF is the model learned from this supervised learning process.

This LGF then be used as a ranking function in an evolutionary algorithm. Take a each member of the population, and apply the LGF to it. Then select the individuals that will form the parents of the next population from the lowest scoring ones on the LGF—these are the ones that are being predicted as being closest to the solution.

2.1 Formalisation

Now we formalise this idea. Consider a search space S consisting of a set of points, which is the node set of a directed graph M_S, which represent the possible moves (mutations) from each point in the search space. Identify one or more of these as goal states; these might be the only goal states, or they might represent a sample of the class of states that the eventual problem is trying to solve.

Now take a set of trajectories $T = \{T_1, T_2, ... T_{n_T}\}$, where each trajectory is a set of points in S, i.e. $T_i = [s_1, s_2, ..., s_{n_{T_i}}]$, where in each of these cases s_1 is a goal state, and where each adjacent pair (s_i, s_{i+1}) are joined by an edge in M_s. Now create a new set X consisting of the pairs (s_i, i) for all the s_i in all members of T.

X can now be used as a training set for a supervised learning algorithm. The trained model from that supervised learning algorithm, $L : S \to \mathbb{Z}^{\geq 0}$, is a function that takes a set in the search space and predicts how many moves are needed to get to the goal state. This function will be used as an alternative kind of fitness function in the experiments below.

3   Example: Applying Deep LGFs to the Rubik's Cube

In [14] we applied the LGF to the problem of unscrambling the Rubik's Cube. We used a number of classifiers from the *scikit-learn* library [2] to implement LGFs, and demonstrated that (1) the LGF can learn to recognise the number of turns that have been made to a cube to a decent level of accuracy; and, (2) that this LGF can then be used to unscramble particular states of the cube in a sensible number of moves. Unscrambling is not one of the non-oracular problems, but it has a complex fitness landscape with many local minima, and so is a good test for these kind of algorithms.

The search space C consists of all possible configurations of coloured facelets on the six faces of the cube, each of which has a 3×3 set of facelets. The move set M is notated by a list of twelve $90°$ moves, $\{F, B, R, L, U, D, F', B', R', L', U', D'\}$ [23], which are functions from C to C.

This paper presents two new aspects compared to the previous one. Firstly, we introduced a new approach to learning the LGFs, based on deep learning [10].

Secondly, we apply a population-based approach to this problem, based around an evolution strategy, rather than the hillclimbing approach used in the previous paper.

3.1   Constructing the LGF

The LGF for this problem is constructed as follows (pseudocode in Algorithm 1). For n_s iterations, start with a solved cube and make $n_{\ell-1}$ moves. Each time a move is made (and in the initial state), the pair consisting of the current state and the number of moves made to get to that state is added to the training set. This is illustrated in Fig. 1.

Algorithm 1. Training set construction for the Rubik's cube

1: **procedure** CONSTRUCTTRAININGSETRUBIK(n_s, n_m)
2:     let $M = \{F, B, R, L, U, D, F', B', R', L', U', D'\}$
3:     let $X = \emptyset$
4:     **for** $s \in [0, \ldots, n_s - 1]$ **do**
5:         let c be a new cube in the solved state
6:         **for** $\ell \in [0, \ldots, n_m - 1]$ **do**
7:             let $X = X \cup \{(c, \ell)\}$
8:             let $m = $ random element from M
9:             let $C = m(c)$
10:         **end for**
11:     **end for**
12:     **return** T
13: **end procedure**

The LGF is then constructed from this training set by applying a supervised learning algorithm, specifically a deep neural network implemented in the *Keras* framework [1] on TensorFlow [3]. The specific network used is illustrated in Fig. 2. This is a fairly standard deep learning network, with dropout [25] used to encourage generalisation and prevent overfitting. The categorical crossentropy function was used for the loss function, and the adam optimizer was applied. Future work will apply meta-learning of parameters and network shape to optimise the model produced [13].

Once an LGF is learned, it can be applied to the task at hand, which is to take a scrambled state of the cube and move through the search space with the aim of finding the solved state. This is done using a variant on evolution strategies. The initial state of the cube is duplicated to fill the population. Then, in each generation a number of mutants are generated by making a random move for each member of the population. Any solutions that are predicted by the LGF to be closer to the solution than the current one are placed in an intermediate population pool, and a new generation created by uniform random sampling with replacement from this pool to bring the population up to full size. This is repeated until one of three states occurs: (1) the solution is found; (2) none of the mutants produce any improvement, in which case the algorithm is restarted; (3) a user-set limit on the number of generations is reached (in the experiments below, this is 100 generations), in which case a fail-state is returned.

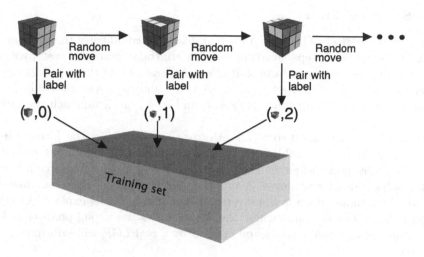

Fig. 1. Construction of the training set (modified from [14]).

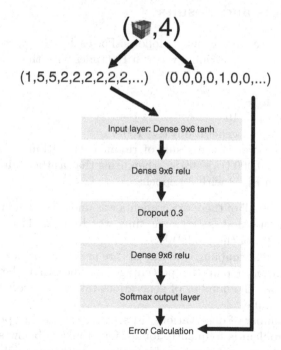

Fig. 2. Keras deep learning network used for training.

This is summarised in pseudocode in Algorithm 2, where the inputs are: n_ℓ, the problem size (number of scrambling twists given); n_p, the population size; θ the maximum number of generations; and, L the LGF function used.

3.2   Sources of Error

Note that if a perfect LGF existed for a problem, we could solve the problem in a minimal number of steps. Starting from an arbitrary scrambled state, we can examine all possible moves from that state. At least one of these will be closer in terms of number of moves to the target state, and so we can move the state of the system to the state which is closest, and repeat until we reach the target state.

In practice, there are two forms of error. The first is in the formation of the training set for the problem. A particular sequence of scrambling moves of length n might, nonetheless, end up with the cube in a state which could have been reached using fewer moves. A simple example of this is where one move is followed by a move which is the inverse of that move (this is explored in more detail in [14]). The second is where the model makes the wrong prediction. For these reasons, the fitness landscape created by a real LGF will still have local minima.

4   Experiments and Results

The experiments were carried out as follows. For each pair $(n_\ell, n_m) \in [2, 13] \times [2, 13]$ where $n_\ell \leq n_m$, Algorithm 2 was run 100 times with the following parameters:

- Size of problem $n_\ell = n_\ell$
- Population size $n_p = 100$
- Maximum number of generations $\theta = 100$
- LGF function used L is the result of running Algorithm 1 with trajectory length n_m and 100,000 trajectories, then using that as the training set for the Keras network in Fig. 2 with 50 epochs.

The total time to run all of these experiments was under three hours, not including time to train the models (training time was between 11 s–59 s per epoch depending on the size of the model).

Results for the unscrambling experiments are presented in two tables. Table 1 shows for each (n_ℓ, n_m) pair the percentage of times that the problem was solved. Table 2 shows the number of generations taken by successful algorithms to unscramble the cube.

There are a number of observations. Firstly, for the smaller problem sizes, a solution to the problem is frequently found; for problems below size 9, at least half of the attempts are successful, and it is very reliable for small problem sizes. Secondly, the size of the model makes little difference—using a larger model than the problem size is of little value. Thirdly, the number of generations needed is

---

Algorithm 2. Scrambling/unscrambling algorithm for the Rubik's cube

---

1: **procedure** ES-LGF-UNSCRAMBLE(n_ℓ, n_p, θ, L)
2:      **let** $M = \{F, B, R, L, U, D, F', B', R', L', U', D'\}$
3:      **let** c be a new cube in the solved state
4:      **for** $\ell = 0; \ell < n_\ell; \ell = \ell + 1$ **do**
5:          **let** $m =$ random element from M
6:          **let** $c = m(c)$
7:      **end for**
8:   ▷ c now in scrambled state
9:      **let** $\ell = n_\ell$
10:     **let** $P = n_p$ copies of c
11:     **for** $t = 0; t < \theta; t = t + 1$ **do**
12:         **let** $P' = \emptyset$
13:         **for** $p \in P$ **do** $m =$ random element from M
14:             **let** $P' = P' \cup m(p)$
15:             **if** $m(p)$ is the solved state **then**
16:                 **return** p ▷ Problem Solved
17:             **end if**
18:         **end for**
19:         **let** $P'' = \emptyset$
20:         **for** $p \in P'$ **do**
21:             **if** $L(p) < \ell$ **then**
22:                 **let** $P'' = P'' \cup p$
23:             **end if**
24:         **end for**
25:         **if** $P'' == \emptyset$ **then**
26:             **let** $P = n_p$ copies of c ▷ Reinitialise
27:             **let** $\ell = n_\ell$
28:         **else**
29:             **let** $P = \emptyset$
30:             **for** $n = 0; n < n_p; n = n + 1$ **do**
31:                 $P = P \cup$ random member of P''
32:             **end for**
33:             **let** $\ell = \ell - 1$
34:         **end if**
35:     **end for**
36:     **return** null   ▷ Timed out
37: **end procedure**

---

small for the lower problem sizes, but increases for large problem sizes; this may be an effect of more re-initialisations needing to be carried out.

Fourthly, note that some of the average lengths in Table 2 are shorter than the problem size. This is because the problems were constructed by scrambling randomly n_ℓ times, but no check was made to ensure that the resulting state could not be solved in less than n_ℓ moves; indeed, doing such a check is rather complex. Therefore, the starting state for some runs may contain a problem that can be solved in fewer than n_ℓ moves.

Table 1. Percentage of times unscrambling problem of each size was solved using a model of each size. Results from 100 runs.

		Size of problem											
		2	3	4	5	6	7	8	9	10	11	12	13
Size of model	2	100	–	–	–	–	–	–	–	–	–	–	–
	3	100	100	–	–	–	–	–	–	–	–	–	–
	4	100	100	100	–	–	–	–	–	–	–	–	–
	5	100	100	100	98	–	–	–	–	–	–	–	–
	6	100	100	100	89	92	–	–	–	–	–	–	–
	7	100	100	100	94	80	70	–	–	–	–	–	–
	8	100	100	100	93	82	71	61	–	–	–	–	–
	9	100	100	100	92	76	57	52	47	–	–	–	–
	10	100	100	100	97	85	75	63	60	38	–	–	–
	11	100	100	99	92	83	73	73	52	37	21	–	–
	12	100	100	100	97	89	73	71	56	37	22	15	–
	13	100	100	100	90	77	61	63	50	37	22	17	6

Table 2. Average number of generations needed to solve problem of each size using trained model of each size. Includes successful solutions only, and includes restarts.

		Size of problem											
		2	3	4	5	6	7	8	9	10	11	12	13
Size of model	2	1.0	–	–	–	–	–	–	–	–	–	–	–
	3	1.0	1.7	–	–	–	–	–	–	–	–	–	–
	4	1.0	1.7	2.6	–	–	–	–	–	–	–	–	–
	5	1.0	1.7	2.8	4.4	–	–	–	–	–	–	–	–
	6	1.0	1.6	2.7	4.3	8.4	–	–	–	–	–	–	–
	7	1.0	1.7	2.8	4.0	6.7	8.1	–	–	–	–	–	–
	8	1.0	1.8	2.8	4.8	7.0	11.8	18.1	–	–	–	–	–
	9	1.0	1.7	2.7	4.1	5.9	7.8	10.0	23.4	–	–	–	–
	10	1.0	1.7	2.8	3.6	6.2	12.9	13.3	20.2	28.8	–	–	–
	11	1.0	1.7	2.7	4.0	6.8	10.8	16.7	21.9	23.5	34.3	–	–
	12	1.0	1.8	2.8	4.2	7.3	11.1	14.7	20.5	30.4	31.4	30.5	–
	13	1.0	1.7	2.8	4.1	5.4	10.5	11.4	16.7	19.2	33.6	25.4	69.8

Tables 3 and 4 compare the results to two experiments in a previous paper [14]. The main experiments in the current paper (Deep LGF + ES) varied from the experiments in this earlier paper (Random Forest LGF + Hillclimbing) in two main ways. Firstly, the models were trained using a random forest classifier (the implementation in the *scikit-learn* package [2]). The tables give the results for models trained on examples with up to 13 moves. Secondly, the unscrambling in the earlier paper was based on a simple hill-climbing approach rather than the ES used in this paper.

These tables also contain a comparison with a baseline experiment also described in detail in the earlier paper [14] (Error + Hillclimbing). This also uses a simple hill-climbing method, but the choice of moves is made by choosing the move that maximises the number of correct facelets. This is more similar to a traditional error-based fitness function.

It is notable that the percentage of successes in the *Deep LGF + ES* approach is considerably higher than the *Random Forest LGF + Hillclimbing* approach. However, the length of the solutions found by the new approach is much larger for larger problem sizes. This may well reflect the use of reinitialisation in the latter approach; in the earlier paper, a search that did not terminate was considered a failure. Both methods clearly outperform the traditional error-based fitness measure, demonstrating the value of this pre-training step.

Table 3. Comparison of three models: deep learning of LGF with evolution strategies, random forest learning of LGF and hillclimbing, and error-based fitness with hillclimbing. Percentage of runs that found the solution.

	Size of problem											
	2	3	4	5	6	7	8	9	10	11	12	13
Deep LGF + ES (this paper)	100	100	100	90	77	61	63	50	37	22	17	6
RF LGF + Hillclimbing [14]	100	100	98	75	62	45	20	17	11	9	7	0
Error + Hillclimbing [14]	62	33	24	10	4	3	2	0	0	0	1	0

5 Related Work

There are similarities between this approach and the idea of a learned value function in reinforcement learning [27]. However, the reinforcement learning approach calculates this by starting from a point in the space and working back from later successes, whereas the approach in this paper constructs trajectories by making moves back from a successful state (similar to the approach taken by McAleer et al. [19]). It would be interesting to see if this approach of backwards synthesis of trajectories could be applied to the learning of value functions in

Table 4. Comparison of three models: deep learning of LGF with evolution strategies, random forest learning of LGF and hillclimbing, and error-based fitness with hillclimbing. Average length to solution for successful runs.

	Size of problem											
	2	3	4	5	6	7	8	9	10	11	12	13
Deep LGF + ES (this paper)	1.0	1.7	2.8	4.1	5.4	10.5	11.4	16.7	19.2	33.6	25.4	69.8
RF LGF + Hillclimbing [14]	1.8	2.6	3.3	3.9	4.2	4.6	4.8	5.5	4.9	4.6	4.9	–
Error + Hillclimbing [14]	2.1	2.2	2.3	2.8	4.5	3.7	2.0	–	–	–	4.0	–

reinforcement learning. It is notable that the idea of learning from a rich set of behaviour trajectories—rather than just from a single measure of quality—is becoming more prominent in machine learning, for example in the work by Bojarski et al. [5] on self-driving cars which learn from examples of human driving.

In the metaheuristics literature the idea of learning from a set of already-solved problems is explored in the idea of *target analysis* [9]. This takes a set of solved problems from a problem class, and uses those known solutions to set the parameters of a metaheuristic. This is different to our approach in that it still relies on the metaheuristic operators to avoid local optima in the landscape, whereas the approach in this paper uses those already-solved problems to construct a new landscape based on a metric which is designed to have fewer such local optima. The idea of learning a metric from a large set of examples is explored in the literature on metric learning [18], and it would be interesting to explore further connections between metric learning and the idea of constructing new fitness functions.

It should be noted that there are algorithms specifically for solving the Rubik's Cube, as summarised in the book by Slocum et al. [24]. However, comparisons with these are less relevant to this paper, which was using the Rubik's Cube as an example to see whether a learning algorithm could learn naïvely from it. The importance of these methods that can learn without explicit human knowledge has been emphasised as an important route towards artificial general intelligence [22].

6   Summary and Future Work

We have introduced the idea of deep learning for learned guidance functions, and shown how these can then be used as fitness drivers in evolutionary computation. This has been applied to a case study of solving a Rubik's Cube, and shown to have a advantages in terms of frequency of finding a solution and the size of the models needed when compared to a random forest-based LGF; however, the number of generations needed is, for more complex problems, larger. It would be interesting to explore the comparative impact of the deep learning aspects and the evolutionary computation aspects by doing more experiments that use these two separately.

There are a number of areas for future work. Firstly, there is much of scope for optimising the deep learning system using automated machine learning approaches both to optimise the parameters and the structure of the system [13]. Secondly, there are a number of further experiments that would investigate the behaviour further: investigating the frequency of and impact of the reinitialisation in this method, using measures of landscape smoothness to understand the effect of the LGF on the landscape, and experimenting with different population sizes. Finally, there are a large number of other problems to which this approach could be applied, e.g. protein folding, and de-noising of audio and video files.

References

1. Keras: The python deep learning library. http://keras.io/. Accessed Jan 2019
2. scikit-learn: Machine learning in python. http://scikit-learn.org/. Accessed Jan 2019
3. Tensorflow: An open source machine learning framework for everyone. http://www.tensorflow.org/. Accessed Jan 2019
4. Asselmeyer, T., Ebeling, W., Rosé, H.: Smoothing representation of fitness landscapes — the genotype-phenotype map of evolution. Biosystems **39**(1), 63–76 (1996)
5. Bojarski, M., et al.: End to end learning for self-driving cars. CoRR abs/1604.07316 (2016). http://arxiv.org/abs/1604.07316
6. Culberson, J., Schaeffer, J.: Pattern databases. Comput. Intell. **14**(3), 318–334 (1998)
7. Dobson, C.M.: Protein folding and misfolding. Nature **426**, 884–890 (2003)
8. Erez, T., Smart, W.D.: What does shaping mean for computational reinforcement learning? In: 2008 7th IEEE International Conference on Development and Learning, pp. 215–219 (2008)
9. Glover, F., Greenberg, H.: New approaches for heuristic search: a bilateral linkage with artificial intelligence. Eur. J. Oper. Res. **39**(2), 119–130 (1989)
10. Goodfellow, I., Bengio, Y., Courville, A.: Deep Learning. MIT Press, Cambridge (2017)
11. Grefenstette, J.: Optimization of control parameters for genetic algorithms. IEEE Trans. Syst. Man Cybern. **16**, 122–128 (1986)
12. Hopgood, A.A., Mierzejewska, A.: Transform ranking: a new method of fitness scaling in genetic algorithms. In: Bramer, M., Petridis, M., Coenen, F. (eds.) SGAI 2008, pp. 349–354. Springer, London (2009). https://doi.org/10.1007/978-1-84882-171-2_26
13. Hutter, F., Kotthoff, L., Vanschoren, J.: AutoML: Methods, Systems, Challenges (2019). Book in preparation. Current draft at https://www.automl.org/book/. Accessed July 2019
14. Johnson, C.G.: Solving the Rubik's Cube with learned guidance functions. In: Proceedings of the 2018 IEEE Symposium Series in Computational Intelligence. IEEE Press (2018)
15. Krawiec, K.: Behavioural Program Synthesis with Genetic Programming. Springer, Cham (2016). https://doi.org/10.1007/978-3-319-27565-9
16. Krawiec, K., Swan, J., O'Reilly, U.M.: Behavioral program synthesis: insights and prospects. In: Riolo, R., Worzel, W., Kotanchek, M., Kordon, A. (eds.) Genetic Programming Theory and Practice XIII. GEVO, pp. 169–183. Springer, Cham (2016). https://doi.org/10.1007/978-3-319-34223-8_10
17. Kreinovich, V., Quintana, C., Fuentes, O.: Genetic algorithms: what fitness scaling is optimal? Cybern. Syst. **24**, 9–26 (1993)
18. Kulis, B.: Metric learning: a survey. Found. Trends® Mach. Learn. **5**(4), 287–364 (2013). https://doi.org/10.1561/2200000019
19. McAleer, S., Agostinelli, F., Shmakov, A., Baldi, P.: Solving the Rubik's Cube Without Human Knowledge. ArXiv e-prints, May 2018
20. Samadi, M., Felner, A., Schaeffer, J.: Learning from multiple heuristics. In: Proceedings of Association for the Advancement of Artificial Intelligence (AAAI-08), pp. 357–362 (2008)

21. Moraglio, A., Krawiec, K., Johnson, C.G.: Geometric semantic genetic programming. In: Coello, C.A.C., Cutello, V., Deb, K., Forrest, S., Nicosia, G., Pavone, M. (eds.) PPSN 2012, Part I. LNCS, vol. 7491, pp. 21–31. Springer, Heidelberg (2012). https://doi.org/10.1007/978-3-642-32937-1_3

22. Silver, D., et al.: Mastering the game of go without human knowledge. Nature 550(7676), 354–359 (2017). https://doi.org/10.1038/nature24270

23. Singmaster, D.: Notes on Rubik's Magic Cube. Enslow Publishing, Hillside (1981)

24. Slocum, J., et al.: The Cube: The Ultimate Guide to the World's Best-Selling Puzzle. Black Dog and Leventhal, New York (2011)

25. Srivastava, N., Hinton, G., Krizhevsky, A., Sutskever, I., Salakhutdinov, R.: Dropout: a simple way to prevent neural networks from overfitting. J. Mach. Learn. Res. 15(1), 1929–1958 (2014)

26. Sturtevant, N.R., Felner, A., Barrer, M., Schaeffer, J., Burch, N.: Memory-based heuristics for explicit state spaces. In: Proceedings of the 21st International Joint Conference on Artifical Intelligence, IJCAI 2009, pp. 609–614, Morgan Kaufmann Publishers Inc. (2009)

27. Sutton, R.S., Barto, A.G.: Reinforcement Learning: An Introduction. MIT Press, Cambridge (1998)

28. Szubert, M., Jaśkowski, W., Liskowski, P., Krawiec, K.: Shaping fitness function for evolutionary learning of game strategies. In: Proceedings of the 15th Annual Conference on Genetic and Evolutionary Computation, pp. 1149–1156. ACM (2013)

29. Vanneschi, L., Castelli, M., Manzoni, L., Silva, S.: A new implementation of geometric semantic GP and its application to problems in pharmacokinetics. In: Krawiec, K., Moraglio, A., Hu, T., Etaner-Uyar, A.Ş., Hu, B. (eds.) EuroGP 2013. LNCS, vol. 7831, pp. 205–216. Springer, Heidelberg (2013). https://doi.org/10.1007/978-3-642-37207-0_18

30. Ware, J.M., Wilson, I.D., Ware, J.A.: A Knowledge based genetic algorithm approach to automating cartographic generalisation. In: Macintosh, A., Ellis, R., Coenen, F. (eds.) Applications and Innovations in Intelligent Systems X, pp. 33–49. Springer, London (2003). https://doi.org/10.1007/978-1-4471-0649-4_3

31. Widera, P., Garibaldi, J.M., Krasnogor, N.: GP challenge: evolving energy function for protein structure prediction. Genet. Program. Evolvable Mach. 11(1), 61–88 (2010)

Monotonicity Detection and Enforcement in Longitudinal Classification

Sergey Ovchinnik[✉], Fernando E. B. Otero, and Alex A. Freitas

School of Computing, University of Kent, Canterbury, UK
{S.Ovchinnik,F.E.B.Otero,A.A.Freitas}@kent.ac.uk

Abstract. Longitudinal datasets contain repeated measurements of the same variables at different points in time, which can be used by researchers to discover useful knowledge based on the changes of the data over time. Monotonic relations often occur in real-world data and need to be preserved in data mining models in order for the models to be acceptable by users. We propose a new methodology for detecting monotonic relations in longitudinal datasets and applying them in longitudinal classification model construction. Two different approaches were used to detect monotonic relations and include them into the classification task. The proposed approaches are evaluated using data from the English Longitudinal Study of Ageing (ELSA) with 10 different age-related diseases used as class variables to be predicted. A gradient boosting algorithm (XGBoost) is used for constructing classification models in two scenarios: enforcing and not enforcing the constraints. The results show that enforcement of monotonicity constraints can consistently improve the predictive accuracy of the constructed models. The produced models are fully monotonic according to the monotonicity constraints, which can have a positive impact on model acceptance in real world applications.

1 Introduction

Longitudinal data mining is a branch of data mining that is concerned with longitudinal datasets, where repeated measurements of the same variables are taken at different points in time. Such datasets can provide deeper insight into the nature of the data being explored and thus can be used to construct predictive models that not only take into account the individual attribute values, but also the changes that occurred in those values over time and general time-based trends. Longitudinal data mining is becoming increasingly important in the context of human ageing research (the target domain in this work) with more and more datasets becoming available [10,17].

Monotonic relations are relations between attributes in data that occur when the value of one attribute always changes in the same direction (increasing or decreasing) as the value of another does (or stays the same). Monotonic relations often represent natural dependencies or correlations that occur in data, such as a relation between a patient's blood cholesterol level and probability of chronic heart disease.

© Springer Nature Switzerland AG 2019
M. Bramer and M. Petridis (Eds.): SGAI-AI 2019, LNAI 11927, pp. 63–77, 2019.
https://doi.org/10.1007/978-3-030-34885-4_5

Monotonicity constraints are the most common domain constraints used in model construction and can have a significant effect on both the comprehensibility and the acceptability of a model [11]. While it is possible for monotonic constraints to improve the predictive accuracy of the model by improving generalization [3,8], some practical experiments have shown the opposite effect [2].

There are currently many examples in the literature of longitudinal data mining methodologies [16] and many examples of use of monotonic relations in data mining [4]. There is, however, no example of the two approaches being used together in a single study. In this paper we propose a new methodology that automatically detects monotonic relations in longitudinal data and uses these in the construction of a longitudinal classification model. The proposed methodology utilises the longitudinal nature of the data by detecting monotonic relations that occur within individuals across different time points, which is a type of monotonic relation unexplored in the literature.

The dataset used in this study was created from data of the English Longitudinal Study of Ageing (ELSA) [7]. The attributes used were mainly from the "Nurse Visit" section of ELSA, representing various health-related measurements across four time points (referred to as "Waves" in ELSA). The class attributes used in this study were binary attributes representing whether an individual had a particular age-related disease. Ten age-related diseases were used as class attributes to be predicted, and were addressed as ten separate classification problems. A series of experiments was run using each of the classification problems to determine the effects of adding the proposed monotonicity detection approaches on the predictive accuracies of the constructed models.

The remainder of this paper is organized as follows. Section 2 presents the background on longitudinal classification, monotonic classification, and the XGBoost classification algorithm used in this work. Section 3 describes the experimental methodology and dataset creation. Section 4 reports the results obtained by using the proposed methods to detect monotonicity constraints that are exploited by the XGBoost algorithm, a state-of-the-art classification algorithm. Finally, Sect. 5 presents our conclusions and suggests future work.

2   Background

2.1   Longitudinal Classification

In recent years, a number of approaches for longitudinal classification were proposed. So far, most longitudinal classification studies use conventional non-longitudinal classification algorithms and rely heavily on data pre-processing algorithms that transform the longitudinal datasets to allow conventional algorithms to be used for class prediction [16].

A recent study by Zhang et al. [19] used a conventional non-longitudinal decision tree algorithm to make predictions based on longitudinal data. Their approach used a data pre-processing algorithm that combined the data from two consecutive waves into a single dataset, disregarding the time indexes of the features. A C5.0 decision tree classifier was built to predict the value of the class attribute in the first of the two waves using predictor attributes from both waves. A similar approach was used earlier by Mo et al. [12] where data from two waves was merged and the class attribute from the first wave was predicted using the predictor attributes of the second wave. The study used five non-longitudinal classification algorithms to build prediction models and evaluated their performance.

Niemann et al. [13] proposed an approach for longitudinal classification that used a pre-processing step to cluster all data instances based on their attribute values and generated new predictor attributes based on cluster data. After the clustering is completed and cluster data is added to every instance in each wave, the dataset is transformed by combining all waves into a single dataset, similarly to the two previous studies, omitting the time indexes. A number of non-longitudinal classification algorithms are used to construct the classification models and evaluate their performance.

Overall, the longitudinal classification literature is dominated by studies using data pre-processing methods to transform the longitudinal data to allow the use of conventional non-longitudinal classification algorithms. It is interesting to note that there is no example in the literature of a longitudinal classification approach enforcing monotonicity constraints.

2.2   Monotonic Classification

In recent years, many new monotonic classification algorithms have been developed, using various approaches to monotonicity enforcement [4].

Some applications use data pre-processing approaches to make the training data fully monotonic. This is done by relabeling the input dataset to enforce full monotonicity according to pre-defined monotonicity constraints. A set of algorithms for monotonic dataset relabeling was described by Pijls and Potharst [14]. The *Naive Relabel* is a greedy algorithm for relabeling datasets that produces fully monotonic outputs, but does not guarantee an optimal solution to the relabeling problem. The *Borders* algorithm is an extension of Naive Relabel that minimises the differences between the new and original labels and uses a simpler approach for selecting the new label values. The *Antichain* algorithm is a further extension to the Borders algorithm that minimises the total number of relabelings by constructing a monotonicity violation graph and finding the maximum antichain in it. The Antichain approach produces a fully monotonic dataset with a minimal number of relabelings.

Duivesteijn and Fielders [8] proposed an algorithm for monotonic classification based on the k-nearest neighbors (kNN) classification algorithm. The proposed Monotone kNN (MkNN) algorithm uses a procedure for re-labeling the instances in the training set to ensure full monotonicity before the kNN model is created. The algorithm used a monotonicity violation graph (MVG) as a representation of all instances within the training set and the ordinal relations between them. The graph is then used to determine the optimal set of instances to be re-labeled and the relabeling step is done. The authors argue that since the kNN algorithm uses the training data as classification model, monotonising the training data at the pre-processing step is sufficient to produce a fully monotonic classification algorithm. Overall, monotonicity enforcement has improved the predictive accuracy of the kNN classifiers and a positive effect on model acceptability was suggested.

Some applications use model post-processing approaches to alter the model trained on non-monotonic data to make the model fully monotonic. This is done by altering the model after the training is completed to enforce full monotonicity in the output of the model. Verbeke et al. [18] proposed a post-processing algorithm to create rule-based and tree-based models. The proposed RUle LEarning of ordinal classification with Monotonicity constraints (RULEM) algorithm can guarantee full monotonicity of the constructed model by applying post-processing changes to any model constructed by a decision tree or rule induction classification algorithm. It evaluates the monotonicity of a rule set by generating a decision grid based on the rules and evaluating the Conflict score (C-score) of each cell on the grid and detects monotonicity violations. It then adds complementary rules to the rule set to resolve the monotonicity violations. The results of the experiments indicate that the proposed approach preserves the predictive power of the original rule induction techniques while guaranteeing monotone classification, at the cost of a small increase in the size of the rule set.

There is a small number of approaches that incorporate monotonic constraints on the model construction stage, thus using the monotonic constraints in training and producing fully monotonic models based on non-monotonic data and some pre-defined constraints. Zhu et al. [20] proposed a neural network-based monotonic classification algorithm, called Monotonic Classification Extreme Learning Machine (MCELM). The proposed algorithm is an extension of Extreme Learning Machine (ELM) [9]—a single hidden layer feed-forward neural network learning algorithm. The proposed algorithm approaches the classification model construction task as a quadratic programming problem, where the training error rate is used as the objective for optimisation. The algorithm can ensure that the model produced by ELM is fully monotonic and does not require training data to be fully monotonic. A similar approach was taken by Chen and Li [5] using a Support Vector Machine (SVM)-based classification algorithm. In this study, a Monotonicity Constrained Support Vector Machine (MC-SVM) classification algorithm was proposed for monotonic classification of financial credit rating data. It uses a quadratic programming approach in a similar fashion to MCELM, and approaches the classifier construction as an optimisation problem with pre-defined monotonicity constraints being added as conditions to the problem. This approach produces fully monotonic models but has the drawback of requiring a fully monotonic set of training data.

2.3   Monotonicity Measures

There are two main monotonicity measures that can be used for estimating monotonicity in datasets and classification models: Non-Monotonicity Index (NMI) and Spearman's rank correlation coefficient.

The Non-Monotonicity Index (NMI) is a monotonicity measure originally introduced for determining the degree of monotonicity that a decision tree model exhibits in relation to a pre-defined set of monotonic constraints [1]. NMI is a measure of how "non-monotonic" a given set of examples is in relation to a certain monotonic constraint (or a set of constraints). In the original paper, the measure was used to compare pair-wise all paths from the root to the leaves of a decision tree and calculate the proportion of such pairs that violated a pre-defined set of constraints. NMI is defined as a measure that ranges between 0 and 1, where low values (around 0) represent strong monotonic relations, middle values (around 0.5) represent no monotonic relation, and high values (around 1) represent an inverted monotonic relation that is the opposite of the one being evaluated.

The monotonic relation between two attribute value pairs (x_i, y_i) and (x_j, y_j) is evaluated using the following function, which takes the value 1 if the two attribute pairs contradict the monotonic relation and 0 otherwise:

$$non\_monotonic((x_i, y_i), (x_j, y_j)) \tag{1}$$

For example, if the positive monotonic relation is estimated, then the two value pairs $(1, 6)$ and $(4, 8)$ would have $non\_monotonic$ value of 0, while two value pairs $(1, 6)$ and $(4, 2)$ would have $non\_monotonic$ value of 1. NMI can then be estimated using the following formula:

$$NMI = \frac{\sum_{i=1}^{k} \sum_{j=1}^{k} non\_monotonic((x_i, y_i), (x_j, y_j))}{k \times (k - 1)} \tag{2}$$

where k is the number of instances, $i \neq j$.

The Spearman's rank correlation coefficient is a mathematical measure that estimates how well the relationship between two variables can be described using a monotonic function. It assesses the degree of the correlation between two variables by first converting each variable to a ranked variable. It then applies the Pearson's correlation coefficient to the two ranked variables to estimate the degree of linear correlation between them.

The Pearson's correlation coefficient is estimated using the covariance of two attributes X and Y divided by the product of their standard deviations (σ_X and σ_Y).

$$Pearson_{X,Y} = \frac{cov(X, Y)}{\sigma_X \times \sigma_Y} \tag{3}$$

While the NMI monotonicity measure was used in a large portion of monotonic classification studies, Spearman is currently under-explored by the monotonic classification literature despite being the main mathematical measure for estimating the monotonic relation between two variables.

2.4 The XGBoost Tree Boosting Algorithm

XGBoost is a highly accurate, scalable tree boosting system that uses the gradient boosting approach with tree-based classifiers serving as weak learners [6].

XGBoost has become a popular approach for data mining in recent years with many studies conducted using it as the main machine learning tool.

XGBoost supports monotonicity constraint enforcement during model construction, which allows users to add monotonic constraints to a set of predictor attributes to produce models that follow those constraints. The constraints are enforced during the model construction using a simple yet effective method of restricting the output values of the branches following a split on a constrained attribute. Using this approach, XGBoost can guarantee that after the value on an attribute is checked against the threshold, the outputs of all leaf nodes under the left branch will always be lower than outputs of all leaf nodes under the right branch, thus ensuring full monotonicity of the model. XGBoost always produces a fully monotonic model without requiring any data pre-processing steps to be taken, making it applicable to large non-monotonic datasets.

XGBoost has a built-in method for handling missing values in data. During the construction of tree models, each split in the tree has a default direction assigned for the instances where the attribute being split has no value. This allows the XGBoost algorithm to effectively classify instances with missing values by simply making default decisions where a value test can not be performed. This property is especially important when working with ELSA data, since it contains a large amount of missing attribute values.

XGBoost is highly customisable and allows creation of boosted models with any number of tree classifiers, and the maximum size of tree classifiers can be adjusted. XGBoost can be used for both regression and classification problems with minor parameter adjustments. Although XGBoost uses a combination of weak classification models and produces a non-interpretable ensemble model, it has a built-in measure of attribute importance which can be accessed directly form the model. This provides an insight on which attributes are involved in the predictions and scores them based on their impact.

3   Methodology

3.1   Quantitative Measures for Monotonicity Detection

Two quantitative measures are used in the proposed approach to evaluate the strength of monotonic relations between attributes: the Non-Monotonicity Index (NMI) and the Spearman's correlation coefficient.

Despite being originally developed as a measure for evaluating the degree of monotonicity of predictive models, NMI has also proven useful in detecting monotonic relations in data. In data, a similar approach can be taken by comparing the data instances pair-wise and calculating the proportion of those that violate an assumed monotonicity constraint. In the task of full monotonicity detection, the detection algorithm can be used to iterate through possible monotonic relations in the data and then estimate the value of NMI to asses if those relations exist.

Since in this study we are only concerned with monotonic relations between pairs of attributes where one attribute is the class, a full monotonicity scan only requires the monotonicity detection algorithm to iterate through all pairs between predictor attributes and the class in a dataset and estimate the strength of their monotonic relation using NMI. Thus, a dataset with n predictor attributes would only require n NMI estimations.

NMI serves as a good monotonicity detection measure in many cases, but it has a flaw that causes it to become unusable in some cases. NMI always has to assume that a pair of examples is monotonic if the values of at least one attribute in a pair are equal. For example, the attribute pairs $(1, 6), (1, 3)$ and $(1, 12)$ would all be considered monotonic with each other since the value of the first attribute is the same. This causes no trouble on numeric attributes with barely any repeating values, but can have a huge impact on attributes with small domain space (e.g. binary attributes) and attributes that have many repeated values. Since NMI has to make an assumption that two examples with repeated attribute value are monotonic, it can not accurately estimate monotonicity when one or both attributes are largely dominated by a frequent repeated value. For example, a binary attribute that has 95% positive values and 5% negative values will always have very low NMI even when it is estimated against random noise.

As a solution for this issue, we propose an Entropy-Adjusted Non-Monotonicity Index (EANMI). It uses an entropy-based coefficient to adjust the monotonicity measure and increase the degree of non-monotonicity for the attributes that are largely dominated by a single value (and thus have low entropy). The adjustment uses the entropy of an attribute and the maximum entropy of the attribute. The maximum entropy is estimated as the maximum entropy an attribute can have, provided it has the same domain of values. For each pair of a predictor attribute x and the class attribute y, the adjustment is made only for x (considering that y is fixed as the second attribute in all attribute pairs used for monotonicity detection).

$$Entropy(X) = -\sum_{i=1}^{n} P(x_i) \times log_2 P(x_i) \tag{4}$$

$$Max\_Entropy(X) = log_2(n) \tag{5}$$

$$EANMI_{X,Y} = 1 - (1 - NMI_{X,Y}) \times \frac{Entropy(X)}{Max\_Entropy(X)} \tag{6}$$

where n is the number of unique values of x, x_i is the ith unique value of X, $P(x_i)$ is the relative frequency (empirical probability) of value x_i.

The Spearman's correlation coefficient can also be used as a monotonicity estimation measure using the same approach of estimating the strength of monotonic relation between two attributes in a dataset. Since it only estimates the strength of the linear correlation between ranked values of the attributes, no additional adjustment is required.

3.2   The Proposed Longitudinal Monotonicity Detection Approaches

Two longitudinal monotonicity techniques are used in this project:

- **Timeless** monotonicity detection is a method for detecting general trends occurring between attributes in the data. This approach ignores the longitudinal aspect of the dataset and combines all data entries from different waves into a single non-longitudinal dataset. It can then detect monotonic relations between attributes in the resulting dataset. This approach can detect strong correlations in data that occur regardless of time and individual effects. It is intended to be used iterating through all attribute pairs to provide a full insight into monotonic relations that occur in the dataset, although in the context of classification, only the attribute pairs containing the class attribute are of interest. A natural language example of such relation can be: "The higher a patient's blood sugar levels are, the higher their likelihood of diabetes is".
- **Time-Index Based Individual-wise (TIBI)** monotonicity detection is a method for detecting the time-based attribute trends that occur in measurements taken for a certain individual. This approach takes the different values of an attribute across time for each individual and estimates how those values have changed over time. It can provide an insight into time-based trends a certain individual may have and the strength measures of the monotonic relations can be used as additional predictive attributes. In a monotonicity detection task, it is intended to be used iterating through all individuals and all longitudinal attributes to cover all possible relations of this type. A natural language example of such relation can be: "Individual 12345 has their blood sugar levels steadily increasing over time". Note that this method ignores the class labels of examples and requires the data to be present for at least three waves in order to be significant.

3.3   Datasets

The dataset used in these experiments was constructed using biomedical data from ELSA [7]. Predictive attributes were created from the "Nurse Visit" data portion of the ELSA database. Most attributes use raw values of ELSA variables representing various patient health measurements such as blood test results and physical performance tests. There are 10 class attributes, each containing binary values representing either the presence or absence of a certain age-related disease in the final wave (Wave 8 in these experiments). A separate classification problem was constructed for each class attribute. Since most of these attributes in ELSA are only recorded on even numbered waves, only the data from waves 2, 4, 6 and 8 was used. A full description of attributes used and their meaning can be found in a related study that previously used the same data preparation techniques in the context of automatic feature selection [15].

The 10 classification problems used for experiments each contained records for 7097 individuals participating in the ELSA study. Each instance contains 143 attribute values in total (considering different values of an attribute across all waves) and a single class label. The 10 classification problems are presented in Table 1 along with the proportion of positive class values (presence of the disease) in each problem.

Table 1. Frequencies of positive class values

Class attribute	Number of positive instances	Frequency
Angina	258	3.64%
Arthritis	3021	42.57%
Cataract	2322	32.72%
Dementia	148	2.09%
Diabetes	946	13.33%
High blood pressure	2854	40.21%
Heart attack	401	5.65%
Osteoporosis	654	9.22%
Parkinson's	66	0.93%
Stroke	421	5.93%

3.4 Experimental Setup

For each of the classification problems described in the previous section, a separate set of experiments was conducted, thus producing separate results for each class attribute used. Each set of experiments consisted of four separate experiments:

- One was performed on the baseline dataset without any changes (Baseline experiment).
- One experiment which included detection of Timeless monotonic relations using Entropy-Adjusted NMI (EANMI). Only the relations between the class attribute and all other attributes were used. The entropy adjustment was only made for each predictor (non-class) attribute. Only strong monotonicity constraints (with EANMI < 0.15, a threshold determined in preliminary experiments) were used as monotonicity constraints for the XGBoost algorithm.
- One experiment was performed with an addition of TIBI attributes representing monotonic trends in values of longitudinal attributes between waves. The TIBI attributes were detected using the Spearman's correlation coefficient.
- The final experiment introduced both the TIBI attributes and Timeless monotonic constraints. It is important to note that the Timeless constraints were introduced after the TIBI attributes were added, thus allowing those attributes to be considered for constraints as well.

During each experiment, a well-known 10-fold cross-validation approach was used to estimate the average accuracy of the XGBoost model built using the created dataset and monotonicity constraints if any (depending on the experiment). In order to get a reliable estimation of average predictive accuracy of the models, the cross validation process was repeated 30 times (using different random seeds for cross validation) and the average predictive accuracy was measured. The predictive accuracy measure used in model training and evaluation was area under ROC curve. In all experiments, the following parameters were used for XGBoost: num_round=10, max_depth=10, objective="binary:logistic", eval_metric="auc", eta=1.0. The parameter values were selected based on parameter descriptions in the XGBoost documentation; no attempt was made to optimise the parameters for this specific task.

4   Results of the Experiments and Comparative Analysis

4.1   Predictive Accuracies of Constructed Models

The results for the four sets of experiments over the ten classification problems were collected. Table 2 shows the average area under ROC curve ($\overline{\text{AUROC}}$) values for each set of experiments. In addition, the average rank value for each monotonicity type combination is included.

Table 2. $\overline{\text{AUROC}}$ values for each set of experiments. The highest $\overline{\text{AUROC}}$ value for each dataset is shown in bold.

Class attribute	Baseline	Timeless	TIBI	TIBI+Timeless
Angina	0.545	**0.682**	0.660	0.668
Arthritis	0.610	0.610	0.610	**0.611**
Cataract	**0.655**	**0.655**	**0.655**	**0.655**
Dementia	0.755	**0.767**	0.750	0.758
Diabetes	0.825	**0.829**	0.824	**0.829**
High blood pressure	**0.704**	**0.704**	**0.704**	**0.704**
Heart attack	0.679	0.696	0.688	**0.698**
Osteoporosis	0.666	**0.677**	0.664	0.670
Parkinson's	0.575	**0.621**	0.578	0.606
Stroke	0.666	**0.681**	0.673	0.680
Average rank	3.3	1.65	3.2	1.85

Table 3. Results of the Friedman test with post-hoc Holm test. Statistically significant results at the 5% significance level are shown in bold, indicating that the result of a particular approach is statistically significantly worse than the control approach.

Approach	Average rank	p-value	Holm
Timeless (Control)	1.65	-	-
Timeless+TIBI	1.85	0.729	0.05
TIBI	**3.2**	**0.007**	**0.025**
Baseline	**3.3**	**0.004**	**0.017**

From Table 2 we can see that the introduction of monotonicity constraints led to an improvement of the AUROC or had no substantial negative effect across all classification problems. Both approaches enforcing monotonicity constraints (Timeless and TIBI+Timeless) achieved the best rankings. The use of monotonicity-based TIBI attributes alone had no significant effects.

Further statistical analysis was performed on the $\overline{\text{AUROC}}$ rankings, where Table 3 shows the results of the non-parametric Friedman test with the Holm post-hoc test—statistically significant differences at the 5% significance level are shown in bold. Both TIBI and Baseline approaches are statistically significantly worse than Timeless, the combination with the best ranking (control).

Table 4. Average number [standard deviation] of Timeless monotonicity constraints used by XGBoost per classification problem

Class attribute	Number of constraints
Angina	65.0 [0.50]
Arthritis	0.003 [0.005]
Cataract	0.0 [0.0]
Dementia	73.06 [0.50]
Diabetes	20.12 [0.39]
High blood pressure	0.0 [0.0]
Heart attack	61.89 [0.50]
Osteoporosis	39.42 [0.46]
Parkinson's	80.87 [0.49]
Stroke	61.61 [0.50]

4.2   Monotonicity Constraints and Their Effects on Model Sizes

Monotonic relations were detected separately in each training set prior to the experiments and then used as monotonicity constraints during model construction. The results have shown that no monotonic relations were detected between TIBI attributes and the class in any of the TIBI experiments. Table 4 shows the average number of monotonicity constraints used by XGBoost for each of the classification problems as well as the corresponding standard deviation (over all training sets produced by cross-validation iterations with different random seeds) of each measurement.

It can bee seen from the Table 4 that some classification problems used a large number of monotonicity constraints while others used none at all. Standard deviations remain very low for each measurement, meaning that there was only a small variation in number of detected constraints between different training sets.

The number of constraints can be correlated to the percentage of positive class labels in each dataset as shown in Table 1. Generally, the classification problems that used class attributes with lower number of positive class labels had a larger number of monotonic constraints. The reason for this trend may be related to the adjustment used by EANMI, which took into account the entropies of predictor attributes but not the entropy of the class. Therefore, class attributes with lower entropy generally had a high chance of having a strong monotonic relation ($EANMI < 0.15$) and thus had more monotonic constraints.

The average model sizes were measured for each of the experiments to determine the effect of introduction of monotonic approaches to the classification task. Overall, the introduction of both Timeless monotonicity constraints and TIBI attributes resulted in a small decrease in model size across all experiments. The decrease was consistent across all classification problems, yet not very significant: Introduction of Timeless constraints decreased the model size on average by 13% and introduction of TIBI attributes resulted in a 2% decrease in average model sizes. In the experiments where both approaches were used, the model size effects were similar to that of just using Timeless constraints.

4.3 Feature Importance

The average feature importance was estimated for each feature in each experiment using the built-in feature importance measure of XGBoost (based on average predictive accuracy increase) and the most important features were analysed. The results were sensible in most experiments: in Diabetes experiments the most important features were patient blood glucose levels; in HBP experiments the blood pressure features were most important; blood cholesterol levels had high importance in the Angina, Heart Attack and Stroke experiments. In most experiments, the age feature was among the top five most important features and the sex feature generally had a high feature importance in all models.

Interestingly, some of the TIBI features achieved very high feature importance in some of the TIBI experiments. In the Cataract experiments, the TIBI feature for diastolic blood pressure has achieved 4th highest feature importance; the TIBI feature for blood total cholesterol level had high importance in Heart Attack and Stroke TIBI experiments, and in the Heart Attack experiment with TIBI+Timeless approach it was the most important feature.

Some categorical ordinal attributes were also highly important in classification models constructed using training sets with TIBI features. In the Angina experiments, the TIBI feature for the outcome of side-by-side stand test was the feature with the highest average importance; a TIBI feature of a binary feature representing whether the patient had any respiratory infection in the last 3 weeks was the 4th most important feature in Heart Attack TIBI experiments.

Table 5 shows the features that achieved high feature importance in the constructed models across all experiments for a given class. The features in bold were often detected as being monotonic with the class and were used as monotonic constraints in Timeless and TIBI+Timeless experiments.

Table 5. High-importance features for each classification problem. The features that were constrained by Timeless constraints are displayed in bold.

Class attribute	Common features
Angina	**Age, Arterial pressure, Cholesterol level,** Chair rises*, Side-by-side stands*
Arthritis	Age, Chair raises*, Leg raises*, Main hand grip*, Hip measurement
Cataract	Age, Leg raises with eyes open*, Diastolic blood pressure
Dementia	**Age,** Clotting disorder, **Blood ferritin level, Grip strength***
Diabetes	Fasting blood glucose level, **LDL cholesterol level, Waist measurement**
High blood pressure	Age, Systolic blood pressure, Diastolic blood pressure
Heart attack	**Cholesterol level, LDL cholesterol level, Arterial pressure**
Osteoporosis	**Age, Main hand grip*, Weight**
Parkinsons	Blood fibrinogen level, **White blood cell count, Non-dominant hand grip***
Stroke	**Age, Cholesterol level, LDL cholesterol level,**

*Outcomes of physical exercise tests

5 Conclusion

A set of experiments was conducted using the proposed monotonicity detection approaches and their effect on the predictive accuracies of the constructed classification models was evaluated. Enforcement of monotonicity constraints detected using the proposed Entropy Adjusted Non-Monotonicity Index was shown to generally result in a significant improvement of the predictive accuracy of the model without any significant negative effects. The addition of Time-Index Based Individual-wise (TIBI) monotonic attributes was shown to have a very minor effect on the constructed models. TIBI attributes, despite being frequently used in some classification models, were not detected as being monotonic with the class attributes and thus have not been used as monotonicity constrained attributes in any of the models.

Overall, our approach used the longitudinal dataset to make class predictions and effectively detected and enforced monotonicity constraints. The proposed approach for automatic monotonicity detection in datasets and enforcement in classification models worked well in this context, but further studies are needed to determine the optimal monotonicity detection approach and to define methodologies for longitudinal monotonicity detection more appropriate for general use. Additionally, it would be interesting to evaluate the use of the entropy adjustment on the class attribute to cope with class imbalance.

References

1. Ben-David, A.: Monotonicity maintenance in information-theoretic machine learning algorithms. Mach. Learn. **19**(1), 29–43 (1995). https://doi.org/10.1023/a:1022655006810
2. Ben-David, A., Sterling, L., Tran, T.: Adding monotonicity to learning algorithms may impair their accuracy. Expert Syst. Appl. **36**(3), 6627–6634 (2009). https://doi.org/10.1016/j.eswa.2008.08.021
3. Brookhouse, J., Otero, F.E.B.: Monotonicity in ant colony classification algorithms. In: Dorigo, M., et al. (eds.) ANTS 2016. LNCS, vol. 9882, pp. 137–148. Springer, Cham (2016). https://doi.org/10.1007/978-3-319-44427-7_12
4. Cano, J.R., Gutiérrez, P.A., Krawczyk, B., Woźniak, M., García, S.: Monotonic classification: an overview on algorithms, performance measures and data sets. Neurocomputing **341**, 168–182 (2019). https://doi.org/10.1016/j.neucom.2019.02.024
5. Chen, C.C., Li, S.T.: Credit rating with a monotonicity-constrained support vector machine model. Expert Syst. Appl. **41**(16), 7235–7247 (2014)
6. Chen, T., Guestrin, C.: XGBoost: a scalable tree boosting system. In: Proceedings of the 22nd ACM SIGKDD International Conference on Knowledge Discovery and Data Mining - KDD 2016, pp. 785–794. ACM Press (2016). https://doi.org/10.1145/2939672.2939785
7. Clemens, S., et al.: English longitudinal study of ageing: waves 0-8, 1998–2017 (2019). https://doi.org/10.5255/ukda-sn-5050-16
8. Duivesteijn, W., Feelders, A.: Nearest neighbour classification with monotonicity constraints. In: Daelemans, W., Goethals, B., Morik, K. (eds.) ECML PKDD 2008. LNCS (LNAI), vol. 5211, pp. 301–316. Springer, Heidelberg (2008). https://doi.org/10.1007/978-3-540-87479-9_38
9. Huang, G.B., Zhu, Q.Y., Siew, C.K.: Extreme learning machine: theory and applications. Neurocomputing **70**(1–3), 489–501 (2006). https://doi.org/10.1016/j.neucom.2005.12.126
10. Kaiser, A.: A review of longitudinal datasets on ageing. J. Popul. Ageing **6**(1–2), 5–27 (2013). https://doi.org/10.1007/s12062-013-9082-3
11. Martens, D., Baesens, B.: Building acceptable classification models. In: Stahlbock, R., Crone, S., Lessmann, S. (eds.) Data Mining. Annals of Information Systems, vol. 8, pp. 53–74. Springer, Boston (2009). https://doi.org/10.1007/978-1-4419-1280-0_3
12. Mo, J., Siddiqui, S., Maudsley, S., Cheung, H., Martin, B., Johnson, C.A.: Classification of Alzheimer Diagnosis from ADNI plasma biomarker data. In: Proceedings of the International Conference on Bioinformatics, Computational Biology and Biomedical Informatics - BCB 2013. ACM Press (2013)
13. Niemann, U., Hielscher, T., Spiliopoulou, M., Volzke, H., Kuhn, J.P.: Can we classify the participants of a longitudinal epidemiological study from their previous evolution? In: 2015 IEEE 28th International Symposium on Computer-Based Medical Systems. IEEE, June 2015. https://doi.org/10.1109/cbms.2015.12
14. Pijls, W., Potharst, R.: Repairing non-monotone ordinal data sets by changing class labels. Technical report, Erasmus University Rotterdam, December 2014
15. Pomsuwan, T., Freitas, A.A.: Feature selection for the classification of longitudinal human ageing data. In: 2017 IEEE International Conference on Data Mining Workshops (ICDMW). IEEE, November 2017. https://doi.org/10.1109/icdmw.2017.102

16. Ribeiro, C., Freitas, A.A.: A mini-survey of supervised machine learning approaches for coping with ageing-related longitudinal datasets. In: 3rd Workshop on AI for Aging, Rehabilitation and Independent Assisted Living (ARIAL), held as part of IJCAI-2019 (2019)

17. Ribeiro, C.E., Brito, L.H.S., Nobre, C.N., Freitas, A.A., Zárate, L.E.: A revision and analysis of the comprehensiveness of the main longitudinal studies of human aging for data mining research. Wiley Interdiscip. Rev. Data Min. Knowl. Discov. **7**(3), e1202, March 2017. https://doi.org/10.1002/widm.1202

18. Verbeke, W., Martens, D., Baesens, B.: RULEM: a novel heuristic rule learning approach for ordinal classification with monotonicity constraints. Appl. Soft Comput. **60**, 858–873 (2017). https://doi.org/10.1016/j.asoc.2017.01.042

19. Zhang, Y., Jia, H., Li, A., Liu, J., Li, H.: Study on prediction of activities of daily living of the aged people based on longitudinal data. Procedia Comput. Sci. **91**, 470–477 (2016). https://doi.org/10.1016/j.procs.2016.07.122

20. Zhu, H., Tsang, E.C., Wang, X.Z., Ashfaq, R.A.R.: Monotonic classification extreme learning machine. Neurocomputing **225**, 205–213 (2017). https://doi.org/10.1016/j.neucom.2016.11.021

Understanding Structure
of Concurrent Actions

Perusha Moodley[1]([✉])[iD], Benjamin Rosman[2,3][iD], and Xia Hong[1][iD]

[1] University of Reading, Reading, UK
perusha.moodley@pgr.reading.ac.uk
[2] University of the Witwatersrand, Johannesburg, South Africa
[3] CSIR, Johannesburg, South Africa

Abstract. Whereas most work in reinforcement learning (RL) ignores the structure or relationships between actions, in this paper we show that exploiting structure in the action space can improve sample efficiency during exploration. To show this we focus on concurrent action spaces where the RL agent selects multiple actions per timestep. Concurrent action spaces are challenging to learn in especially if the number of actions is large as this can lead to a combinatorial explosion of the action space.

This paper proposes two methods: a first approach uses implicit structure to perform high-level action elimination using task-invariant actions; a second approach looks for more explicit structure in the form of action clusters. Both methods are context-free, focusing only on an analysis of the action space and show a significant improvement in policy convergence times.

Keywords: Concurrent actions · Reinforcement learning · Structure · Action elimination · Clustering

1 Introduction

In reinforcement learning (RL) complex environments are often modelled using games such as Atari [1], Go [13] and StarCraft [16] as proxies for learning how to behave in the real world. Many of these games can handle multiple actions per time step, but most algorithms unroll the possible combinations of actions and treat each combination as an individual action (or primitive action) during learning [8,17]. This approach has been successful in many complex environments but as environments become more specialised, integrated and relevant to the real world it becomes increasingly important to learn something of the structure of the action space to improve exploration times and leverage relationships or causal patterns.

This paper looks specifically at environments where the RL agent can take multiple simultaneous discrete actions in a timestep, also referred to as concurrent action environments. These environments may apply the actions concurrently or sequentially but will return a single response to the concurrent

© Springer Nature Switzerland AG 2019
M. Bramer and M. Petridis (Eds.): SGAI-AI 2019, LNAI 11927, pp. 78–90, 2019.
https://doi.org/10.1007/978-3-030-34885-4_6

action request from the agent, for example, action set A = (jump, kick) elicits a response (next-state=position-x, reward=0.01) from the environment. Rohanimanesh et al. [10] define concurrent actions and a generalised framework for working in such environments. The action space consists of a pool of primitive actions from which the agent must select one or more actions to send to the environment. There is potential for interactions, relationships and influence between actions, for example jumping and kicking vs just kicking may trigger better rewards.

Concurrent action settings are becoming more relevant as RL environments become more complex with actions that interact and may be applied concurrently, for example Atari [1] and StarCraft II [16] environments. Concurrent actions are possible in a single agent and a multi-agent reinforcement learning (MARL) context. While exploration in a concurrent action MARL environment [3,4] is an interesting area it is out of scope in this paper.

A concurrent action environment is complex because the computation time required to explore all state-action-sets increases combinatorially with the number of actions [14]. It is desirable to reduce the amount of exploration required, either by using prior knowledge or some intelligence about the environment. An important aspect of these environments is the possibility of relations and interactions between actions. Treating action combinations as primitive actions ignores potentially valuable information, such as whether some actions work particularly well with other actions, or whether some combinations of actions are redundant.

Some work in concurrent action spaces has focused on addressing these problems by reducing the size of the space using action elimination and prior knowledge [11,18]. Other groups have looked at various representations of the action space to reveal relationships and structure between actions either by factorisation, encoding or embeddings [2,12,15,17].

The scope of this work is the single agent concurrent action environment where the agent takes multiple discrete actions per timestep, or an action set. In this paper, we propose extracting structure from the action space to better inform exploration and improve sample efficiency. Two mechanisms are compared: explicit structure in the form of clusters in action space and implicit structure exposed by task-invariant actions. Both are unsupervised approaches focused purely on the action space, i.e. context-less.

Frequently used actions are collected from successful trajectories in a pretraining phase. The frequency of the action set is used as an indicator of how useful it is for a task. The most frequent action sets across multiple tasks are collected, representing a set of task-invariant action sets, and used as a prior during exploration in the second phase of training. The task invariant action sets indicate some underlying structure that action elimination can expose and leverage.

The frequency data is also used to learn more explicit structural information using spectral clustering [6] to partition the action space and reveal clusters of actions that work well together.

The contributions in this work are:

1. Using action elimination to reduce the exploration space in a concurrent action environment (Sect. 4).
2. Finding explicit structure in the concurrent action space using spectral clustering (Sect. 5).

These approaches were inspired by observations of how actions interact and influence other actions in the real world and how we, as humans, learn to select actions. We have a distinct advantage because we have a vast amount of pre-processed and distilled experience. When we need to learn something new we are very reliant on existing abstractions and structure. We also always apply relevance filters, often but not always, filtering by context. We are able to apply actions/skills learnt in one context to a completely new context without ever having seen the new context. This implies an abstraction of the mechanism in the action itself.

Section 2 looks at related research. Section 3 reviews the reinforcement learning framework and how it is used in the concurrent action problem setting. Section 4 expands the action elimination algorithm proposed to reduce exploration space while Sect. 5 looks at explicit structure as a means to enhance exploration. Section 6 provides details of the experiments and results. Finally, Sect. 7 concludes and discusses future work.

2 Related Work

Several papers combine learning factors for action composition in concurrent environments although the approaches for obtaining the factors and methods of composition differ. Wang and Yu [17] decompose an action into sub-action components and focus on learning the relationships between sub-actions. They use a novel structure to model the parameters of the sub-action components in a maximum a posteriori setting to learn the relations between sub-actions. Similarly Sharma et al. [12] decompose every action into a set of action-factors forming a factored action representation. The agent learns how to compose concurrent sets of actions based on the factors. Harmer et al. [5] also adopt the composition approach and propose a network architecture that outputs multiple actions per timestep in a deep RL setting. The network is trained using auxiliary signals from experts resulting in an online approach, one of the few online models. The agent benefits from having a concurrent action structure as it can model and learn from experts without restriction. This approach seems very effective but requires expert data versus self learning.

Rosman et al. [11] and Zahavy et al. [18] look at action elimination and prior knowledge to bias the agent's learning of new behaviours. In Rosman et al. action priors are modelled using Dirichlet distributions where the concentration parameters are the counts for a task. Zahavy et al. propose reducing the size of the relevant action set per state by using a separate network, a bandit trained using an elimination signal, to control which actions to eliminate in the main RL

Deep Q-Network agent. The motivation is to remove unnecessary actions and improve sample efficiency.

Some interesting work that focuses specifically on structure in action space comes from Tennenholtz et al. [15]. They developed an action-context embedding representation, Act2Vec, modelled on word embeddings using skip-grams [7]. The action embedding is used to enhance Q-function learning and to cluster similar actions together, thereby reducing the exploration space. The embeddings are generated from optimal demonstrator trajectory data. The paper uses this representation and a new measure of similarity to consider a broad spectrum of analysis that includes concurrent actions and exploration across clusters. Chandak et al. [2] also learn a lower dimensional action representation and a transform function between the representation policy and original policy. The embedding is used for training the agent in the lower dimensional space and makes use of underlying structure, similar to Tennenholtz et al.

Our paper has expanded on some of the ideas in Rosman et al. [11] but in a concurrent action setting specifically extracting task-invariant structure into a prior for action exploration. There are a few similarities in approach with Tennenholtz et al. They use supervised embedding and clustering of action space vs our unsupervised, count-based spectral clustering approach; we both look at the action-only context; the use of the clusters during exploration is also different. Tennenholtz et al. cluster to prevent redundant selections of actions whereas we cluster effective combinations with positive interactions.

3   Preliminaries

This work considers the setting of a standard Markov Decision Process (MDP) [14], defined by (S, A, T, R, γ) where S refers to the set of states, A the set of n primitive actions defined by $\{a_0, a_1, ..., a_n\}$, T the transition function $T : S \times A \times S \to [0, 1]$ defines the probability of moving from a state s to the next state s' after taking action a, R the reward function $R : S \times A \to \mathbb{R}$ such that $R(s, a)$ is the expected reward received when taking action a at state s and $\gamma \in [0, 1]$ is the discount factor.

The focus of this paper is concurrent actions as opposed to primitive actions. A concurrent action is represented as a set of actions $A_i \subset A$ containing np primitive actions. In this paper we focus primarily on the case where $np = 2$, so the agent takes two actions (hereafter referred to as an action set) per timestep $\{a_{i0}, a_{i1}\}$ where $a_{i0}, a_{i1} \in A$.

In the normal RL framework a stochastic policy $\pi : S \times A \to [0, 1]$ is defined where $\pi(s, a)$ is the probability of selecting an action a in state s and $Q^\pi(s, a)$ holds the value of each state-action pair under the policy π.

In the concurrent action environment the Q-value function holds the values of the action set, A_i, at each state. The goal is to find the optimal action set A_i that yields the highest value at any state s. While there is no restriction on how actions are selected, the actions are evaluated at the action set level.

Action selection generally takes place in the explore/exploit phase where the agent's accumulated knowledge of the environment is utilised or it is forced to explore new state-action-set combinations. Exploration can take a long time in a concurrent action space with a large number of actions. The next section expands the proposed ideas of learning structure in the action space to improve the sample efficiency of the exploration process.

4 Implicit Structure: Action Elimination Using Task Invariance

This approach collects samples from successful trajectories across multiple tasks to extract or filter the most frequently used action sets.

The intuition is that high frequency action sets are probably more useful and could be used as a basis for elimination. To reduce bias a pre-training process is performed over multiple tasks to extract a set of task invariant action sets that are referenced during exploration. The motivation is to remove useless action sets by favouring the task-invariant sets thereby reducing the size of the exploration space and making exploration more efficient.

Algorithm 1. Processing Count Data

---

1. Generate *Counts* **matrix**
Generate trajectories using RL algorithm (eg. Q-learning)
Collect count of each action set selected per state for successful episodes

Average over multiple runs to generate a count matrix by state and action set, $Counts(s, a, a)$

2. Process Action Counts
Hyperparameters: threshold t, no. of top counts NC
Reshape *Counts* from $SxNxN$ to SxN^2, unrolling action sets per state

2.a. Process Action Elimination Count Matrix
Set threshold $t > 0$ and NC to low number
Apply threshold filter to *Counts* and accumulate only the remaining top NC action counts across all states
Normalise the vector formed: $probs(A_i)$

2.b. Process Clustering Count Matrix
Set threshold $t = 0$ and increase NC
Apply threshold filter to *Counts* and accumulate the top NC action counts across all states
Reshape to form matrix W with dimensions N x N
Return Vector $probs(A_i)$ with dim $1xN^2$ or in matrix form, W, with dim N x N, where N is no. of primitive actions

---

To collect the common or frequent action sets, a configurable environment is needed to easily create multiple tasks. Algorithm 1 describes how the count data is processed for both the action elimination method of this section (step 2a) and the clustering method of the next section (step 2b).

In a pre-training phase, a Q-learning algorithm is used to generate trajectories. The Q-function holds the value of each state-action set pair, $Q(s, A_i)$ where A_i is the set of two actions $\{a_{i0}, a_{i1}\}$. Successful trajectories are collected where the goal state is reached before the maximum allowed step count (a hyperparameter).

The algorithm describes how the counts per action set are collected for a task. Only the most frequently used action sets are retained, controlled by a threshold hyperparameter, t. Counts below this threshold will be filtered out, effectively pruning the action sets. The result is a distilled action set usage vector representing each task. Note this approach holds count data by action set and not by action primitives.

Algorithm 2. Exploration with Action Elimination Prior

Given: $probs(A_i)$, $Q(s, A_i)$

If Explore:
    Sample an action set from $probs(A_i) \rightarrow A_i$
Else if Exploit:
    Find action set with max value in $Q(s, A_i) \rightarrow A_i$
Return A_i

This process is repeated for multiple tasks to build up a collection of invariant action sets for this domain. The action set counts are averaged across all tasks to produce a vector of importance weightings for each action set, which is then injected into the exploration process as prior knowledge. Algorithm 2 briefly illustrates how the action elimination prior is used to impact action selection in a basic Q-learning algorithm.

Averaging the counts over multiple tasks makes this a context-free approach, i.e. there is no direct association with states at this time. Experiments show that the training time is improved with this general context-free reduction of the action space.

The next section looks at an approach that finds and exploits explicit structure in concurrent action spaces.

5 Explicit Structure: Clustering of Action Space

The previous approach treats action sets as primitives, i.e. expands the action space to include all possible combinations of actions, then learns the best policy using a standard Q-learning algorithm. The general reduction in the number of eligible action sets is effective at improving time to convergence but the approach does not explicitly learn about the relationship between actions and is potentially discarding valuable information.

This second approach learns explicit structure in the action space in the form of clusters. The premise is that high counts of some action sets imply an underlying relationship or affinity between the primitive actions in those sets, that can be used to separate the action space into clusters. During exploration and action selection the agent would select from within these clusters on the basis that there is a higher likelihood of picking an effective action set.

Algorithm 3. Spectral Clustering of Actions

Requires:
Count matrix for action sets, W, with dim N x N, where N is no. of primitive actions

1. Prepare Affinity Matrix:
Check Symmetry, zero diagonals

2. Apply Spectral Clustering algorithm [9]
Degree matrix: D where d_{ii} is the diagonal sum of row $W[i]$
Normalised Laplacian: $L = D^{-1/2}WD^{-1/2}$
V is a matrix formed from the top k of eigenvectors of L
Y is the matrix V normalised
Apply k-means to Y for k clusters and create list of clusters, C

3. Post Process Clusters
Remove clusters with low silhouette score
Remove single item sets
Return List of clusters C

Algorithm 3 describes how the spectral clustering algorithm in Ng et al. [9] is applied to cluster actions using a count matrix.

As in the previous approach frequent action sets are collected from successful trajectories using a Q-learning algorithm in a pre-training phase. Algorithm 1, step 2b describes the generation of the count matrix from trajectory data. The threshold and top counts hyperparameters are used to control the sparsity of the matrix.

As before this process is repeated across multiple tasks. An assumption of this work is that the partitioning of the action space does not change with the task however this will be considered in future work. A count matrix of dimension $N \times N$ is passed as input to Algorithm 3.

Spectral clustering is a clustering method that separates data using the eigenvectors of the Laplacian of an affinity matrix [6]. The affinity matrix should reflect the similarity (or affinity) of the component elements. The count matrix is used as the basis for an affinity matrix and spectral clustering is performed to find clusters in the action space. The count matrix may be viewed as a graph where each action is a node and the edge is the strength of the relationship between actions, the strength reflected by the count.

The spectral clustering algorithm applied [9] describes some conditions that the affinity matrix should meet. The first step in Algorithm 3 transforms the count matrix into the appropriate form. In step 2 the eigenvalues and eigenvectors of the normalised Laplacian are calculated; typically cluster blocks are revealed in this step. K-means clustering is used to group the top eigenvectors. The number of clusters k is a hyperparameter, however it is also determinable using an eigengap heuristic [9]. A final post processing step uses a cluster measure to check the validity of each cluster and retains only the most confident clusters.

Spectral clustering was applied on this data although another clustering method could be used instead. Spectral clustering works well on correlated data and the count matrix forms a natural affinity matrix.

Once the clusters are determined, this structural information is built into the action selection method of the exploration process. Algorithm 4 briefly shows how the clusters are used during exploration to compose an action set.

Algorithm 4. Action Selection - Clustering

Given: List of clusters C, $Q(s, A_i)$, no. of actions in a set np
If Exploration:
    Sample a cluster c_i from C randomly
    Select np actions from within $c_i \rightarrow A_i$
Else if Exploitation:
    Find action set with max value in $Q(s, A_i) \rightarrow A_i$
Return A_i

---

6 Experiments

Experiment Setup: A basic four room grid environment was used, Fig. 1. The key requirement was an easily configurable environment for generating multiple tasks. In this environment the doors, start state (S) and goal state (G) are easily changed to create different tasks. A single goal state (G) is located in one of the rooms for each task. The set of primitive actions is fixed across all tasks: 6 actions viz. {U-Up, D-Down, L-Left, R-Right, O-Open, E-Enter}. There is a per-step penalty of -0.01 and the goal state has a reward of 10. There are no rewards associated with the doors. For each room configuration the agent was run for 50 runs of 100 episodes; each episode was truncated after 100 steps. Several different room configurations were generated to mimic different tasks using the same set of actions.

Agent: The agent is configured to take 2 actions per timestep. There are no limitations on the composition of the action sets so useless action sets such as {U,D} are possible. A basic Q-learning algorithm was implemented. It should be noted that other algorithms such as SARSA or Policy Gradients [14] would work too as both methods are algorithm agnostic. In the data collection pre-training phase the agent was designed to select an action set of two actions per step by either exploring or exploiting. Exploration involves selecting two primitive actions randomly with probability ϵ to create an action set. ϵ starts high at 0.9 and was annealed to 0. Exploitation is unchanged and performs a lookup of the maximum value action set in the Q-value function for any state.

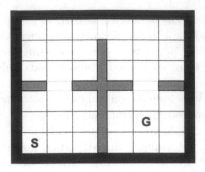

Fig. 1. Four room grid world

6.1   Implicit Structure - Action Elimination

Eight tasks were chosen at random, each with a different room configuration. The agent was pre-trained using the Q-learning algorithm and counts of action sets by state were collected over the total runs and averaged. The counts were aggregated across all states for each action set and normalised resulting in a vector of proportional representation for all action sets. The threshold hyper-parameter was set to 7 and the number of top actions to 2 to generate a very sparse count matrix.

A sample of the resulting vector of proportions for the action sets is illustrated as heatmap in Fig. 2. Each location on the grid is an action set, for example the first block on the top left is the action set (Up, Up). The colour intensity reflects how often that action set has been used in successful trajectories. The (Open, Enter) action set is relatively frequent, as is the (Down, Down) action set. The heatmap shows some of the bias that creeps in with only 8 tasks. Increasing the number of tasks during the first phase of training should help to reduce this.

The vector of proportions is injected into the exploration process as prior knowledge in the same domain but for a completely different set of tasks. Figure 3 compares the time to convergence for four randomly selected new tasks before

	U	D	L	R	O	E
U	0.039	0.018	0.034	0.022	0	0
D	0	0.14	0.027	0.02	0	0
L	0.014	0.05	0.04	0	0.004	0
R	0.028	0.018	0	0.01	0	0
O	0	0	0	0	0	0.54
E	0	0	0.004	0	0	0

Fig. 2. Sample of a heatmap for action sets

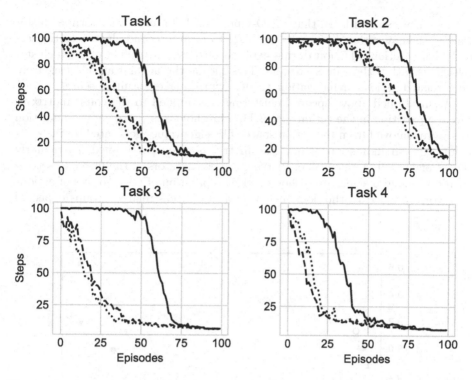

Fig. 3. Comparison of task convergence for pre-training(solid), clustering approach (dots), action elimination (dashed) for 4 random tasks

and after applying action elimination. The graphs show a reduction in average steps to convergence implying that basic action elimination during exploration is effective in concurrent action spaces.

The results show that using the frequency of actions selected across tasks as a basis for eliminating less useful action sets, without any contextual reference to the state, is sufficient to result in a decent performance improvement.

6.2 Explicit Structure - Clustering

The purpose of these experiments is to learn some structural aspects from the domain's action space that will improve the convergence times of other tasks in the same domain. To better illustrate this, the environment is designed with natural clusters in the action space. In particular a very specific set of actions was required to move through the doors in the four rooms environment, viz. (O, E) in a single timestep. Once again there were two phases: phase one was data collection pre-training phase across multiple tasks using a Q-learning algorithm with ϵ-greedy exploration; phase two was training under the new exploration model (Algorithm 4).

The agent should learn that the O-Open and E-Enter actions form a cluster leaving the navigation actions $\{U, D, L, R\}$ to form a second cluster. In the second phase, action selection during exploration was constrained to intra-cluster selections rather than inter-clusters. This means the agent was selecting from door-related actions or navigation actions, which makes intuitive sense.

As mentioned above spectral clustering was applied to the count matrix to reveal a partition in the action space. The threshold was set to zero so no action sets were removed from the action space. The eigenvalues generated by the algorithm give an indication of how the matrix may be partitioned, particularly the second smallest eigenvalue. Plotting the eigenvectors of the first and second smallest non-zero eigenvalues shows a clear separation of the two sets of actions that corresponded to the door-related and navigation related groups expected (Fig. 4).

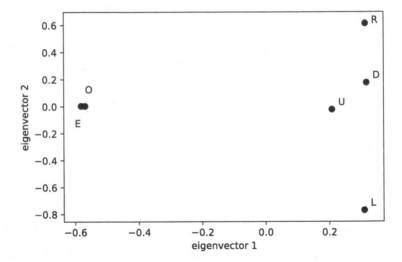

Fig. 4. Plotting the top eigenvectors shows separation of the Open, Enter actions and the navigation actions Up, Down, Left, Right

The action selection method in Algorithm 4 was applied to select actions from within the two clusters when creating action sets during exploration. The resulting comparative graphs in Fig. 3 over four randomly generated new tasks show an improvement in learning times, similar to the action elimination.

The significant improvement in convergence times after structure is applied, even with the randomness of choosing a cluster and then selecting actions within the cluster, highlights just how much time is typically lost by the agent in an $\epsilon-$greedy exploration process.

The performance of the clustering approach could be improved by knowing which cluster to select based on the state, for example selecting from the door-related actions when at a door state and navigation-related actions otherwise.

This contextual approach should have a positive impact on learning, however it is interesting to observe that just an analysis of the action space can produce a useful reduction in training time that is once again invariant across tasks.

7   Conclusion and Future Work

This paper proposed two approaches for using structure to improve sample efficiency during exploration in concurrent action environments including action elimination and clustering. Count data from successful trajectories were used as a basis for extracting prior knowledge across multiple tasks in the same domain. The priors were used to enhance a Q-learning algorithm and showed significant improvements in policy convergence times. Given that these are context free mechanisms there is room for improvement by bringing in context.

Some of the key limitations to these approaches include the need for a pre-training phase which means the methods are not online. There is also a need for successful trajectory data which limits these approaches to environments that are solvable by other means. Other work such as Tennenholtz et al. [15] and Harmer et al. [5] use demonstrator or expert trajectories which could work here too.

Future work would look into online methods that would remove the pre-training phase and not require solved trajectories. This will impact the scalability of these approaches. Secondly the use of context to better select clusters of actions will be considered.

References

1. Bellemare, M.G., Naddaf, Y., Veness, J., Bowling, M.: The arcade learning environment: an evaluation platform for general agents. In: Proceedings of the 24th International Conference on Artificial Intelligence, pp. 4148–4152. IJCAI 2015, AAAI Press (2015). http://dl.acm.org/citation.cfm?id=2832747.2832830
2. Chandak, Y., Theocharous, G., Kostas, J., Jordan, S., Thomas, P.: Learning action representations for reinforcement learning. In: Chaudhuri, K., Salakhutdinov, R. (eds.) Proceedings of the 36th International Conference on Machine Learning. Proceedings of Machine Learning Research, vol. 97, pp. 941–950. PMLR, Long Beach, California, USA (09–15 June 2019). http://proceedings.mlr.press/v97/chandak19a.html
3. Claus, C., Boutilier, C.: The dynamics of reinforcement learning in cooperative multiagent systems. AAAI/IAAI (1998)
4. Dimakopoulou, M., Van Roy, B.: Coordinated exploration in concurrent reinforcement learning. In: Dy, J., Krause, A. (eds.) Proceedings of the 35th International Conference on Machine Learning. Proceedings of Machine Learning Research, vol. 80, pp. 1271–1279. PMLR, Stockholmsmässan, Stockholm Sweden (2018)
5. Harmer, J., et al.: Imitation learning with concurrent actions in 3D games. In: 2018 IEEE Conference on Computational Intelligence and Games, CIG 2018, Maastricht, The Netherlands, August 14–17, 2018, pp. 1–8 (2018). https://doi.org/10.1109/CIG.2018.8490398

6. Luxburg, U.: A tutorial on spectral clustering. Stat. Comput. **17**(4), 395–416 (2007). https://doi.org/10.1007/s11222-007-9033-z
7. Mikolov, T., Chen, K., Corrado, G., Dean, J.: Efficient estimation of word representations in vector space. CoRR abs/1301.3781 (2013). http://dblp.uni-trier.de/db/journals/corr/corr1301.html/abs-1301-3781
8. Mnih, V., et al.: Asynchronous methods for deep reinforcement learning. In: Proceedings of the 33rd International Conference on International Conference on Machine Learning, vol. 48, pp. 1928–1937. ICML 2016, JMLR.org (2016). http://dl.acm.org/citation.cfm?id=3045390.3045594
9. Ng, A.Y., Jordan, M.I., Weiss, Y.: On spectral clustering: analysis and an algorithm. In: Dietterich, T.G., Becker, S., Ghahramani, Z. (eds.) Advances in Neural Information Processing Systems, vol. 14, pp. 849–856. MIT Press, Cambridge (2002). http://papers.nips.cc/paper/2092-on-spectral-clustering-analysis-and-an-algorithm.pdf
10. Rohanimanesh, K.: Concurrent decision making in Markov decision processes. Citeseer (2006)
11. Rosman, B., Ramamoorthy, S.: Action priors for learning domain invariances. IEEE Trans. Auton. Ment. Dev. **7**(2), 107–118 (2015)
12. Sharma, S., Suresh, A., Ramesh, R., Ravindran, B.: Learning to factor policies and action-value functions: factored action space representations for deep reinforcement learning. CoRR abs/1705.07269 (2017). http://arxiv.org/abs/1705.07269
13. Silver, D., et al.: Mastering the game of go without human knowledge. Nature **550**, 354 (2017). https://doi.org/10.1038/nature24270
14. Sutton, R.S., Barto, A.G.: Reinforcement Learning: An Introduction. MIT Press, Cambridge (1998). http://www.cs.ualberta.ca/ sutton/book/the-book.html
15. Tennenholtz, G., Mannor, S.: The natural language of actions. In: Chaudhuri, K., Salakhutdinov, R. (eds.) Proceedings of the 36th International Conference on Machine Learning. Proceedings of Machine Learning Research, vol. 97, pp. 6196–6205. PMLR, Long Beach, California, USA (09–15 Jun 2019). http://proceedings.mlr.press/v97/tennenholtz19a.html
16. Vinyals, O., et al.: Starcraft II: a new challenge for reinforcement learning. CoRR abs/1708.04782 (2017). http://arxiv.org/abs/1708.04782
17. Wang, H., Yu, Y.: Exploring multi-action relationship in reinforcement learning. In: Booth, R., Zhang, M.-L. (eds.) PRICAI 2016. LNCS (LNAI), vol. 9810, pp. 574–587. Springer, Cham (2016). https://doi.org/10.1007/978-3-319-42911-3_48
18. Zahavy, T., Haroush, M., Merlis, N., Mankowitz, D.J., Mannor, S.: Learn what not to learn: action elimination with deep reinforcement learning. In: Bengio, S., Wallach, H., Larochelle, H., Grauman, K., Cesa-Bianchi, N., Garnett, R. (eds.) Advances in Neural Information Processing Systems 31, pp. 3562–3573. Curran Associates, Inc. (2018). http://papers.nips.cc/paper/7615-learn-what-not-to-learn-action-elimination-with-deep-reinforcement-learning.pdf

Agents, Knowledge Acquisition and Ontologies

Demonstrating the Distinctions Between Persuasion and Deliberation Dialogues

Yanko Kirchev, Katie Atkinson[✉], and Trevor Bench-Capon

Department of Computer Science, University of Liverpool, Liverpool, UK
katie@liverpool.ac.uk

Abstract. A successful dialogue requires that the participants have a shared understanding of what they are trying to achieve, individually and collectively. This coordination can be achieved if both recognise the type of dialogue in which they are engaged. We focus on two particular dialogue types, action persuasion and deliberation dialogues, which are often conflated because they share similar speech acts. Previously, a clear distinction was made between the two in terms of the different pre- and post-conditions used for the speech acts within these dialogues. This prior work gave formal specifications of the dialogue moves within the dialogues but offered no evaluation through implementation. In this paper, we present an implementation to demonstrate that the two dialogue types described in this way can be realised in software to support focussed communication between autonomous agents. We provide the design and implementation details of our new tool along with an evaluation of the software. The tool we have produced captures the distinctive features of each of the two dialogue types, to make plain their differences and to validate the speech acts for use in practical scenarios.

Keywords: Argumentation · Dialogue · Deliberation · Persuasion

1 Introduction

Dialogues with computers are becoming an increasingly popular way of interacting with members of the public (e.g. [5,7,11]) for giving advice, soliciting opinions, and e-participation generally. When modelling dialogues, it is important to be aware of the type of dialogue that one is dealing with. Dialogues are essentially cooperative acts between the participants, and it is therefore important that they are both playing by the same rules. These rules derive from the particular type of dialogue they are engaged in. Without a mutual understanding of the type of dialogue, participants will be at cross purposes, leading to misunderstandings and breakdown of the dialogue.

© Springer Nature Switzerland AG 2019
M. Bramer and M. Petridis (Eds.): SGAI-AI 2019, LNAI 11927, pp. 93–106, 2019.
https://doi.org/10.1007/978-3-030-34885-4_7

The notion of dialogue types can be found in [10], where five types were introduced. We will be concerned with two of these: persuasion and deliberation[1]. These two dialogues types are especially important in e-participation [2]. Persuasion is required to explain and defend policies, and deliberation is required in order to undertake public consultations. In [10], Walton and Krabbe characterise their dialogue types according to three aspects: the initial situation, the collective goal, and the individual goals of the participants.

- *Initial Situation*: For persuasion, the initial situation is a disagreement: the agents do not agree as to the best option. In deliberation, it is one of uncertainty: while the individuals may (or may not) have their own opinions about the best option, they do not know which option is collectively acceptable.
- *Collective Goal*: For both dialogue types, the collective goal is to come to an agreement as to what should be done, but there is a difference in what can be agreed. In persuasion, this is limited to the option proposed by the persuader being accepted by the persuadee; in deliberation, agreement can be to any option that is acceptable to the group as a whole. This is done by producing a rule expressing their collective preference, which can then be used to identify the most acceptable option for the group.
- *Individual Goals*: In persuasion, the individual goals are different: the persuader wishes to convince the other, whereas the persuadee, if cooperative, wishes to explore the possibility that its currently preferred option is not in fact best for it in the light of information known to the persuader. If uncooperative, the persuadee may wish to defend its own option or even convert the persuader. In a deliberation, the individual goals are the same for all participants: all participants wish to determine which option is the best for them collectively.

This characterisation does highlight some important differences between the dialogues. To an observer who has no access to the inner states of the participants, however, it may be difficult to tell which sort of dialogue is taking place. This is because the speech acts used are the same in both dialogue types. Although this is so, the force of the speech acts differs: the dialogue types determine how the acts are to be interpreted. The pragmatic effects of the various utterances differ: the *conversational implicatures* [6] of the utterances differ according to the dialogue type.

This aspect was explored in [1], where the various speech acts were described in terms of pre- and post-conditions. Each speech act has some of these common to both dialogue types, representing the semantic aspects of the act, but also additional different conditions for deliberation and persuasion which represent the pragmatic aspects of the act in the specific context. These pre-conditions show what should hold for the utterance to be legally made in the given dia-

---

[1] Further in this paper, we will focus on persuasion and deliberation about *actions*. Although [10] might seem to suggest that persuasion concerns only propositions and not actions, persuading people to do something is such an everyday occurrence that we may regard persuasion about action as a *bona fide* dialogue type.

logue type and what should be understood from the utterance in the different dialogues.

Although [1] gave full definitions of the pre- and post-conditions for the speech acts of persuasion and deliberation dialogues, there was no implementation, and hence no practical evaluation. Therefore, our aims were:

- To implement and so evaluate the sets of speech acts proposed in [1] to demonstrate their adequacy or, if necessary, to refine them to provide an adequate set of speech acts;
- To provide a tool which will explicitly show the differences between the dialogue classes, allowing users to compare them and explore the different effects of the various speech acts.

The rest of the paper is structured as follows. In Sect. 2, we discuss the various speech acts. The evaluation in fact showed that two speech acts additional to those given in [1] are required. Section 3 describes the design of the tool, and Sect. 4 the realisation of this design. Section 5 describes how the tool can be used to input a situation and generate persuasion and deliberation dialogues, illustrated with the example from [1]. This example involves a scenario, expressed as a logic program, in which three agents are choosing a restaurant to dine out in and each agent has its own individual preferences. Our example dialogues show the differences in the commitment stores that result from the speech acts being deployed within the two different dialogue contexts. Section 6 shows the methods used to evaluate the tool, and Sect. 7 offers some discussion and concluding remarks.

2   Speech Acts

The protocols for the two dialogue types are distinguished by specifying different pre- and post-conditions for the speech acts depending upon which of the two dialogues they are used within. Each agent is defined to have a 'commitment store' [10]: a set of statements to which they become publicly committed during the course of a dialogue. The pre-conditions determine the pre-requisites that need to be satisfied in terms of available knowledge and prior commitments of dialogue participants in order for the speech acts to be used legally. The post-conditions determine the updates on the agents' commitment stores that occur immediately after the enactment of the move. Our implementation initially follows [1] by using the speech acts set out in Prakken's dialogue system [9]. These speech acts are:

- *Claim*: used to assert a fact;
- *Why*: used to ask for a justification of a claim;
- *Since*: used to provide a justification for a claim;
- *Concede*: used to accept a claim;
- *Retract*: used to withdraw a claim;
- *Question*: used to seek a piece of information.

Prakken also sets out a protocol in the form of a set of rules by which a dialogue proceeds. The protocol specifies the speech acts permitted at any given point during the dialogue, the effects of utterances on the participants' commitments, the outcome of the dialogue, the turn-taking function, and the termination criteria. Our tool demonstrates the changes in the commitment stores of the agents as the dialogues proceed towards termination. The above set of speech acts is set out formally in [1].

2.1 Refinement of Speech Acts

Designing and implementing software to execute the persuasion and deliberation dialogues required the speech acts to be operationalised. Through designing the software, it became apparent that refinements were needed to two of the original speech acts from [1]. The *claim* speech act, used by opponents in the persuasion dialogue and all agents in the deliberation dialogue, turned out to be too restrictive; one of its pre-conditions allows for assertions to be made only about options that the agents find acceptable, thus rendering the agents incapable of making objections towards options that they do not find acceptable or of making claims about options they do not find acceptable.

A similar observation can be made about the *since* move in deliberation: some of its pre- and post-conditions are implied by, or clash with, other conditions. Moreover, deliberation changes the speech act's purpose to move previously proposed criteria into the body of the rule expressing the agreed preference, making agents in deliberation incapable of simply justifying previously made claims without changing the preference rule, which is the role of the *since* move in the other types of dialogues.

Given the above observations revealed through the implementation exercise, both the *claim* and *since* speech acts require modifications in order for the aforementioned difficulties to be overcome. The *claim* speech act has thus been modified by replacing its problematic pre-condition with a *preferable* function, which consequently allows opponents in persuasion and all agents in deliberation to make assertions about their initial preferences, even in the cases where they do not find them completely acceptable. Furthermore, a new speech act is introduced, *counterclaim*, which allows all types of agents to make objections against options that they do not find acceptable. Finally, the *since* speech act for deliberation has been split into two distinct acts: the general *since* move remains unchanged and is used to justify a previously made claim, but a new *concede-since* speech act is introduced that is only used to move previously proposed criteria into the body of the agreed preference rule.

The refinements made to the speech acts, as described in this section, were found to be required to enable the sample dialogues given in [1] to be automated in an implementation. In the next section, we provide the design for the programs to realise the dialogues in software.

3   Design

The tool allows for the simultaneous generation of customisable persuasion and deliberation dialogues, which are set in the same restaurant selection scenario that was introduced in [1], where three agents try to decide on a place in which to dine. Consequently, the tool is called *Diners' Discourse*, and this section describes the object-oriented components used in the protocols.

The class diagram in Fig. 1 illustrates the entities that the tool encapsulates and also provides insight on the relationships between the various objects that are created during a single lifecycle.

3.1   Agent Class

The *Agent* class represents a participant in a dialogue, and every agent has the following attributes: a *name*; an *initialPreference*, which is a restaurant that the agent introduces to the dialogue as their preferred option regardless of whether they find it acceptable; a *knowledgeBase*, which is a static collection of Prolog facts and rules that specify the available knowledge of the agent about the world; and a *commitmentStore*, which is an initially empty set of statements that is populated with the statements to which the agent becomes committed in the course of a dialogue.

Alongside that, each *Agent* instance also includes a *doesPrefer* method, which corresponds to the *preferable* function discussed in the previous section, and which takes a restaurant name as an argument and returns *true* only if it matches the agent's initial preference or if the agent finds it acceptable.

3.2   Dialogue Class

The *Dialogue* class is abstract and represents a generic dialogue. Every dialogue has three participants stored in the *agents* attribute, and its conversational script is continuously expanded in the *text* attribute as the participants perform various moves.

The class also implements methods that correspond to the general specifications of the speech acts that are common to both persuasion and deliberation. In addition to that, it records the evolution of the commitment stores of the participating agents throughout the course of the dialogue by utilising the *saveCommitmentStores* method and the *commitmentStoreHistory* attribute. Moreover, the abstract *isOver* method returns a Boolean value that determines whether the dialogue is in an end state.

3.3   PersuasionDialogue Class

The *PersuasionDialogue* class extends the abstract *Dialogue* class and represents a persuasion dialogue. As such, it features an additional *proponent* attribute, which points to one of the objects in *agents* and which indicates the designated persuader of the dialogue.

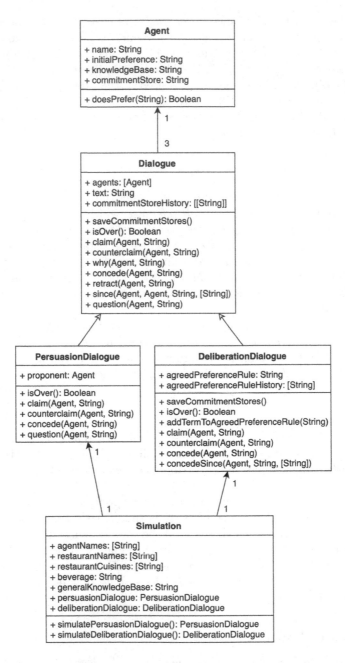

Fig. 1. Class diagram

The *isOver* method of the parent class receives a dialogue instance and returns *true* only if every agent is committed to the statement that the initial preference of the proponent is acceptable. Moreover, the *claim, counterclaim, concede*, and *question* methods are overridden to feature the additional pre- and post-conditions required by persuasion.

3.4   DeliberationDialogue Class

The *DeliberationDialogue* class extends the abstract *Dialogue* class and represents a deliberation dialogue. As such, it features an additional *agreedPreferenceRule* attribute, which represents the collective preference rule of what constitutes an acceptable restaurant that the agents construct during the course of the dialogue, and its evolution is recorded in the *agreedPreferenceRuleHistory* attribute.

The class also overrides the *claim, counterclaim*, and *concede* methods to feature the additional pre- and post-conditions required by deliberation and also implements a *concedeSince* method, which corresponds to the deliberation-exclusive *concede-since* speech act. Moreover, a method *addTermToAgreedPreferenceRule* is utilised by the *concede* and *concedeSince* methods to add the locution used with them to the body of the agreed preference rule.

DeliberationDialogue also implements the *isOver* method of its parent class, and, in this case, it returns *true* only if all agents agree on the same option being acceptable and if the acceptability of the agreed option can be demonstrated from the collective commitment store of the participating agents in conjunction with the agreed preference rule, minus any private preference commitments.

3.5   Simulation Class

Simulation is a concept class that represents the lifecycle of one persuasion and one deliberation dialogue from their initialisation, through their execution, until they reach their final states. It contains a *generalKnowledgeBase* attribute, which is a refined template of the collective facts and rules of the participating agents from the model dialogues in [1]. The placeholder values in it are populated with the data from the *restaurantNames, restaurantCuisine*, and *beverage* attributes, and the populated general knowledge base along with the *agentNames* attribute is then used by the *createPersuasionDialogue* and *createDeliberationDialogue* methods to create three *Agent* objects each and to distribute the facts and rules amongst them.

Thereafter, *PersuasionDialogue* and *DeliberationDialogue* instances are created and predefined sequences of speech acts are performed on them. They are assigned to the appropriate *persuasionDialogue* and *deliberationDialogue* attributes after the *isOver* methods check that they have reached an end state.

In the next section, we cover the implementation details of the protocols and also present a web application that is provided as a user interface for the tool.

4   Realisation

The protocols are written in JavaScript and run on the Node.js environment with the help of the Tau Prolog module, which provides native knowledge representation without requiring Prolog itself. A graphical web interface allows for a user-friendly interaction with the tool and is constructed using the React.js framework together with Carbon Design's React components and supporting technologies such as HTML5 and CSS3.

4.1   Project Architecture

The project's software architecture is shown in Fig. 2 and can also be further examined on its GitHub repository[2]. As can be seen, the front-end is written as modular components, each of which has a distinct purpose within the system

Fig. 2. Project architecture

_____
[2] See: github.com/yankirchev/diners-discourse.

and is contained within the *src* folder, whereas the *protocols* subfolder contains the back-end files, each of which corresponds to a class in Fig. 1. Moreover, the protocols are supported by unit tests under *test*, which verify the soundness of the implementation, and additional helper files under *utils*.

4.2   Interface

The web interface of *Diners' Discourse* features a single, dynamic page, the view of which changes based on the selected tab of the content switcher in its top centre. The three available views are *Home*, which contains a welcome message and a demo dialogue; *Background*, which contains the purpose of, and the technologies used by, the application along with a glossary; and *Generate*, where the persuasion and deliberation dialogues are customised, generated, and presented to the users.

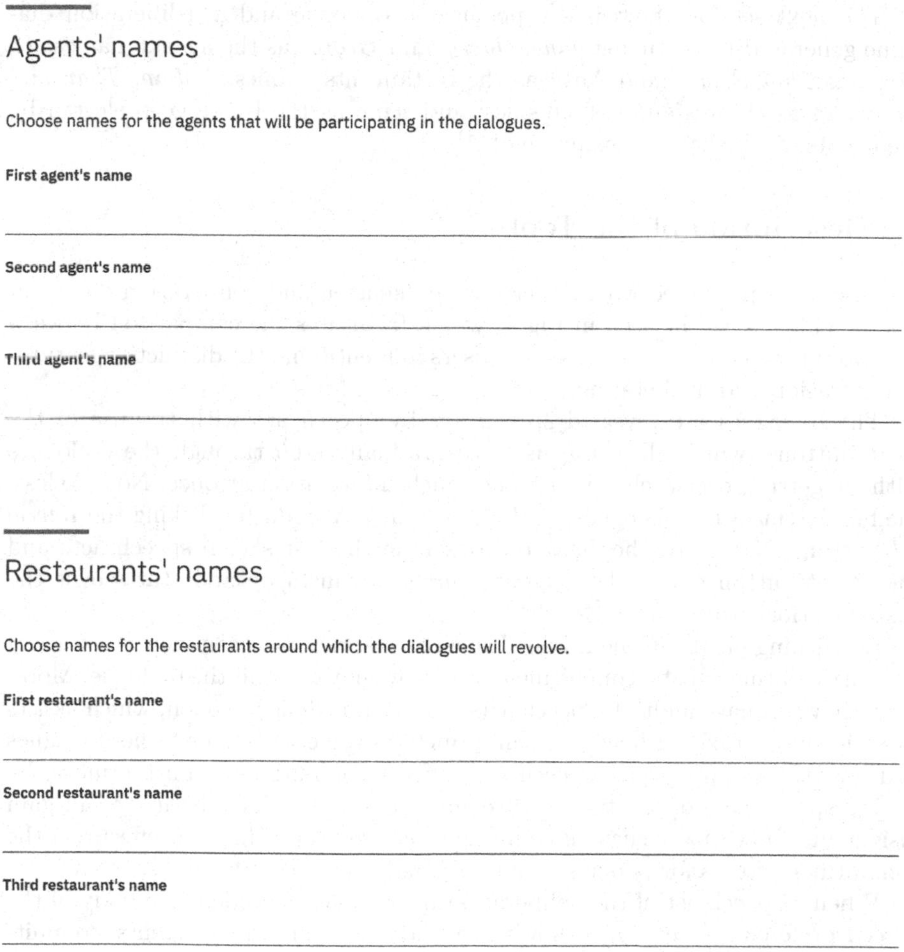

Agents' names

Choose names for the agents that will be participating in the dialogues.

First agent's name

_____

Second agent's name

_____

Third agent's name

_____

Restaurants' names

Choose names for the restaurants around which the dialogues will revolve.

First restaurant's name

_____

Second restaurant's name

_____

Third restaurant's name

_____

Fig. 3. First part of the input form

While this subsection focuses on the *Generate* tab, as it contains the main functionality of the application, the tool is available to be further examined in the public domain at the URL given in footnote 2.

The *Generate* tab presents the users with an input form, as can be seen in Figs. 3 and 4, which collects the required data for the customisation of the dialogues. The users are allowed to choose the names of the participating agents, the names and the cuisines of the restaurants, and the beverage that is preferred by the agents. The choices in regard to the names are entirely up to the users. However, for the cuisines of the restaurants and the beverage preferred by the agents, the choices are restricted. This restriction is so that the categories make sense in terms of the agent preferences, which are taken from [1].

The form also features a *Generate* button at the very bottom, which, when clicked, prompts *Diners' Discourse* to create a *Simulation* instance by populating the *agentNames*, *restaurantNames*, *restaurantCuisines*, and *beverage* attributes using the user input.

The next section showcases a persuasion dialogue and a deliberation dialogue generated by inputting *Jane*, *Harry*, and *George* as the agents' names; *La Zingara*, *Thai Palace*, and *Nosh* as the restaurants' names; *Italian*, *Thai*, and *American* as the restaurants' cuisines; and *wine* as the beverage preferred by the agents, as in the main example of [1].

5   Description of the Tool

The users are presented with the custom persuasion and deliberation dialogues side by side, as can be seen in Fig. 5, which facilitates the comparison between the two types and therefore assists the users in identifying the distinctive features of persuasion and deliberation.

The dialogues are revealed speech act by speech act with the use of the *Next* buttons, which allow the users to gradually step through the dialogues without getting overwhelmed with too much information at once. Nonetheless, the full extent of the dialogues can be shown at any point by clicking the *Reveal all* buttons. Naturally, the *Back* buttons hide the last shown speech acts and the *Reset* button erases the current *Simulation* instance and starts over the customisation process again.

By clicking on any of the revealed speech acts, the users can view the state of the participating agents' commitment stores at that point in the dialogue. Moreover, they can have multiple speech acts of the same dialogue open, which assists them in understanding how the commitments evolve throughout the dialogues and how the use of specific speech acts affects commitments. Furthermore, by having speech acts of the two types expanded side by side, the users can gain insight into how moves such as *claim* and *question* have different effects on the commitment stores for persuasion and deliberation.

When a speech act of the deliberation dialogue is expanded, the body of the agreed preference rule is also shown alongside the state of the agents' commitments. This lets the users observe how the rule is constructed throughout the

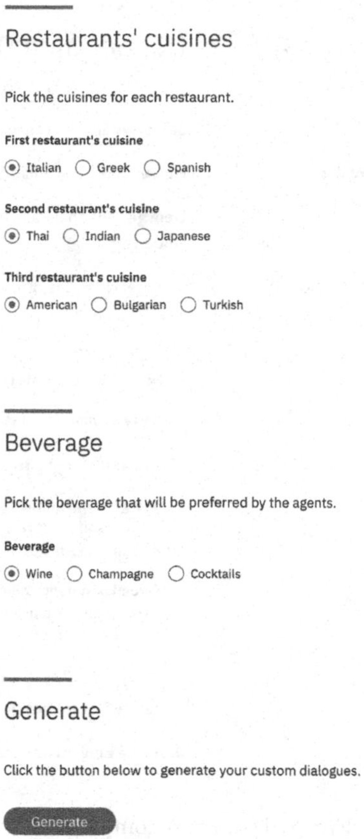

Restaurants' cuisines

Pick the cuisines for each restaurant.

First restaurant's cuisine

◉ Italian   ○ Greek   ○ Spanish

Second restaurant's cuisine

◉ Thai   ○ Indian   ○ Japanese

Third restaurant's cuisine

◉ American   ○ Bulgarian   ○ Turkish

Beverage

Pick the beverage that will be preferred by the agents.

Beverage

◉ Wine   ○ Champagne   ○ Cocktails

Generate

Click the button below to generate your custom dialogues.

Generate

Fig. 4. Second part of the input form

dialogue and how speech acts such as *concede* and *concede-since* determine the joint rule's final structure.

6   Testing and Evaluation

The dialogues in Fig. 5 closely adhere to those in [1] from which the protocols' formal definitions have been derived, indicating that the tool implements the dialogues as conceived in [1].

In order to demonstrate the close resemblance, we compare the structure of the two dialogues and the use of particular speech acts instead of their scripts, as the protocols do not use a natural language engine to produce the text of the dialogues. Ultimately, it is not essential that the dialogues match word for word, but rather that the same arguments by the same agents appear in both dialogues in the same context and that they reach the same conclusions.

While the resulting implemented dialogues feature some additional speech acts, these additions complement the general conduct of the dialogues and

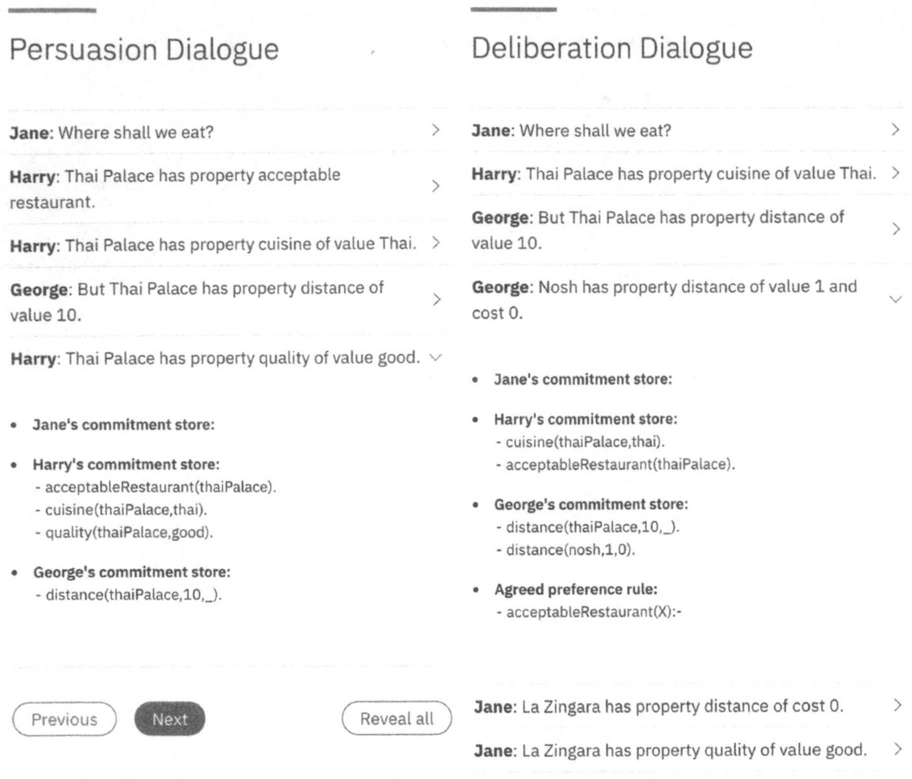

Persuasion Dialogue	Deliberation Dialogue
Jane: Where shall we eat? >	**Jane**: Where shall we eat? >
Harry: Thai Palace has property acceptable restaurant. >	**Harry**: Thai Palace has property cuisine of value Thai. >
Harry: Thai Palace has property cuisine of value Thai. >	**George**: But Thai Palace has property distance of value 10. >
George: But Thai Palace has property distance of value 10. >	**George**: Nosh has property distance of value 1 and cost 0. ⌄
Harry: Thai Palace has property quality of value good. ⌄	

Persuasion Dialogue:
- Jane's commitment store:
- Harry's commitment store:
  - acceptableRestaurant(thaiPalace).
  - cuisine(thaiPalace,thai).
  - quality(thaiPalace,good).
- George's commitment store:
  - distance(thaiPalace,10,_).

Deliberation Dialogue:
- Jane's commitment store:
- Harry's commitment store:
  - cuisine(thaiPalace,thai).
  - acceptableRestaurant(thaiPalace).
- George's commitment store:
  - distance(thaiPalace,10,_).
  - distance(nosh,1,0).
- Agreed preference rule:
  - acceptableRestaurant(X):-

Previous Next   Reveal all

Jane: La Zingara has property distance of cost 0. >

Jane: La Zingara has property quality of value good. >

Fig. 5. Dialogues comparison

support the agents in arriving at their goals, which in turn make the generated persuasion and deliberation dialogues more complete versions of the model ones.

Aside from sounding less natural because of the computer-generated phrases, the produced dialogues are largely analogous to the model ones: in both sets of dialogues, the same agents have the same goals and execute the same moves towards achieving them. Moreover, the outcomes of the generated dialogues are the same as those of the model ones.

Ultimately, this corroborates the implemented protocols' integrity and effective application in a practical setting, meeting our aims for the work.

6.1   Unit Testing

In order to verify the correctness of the protocols' implementation, it is necessary to demonstrate that it exhibits the behaviour that the specifications of the speech acts describe for persuasion and deliberation. More precisely, we need to demonstrate that the pre-conditions of each speech act are adhered to when used in any situation and that the post-conditions occur thereafter as well.

Consequently, every pre-condition is implemented so that it throws an error with an identifying description when it is not satisfied, and a positive and a negative test is written for each. The positive test ensures that the pre-condition does not throw an error when the speech act is used legally, whereas the negative test ensures that the pre-condition throws an error when the speech act is used illegally. The tests fail only if the speech acts exhibit behaviour that deviates from the expected results.

The post-conditions only have a positive test each: although they are called conditions, their function is to update the commitment stores of the agents. Therefore, their tests ensure that the commitments are amended as required given that the pre-conditions are satisfied. The tests fail only if the state of the commitment stores deviates from the expected results.

Thereafter, custom simulations of persuasion and deliberation dialogues are carried out separately for each pre- and post-condition, which are similar in function to the *Simulation* class described in Subsect. 3.5. A total of 125 unit tests were written using the Jest framework for JavaScript and all were passed successfully. The unit tests take just over a second to execute, with each of them averaging ~11.13 ms to run. This indicates the efficiency of the implemented protocols, which is an important factor in multi-agent communications where parties are expected to react quickly to an evolving situation.

The exhaustive number of unit tests along with their affirmative results corroborate the notion that any dialogues produced by the protocols are valid with respect to our expectations about persuasion and deliberation. Since each pre- and post-condition of every speech act is tested individually, the tests also ensure that the results of the conditions are independent of each other. Furthermore, the positive tests demonstrate that the legal use of the speech acts has the intended effect on the dialogue, while the negative tests show that no deviation from what is required of the speech acts is allowed.

7 Discussion and Concluding Remarks

We have described a tool that has been implemented to realise automated communication between several agents within action persuasion and deliberation dialogues. Our tool explicitly shows to users the differences between the dialogue types and enables exploration of the different effects of the various speech acts available. Whilst the software relied on the formal specification given in [1], the implementation exercise revealed refinements required to the underlying speech act specifications to enable accurate, realistic dialogues to be produced. The evaluation has demonstrated that the implementation exercise has been successful and we are encouraged that the distinctive features manifest in the two types of dialogue can be captured in tools for automated communication.

In implementing the two dialogue types, we have extended the speech acts based on [9] that were used in [1] to include two additional acts tailored for these dialogue types. We have shown that these speech acts enable dialogues of both types to be conducted. They can therefore form the basis of further implementations designed to address particular e-participation tasks. These tasks include the presentation and justification of policies, which require the user to be persuaded, and deliberations such as consultation about the suitability of a range of options, intended to gauge which options have public support, and to enable progress towards a consensus about the preferred option. Thus, although the particular tool described here is intended primarily to teach the differences between to two types of dialogue, the implementation can form the basis for the realisation of a range of e-participation applications.

Future work will focus on two aspects. On a practical level, we will adapt the tool so that the speech acts can be used to implement some specific tasks, such as the e-participation tasks mentioned above. Of course, any fielded application of such dialogue agents would need careful consideration of the ethical issues, particularly as "fake news" and campaigns of disinformation become more prevalent. Consideration of ethical issues associated with conversational agents are discussed in [8]. At a more theoretical level, we will investigate how the speech acts of the dialogue types discussed here relate to other dialogue types, such as inquiry [4] and examination [3].

References

1. Atkinson, K., Bench-Capon, T., Walton, D.: Distinctive features of persuasion and deliberation dialogues. Argum. Comput. **4**(2), 105–127 (2013)
2. Bench-Capon, T., Atkinson, K., Wyner, A.: Using argumentation to structure e-participation in policy making. In: Hameurlain, A., Küng, J., Wagner, R., Decker, H., Lhotska, L., Link, S. (eds.) Transactions on Large-Scale Data- and Knowledge-Centered Systems XVIII. LNCS, vol. 8980, pp. 1–29. Springer, Heidelberg (2015). https://doi.org/10.1007/978-3-662-46485-4_1
3. Bench-Capon, T., Doutre, S., Dunne, P.E.: Asking the right question: forcing commitment in examination dialogues. In: Besnard, P., Doutre, S., Hunter, A. (eds.) Proceedings of COMMA 2008, vol. 172, pp. 49–60. IOS Press (2008)
4. Black, E., Hunter, A.: An inquiry dialogue system. Auton. Agents Multi Agent Syst. **19**(2), 173–209 (2009). https://doi.org/10.1007/s10458-008-9074-5
5. Chalaguine, L.A., Hamilton, F.L., Hunter, A., Potts, H.W.: Argument harvesting using chatbots. In: Proceedings of COMMA 2018, pp. 149–160. IOS Press (2018)
6. Grice, H.P.: Logic and conversation. In: Cole, P., Morgan, J.L. (eds.) Syntax and Semantics, vol. 3, pp. 41–58. Academic Press, New York (1975)
7. Morgan, J., Paiement, A., Seisenberger, M., Williams, J., Wyner, A.: A chatbot framework for the children's legal centre. In: Proceedings of JURIX 2018, pp. 205–209 (2018)
8. Olszewska, J.I., et al.: Robotic ontological standard development life cycle. In: IEEE International Conference on Robotics and Automation 2018: Workshop on Elderly Care Robotics: Technology and Ethics (2018)
9. Prakken, H.: Formal systems for persuasion dialogue. Knowl. Eng. Rev. **21**(2), 163–188 (2006)
10. Walton, D., Krabbe, E.: Commitment in Dialogue: Basic Concepts of Interpersonal Reasoning. SUNY Press, New York (1995)
11. Wardeh, M., Wyner, A., Atkinson, K., Bench-Capon, T.: Argumentation based tools for policy-making. In: Proceedings of the Fourteenth International Conference on Artificial Intelligence and Law, pp. 249–250. ACM (2013)

Ontology-Driven, Adaptive, Medical Questionnaires for Patients with Mild Learning Disabilities

Ryan Colin Gibson[1]([✉]) [iD], Matt-Mouley Bouamrane[2] [iD],
and Mark D. Dunlop[1] [iD]

[1] University of Strathclyde, Glasgow, UK
ryan.gibson@strath.ac.uk
[2] University of Edinburgh, Edinburgh, UK

Abstract. Patients with Learning Disabilities (LD) have substantial and unmet healthcare needs, and previous studies have highlighted that they face both health inequalities and worse outcomes than the general population. Primary care practitioners are often the first port-of-call for medical consultations, and one issue faced by LD patients in this context is the very limited time available during consultations - typically less than ten minutes. In order to alleviate this issue, we propose a digital communication aid in the form of an ontology-based medical questionnaire that can adapt to a patient's medical context as well as their accessibility needs (physical and cognitive). The application is intended to be used in advance of a consultation so that a primary care practitioner may have prior access to their LD patients' self-reported symptoms. This work builds upon and extends previous research carried out in the development of adaptive medical questionnaires to include interactive and interface functionalities designed specifically to cater for patients with potentially complex accessibility needs. A patient's current health status and accessibility profile (relating to their impairments) is used to dynamically adjust the structure and content of the medical questionnaire. As such, the system is able to significantly limit and focus questions to immediately relevant concerns while discarding irrelevant questions. We propose that our ontology-based design not only improves the relevance and accessibility of medical questionnaires for patients with LDs, but also provides important benefits in terms of medical knowledge-base modularity, as well as for software extension and maintenance.

Keywords: OWL ontologies · Adaptive questionnaire · Intelligent software development · Knowledge-base modularity · Human-computer interaction · Accessibility · Digital communication aids · Learning Disabilities

1 Introduction

Computer-based medical Information Collection Systems (ICS) can provide a range of benefits in comparison to conventional data extraction practices such as face-to-face interviews. These benefits include more accurate, structured and detailed data [1]; as well as allowing medical professionals to focus on providing patient-centered care,

© Springer Nature Switzerland AG 2019
M. Bramer and M. Petridis (Eds.): SGAI-AI 2019, LNAI 11927, pp. 107–121, 2019.
https://doi.org/10.1007/978-3-030-34885-4_8

rather than conducting data collection tasks. ICS can also play an important role with regards to 'hard to reach' populations, such as individuals with learning disabilities (LDs). For example, medical professionals remain undertrained on the health and communication needs of patients with LDs [2], and this affects their ability to diagnose conditions that are commonly overshadowed within the LD population. In contrast, these symptoms may be embedded in ICS (such as [3–5]) that dynamically adjust to a patient's individual medical context, therefore identifying such conditions on a more consistent basis. Furthermore, systems such as [6, 7] can present information to people with LDs in the format most suited to their own needs, thus increasing their ability to communicate about their health.

As such, adaptive ICS are particularly useful for patients with LDs since the medical conditions and specific needs of this population are heterogeneous and wide-ranging - meaning a 'one-size-fits-all' model is simply unfeasible. Consequently, developing a multitude of questionnaires to cater for every possible scenario would be unmanageable and would not scale [6, 7].

In this paper we expand upon previous research on adaptive medical questionnaires (primarily [3–5, 8]), by combining the use of 2 distinct ontologies into a single system, so that the proposed ICS can adapt to both the medical and accessibility needs of a patient with mild LD. An ontology is a formal description of a domain that models a set of concepts within this domain, as well as the relationships that exist between them. They have an important role in the healthcare as they enable complex concepts, such as patient data, to be captured and reused in a generic way.

Our system first mitigates the potential accessibility barriers experienced by a patient by mapping their cognitive and physical impairments to alterations in the user interface (e.g. changing the background color or prioritizing the use of audio feedback). A second medical ontology is then used to dynamically change the structure and content of a medical questionnaire so that it limits and focuses its scope to questions that are deemed immediately relevant to the patient's health status.

The remainder of this paper is structured as follows: we present the background and related work in the next Sect. 2; the methodology in Sect. 3; the ontology development in Sect. 4, the adaptive engine in Sect. 5 and conclude with a scenario-based evaluation in Sect. 6.

2   Background and Related Work

Learning Disabilities
In this work, we consider "learning disability" using the World Health Organization (WHO) definition[1]: *"they have a significantly reduced ability to understand new or complex information and to learn and apply new skills. This results in a reduced ability to cope independently and begins before adulthood with a lasting effect on development."* LDs can also have a significant impact on an individual's capacity to interact with digital technologies as is discussed in depth in [6, 7].

---

[1] WHO: Definition: intellectual disability, https://bit.ly/2qFOwFX (2010).

Adaptive Questionnaires

Bouamrane et al. were the first to propose the use of ontologies to drive the adaptive behavior of medical questionnaires during preoperative assessment [3–5]. Their ontology-based questionnaire updates its structure depending on the input received from the patient, thus removing questions that are of no relevance to the risk assessment while expanding on those deemed to be important. The system can thus capture finer-grained information providing it is relevant to the patient's specific medical context.

Benmimoune et al. [8] subsequently extended this framework to implement questionnaires which are not 'hard-coded' to a specific domain. They proposed a further ontology that gives meaning to a specific question by relating it to a concept within a particular healthcare domain such as "digestive surgery". The patient's interactions with the system (i.e. the questions presented/answers received) are also captured via an Interrogations History Ontology. This process is facilitated by a questionnaire engine (similar to that in [3–5]) which interprets the structure of the Questionnaire Ontology and stores the results in the Interrogations History Ontology.

Accessible Interfaces

With regards to the use of ontologies and knowledge-base to address the accessibility requirement of users with additional needs, Yesilada et al. [9] developed a semi-automated annotation tool that uses an ontology to translate web elements into "travel" concepts. These concepts assist users with visual impairments when navigating internet content. Obrenovic et al. [10] also employed ontologies to assist researchers in the creation of multimodal interfaces. Three sets of logically related ontologies were developed to capture basic concepts that may affect how an interface is utilized, including: the computing environment; the capabilities of the user; and the context of the user's surroundings. A fourth ontology is then used to import and connect the concepts from these domains to support the definition of interaction on multiple levels. Developers may then view how their design choices impact various human factors. Castillejo et al. also proposed an ontology that captures 3 sets of characteristics: the user's characteristics, the environment's characteristics, and the device's characteristics [11]. Rule sets are then executed to enact adaptions to a mobile device based on these characteristics.

Karim and Tjoa [12, 13] proposed using ontologies to formally describe a mapping between a user's impairments and the available interface characteristics (e.g. low visual acuity to text size). This was achieved via a class-subclass hierarchy and the use of description logic statements to compute automatic interface adaptions. Finally, in contrast to the previous approaches, Marino et al. [14] proposed a model which focuses on enhancing a user's capabilities as opposed to mitigating the impact of disabilities.

3   Methodology

Our system consists of 3 entities, as shown in Fig. 1: an ontology to model the accessibility needs of the patient; a second ontology to model the medical needs of the patient; and a Java Adaptive Engine to accept user input and interact with the ontologies as appropriate. We made a deliberate decision to separate the 2 ontologies to ensure they may be used as stand-alone resources and can be updated and maintained separately, which is considered as best-practice design in ontology and software engineering [15]. Both the accessibility preferences and medical questionnaire ontologies were modelled using the Web Ontology Language (OWL), and the Protégé-OWL development tool [16]. The java adaptive engine was implemented using the OWL API [17].

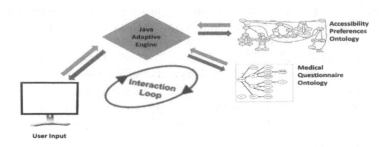

Fig. 1. System architecture for the adaptive questionnaire.

Accessibility & Medical Ontology

The primary intention of the accessibility ontology is to model common impairments experienced by people with LDs (both physical and cognitive) and map these to potential adaptations in the interface employed. We identified and modelled these impairments using the International Classification of Functioning, Disability and Health (WHO-ICF) framework proposed by the World Health Organization[2]. Forward engineering was then used to semantically link these impairments to appropriate changes in the interface based on the Web Content Accessibility Guidelines[3]. This ontology requires the user to input their accessibility needs via a questionnaire (as opposed to an automated process that utilizes other resources) meaning it should be completed in conjunction with a carer or care assistant (e.g. practice nurse).

We used published guidelines regarding the health needs of people with LDs in order to design the questions to be embedded within the ICS; specifically, the "Learning Disability Health Toolkit"[4] (LDHT) as it contains information on the most common symptoms experienced by LD patients. We used forward engineering to model the medical symptoms contained within the LDHT, as well as their relationship to other body parts or conditions in the medical ontology. We began by modelling the symptoms related to a single condition contained within the toolkit and iteratively refined the emerging properties as further conditions were added. The concepts were modelled as classes and subclasses, instead of instances, to aid in maintenance as we expect such concepts to change frequently as new guidelines are released. Since the

---

[2] https://www.who.int/classifications/icf/en/.

[3] https://www.w3.org/WAI/standards-guidelines/wcag/.

[4] Turning Point: Learning Disability Health Toolkit, https://bit.ly/2JgecS0 (2016).

needs of people with LDs differ dramatically from other populations, we were unable to identify (and therefore reuse) appropriate conceptualizations that met our goals. As such, it was necessary to develop the 2 ontologies described in the next section.

Java Adaptive Engine

Rather than utilizing a reasoner to classify the behavior of the ontologies, we have developed a rule-based Java Adaptive Engine to decouple the handling of the user-input and the traversal of the ontologies from the actual ontologies. This also promotes convenient maintainability as changes can be made to the questionnaires without affecting the Java Adaptive Engine and vice-versa, allowing for lesser system complexity and higher modularity as recommended in [15].

4   Ontologies Development

4.1   Medical Questionnaire Ontology

The ontology aims to model two distinct aspects: (1) the structure of the questionnaire and (2) the adaptive behavior of the questionnaire. These fundamental principles are based on previous work [3–5], and have been adapted to cater to the concepts that emerged whilst modelling the conditions contained in the LDHT. A high-level overview of the developed classes may be found in Fig. 2.

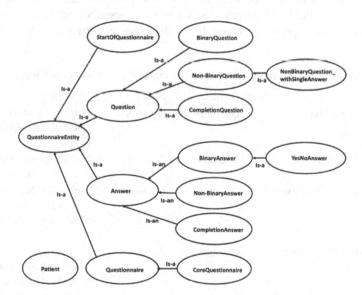

Fig. 2. Overview of the classes contained in the medical questionnaire ontology.

- *Questionnaire:* Comprised of thematically related *Question* classes.
- *CoreQuestionnaire:* Comprised of *Question* classes that are used to determine whether the primary *Questionnaire's* (equating to the body parts and conditions found in the LDHT) are presented to the patient. All *Question's* contained within are adaptive thus heavily restricting the number of *Questionnaires* parsed.

- **StartOfQuestionnaire:** Points to the *Questionnaire* class containing the first *Question* to be presented to the user - primarily *CoreQuestionnaire*, see Sect. 5.
- **Question:** Captures the information used to determine the runtime behavior of the questionnaire implementation. This includes: the set of possible *Answers* for a *Question*; and the set of potential actions that may occur upon receiving user input. 3 types of *Questions* are included: (1) *BinaryQuestion* provides exactly two *Answers* to the user, with the option to select one of these *Answers*. (2) *NonBinaryQuestion* presents 3 or more *Answers*, with *NonBinaryQuestion_withSingleAnswer* permitting the user to select just one of these *Answers*. (3) Finally, *CompletionQuestion* requires the user to input free text when answering *Questions* that have no defined *Answers*. All *Questions* are characterized by a questionContent property to display the question text and a questionPriority property to determine the order in which the *Questions* contained within a *Questionnaire* are presented.
- **Answer:** Mirrors the *Question* classes whilst encapsulating the information required by the user interface to display the *Answer* i.e. an answerContent property.
- **Patient:** Encapsulates the patient's personal information (gender, age, impairments) which facilitates the restriction of a specific *Question* or *Questionnaire*.

Medical Questionnaire Properties
Object properties are fundamental in defining both the structure of the questionnaire implementation and its run-time behavior. As such, two main sets of properties have been defined, structural and adaptive, and these are described in Table 1 using the acronyms S and A respectively. Examples of their use are provided in Sect. 5.

Table 1. Object properties included in medical questionnaire ontology.

Property	Type	Domain	Range	Description
containsQuestionAbout	S	Questionnaire	Question	Determines which Questions are contained within a Questionnaire
hasExpectedAnswers	S	Question	Answer	Links a Question class to its Answer classes
hasAlwaysRelatedQuestion	S	Question	Question	Links two Question classes provided one is always followed by the other
ifAnswerToThisQuestionIs	A	Question	Answer	Declares Question is adaptive. Links Question to further Question classes depending on the Answer received
thenGoToQuestion	A		Question	Links a follow-up question to a specific answer
hasAssociatedQuestionnaire	A	Question	Questionnaire	Links a Question to a follow-up Questionnaire

Three specialized adaptive properties have also been defined to restrict the presentation of *Questions* based on the user's age (onlyIfAgeIs), sex (onlyIfSexIs), and impairments (onlyIfImpairmentIsNotApplicable). The latter depends on the information extracted from the Accessibility Preferences Ontology described in Sect. 4.2.

4.2 Accessibility Ontology

A wide range, and combination of, impairments must be addressed to ensure the system is accessible to the LD population. The accessibility preferences ontology achieves this by extracting the cognitive/physical impairments experienced by the patient, before mapping these to a model of interface changes that mitigate their effect (similar to [12]).

A high-level overview of the ontologies structure may be found in Fig. 3. Its basic composition is similar to that of the medical questionnaire ontology described in Sect. 4.1, with adjustments being made to capture the concepts included in the WHO-ICF framework. The new classes that emerged as a result of this process are as follows:

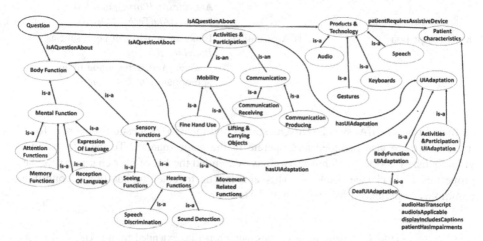

Fig. 3. Overview of the Accessibility Preferences Ontology. The hearing functions concept has been extended to demonstrate the effect a UIAdaptation may have on PatientCharactersistics.

- *BodyFunctions:* Captures the potential options (impairments) that may be presented to the user related to an individual's functioning of the body. This includes both mental functions, and sensory functions. An impairmentDescription annotation is used to describe the impairment in a textual format.
- *ActivitesAndParticipation:* Essentially the same as *BodyFunctions* except that it captures impairments that may affect an individual's ability to complete everyday tasks. This includes mobility and communication.
- *ProductsAndTechnology:* Captures the potential assistive devices required by the user to operate digital technologies. Such devices were extracted from [14] and grouped under the following concepts: Audio, Gestures, Keyboard and Screen.

- **UIAdaptation:** Models the interface adaptations that should occur once the user has indicated that they have an impairment or that they require an assistive device.
- **PatientCharacteristics:** Encapsulates the individual's user interface preferences, which have been previously captured via the UIAdaptation classes.

Accessibility Ontology Properties

Two sets of properties have been defined: object properties that determine the structure and run-time behavior of the questionnaire; and data properties that capture the individual's user interface preferences. Table 2 contains a description of the newly developed object properties, with examples of their use being found in Sect. 5.

Table 2. Object properties included in accessibility preferences ontology.

Property	Domain	Range	Description
isAQuestionAbout	Question		Links a *Question* to a relevant option class i.e. a subclass of *BodyFunctions*, *ActivitiesAndParticipation*, or *ProductsAndTechnology*
hasUIAdaptation		UIAdapatation	Links an impairment i.e. a subclass of *BodyFunctions* or *ActivitiesAndParticipation* to an appropriate *UIAdaptation*

In addition, the ifAnswerToThisQuestionIs and thenGoToQuestion properties found in Sect. 4.1 are also included and operate in the same manner. To capture the individual's user interface preferences, we have extended the list of user characteristic data properties in [11] (see Table 3). This enables us to cater to additional conditions commonly experienced by people with LDs.

Table 3. PatientCharacteristics data properties extended from [11].

Subclass	Property name	Description
Audio	audioHasTranscript	A Boolean value that describes whether an accompanying transcript should be provided in addition to audio feedback
Interface	interfaceEnablesScrolling	A Boolean value that indicates whether scrolling is enabled
	interfaceEnablesSwiping	A Boolean value that captures whether swiping is enabled
	interfaceTouchStrategy	This property models the preferred touch input method with the following possibilities: "default" and "end-tap"
	interfaceTracksAttention	A Boolean value which indicates whether an eye-tracker may be utilized to determine if the system is in possession of the user's attention

(continued)

Table 3. (*continued*)

Subclass	Property name	Description
Patient	patientHasImpairments	A list of impairments that affect the individual
	patientRequiresAssistiveDevice	A list of assistive devices required by the individual to operate digital technologies effectively
View	viewIncludesCaptions	A Boolean value indicating whether videos should include captions
	viewIncludesGIFS	A Boolean value describing whether GIFs are appropriate to the individual
	viewIncludesProgess	A Boolean value which captures whether the individual's progress should be recorded and returned

5 System Implementation – Java Adaptive Engine

5.1 Java Engine

As shown in Fig. 1, the Adaptive Engine is decoupled from the underlying questionnaire models. Consequently, we had a significant amount of discretion regarding the implementation of the engine, and ultimately chose to develop the questionnaire as a stack, similar to the approach adopted by Bouamrane et al. [3–5].

The engine first calls the method required to traverse the Accessibility Preferences Questionnaire Ontology and carries out the following 5 stage process: (1) the initial *Question* classes are loaded into the stack in order of priority. (2) The *Question* at the top of the stack is popped and presented to the patient, along with the potential options that the user may select from. These options are identified via the direct subclasses of the object contained in the current *Question's* "isAQuestionAbout" superclass. As such, they may be a subclass of *ActivitesAndParticipation*, *BodyFunction*, or *ProductsAndTechnology*. (3) An appropriate *Answer* is extracted from the user and subsequently mapped to changes in the interface via the filler contained in the selected *Answer's* "hasUIAdaption some *UIAdaptation*" superclass. The annotation properties held in the *UIAdaptation* class are then used to update those held in *PatientCharacteristics*.

(4) The engine then checks to see if the current *Question* is adaptive i.e. whether it is a subclass of "(ifAnswerToThisQuestionIs some *Answer*) and (thenGoToQuestion some *Question*). If the *Question* is not adaptive, or the input received from the user does not trigger further questions, the system moves on to stage 5. Otherwise, an additional *Question* is added to the top of the stack via the "thenGoToQuestion some *Question*" superclass. (5) Steps 2 to 5 are repeated until the stack becomes empty.

The Java Engine then calls the method used to traverse the Medical Questionnaire Ontology and subsequently passes in the information held in *PatientCharacteristics'* patientHasImpairments data property. This parameter is used to update the hasImpairments property contained in the Medical Questionnaire's *Patient* class, which facilitates the restriction of *Questions* based on the user's physical or cognitive disabilities. The following 5 steps are then carried out.

(1) the starting *Questionnaire* is identified by examining *StartOfQuestionnaire* and extracting the filler from its superclass "hasAssociatedQuestionnaire some Question-naire". (2) The *Questionnaire's* "containsQuestionAbout some *Question*" superclass is then examined with all direct subclasses of the filler being added to the stack in order of priority, provided they satisfy all restrictions placed on it e.g. a *Question* may not be added if it is a subclass of "onlyIfSexIs some Female" and the patient is male.

(3) The *Question* at the top of the stack is popped and presented to the patient along with the set of possible answers the user may select from. These options constitute the direct subclasses of the filler included in the *Question's* "hasExpectedAnswer some *Answer*" superclass. (4) Once an appropriate *Answer* has been received from the patient, the Java engine stores the *Question/Answer* pairing and subsequently checks to see if the current *Question* is adaptive i.e. whether its superclasses includes "ifAnswerToThisQuestionIs some *Answer*." If the *Question* is not adaptive or the *Answer* received by the user does not trigger its adaptive properties, then the system moves on to stage 5. If the current *Question* is adaptive and requires a single *Question* to be added to the stack, then this is pushed to the top via "thenGoToQuestion some *Question*", provided it meets all restrictions placed on it. If multiple *Questions* are

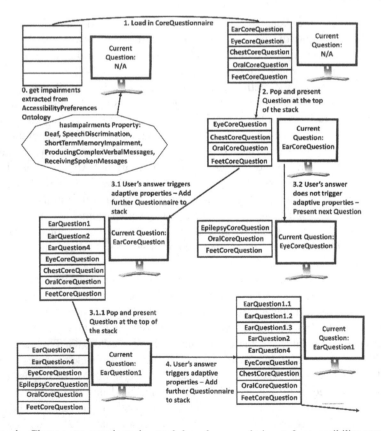

Fig. 4. Changes to questionnaire stack based on user's input & accessibility needs.

required to be added e.g. those contained in a *Questionnaire*, then this is done in a similar process to that described in stage 2. (5) Stages 3–5 are repeated until the stack becomes empty.

5.2 Dynamic Changes to Stack

We will now present an example of how the Medical Questionnaire stack reacts to the patient's input, to show the importance of *CoreQuestionnaire* and onlyIfImpairmentIsNotApplicable in reducing the number of irrelevant *Questions* presented.

The initialization phase is shown in step 0 of Fig. 4 and involves the hasImpairments property of the *Patient* class being updated with the impairments identified by the Accessibility Preferences ontology. The Java Engine then pushes all *Questions* contained in *CoreQuestionnaire* (step 1) to the stack in order or priority, since this is identified as the starting *Questionnaire*. *CoreQuestionnaire* encapsulates the *Question* classes that link to further *Questionnaires* containing queries on specific body parts or conditions. All *Questions* are adaptive meaning an entire *Questionnaire* can be bypassed based on a single response received from the patient. For example, in step 3 of Fig. 4 the user is required to answer the current *Question* displayed - in this case *EarCoreQuestion*. The questionContent annotation attached to this class is presented on the screen along with the possible answers. If the user selects the option "No", the system simply presents the next *Question* at the top of the stack, see step 3.2 in Fig. 4. Consequently, the class *EarQuestionnaire* is never parsed by the Java Engine or presented to the user.

Step 3.1 in Fig. 4 demonstrates what occurs if the patient's answer triggered the adaptive properties of *EarCoreQuestion*. All *Questions* contained in *EarQuestionnaire* is added to the stack except from *EarQuestion3*. *EarQuestion3* is not parsed as it is a subclass of "onlyIfImpairmentIsNotApplicable some Deaf" and the condition "Deaf" is included in *Patient's* hasImpairments property. *Questions* that are not a subclass of *CoreQuestionnaire* may also cause additional *Questions/Questionnaires* to be added to the stack, as shown in step 4 of Fig. 4.

6 Scenario Based Evaluation

In a similar approach to [11], we have used scenarios to demonstrate the scope of adaptation that occurs when the Medical Questionnaire Ontology responds to the accessibility and medical needs of users. A more empirical evaluation was not appropriate at this stage due to the lack of available clinical alternative and augmentative communication applications for people with LDs. Previous research such as [6, 7] has focused on extracting design requirements from experts, as opposed to target stakeholders; thus, embedding the questionnaire within such technologies could negatively influence the results obtained, if the user interface is inappropriate for the participants needs. Currently, the Medical Questionnaire Ontology is populated with 110 *Questions* across 9 distinct *Questionnaires* capturing conditions of the mouth, feet, chest, ears and eyes, as well as the patient's mental wellbeing, toiletry habits, weight trends, and general health.

Table 4. Important sections of the proposed user interface model for scenarios 1 and 2.

Scenario 1		Scenario 2	
Property	Value	Property	Value
viewHasPageLayout	Right-aligned	viewHasTextSize	14
patientRequiresAssistiveDevice	SpeechRecognition	viewIncludesCaptions	True
interfaceAcceptsAudioInput	True	patientRequiresAssistiveDevice	ScreenMagnifier
viewHasTextSize	10	interfaceAcceptsAudioInput	True
interfaceTouchStrategy	End-tap	interfaceTracksUserAttention	True
patientHasImpairments	ComplexMotorFunctions, LeftFieldLoss, TappingAccuracy	patientHasImpairments	Deaf, SpeechDiscrimination, ShortSighted, AttentionDeficit, ShortTermMemory, Producing&ReceivingVerbalMessages
		audioIsApplicable	False
		viewIncludesProgress	True

Scenario 1

Jane currently works for a national advocacy charity. The left-hand side of her vision is impaired meaning she finds it difficult to interact with applications that have been developed in the standard, justified format. Jane has a slight motor impairment; however, this does not affect her ability to interact with digital technologies on an everyday basis. Nonetheless, when she becomes tired her touch accuracy reduces significantly, at which point she prefers to interact with the user interface via speech.

Table 4 includes the most relevant sections of Jane's user interface model proposed by the Accessibility Preferences Ontology. The main adaptation to the default interface is captured via the viewHasPageLayout property, which aligns the elements to the right-hand side of the screen. Since her visual acuity is unaffected the default text-size is reduced to assist this process. Regarding Jane's motor impairments, the model has suggested that touch input should only register once an action has been completed, whilst audio input is also a recommended as an interaction modality.

Jane's Medical Needs: *Jane has recently secured a promotion at the advocacy charity meaning her responsibilities have increased substantially over the last few weeks. This increased workload is becoming overwhelming and has had a significant impact on 3 areas of Jane's life – her social routine, relationship with peers, and mental wellbeing. She is currently experiencing the following primary symptoms: difficulty sleeping due to heightened stress and anxiety; a decrease in attentiveness; irritation; and isolation.*

In this instance, just one of the *Questions* contained in *CoreQuestionnaire* has its adaptive properties triggered - *MentalWellbeingCoreQuestion*. Consequently, only the mental wellbeing *Questionnaire* is presented to Jane in addition to the initial 9 *Questions* contained in the *CoreQuestionnaire*. The mental wellbeing *Questionnaire* includes a total of 15 *Questions* of which 6 are dependent on the adaptive properties of 2 separate *Questions* – *SocialRoutineQuestion* and *SleepingRoutineQuestion*. These adaptive properties are triggered, meaning a total of 23 Questions from a possible 110 (20.91%) are presented to Jane.

Scenario 2

John is deaf and therefore has a dependence on visual methods to receive information. Despite this reliance, he is short-sighted and finds it difficult to read small text. In addition, the patient's LD affects their capacity to understand obscure or abstract information and significantly impedes their attention span and short-term memory. He is able to express simple concepts - such as yes or no - via the use of speech yet struggles to convey more complex words/sentences coherently.

The primary adaptations that occur (see Table 4) relate to the user's inability to detect sounds. The audioIsApplicable property states that sound is not a viable method used to provide feedback. Despite this, John has indicated that he is able to use speech to communicate simple needs, hence why the interfaceAcceptsAudioInput value is True. viewIncludesCaptions expresses the need to provide captions alongside any media content. Several adaptations also occur to combat John's short attention span, along with an increase in text size to overcome his short sightedness.

John's Medical Needs: *Regarding John's current health status, he has been confined to his bed over the last few days with a high fever and a feeling of nausea. When active, the patient has been experiencing dizzy spells and cannot stay on his feet for too long. John has found it hard to sleep due to an aching pain emanating from his inner right ear, yet he finds it difficult to communicate this pain.*

In this instance, 2 of the 9 *Questions* contained in *CoreQuestionnaire* has its adaptive properties triggered – *GenerallyUnwellCoreQuestion* and *EarCoreQuestion*. The generally unwell *Questionnaire* includes 7 *Questions*, of which none are adaptive, meaning all are parsed by the system. On the other hand, *EarQuestionnaire* is made up of 9 *Questions*, with 4 of these being dependent on the user's ability to hear. Since John has indicated that he is deaf, these 4 *Questions* are not presented. Therefore, John is required to answer a total of 21 *Questions* (19.09%).

7 Conclusion and Future Work

We have proposed a model for an adaptive questionnaire for patients with learning disabilities that responds to both the accessibility needs of patients (physical and cognitive) as well as their clinical context. In that model, an individual's accessibility profile (i.e. the presence of impairments) is used to customize the interaction and interface to the user's needs. The model also adapts the structure and content of the questionnaire to the patient's specific clinical context to ensure that only relevant questions are asked or expanded on. This is the first research conducted to apply these technologies to the domain of medical data collection for patients with LDs. Opportunities for future work include: expanding our questionnaire to incorporate further conditions; implementing the functionality required to map the extracted accessibility profile to the elements included in the interface; adding further decision support functionalities as in [18] and conducting user evaluations to determine whether the system meets the care needs of patients with LDs and medical practitioners.

References

1. Bachman, J.W.: The patient-computer interview: a neglected tool that can aid the clinician. Mayo Clin. Proc. **78**, 67–78 (2003). https://doi.org/10.4065/78.1.67
2. Afia, A., et al.: Discrimination and other barriers to accessing health care: perspectives of patients with mild and moderate intellectual disability and their carers. PloS one **8**(8), e70855 (2013). https://doi.org/10.1371/journal.pone.0070855
3. Bouamrane, M.-M., Rector, A., Hurrell, M.: Gathering precise patient medical history with an ontology-driven adaptive questionnaire. In: 21st IEEE Symposium on Computer-Based Medical Systems, Jyvaskyla, pp. 539–541 (2008). https://doi.org/10.1109/cbms.2008.24
4. Bouamrane, M.-M., Rector, A., Hurrell, M.: Ontology-driven adaptive medical information collection system. In: An, A., Matwin, S., Raś, Z.W., Ślęzak, D. (eds.) ISMIS 2008. LNCS (LNAI), vol. 4994, pp. 574–584. Springer, Heidelberg (2008). https://doi.org/10.1007/978-3-540-68123-6_62
5. Bouamrane, M.-M., Rector, A., Hurrell, M.: Using ontologies for an intelligent patient modelling, adaptation and management system. In: Meersman, R., Tari, Z. (eds.) OTM 2008. LNCS, vol. 5332, pp. 1458–1470. Springer, Heidelberg (2008). https://doi.org/10.1007/978-3-540-88873-4_36
6. Gibson, R.C., Bouamrane, M.-M., Dunlop, M.: Mobile support for adults with mild learning disabilities during clinical consultations. In: MobileHCI 2018, Spain. ACM Press (2018). https://doi.org/10.1145/3229434.3229469
7. Gibson, R.C., Bouamrane, M.-M., Dunlop, M.: Design requirements for a digital aid to support adults with mild learning disabilities during clinical consultations: qualitative study with experts. JMIR Rehabil. Assist. Technol. **6**, e10449 (2019). https://doi.org/10.2196/10449
8. Benmimoune, L., Hajjam, A., Ghodous, P., Andres, E., Hajjam, M.: Ontology-based contextual information gathering tool for collecting patients data before, during and after a digestive surgery. In: Khan, S.U., Zomaya, Albert Y., Abbas, A. (eds.) Handbook of Large-Scale Distributed Computing in Smart Healthcare. SCC, pp. 623–635. Springer, Cham (2017). https://doi.org/10.1007/978-3-319-58280-1_23
9. Yesilada, Y., Harper, S., Goble, C.A., Stevens, R.R.: Ontology based semantic annotation for enhancing mobility support for visually impaired web users. In: Proceedings of the K-CAP 2003 Workshop on Knowledge Markup and Semantic Annotation (2003)
10. Obrenovic, Z., Starcevic, D., Devedzic, V.: Using ontologies in design of multimodal user interfaces. In: INTERACT 2003, Zurich, Switzerland. pp. 535–542. IOS Press (2003)
11. Castillejo, E., Almeida, A., López-de-Ipiña, D.: Ontology-based model for supporting dynamic and adaptive user interfaces. Int. J. Hum. Comput. Interact. **30**, 771–786 (2014)
12. Karim, S., Tjoa, A.M.: Towards the use of ontologies for improving user interaction for people with special needs. In: Miesenberger, K., Klaus, J., Zagler, Wolfgang L., Karshmer, Arthur I. (eds.) ICCHP 2006. LNCS, vol. 4061, pp. 77–84. Springer, Heidelberg (2006). https://doi.org/10.1007/11788713_12
13. Karim, S., Tjoa, A.M.: Connecting user interfaces and user impairments for semantically optimized information flow in hospital information systems. In: Proceedings of I-MEDIA 2007 and I-SEMANTICS 2007 (2007)
14. Marino, B.D.R., Rodriguez-Fortiz, M.J., Torres, M.V.H., Haddad, H.M.: Accessibility and activity-centered design for ICT users: ACCESIBILITIC ontology. IEEE Access **6** (2018). https://doi.org/10.1109/access.2018.2875869
15. Happel, H.-J., Seedorf, S.: Applications of ontologies in software engineering. In: Semantic Web Enabled Software Engineering (SWESE) (2006)

16. Knublauch, H., Fergerson, Ray W., Noy, Natalya F., Musen, Mark A.: The Protégé OWL plugin: an open development environment for semantic web applications. In: McIlraith, Sheila A., Plexousakis, D., van Harmelen, F. (eds.) ISWC 2004. LNCS, vol. 3298, pp. 229–243. Springer, Heidelberg (2004). https://doi.org/10.1007/978-3-540-30475-3_17
17. Horridge, M., Bechhofer, S., Noppens, O.: Igniting the OWL 1.1 touch paper: the OWL API. In: OWLED (2007)
18. Bouamrane, M.M., Rector, A., Hurrell, M.: Using OWL ontologies for adaptive patient information modelling and preoperative clinical decision support. Knowl. Inf. Syst. **29**, 405–418 (2011)

Exposing Knowledge: Providing a Real-Time View of the Domain Under Study for Students

Omar Zammit[1]([⊠]), Serengul Smith[2]([⊠]), Clifford De Raffaele[1]([⊠]), and Miltos Petridis[2]([⊠])

[1] Middlesex University Malta, Pembroke, Malta
ozammit@ieee.org, cderaffaele@ieee.org
[2] Middlesex University, London, UK
{s.smith,m.petridis}@mdx.ac.uk

Abstract. With the amount of information that exists online, it is impossible for a student to find relevant information or stay focused on the domain under study. Research showed that search engines have deficiencies that might prevent students from finding relevant information. To this end, this research proposes a technical solution that takes the personal search history of a student into consideration and provides a holistic view of the domain under study. Based on algorithmic approaches to assert semantic similarity, the proposed framework makes use of a user interface to dynamically assist students through aggregated results and wordcloud visualizations. The effectiveness of our approach is finally evaluated through the use of commonly used datasets and compared in line with existing research.

Keywords: Search engine keywords · Similarity analysis · Text enrichment

1 Introduction

Confidence in search engines has increased, some Internet users nowadays tend to give high veracity to a website because of its inclusion or high ranking in a search engine result [1]. With the amount of information that exists on-line it is more difficult for users to find accurate information [2] and therefore it is impossible for an Internet user to find information without the use of a search engine [3]. Unfortunately, search engines have deficiencies. Search engines tend to be biased and favour certain web sites over others [4]. Discrepancies between search engine results make it difficult for Internet users to decide which search engines to trust. It is already challenging for Internet users to judge the relevance of on-line content [5] and ignore fake news [6] let alone having such inconsistency and doubts about validity.

By design, search engines are targeting a generic audience and search results might not be suitable for a specific group of people [7] like students. We are

© Springer Nature Switzerland AG 2019
M. Bramer and M. Petridis (Eds.): SGAI-AI 2019, LNAI 11927, pp. 122–135, 2019.
https://doi.org/10.1007/978-3-030-34885-4_9

focusing on providing a better search experience to students while they are doing research, and try to overcome some of the deficiencies imposed by search engines. To achieve this we are proposing a solution that aims to help students focus more on the domain they are studying by exposing them to various resources related to the domain. The solution takes into consideration previously searched queries related to the current domain being studied using a combination of similarity analysis techniques. A bag-of-words is created that is used to query third-party APIs to find relevant papers and construct a wordcloud. The proposed solution includes a graphical user interface that will allow students to have a holistic view of the domain being studied.

This paper proposes a framework that takes into consideration the students' personal search history to provide an integrated and comprehensive view of the search domain. Following a brief review in Sect. 2 on related work, the paper presents in detail the proposed framework design and implementation in Sect. 3. Section 4 presents and discusses the results obtained from the implementation when the framework was compared with existing solutions. Lastly, a conclusion is drawn in Sect. 5.

2   Current Solutions

Various solutions are trying to assist students in their study. Some suggest to move away from a 'search engine' and focus on an 'educational search engine' targeting a particular domain [7]. Such approach is problematic since students tend to rely on search engines before libraries to search a new term or when they are unfamiliar with a new topic [8], and therefore it might be challenging to convince them to move away from search engines. Some focused their studies on users URL visited or browsing clicks to understand browsing habits [7,9–11]. We are taking a similar approach but we are focusing mainly on the keywords visited by the student since these are the entry point of a web search session. A web search session starts with a student issuing a query, the query is processed and the result may surface a website. Students will validate the result and visit the website (see Fig. 1) [12]. Entities are bidirectional, students can start with a query and can continue formulating different queries until the required result is obtained [9]. Queries are often appended

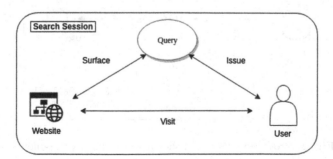

Fig. 1. A web search session as explained in [12]

to URLs [13] and some studies already showed that such data can be used to learn about users browsing behaviour [14] or to understand how students search with the purpose of learning. Usta et al. (2014) focused on secondary school students search behaviour in a learning environment and compared such behaviour with general web search engines trends. Vidinli and Ozcan (2016) proposed a general modular framework for query suggestion algorithm development to overcome the issue that search engines are targeting a very diverse population. Their research focused mainly on secondary school students since such students have difficulty in formulating queries. The only issue with such a framework is that they are targeting secondary school students only.

Smith et al. (2017) did an exploratory study on query auto-completion usage during a search session with assigned tasks. To monitor user activity they used a modified version of CrowdLogger[1], a Google Chrome extension that collects searched keywords. Keywords where re-submitted using Google QAC API and all **Search Engine Results Pages** (SERP) were scraped and cleaned from images and other elements before displaying them to the user. Such an approach can be used to collect data and evaluate a system that its main aim is to learn more about browsing habits. We opted to take a seamless approach, instead of forcing students to install external plugins, we are reading keywords directly from the browser local history database. In Bast and Weber (2006) the authors mined query logs and used query frequency to predict query completion and rank suggestions [15].

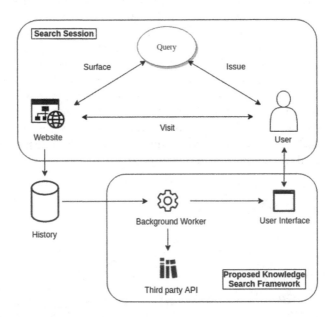

Fig. 2. Proposed framework showing additional components

---

[1] https://crowdlogger.cs.umass.edu/.

3   Proposed Knowledge Search Framework

Keywords search terms play an important role to understand user's psychology [16] and thus we are using keywords searched by the student to understand which domains relate to the student. Past students keywords are taken into consideration since these requests determine the context of the research [17,18]. To improve student experience we are extending the search session as described in Kim et al. (2012) by adding an additional framework (see Fig. 2). Internet browsers, like Google Chrome, are storing history data on the local computer in SQLite databases [16] for reference. Such databases contain data about URLs visited by the student and keywords searched online.

3.1   Background Worker

We implemented a background worker to extract information from the local history files and predict suitable content. To achieve this the SQLite history file is copied into an accessible location (since this cannot be read while being used by the browser) and SQL statements are executed to extract keywords currently being searched by the student (refer to Listing 1.1 for an SQL example to retrieve data).

Listing 1.1. Query to get all keywords searched by the user from Google Chrome

```
1  select * from urls
2  inner join keyword_search_terms
3  on urls.id = keyword_search_terms.url_id
4  where urls.last_visit_time > ?
5  order by urls.last_visit_time asc limit ?;
```

Text Enrichment Using Third-Party API. Keywords are not enough to determine what students are searching for. Search queries tend to be short ambiguous and under specified [19]. Having short text is less effective due to its brevity and less sparsity of words and when dealing with such data, enriching the semantics using external entities is essential [20]. Various studies used third party like Wikipedia to enrich text or find similarity between keywords [10,20–23].

We implemented text enrichment in the background worker so that more insight is known about the domain related to the keywords submitted by the student. For each keyword searched by the student that is stored in the local history, a Google search URL is created (see Listing 1.2) and sent to Google.

Listing 1.2. Google request URL format

```
1  url = f"https://www.google.com.mt/search?" \
2        f"q={keyword}&oq={keyword}&client=ubuntu"
```

The HTML response contains search results in the form of HTML anchor tags consisting of a URL to an external source and a short description (anchor text). The background worker will parse the response and identify anchor tags. Since results may contain trending and e-commerce anchor tags other than sponsored links [21], Python libraries based on Levenshtein distance[2] were used to determine if the anchor tag is relevant to the keyword being searched. This was done by comparing the anchor tag description to the keyword itself.

Levenshtein distance is the number of deletions, insertions or substitutions required to transform a source string s into a target string t [24]. Computed as:

Step 1: Let n be the length of s and m be the length of t.
Step 2: If $min(n, m) = 0$ then $lev = max(n, m)$. No more steps.
Step 3: Create a matrix d containing $0..m$ rows and $0..n$ columns.
Step 4: Set the first row to $0..n$ and first column to $0..m$.
Step 5: Process each $s[i]$ value from 1 to n
Step 6: Process each $t[i]$ value from 1 to m
Step 7: If $s[i] = t[i]$ then $cost = 0$
Step 8: If $s[i] \neq t[i]$ then $cost = 1$
Step 9: Set $d[i, j]$ as follows:

$$d[i, j] = min \begin{cases} d[i-1, j] + 1 \\ d[i, j-1] + 1 \\ d[i-1, j-1] + cost \end{cases} \tag{1}$$

Step 10: Repeat from step 5 until $d[n, m]$ value is found.
Step 11: $lev = d[n, m]$

The smaller the Levenshtein distance between the keyword and the anchor text description, the more similar the two strings are [24]. Once anchor texts having a high degree of similarity are identified, a web request is done for each anchor tag link and a bag-of-words based on their HTML content is created. Each HTML response obtained from anchor tags link was cleaned as described by Hu et al. (2013), that is, removing HTML tags from the response, identify tokens, removing stop words and eliminating punctuation [25]. The normalization steps [26] done in this research are similar to the steps suggested by Gowtham et al. (2014), the only difference is that we used the Python Natural Language Toolkit, since this includes functions to convert text to tokens, has a list of stop words, can perform part of speech tagging and can convert a word to its lemma [27]. The toolkit contains an implementation of the WordNet lexical database [28] that we used to check the validity of the words since it models the lexical knowledge of an English native speaker and defines Nouns and Verbs in a well-defined hierarchy [28–30]. The majority of queries submitted by users over the internet are a structured collection of noun-phrases, in fact, 70% of the query terms are made up mainly of nouns and proper nouns [31] while other words like helping verbs and pronouns are considered as stop-words [21]. As stated

---

[2] https://github.com/seatgeek/fuzzywuzzy.

by Barr et al. (2008) part-of-speech tagging on query keywords can be significant when extracting features in machine learning. We considered this fact and in addition to text normalization, tokens that are not nouns and verbs were removed from the bag-of-words. Once text enrichment is done, a local database is created that stores all keywords searched by the user and their respective bag-of-words. We took this approach so that text enrichment is only done once for a given keyword.

3.2   User Interface

When dealing with large amount of data, the focus point should not just be the collection of data but the analysis and the ability to find meaningful results from it [32]. In order to assist students a user interface was created that will allow the students to view the results and the predictions computed by the background worker (see Fig. 3). The user interface is divided as follows:

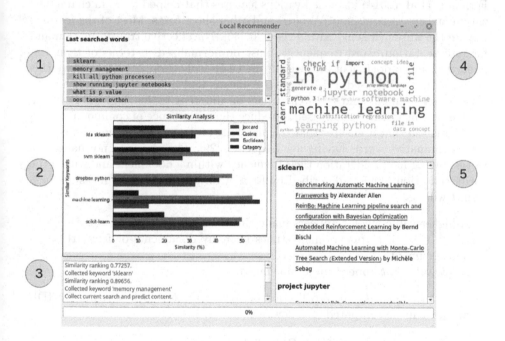

Fig. 3. Evaluation user interface to display predicted data

1. *Current Search*: Provides a list of the last keywords searched by the student.
2. *Similar Searches*: Previously searched keywords refer to Sect. 3.3.
3. *System Logs*: Contains system logs.
4. *Domain Wordcloud*: Representation of the most commonly used **ngrams** in the domain being searched.
5. *Academic References*: Paper recommendation.

The framework visually exposes students to new terminologies, by including a wordcloud containing bigrams extracted from the bag-of-words associated with each similar keyword identified. Bigrams were first searched in Wikipedia to ensure their validity and submitted to the Arxiv database [33] to retrieve papers related to the domain being searched by the student.

3.3   Similarity Analysis

Feature Extraction for Similarity Analysis. In order to find similar keyword searches similarity analysis was used. Hansen and Jaumard (1997) stated that in order to group data, a dataset $O = \{O_1, O_2, ..., O_n\}$ of N entities is needed [34]. The dataset is made up of the keywords searched by the user and their respective bag-of-words. To classify samples O, one should identify p characteristics of each sample and end up with a matrix X of $N \times p$. Since these characteristics define and will determine the dissimilarities between entities. Fernando et al. (2014) identified various features that helped them in characterization and categorization of Weblogs and other short texts. Most of the features rely on the words (tokens) within the text [35]. For effective transformation and for representation, word frequencies must be normalized in terms of their frequency within a document and within the entire collection [29]. To achieve this Bafna et al. (2016) used TF-IDF with K-means and hierarchical algorithms to classify news, emails and research papers on different topics [36]. TF-IDF was used since this is a technique used to reduce the importance of common terms in a collection so that it ensures that the matching of documents is more influenced by discriminative words having low frequency [29]. The aim is to normalize the words, taking in consideration their frequency within a document and within the entire collection [29]. As described by Erra et al. (2015) TF-IDF measure for a term t will be:

- A higher value when t appears many times within few documents.
- A low value if t appears many times in many documents or fewer times in one document.
- A low value if t appears in all documents.

Let $D = \{d_1, d_2, ..., d_n\}$ be a collection of documents or block of texts. TF-IDF for word t can be computed as follows:

$$tfidf(t, d, D) = tf(t, d) \times idf(t, D) \tag{2}$$

where $tf(t, d)$ is the number of instances of t in a document d. And $idf(t, D)$ which is the inverse document frequency can be described as [37]:

$$idf(t, D) = \log_{10}\left(\frac{|D|}{|\{d|t \in d\}|}\right) \tag{3}$$

Where the total amount of documents D is divided by the number of documents containing term t.

In this research each bag-of-word for a given keyword was treated as a document and converted into a TF-IDF matrix.

In order to find similar keywords, we used three similarity measures. Cosine similarity, Euclidean distance and Jaccard similarity. The first two measures take as an input the TF-IDF vector to compute the similarity, while the latter takes the actual bag-of-words. Every time a student searches a new keyword, the background worker will detect the keyword and creates a bag-of-words and a TF-IDF vector. Cosine similarity, Euclidean distance and Jaccard similarity are computed comparing the searched keyword bag-of-words with existing keywords. Similar keywords are selected as follows:

- Let $C = \{x : x$ keyword having high Cosine similarity$\}$
- Let $J = \{x : x$ keyword having high Jaccard similarity$\}$
- Let $E = \{x : x$ keyword having high Euclidean distance$\}$
- Display only entries from $C \cap J$, $C \cap E$ and $E \cap J$.

Cosine Similarity. Cosine similarity can be used with TF-IDF to measure the similarity between two vectors since such measure is suitable because it focuses on the orientation of the document rather than the magnitude [38]. Cosine similarity ranges from -1 (exactly opposite), to 1 (exactly the same) [38].

$$similarity = \cos(\theta) = \frac{A \cdot B}{\|A\| \times \|B\|} = \frac{\sum_{i=1}^{n} A_i B_i}{\sqrt{\sum_{i=1}^{n} A_i^2} \sqrt{\sum_{i=1}^{n} B_i^2}} \qquad (4)$$

Euclidean Distance. If $X_i = (x_{i,1}, ..., x_{i,D})$ and $X_j = (x_{j,1}, ..., x_{j,D})$ are D-dimensional vectors representing two bag-of-words for two keywords that need to be compared. Since distance range can vary, normalization of the result was done using $\frac{1}{1+\eta}$. The Euclidean distance η between both vectors is computed as [39]

$$\eta = \sqrt{\sum_{d=1}^{D} (x_{i,d} - x_{j,d})^2} \qquad (5)$$

Jaccard Similarity. Jaccard similarity can determine the similarity between two data sets and is computed by dividing the number of features that are common between two datasets by the number of features that are not common [40]. Let A and B be two bag-of-words for two keywords that need to be compared. Jaccard similarity can be computed as.

$$Jaccard(A, B) = \frac{|A \cap B|}{|A \cup B|} \qquad (6)$$

Weighted Score Based Aggregation. A weighted score based aggregation was used as suggested by Vidinli and Ozcan (2016) to aggregate the three algorithms used and compute the final similarity score. A score is assigned for each keyword searched by the student from the local database. The top 10 keywords having the highest scores are displayed in the user interface and presented to the student as top similar keywords. Each similarity score V was assigned a coefficient k and the final score was computed as.

$$Score = k_{cos} \times V_{cos} + k_{jak} \times V_{jak} + k_{euc} \times V_{euc} \tag{7}$$

4   Evaluation

In order to evaluate the proposed solution and assess the semantic relationship validity, a quantitative methodology was adopted whereby the effectiveness of our approach was mathematically measured and statistically analysed based on datasets used by **Mturk-771**[3] [41], **Rel-122**[4] [42] and **WordSimilarity-353**[5] [17], since these are some of the most commonly used datasets for similarity analysis [43]. Datasets are composed of two terms and their similarity score based on human judgment. A grid search [44] approach similar to the one described by Buitinck et al. (2013) was conducted on each dataset to determine the best similarity coefficient and to validate the results obtained. A nested loop was created that allowed to iterate through 11 coefficient values (from 0 to 2 with 0.2 increments) for each similarity analysis totalling a 11^3 combinations. Within each combination, a similarity score was computed by our system for each word pair in the dataset. Pearson product-moment correlation coefficient [45] and Spearman rank-order correlation coefficient [46] were used to compare the similarity score obtained by our system with respect to the datasets human judgment score. For every grid search iteration, the highest Pearson and Spearman rank was noted together with the iteration coefficients and tabulated in Table 1.

Table 1. Grid search results for all datasets

WordSimilarity-353 grid search results				
Cosine coefficient	Jaccard coefficient	Euclidean coefficient	Pearson	Spearman
1.4	0	0	**0.4568**	0.5664
1.8	0	1.2	0.4370	**0.5687**
Mturk-771 grid search results				
Cosine coefficient	Jaccard coefficient	Euclidean coefficient	Pearson	Spearman
0.8	0	0	**0.4419**	**0.5283**
Rel-122 grid search results				
Cosine coefficient	Jaccard coefficient	Euclidean coefficient	Pearson	Spearman
2	0	0	**0.4389**	0.4699
0.6	0	0.2	0.3389	**0.4796**

---

[3] http://www2.mta.ac.il/~gideon/mturk771.html.
[4] http://www.cs.ucf.edu/~seansz/rel-122/.
[5] http://www.cs.technion.ac.il/~gabr/resources/data/wordsim353/.

Results in Table 1 show that Jaccard similarity did not contribute in improving the accuracy of the analysis, whilst the Euclidean distance contributed in improving the Spearman Correlation for some datasets. In order to evaluate our approach, we compared our similarity results to existing research mainly focusing on the work done by Li et al. (2017). In their research these authors used Wikipedia features to find the similarity between terms and they compared their results with existing benchmarks.

Table 2. Comparison of Pearson and Spearman as Li et al. (2017)

Dataset	Pearson		Spearman	
	Benchmark	Our System	Benchmark	Our System
Mturk-771	**0.56**	0.44	**0.62**	0.53
Rel-122	**0.64**	0.44	**0.65**	0.47
WordSimilarity-353	**0.56**	0.46	**0.76**	0.57

As shown in Table 2, albeit the obtained results values are lower than the benchmarks identified in Li et al. (2017), this does not imply that the proposed solution is inadequate in its ability to assist students. One should note that the evaluation results are measuring the ability of our system to compute the similarity between two resultant keywords or for a given word search, and only strictly score on the ability to retrieve a preset keyword from the tuples within the dataset. Conversely however, in the context of aiding student learning and searching, our framework is able to take into consideration a range of relevant keywords for each search and to this end our similarity analysis is configured to return top 10 similar keywords. Thus, robustness of returned results is inherently provided through our framework since the top 10 similar keywords returned for each query incorporate both similarities based on human judgement (in line with the dataset) as well as contextually relevant keywords which are extracted through similar analysis which in most instances are not covered by the limited combination of tuples present within these datasets.

5 Conclusion

Retaining focus whilst undertaking research and finding relevant information is proving evermore difficult for students due to current limitations with query formulation and search engines deficiencies. Thus, this paper takes advantage of the browsing history database to extract keywords and try to understand what students are searching for. We proposed a solution that captures the keywords searched by the student in real-time and provides a holistic view of the domain under study. For a given keyword, using various similarity analysis, we are identifying similar previously searched keywords, creating a domain wordcloud and retrieve academic papers related to the domain under study. Results and predictions are aggregated and presented to the student within a user interface that can be used alongside the Internet browser.

The evaluation performed showed that Cosine similarity and Euclidean distance contributed in increasing the accuracy of the proposed solution while Jaccard similarity did not contribute. Moreover, the proposed solution provides a more comprehensive output with respect to current systems since the framework displays the top 10 relevant keywords for each search through the use of a supporting wordcloud. This methodology ensures that students can review both similar data tuples commonly found within datasets as well as contextually relevant keywords pertinent to their research domain.

References

1. Bartlett, J., Miller, C.: Truth, Lies and the Internet a Report into Young People'S Digital Fluency (2011). http://www.demos.co.uk/files/Truth_-_web.pdf
2. Kraft, R.: A machine learning approach to improve precision for navigational queries in a Web information retrieval system (2002)
3. Chiru, C.: Search engines: ethical implications. Econ. Manag. Financ. Mark. **11**(1), 162–167 (2016)
4. Introna, L.D., Nissenbaum, H.: Shaping the web: why the politics of search engines matters. Inf. Soc. **16**(3), 169–185 (2000). https://doi.org/10.1080/01972240050133634
5. Leeder, C.: Student misidentification of online genres. Libr. Inf. Sci. Res. **38**(2), 125–132 (2016). https://doi.org/10.1016/j.lisr.2016.04.003
6. Tredinnick, L., Laybats, C.: Evaluating digital sources: trust, truth and lies. Bus. Inf. Rev. **34**(4), 172–175 (2017). https://doi.org/10.1177/0266382117743370
7. Vidinli, I.B., Ozcan, R.: New query suggestion framework and algorithms: a case study for an educational search engine. Inf. Process. Manag. **52**(5), 733–752 (2016). https://doi.org/10.1016/j.ipm.2016.02.001
8. Cheng, Y.H., Tsai, C.C.: Online research behaviors of engineering graduate students in Taiwan. Educ. Technol. Soc. **20**(1), 169–179 (2017)
9. Usta, A., Altingovde, I.S., Vidinli, I.B., Ozcan, R., Ulusoy, Ö.: How K-12 students search for learning? Analysis of an educational search engine log. In: SIGIR 2014 - Proceedings of the 37th International ACM SIGIR Conference on Research and Development in Information Retrieval, pp. 1151–1154 (2014). https://doi.org/10.1145/2600428.2609532
10. Smith, C.L., Gwizdka, J., Feild, H.: The use of query auto-completion over the course of search sessions with multifaceted information needs. Inf. Process. Manag. **53**(5), 1139–1155 (2017). https://doi.org/10.1016/j.ipm.2017.05.001
11. Feild, H., Allan, J., Glatt, J.: CrowdLogging: distributed, private, and anonymous search logging. In: SIGIR 2011 - Proceedings of the 34th International ACM SIGIR Conference on Research and Development in Information Retrieval, pp. 375–384 (2011). https://doi.org/10.1145/2009916.2009969
12. Kim, J.Y., Collins-Thompson, K., Bennett, P.N., Dumais, S.T.: Characterizing web content, user interests, and search behavior by reading level and topic. In: WSDM 2012 - Proceedings of the 5th ACM International Conference on Web Search and Data Mining, pp. 213–222. ACM, New York (2012). https://doi.org/10.1145/2124295.2124323

13. West, A.G., Aviv, A.J.: Measuring privacy disclosures in URL query strings. IEEE Internet Comput. **18**(6), 52–59 (2014). https://doi.org/10.1109/MIC.2014.104

14. Tikhonov, A., Prokhorenkova, L.O., Chelnokov, A., Bogatyy, I., Gusev, G.: What can be found on the web and how: a characterization of web browsing patterns. In: Proceedings of the 2015 ACM Web Science Conference, pp. 1–10 (2015). https://doi.org/10.1145/2786451.2786468

15. Bast, H., Weber, I.: Type less, find more: fast autocompletion search with a succinct index. In: Proceedings of the Twenty-Ninth Annual International ACM SIGIR Conference on Research and Development in Information Retrieval, vol. 2006, pp. 364–371. ACM (2006)

16. Rathod, D.: Web browser forensics: Google Chrome available online at www.ijarcs. info. Int. J. Adv. Res. Comput. Sci. **8**, 5–9 (2017). https://doi.org/10.26483/ijarcs. v8i7.4433

17. Finkelstein, L., et al.: Placing search in context: the concept revisited. In: Proceedings of the 10th International Conference on World Wide Web, WWW 2001, vol. 20(1), pp. 406–414 (2001). https://doi.org/10.1145/371920.372094

18. Bharat, K.: SearchPad: explicit capture of search context to support Web search. Comput. Netw. **33**(1), 493–501 (2000). https://doi.org/10.1016/S1389-1286(00)00047-5

19. Pound, J., Hudek, A.K., Ilyas, I.F., Weddell, G.: Interpreting keyword queries over web knowledge bases. In: ACM International Conference Proceeding Series, pp. 305–314 (2012). https://doi.org/10.1145/2396761.2396803

20. Shirakawa, M., Nakayama, K., Hara, T., Nishio, S.: Wikipedia-based semantic similarity measurements for noisy short texts using extended Naive Bayes. IEEE Trans. Emerg. Top. Comput. **3**(2), 205–219 (2015). https://doi.org/10.1109/TETC.2015.2418716

21. Rajeshwarkar, A., Nagori, M.: Optimizing search results using Wikipedia based ESS and enhanced TF-IDF approach. Int. J. Comput. Appl. **144**(12), 23–28 (2016). https://doi.org/10.5120/ijca2016910498

22. Banerjee, S., Ramanathan, K., Gupta, A.: Clustering short texts using wikipedia. In: Proceedings of the 30th Annual International ACM SIGIR Conference on Research and Development in Information Retrieval, SIGIR 2007, pp. 787–788 (2007). https://doi.org/10.1145/1277741.1277909

23. Ferragina, P., Scaiella, U.: TAGME: On-the-fly annotation of short text fragments (by Wikipedia entities). In: Proceedings of the International Conference on Information and Knowledge Management, pp. 1625–1628 (2010). https://doi.org/10.1145/1871437.1871689

24. Haldar, R., Mukhopadhyay, D.: Levenshtein Distance Technique in Dictionary Lookup Methods: An Improved Approach. Computing Research Repository - CORR (2011). http://arxiv.org/abs/1101.1232

25. Hu, X., Tang, J., Gao, H., Liu, H.: Unsupervised sentiment analysis with emotional signals. In: WWW 2013 - Proceedings of the 22nd International Conference on World Wide Web, pp. 607–617 (2013). https://doi.org/10.1145/2488388.2488442

26. Gowtham, S., Goswami, M., Balachandran, K., Purkayastha, B.S.: An approach for document pre-processing and K Means algorithm implementation. In: Proceedings of the 2014 4th International Conference on Advances in Computing and Communications, ICACC 2014, pp. 162–166. IEEE (2014). https://doi.org/10.1109/ICACC.2014.46

27. Loper, E., Bird, S.: NLTK: The Natural Language Toolkit (2002). https://doi.org/10.3115/1118108.1118117, http://arxiv.org/abs/cs/0205028

28. Kilgarriff, A., Fellbaum, C.: WordNet: an electronic lexical database. Language **76**(3), 706 (2000). https://doi.org/10.2307/417141
29. Patil, L.H., Atique, M.: A novel approach for feature selection method TF-IDF in document clustering. In: Proceedings of the 2013 3rd IEEE International Advance Computing Conference, IACC 2013, pp. 858–862. IEEE (2013). https://doi.org/10.1109/IAdCC.2013.6514339
30. Miller, G.A.: WordNet: a lexical database for English. Commun. ACM **38**(11), 39–41 (1995). https://doi.org/10.1145/219717.219748
31. Barr, C., Jones, R., Regelson, M.: The linguistic structure of English web-search queries. In: EMNLP 2008–2008 Conference on Empirical Methods in Natural Language Processing, Proceedings of the Conference: A Meeting of SIGDAT, a Special Interest Group of the ACL, EMNLP 2008, pp. 1021–1030. Association for Computational Linguistics, Stroudsburg (2008). https://doi.org/10.3115/1613715.1613848
32. Aljrees, T., Shi, D., Windridge, D., Wong, W.: Criminal pattern identification based on modified K-means clustering. In: Proceedings of the International Conference on Machine Learning and Cybernetics, South Korea, vol. 2, pp. 799–806 (2017). https://doi.org/10.1109/ICMLC.2016.7872990
33. McKiernan, G.: arXiv.org: the Los Alamos National Laboratory e-print server. Int. J. Grey Liter. **1**(3), 127–138 (2000). https://doi.org/10.1108/14666180010345564
34. Hansen, P., Jaumard, B.: Cluster analysis. Math. Program. **79**(1–3), 191–215 (1997). https://doi.org/10.1007/BF02614317
35. Perez-Tellez, F., Cardiff, J., Rosso, P., Pinto, D.: Weblog and short text feature extraction and impact on categorisation. J. Intell. Fuzzy Syst. **27**(5), 2529–2544 (2014). https://doi.org/10.3233/IFS-141227
36. Bafna, P., Pramod, D., Vaidya, A.: Document clustering: TF-IDF approach. In: International Conference on Electrical, Electronics, and Optimization Techniques, ICEEOT 2016, pp. 61–66 (2016). https://doi.org/10.1109/ICEEOT.2016.7754750
37. Erra, U., Senatore, S., Minnella, F., Caggianese, G.: Approximate TF-IDF based on topic extraction from massive message stream using the GPU. Inf. Sci. **292**, 143–161 (2015). https://doi.org/10.1016/j.ins.2014.08.062
38. Chaithanya, K., Reddy, P.V.: A novel approach for document clustering using concept extraction. Int. J. Innov. Res. Adv. Eng. (IJIRAE) **3** (2016). www.ijirae.com
39. Mesquita, D.P., Gomes, J.P., Souza Junior, A.H., Nobre, J.S.: Euclidean distance estimation in incomplete datasets. Neurocomputing **248**, 11–18 (2017). https://doi.org/10.1016/j.neucom.2016.12.081
40. Niwattanakul, S., Singthongchai, J., Naenudorn, E., Wanapu, S.: Using of Jaccard coefficient for keywords similarity. Lecture Notes in Engineering and Computer Science, vol. 1, pp. 380–384 (2013)
41. Halawi, G., Dror, G., Gabrilovich, E., Koren, Y.: Large-scale learning of word relatedness with constraints. In: Proceedings of the ACM SIGKDD International Conference on Knowledge Discovery and Data Mining, pp. 1406–1414. ACM (2012). https://doi.org/10.1145/2339530.2339751
42. Szumlanski, S., Gomez, F., Sims, V.K.: A new set of norms for semantic relatedness measures. In: Proceedings of the Conference on ACL 2013–51st Annual Meeting of the Association for Computational Linguistics, vol. 2, pp. 890–895 (2013)
43. Li, P., Xiao, B., Ma, W., Jiang, Y., Zhang, Z.: A graph-based semantic relatedness assessment method combining wikipedia features. Eng. Appl. Artif. Intell. **65**, 268–281 (2017). https://doi.org/10.1016/j.engappai.2017.07.027

44. Buitinck, L., et al.: API design for machine learning software: experiences from the Scikit-learn project. In: ECML PKDD Workshop: Languages for Data Mining and Machine Learning, pp. 108–122 (2013). http://arxiv.org/abs/1309.0238
45. Dillon, M.: Introduction to modern information retrieval (1983). https://doi.org/10.1016/0306-4573(83)90062-6
46. Spearman, C.: The proof and measurement of association between two things. Am. J. Psychol. **100**(3/4), 441 (1987). https://doi.org/10.2307/1422689

Short Technical Papers

A General Approach to Exploit Model Predictive Control for Guiding Automated Planning Search in Hybrid Domains

Faizan Bhatti[✉], Diane Kitchin, and Mauro Vallati

School of Computing and Engineering, University of Huddersfield, Huddersfield, UK
{faizan.bhatti,d.kitchin,m.vallati}@hud.ac.uk

Abstract. Automated planning techniques are increasingly exploited in real-world applications, thanks to their flexibility and robustness. Hybrid domains, those that require to reason both with discrete and continuous aspects, are particularly challenging to handle with existing planning approaches due to their complex dynamics. In this paper we present a general approach that allows to combine the strengths of automated planning and control systems to support reasoning in hybrid domains. In particular, we propose an architecture to integrate Model Predictive Control (MPC) techniques from the field of control systems into an automated planner, to guide the effective exploration of the search space.

Keywords: Automated planning · Model Predictive Control · Hybrid reasoning

1 Introduction

The application of automated planning to real-world domains has always been a matter of great interest for the research community, and is supported by the large set of available planning engines and knowledge engineering approaches. A very common yet challenging feature of real-world applications is the presence of both Boolean and numeric resources and continuous update processes as part of the problem, which makes them hybrid in nature. Planners at the state-of-the-art, rely on the discretisation of dynamic equations of the continuous part of the domain. Due to this discretisation issue, tackling the continuous aspects of hybrid domains is a challenging task for automated planners. On the other hand, planning approaches are extremely performant in dealing with discrete variables, and discontinuities.

In contrast with automated planning, Control Theory is a particularly effective approach for controlling dynamical systems with continuous aspects. Control System techniques are efficient in presence of linear continuous processes or linear-time-invariant (LTI) systems but when there is some non-linearity, it

© Springer Nature Switzerland AG 2019
M. Bramer and M. Petridis (Eds.): SGAI-AI 2019, LNAI 11927, pp. 139–145, 2019.
https://doi.org/10.1007/978-3-030-34885-4_10

becomes a difficult problem for control system engineers to solve. Given the complementary strengths of control theory techniques and automated planning, it naturally raises the possibility of combining them for better dealing with applications where hybrid reasoning is needed. The idea has been initially explored by Jimoh [7]. However, the work of Jimoh is domain-specific, and can not be transferred or re-used in different application domains.

In this paper, we propose a general approach to exploit Model Predictive Control (MPC) [2] for guiding automated planning search in hybrid domains. More specifically, we propose an architecture that allows to use MPC techniques from the field of control systems, for calculating a heuristic for the continuous part of a domain model. The heuristic is then exploited by the planner, that has therefore a better overall view of both continuous and discrete elements of the problem at hand. Our experimental analysis, that focuses on a well-known benchmark domain for hybrid PDDL+ planners, demonstrates that our domain-independent approach can improve the planning performance of state-of-the-art planners on this complex type of problems.

2   Background

Automated Planning is a deliberation process which looks at finding a sequence of actions suitable for transforming a given initial state of a system under consideration into a desired goal state. A *planning domain model* is specified by the set of available actions and their consequences whereas a *planning problem* is composed by the domain model, and a description of the initial state, involved objects, and the desired goal. A *solution plan* is a sequence of actions such that their consecutive application, starting from the initial state, results in a state that satisfies the goal [12].

PDDL+ [5], an extension to McDermott's PDDL [8], introduced new modelling features which make it possible to model continuous numeric change in a more realistic way. It introduced the concept of autonomous *processes* and *events*. In PDDL+, a process represents a continuous numeric change with time while maintaining the logical state of the system. A process is autonomous in nature and is not under the direct control of the executive. Similar to processes, events are not under the direct control of the executive. They can be a consequence of a change in the state of the world. Whenever its preconditions are satisfied, an event must occur. The concept of autonomous continuous process made it possible to model many real life problems which were not realisable before. UPMurphi [4], Discretised Nonlinear Heuristic Planner (DiNo) [9], COLIN [3], SMTPlan+ [1] and Expressive Numeric Heuristic Search Planner (ENHSP) [11] are some of the significant planners developed after the introduction of PDDL+.

Model Predictive Control does not refer to a unique control algorithm, but indicates a family of approaches sharing the same philosophy. It starts with the dynamical model of the system and the initial state. At every time step, it calculates the suitable control actions, by solving an open-loop optimisation problem for a given prediction horizon. The prediction output is a sequence of next states and an array of suitable inputs for the system. Only the first control input is picked and applied, so the system can reach the first predicted state. The difference between the predicted state and the actual state is fed back to the controller for correction. This whole process is repeated at every new state.

3   Using MPC to Guide Automated Planning Search

The proposed approach relies on the idea of using MPC for guiding the planning search. In a nutshell, MPC provides a sort of heuristic that can give useful information to the search of a solution, on a given hybrid problem. Figure 1 depicts the working principle of our approach. The dynamic equations which are related and collectively form a composite entity, which we call a *plant*, are identified and separated. A plant, in this context, is a relatively independent sub-system of the one bigger system. Once a plant is created, the prediction matrices are calculated on the basis of the dynamic model of the plant, which in turns help to calculate the future control moves on the basis of the defined control law.

A general discrete model of a linear-time-invariant system in absence of any input disturbance is given by the following equations.

$$x_{k+1} = Ax_k + Bu_k, \tag{1}$$

$$y_k = Cx_k + d_k, \tag{2}$$

where x_k is the state vector of the plant, u_k is the control input, y_k is the output, A is the state co-efficient matrix, B is the input co-efficient matrix, C is the output co-efficient matrix, and d_k is the output disturbance at time step k. The discrete model of an LTI system is inherently a one-step-ahead prediction model [10]. Therefore, the output of the system at instance $k+1$ can be determined as

$$y_{k+1} = CAx_k + CBu_k + d_k. \tag{3}$$

The best guess for disturbance is $d_{k+1} = d_k$. Equations (1) & (3) represent one-step-ahead relations of state and output vectors. These equations can be used recursively to find any number of step-ahead prediction. In order to calculate the optimum value of future input and in turn the optimum plan, we need to define a control law. We define our performance index or the cost function as a simple quadratic function of error (distance of current state from goal) and the control effort.

$$J = \sum_{k=1}^{N_p}(e_k^T e_k + u_k^T R u_k). \tag{4}$$

Here R is the weighting matrix and defined as positive definite. The error e_k is the difference between the reference value r_k and the actual output y_k. Minimisation of the above performance index with respect to u_k gives us an unconstrained control law for MPC. The addition of constraints from the PDDL+ model makes

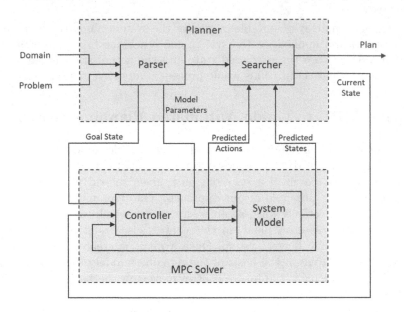

Fig. 1. The proposed architecture to exploit MPC in automated planning.

it a standard quadratic optimisation problem subject to linear constraints and any off-the-shelf quadratic optimiser can be used to solve this quadratic.

To apply MPC in planning we assume that any state of the system is a pair $S = \langle P, N \rangle$, where P is a set of atomic propositions and N is a sequence of numeric values assigned to numeric variables. The input to the planning system is the initial state $I = \langle I_P, I_N \rangle$, the goal condition $G = \langle G_P, G_N \rangle$, the domain model DM and the prediction horizon N_p. Where G_P is a set of atomic propositions and G_N is a set of conditions on numeric variables. A node in the search space consists of state S and a path from initial state to the current node which is a partial plan. The search for the solution starts with expanding the nodes from the initial state in classical manner until the preconditions for the processes of the plant are satisfied. As soon as the preconditions for the process are satisfied, MPC solver starts running at that node, considering it as its initial state. The output of MPC solver is a sequence of future actions to be selected and next predicted states as the outcome of those actions. Therefore, it acts as a guide for search. The next node for expansion is selected by finding the node which is nearest to the proposed trajectory of the MPC. If more than one nodes are at the same distance, then any node is selected randomly, since MPC has the tendency to correct itself. Once the next node for the expansion has been chosen, the frontier of search is extended by expanding the chosen node. At this stage, the MPC once again predicts for a new improved trajectory. This process keeps repeating until a solution to G_N is found or the preconditions for processes no longer hold. If G_N is found, the other part of the goal, G_p is searched in classical way. The selection of one node appears to create incompleteness but it limits the search space by pruning a lot of branches and as a result, reduces the search effort.

4   Experimental Analysis

The objective of this experimental analysis is to evaluate the feasibility of using MPC in planning as a heuristic for the continuous processes and to check the generality of our methodology. We focus on the well-known Car domain, that is traditionally used for benchmarking the performance of PDDL+ planners, including DiNo [9] and ENHSP [11]. The experiments were carried out in Java NetBeans 8.2 on a machine with Intel(R) Core(TM) i7-8700 CPU, 3.2 GHz processor and 16 GB RAM. We used IBM CPLEX [6] optimiser for solving the quadratic during the MPC prediction process. While experimenting with different planners, we found ENHSP to be the most efficient planner on these benchmarks. Therefore, our results in this paper are presented in comparison with ENHSP only.

Table 1. Performance achieved by ENHSP, and the same planner exploiting the proposed approach (MPC) on instances of the Car domain.

Disp.	Vel. limit	Acc. limit	Planner	Duration	Plan length	Nodes exp	Time (mSec)
30	-10	-2.0	ENHSP	11.0	19	32	230
	$+10$	$+2.0$	MPC	12.0	24	28	270
30	-10	-4.0	ENHSP	11.0	17	32	230
	$+10$	$+4.0$	MPC	7.0	25	29	250
30	-10	-8.0	ENHSP	11.0	17	32	235
	$+10$	$+8.0$	MPC	6.0	36	40	245
30	-10	-10.0	ENHSP	11.0	17	32	235
	$+10$	$+10.0$	MPC	6.0	40	44	245
100	-10	-10.0	ENHSP	17.0	27	47	245
	$+10$	$+10.0$	MPC	13.0	47	51	265
200	-10	-10.0	ENHSP	27.0	39	519	315
	$+10$	$+10.0$	MPC	23.0	57	61	300
500	-10	-10.0	ENHSP	56.0	68	17516	1720
	$+10$	$+10.0$	MPC	53.0	87	91	430
1000	-20	-10.0	ENHSP	61.0	71	28512	2440
	$+20$	$+10.0$	MPC	56.0	100	104	445

Table 1 shows the comparison of ENHSP with MPC in terms of the number of nodes expanded, the duration of the plan, the number of actions (plan length), and the CPU-time needed to find a solution. In the first 4 instances we kept goal distance and velocity constant, while modifying the acceleration limit. Results on those instances shows that the use of our framework does not significantly increase runtime on easy instances, and allows to find solutions of comparable quality. Changing the goal requirement and relaxing the velocity limits shows that the use of MPC allows to outperform ENHSP in terms of expanded nodes, planning time and quality of the generated plans. This is due to the fact that

MPC is an optimal control method, so on complex instances it can help in identifying better solutions. An important point to note in results is that the number of nodes expended by MPC approach are always plan length plus 4. As this car domain is a hybrid domain, these 4 nodes refer to the searching for discrete part of the domain, whereas for the continuous part, no node has been expanded which is not part of the final solution plan. This suggests that our approach can dramatically reduce the search space exploration, and is reflected in the reduced runtime on larger and more complex instances.

5   Conclusion

In this paper, we introduced an approach for exploiting MPC to guide AI planning forward chaining search in general PDDL+ hybrid domains. We demonstrated the effectiveness of the proposed approach on a well-known benchmark domain, that involves coupled equations. Despite a limitation in the implementation that no heuristic has been used for the discrete part of hybrid domain, experimental results showed that our approach can outperform a PDDL+ state-of-the-art planner. The simplicity of our approach is that it can be augmented with any other state of art heuristic search method for classical planning to create a complete hybrid planner. Future works will be focused in considering more benchmarks to better evaluate our approach and in adding a state of the art heuristic to further improve the performance.

References

1. Cashmore, M., Fox, M., Long, D., Magazzeni, D.: A compilation of the full PDDL+ language into SMT. In: Workshops at the Thirtieth AAAI Conference on Artificial Intelligence (2016)
2. Clarke, D.W., Mohtadi, C., Tuffs, P.: Generalized predictive control Part I. The basic algorithm. Automatica $23(2)$, 137–148 (1987)
3. Coles, A.J., Coles, A.I., Fox, M., Long, D.: Colin: planning with continuous linear numeric change. J. Artif. Intell. Res. 44, 1–96 (2012)
4. Della Penna, G., Magazzeni, D., Mercorio, F., Intrigila, B.: UPMurphi: a tool for universal planning on PDDL+ problems. In: Nineteenth International Conference on Automated Planning and Scheduling (2009)
5. Fox, M., Long, D.: Modelling mixed discrete-continuous domains for planning. J. Artif. Intell. Res. 27, 235–297 (2006)
6. ILOG, IBM: CPLEX optimizer. En ligne (2012). http://www-01.ibm.com/software/commerce/optimization/cplex-optimizer
7. Jimoh, F.: A synthesis of automated planning and model predictive control techniques and its use in solving urban traffic control problem. Ph.D. thesis, University of Huddersfield (2015)
8. McDermott, D., et al.: PDDL-The planning domain definition language (1998)
9. Piotrowski, W.M., Fox, M., Long, D., Magazzeni, D., Mercorio, F.: Heuristic planning for hybrid systems. In: Thirtieth AAAI Conference on Artificial Intelligence (2016)

10. Rossiter, J.A.: Model-Based Predictive Control: A Practical Approach. CRC Press, Boca Raton (2003)
11. Scala, E., Haslum, P., Thiébaux, S., Ramirez, M.: Interval-based relaxation for general numeric planning. In: Proceedings of the Twenty-Second European Conference on Artificial Intelligence, pp. 655–663. IOS Press (2016)
12. Vallati, M., Chrpa, L., Kitchin, D.: ASAP: an automatic algorithm selection approach for planning. Int. J. Artif. Intell. Tools **23**(06), 1460032 (2014)

A Tsetlin Machine with Multigranular Clauses

Saeed Rahimi Gorji$^{(\boxtimes)}$ (iD), Ole-Christoffer Granmo(iD), Adrian Phoulady(iD),
and Morten Goodwin(iD)

Centre for Artificial Intelligence Research, University of Agder, Grimstad, Norway
{saeed.r.gorji,ole.granmo,morten.goodwin}@uia.no

Abstract. The recently introduced Tsetlin Machine (TM) has provided competitive pattern recognition accuracy in several benchmarks, however, requires a 3-dimensional hyperparameter search. In this paper, we introduce the Multigranular Tsetlin Machine (MTM). The MTM eliminates the *specificity* hyperparameter, used by the TM to control the granularity of the conjunctive clauses that it produces for recognizing patterns. Instead of using a fixed global specificity, we encode varying specificity as part of the clauses, rendering the clauses multigranular. This makes it easier to configure the TM because the dimensionality of the hyperparameter search space is reduced to only two dimensions. Indeed, it turns out that there is significantly less hyper-parameter tuning involved in applying the MTM to new problems. Further, we demonstrate empirically that the MTM provides similar performance to what is achieved with a finely specificity-optimized TM, by comparing their performance on both synthetic and real-world datasets.

Keywords: Tsetlin Machine · Multigranular Tsetlin Machine ·
Learning automata · Classification · Supervised learning ·
Propositional logic

1 Introduction

The Tsetlin Machine (TM) is a new machine learning algorithm that was introduced in 2018 [9]. It leverages the ability of so-called learning automata (LA) to learn the optimal action in unknown stochastic environments [10]. The TM has provided competitive pattern recognition accuracy in several benchmarks, without losing the important property of interpretability [9].

The TM builds upon a long tradition of LA research, involving cooperating systems of LA [11–14]. More recently, LA have been combined with cellular automata (CA), where each CA cell contains one or more LA, which learn in a distributed fashion [3,6,16]. Some noteworthy LA-based classifiers are further

A. Phoulady—Independent researcher

M. Bramer and M. Petridis (Eds.): SGAI-AI 2019, LNAI 11927, pp. 146–151, 2019.
https://doi.org/10.1007/978-3-030-34885-4_11

introduced in [1,2,4,7,17,18]. However, these approaches mainly tackle small-scale pattern classification problems.

In all brevity, a TM consists of m teams of Tsetlin Automata (TA) [15] that interact to solve complex pattern recognition problems. It takes a binary feature vector $X = [x_1, x_2, ..., x_n] \in \{0,1\}^n$ as input, which is further processed by m conjunctive clauses $C_1^+, ..., C_{\frac{m}{2}}^+$ and $C_1^- ..., C_{\frac{m}{2}}^-$. Each clause captures a specific sub-pattern, formulated as a conjunction of literals (binary features and their negations): $x_a \wedge ... \wedge x_b \wedge \neg x_c \wedge ... \wedge \neg x_d$. Half of the clauses are assigned positive polarity. These describe sub-patterns for output $y = 1$. The other half is assigned negative polarity, describing sub-patterns for output $y = 0$. The output $y \in \{0,1\}$ is thus simply decided by a majority vote: $y = (\sum C_j^+ - \sum C_j^- \geq 0)$.

During learning, each team of TA is responsible for a specific clause. There are two TA per feature x_i. One decides whether to include x_i in the clause, while the other decides upon including $\neg x_i$. These decisions are updated based on reinforcement derived from training examples $(\widehat{X}, \hat{y})$, contrasting the current clauses against $(\widehat{X}, \hat{y})$ (see [9] for further details).

Learning in the TM is governed by three hyperparameters: number of clauses m, specificity s, and voting target T, all set by the user [9]. The number of clauses m decides the overall capacity of the TM to represent patterns, with each clause capturing a particular facet of the data. Specificity s, in turn, is used by the TM to control the granularity of the clauses, playing a similar role as so-called *support* in frequent itemset mining. Finally, the voting target T produces an ensemble effect by stimulating up to T clauses to output 1 for each input, but not more than T. This drives the m clauses to distribute themselves uniformly across the patterns present in the data, avoiding local optima. In this paper, we will divide T by the number of clauses m, to obtain a target value relative to the number of clauses.

2   A Tsetlin Machine with Multigranular Clauses

We now introduce the Multigranular Tsetlin Machine (MTM) with the goal of eliminating specificity s as hyperparameter. Specificity controls how fine-grained patterns the TM seeks, and it is thus crucial to set this parameter correctly to maximize the accuracy of the resulting classifier. A poor choice for s can easily result in inferior accuracy.

While s is a global hyperparameter for the TM, to be set by the user, the MTM instead assigns a unique s_j-value local to each clause C_j, $1 \leq j \leq m$. In all brevity, we define a fixed range $[l, u]$ for s_j and then assign s_j a value decided by the clause index j:

$$s_j = (u - l) \cdot \frac{m - j}{m - 1} + l.$$

As seen, specificity values $\{s_j\}$ are decreasing linearly with the clause index j. In this paper, we use the range $l = 2.0$ to $u = 200.0$, which covers a wide range of both coarse and very fine patterns, as this range performs robustly across all of our experiments.

The above multigranular approach has two crucial effects. First, one avoids the need for finding a suitable value for s. Experimenting with different s-values can be computationally expensive, in particular for large datasets. Secondly, patterns of diverse frequencies can more easily be captured by the clauses when the clauses themselves reflect the diversity of the patterns. Indeed, the classic TM may in the worst case spend an unnecessary large amount of clauses to capture frequent patterns, when s has been set to also capture less frequent patterns. This in turn may potentially clutter some clauses with unnecessary literals, making them less readable (of course, these unnecessary literals may also be pruned in a post-processing phase, but at a higher computational cost during learning). As an example, assume the classic TM tries to capture the pattern $x_1 \wedge \neg x_2$ of frequency $\frac{1}{4}$, with an s-value of 16. In this case, the TM will potentially add two extra literals to the target pattern, introducing e.g. $x_1 \wedge \neg x_2 \wedge x_3 \wedge x_4$. Now, to capture the pattern $x_1 \wedge \neg x_2$, the TM must spend four clauses instead of one, that is, one clause per value configuration of x_3 and x_4.

3   Experimental Results

In this section, we present experimental results examining how multigranular clauses affect accuracy and learning speed, in comparison with the classic TM. For the classic TM algorithm, we used a grid search to find the best s-values as well as the threshold parameters. For MTM, however, we only needed to find an appropriate threshold value, using s-values in the form of an arithmetic progression from 2 to 200.

In our first experiment, we consider a problem that intermixes two kinds of patterns of different complexity. In brief, we specify patterns using 6 binary variables $x_1, x_2, \ldots, x_6$. The patterns for output $y = 0$ are either $\neg x_1 \wedge \neg x_2$ or the more elaborate $x_1 \wedge \neg(x_3 \oplus x_4 \oplus x_5 \oplus x_6 \oplus x_7)$, while the patterns for output $y = 1$ are either $\neg x_1 \wedge x_2$ or $x_1 \wedge (x_3 \oplus x_4 \oplus x_5 \oplus x_6 \oplus x_7)$.

Table 1. Accuracy after 200 and 500 epochs for TM and MTM on artificial data.

Clauses	s	Threshold	TM (200)	TM (500)	Threshold	MTM (200)	MTM (500)
10	110	0.1	75.7%	78.2%	0.16	76.1%	78.0%
20	100	0.06	76.6%	78.2%	0.08	78.8%	78.4%
50	50	0.04	88.4%	89.2%	0.04	88.5%	88.2%
100	60	0.03	94.3%	95.9%	0.02	93.2%	95.2%
500	35	0.01	97.8%	98.0%	0.01	98.0%	98.0%

Both the training and test sets consist of 300 randomly generated examples and approximately 25% of the examples fall within each of the four patterns. Table 1 shows the final accuracy for the TM and the MTM after 200 and 500 epochs, averaged over 10 independent experiment runs, alongside the hyperparameter values that led to that result. As seen, both algorithms exhibit similar performances for different number of clauses, however, MTM did not require tuning of s.

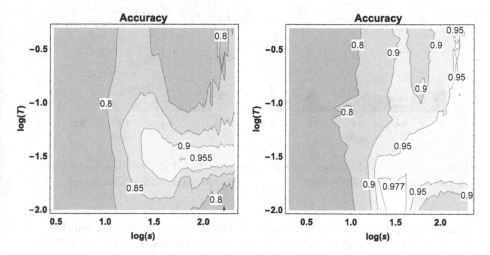

Fig. 1. The TM's performance for XOR with 100 clauses after 500 epochs

Fig. 2. The TM's performance for XOR with 500 clauses after 500 epochs

Figures 1 and 2 depict accuracy as a function of the s and the threshold parameters. As seen, finding high-performing hyperparameter values is not trivial, with the search space varying with the number of clauses employed. In contrast, MTM is optimized only with respect to the threshold.

In our second experiment, we evaluate performance on the Iris flower dataset[1] [5]. This dataset contains measurements for three classes of flowers, 50 instances of each. Each instance consists of four real-valued features. We used five bits to represent each real number (three and two bits for the integer and fractional parts, respectively). We further employed 10 random 80%–20% training-test splits to increase the robustness of the evaluation. The results reported in Table 2 are the average performance of 10 independent experiment runs, for each

Table 2. The accuracy of TM and MTM on the binary Iris dataset

Epoch	TM (100 clauses) ($s = 5, T = 0.2$)	TM (500 clauses) ($s = 5, T = 0.2$)	MTM (100 clauses) ($T = 0.05$)	MTM (500 clauses) ($T = 0.03$)
100	95.1%	95.5%	94.2%	95.0%
200	95.3%	95.6%	94.5%	94.6%
300	95.1%	95.7%	94.5%	94.9%
500	95.2%	95.7%	94.7%	95.0%

[1] https://archive.ics.uci.edu/ml/datasets/iris.

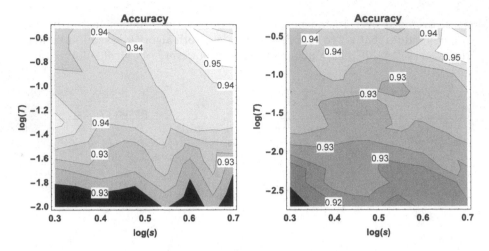

Fig. 3. The TM's performance for Iris with 100 clauses after 500 epochs

Fig. 4. The TM's performance for Iris with 500 clauses after 500 epochs

training-test split. Figures 3 and 4 capture the difficulty of finding suitable values for the hyperparameters, while Table 2 shows how the MTM attains slightly lower accuracy compared to the classic TM, however, by only fine-tuning the threshold value.

Further experiments can be found in the unabridged version of this paper [8].

4   Conclusion

In this work we introduced the multigranular Tsetlin Machine (MTM) to reduce the complexity of the hyperparameter search in Tsetlin Machine (TM) based learning. We achieved this by eliminating the specificity hyperparameter s, instead introducing clauses with unique and diverse local s-values. In our empirical results, it turns out that we actually can obtain similar accuracy as a finely optimized classic TM, however, eliminating the need to consider s. Furthermore, we explored the capability of the MTM to capture patterns of diverse frequencies by using an artificial dataset.

As further research, a natural next step is to work on the theoretical aspects of MTM. Although the theoretical convergence results for TM also should hold for MTM, this needs to be investigated more rigorously. Furthermore, other interesting areas of research could be mechanisms for improving convergence speed. Finally, we intend to investigate the possibility of eliminating the other two remaining hyperparameters as well, making the TM completely parameter-free.

References

1. Afshar, S., Mosleh, M., Kheyrandish, M.: Presenting a new multiclass classifier based on learning automata. Neurocomputing **104**, 97–104 (2013)
2. Aghaebrahimi, M., Zahiri, S., Amiri, M.: Data mining using learning automata. World Acad. Sci. Eng. Technol **49**, 343–351 (2009)
3. Ahangaran, M., Taghizadeh, N., Beigy, H.: Associative cellular learning automata and its applications. Appl. Soft Comput. **53**, 1–18 (2017)
4. Barto, A.G., Anandan, P.: Pattern-recognizing stochastic learning automata. IEEE Trans. Syst. Man Cybern. **3**, 360–375 (1985)
5. Dua, D., Graff, C.: UCI machine learning repository (2017). http://archive.ics.uci.edu/ml
6. Esmaeilpour, M., Naderifar, V., Shukur, Z.: Cellular learning automata approach for data classification. Int. J. Innov. Comput. Inf. Control **8**(12), 8063–8076 (2012)
7. Goodwin, M., Yazidi, A., Jonassen, T.M.: Distributed learning automata for solving a classification task. In: 2016 IEEE Congress on Evolutionary Computation (CEC), pp. 3999–4006. IEEE (2016)
8. Gorji, S.R., Granmo, O.C., Phoulady, A., Goodwin, M.: A Tsetlin machine with multigranular clauses and its applications. Unabridged journal version of this paper (2019, to be submitted)
9. Granmo, O.C.: The Tsetlin Machine - A Game Theoretic Bandit Driven Approach to Optimal Pattern Recognition with Propositional Logic. arXiv preprint arXiv:1804.01508 (2018)
10. Narendra, K., Thathachar, M.: Learning Automata: An Introduction. Prentice-Hall International (1989). https://books.google.no/books?id=ljphQgAACAAJ
11. Rahnamazadeh, A., Meybodi, M.R., Kadkhoda, M.T.: Node classification in social network by distributed learning automata. Information Systems & Telecommunication, p. 111 (2017)
12. Sastry, P., Nagendra, G., Manwani, N.: A team of continuous-action learning automata for noise-tolerant learning of half-spaces. IEEE Trans. Syst. Man Cybern. Part B (Cybern.) **40**(1), 19–28 (2009)
13. Sastry, P., Thathachar, M.: Learning automata algorithms for pattern classification. Sadhana **24**(4–5), 261–292 (1999)
14. Thathachar, M.A., Sastry, P.S.: Learning optimal discriminant functions through a cooperative game of automata. IEEE Trans. Syst. Man Cybern. **17**(1), 73–85 (1987)
15. Tsetlin, M.L.: On behaviour of finite automata in random medium. Avtom I Telemekhanika **22**(10), 1345–1354 (1961)
16. Uzun, A.O., Usta, T., Dündar, E.B., Korkmaz, E.E.: A solution to the classification problem with cellular automata. Pattern Recognit. Lett. **116**, 114–120 (2018)
17. Zahiri, S.H.: Learning automata based classifier. Pattern Recognit. Lett. **29**(1), 40–48 (2008)
18. Zahiri, S.H.: Classification rule discovery using learning automata. Int. J. Mach. Learn. Cybern. **3**(3), 205–213 (2012)

Building Knowledge Intensive Architectures for Heterogeneous NLP Workflows

Kareem Amin[1,3], Stelios Kapetanakis[4(✉)], Nikolaos Polatidis[4],
Klaus-Dieter Althoff[1,2], Andreas Denge[1,3], and Miltos Petridis[5]

[1] German Research Center for Artificial Intelligence, Kaiserslautern, Germany
{kareem.amin,klaus-dieter.althoff,
andreas.dengel}@dfki.uni-kl.de
[2] Institute of Computer Science, University of Hildesheim,
Hildesheim, Germany
[3] Kaiserslautern University, Kaiserslautern, Germany
[4] School of Computing Engineering and Mathematics,
University of Brighton, Brighton, UK
s.kapetanakis@brighton.ac.uk
[5] Department of Computing, Middlesex University, London, UK
m.petridis@mdx.ac.uk

Abstract. Workflows are core part of every modern organization ensuring smooth running operations, task consistency and process automation. Dynamic workflows are being used increasingly due to their flexibility in a working environment where they minimize mundane tasks like long-term maintenance and increase productivity by automatically responding to changes and introducing new processes. Constant changes within unstable environments where information may be sparse, inconsistent and uncertain can create a bottleneck to a workflow in predicting behaviours effectively. Within a business environment, automatic applications like customer support, complex incidents can be regarded as instances of a dynamic process since mitigation policies have to be responsive and adequate to any case no matter its unique nature. Support engineers work with any means at their disposal to solve any emerging case and define a custom prioritization strategy, to achieve the best possible result. This paper describes a novel workflow architecture for heavy knowledge-related application workflows to address the tasks of high solution accuracy and shorter prediction resolution time. We describe how policies can be generated against cases deriving from heterogeneous workflows to assist experts and domain-specific reusable cases can be generated for similar problems. Our work is evaluated using data from real business process workflows across a large number of different cases and working environments.

Keywords: Business processes · Case-Based Reasoning · Deep learning · Natural language processing

© Springer Nature Switzerland AG 2019
M. Bramer and M. Petridis (Eds.): SGAI-AI 2019, LNAI 11927, pp. 152–157, 2019.
https://doi.org/10.1007/978-3-030-34885-4_12

1   Introduction

Knowledge intensive (KI) workflows are common in modern enterprises. KI activities can vary in terms of depth, operation and content and usually the cannot be modeled sufficiently using traditional, static process modelling techniques. Knowledge extraction from heterogeneous natural language (NL) data states a further challenge, since language expressions within business context are usually unstructured, inconsistent and fuzzy. In a Customer Support setting, unsupervised workflow pre-processing aim to learn from any past cases to identify solutions to current problems with customers. Getting this right lead to improved problem-solving ability for an enterprise service and increased satisfaction levels for both a service user and customer. Increasing satisfaction among users improves the likelihood of choosing the same provider again, establishes the brand loyalty and results in a win-win situation for both a customer and a service provider. Recently, the customer experience industry has adopted a data-centric vision in an equivalent way, as companies embrace the power of data to optimize their business workflows and the quality of their services.

Customer support cases usually resemble a series of steps that follow a pre-defined business process. Business processes can be represented as sets of activities with defined temporal relationships and a plethora of constraints. Business processes are highly standardized to be monitored automatically [1, 3, 10] and several standards exist for large scale notation, implementation, transformation and transfer from system to system that work different workflow products and systems [11].

Deep Learning algorithms are effective when dealing with learning from substantial amounts of both structured and unstructured data. While Deep Learning can be applied to learn from large volumes of labeled data, it can also be attractive for learning from substantial amounts of unlabeled/unsupervised data [4–6], making it attractive for extracting meaningful representations and patterns from large Workflow Data.

This paper presents a novel architecture for knowledge intensive workflows management systems using textual CBR and Deep neural networks. This paper is structured as follows: First we describe the related work to our approach. Section 2 presents the relates work; Sect. 3 explains the Deep Knowledge Acquisition Framework. Section 4 presents the carried-out evaluation with domain experts to ensure the efficiency of our proposed approach. Finally, Sect. 5 concludes this work and presents our future directions.

2   Related Work

Case-Based Reasoning (CBR) systems mimic the human approach of recalling past knowledge to solve present problems and follows the Retrieve, Reuse, Revise, Retain cycle [2]. CBR seems an effective way of monitoring business processes [1, 3] if they can be represented as graphs and spatio-temporal [7] or structural similarity measures are applied.

Relevant work to NLP intensive workflows pertains to the categories of text processing, customer support and CBR systems and automation of text relation extraction. Textual CBR supports cases represented as text. Text representation has several challenges since text can be unstructured, can have grammatically incorrect sentences and information can be either hidden or redundant. This research can be compared to the work presented in [19, 20], where hybrid CBR with NLP frameworks were used to process knowledge written in free text. The presented frameworks were not able to process text spanned across different languages since there were several issues related to accurate sentence parsing. We suggest a different approach using Deep Neural Networks to ease the task of finding similarities between workflows and automate the knowledge from textual workflows. Relevant work can also be seen in TRG graph systems where a graph-based representation has been used to represent the chain of reasoning behind a specific analysis as well as facilitate the adaptation of a past analysis to a new problem. The authors have used manually constructed lexico-syntactic patterns developed to extract the relations across text cases.

3   An Architecture for Knowledge Intensive Workflows

DeepKAF consists of three layers, every layer contains several software agents designated for several tasks.

(1) Knowledge Stream: The knowledge stream layer contains two kinds of agents. One is responsible for integrating with knowledge sources. The second agent is connected to the case-base and able to answer the incoming queries.
(2) Knowledge Pre-Processing: The knowledge preprocessing layer contains several agents with implemented DL models that are trained to perform the data preprocessing tasks (e.g., denoising and dimensionality reduction).
(3) Knowledge Processing: The knowledge processing layer is the layer with the CBR logic inside. This layer has agents to do the retrieval based on deep learning models that were built to measure similarities between two different case.

Figure 1 shows the architecture at its most general form prior applying to a problem domain.

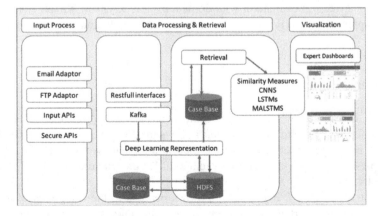

Fig. 1. DeepKAF architecture.

Via DeepKAF an enterprise user can choose how to set up a business workflow using CBR. The architecture is designed for continuous streaming workflows and as such the workflow Data Generation can be connected with streams of emails, ftp requests, secure and plain API calls responsible for generating and simulating business process requests. Previous work [8, 9] has presented the DeepKAF Deep Learning models residing in CNN and LSTM format. This work presents an comprehensive version which works on Siamese Manhattan LSTMs and Autoencoders. Manhattan LSTMs (MaLSTM) model have been introduced by Mueller and Thyagarajan (2016) [8] and have shown high accuracy in finding the Semantic commonalities among sentences across the field baselines.

4   DeepKAF Evaluation

For the evaluation, a multi-language customer support workflow dataset was chosen which was used in previous work [8]. The dataset contains several thousand of case problems written in mixed languages along with their associated solutions and case topology information email threads, sender/ receiver information, department roles, responsible department, previous responsibility holders and others.

DeepKAF was used to audit and identify the current state of a support workflow. Workflows could be generally treated as 'hot', 'cold' or 'neutral' based on the severance of their reported incidents, the priority of the case and the key responsibility of the "affected" person or department. DeepKAF should respond to an investigated workflow by identifying and presenting the most relevant past case/solution from similarly experienced situations using a historical knowledge base. Any retrieved solutions were presented and recommended in real time support cases to a Help-Desk engineer. Work on DeepKAF has already experimenting extensively on trials to improve the accuracy of the framework as well as minimize the efforts to acquire new knowledge [8, 9]. The system has been evaluated based on its ability to provide better solutions in the top 10 proposed ones and by decreasing the probability of not being able to respond.

A Siamese MaLSTM [8] was used to find the most similar workflow cases and propose respective solutions. Three models were used to cover for the autoencoder, Siamese MaLSTM versus Word2Vec [8]. For the autoencoder 150,000 workflow instances were used to be able to compile a low level representation for workflow contents. Word3Vec was used based on the literature training [8] whereas MaLSTM was trained using supervised learning. Hyperparameters were selected and optimized throughout the training process.

DeepKAF was evaluated in terms of the retrieved workflow score across the top 10 retrieved solutions. To evaluate the model, ten thousand workflows were used as a testing sample requiring an imminent solution. DeepKAF used both MaLSTM and MaLSTM+ Skip-through models. Domain experts evaluated the results as coming from the framework. From the business workflow expert evaluation, the framework performance was acceptable since even 'human' support agents have a similar performance.

5 Conclusions

This paper presents a novel architecture for knowledge intensive workflows management systems using textual CBR and Deep neural networks. Automatic policy generation against heterogeneous workflow cases can be possible using DeepKAF and its evaluation results have been seen promising in dynamic workflow applications. DeepKAF has been applied in real time case processing and combines a range of advanced deep learning algorithms and techniques such as adversarial generative networks and Siamese networks. This work has shown that it is possible to have an NLP generic architecture using CBR and deep learning. Our future work will focus on generalizing and expanding DeepKAF to further workflow application areas as well as improve the generalization ability of its models.

References

1. Kapetanakis, S., Petridis, M., Knight, B., Ma, J., Bacon, L.: A case based reasoning approach for the monitoring of business workflows. In: Bichindaritz, I., Montani, S. (eds.) ICCBR 2010. LNCS (LNAI), vol. 6176, pp. 390–405. Springer, Heidelberg (2010). https://doi.org/10.1007/978-3-642-14274-1_29
2. Aamodt, A., Plaza, E.: Case-based reasoning: foundational issues, methodological variations, and system approaches. AI Commun. 7(1), 39–59 (1994)
3. Kapetanakis, S., Petridis, M.: Evaluating a case-based reasoning architecture for the intelligent monitoring of business workflows. In: Montani, S., Jain, L.C. (eds.) Successful Case-based Reasoning Applications-2, pp. 43–54. Springer, Heidelberg (2014). https://doi.org/10.1007/978-3-642-38736-4_4
4. Bengio, Y.: Deep learning of representations: looking forward. In: Dediu, A.-H., Martín-Vide, C., Mitkov, R., Truthe, B. (eds.) SLSP 2013. LNCS (LNAI), vol. 7978, pp. 1–37. Springer, Heidelberg (2013). https://doi.org/10.1007/978-3-642-39593-2_1
5. Bengio, Y., LeCun, Y.: Scaling learning algorithms towards, AI. Large Scale Kernel Machines, vol. 34, pp. 321–360. MIT Press, Cambridge (2007)
6. Bengio, Y., Courville, A., Vincent, P.: Representation learning: a review and new perspectives. IEEE Trans. Pattern Anal. Mach. Intell. 35(8), 17981828. https://doi.org/10.1109/tpami.2013.50
7. Mueller, J., Thyagarajan, A.: Siamese recurrent architectures for learning sentence similarity. In: Proceedings of the Thirtieth AAAI Artificial Intelligence, AAAI 2016
8. Amin, K., Kapetanakis, S., Althoff, K.-D., Dengel, A., Petridis, M.: Answering with cases: a CBR approach to deep learning. In: Cox, Michael T., Funk, P., Begum, S. (eds.) ICCBR 2018. LNCS (LNAI), vol. 11156, pp. 15–27. Springer, Cham (2018). https://doi.org/10.1007/978-3-030-01081-2_2
9. Amin, K., Kapetanakis, S., Althoff, K.D., Dengel, A., Petridis, M.: Dynamic process workflow routing using Deep Learning. In: AI-2018 Thirty-Eighth SGAI International Conference on Artificial Intelligence. Cambridge
10. Bandis, L., Kapetanakis, S., Petridis, M., Fish, A.: An architecture for process mining using CBR on rail transport industry. In: Petridis, M. (ed.) Proceedings of the 22nd UK CBR Workshop, Peterhouse, December 2017, pp. 11–18. Brighton Press (2017)

11. Kapetanakis, S., Petridis, Ma, J., Bacon, L.: Providing explanations for the intelligent monitoring of business workflows using case-based reasoning. In: Roth-Berghofer, T., Tintarev, N., Leake, D.B., Bahls, D. (eds.) Proceedings of the 5th International Workshop on Explanation- Aware Computing Exact, ECAI 2010, Lisbon, Portugal (2010)
12. Mikolov, T., Chen, K., Corrado, G., Dean, J.: Efficient estimation of word representations in vector space. In: Proceedings of the 26th International Conference on Neural Information Processing Systems, NIPS 2013, vol. 2 (2013)
13. Altszyler, E., Sigman, M., Fernndez Slezak, D.: Comparative study of LSA vs Word2vec embeddings in small corpora: a case study in dreams database (2016)
14. Maddern, M., Maull, R., Smart, A.: Customer satisfaction and service quality in UK financial services. Int. J. Prod. Oper. Manag. **27**, 998–1019 (2007)
15. Bach, K., Althoff, K.-D., Newo, R., Stahl, A.: A case-based reasoning approach for providing machine diagnosis from service reports. In: Ram, A., Wiratunga, N. (eds.) ICCBR 2011. LNCS (LNAI), vol. 6880, pp. 363–377. Springer, Heidelberg (2011). https://doi.org/ 10.1007/978-3-642-23291-6_27
16. Richter, M.M., Lenz, M., Bartsch-Sprl, B., Burkhard, H.-D., et al.: Introduction. In: Lenz, M., Bartsch-Spörl, B., Burkhard, H.-D., Wess, S. (eds.) Case Based Reasoning Technology: From Foundations to Applications. LNAI, vol. 1400, p. 1. Springer, Berlin (1998). https:// doi.org/10.1007/3-540-69351-3
17. Kim, Y.: Convolutional neural networks for sentence classification. In: Conference on Empirical Methods in Natural Language Processing (2014)
18. Stram, R., Reuss, P., Althoff, K.-D.: Weighted one mode projection of a bipartite graph as a local similarity measure. In: Aha, D.W., Lieber, J. (eds.) ICCBR 2017. LNCS (LNAI), vol. 10339, pp. 375–389. Springer, Cham (2017). https://doi.org/10.1007/978-3-319-61030-6_26
19. Reuss, P., Witzke, C., Althoff, K.-D.: Dependency modeling for knowledge maintenance in distributed CBR systems. In: Aha, David W., Lieber, J. (eds.) ICCBR 2017. LNCS (LNAI), vol. 10339, pp. 302–314. Springer, Cham (2017). https://doi.org/10.1007/978-3-319-61030-6_21
20. Amin, K., Lancaster, G., Kapetanakis, S., Althoff, K.-D., Dengel, A., Petridis, M.: Advanced similarity measures using word embeddings and siamese networks in CBR. In: Bi, Y., Bhatia, R., Kapoor, S. (eds.) IntelliSys 2019. AISC, vol. 1038, pp. 449–462. Springer, Cham (2020). https://doi.org/10.1007/978-3-030-29513-4_32

WVD: A New Synthetic Dataset for Video-Based Violence Detection

Muhammad Shahroz Nadeem[1][(⊠)], Virginia N. L. Franqueira[2],
Fatih Kurugollu[1], and Xiaojun Zhai[3]

[1] University of Derby, Derby, UK
{m.nadeem,f.kurugollu}@derby.ac.uk
[2] University of Kent, Canterbury, UK
v.franqueira@kent.ac.uk
[3] University of Essex, Colchester, UK
xzhai@essex.ac.uk

Abstract. Violence detection is becoming increasingly relevant in many
areas such as for automatic content filtering, video surveillance and law
enforcement. Existing datasets and methods discriminate between violent and non-violent scenes based on very abstract definitions of violence.
Available datasets, such as "Hockey Fight" and "Movies", only contain
fight versus non-fight videos; no weapons are discriminated in them. In
this paper, we focus explicitly on weapon-based fighting sequences and
propose a new dataset based on the popular action-adventure video game
Grand Theft Auto-V (GTA-V). This new dataset is called "Weapon Violence Dataset" (WVD). The choice for a virtual dataset follows a trend
which allows creating and labelling as sophisticated and large volume,
yet realistic, datasets as possible. Furthermore, WVD also avoids the
drawbacks of access to real data and potential implications. To the best
of our knowledge no similar dataset, that captures weapon-based violence, exists. The paper evaluates the proposed dataset by utilising local
feature descriptors using an SVM classifier. The extracted features are
aggregated using the Bag of Visual Word (BoVW) technique to classify
weapon-based violence videos. Our results indicate that SURF achieves
the best performance.

Keywords: Violence detection · Dataset · Hot and cold weapons ·
Video classification · GTA-V · Computer games · WVD

1 Introduction

One of the fundamental challenges for building violence detection systems is the
subjective nature of violence [2]. Violence can be expressed in verbal, physical
and physiological forms. Particularly, it is a common observation that in acts
of deliberate physical violence, weapons play an important role in causing harm
to others. These weapons are broadly classified as hot (containing gunpowder,
which cause fire and explosion) or cold (do not contain gunpowder) weapons.

© Springer Nature Switzerland AG 2019
M. Bramer and M. Petridis (Eds.): SGAI-AI 2019, LNAI 11927, pp. 158–164, 2019.
https://doi.org/10.1007/978-3-030-34885-4_13

Current work in violence detection, only focuses on discriminating violent scenes against nonviolent. MediaEval has provided a large scale authoritative benchmark for violence detection. However, it is based on Hollywood movies, thus, categorised as containing staged violent videos. Staged sequences lacks the human behaviour and components exhibited during fights in real world settings. Moreover, it is designed to discriminate videos containing violence against non violence. Nievas et al. [5] proposed the Movies and Hockey datasets. These datasets contain fight sequences taken from Hollywood movies and the National Hockey League but do not contain any weapons usage. Further, YouTube is a prominent source to gather real-world video data. However, their policies restrict uploading content which involves violence, gore or disturbing content which can incite others to commit violent acts[1]. These factors greatly restricts gathering data that captures weapon-related violence. Therefore, these existing datasets (1) lack the presence of any type of weapon in fights, (2) contain videos taken from Hollywood movies which are staged, (3) have scalability and ethical issues.

In this paper, these gaps are addressed through a synthetically generated dataset of violent sequences for hot and cold weapons using the photo-realistic game Grand Theft Auto-V (GTA-V), named as "Weapon Violence Dataset" (WVD). The dataset is available on request from the authors. Recently, in computer vision simulated environments, games and frameworks are been used for designing, labelling and gathering data. This virtual data is then used to train algorithms. Autonomous vehicle research is a prime example where synthetic data is utilised [1,3,7]. GTA-V has also been used for synthetic data generation [4,6]. The contribution of the paper include a novel video-based dataset for weapon-based violence. Our dataset contain weapon based violent interactions, governed by game's AI thus are not staged. Further, it solves the ethical or moral implication problem. We evaluated the proposed dataset with an SVM classifier using local feature descriptors which include: Histogram Of Gradients (HOG), Scale-Invariant Feature Transform (SIFT), Speeded Up Robust Features (SURF) and Oriented FAST and Rotated BRIEF (ORB). The low-level features extracted from these are passed to Bag of Visual Words (BoVW) technique used in image recognition to aggregate low-level feature to develop high-level features, on the WVD dataset. Our results indicate that features extracted by SURF are superior in-comparison to the experimented feature extractors. The remaining of the paper is organised as follows.

Section 2 explains the characteristics of our WVD dataset using BoVW. In Sect. 3 we show experimental results on the WVD dataset. Finally, Sect. 4 concludes the paper where we highlight our main contributions and future research directions and goals.

2   Hot vs Cold Weapons Violence Dataset

GTA-V is an open world game, which gives us the freedom to design violent scenarios for violence detection. Several characteristics of this game made it an

---

[1] https://support.google.com/youtube/answer/2802008?hl=en-GB.

ideal candidate for generation of the dataset. Firstly, GTA-V has a strong "mod" (modification) support and community which generate scripts, with them it is possible to change different aspects of the game. Secondly, GTA-V allows to capture the design scenarios under different times of the day, multiple camera angles and a huge array of different weapons, vehicles and objects. Moreover, the ability to place and edit the appearance, fighting styles, stances and health of the Non-Player Characters (NPC). Thirdly, NPCs can fight independently without human supervision or involvement. These factors make GTA-V an ideal candidate to be chosen as a virtual platform for weapon based violence data generation.

The proposed WVD was generated in a three-step process, the first step includes designing violent scenarios through mods which use 'ScriptHookV' and 'ScriptHookDotNet'. Each scenario consisted of two NPCs, which were assigned the roles of the 'aggressor' and the 'victim'. In every scenario, the aggressor NPC is equipped with a weapon (either hot or cold), their combat style was set as either aggressive or defensive. However, in case of hot weapon fights the combat style was set to stationary. The reason for this was to avoid the NPC moving away from the field of capture. In GTA-V's combat engine, we observed that NPCs maintained a specific safe distance while fighting with hot weapons in order to protect themselves. They also ran towards the nearest object in order to take cover. These safety features made capturing the hot violent sequences difficult. As our goal was to focus on fights where the intention of the aggressor is to kill or inflict fatal wounds, also the victim is unarmed this removes the necessity of maintaining a safe distance or taking cover. Due to this, the fighting style stationary was fixed. Depicting the roles of aggressor and victim. The victim NPC were unarmed and were assigned different combat styles however, they had to rely just on their fists to fight the aggressor. The scenarios were set up in urban, industrial and rural settings. The weapons utilised are mentioned in Table 1.

Table 1. The list of weapons used in the dataset.

Hot weapons		
AP Pistol (OTs-33 Pernach or HK Mark 23)	Combat Pistol (HK P2000)	Pump Shotgun (M590A1)
Bullpup Rifle (QBZ-95)	Carbine Rifle (HK416, LR-300)	Assault Shotgun (UTAS UTS-15)
Micro SMG (IMI Uzi)	SMG (HK MP5)	MG (PK)
Combat MG (M249)		
Cold weapons		
Baseball Bat	Broken Bottle	Crowbar
Hammer	Hatchet	Knife
Pipe Wrench	Machete	Golf Club

Once the scenarios were set up, the second step was to run these scenarios. It must be noted that no human supervision or assistance was used during the duration of the fights. This meant that we had no control over the fight and its end result. The mechanics of the game set the rules and the outcome of fights. This meant that running a particular scenario multiple times would result in different actions taken by both the aggressor and victim NPC. Moreover, we had no control over the positioning of the NPCs during the fights. Due to this, NPCs' had variations in the position and depth of their fights. However, due to the visible advantages of the weapon, that the aggressor NPC had of extended range and damage, resulted in aggressor winning the fight. These scenarios were set up under different times of the day which include Morning, Midday, Midnight, Dusk, Afternoon and Sunset. The final step required human supervision where the captured sequence was viewed by human observers for anomalies. For each captured video, unwanted frames were removed. Figure 1 shows a sample of frames captured from hot weapon fights. Here we can observe the visible presence of blood and gunfire. While Fig. 2 illustrates cold weapons with 'swinging' and 'shoving' actions being performed against the victim.

Fig. 1. Frame sequences capturing fights with hot weapons, exhibit the presence of blood, gun fire and close quarter combat.

3 Experimental Evaluation

In this paper, we selected the appearance-based visual features following the example of Nievas et al. [5] on the WVD dataset. For low-level feature extraction, the descriptors selected include HOG, SIFT, SURF and ORB. The features extracted from these descriptors are used to generate the vocabulary using K-Means. Finally, an SVM classifier is trained to distinguish between Hot and Cold fights. For experimental purposes, the frames were resized from a 800 × 500 × 3 dimensional frame to 400 × 250 × 3. This resulted in two variants of our dataset with 5.34 GB and 1.52 GB in size. We utilised the reduced set for training.

A total of 40,845 frames were extracted from the videos in WVD. This resulted in multiple frames from each scenario with different levels of NPC depth, weapon occlusion and fight styles.

Fig. 2. Frame sequences capturing fights with cold weapons, exhibit the presence of swinging, shoving from cold weapons

The WVD dataset was divided into 70% training and 30% testing sets. Each of the methods took approximately two to three days to train on an Intel Xeon W-2123 3.60 GHz with 64 GB of RAM on the resized version of the dataset. First, low-level features are extracted from individual frames by local feature descriptors. These low-level features are aggregated to develop higher-level feature representation through clustering techniques. Afterward, the SVM classifier is trained upon these high-level features. As HOG, SIFT, SURF and ORB all extract low-level features. Thus combining them together would result in high number of features, which would have increased the computational complexity. Further, all such features would be aggregated during BoVW representation. The goal was to evaluate the quality of the features rather than the quantity. Due to this reason, we did not combined these feature extractors.

Based on experimental evaluation, SURF performed better than all the other feature extractors. SIFT and HOG had similar performance, while with slight variations in F1 scores. However, SIFT has lower precision and high recall for hot weapon fights, compared to HOG, which has higher precision and lower recall. SIFT was much more computationally friendlier in comparison to HOG, which was found to be the most memory hungry. ORB performed poorly amongst all the local feature descriptors. Results indicate that SURF has the highest precision while HOG has the highest recall for cold fights. Overall, hot weapon fights have a lower precision rate in comparison to cold weapon fights as shown in Table 2. This shows that the classifiers are more confused when it comes to identifying hot weapon fights.

Table 2. The reported precision, recall, F1-scores and accuracy (ACC) are shown for the selected feature extractors.

SIFT	Precision	Recall	F1 Score
Cold	0.90	0.79	0.84
Hot	0.68	0.84	0.75
ACC			0.81

ORB	Precision	Recall	F1 Score
Cold	0.87	0.76	0.81
Hot	0.65	0.80	0.72
ACC			0.78

SURF	Precision	Recall	F1 Score
Cold	0.92	0.91	0.91
Hot	0.84	0.85	0.84
ACC			0.89

HOG	Precision	Recall	F1 Score
Cold	0.82	0.92	0.86
Hot	0.78	0.65	0.71
ACC			0.81

4   Conclusion and Future Work

In this paper, we presented a new synthetic virtual dataset called WVD built for hot and cold weapon-based violence using the photo-realistic game GTA-V. The dataset focuses explicitly on fights with different weapon types between individuals, something not discriminated in authoritative datasets for violence detection such as the "Hockey Fight" and "Movies". To the best of our knowledge, this is the first synthetic dataset for this problem which is not based on Hollywood movies and contains a range of weapon-based violence. Our approach is scalable and does not suffer from any ethical implications associated with violence. Further experiments are performed using the BoVW approaches using four different local feature descriptors. Our experimental results indicate that SURF is by far the better feature descriptor achieving a F1 score of 0.91 for cold and 0.84 for hot weapon fights. This means that WVD retains enough visual information. In this paper, we only focused on appearance-based visual features. To further evaluate the dataset, we aim to combine motion-based features with visual features. Furthermore, we also aim to diversify our dataset by adding 'no-violence' class as a control group and capturing scenarios for these classes under different camera angles and multiple weather settings.

References

1. Caesar, H., et al.: nuScenes: a multimodal dataset for autonomous driving. arXiv preprint arXiv:1903.11027 (2019)
2. Demarty, C.H., Penet, C., Soleymani, M., Gravier, G.: VSD, a public dataset for the detection of violent scenes in movies: design, annotation, analysis and evaluation. Multimed. Tools Appl. **74**(17), 7379–7404 (2015)
3. Dosovitskiy, A., Ros, G., Codevilla, F., Lopez, A., Koltun, V.: CARLA: an open urban driving simulator. arXiv preprint arXiv:1711.03938 (2017)
4. Huang, P.H., Matzen, K., Kopf, J., Ahuja, N., Huang, J.B.: DeepMVS: learning multi-view stereopsis. In: Proceedings of the IEEE Conference on Computer Vision and Pattern Recognition, pp. 2821–2830 (2018)

5. Bermejo Nievas, E., Deniz Suarez, O., Bueno García, G., Sukthankar, R.: Violence detection in video using computer vision techniques. In: Real, P., Diaz-Pernil, D., Molina-Abril, H., Berciano, A., Kropatsch, W. (eds.) CAIP 2011. LNCS, vol. 6855, pp. 332–339. Springer, Heidelberg (2011). https://doi.org/10.1007/978-3-642-23678-5_39

6. Richter, S.R., Vineet, V., Roth, S., Koltun, V.: Playing for data: ground truth from computer games. In: Leibe, B., Matas, J., Sebe, N., Welling, M. (eds.) ECCV 2016. LNCS, vol. 9906, pp. 102–118. Springer, Cham (2016). https://doi.org/10.1007/978-3-319-46475-6_7

7. Ros, G., Sellart, L., Materzynska, J., Vazquez, D., Lopez, A.M.: The synthia dataset: a large collection of synthetic images for semantic segmentation of urban scenes. In: Proceedings of the IEEE Conference on Computer Vision and Pattern Recognition, pp. 3234–3243 (2016)

Application Papers

Evolving Prediction Models with Genetic Algorithm to Forecast Vehicle Volume in a Service Station (Best Application Paper)

Himadri Sikhar Khargharia[1,2](✉), Siddhartha Shakya[1,2],
Russell Ainslie[1,2], and Gilbert Owusu[1,2]

[1] EBTIC, Khalifa University, Abu Dhabi, UAE
{himadri.khargharia, sid.shakya}@ku.ac.ae,
{russell.ainslie, gilbert.owusu}@bt.com
[2] British Telecom, Ipswich, UK

Abstract. In the service industry, having an efficient resource plan is of utmost importance for operational efficiency. An accurate forecast of demand is crucial in obtaining a resource plan which is efficient. In this paper, we present a real world application of an AI forecasting model for vehicle volumes forecasting in service stations. We improve on a previously proposed approach by intelligently tuning the hyper parameters of the prediction model, taking into account the variability of the vehicle volume data in a service station. In particular, we build a Genetic algorithm based model to find the topology of the neural network and also to tune additional parameters of the prediction model that is related to data filtration, correction and feature selection. We compare our results with the results from ad hoc parameter settings of the model from previous work and show that the combined genetic algorithm and neural network based approach further improves forecasting accuracy which helps service stations better manage their resource requirements.

Keywords: Forecasting · Neural network · Genetic algorithm

1 Introduction

The service industry expands across various domains like telecoms, retail, banking and utilities. In the service industry customer satisfaction is a key factor. There are various metrics which help to evaluate customer satisfaction, such as turnaround time, quality of service, efficiency of the service, etc. Higher customer satisfaction will lead to repeat business and increased revenue. It is therefore necessary for the service providers to effectively plan the utilization of their resources, in order to attain maximum operational efficiency for greater revenue generation [1, 2].

Attaining operational efficiency, with maximized utilization of resources and minimized wastage, needs an accurate forecast of the demand [3]. A clear view of demand is available when there is an existence of a contract which states a certain set of services are required for a certain period of time. In cases where this isn't available, the historical pattern of demand and other correlated factors are needed for predicting it.

© Springer Nature Switzerland AG 2019
M. Bramer and M. Petridis (Eds.): SGAI-AI 2019, LNAI 11927, pp. 167–179, 2019.
https://doi.org/10.1007/978-3-030-34885-4_14

In the case of an IoT enabled service station, which may include various installations, like retail stores, fuelling stations, telecoms etc., usually the demand states the volumes of customers entering the service stations. There are various devices or sensors which are installed to detect this volume, these devices, or sensors, include wireless magnetometers, wireless ultrasonic sensors, radar sensors, optical sensors and CCTV cameras, all of which keep track of customers entering or leaving the premises and thus end up generating a huge volume of historical data [4–6]. This historical data collected can be used to determine the pattern of demand in the past and can help with forecasting the future demand.

In [3] an application of demand forecasting for a service station is presented. A set of experiments were run for forecasting the demand of a fuelling station in various bays, like auto car washing, lube counter, oil change, parking area for retail, fuelling station, etc. The historical data of the vehicle volume along with highly correlated weather inputs were used to train the model. As part of the experimental results it was concluded that for the specific problem of predicting the demand of fuelling stations, a neural network based model gave the best accuracy with the documented set of hyper parameters. The model was built into a tool that predicts demand on a regular basis. While the results were encouraging, the hyper-parameter tuning was an issue, particularly when there was a large number of neural network models to be built for predicting the demand for different stations and for different periods. Furthermore, the parameter tuning was done using an ad-hoc approach, leaving room for further improvements to obtain better accuracy. This paper is a continuation of that work. The goal is to intelligently determine the optimal set of hyper parameters for the neural network models, as well as the data correction and filtering models. In particular, we built a genetic algorithm based model tuner for this purpose. Such approach to finding better neural network models has been studied in the past for other use cases and with good results reported [7–9]. The aim here is to apply that to service station forecasting and improve the performance of the forecasting tool currently being used by our partner organisation.

The paper is divided into 5 sections. Section 2 presents a background study of similar approaches. Section 3 describes the genetic algorithm approach for optimising the set of hyper parameters for the vehicle volume forecasting model. It also describes the model used to evaluate the forecasts produced using the neural networks based on an analysis of the historical data. Section 4 describes the experiments for comparing the proposed approach with the ad hoc approach from [3], and presents the results. Section 5 concludes the paper.

2   Background

Forecasting is predicting future values based on the available data (both historical and current) along with a certain set of correlated features as inputs. Various mechanisms like moving average, ARIMA, ElasticNet, KNN Regressor, SVR, neural network, etc. [29–32] can be used for predicting the future value. For a neural network model, this could involve different types, such as feed forward, recurrent, convolutional, etc.

There have been many successful applications of neural networks in real world prediction problems. In [10, 11], a work demand prediction for service providers along with optimal resource planning allocation using neural networks are detailed. In [12], a building energy prediction model was built using a neural network. Work on traffic volume forecasting [13] and future trading volume forecasting [20] are some other examples of neural networks in the time series forecasting domain. Neural networks for stock market price prediction have been considered by R. Lawrence [21].

One of the key contributors to the success of any neural network prediction model is how well its topology is designed. Also the effectiveness of the input data in terms of reduced noise and correctly selected features contribute to its success. Setting the correct parameters for the topology design and data filtration can sometimes be a complex task, particularly when there are large numbers of prediction models to be built. This requires an automated approach to setting these parameters. Evolutionary algorithms have been used in the past to optimize the parameters of prediction models, including optimising the artificial neural networks, in terms of their weights, the network architecture, the learning rules, etc. [14]. Genetic algorithms (GA) are a well-known evolutionary algorithm which is originally motivated from biology analogy [15] and have been successfully applied in many real world optimisation problems [24–26]. In [22], a prediction model is presented that predicts the outcome in critically ill patients using neural networks synthesized by a genetic algorithm and decide whether a patient is to be admitted to intensive care using this approach. [23] use neural networks tuned by genetic algorithms to predict the deformation modulus of rock masses.

3   Model Formulation

A historical dataset of around 1 year for three service stations, referred to as station 1, station 2 and station 3, was provided by our partner telecoms company for the purpose of investigating the forecasting model. This is a univariate time series continuous data, which is the count of the vehicle volume from the sensors installed in different bays in the stations. In [3] an earlier set of data for 6 months duration was used. Figure 1 shows the time series data for the petrol pump bay for all three stations of 1 year duration. It can be seen that station 2 has bigger volume of vehicles when compared to station 1 and station 3. There is a dip of vehicle volume in station 1 after April 2019. In all the three stations during weekends or bank holidays there is a decrease of the volume of vehicles.

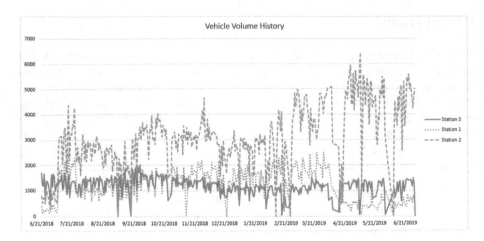

Fig. 1. Historical Vehicle Volume for Station 1, 2 and 3 for petrol pump bay.

Weather plays an important role in people's movement, hence can have an impact in the traffic volume. An extended set of weather data is collected for the whole year as an additional parameter that could contribute to the vehicle volume forecasting. It consists of mean, max and min of temperature, humidity and heat index. The weather data for temperature, humidity and heat index are plotted in Fig. 2 for the duration of 1 year. It can be seen that the Humidity is quite high when the temperature decreases and slightly decreases when the temperature increase. The heat index increases and decreases with the increase and decrease of temperature.

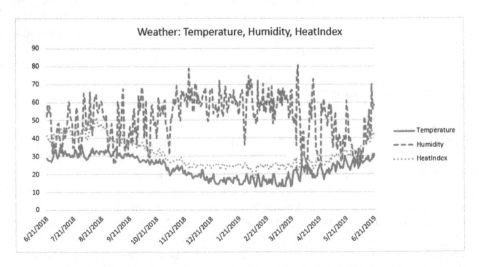

Fig. 2. Weather data with mean Humidity, Heat Index and Temperature.

Figure 3 shows the average number of visitors for each day of the week for all of the three stations. It can be noticed that the number of visitors varies among different day of the week. This led us to build a prediction model for each day of the week separately instead of building a single prediction model that predicts all days of week. This allows us to explicitly reduce the noise that would be introduced if we combine all days of the week into a single predictor that would require complex training and parameter identification.

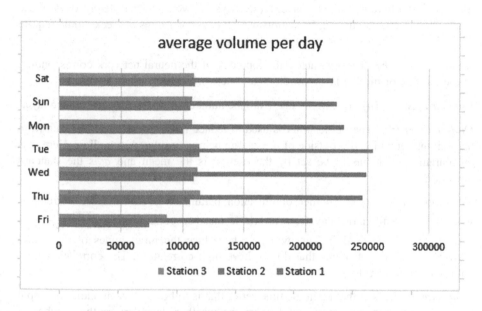

Fig. 3. Average volume of vehicle per day for 3 stations.

3.1 Neural Network Based Prediction Model

An artificial neural network is a supervised learning algorithm that learns the function:

$$f(\cdot): R^m \to R^o \tag{1}$$

where m and o are the input and the output dimensions. Given a set of inputs $X = x_1, x_2, x_3, \ldots, x_m$ and a target Y it can learn non-linear function approximation and regression. A neural network consists of nodes, an input layer, hidden layer and output layer. Each node in the hidden layer converts the value from the previous layer with a weighted linear summation $w_1 x_1 + w_2 x_2 + w_3 x_3 + \ldots + w_m x_m$ followed by a non-linear activation function, $(\cdot): R \to R'$. The output layer takes the input from the hidden layer and transforms them to the output values.

For the purpose of our paper and following [3], we use a feed forward neural network model with the resilient back propagation algorithm [27]. We also use the early stopping strategy to avoid overfitting [28]. It subdivides the data from the training set into training and validation set. This validation set is used to evaluate the accuracy of the model. Once the accuracy of the model stops improving and starts to decrease this indicates overfitting and the training process is stopped. The activation function of the nodes are of sigmoid form [19]. We restrict the neural network model to support a maximum of 6 hidden layers and 12 nodes for each layer.

Below are the descriptions of all the parameters for the prediction model that have to be optimally set to get the best accuracy from the model. These include the parameter related to the core neural network topology, as well as parameters related to data filtering and correction models. They can be different for each neural network trained - for different stations, for different bays, as well as for different days of the week. As an example, having 50 stations with 5 bays for 7 days of week would require $50 \times 5 \times 7 = 1750$ individual models to be trained.

Hidden Layers (h): These relate to the topology of the neural network corresponding to the number of hidden layers in the neural network model.

Number of Nodes [n_1, n_2, ...n_h]: These are the number of nodes for each hidden layer.

Outlier Filter (α): The outlier filter is used to reduce noise in the data. The data from the training set which lies outside of $\mu \pm \alpha\sigma$ are being considered as outliers. Here, α is the parameter that has to be set by the user, μ is the mean and σ is the standard deviation.

Correlation Filter (β): Another optimization parameter is the distance correlation value [16]. We filter out any features whose distance correlation $\frac{dCov(X,Y)}{\sqrt{(dVar(X)dVar(Y))}}$ is greater than a threshold β. This will help to reduce the input nodes of the neural network by filtering features that do not have high correlation. The correlation filter value ranges from 0 to 1.

Input Lag (l): This is the lag in the time series that is to be used as an additional input to the model. For example Input lag for the weather data defines the number of previous day's data that will be used in the feature set to predict current day's vehicle volume. In other word, it tests whether there is any effect of past temperatures on today's volume in addition to today's temperature. For example, if input lag of 2 is used, it means mean temperature from current day as well as mean temperature from yesterday and day before yesterday will be part of feature set for predicting today's vehicle volume.

Duration Days (d): This field states how many days of the target variables historical values are part of the input feature set. If the duration days is 2, then the vehicle volume from past two days will be part of the feature set. These are also known as auto regressive inputs.

Duration Weeks (w): This field states how many target variable data points from previous weeks for any specific day-of-the-week from historical data is being fed as an additional input. If the duration weeks is 2, then vehicle volume for past 2 Sundays will be part of the feature set for the neural network model for Sundays, past two Tuesdays for the neural network model for Tuesdays, and so on.

Setting optimal values for each of the above parameters to get the best prediction for a large number of models soon becomes infeasible, particularly when they need to be retrained periodically. Below we describe how a GA is built to automatically tune the parameters for these models.

3.2   Genetic Algorithm

As described before, genetic algorithms are a member of a class of population based optimisation algorithms where a population of strings called chromosomes are used to represent a solution. Using concepts such as crossover and mutations, the recombination of the strings are carried out with the search being guided by the results of the objective function f for each string in the population. Strings with higher fitness are given more opportunity to breed. In a discreet search space X and a function $f : X \rightarrow \mathbb{R}$. The general problem is $\min_{x \in X} f$. Genetic algorithms allow separation of the representation of the problem from the actual variables with which it was originally formulated with concepts like *genotype* (encoded representation of the variable) and *phenotype* (the set of actual variables). So, if the vector x is represented by a string s of length l, made up of symbols drawn from alphabet A, using a mapping $c : A' \mapsto x$, we then need to use a search space $s \subseteq A'$ as some image of A' under c may represent invalid solution.

The optimization problem then becomes $\min_{s \in S} g(s)$ where the function $g(s) = f(c(s))$. Fitness may not necessarily be $f(c(s))$ but $h(f(c(s)))$ where $h : \mathbb{R} \mapsto \mathbb{R}^+$ is a monotonic function used to eliminate the problem of 'negative' fitness [15].

We consider a generic GA with a population string consisting of 1's and 0's (binary representation). Each parameter of the prediction model as described in Sect. 3.1 is represented by a set of binary bits. Table 1 describes the solution length and the number of bit size for each parameter with *min* and *max* values defining ranges for each of them. The *min* and *max* are used to normalize the binary bits, 2^r, where r is the bit size, to decimal numbers within that range.

Table 1. Bit Size r, Min and Max value for each variable

Variable name	R	Min value	Max value
Hidden Layer (h)	3	1	6
Hidden Layer 1 – Nodes (n_1)	4	1	13
Hidden Layer 1 – Nodes (n_2)	4	0	13
Hidden Layer 1 – Nodes (n_3)	4	0	13
Hidden Layer 1 – Nodes (n_4)	4	0	13
Hidden Layer 1 – Nodes (n_5)	4	0	13
Hidden Layer 1 – Nodes (n_6)	4	0	13
Input Lag (l)	3	0	7
Duration Days (d)	3	0	7
Duration Weeks (w)	2	0	3
Correlation Filter (β)	3	0.0	1.0
Outlier Filter (α)	2	0	3
Total number of bits	**40**		

The solution length, which is same as the total number of bits is 40. For example a chromosome, $x = $ **010**0111**0101**00000000000000000000000**100**001 can be divided as 010 (h is 2), 0111 (n_1 is 7), 0101 (n_2 is 5), 0000 (n_3 is 0), 0000 (n_4 is 0), 0000 (n_5 is 0), 0000 (n_6 is 0), 000 (l is 0), 000 (d is 0), 01 (w is 1), 000 (β is 0.0), 01 (α is 1).

The pseudocode of the developed GA is described below. It is important to note that this is done for each prediction model resulting from the combination of stations, bays, and day of the week:

1. Generate a population of solution P of size m. Where each solution x in P is generated randomly.
2. Decode each solution x in P to get the parameters and evaluate it by building and training a neural network model based on the decoded parameters. The fitness of the solution is defined by the MAPE error.
3. Create a breeding pool by selecting N solutions from P using a selection operator.
4. Perform a crossover operation on the solutions in the breeding pool to generate new solutions.
5. Perform a mutation operation on the new solutions where one or more randomly selected values of some solutions are given new values with very small probability values.
6. Replace P with new solutions and repeat the steps from Step 2 until maximum generation is reached.

At the end of each GA run, we get a setting for a specific model.

4 Experiment Setup and Analysis of Results

In this section we report the comparison of prediction accuracy (Mean Absolute Percentage Error or MAPE result) using the ad hoc approach as reported in [3] and the proposed GA approach. The ad-hoc approach is an experimental design method where a range was specified for each parameter and a relatively higher step value was used to get the test sequence within the range. Each combination of sequence for each parameter was tested and the best performing settings was recorded [3].

For GA, parameters such as population size, maximum generations and type of genetic operators were set empirically where multiple experiments were run with many different settings and the one that found the best result was used. Particularly, a "*tournament*" selection was used as the selection operator (*so*) involving running a tournament among 2 chromosomes chosen at random from the population and the one with the smaller MAPE error is selected for crossover [17]. Similarly, single point (one point) crossover [18] with Crossover Probability (*cp*) of 0.6 was used, and one bit mutation with Mutation Probability (*mp*) of *0.1* was used. The population size (*m*) was set to 500, maximum generations (*g*) was set to 80.

4.1 Comparison of Accuracy Using MAPE

The purpose of this experiment is to compare the MAPE results given by the ad hoc approach of selecting parameters to the genetic algorithm approach. We did 10 iterations for the GA and calculated the average MAPE found. The results are presented in

Table 2, where the average day-wise MAPE results for the two approaches is provided for the three stations. Also, Table 3, presents the overall MAPE across all the stations by computing the average for each of the station across the whole week.

Table 2. Comparison of MAPE results for each day using ad hoc and GA approach.

Day of week	Station	MAPE – ad hoc	MAPE GA
Fri	Station 1	7.36	1.49
	Station 2	14.53	7.06
	Station 3	8.99	1.32
Sat	Station 1	13.96	5.82
	Station 2	13.19	4.75
	Station 3	5.03	1.42
Sun	Station 1	12.97	5.01
	Station 2	21.83	4.68
	Station 3	6.26	0.58
Mon	Station 1	6.22	5.23
	Station 2	12.48	0.32
	Station 3	2.29	1.92
Tue	Station 1	17.31	0.78
	Station 2	10.83	2.51
	Station 3	4.39	1.78
Wed	Station 1	25.97	5.45
	Station 2	15.65	5.13
	Station 3	12.02	11.48
Thu	Station 1	9.44	3.47
	Station 2	7.4	7.08
	Station 3	10.63	1.32

Table 3. Comparison of average MAPE.

Stations	MAPE – Ad hoc	MAPE - GA
Station 1	13.31	3.89
Station 2	13.70	4.50
Station 3	7.08	2.83
Average	**11.36**	**3.74**

As mentioned previously the lower the MAPE, higher the accuracy. It can be noticed in Table 1 that the error for GA is less than that of the ad hoc approach for each day of the week for all the stations. The overall MAPE as shown in Table 2 for the 3 stations for ad-hoc approach is 11.36%, i.e. with an accuracy of 88.64% and using the GA approach it is 3.74% with accuracy of 96.26%. This suggest that the accuracy of the prediction model could be increased by ∼7% by using settings generated by the GA compared to the ad hoc method from [3].

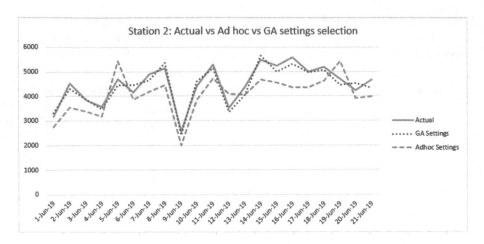

Fig. 4. Actual vs Predicted using ad hoc selection and GA selection for station 2.

Also in Fig. 4, the actual against the predicted value of both the ad hoc and the genetic algorithm approach is plotted for station 2 and for petrol island bay. Station 2 has an average MAPE of 4.50 for GA approach and 13.70 using the ad hoc approach. It can be noticed that the prediction produced by GA approach is much closer to the actual in comparison to the ad hoc approach.

4.2   Comparison of Produced Parameter Settings

We find it also interesting to compare the parameters typically suggested by the GA approach to that used by ad hoc approach. This is to see the difference in topology and data filtering approach of GA against the ad hoc approach. For the GA, the comparison is done against the settings that gave the best MAPE out of the 10 iterations.

As an example, for a Friday for station 1, the ad hoc setting was $h = 1$, $nl = 11$, $l = 3$, $d = 3$, $w = 1$, $\beta = 0.6$, $\alpha = 0$ with MAPE of 7.36, in comparison to the GA approach where $h = 1$, $nl = 2$, $l = 1$, $d = 3$, $w = 2$, $\beta = 0.7$, $\alpha = 2$ was used with a MAPE of only 1.49. The number of hidden layers was the same with 1 hidden layer, but the number of nodes in hidden layer of 2 was much lower with the GA approach than 11 used by the ad hoc approach. Also GA approach found that the target feature from past 2 weeks was necessary while in ad hoc approach past 1 week was used. GA approach also found that β (correlation filter) = 0.7, α (outlier filter) = 2 was required while compared to $\beta = 0.6$, $\alpha = 0$ by the ad hoc approach. It clearly shows that there are settings, as done in ad hoc approach, was not able to find while the GA evolved to those settings giving a much better prediction model.

4.3   Typical GA Evolution of Model

In this section we show a typical evolution of prediction model as done by the GA, by plotting the average fitness of the population against the fitness of the best solution in the population (maximum fitness) for a prediction instance (Fig. 5). The fitness here means the calculated accuracy of prediction as GA generation progresses. We can see that typically, and as expected, the GA starts with lower quality solutions in the population with lower average fitness. However as generations progress, the population evolves to better solutions and both average fitness and the best solution fitness increases. By 80 generations the population fully converges. This plotting shows that there is a gain in running GA, as typical random solutions in first few generations does not achieve best settings.

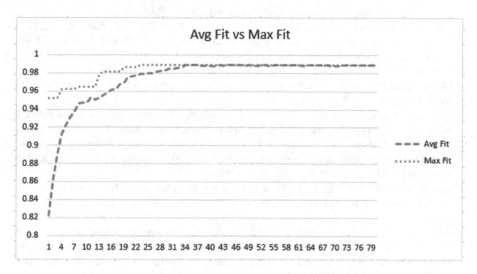

Fig. 5. Average Fitness against Maximum Fitness for Station 1 for 80 generations.

5 Conclusion

In this paper our goal was to enhance the accuracy of the prediction model and find the best configuration settings for the neural network prediction model to predict the visitor demand in service stations. We compared the MAPE of the neural network model prediction using settings suggested by the approach from [3] and settings which are found to be optimal by the genetic algorithm. We have seen that the settings selected by the genetic algorithm has much lower MAPE and thus higher accuracy than the settings selected using adhoc approach, with average improvement of about 7%. The proposed Genetic algorithm approach to evolving the parameters of the prediction model is updated into previously built tool in [3] and is being trialled by our partner telecom. The GA module is triggered every fortnight for selecting the optimal parameter settings, which are used for training the prediction model on a weekly basis. The results are encouraging, and is likely to improve their service offerings, by better management of resource against much more accurately forecasted demand.

References

1. Balwani, S.S.V.: Operational efficiency through resource planning optimization and work process improvement. Ph.D. dissertation, Massachusetts Institute of Technology (2012)
2. Madanhire, I., Mbohwa, C.: Enterprise resource planning (ERP) in improving operational efficiency: case study. Proc. CIRP **40**, 225–229 (2016)
3. Khargharia, H.S., Shakya, S., Ainslie, R., AlShizawi, S., Owusu, G.: Predicting demand in IoT enabled service stations. In: 2019 IEEE Conference on Cognitive and Computational Aspects of Situation Management (CogSIMA), pp. 81–87. IEEE (2019)
4. Ashraf, A., Baldwin, D.: Vehicle detection system, 17 April 2012. US Patent 8,157,219
5. Schmidt, C., Bauer, S.: Parking control device, 20 June 2013. US Patent App. 13/723,016
6. Huang, Y.: RFID based parking management system, 5 July 2011. US Patent 7,973,641
7. Sheikhpour, S., Sabouri, M., Zahiri, S.-H.: A hybrid Gravitational search algorithm— Genetic algorithm for neural network training. In: 2013 21st Iranian Conference on Electrical Engineering (ICEE). IEEE (2013)
8. Tsai, J.-T., Chou, J.-H., Liu, T.-K.: Tuning the structure and parameters of a neural network by using hybrid Taguchi-genetic algorithm. IEEE Trans. Neural Netw. **17**(1), 69–80 (2006)
9. Jaddi, N.S., Abdullah, S., Hamdan, A.R.: Taguchi-based parameter designing of genetic algorithm for artificial neural network training. In: 2013 International Conference on Informatics and Creative Multimedia. IEEE (2013)
10. Ainslie, R., McCall, J., Shakya, S., Owusu, G.: Predictive planning with neural networks. In: 2016 International Joint Conference on Neural Networks (IJCNN), pp. 2110–2117. IEEE (2016)
11. AlShizawi, S., Shakya, S., Sluzek, A.S., Ainslie, R., Owusu, G.: Predicting fluid work demand in service organizations using AI techniques. In: Bramer, M., Petridis, M. (eds.) SGAI 2018. LNCS (LNAI), vol. 11311, pp. 266–276. Springer, Cham (2018). https://doi. org/10.1007/978-3-030-04191-5_24
12. Ekici, B.B., Aksoy, U.T.: Prediction of building energy consumption by using artificial neural networks. Adv. Eng. Softw. **40**(5), 356–362 (2009)
13. Yun, S.-Y., Namkoong, S., Rho, J.-H., Shin, S.-W., Choi, J.-U.: A performance evaluation of neural network models in traffic volume forecasting. Math. Comput. Model. **27**(9–11), 293–310 (1998)
14. Yao, X.: Evolutionary artificial neural networks. Int. J. Neural Syst. **4**(03), 203–222 (1993)
15. Reeves, C.R.: Genetic algorithms. In: Gendreau, M., Potvin, J.-Y. (eds.) Handbook of Metaheuristics, pp. 109–139. Springer, Boston (2010). https://doi.org/10.1007/978-3-319-91086-4
16. Distance correlation: Wikipedia. https://en.wikipedia.org/wiki/Distance_correlation
17. Selection: Wikipedia. https://en.wikipedia.org/wiki/Selection_(genetic_algorithm)
18. Crossover: Wikipedia. https://en.wikipedia.org/wiki/Crossover_(genetic_algorithm)
19. Sigmoid function: Wikipedia. https://en.wikipedia.org/wiki/Sigmoid_function
20. Kaastra, I., Boyd, M.S.: Forecasting futures trading volume using neural networks. J. Future Mark. **15**(8), 953–970 (1995)
21. Lawrence, R.: Using neural networks to forecast stock market prices. University of Manitoba, p. 333 (1997)
22. Dybowski, R., Gant, V., Weller, P., Chang, R.: Prediction of outcome in critically ill patients using artificial neural network synthesised by genetic algorithm. The Lancet **347**(9009), 1146–1150 (1996)
23. Majdi, A., Beiki, M.: Evolving neural network using a genetic algorithm for predicting the deformation modulus of rock masses. Int. J. Rock Mech. Min. Sci. **47**(2), 246–253 (2010)

24. Starkey, A.J., Hagras, H., Shakya, S., Owusu, G.: A genetic algorithm based system for simultaneous optimisation of workforce skills and teams. KI-Künstliche Intelligenz 32(4), 245–260 (2018)
25. Starkey, A.J., Hagras, H., Shakya, S., Owusu, G.: A genetic algorithm based approach for the simultaneous optimisation of workforce skill sets and team allocation. In: Bramer, M., Petridis, M. (eds.) Research and Development in Intelligent Systems XXXIII, pp. 253–266. Springer, Cham (2016). https://doi.org/10.1007/978-3-319-47175-4_19
26. Petrovski, A., Shakya, S., McCall, J.: Optimising cancer chemotherapy using an estimation of distribution algorithm and genetic algorithms. In: Proceedings of the 8th Annual Conference on Genetic and Evolutionary Computation. ACM (2006)
27. Resilient Back Propagation: Wikipedia. https://en.wikipedia.org/wiki/Rprop
28. Early Stopping: Wikipedia. https://en.wikipedia.org/wiki/Early_stopping
29. Nau, R.: Introduction to ARIMA: nonseasonal models, Fuqua School of Business Duke University. https://people.duke.edu/rnau/411arim.htm
30. Yu, G., Zhang, C.: Switching ARIMA model based forecasting for traffic flow. In: 2004 IEEE International Conference on Acoustics, Speech, and Signal Processing, vol. 2, pp. ii-429. IEEE (2004)
31. Nava, N., Di Matteo, T., Aste, T.: Financial time series forecasting using empirical mode decomposition and support vector regression. Risks 6(1), 7 (2018)
32. Pedregosa, F., et al.: Scikit-learn: machine learning in Python. J. Mach. Learn. Res. 12, 2825–2830 (2011)

Medical Applications

Are You in Pain? Predicting Pain and Stiffness from Wearable Sensor Activity Data

Niladri Sett[1(✉)], Brian Mac Namee[1], Francesc Calvo[2], Brian Caulfield[1],
John Costello[1], Seamas C. Donnelly[3], Jonas F. Dorn[2], Louis Jeay[4],
Alison Keogh[1], Killian McManus[1], Ronan H. Mullan[3], Emer O'Hare[2],
and Caroline G. M. Perraudin[2]

[1] Insight Centre for Data Analytics, University College Dublin, Dublin, Ireland
niladrisett@gmail.com
[2] Digital Development, Novartis Pharma AG, Basel, Switzerland
[3] Tallaght Hospital, Trinity College Dublin, Tallaght, Ireland
[4] Telecom SudParis, Evry, France

Abstract. Physical activity (PA) is a key component in the treatment of a range of chronic health conditions. It is therefore important for researchers and clinicians to accurately assess and monitor PA. Although advances in wearable technology have improved this, there is a need to investigate PA in greater depth than the sum of its total parts. Specifically, linking deep PA data to patient outcomes offers a valuable, and unexplored use for wearable devices. As a result, this paper extracts useful features from accelerometer data (Actigraph GT3X Link), and applies machine learning algorithms to predict daily pain and stiffness. This was applied to a population of 30 arthritis patients and 15 healthy volunteers. Participants were provided with an Actigraph and asked to wear it continuously for 28 days. Results demonstrate that it is possible to predict both pain and stiffness of patients using the extracted accelerometer features.

Keywords: Machine learning · Accelerometer · Arthritis · Physical activity · Predict pain and stiffness

1 Introduction

Recent advances in wearable sensor technology and data analysis are providing researchers with unprecedented access to large volumes of objectively measured, remotely captured participant health data, removing the previously accepted ambiguity that shrouded the reliability of some clinical trial outcomes such as physical activity (PA). Traditionally, PA outcomes relied on self-report measures [19], however wearable devices like Actigraph GT3X Link are now been used to reliably measure PA in a range of clinical populations [2,5,21].

© Springer Nature Switzerland AG 2019
M. Bramer and M. Petridis (Eds.): SGAI-AI 2019, LNAI 11927, pp. 183–197, 2019.
https://doi.org/10.1007/978-3-030-34885-4_15

However, despite the benefits offered by these sensors, to date, most research has utilised the data generated from the proprietary algorithms, specific to each device, to quantify PA for their outcome measures [1,19]. While these have been shown to be valid, the value and potential of the raw data provided by these devices has not yet been fully realized. Indeed, the need for researchers to both access and utilize the raw data from wearable devices has recently been endorsed [19], highlighting the need for research to investigate what additional learnings can be gained from previously validated devices. The purpose of this study was therefore to use raw data gathered from the ActiGraph GT3X Link in the assessment of PA. Specifically, the raw data was converted to 60 s epoch data using ActiLife software which contains step counts, x, y and z axes activity counts, and the number of seconds considered standing within the epoch. Based on these measures several derived measures like energy expenditure, 60 s epoch activity intensity, time since last activity and steps were calculated for each 60 s epoch. Actigraphy variables were calculated to describe 60 s epoch measures during or across the day, or across different days.

To establish the utility of the derived actigraphy variables, it is important to test in a clinical population. Musculoskeletal disorders, such as arthritis, are estimated to cause 21.3% of the total years lived with disability, and are ranked as the fourth greatest health burden on the world's population [24]. Measures such as pain and stiffness are common outcome measures in arthritis and are frequently listed as barriers to treatment, resulting in less activity, higher disability and lower functional status [12,15]. As a result, there is a need to quantify the impact of PA on pain, stiffness, and function using objectively measured PA data [12]. Linking this data to measures such as pain and stiffness may provide important insights into disease trajectories, and may help predict symptom flare-ups [18]. Therefore, this study builds machine learning models using the actigraphy variables as features to predict self reported pain and stiffness in arthritis patients. High accuracy of prediction results demonstrates the usefulness of the derived actigraphy variables in prediction of self reported outcome.

The remainder of this paper is organized as follows. Section 2 discusses the related work. Section 3 describes the participants and how data was acquired. Section 4 describes the transformation process of the actigraphy data which include preprocessing and generation of 60 s epoch measures. Section 5 introduces the derived actigraphy variables. Section 6 defines the problem of predicting pain and stiffness and describes the method and results of predicting pain and stiffness. Section 7 concludes the paper.

2   Related Work

Recently, researchers have attempted to find associations between objective measures of PA and pain [10,13,14,16,17,25]. Pan et al. [16] found that a greater number of painful sites in musculoskeletal pain is associated with increased low intensity PA and reduced moderate to vigorous PA. Locks et al. [13] investigated whether temporal patterns of static standing influence lower extremity pain among blue-collar workers, and concluded that short bouts of static standing and total static standing time during leisure are associated with knee and hip pain. Naugle et al. [14] tried to predict conditioned pain modulation and pain facilitation on the temporal summation in healthy older adults using three PA measures: sedentary time, light physical activity, and moderate to vigorous physical activity. They concluded that less sedentary time and greater light physical activity per day is associated with greater pain inhibitory capacity, and greater moderate to vigorous physical activity is associated with less temporal summation of pain. Kichline et al. [10] found that a previous day's moderate to vigorous physical activity is associated with pain severity in youths. Perraudin et al. [17] showed that the duration of a standard motor task, known as the Five Times Sit to Stand test is associated with pain and stiffness intensity in arthritis patients. Zhaoyang et al. [25] found that sedentary behavior may be related to less pain in the short term in arthritis patients. Where all these studies attempted to find association of few aggregated PA measures with pain, this paper extracts fine grained features from raw accelerometer data and applies machine learning algorithms to predict pain and stiffness. To the best of our knowledge, there exists no such study which uses fine grained accelerometer features to predict pain and stiffness. For example, although our work uses the same data as described in Perraudin et al. [17], the approach of Perraudin et al. sampled the data based on Five Times Sit to Stand test duration, while this work considers activity data from a full day to extract features.

Human activity recognition [11] is the most popular research area to which machine learning on features extracted from raw accelerometer data has been applied. It is a classification task which aims at identifying daily activities—like sitting, walking, running, standing—given accelerometer readings from a specified time. Several summary statistics like mean, variance, interquartile range, mean absolute deviation, correlation between axes, kurtosis, etc. derived from sampled accelerometer readings of acceleration in the axes have been used as features in activity recognition. Frequency domain features such as energy, and coefficients of autoregressive models have also been used as features in activity recognitions [11]. Where activity recognition requires handling variability in acceleration signals in the axes, predicting outcome like pain and stiffness from PA is a completely different application area where the amount of PA at different times in a day and across multiple days can be the main discriminating factors. So, we defined several 60 s epoch measures and engineered actigraphy variables to describe 60 s epoch measures during or across the day, or across different days.

3   Participants and Data Acquisition

This section describes the participant recruitment process and how data was acquired. The same data used in this study has been described previously by Perraudin et al. [17] who investigated the association between a standard motor task—known as the *five times sit to stand* test—with morning pain and stiffness.

3.1 Participants and Recruitment Procedure

This study was carried out in two settings. Healthy volunteers (HVs) were recruited through University College Dublin (UCD) and the arthritis patient cohort was recruited through Tallaght Hospital via Trinity College Dublin (TCD). Patients underwent clinical assessment in Tallaght hospital, while healthy volunteers had a clinical assessment at UCD. Subsequent sensor deployment and app installation, either on participant's own or provisioned phone, took place in the participants' home (or in UCD for some HVs). 30 participants fulfilling criteria of different varieties of arthritis patients were recruited. 15 additional age/gender matched participants were recruited as HV cohort, for an overall total of 45 participants. Informed written consent was obtained prior to inclusion following ethical approval by the institutional ethics committee.

3.2 Data Collection

All participants were provided with a CentrosHealth[1] application for use on a smartphone to rate the degree of joint pain in the morning while walking and stiffness severity upon waking up, together with a wrist-worn Actigraph Link activity monitor during the 4-week study. The participants were expected to wear the activity monitor continuously (day and night except when showering and charging). Participants had to charge the activity monitors but otherwise they worked automatically. Pain was recorded on a 0–10 scale, where 0 represented no pain. Stiffness was recorded on a 0–4 scale, where 0 represented no stiffness. If the participant had not completed the pain and stiffness rating, a reminder was set at 10:00 and 11:00. Participants who did not provide a rating by midday could not do so for that and their ratings were considered missing.

4   Transformation of Actigraph Data

This section describes the transformation of the raw data collected from the Actigraph devices to a clean representation that could be used for analysis. This included calibration, 60 s epoch generation, missing data handling, non-wear and sleep-time detection, and normalization of data to *data analysis days*. Following this a collection of measures were derived from the 60 s epoch data.

Calibration and 60 s Epoch Data Generation. Actigraph raw accelerometer data gives measurements of the movements at the wrist in the x, y, and z axes. The movements at the wrist indicates the activity levels of the participant. The raw accelerometer data was collected at 30 Hz. To reduce variability introduced by sensors, raw data from Actigraph devices was re-calibrated. The calibration method used was adapted from [6] and applied to the raw accelerometer 30 Hz signals on x, y, and z axes. The calibrated acceleration data was

---
[1] Currently ClinicalInk ENGAGE: https://www.clinicalink.com/engage/.

imported back into the ActiLife software to get the corrected 60 s epoch step and activity counts for the x, y, and z axes.

Activity counts are calculated by a proprietary algorithm used in the ActiLife software that first applies a band-pass filter to the sensor data, eliminating both very slow and very rapid changes in acceleration, after which each value above a certain threshold is counted. The Actilife software application also produced step counts calculated using the calibrated accelerometer 30 Hz signals from the y-axis. It also generated a count of the number of seconds spent standing, sitting and lying for each epoch. It was determined that readings for sitting and lying were too inaccurate and were discarded, however, standing readings were retained.

Transforming Study Days to Data Analysis Days. To facilitate sleep detection, and for more convenient visualization, study days were converted to *data analysis days* (DADs). A data analysis day starts at 18:00.033, and ends at 18:00:000 on the following day. The day at which recording starts is set to DAD 0, so that DAD 1 is the first day within the study with 24 h of data (assuming full compliance; all deployments were completed before 18:00).

Generating Non-wear Times. Each 60 s epoch of activity data was classified as an epoch during which the Actigraph was worn or not-worn. A modified version of the Choi [4] wear time validation algorithm was used to detect sections of non-wear and these epochs were marked as non-wear epochs.

Generating Sleep Times. To identify sleep periods we applied the Cole-Kripke [8] algorithm which classified epochs as sleep or non-sleep. To combine connected epochs of sleeping together into continuous sleep periods we applied the Tudor-Locke [23] algorithm. The Tudor-Locke algorithm was applied multiple times in parallel using different values of different sizes for its minimum sleep onset time, maximum permitted wake during sleep, and minimum sleep period duration parameters. For example, minimum sleep period duration parameters ranged from 40 min to 200 min. The multiple parallel runs were merged to find overlapping periods of sleep and these were used as a final sleep periods.

Missing Data. Each DAD was split into periods of interest for analysis (refer to Sect. 5.1). If any period contained less than 80% or fewer than 4 out of 5 epochs with data, it was excluded from analysis.

4.1   Generating 60 s Epoch Measures

Raw 60 s epoch data contained step counts, x, y and z axes activity counts, and the number of seconds considered standing within the epoch. Based on these measures the following derived measures were also calculated for each 60 s epoch.

Vector Magnitude of Triaxial Activity Counts. The activity counts used for analysis are the activity counts calculated on the calibrated data from three perpendicular axes. The vector magnitude activity count is calculated using the square root of the summed squares of the activity counts from the three axes to give a single total activity measure.

Energy Expenditure Estimates. Two types of measures were generated to estimate energy expenditure, Kilo Calories (Kcal) and Metabolic Equivalent (MET). MET is a means of expressing energy expenditure in a way comparable among persons of different weight, and Kcal uses a person's body weight to calculate the amount of energy expended in standard energy units.

Kcal estimates were calculated using Freedson VM3 combination [20]. Freedson VM3 combination uses a combination of two energy expenditure calculation methods. The first method, Williams work energy, is used to capture low intensity activity, where low intensity activity is defined as activity below 2453 activity counts/60 s. A second method, Freedson VM3 [20], is used for higher intensity activity. These calculations can be summarized as follows:

< 2453 activity counts per min $BodyMass \times (ActivityCount \times 0.00000191)$

> 2453 activity counts per min $BodyMass \times 0.087512 + (ActivityCount \times 0.001064) - 5.500229$

MET energy expenditure was calculated as $1.602 + (ActivityCount \times 0.000638)$ for > 0 activity counts/min [7].

60 s Epoch Activity Intensity. In order to label the intensity of activity within an epoch a set of activity cut points were used to classify activity intensity. Validated activity intensity count cut points for wrist worn activity sensors are unavailable in the literature so arbitrary weighted estimates of Freedson cut points [20] were used to account for upper body extremity activity. The cut points for activities and steps are shown in Table 1. Each 60 s epoch was labeled with one of these intensities.

Table 1. 60 s Epoch activity intensity level cut points for activity counts and steps

Activity count cut point (activity counts/min)	Step cut point (steps/min)	Activity intensity level
0–1800	0–30	Inactive/Very Sedentary
1801–2690	30–80	Light/Sedentary
2691–6166	81–150	Moderate
6166–9641	>150	Vigorous/Hard
>2691	>81	Moderate to vigorous
>9642		Very hard

Time Since Last Activity and Steps. In order to measure periods of long rest, a measure of the time since last activity can be added to each epoch indicating how long ago the last epoch with activity happened. When calculating time since last activity, a threshold of 100 activity counts per minute was used to determine inactive epochs, i.e. epochs without activity above what is considered as sensor noise. The time since 60 s epoch activity counter is reset to zero at the first insignificant epoch seen; the epoch counter is then incremented for every subsequent insignificant activity 60 s epoch until reset to zero by activity. When counting inactivity using steps, no similar insignificant activity threshold was required as the proprietary Actilife step calculation applied insignificant activity thresholds as an intrinsic element of its step calculation and so a step count of 0 is considered inactivity.

Linear Regression Residuals of Steps on Activity. A linear regression model of steps against activity was calculated individually for each participant. For each 60 s epoch, the residual between the value for steps based on measured activity predicted by this model and the actual value recorded was captured. The intuition behind this measure is that it gave an indication of upper body extremity activity not associated with steps, as the naive linear regression model is likely to overestimate step counts compared to the more sophisticated step count estimation algorithm used by Actigraph. In this paper, we refer this as step_acti_resid.

5   Generating Actigraphy Variables from 60 s Epoch Measures

Using the basic 60 s epoch measures described in the previous section a suite of richer actigraphy variables can be calculated. This section describes these in detail. The actigraphy variable sets can be classified into two groups: intra-DAD and inter-DAD. The intra-DAD variables are calculated from the actigraphy data over the current DAD, while inter-DAD variables are calculated over the actigraphy data from multiple DADs.

5.1   Intra-DAD Measures

Using the fully calculated 60 s epoch data, the DAD was split into periods of interest for analysis. The interesting DAD periods that were used in the analysis were as follows:

- Full DAD: A complete DAD covering 24 h from 18:00 on one day to 18:00 the following day.
- 11-to-3: The midday period from 11:00 to 15:00 within a DAD.
- Post Waking: Any DAD for which a sleep time was calculated allowed the period immediately following waking to be identified. The length of this period could be varied from 15 min to 240 min. This is the period of most interest within the study.

- Pre Sleeping: Any DAD for which a sleep time was calculated allowed the period immediately preceding sleeping to be identified. The length of this period could be varied from 15 min to 240 min.
- Midday: A period of a specified length (lengths from 15 min to 240 min were used) centered around 13:00 within a DAD.
- Post-wake Hours: Individual hours after a participant wakes. These can be the first hour (1 h), second hour (1 to 2 h), third hour (2 to 3 h), fourth hour (3 to 4 h), or fifth hour (4 to 5 h) before waking.
- Pre-sleep Hours: Individual hours before a participant sleeps. These can be the first hour (1 h), second hour (1 to 2 h), third hour (2 to 3 h), fourth hour (3 to 4 h), or fifth hour (4 to 5 h) before sleep.

For each of these intra-DAD periods a collection of actigraphy measures were generated, typically by calculating summary statistics of one of the 60 s epoch measures within the time period. These are explained in detail in the remainder of this section.

60 s Epoch Measure Summary Statistics. To perform basic analysis across DAD periods the 60 s epoch measures, described in Sect. 4.1 were aggregated across each period using appropriate summary statistics. The summary statistics used were sum, mean, standard deviation, peak, kurtosis, and median. To combat noise within the 60 s epoch data these summary statistics were always calculated against a 5 min epoch (calculated by summing 60 s epoch measure's values from the 60 s epoch data).

Full DAD Intensity and Standing Durations. For each DAD the total number of seconds in which activity in each of the activity intensity bands described in Table 1 was counted. The total time recognised as standing was also counted.

Comparison to Participant Median. As a normalization effort across the full time period of the study a median value for each actigraphy measure (e.g. steps, Kcal, activity), for each DAD period (e.g. post-waking) was calculated. Based on this the amount of time spent above or below that median value (mins_above_median and mins_below_median) in a specific time period can be recorded. The intuition behind this measure is that this would indicate participants struggling with symptoms on a particular day.

Percent of Time Period. As another normalization effort it is possible to transform the activity, calories, or steps within a particular time period into a percentage of the activity, calories or steps in a larger time period (for example the full DAD). This could be done for any time period but in this study is done only for the full DAD and for certain pre-sleep, midday, post-wake combinations.

Full DAD Activity Intensity Bouts. Prolonged bouts of activity at a particular intensity level (as defined in Table 1) are an interesting phenomenon to measure. The number of bouts over a minimum duration that occur for each activity intensity level across a DAD was recorded.

Naming Intra-DAD Measures. In total ~1600 period-based actigraphy measures were calculated for each DAD. Table 2 describes these. Each is based on a period, a duration (except for measures calculated over a full DAD), a summary statistic, and a 60s epoch measure. We name these measures be concatenating these components together. For example, *presleep_60m_maximum_steps* refers

Table 2. Period-based actigraphy measure labels. Each measure is defined by a period, a duration (not required for full_DAD periods), a summary statistic, and a 60 s epoch measure.

Period	Duration	Summary statistic	60s Epoch measure
full_DAD		sum, mean, standard_deviation, maximum, kurtosis, median, mins_above_median, mins_below_median	activity, steps, Kcal, MET, mins_since_activity, mins_since_step, step_acti_resid, standing
11_to_3		sum, mean, standard_deviation, maximum, kurtosis, median	activity, steps, Kcal, MET, mins_since_activity, mins_since_step, step_acti_resid, standing
postwake, presleep, midday	15 min, 30 min, 60 min, 120 min, 240 min	sum, mean, standard_deviation, maximum, kurtosis, median, percent_of_DAD	activity, steps, Kcal, MET, mins_since_activity, mins_since_step, step_acti_resid, standing
postwake, presleep,	1 h, 1 to 2 h, 2 to 3 h, 3 to 4 h, 4 to 5 h	sum, mean, standard_deviation, maximum, kurtosis, median, mins_above_median, mins_below_median, percent_of_DAD	activity, steps, Kcal, MET, mins_since_activity, mins_since_step, step_acti_resid, standing
postwake, presleep	1 h, 1 to 2 h, 2 to 3 h, 3 to 4 h, 4 to 5 h	count	hard, moderate, sedentary, very_sedentary, very_hard
full_DAD		count	hard, moderate, sedentary, very_sedentary, very_hard
full_DAD	2 min, 5 min, 10 min	bout_count	hard, moderate, sedentary, very_sedentary, very_hard, moderate_to_vigorous

to the maximum value for step count seen in the 60 min prior to sleep while *full_DAD_5m_bout_count_very_hard* refers to the number of bouts of at least 5 min duration of very hard activity.

5.2   Inter-DAD Measures

Inter-DAD measures were derived using the actigraphy data covering multiple days. Five inter-DAD Measures were derived using combinations of the full_DAD_sum_activity measures of the current day, the previous day and the following day. These combinations included basic activity counts for the two extra days, sums of activity across combinations of days, and ratios between activity sums on different days. The 5 measures calculated are:

1. full_DAD_prev_sum_activity: The sum of activity for the previous day.
2. full_DAD_next_sum_activity: The sum of activity for the next day.
3. full_DAD_prev_curr_next_sum_activity: The total sum of activity for the previous, current, and next days.
4. full_DAD_curr_prev_sum_activity_ratio: The ratio between the total activity on the current and previous days.
5. full_DAD_curr_next_sum_activity_ratio: The ratio between the total activity on the current and next days.

These measures were designed to capture significant changes between activity levels on subsequent days as these might be likely indicators of pain and stiffness levels.

6   Predicting Morning Pain and Stiffness

The actigraphy variables were used as features to build regression and classification models to predict pain and stiffness. The prediction problem is to predict the pain and stiffness given the activity monitor data. The actigraphy variables were used as features for predicting each day's pain and stiffness. The prediction problem was posed as regression as well as binary classification problem. In the regression problem, the problem is to predict the pain and stiffness rating given by the participant. In the classification problem the ratings were converted into two labels: *low* and *high*. For pain ratings of 0–4 were considered *low* and ratings of 6–10 were considered *high*. Ratings of 5 were considered neutral and were discarded. Similarly, stiffness ratings were converted into *low* (0–1) and *high* (3–4), again ratings of 2 were considered neutral and discarded.

6.1   Feature Selection and Modelling Algorithms

A significant question in this investigation was which types of features would be most effective for the different prediction problems—for example basic features, intra-DAD features or inter-DAD features? However, as there were approximately 1600 intra-DAD variables, feature selection was used to isolate the most important features from this large set. A rank and prune [9] approach using a univariate Pearson correlation measure to find the intra-DAD actigraphy variables most associated with pain and stiffness. The 45 measures most closely correlated with pain (and stiffness) were first selected and then this list was pruned to remove measures that were very closely correlated with each other (again based on Pearson correlations). For predicting pain 11 of the intra-DAD actigraphy measures were selected by the feature selection process:

- full_DAD_mins_below_median_Kcal
- full_DAD_maximum_Activity
- full_DAD_kurtosis_Activity
- full_DAD_kurtosis_steps
- full_DAD_standard_deviation_step_acti_resid
- full_DAD_maximum_steps
- midday_60m_percent_of_DAD_mins_since_activity
- postwake_15m_mean_Kcal
- postwake_15m_mean_activity
- postwake_240m_kurtosis_Kcal
- presleep_3to4h_standard_deviation_step_acti_resid

For stiffness prediction 14 of the intra-DAD actigraphy features were selected by the feature selection process:

- full_DAD_kurtosis_MET
- full_DAD_maximum_step_acti_resid
- full_DAD_kurtosis_Steps
- full_DAD_standard_deviation_step_acti_resid
- full_DAD_maximum_steps
- postwake_15m_mean_Kcal
- postwake_15m_mean_activity
- postwake_15m_median_Kcal
- postwake_15m_mean_standing
- postwake_60m_percent_of_DAD_mins_since_activity
- postwake_4to5h_mean_Kcal
- postwake_4to5h_kurtosis_Kcal
- postwake_4to5h_standard_deviation_step_acti_resid
- full_DAD_5m_bout_count_moderate_to_vigorous

Random forest regression [3] models were used for the regression tasks and *random forest classification* [3] models were used for the classification tasks. Random forest models were used as they have been shown to perform well across diverse prediction problem types, are robust to overfitting, and do not require very large training datasets.

6.2   Evaluation Method

To evaluate the performance of different models built, *leave-one-subject-out* cross validation [22] was used. All results reported are averaged over the folds of the cross validation experiments. To search for the best hyper-parameters for the models a grid search was performed. Three hyper-parameters were tuned: number of trees (varied from 10 to 300), maximum depth of the trees (varied from 5 to 20) and number of features to consider when looking for the best split (all features, square root of the number of features *log* of the number of features). After the best hyper-parameters were found using the grid search, multiple models were built using multiple random seeds and the mean of the performance is shown in result.

To evaluate the regression models we used *mean absolute error* (MAE) [9] mainly to aid interpretation of model performance. To evaluate the classification models we used *area under the ROC curve* (AUC) [9] as the class distributions in the datasets are skewed towards *low* pain and stiffness responses.

6.3   Results

This section describes the results of the evaluation experiments for the models predicting pain and stiffness. In total, there were 1045 rows (i.e., DADs) in the experiments for 44 participants (one patient dropped out).

Predicting Pain. We performed experiments with different feature sets and combination of multiple feature sets to evaluate the performance of the engineered features. The feature sets considered are:

- **Basic:** five features measuring the sum of activity, time standing, Kcal, MET and steps over a full day (full_DAD_sum_activity, full_DAD_sum_standing, full_DAD_sum_Kcal, full_DAD_sum_MET, and, full_DAD_sum_steps).
- **Intra-DAD:** The 11 intra-DAD actigraphy features selected as described in Sect. 6.1.
- **Inter-DAD:** The inter-DAD features.

Table 3 summarizes the regression and classification results. Mean and standard deviation results are given across over folds and multiple runs of the experiment. The result shows that the intra-DAD features perform better than the basic features in both of regression and classification, which shows the effectiveness of the engineered features. The best performing model for regression is Intra-DAD (MAE 1.88) which outperforms the Basic model by 13%, and the best performing model for classification is Basic+Intra-DAD+Inter-DAD (AUC 0.79) which outperforms the Basic model by 27%.

Table 3. Regression and classification results for predicting pain

Model	Regression (MAE)	Classification (AUC)
Basic	2.16 (±1.24)	0.62 (±0.22)
Intra-DAD	**1.88** (±1.01)	0.76 (±0.18)
Inter-DAD	2.16 (±1.21)	0.54 (±0.22)
Basic+Intra-DAD	1.89 (±1.01)	0.78 (±0.18)
Basic+Inter-DAD	2.17 (±1.24)	0.56 (±0.23)
Intra-DAD+Inter-DAD	1.92 (±1.08)	0.77 (±0.17)
Basic+Intra-DAD+Inter-DAD	1.92 (±1.06)	**0.79** (±0.18)

Predicting Stiffness. For predicting stiffness, combinations of the same three feature groups described in the previous section (Basic, Intra-DAD (this time with 14 selected features), and Inter-DAD) were evaluated. Table 4 summarizes the results for predicting stiffness. Like pain, also in case of stiffness, the intra-DAD features outperform the basic features in both of regression and classification, which shows the effectiveness of the engineered features. The best performing model for both regression and classification is Intra-DAD (MAE 0.74 for regression and AUC 0.76 for classification) which outperforms the Basic model by 11% in regression and 33% in classification.

Table 4. Regression and classification results for predicting stiffness

Model	Regression (MAE)	Classification (AUC)
Basic	0.83 (±0.36)	0.57 (±0.25)
Intra-DAD	**0.74** (±0.28)	**0.76** (±0.19)
Inter-DAD	0.84 (±0.35)	0.49 (±0.21)
Basic+Intra-DAD	**0.74** (±0.29)	0.75 (±0.19)
Basic+Inter-DAD	0.83 (±0.36)	0.53 (±0.23)
Intra-DAD+Inter-DAD	0.75 (±0.28)	0.75 (±0.19)
Basic+Intra-DAD+Inter-DAD	**0.74** (±0.29)	0.75 (±0.19)

7   Conclusions and Future Work

This paper has described how raw accelerometer data (Actigraph GT3X Link) was processed and features were extracted to access PA. It was investigated how useful these features are in predicting patient reported outcomes. As arthritis is a leading health burden on the world's population, and PA is correlated with pain and stiffness an arthritis patient face, these features were used to build machine learning models to predict daily pain and stiffness of arthritis patients.

Data were collected from 30 arthritis patients and 15 healthy volunteers. They were asked to wear Actigraph for 28 days and rate their pain and stiffness level every day in the morning. The results have demonstrated that the extracted features are useful to predict both pain and stiffness.

In future, the study can be performed with larger number of participants to validate the proposed methods. Also, the derived actigraphy variables can be used for other prediction tasks than stiffness and pain.

References

1. Ainsworth, B., Cahalin, L., Buman, M., Ross, R.: The current state of physical activity assessment tools. Prog. Cardiovasc. Dis. **57**(4), 387–395 (2015)
2. Anderson, J., Green, A., Yoward, L.: Validity of the actigraph GT3X accelerometer in quantification of step count in hospitalised adults recovering from critical illness. Physiotherapy **105**, e179–e180 (2019)
3. Breiman, L.: Random forests. Mach. Learn. **45**(1), 5–32 (2001)
4. Choi, L., Liu, Z., Matthews, C.E., Buchowski, M.S.: Validation of accelerometer wear and nonwear time classification algorithm. Med. Sci. Sport. Exerc. **43**(2), 357 (2011)
5. Evenson, K.R., Goto, M.M., Furberg, R.D.: Systematic review of the validity and reliability of consumer-wearable activity trackers. Int. J. Behav. Nutr. Phys. Act. **12**(1), 159 (2015)
6. van Hees, V.T., et al.: Autocalibration of accelerometer data for free-living physical activity assessment using local gravity and temperature: an evaluation on four continents. J. Appl. Physiol. **117**(7), 738–744 (2014)
7. Hendelman, D., Miller, K., Baggett, C., Debold, E., Freedson, P.: Validity of accelerometry for the assessment of moderate intensity physical activity in the field. Med. Sci. Sport. Exerc. **32**(9), S442–S449 (2000)
8. Jean-Louis, G., Kripke, D.F., Cole, R.J., Assmus, J.D., Langer, R.D.: Sleep detection with an accelerometer actigraph: comparisons with polysomnography. Physiol. Behav. **72**(1–2), 21–28 (2001)
9. Kelleher, J.D., Mac Namee, B., D'arcy, A.: Fundamentals of Machine Learning for Predictive Data Analytics: Algorithms, Worked Examples, and Case Studies. MIT Press, Cambridge (2015)
10. Kichline, T., Cushing, C.C., Ortega, A., Friesen, C., Schurman, J.V.: Associations between physical activity and chronic pain severity in youth with chronic abdominal pain. Clin. J. Pain **35**(7), 618–624 (2019)
11. Lara, O.D., Labrador, M.A.: A survey on human activity recognition using wearable sensors. IEEE Commun. Surv. Tutor. **15**(3), 1192–1209 (2012)
12. Liu, S.H., Driban, J.B., Eaton, C.B., McAlindon, T.E., Harrold, L.R., Lapane, K.L.: Objectively measured physical activity and symptoms change in knee osteoarthritis. Am. J. Med. **129**(5), 497–505.e1 (2016)
13. Locks, F., Gupta, N., Madeleine, P., Jørgensen, M.B., Oliveira, A.B., Holtermann, A.: Are accelerometer measures of temporal patterns of static standing associated with lower extremity pain among blue-collar workers? Gait Posture **67**, 166–171 (2019)
14. Naugle, K.M., Ohlman, T., Naugle, K.E., Riley, Z.A., Keith, N.R.: Physical activity behavior predicts endogenous pain modulation in older adults. Pain **158**(3), 383–390 (2017)

15. Neogi, T.: The epidemiology and impact of pain in osteoarthritis. Osteoarthr. Cartil. **21**(9), 1145–1153 (2013). Pain in Osteoarthritis

16. Pan, F., Byrne, K.S., Ramakrishnan, R., Ferreira, M., Dwyer, T., Jones, G.: Association between musculoskeletal pain at multiple sites and objectively measured physical activity and work capacity: results from UK biobank study. J. Sci. Med. Sport. **22**(4), 444–449 (2019)

17. Perraudin, C.G., et al.: Observational study of a wearable sensor and smartphone application supporting unsupervised exercises to assess pain and stiffness. Digit. Biomark. **2**(3), 106–125 (2018)

18. Phillips, S.M., Cadmus-Bertram, L., Rosenberg, D., Buman, M.P., Lynch, B.M.: Wearable technology and physical activity in chronic disease: opportunities and challenges. Am. J. Prev. Med. **54**(1), 144–150 (2018)

19. Reeder, B., David, A.: Health at hand: a systematic review of smart watch uses for health and wellness. J. Biomed. Inform. **63**, 269–276 (2016)

20. Sasaki, J.E., John, D., Freedson, P.S.: Validation and comparison of actigraph activity monitors. J. Sci. Med. Sport. **14**(5), 411–416 (2011)

21. Schaffer, S.D., Holzapfel, S.D., Fulk, G., Bosch, P.R.: Step count accuracy and reliability of two activity tracking devices in people after stroke. Physiother. Theory Pract. **33**(10), 788–796 (2017)

22. Steyerberg, E.W., Harrell Jr., F.E., Borsboom, G.J., Eijkemans, M., Vergouwe, Y., Habbema, J.D.F.: Internal validation of predictive models: efficiency of some procedures for logistic regression analysis. J. Clin. Epidemiol. **54**(8), 774–781 (2001)

23. Tudor-Locke, C., Barreira, T.V., Schuna Jr., J.M., Mire, E.F., Katzmarzyk, P.T.: Fully automated waist-worn accelerometer algorithm for detecting children's sleep-period time separate from 24-h physical activity or sedentary behaviors. Appl. Physiol. Nutr. Metab. **39**(1), 53–57 (2013)

24. Woolf, A.D.: Global burden of osteoarthritis and musculoskeletal diseases. BMC Musculoskelet. Disord. **16**(1), S3 (2015)

25. Zhaoyang, R., Martire, L.M.: Daily sedentary behavior predicts pain and affect in knee arthritis. Ann. Behav. Med. **53**, 642–651 (2018)

Motif Discovery in Long Time Series: Classifying Phonocardiograms

Hajar Alhijailan[1,2]([⊠]) [iD] and Frans Coenen[1] [iD]

[1] Department of Computer Science, University of Liverpool, Liverpool, UK
{h.alhijailan,coenen}@liverpool.ac.uk
[2] College of Computer and Information Sciences, King Saud University,
Riyadh, Saudi Arabia
halhujailan@ksu.edu.sa

Abstract. A mechanism is presented for classifying phonocardiograms (PCGs) by interpreting PCGs as time series and using the concept of motifs, times series subsequences that are good discriminators of class, to support nearest neighbour classification. A particular challenge addressed by the work is that PCG time series are large which renders exact motif discovery to be computationally expensive; it is not realistic to compare every candidate time series subsequence with every other time series subsequence in order to discover exact motifs. Instead, a mechanism is proposed the firstly makes use of the cyclic nature of PCGs and secondly adopts a novel time series pruning mechanism. The evaluation, conducted using a canine PCG dataset, illustrated that the proposed approach produced the same classification accuracy but in a significantly more efficient manner.

Keywords: Phonocardiograms · Time series segmentation · Frequent motif discovery · Time series analysis · Classification

1 Introduction

A phonocardiogram (PCG) is a recording of the sound of the heart; it is essentially an univariate time series [1,13,22]. The sound is cyclic and comprises two phases (S1 and S2), the Systole phase when the heart contracts, and the Diastole when the heart relaxes. The systole phase starts and ends with two sound components, when the *atrioventricular* valves close and when the aortic and pulmonary valves close respectively. The diastole phase is marked by the relative absence of sound. There will also be unwanted background noise and, in an unhealthy heart, what are known as murmurs, indicators of abnormal activity. A PCG is collected using a phonocardiograph, more commonly known as an electronic or digital stethoscope [8]. By analysing PCGs, it is possible to detect heart conditions of various sorts; this process can be automated using machine learning techniques, typically supervised learning (classification).

A common method of classifying time series where repeating patterns are known to exist is Motif Discovery [7,10,28,29]. The idea is to discover and store

© Springer Nature Switzerland AG 2019
M. Bramer and M. Petridis (Eds.): SGAI-AI 2019, LNAI 11927, pp. 198–212, 2019.
https://doi.org/10.1007/978-3-030-34885-4_16

reoccurring patterns, known as *motifs* which are representative of class-labels [15,17]. A good motif, in the context of this paper, is one that appears frequently and at the same time is associated with only a single class. The discovered motifs can then be used to label (classify) previously unseen time series [1,22,28]. However, finding motifs that are good representatives of class-labels is computationally challenging, especially given long time series (as in the case of PCG data). Exact motif discovery requires the comparison of every candidate time series subsequence with every other subsequence that exists in the dataset; a computationally expensive enterprise. One solution is to adopt an approximate approach [22]. Another is to reduce the complexity of the motif discovery process by preprocessing the time series so as to reduce the number of computations needed later in the process.

In this paper, an exact PCG motif discovery mechanism is presented which is effective in terms of classification accuracy and is efficient in terms of runtime. The idea is to limit the number of time series subsequences to be considered by first identifying cycles, using a PCG segmentation mechanism founded on the approach presented in [12], but with modifications. Next, to prune cycles that will not result in good motifs using a novel "zero motif" mechanism. Then, to process the retained candidate motifs further so as to extract good discriminators of class. The approach was evaluated using a canine PCGs dataset comprised of four classes. The first three classes described stages of Mitral Valve disease, as defined by the the European College of Veterinary Internal Medicine [2,23], and the fourth was a control class (no disease). The evaluation results obtained indicated that the proposed mechanisms was more efficient than alternative algorithms considered, whilst obtaining the same accuracy.

The rest of this paper is organised as follows. Section 2 gives a review of previous work regarding the research domain. The proposed PCG frequent motif selection and extraction mechanism, and its processes, are then presented in Sect. 3. Section 4 considers the evaluation strategy, followed by presentation and discussion of the results. The paper is completed with some concluding remarks in Sect. 5.

2   Previous Work

Time series analysis is concerned with the processing of time series data so as to extract knowledge. Typical applications include the discovery of distinguishing patterns, the clustering of time series collections and the modelling of the domain from which the time series are drawn. In the case of pattern identification, one type of pattern, and that of interest with respect to the work presented in this paper, is the *motif* [5,11,14]. A motif is a reoccurring subsequence in a time series that is a good indicator of class. A subsequence (candidate motif) is said to be reoccurring, and hence a motif, if there is at least one non-trivial match with another subsequence in a given time series according to some predefined similarity threshold [20,27]; a "trivial match" is where two subsequences overlap. To measure how well two subsequences match, a distance function is required.

Euclidean Distance (ED) is widely used in the literature with some evidence suggesting its competitiveness with, or superiority to, other more complex measures [9]. The "brute force" approach to identifying motifs entails a significant computational overhead. A number of more efficient, but approximate, motif discovery algorithms have therefore been proposed [18,19,22], while a tractable exact algorithm remains a research challenge [3,22]. The later is, in part, the research focus of this paper. The exact algorithm presented in [22], the MK algorithm, is of particular relevance to this paper because it is used as a comparator approach with which to compare the operation of the proposed approach.

The efficiency of motif discovery algorithms, exact or approximate, can be enhanced by preprocessing the input data. This is typically conducted using knowledge of the application domain to reduce the number of calculations to be considered, usually by considering the characteristics of the subsequences to be considered. The simplest technique is to restrict the comparisons to potential non-trivial matches [5]. This technique is widely used in many proposed motif discovery algorithms [5,22] and is adopted with respect to the work presented in this paper. For some applications, it is possible to exclude some sequences because they are known in advance not to be relevant, but this requires very specific domain knowledge. Another technique for reducing the complexity of the motif discovery process is to adopt the concept of "early abandonment" whereby a similarity comparison is stopped when the dissimilarity between two potential motifs being compared reaches a pre-specified threshold at which point it can be safely assumed that the two subsequences cannot be motifs. The threshold can be user-defined; or, as in the case of [22], derived.

There has been considerable work directed at analysing PCG data, although not in terms of motif discovery, for the purpose of PCG classification. A segmentation process is typically applied first to identify cycles. This is usually achieved with respect to a reference signal, either an ECG signal recorded at the same time and/or a Carotid Pulse (CP) [16,24,25]. In the case of the PCG signals collected using electronic stethoscopes, the application focus of the work presented in this paper, no such reference signal is typically available. In such cases, the components of the PCG signal can still be extracted by processing the signal. This is usually achieved according to the "energy" of the signal and one or more *energy thresholds* [4,12]. The well-known Shannon Energy is frequently used [21] as it maintains time series features. However, there are situations where not all of the features are needed, as in the case of the work presented in this paper, in which case alternative energy methods can be used as long as the required salient features are preserved. Extracting the cardiac components from PCGs using empirically defined static thresholds is usually inappropriate because of the varying amplitudes recorded. This is due to difference between subjects in: the thickness of the chest wall [32], subject age [30], subject mood [30] and further subjective factors [30]. The alternative is to use dynamically computed thresholds [4,12]; this is the approach adopted with respect to the work presented in this paper.

3   PCG Frequent Motif Selection and Extraction

This section presents the proposed PCG frequent motif selection and extraction process. The input is a set of time series $T = \{\langle P_1, c_1 \rangle, \langle P_2, c_2 \rangle, \dots \}$. The output is a set of motifs, H''; a set of frequently occurring PCG cycles that are considered to be good discriminators of class. These motifs can then be used to classify previously unseen PCGs. The proposed mechanism is a three stage process:

1. Cycle segmentation.
2. Candidate motif selection.
3. Frequent motif extraction.

In the first stage, the set T is processed to produce the set H, a set of heartbeat cycle and class pairs $\langle h_i, c_i \rangle$. In the second stage, the set H is pruned by removing infrequent cycles so as to produce a set of cycles H'. This is then further processed in Stage 3 to identify the set of k motifs, the most frequent cycles within H' that are good discriminators of class; these are held in a set H'' which can be then used as a "data bank" in a Nearest Neighbour Classification (NNC) model which in turn can be used to label previously unseen time series. Each stage is discussed in further detail in the following three subsections, Subsects. 3.1 to 3.3.

3.1   Cycle Segmentation

PCGs cycles comprises: (i) a heartbeat, (ii) some murmurs and clicks, if diseased, and (iii) noise. A cycle is measured from the start of the S1 component to the start of the following S1 component. The idea was to segment a training set of labelled PCGs into a collection of cycles and then to group the cycles according to class-labels. This idea is common in the Signal Processing field and has been applied to PCG signals to, for example, study the duration of S1 or to find "click positions" [21,30]. The proposed mechanism differs from this previous work; the focus is on "whole cycles" rather than their components. The mechanism, is founded on that presented in [12], but with modifications, and operates using a dynamic threshold, computed for each PCG signal, so as to detect the beginning of cycles.

The process is as follows. For each point series $P_i = \{p_{i_1}, p_{i_2}, \dots \} \in T$ the *standardised signal energy envelope* (V) is calculated according to the signal (time series) energy E which is standardised to give E'. The energy $E = \{e_1, e_2, \dots \}$ is computed by squaring the amplitude values (p_{i_j}) in P_i, for each $e_j \in E$, using Eq. 1. There are many other ways to calculate the energy of a signal, such as using absolute value, Shannon entropy or Shannon energy [12]. As the aim in the context of the work presented in this paper is to detect the beginning of cycles, the start of the S1 component, usually the component with highest amplitude (the loudest) [8], the above method of calculating the energy was adopted because samples with high amplitude will be favoured over those with low amplitude. This will in turn facilitate S1 detection. The standardised energy e'_j, given a value e_j, is then calculated using Eq. 2, where μ_e and σ_e are the mean and standard deviation of E respectively.

$$e_j = p_{i_j}^2 \tag{1}$$

$$e'_j = \frac{e_j - \mu_e}{\sigma_e} \tag{2}$$

The set of standardised energy values, $E' = \{e'_1, e'_2, \dots\}$ are then used to define the envelope V, which is then used to detect the beginning of cycles using an amplitude "cut-off" value t. The process is illustrated in Fig. 1. The process starts by identifying the oscillation in V with the highest energy value, the dotted oscillation in Fig. 1(a). Then, a predefined α threshold, a percentage of the width of the oscillation with the highest amplitude (the start and end of an oscillation can be identified from trend changes in V), is used to determine the value for t, the dash-dotted line shown in Fig. 1(b) (and Fig. 1(c)). The value for t is used to find ascending intersection points in V as shown in Fig. 1(c). All oscillations in the energy envelope V whose amplitude falls bellow t are ignored, because they are deemed to be S2s, clicks and murmurs. Using this process, some ascending intersection points demarcating S2 components will still be retained, as illustrated in Fig. 1(c). To remove these, the distance between intersection points is considered, if this falls below the average distance then we have an S2 intersection point which should be ignored. The retained points are then used to "track" back along the energy envelope V until a change in trend is discovered; this marks the start of an S1 component and thus the start of a cycle, the cycle ends with the start of the following S1 component. In this manner a set of cycles (heartbeats), $H = \{\langle h_1, c_1 \rangle, \langle h_2, c_2 \rangle, \dots\}$, for the given collection of time series (PCGs) T, is obtained. Note that each heartbeat h_j has a class-label c_j associated with it where c_j is taken from a set of class-labels C.

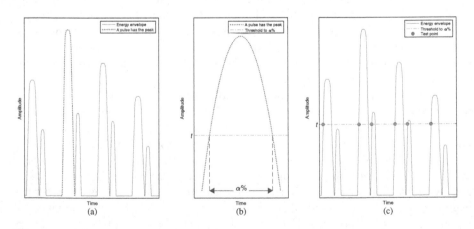

Fig. 1. Dynamic t value calculation using a PCG envelope signal: (a) example PCG envelope with the highest amplitude oscillation highlighted, (b) t value calculation and (c) intersect points.

3.2   Candidate Motif Selection

In Stage 2, the collection of heartbeats (cycles) H, generated during Stage 1, each with an associated class-label, is pruned by removing cycles that are infrequent so as to retain a set of candidate frequent cycles, H'. The assumption was that frequent cycles were likely to be better indicators of class than infrequent cycles. To find cycle frequency, a novel mechanism was adopted whereby a hypothetical cycle, r, referred to as the "zero motif", holding only zero values was used, $r = \{r_j : r_j = 0, j = 1 \text{ to } j = |h| \ \forall h \in H\}$. The similarity between each heartbeat $h_i \in H$, and r was calculated using a Euclidean Distance similarity function (Eq. 3). However, given that r is a vector of zeros, the similarity function could be simplified to give Eq. 4. Since the length ($|h_i|$) of each cycle h_i is not fixed, the similarity value was normalised by dividing it by cycle length (Eq. 5).

$$d(r, h_i) = \sqrt{\sum_{j=1}^{j=\omega} (r_j - h_{i_j})^2} \tag{3}$$

$$d_r(h_i) = \sqrt{\sum_{j=1}^{j=\omega} h_{i_j}^2} \tag{4}$$

$$d_r(h_i) = \frac{\sqrt{\sum_{j=1}^{j=\omega} h_{i_j}^2}}{|h_i|} \tag{5}$$

The obtained similarity values were used to define a Gaussian distribution, with bins holding similarity values arranged along the x-axis, for which the mean (μ_d) and sigma (σ_d) values were calculated. The cycles associated with bins falling within a given number of standard deviations, defined by a parameter ζ, were then retained to give a set H' ($H' \subset H$).

3.3   Frequent Motif Extraction

The third and final stage in the proposed process, given a set of candidate frequent cycles H', is to identify the most frequent cycles (motifs) that are deemed to be the best discriminators and store these in a set H''. Frequent motifs were defined using a threshold σ; if the frequency count of a cycle was greater than σ, the cycle was considered to be frequent and we have a candidate motif. Preliminary experiments, not reported here, indicated that the number of remaining cycles in H' could still be large and that not necessarily all of them would be good discriminators of class. An optional mechanism for limiting the number of candidate frequent cycles to be considered was thus introduced using a parameter max, whereby the max most frequent candidates from the set H' was chosen. If this option was not chosen, all the frequent candidates in the set H' would be considered. We distinguish the two approaches as the Max and All approaches respectively.

The cycles associated with each class was processed in turn by creating a subset A from H' comprised of cycles that belong to c_i. Next, the frequency count f_i for each cycle $h_j \in A$ was determined using Euclidean Distance as the similarity measure and a threshold λ to define whether two cycles were similar or not; if the Euclidean distance between two cycles was less than λ, the two cycles were deemed to be similar. In this manner, a frequency count for each $h_i \in A$ was obtained. In each case, if the count was less than $\sigma\%$ of $|A|$, the cycle was removed from the subset A. Note that if a high σ threshold value is used, the set A may become empty, thus the value for σ must be selected appropriately. The set A is then ordered according to the frequency count. If the Max approach has been adopted only the max most frequent cycles in A are retained, otherwise all the cycles in A are retained. Whatever the case, the next step was to select the k most "discriminative" motifs from the set A. The most discriminative motifs are considered to be the most frequently occurring cycles which are associated with only one class (there are no similar cycles associated with other classes). It is then necessary to compare each cycle in A with all other cycles in H' (similarity is measured in the same way as before using Euclidean Distance and the λ threshold). The identified discriminative cycles are stored in the set H''. This set can then be used as the "data bank" in a Nearest Neighbour Classification (NNC) model.

4   Evaluation

This section presents the evaluation of the proposed mechanism. For the evaluation, a dataset of canine PCGs was used; this is described in Subsect. 4.1. Subsect. 4.2 presents the experimental set-up in terms of the parameters used. The following three subsections, Subsects. 4.3 to 4.5, report on experiments designed to evaluate the operation of the cycle segmentation subprocess, the candidate motif selection subprocess and the frequent motif extraction subprocess respectively. Subsects. 4.6 and 4.7 consider the runtime and accuracy of the proposed mechanism in comparison with two competitor approaches.

4.1   Evaluation Data

The dataset used for the evaluation was a set of 59 PCGs, encapsulated as WAVE files, collected using an electronic stethoscope, from animals with and without Mitral Valve disease. The average length of a single (PCG) point series was approximately $800K$ points. Each point series had a class-label associated with it selected from the class attribute set $\{B_1, B_2, C, Control\}$. The first three class attributes represented the three stages of Mitral Valve disease according to the European College of Veterinary Internal Medicine (ECVIM) classification [2,23]. The last class attribute was the control class, no disease.

4.2   Experimental Set-Up

Recall that the proposed mechanism required six parameters: λ, σ, ζ, max, k and α. The selected values for these parameters all affect the number of frequent motifs identified and consequently the quality of any further utilisation of the motifs. Clearly, the higher the σ frequency threshold value, the fewer motifs that would be identified because the criteria for frequency would become stricter as σ increased. Inversely, the higher the similarity λ threshold value, the greater the number of motifs that would be identified because the criteria for similarity would become less strict as λ increased. As the value for ζ is increased, the number of selected motifs would also increase, but the average frequency of occurrence would decrease. The values for max and k would also affect the number of identified candidate frequent motifs and, it was conjectured, would thus also influence the number of frequent motifs eventually selected. For the experiments, ranges of values for λ and σ were used, $\{17e5, 91e5, 164e5, 238e5\}$ and $\{0.1, 1\}$ respectively. Similarly, a range of three values was used for both ζ and k, $\{1, 2, 3\}$ and $\{10, 20, 30\}$ respectively. The value for max was set to 60 although any value greater than k could have been used. The α parameter, the oscillation-width threshold to decide where the t cut-off was located, was fixed at 70%; this was the value was suggested in [12].

4.3 Cycle Segmentation Subprocess Evaluation

As noted earlier, the proposed cycle segmentation subprocess used a dynamic cut-off value t, computed using a user-specified α threshold that expressed a percentage-width of the oscillation with the highest amplitude in a given time series. A method also adopted in [12] where $\alpha = 70$ was suggested to detect the S1 and S2 PCG components. The focus with respect to this paper was to detect the start of cycles, the start of the S1 component, therefore $\alpha = 70$ was used to detect all S1 components (and some S2 components which were discarded later). An example of the results obtained is given in Fig. 2 using a fragment of one of the evaluation PCG time series. In Fig. 2(a), the envelope signal is given for the raw signal given in Fig. 2(b). From the figure, it can be seen that all S1s are identified (and in this case no S2s because these are all below the "cut-off" line)

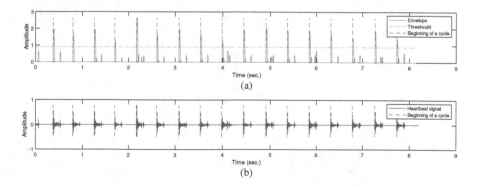

Fig. 2. Extraction of cardiac cycles from the signal energy envelope; (a) envelope PCG signal with "cut-off" line, and (b) raw PCG signal with "start points".

but no noise points. Using $\alpha = 70$, applied to the evaluation dataset, resulted in the identification of 2139 cardiac cycles, an average of 36.25 cycles per PCG (time series), stored in the set H.

4.4   Candidate Motif Selection Subprocess Evaluation

The Candidate Frequent Cycle Selection subprocess was used to identify and select the most frequent cycles in H, and prune the remainder. The proposed method involved determining the Gaussian distribution of the similarity values (distances), calculated using a novel zero motif approach, and then selecting those that were within a number of standard deviations as prescribed by the user-supplied ζ threshold. The effectiveness is illustrated in Fig. 3 which shows the distribution of distances for each class in the evaluation dataset. A normal distribution (bell-shape) curve can be fitted to these distributions (the solid line in the figure). The "68.3-95.5-99.7 empirical rule" was adopted, which assumes that 68.27%, 95.45% and 99.73% of the distances fall with 1, 2 and 3 standard deviations respectively from the mean (μ_d), to select frequent cycles and store them in a set H'.

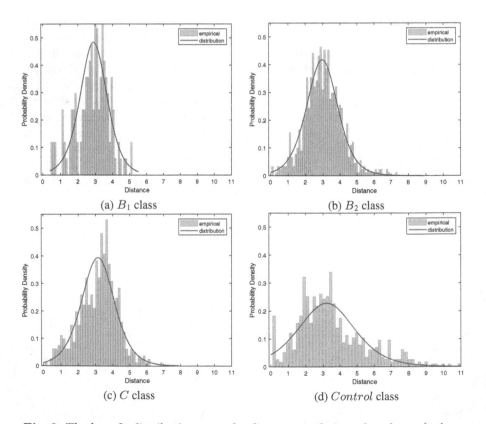

Fig. 3. The best-fit distribution curve for distance similarity values for each class.

4.5   Frequent Motif Extraction Subprocess Evaluation

During the Frequent Motif Extraction subprocess, cycles were ordered according to their frequency within the set H' and then either: (i) a given number (max) of the most frequent cycles were selected or (ii) all cycles were considered. The retained cycles were then processed to determine discriminating cycles, the motifs. The k most frequent best discriminating cycles were then retained, these were then the set of motifs to be used for classification purposes. Evaluation of the process indicated that using the Max approach, some classes had no motifs associated with them at all. A modification was therefore made to the Max approach to ensure that each class had at least one motif associated with it. This change solved the problem.

4.6   Runtime Evaluation

To determine the runtime complexity, 18 sets of experiments were conducted using $\zeta = \{1, 2, 3\}$, $k = \{10, 20, 30\}$ and either the All or Max approach. Experiments, not reported here, were also conducted using a range of λ and σ values, but it was found that this did not affect the runtime, so the results are presented here in the context of the ζ and k parameters, and the approach used. The results are presented in Table 1, these are average runtimes obtained using five evaluation runs. In the table, runtimes are presented for: (i) Cycle Segmentation, (ii) Candidate Motif Selection and (iii) Frequent Motif Extraction. The last column in the table presents the average runtime to process a single PCG time series (the sum of the values in the previous three columns divided by 59, the number of records in the test dataset).

Table 1. Runtime for PCG frequent motif selection and extraction (seconds).

ζ	k	Cycle extraction	Candidate motif selection	Frequent motif extraction		Average	
				All	Max	All	Max
1	10	15.97	184.03	10.55	15.10	3.57	3.57
	20			11.67	11.40	3.59	3.58
	30			12.43	11.12	3.60	3.58
2	10		184.05	12.10	29.94	3.60	3.90
	20			13.94	24.58	3.63	3.81
	30			15.29	23.78	3.65	3.65
3	10		184.06	11.87	35.77	3.59	4.00
	20			14.02	31.34	3.63	3.92
	30			15.67	30.34	3.66	3.90

From the table, it can be seen that the difference between the runtimes, using different ζ values, when selecting candidate frequent cycles, was negligible.

As anticipated, the larger the k value, the more runtime that was required to discover the frequent motifs using the All approach and the less runtime that was required to discover the frequent motifs using the Max approach. The reason for the difference in runtime between the All and Max approaches was unclear: most of the Max experiments required a longer runtime, however two of them ($\zeta = 1$ with $k = 20$ and $\zeta = 1$ with $k = 30$) featured a runtime that was less than the All approach. As also anticipated, when using the Max approach the runtime increased as ζ increased because a larger number of cycles required processing. However, the total runtime required for a single time series to be processed, on average, was similar in all cases.

The average runtime for the combination of parameters that gave the best accuracy (accuracy is discussed in further detail in the next subsection) was 3.65 s/record which is much faster compared with the motif discovery mechanisms and algorithms reported in [1] and [22] where best accuracy runtimes of 700.20 s/record and 4500.00 s/record were recorded respectively. Note that the proposed algorithm, and the two comparator algorithms, were implemented using the Java programming language and run on an iMac Pro (2017) computer with 8-Cores, 3.2 GHz Intel Xeon W CPU and 19 MB RAM.

4.7   Classification Accuracy

The experimental results presented in the previous subsection demonstrated that the proposed process speeded up the runtime compared with the comparator mechanisms considered. However, for this speed up to be of value, the accuracy should not be adversely affected. The experiments reported on in this subsection sought to investigate this. The parameter settings used were as follows:

- $\zeta = \{1, 2, 3\}$.
- $k = \{10, 20, 30\}$.
- $max = 60$.
- $\langle \lambda, \sigma \rangle = \{\langle 17e5, 0.1\rangle, \langle 91e5, 0.1\rangle, \langle 164e5, 0.1\rangle, \langle 238e5, 0.1\rangle, \langle 238e5, 1\rangle\}$.
- Discrimination approach = { All , Max }.

The adopted process for classifying previously unseen cycles (motifs) was the well-known Nearest Neighbour Classification (NNC) method [6], because this was frequently used in the context of time/point series analysis [26,31]. For the experiments, $k_{NNC} = 1$ and $k_{NNC} = 3$ were used. The dataset was divided into training and testing subsets and five cross validation was applied. The idea was that the accuracy of the classification would provide an indicator of the quality of the proposed approach; the metric used were accuracy (Acc.).

Given that each query PCG to be labelled comprised a number of cycles, each of which would be labelled separately, there was a chance that more than one class-label would be associated with the query PCG. To select the most "appropriate" class-label, three different methods were considered: (i) Shortest Distance (SD), (ii) Shortest Total Distances (STD) and (iii) Highest Votes (HV). The SD method simply chooses the class-label associated with the most similar motif. The STD method chooses the class-label associated with the lowest accumulated distance. The HV method chooses the most frequently occurring class-label. In each case, if more than one class-label was nominated, one of the other class selection methods was applied.

Analysis of the results indicated some interesting patterns. It was found that $\zeta = 2$ usually produces the best accuracy regardless of the k_{NNC} value, approach or classification method used. The best results, with regard to the $\langle \lambda, \sigma \rangle$ combinations considered, are presented in Table 2. The table includes the average runtimes recorded (secs). The best obtained accuracy was 72.0% when $\langle \lambda, \sigma \rangle = \langle 164e5, 0.1 \rangle$, the Max approach, the HV classification method, $\zeta = 2$, $k = 30$ and $k_{NNC} = 3$; a runtime of only 3.65 s/record was recorded. Comparing this best recorded accuracy with that obtained using the comparator mechanism described in [1], and the motif discovery approach presented in [22], it was found that the same level of accuracy was obtained but much more efficiently.

Table 2. The best classification accuracy results.

$\langle \lambda, \sigma \rangle$		Parameters					Results	
λ	σ	Discrim. approach	Class. method	ζ	k	k_{NNC}	Acc.	Runtime (Sec.)
17e5	0.1	All	HV	3	10	1	0.667	3.59
91e5	0.1	Max	HV	3	20	3	0.704	3.92
164e5	0.1	Max	HV	2	30	3	0.720	3.65
238e5	0.1	Max	HV	2	30	3	0.695	3.65
238e5	1	Max	HV	2	30	3	0.695	3.65

5   Conclusions

An approach to PCG classification, using the concept of Motifs has been described. The proposed process addresses the challenge of finding discriminative motifs in long time series using three pipelined mechanisms: (i) cycle segmentation and (ii) candidate motif selection and (iii) frequent motif extraction. The first mechanism, has been relatively well studied, but as a means of analysing PCG cycles and not as precursor to motif discovery. The second mechanism featured a novel approach, that did not require every candidate frequent subsequence to be compared to every other subsequence, to prune time series subsequences (cycles) that could not be considered to be frequent. The third involved the extraction of motifs that were good discriminators of class from the retained candidate frequent motifs. The performance of the proposed approach was analysed in terms of runtime and the quality of the identified motifs in the context of a classification scenario, with respect to two comparator algorithms. The results obtained demonstrated a similar classification accuracy, but a significant runtime improvement.

References

1. Alhijailan, H., Coenen, F., Dukes-McEwan, J., Thiyagalingam, J.: Segmenting sound waves to support phonocardiogram analysis: the PCGseg approach. In: Geng, X., Kang, B.-H. (eds.) PRICAI 2018. LNCS (LNAI), vol. 11013, pp. 100–112. Springer, Cham (2018). https://doi.org/10.1007/978-3-319-97310-4_12
2. Atkins, C., et al.: Guidelines for the diagnosis and treatment of canine chronic valvular heart disease. J. Vet. Intern. Med. **23**(6), 1142–1150 (2009). https://doi.org/10.1111/j.1939-1676.2009.0392.x
3. Bagnall, A., Hills, J., Lines, J.: Finding motif sets in time series. CoRR, July 2014
4. Cherif, L.H., Debba, S.: Variability of pulmonary blood pressure, splitting of the second heart sound and heart rate. J. Clin. Exp. Cardiol. **8**(10), 1–3 (2017). https://doi.org/10.4172/2155-9880.1000550
5. Chiu, B., Keogh, E., Lonardi, S.: Probabilistic discovery of time series motifs. In: Proceedings of the Ninth ACM SIGKDD International Conference on Knowledge Discovery and Data Mining, KDD 2003, pp. 493–498. ACM, New York (2003). https://doi.org/10.1145/956750.956808
6. Dasarathy, B.V.: Nearest Neighbor (NN) Norms: NN Pattern Classification Techniques. IEEE Computer Society Press Tutorial, IEEE Computer Society Press, the University of Michigan (1991)
7. Dau, H.A., Keogh, E.: Matrix profile V: a generic technique to incorporate domain knowledge into motif discovery. In: Proceedings of the 23rd ACM SIGKDD International Conference on Knowledge Discovery and Data Mining, KDD 2017, pp. 125–134. ACM, New York (2017). https://doi.org/10.1145/3097983.3097993
8. Delgado-Trejos, E., Quiceno-Manrique, A., Godino-Llorente, J., Blanco-Velasco, M., Castellanos-Dominguez, G.: Digital auscultation analysis for heart murmur detection. Ann. Biomed. Eng. **37**(2), 337–353 (2009). https://doi.org/10.1007/s10439-008-9611-z
9. Ding, H., Trajcevski, G., Scheuermann, P., Wang, X., Keogh, E.: Querying and mining of time series data: experimental comparison of representations and distance measures. Proc. VLDB Endow. **1**(2), 1542–1552 (2008). https://doi.org/10.14778/1454159.1454226
10. Gao, Y., Lin, J., Rangwala, H.: Iterative grammar-based framework for discovering variable-length time series motifs. In: IEEE International Conference on Data Mining, pp. 111–116. IEEE, November 2017. https://doi.org/10.1109/ICDM.2017.20
11. Guéhéneuc, Y.G., Antoniol, G.: DeMIMA: a multilayered approach for design pattern identification. IEEE Trans. Softw. Eng. **34**(5), 667–684 (2008). https://doi.org/10.1109/TSE.2008.48
12. Hamza Cherif, L., Debbal, S.M., Bereksi-Reguig, F.: Segmentation of heart sounds and heart murmurs. J. Mech. Med. Biol. **8**(4), 549–559 (2008). https://doi.org/10.1142/S0219519408002759
13. Hannan, E.J.: Time Series Analysis. Chapman and Hall, London (1960)
14. Hutchins, L.N., Murphy, S.M., Singh, P., Graber, J.H.: Position-dependent motif characterization using non-negative matrix factorization. Bioinformatics **24**(23), 2684–2690 (2008). https://doi.org/10.1093/bioinformatics/btn526
15. Krejci, A., Hupp, T.R., Lexa, M., Vojtesek, B., Muller, P.: Hammock: a hidden markov model-based peptide clustering algorithm to identify protein-interaction consensus motifs in large datasets. Bioinformatics **32**(1), 9–16 (2016). https://doi.org/10.1093/bioinformatics/btv522

16. Lehner, R.J., Rangayyan, R.M.: A three-channel microcomputer system for segmentation and characterization of the phonocardiogram. IEEE Trans. Biomed. Eng. **34**(6), 485–489 (1987). https://doi.org/10.1109/TBME.1987.326060
17. Li, N., Crane, M., Gurrin, C., Ruskin, H.J.: Finding motifs in large personal lifelogs. In: Proceedings of the 7th Augmented Human International Conference 2016, pp. 1–8. ACM, New York (2016). https://doi.org/10.1145/2875194.2875214
18. Lin, J., Keogh, E., Lonardi, S., Patel, P.: Finding motifs in time series. In: Proceedings of the Eighth ACM SIGKDD International Conference on Knowledge Discovery and Data Mining, pp. 53–68 (2002)
19. Lin, J., Keogh, E., Wei, L., Lonardi, S.: Experiencing SAX: a novel symbolic representation of time series. Data Min. Knowl. Discov. **15**(2), 107–144 (2007). https://doi.org/10.1007/s10618-007-0064-z
20. Milo, R., Shen-Orr, S., Itzkovitz, S., Kashtan, N., Chklovskii, D., Alon, U.: Network motifs: simple building blocks of complex networks. Science **298**(5594), 824–827 (2002). https://doi.org/10.1126/science.298.5594.824
21. Mubarak, Q., Akram, M.U., Shaukat, A., Ramazan, A.: Quality assessment and classification of heart sounds using PCG signals. In: Khan, F., Jan, M.A., Alam, M. (eds.) Applications of Intelligent Technologies in Healthcare. EICC, pp. 1–11. Springer, Cham (2019). https://doi.org/10.1007/978-3-319-96139-2_1
22. Mueen, A., Keogh, E., Zhu, Q., Cash, S., Westover, B.: Exact discovery of time series motifs. In: Proceedings of the 2009 SIAM International Conference on Data Mining, pp. 473–484 (2009). https://doi.org/10.1137/1.9781611972795.41
23. Nakamura, K., et al.: Left atrial strain at different stages of myxomatous mitral valve disease in dogs. J. Vet. Intern. Med. **31**(2), 316–325 (2017). https://doi.org/10.1111/jvim.14660
24. Oliveira, J., Sousa, C., Coimbra, M.: Coupled hidden Markov model for automatic ECG and PCG segmentation. In: 2017 IEEE International Conference on Acoustics, Speech and Signal Processing (ICASSP), pp. 1023–1027, March 2017. https://doi.org/10.1109/ICASSP.2017.7952311
25. Ramli, D., Hooi, M., Chee, K.: Development of heartbeat detection kit for biometric authentication system. Procedia Comput. Sci. **96**, 305–314 (2016). https://doi.org/10.1016/j.procs.2016.08.143
26. Stojanović, M.B., Božić, M.M., Stanković, M.M., Stajić, Z.P.: A methodology for training set instance selection using mutual information in time series prediction. Neurocomputing **141**(Supplement C), 236–245 (2014). https://doi.org/10.1016/j.neucom.2014.03.006
27. Thijs, G., et al.: A Gibbs sampling method to detect overrepresented motifs in the upstream regions of coexpressed genes. J. Comput. Biol. **9**(2), 447–464 (2004). https://doi.org/10.1089/10665270252935566
28. Torkamani, S., Lohweg, V.: Survey on time series motif discovery. Wiley Interdiscip. Rev. Data Min. Knowl. Discov. **7**(2), 1–8 (2017). https://doi.org/10.1002/widm.1199
29. Vahdatpour, A., Amini, N., Sarrafzadeh, M.: Toward unsupervised activity discovery using multi-dimensional motif detection in time series. In: Proceedings of the 21st International Joint Conference on Artificial Intelligence, IJCAI 2009, pp. 1261–1266. Morgan Kaufmann Publishers Inc., San Francisco (2009)
30. Vaswani, A., Khaw, H.J., Dougherty, S., Zamvar, V., Lang, C.: Cardiology in a Heartbeat. Scion Publishing Limited, Banbury (2015)

31. Wang, X., Fang, Z., Wang, P., Zhu, R., Wang, W.: A distributed multi-level composite index for KNN processing on long time series. In: Candan, S., Chen, L., Pedersen, T.B., Chang, L., Hua, W. (eds.) DASFAA 2017. LNCS, vol. 10177, pp. 215–230. Springer, Cham (2017). https://doi.org/10.1007/978-3-319-55753-3_14
32. Zhao, Y., et al.: Measurement of two new indicators of cardiac reserve in humans, rats, rabbits, and dogs. J. Biomed. Sci. Eng. **6**(10), 960–963 (2013). https://doi.org/10.4236/jbise.2013.610118

Exploring the Automatisation of Animal Health Surveillance Through Natural Language Processing

Mercedes Arguello-Casteleiro[1]([⊠]), Philip H. Jones[2], Sara Robertson[2], Richard M. Irvine[2], Fin Twomey[2], and Goran Nenadic[1]

[1] School of Computer Science, University of Manchester, Manchester, UK
m.arguello@manchester.ac.uk
[2] Surveillance Intelligence Unit, APHA Weybridge, New Haw, Addlestone, Surrey KT15 3NB, UK

Abstract. The Animal and Plant Health Agency (APHA) conducts post-mortem examinations (PMEs) of farm animal species as part of routine scanning surveillance for new and re-emerging diseases that may pose a threat to animal and public health. This paper investigates whether relevant veterinary medical terms can be automatically identified in the free-text summaries entered by Veterinary Investigation Officers (VIOs) on the PME reports. Two natural language processing tasks were performed: (1) named entity recognition, where terms within the free-text were mapped to concepts in the Unified Medical Language System (UMLS) Metathesaurus; and (2) semantic similarity and relatedness also using UMLS. For this pilot study, we focused on two diagnostic codes: salmonellosis (*S.* Dublin) and Pneumonia NOS (Not Otherwise Specified). The outputs were manually evaluated by VIOs. The results highlight the potential value of natural language processing to identify key concepts and pertinent veterinary medical terms that can be used for scanning surveillance purposes using large, free-text data. We also discuss issues resulting from the inherent bias of UMLS to human medical terms and its use in animal health monitoring.

Keywords: NLP · UMLS · Animal health · Scanning surveillance

1 Introduction

The UK Animal and Plant Health Agency (APHA) [1] carries out veterinary scanning surveillance activities for the timely detection, investigation and characterisation of new and re-emerging diseases and threats to animal and public health, including monitoring changes to the patterns and trends of endemic diseases in livestock. Animals submitted to the Veterinary Investigation Centre (VIC) network for post-mortem examination (PME) are examined by Veterinary Investigation Officers (VIOs). The results of the examination are presented in a report and allocated a Veterinary Investigation Diagnosis Analysis (VIDA) [2] code. Results of such an examination provide valuable clinical information that can be used to build a national picture of livestock diseases and facilitate surveillance.

© Springer Nature Switzerland AG 2019
M. Bramer and M. Petridis (Eds.): SGAI-AI 2019, LNAI 11927, pp. 213–226, 2019.
https://doi.org/10.1007/978-3-030-34885-4_17

During the course of a case investigation, a large amount of information is collected and recorded, much of which is in the form of free-text. In addition, at the end of a case, the VIO has the opportunity to enter a field of text ('surveillance highlights') that describes and highlights pertinent issues relevant to the case. This field – if entered – contains information about the presentation, findings and interpretation (including diagnoses if appropriate). However, as the information is free-text, additional efforts are required to transform unstructured reports into structured data that can be used for surveillance. Processing all such data manually is not feasible, given an increasing number of such resources and an increasing demand for real-time surveillance. Therefore, there is a need to explore automated means to deliver continued effective and efficient surveillance of livestock diseases. The development of natural language processing (NLP) methods [3] that can be used to extract pertinent information from the free-text records relating to livestock diseases would enable hitherto unaccessible data sources to be processed for scanning surveillance activities in an efficient and systematic manner.

The main objective of this study was to examine the feasibility of using 'surveillance highlights' to determine whether clinically-pertinent and 'sensible' veterinary medical terms could be identified in free-text automatically. We specifically focused on surveillance highlights from 2015 to 2017 for cattle, sheep and pigs. These data were likely to contain a representative sample of veterinary clinical free-text that would be pertinent to national scanning surveillance activities in livestock but would not include sensitive personal identifiers relating to the farm of origin or the veterinary practice that referred the case.

1.1   Study Scope: Salmonellosis (*S.* Dublin) and Pneumonia NOS

To identify whether relevant terms/concepts can be identified in the 'surveillance highlights' free-text, and to what extent those terms/concepts can be characterised, the study focuses on two diseases within the scope of the veterinary scanning surveillance activities performed by APHA.

Salmonellosis [4, 5] is a zoonotic disease, i.e. an infectious disease transmissible from animals (poultry, farm animals) to humans. *Salmonella* organisms cause food poisoning [5], and although most cases of salmonellosis are self-limiting, in some patients, infection can be life-threatening [4]. Hence, detection of salmonellosis is an important component of national and regional surveillance systems for foodborne diseases [4, 5] that pose risks to public health.

There is only one or a few *Salmonella* species of interest, most notably *Salmonella enterica*. However, there are many different subtypes (serovars) that can cause disease in animals and humans. This study focuses on *Salmonella enterica* subspecies *enterica* serovar Dublin, which is shortened to *S.* Dublin. Based on APHA data, *S.* Dublin is a common diagnosis in cattle, appearing in more than 25% of entered surveillance highlights.

We also focused on the VIDA code Pneumonia NOS (pNOS). This VIDA code was used to describe pneumonia caused by an agent that was not listed or contained within other specific codes. In such cases, the name of the causative agent should be entered in the free-text field and, therefore, NLP methods present an opportunity to be able to automatically extract recorded causative agents. We therefore included pNOS to explore the potential for some of the pneumonia NOS cases to represent a possible change in the epidemiology of respiratory disease, both in terms of agents causing pneumonia and the presenting clinical signs. This could indicate the detection of a new or re-emerging threat, the first indication of an increase in importance of some previously uncommon agent causing pneumonia or a change in the clinical presentation of an existing endemic pathogen.

2 Materials and Method

2.1 Materials

Two datasets were extracted from the PME database:

- A subset of 124 records from the surveillance highlights 2015–2017 (cattle, sheep, pigs) dataset with VIDA code for *S*. Dublin. Among the 124 records: 121 (98%) were cattle; 3 (2%) were sheep; and none was pigs.
- A subset of 911 records from the surveillance highlights 2015-2017 (cattle, sheep, pigs) dataset with VIDA code for Pneumonia NOS. Among the 911 records: 500 (55%) were cattle; 338 (37%) were sheep; and 73 (8%) were pigs.

Unstructured text of the surveillance highlights is already de-identified and two free-text datasets were created (one for *S*. Dublin and one for Pneumonia NOS). An example of the free-text for a surveillance highlight is the following:

"Salmonella Dublin was isolated from the faeces sample from a four-month-old calf. The history was one of malaise with two sudden deaths in a group of fattening bull calves."

2.2 Lexical Analysis of APHA 'Surveillance Highlights' Free-Text Datasets

By splitting the free-text by white space, we obtained tokens (linguistic units). Punctuation marks, digits, and stopwords were not removed. Hence, in this study, a token could be a single character (e.g. ",") or a combination of characters (e.g. "pneumonia"). Under the lexical statistics, we studied the token frequency distributions. We counted all tokens that appeared in each free-text dataset (one for *S*. Dublin and one for Pneumonia NOS) and built a frequency list, and then, we ranked the tokens in an increasing rank (from the most frequent to the least frequent).

In general English, it has been observed that relatively few words (*the, of, and, to, a, in that, is, was, it*) are used very frequently, while most words occur rarely – this is known as Zipf's law [6]. According to Zipf's law, the frequency of a word is likely to be inversely proportional to its rank in frequency. This can be expressed mathematically as: $f = C/r$ where f is the frequency of the work; r is the rank in a list of words; and C is a constant. When plotting the log of word frequency against the log of word rank, a straight line with the slope -1 indicates that Zipf's law is followed.

Following Sinclair [7], we performed a comparison of token frequency in a general English corpus, i.e. the Brown corpus of American English [8], and the two APHA free-text datasets (where each dataset is considered as a corpus). We checked whether Sinclair's assumptions [7] held, namely:

- A specialised corpus will have a greater concentration of vocabulary than a general reference corpus.
- Both the number of tokens and the proportion of tokens occurring only once are expected to be less in a specialised corpus than in the general corpus.

Also adhering to Sinclair [7], we obtained some text analytics statistics that can be "useful in comparing texts, or searching for texts with particular characteristics" [7].

2.3   NLP Tasks: Named-Entity Recognition and Similarity and Relatedness

Two NLP tasks were intended to identify insights about the content within the APHA surveillance highlights free-text datasets. An outline of the free-text processing appears in Fig. 1. The 3D boxes highlight the two NLP tasks proposed: named entity recognition task [3] and semantic similarity and relatedness task [9]. As part of a task, some pre-processing and/or post-processing was needed (i.e. the other boxes). The grey boxes indicated either the input/output or the concrete tools. The processing of the unstructured text employs different NLP tools: Natural Language Toolkit (NLTK) [10], MetaMap [11], and one of the two UMLS APIs [12].

Name Entity Recognition (NER) Task. Two NLP tools widely used and known for extracting information from clinical texts are MetaMap and cTAKES [13]. Recently, Reategui and Ratte [14] have shown a similar performance between MetaMap and cTAKES when applied to human clinical text from the i2b2 (informatics for integrating biology and the bedside) datasets [15]. In this study we used MetaMap (developed by US National Library of Medicine) to map APHA surveillance highlights free-text to concepts in the UMLS Metathesaurus [16]. In May 2019, the UMLS Metathesaurus contained close to 3.8M biomedical/clinical concepts with 210 sources contributing to concept names – including SNOMED CT [17] and the Veterinary Extension for SNOMED CT (VetSCT) [18].

Every UMLS Metathesaurus concept has a Concept Unique Identifier (CUI) that uniquely identifies the biomedical/clinical concept. Categorisation is straightforward as the UMLS Metathesaurus concepts are already classified into a set of 134 broad categories called Semantic Types [19]. A UMLS Metathesaurus concept can have one or more UMLS Semantic Types. In turn, the 134 UMLS Semantic Types are further grouped into 15 UMLS Semantic Groups [19].

Only 11 of the total 134 UMLS Semantic Types were selected for this study, belonging to 2 UMLS Semantic Groups. The 11 UMLS Semantic Types selected acted as a filtering mechanism to obtain those UMLS Metathesaurus concepts that may have a more clinically-pertinent and 'sensible' veterinary medical relevance for APHA scanning surveillance activities.

The 11 UMLS Semantic Types selected were:

- From the UMLS Semantic Group *Disorders* (DISO): Disease or Syndrome; Pathologic Function; Sign or Symptom; Injury or Poisoning; Congenital Abnormality; Anatomical Abnormality; and Acquired Abnormality.
- From the UMLS Semantic Group *Living Beings* (LIVB): Fungus; Bacterium; Eukaryote; and Virus.

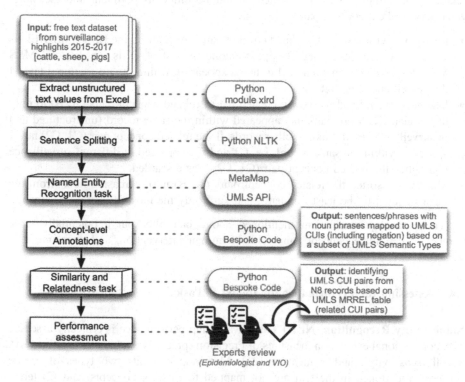

Fig. 1. Outline of the unstructured text processing including NLP tasks (3D boxes).

Using a UMLS API it is possible to map one UMLS Metathesaurus concept (i.e. one UMLS CUI) to none, one, or more than one identifier in a specific terminology, such as SNOMED CT. We investigated how many UMLS CUIs extracted from the surveillance highlights could be mapped to SNOMED CT and VetSCT terminologies.

Semantic Similarity and Relatedness Task. We followed Pedersen et al. [9] and considered that "*similarity is a special case of relatedness that is tied to the likeness (in the shape or form) of the concepts*" [9]. An example of relatedness would be: "congestive heart failure" and "pulmonary edema".

The UMLS MRREL table [16] contains both hierarchical and non-hierarchical information of related UMLS Metathesaurus concept pairs (i.e. CUI pairs). However, if none of the current 210 underlying terminologies in the UMLS Metathesaurus, like

SNOMED CT, has pairwise relations between two concepts, such as ("congestive heart failure", "pulmonary edema"), it will not be included in the MRREL table.

A number of semantic similarity measures and tools use the information within the UMLS MRREL table, such as the well-known tool UMLS-Similarity [20]. An in-depth investigation of semantic similarity measures was not conducted; instead just a reading of concept pairs (UMLS CUIs) within the UMLS MRREL table was done.

We proposed a three-step mechanism to obtain concept pair candidates for APHA scanning surveillance activities, which should be clinically-pertinent and 'sensible' veterinary medical concept pairs:

- Firstly, we retrieved all the related concept pairs (A, B) from the UMLS MRREL as far as both concepts A and B appear among the list of CUIs (i.e. list of UMLS Metathesaurus concepts mapped to terms appearing within the unstructured text of the surveillance highlights).
- Secondly, we refined the newly created list of related concept pairs (A, B) to only those related concept pairs that appeared within the same record (unstructured text of surveillance highlights). In other words, if the related concept pair (C1, C2) never appeared within the same record, i.e. C1 and C2 appeared in different surveillance highlights, the related concept pair (C1, C2) was discarded.
- Thirdly, we sorted the related concept pairs (A, B) into increasing rank (from the most frequent to the least frequent), and kept only the most frequently occurring.

The three-step mechanism mentioned above can filter out a potentially large number of candidate concept pairs without human intervention, and therefore, it is scalable.

2.4   Assessing the Performance for the NLP Tasks

Name Entity Recognition (NER) Task. MetaMap performance is typically assessed with conventional evaluation measures of Precision (predictive value of a positive test), Recall (sensitivity), and F measure [21]. MetaMap commits two types of errors: (1) terms mentioned in the text are not mapped to existing concepts; and (2) terms mentioned in the text are erroneously mapped to concepts. As the unstructured text of surveillance highlights was not annotated manually with UMLS concepts, we did not know which CUIs were missing. Hence, we only calculated precision as TP/(TP + FP) [21], which accounts for error type 2.

As in Pratt and Yetisgen-Yildiz [22], we performed a weaker calculation of MetaMap precision, where exact matches (single CUI mapped) and partial matches (multiple CUIs mapped) were equally counted, i.e. both were considered as True Positives (TPs). An incorrectly mapped CUI was interpreted as False Positive (FP).

Semantic Similarity and Relatedness Task. Two domain experts (a veterinary epidemiologist and a VIO) performed a review of the most frequent candidates for similar and related UMLS Metathesaurus concept pairs. The aim was to obtain a qualitative assessment, i.e. a preliminary impression of the usefulness for APHA scanning surveillance activities, of the UMLS Metathesaurus concept pairs resulting from the three-step mechanism proposed.

3 Results

3.1 Lexical Analysis of APHA Surveillance Highlights Free-Text Datasets

Figure 2 investigates whether the *S.* Dublin dataset and the Pneumonia NOS dataset followed Zipf's Law [6], i.e. whether the frequency of occurrence of tokens was inversely related to their frequency rank. From Fig. 2 it can be concluded that both datasets approximately adhered to Zipf's Law.

Figure 3 provided a more detailed investigation of Zipf's Law, which corroborates the observation that relatively few words (*the, and, of, was, were, this*) are used very frequently.

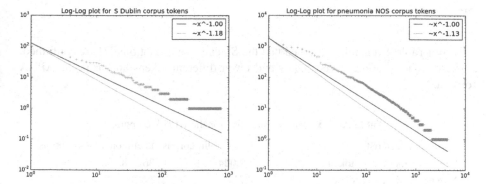

Fig. 2. Plotting the log of token frequency against the log of token rank (lower line), a straight line with the slope −1 is also plotted (higher line).

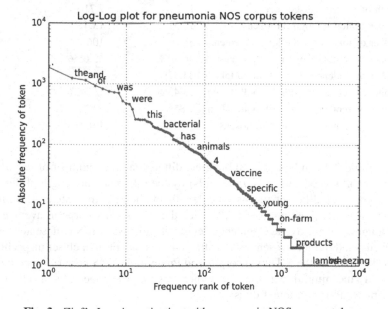

Fig. 3. Zipf's Law investigation with pneumonia NOS corpus tokens

Table 1. Comparison of token frequencies in a general corpus (i.e. Brown corpus [8]) and the two specialised APHA corpora (*S.* Dublin and Pneumonia NOS). The last two columns show the proportional difference % between an APHA corpus characteristic and the Brown corpus characteristic (general corpus), e.g. the proportion of single token occurrence.

Corpus characteristic	Brown corpus	S. Dublin corpus [%]	Pneumonia NOS corpus [%]
Number of different tokens	49,815	717 [1.44%]	3,920 [7.87%]
Tokens occurring once	22,010	474 [2.15%]	1,992 [9.05%]
Tokens occurring twice	7,190	114 [1.59%]	585 [8.14%]
Tokens occurring $\geq$ 20 times	5,011	13 [0.26%]	269 [5.37%]
Tokens occurring $\geq$ 200 times	487	0 [0.00%]	22 [4.52%]

From Table 1 it can be observed that the Sinclair's expectations [7] are confirmed: a greater concentration of vocabulary and fewer different tokens appear in the APHA corpora.

Table 2. Text analysis statistics for the APHA corpora.

Corpus characteristic	S. Dublin corpus	Pneumonia NOS corpus
Length of the text in tokens	2,024	36,338
Number of different tokens	717	3,920
Length of the text in characters	10,991	212,658
Average token length	6.13	7.57
Longest token	43	45
Length of the text in sentences	162	2,710
Average sentence length in tokens	12.51	13.42
Number of tokens for the longest sentence	56	106
Number of sentences with $\leq$ 10 tokens	46.30%	45.65%
Number of sentences with 10 to 20 tokens	34.57%	29.89%
Number of sentences with 20 to 30 tokens	15.43%	16.68%
Number of sentences with 30 to 40 tokens	1.85%	5.87%
Number of sentences with $\geq$ 40 tokens	1.85%	1.92%

From Table 2 it can be observed the great difference in the number of records (124 *S.* Dublin records versus 911 pNOS records) by the difference in: length of the text in tokens; number of different tokens; and length of the text in sentences. Some key corpus characteristics are almost identical for the two APHA corpora: average token length; longest token; average sentence length in tokens; number of sentences with $\leq$ 10 tokens; and number of sentences with $\geq$ 40 tokens. From a closer inspection, the longest token in both the *S.* Dublin corpus and Pneumonia NOS corpus turned out to be not clinically meaningful (e.g. some idiosyncrasies like webpage links or repeating the same character to create a text division).

3.2 NLP Tasks: Name-Entity Recognition and Similarity and Relatedness

Name Entity Recognition (NER) Task. We used as input for MetaMap the 162 sentences from *S*. Dublin corpus and the 2,710 sentences from the Pneumonia NOS corpus reported in Table 2. Table 3 shows the distinct number of UMLS Metathesaurus concepts identified by MetaMap belonging to the 11 UMLS Semantic Types considered of interest for APHA scanning surveillance activities.

Table 3. Number of UMLS Metathesaurus concepts for the 11 UMLS Semantic Types selected

UMLS Semantic Type [group]	S. Dublin corpus	Pneumonia NOS corpus
T047|Disease or Syndrome [DISO]	21	261
T046|Pathologic Function [DISO]	3	68
T184|Sign or Symptom [DISO]	18	54
T037|Injury or Poisoning [DISO]	3	21
T019|Congenital Abnormality [DISO]	0	9
T190|Anatomical Abnormality [DISO]	0	7
T020|Acquired Abnormality [DISO]	1	7
T004|Fungus [LIVB]	1	3
T007|Bacterium [LIVB]	4	64
T204|Eukaryote [LIVB]	4	37
T005|Virus [LIVB]	3	20

The number of UMLS CUIs extracted by MetaMap from the sentences within the surveillance highlights: 58 UMLS CUIs (4 were negated) for *S*. Dublin corpus; and 545 UMLS CUIs (69 were negated) for Pneumonia NOS corpus. We report below the number of unique UMLS CUIs and how they were mapped to SNOMED CT and VetSCT terminologies:

- A total of 56 unique UMLS CUIs for S. Dublin corpus; 41 of which were mapped to SNOMED CT and only 11 were mapped to VetSCT.
- A total of 490 unique UMLS CUIs for Pneumonia NOS; 371 of which were mapped to SNOMED CT and only 73 were mapped to VetSCT.

The typical case was a UMLS CUI being mapped to VetSCT if it also mapped to VetSCT. For example: C1260880\|Rhinorrhea is mapped to both terminologies.

Table 4. Related UMLS Metathesaurus concept pairs (A, B) for the S. Dublin corpus.

UMLS CUI|concept name A	UMLS CUI|concept name B	Number records
C1457887|Symptoms	C0011991|Diarrhea	2
C0035204|Respiration Disorders	C0032285|Pneumonia	2
C0035242|Respiratory Tract Diseases	C0035204|Respiration Disorders	2
C1260880|Rhinorrhea	C0035242|Respiratory Tract Diseases	1

Semantic Similarity and Relatedness Task. Tables 4 and 5 exemplify the related UMLS Metathesaurus concept pairs (A, B) obtained with the three-step mechanism proposed (see Subsect. 2.3 for details).

Table 5. Related UMLS Metathesaurus concept pairs (A, B) for the Pneumonia NOS corpus.

UMLS CUI|concept name A	UMLS CUI|concept name B	Number records
C0018893|Helminths	C0018889|Helminthiasis	37
C3249881|Infection - suppurative	C3203360|Suppuration	24
C3714514|Infection	C0009450|Communicable Diseases	23
C0035242|Respiratory Tract Diseases	C0035204|Respiration Disorders	20
C0319157|AS virus	C0042776|Virus	14
C0235394|Wasting	C0006625|Cachexia	12
C0004623|Bacterial Infections	C0004611|Bacteria	8
C4050015|Viruses ingredient	C0042776|Virus	8
C1299919|Enteric coccidiosis	C0009187|Coccidiosis	7
C0032285|Pneumonia	C0000833|Abscess	8
C0032285|Pneumonia	C0004623|Bacterial Infections	7
C0032285|Pneumonia	C0006285|Bronchopneumonia	6

3.3   Assessing the Performance of the NLP Tasks

Name Entity Recognition (NER) Task. A systematic estimation of precision proved too time-consuming and labour-intensive as more than 500 UMLS Metathesaurus concepts were extracted by MetaMap from the surveillance highlights corpus for the 11 UMLS Semantic Types under study. It was observed that multiple sentences within the surveillance highlights free-text of a record might mention the same UMLS CUI. A less rigorous estimation of lexical precision was calculated considering:

- Only the CUIs that were more frequently mentioned per total number of records.
- Only as FP the UMLS CUIs that had no sentences with at least one TP.

The criterion outlined above favoured quality over quantity, i.e. a thorough investigation of fewer UMLS CUIs considering all the sentences where they appear. Hence, a total of 784 sentences, associated with the 34 UMLS CUIs most frequently extracted, were manually inspected by a veterinary epidemiologist.

The veterinary epidemiologist recorded 'yes' for a sentence if the UMLS CUI presence or absence (some UMLS CUIs were interpreted as negated by MetaMap) was correctly mapped considering the true clinical meaning of the sentence. A UMLS CUI was considered incorrect when unrelated to the text or when negation was incorrectly interpreted. An example of the latter is when the identified disease was not present in the animal being examined (e.g. "vaccination against disease X" does not mean presence of disease X).

Tables 6 and 7 illustrate respectively UMLS CUIs that were most frequent in the *S*. Dublin records and Pneumonia NOS records.

Table 6. MetaMap performance: 7 most frequent UMLS CUIs for S. Dublin corpus.

UMLS CUI|concept name [Semantic Type]	Number records	Sentences appraised "y"	Sentences appraised "n"
C0036111 |Salmonella [T007]	5	6	0
C0011991 |Diarrhea [T184]	2	2	0
C0012634 |Disease [T047]	2	0	2
C0023380 |Lethargy [T184]	2	3	0
C0032285 |Pneumonia [T047]	2	3	0
C0035204 |Respiration Disorders [T047]	2	2	0
C0035242 |Respiratory Tract Diseases [T047]	2	2	0

Table 7. MetaMap performance: 12 most frequent UMLS CUIs for Pneumonia NOS corpus.

UMLS CUI|concept name [Semantic Type]	Number records	Sentences appraised "y"	Sentences appraised "n"
C0032285 |Pneumonia [T047]	72	74	3
C0342895 |Fish-Eye Disease [T047]	45	0	47
C0012634 |Disease [T047]	39	8	42
C0231218 |Malaise [T184]	39	24	17
C0018889 |Helminthiasis [T047]	37	8	30
C0018893 |Helminths [T204]	37	9	37
C0751785 |Unverricht-Lundborg Synd. [T047]	36	0	39
C3714514|Infection [T046]	29	24	0
C0006285|Bronchopneumonia [T047]	28	30	0
C3203360|Suppuration [T046]	24	25	0
C3249881|Infection - suppurative [T047]	24	25	0
C0009450|Communicable Diseases [T047]	23	20	0

Rows in grey in Tables 6 and 7 indicate that the UMLS CUI extracted by MetaMap has no sentences with at least one recorded "y", and thus, was interpreted as FP. The relaxed calculation of the lexical precision yielded:

- 86% for the *S*. Dublin corpus, so the seven UMLS CUIs most frequently extracted have been quite correctly mapped to text.
- 85% for the Pneumonia NOS corpus, meaning that the 27 UMLS CUIs most frequently extracted have been quite correctly mapped to text.

Semantic Similarity and Relatedness Task. For the S. Dublin corpus, we limited the investigation to the UMLS Metathesaurus concepts pairs showed in Table 4. For Pneumonia NOS, a total of 29 UMLS Metathesaurus concepts pairs were investigated that were the most frequent. Overall, all the UMLS Metathesaurus concepts pairs were assessed as plausible by both the veterinary epidemiologist and a VIO.

S. Dublin is an enteric infection in cattle and is often associated with diarrhoeal signs. However, it has also been reported that infected animals can present with pneumonia and septicaemia rather than the more typical diarrhoea presentation, especially in older calves [23, 24]. Therefore, the concepts "pneumonia" and "diarrhoea" found in the S. Dublin records (Table 4) are feasible and plausible.

The expert review for Pneumonia NOS considers appropriate most of the UMLS Metathesaurus concept pairs with the following qualifications: "wasting" could easily be found in cases of pneumonia if the condition was chronic; and "coccidiosis" and "pneumonia" were not necessarily causatively linked but it would not be uncommon or unusual for two conditions to be identified in the same animal.

4   Discussion

Although the amount of data being fully analysed is modest (784 sentences); studies published on public health surveillance have used a similar amount of data [25].

Two UMLS terminologies, SNOMED CT and VetSCT, have been considered in more detail. In the UK, the National Health Service (NHS) is moving towards the adoption of SNOMED CT as the only terminology across health and care settings [26]. Hence, SNOMED CT is becoming key for NHS information exchange and relevant for UK public health. In the same vein, the Veterinary Extension for SNOMED CT (VetSCT) is key for veterinary and public health.

It is important to note that UMLS has a very strong bias towards human medicine and, although specific veterinary terms are included in the veterinary extension to SNOMED CT, there were still some common and, perhaps, slightly surprising concepts that were incorrectly highlighted.

In general, there were several distinct situations where the UMLS Metathesaurus concepts we considered as incorrectly mapped to text by MetaMap:

- Comments in the text that recorded preventive treatments for a disease were often identified as a concept relating to the disease itself. For example, a comment that stated 'the animal was vaccinated against BVD (bovine viral diarrhoea)' was associated with a concept related to BVD even though the disease itself was not present. In some respects, this may be considered as a correctly identified concept but, in terms of future analysis that may use the presence of a concept to reflect disease prevalence, this was, in this study, considered to as an incorrectly identified concept. Similarly, the administration of anthelmintic drugs – often referred to as 'worming' – was often identified as a concept related to helminthiasis; again, in the context of this study, this was considered to be an incorrect classification.
- A word or phrase might be associated with a specific concept in human medicine but should be associated with a different concept in veterinary medicine.

For example, in this study, the term 'ill thrift' was often associated with a concept relating to the patient being 'ill'. Sometimes 'ill' was indeed used in this context. However, in veterinary medicine, 'ill thrift' is a common phrase used to describe an animal with low body weight. Similarly, the term 'condition' was often identified as a concept relating to 'a sickness' or 'an illness'. The word was occasionally used in a similar way in the veterinary narratives but, more commonly, the word 'condition' was used to describe the body weight of an animal (for example 'the animal was in good/poor condition').

- There were some cases where a non-medical word or phrase was incorrectly identified as a medical concept. For example, the word 'fed' (e.g. 'the cows were fed silage') was often identified as the medical abbreviation for "fish eye disease". Similarly, the abbreviation for post-mortem examination, namely PME, was identified as a concept relating to Unverricht-Lundborg Syndrome (i.e. "progressive myoclonus epilepsy") while the word 'graze' (meaning 'to eat grass') was identified as a concept relating to skin abrasions. In addition, although anatomical concepts were not included in this study, it is interesting to note that the word 'calf' (meaning a young bovine) was often associated with an anatomical concept relating to the lower leg of a human.
- In some cases, comments explicitly stating that a disease was not present (e.g. 'tests were negative for disease A, disease B and disease C') failed to negate the concepts relating to the specific diseases appropriately.

5   Conclusion

The results of this pilot study with two PME datasets highlight the potential value of applying NLP methodologies to extract and identify pertinent veterinary medical terms that can be used for scanning surveillance purposes using large, unstructured, free-text data. We note that the UMLS Metathesaurus was used 'as is' and inevitably there were some issues resulting from the inherent bias to human medical terms. Nevertheless, many of the concepts identified were entirely appropriate to the disease process being described. With additional refining to a veterinary-specific corpus, it is likely that the value of the work described can be improved to identify context-specific mentions of pertinent terms, and will prove valuable for semantic indexing and scanning surveillance activities for veterinary public health.

Acknowledgements.   This project was funded by the N8 Research Partnership through an AgriFood pump-priming award from the University of Manchester. The authors would also like to thank the Animal and Plant Health Agency (APHA) for providing a suitable free-text dataset.

References

1. UK APHA. https://www.gov.uk/government/organisations/animal-and-plant-health-agency
2. VIDA. http://apha.defra.gov.uk/documents/surveillance/pub-surv-vida2018.pdf

3. Nadkarni, P.M., Ohno-Machado, L., Chapman, W.W.: Natural language processing: an introduction. J. Am. Med. Inform. Assoc. **18**(5), 544–551 (2011)
4. WHO salmonella. https://www.who.int/zoonoses/diseases/en/
5. UK Zoonotic diseases. https://www.gov.uk/government/publications/list-of-zoonotic-diseases/list-of-zoonotic-diseases
6. Zipf, G.K.: Human Behavior and the Principle of Least Effort: An Introduction to Human Ecology. Addison-Wesley, Cambridge (1949)
7. Sinclair, J.: Corpus, Concordance, Collocation. Oxford University Press, Oxford (1991)
8. Francis, W.N., Kučera, H.: A Standard Corpus of Present-Day Edited American English, for use with Digital Computers (Brown). Brown University, Providence (1979)
9. Pedersen, T., Pakhomov, S.V., Patwardhan, S., Chute, C.G.: Measures of semantic similarity and relatedness in the biomedical domain. J. Biomed. Inform. **40**(3), 288–299 (2007)
10. NLTK. https://www.nltk.org
11. MetaMap. https://metamap.nlm.nih.gov
12. UMLS API. https://documentation.uts.nlm.nih.gov
13. cTAKES. https://ctakes.apache.org
14. Reátegui, R., Ratté, S.: Comparison of MetaMap and cTAKES for entity extraction in clinical notes. BMC Med. Inform. Decis. Mak. **18**(3), 74 (2018)
15. i2b2 Obesity challenge data. https://www.i2b2.org/NLP/Obesity/
16. UMLS Metathesaurus. https://www.ncbi.nlm.nih.gov/books/NBK9685/
17. SNOMED CT. http://www.snomed.org
18. VetSCT. https://vtsl.vetmed.vt.edu
19. McCray, A.T., Burgun, A., Bodenreider, O.: Aggregating UMLS semantic types for reducing conceptual complexity. Stud. Health. Technol. Inform. **84**, 216 (2001)
20. McInnes, B.T., Pedersen, T., Pakhomov, S.V.: UMLS-Interface and UMLS-Similarity: open source software for measuring paths and semantic similarity. In: AMIA Annual Symposium Proceedings, vol. 2009, p. 431 (2009)
21. Manning, C.D., Schütze, H.: Foundations of Statistical Natural Language Processing. MIT Press, Berkeley (1999)
22. Pratt, W., Yetisgen-Yildiz, M.: A study of biomedical concept identification: MetaMap vs. people. In: AMIA Annual Symposium Proceedings, pp. 529–533 (2003)
23. Harvey, R.R., et al.: Epidemiology of Salmonella enterica serotype Dublin infections among humans, United States, 1968–2013. Emerg. Infect. Dis. **23**(9), 1493 (2017)
24. McDonough, P.L., Fogelman, D., Shin, S.J., Brunner, M.A., Lein, D.H.: Salmonella enterica serotype Dublin infection: an emerging infectious disease for the northeastern United States. J. Clin. Microbiol. **37**(8), 2418–2427 (1999)
25. Alvaro, N., Miyao, Y., Collier, N.: TwiMed: Twitter and PubMed comparable corpus of drugs, diseases, symptoms, and their relations. JMIR Public Health Surveill. **3**(2), e24 (2017)
26. NHS 2020. https://www.gov.uk/government/publications/personalised-health-and-care-2020

Applications of Evolutionary Algorithms

GenMuse: An Evolutionary Creativity Enhancement Tool

Massimo Salomoni and Jenny Carter(✉)

University of Huddersfield, Huddersfield, UK
j.carter@hud.ac.uk

Abstract. Creativity is often defined as the creation of something novel through the use of imagination. But for all artists, creativity is also the exploration of new and unknown areas within their specific art. Is it possible to stimulate creativity through a system that creates inspiring original music, and that is also able to learn the personal tastes of its user? Within the project, an evolutionary approach was used in an attempt to stimulate musical creativity by supplying a composer with software that can compose short musical patterns called riffs. The software, called GenMuse, evolves populations of riffs, and makes use of a feed-forward artificial neural network to learn how to autonomously evaluate the evolved riffs to satisfy the tastes of the composer. The results show that the approach is worthy of further investigation. The genetic algorithm produced interesting results that, according to our evaluation parameters, could be included "as is" in a musical composition, and the neural network was able to evaluate the riffs with a good success ratio.

Keywords: Creativity · Genetic Algorithms · Neural networks · Music

1 Introduction

As AI techniques are directly related to mathematics and statistics, they also lend themselves to the creation and manipulation of music. In this project, Genetic Algorithms (GAs) and Artificial Neural Networks (ANNs) were integrated within a piece of software to generate original sound-bites of music (riffs). These two tools were chosen because they offer great capacity for exploring the possible solutions (GAs), and are able to classify those solutions and discover the hidden patterns (ANNs).

The aim was not to create perfectly functioning riffs and melodies that could be used as they were, but rather to provide an aid to creative people, who make music for passion or profession, in need of inspiration for their own compositions. This can, therefore, be regarded as an attempt to develop a Creativity Enhancement Tool.

2 The System

The system created for this project was divided into three distinct parts:

© Springer Nature Switzerland AG 2019
M. Bramer and M. Petridis (Eds.): SGAI-AI 2019, LNAI 11927, pp. 229–240, 2019.
https://doi.org/10.1007/978-3-030-34885-4_18

(1) the process of generation and classification of the riffs, where a user judged the quality of each riff generated, making them evolve into a number of new populations;
(2) the neural network training phase, where the neural network was trained to be able to identify the parameters that make a riff pleasant to the user;
(3) the phase of use, where the properly trained neural network replaced the user at the classification stage, allowing the system to propose new riffs to the user, which should match his musical tastes.

3   The Methodologies

3.1   Genetic Algorithms

The majority of systems that integrate AI and music creation are knowledge based systems, thus they allow for composition that is mostly controlled by a set of rules [1], in order to remain within some canons of composition that constitute the cultural background to Western music. Their main limitation, however, is the inability to create original melodies, completely unbalancing the trade-off between originality and "correctness of composition" (hence predictability), in favour of the latter. They tend to be focused on the "structure" part.

By their very nature, GAs are capable of producing unexpected results, and in recent decades their use has taken hold in many fields where creativity is important, and music is no exception. [2] used a set of mutation functions applied to a genetic algorithm to create original music. The Vox Populi system [3] develops sequences of chords in an evolutionary manner. Another example of the use of GAs in music is AMUSE [4] which evolves melodies starting from a specific harmonic structure.

[5] used a genetic algorithm to compose music. It used position-based representation of rhythm as well as relative representation of pitches. This strategy included a pre-defined rhythm being utilized to create the initial population which give a good starting solution. This approach is similar to the one used for this project, allowing the users to define some characteristics of the initial population to avoid starting from a completely random set of chromosomes, but uses a GA and not an IGA to generate the populations.

A novel promising approach [6] uses Memetic Algorithms (MAs) to create music. MAs are a hybrid which involve traditional Genetic Algorithms plus local search for optimal solutions applied to sub-sections of the main problem. Such approach would help the initial GA to evolve to optimal solutions in a shorter time compared to the standard way of evolving a chromosomes population.

[7] makes use of multi-objective genetic algorithms, a kind of GA that uses more than one fitness function to evaluate the population, to produce harmonies and melodies in parallel.

3.2   Interactive Genetic Algorithms (IGAs)

This is a widely used approach to genetic algorithms, where the fitness function is replaced by interaction with a human operator who takes care of the evaluation. This is the case of this project, in which human users were asked to give their opinion on a population of riffs that evolves over time. There are a good number of (IGA) applications used for the creation of original music, for example, [8] used IGAs for composing original and complex rhythms, using both a human judge and a number of functions based on the characteristics of the rhythms proposed, to evaluate the performance of the system. The system that at present seems to have achieved the best results in terms of application of IGAs in situations of actual performance is GenJam [9], which can simulate a jazz musician during a live performance, and play in a duet with a human musician.

The main limitation of IGAs for creating music is the bottleneck constituted by the fatigue of the user. Therefore, in this project a simple procedure was implemented to reduce fatigue: the user was simply allowed to save and resume the process at a later time. Another limit of IGAs is subjectivity of judgment. In the case of this project, however, subjectivity was not seen to be a limit, but instead created added value since the system created riffs that should not be "universally accepted" but should conform to the user's taste. Subjectivity, in this case, becomes originality.

3.3   Neural Networks

The advantage of artificial neural networks lies mainly in the fact that these can be used to understand the behaviour of a system by using just the observations on the data from the output of that system and the variables that are part of it, without knowing the type of relationship between the variables and the output. This feature makes it possible to model complex systems that could not be modelled using a deterministic approach. When provided with a set of characteristics (*inputs*) and a corresponding classification (*output*) that is known *a priori*, it is possible to teach the ANN how to identify, for example, whether a given element with certain characteristics belongs to class A or B.

The learning process of an ANN can be defined as the search for a set of internal weights which are able to simulate a complex function that should be as close as possible to the optimal function. The training consists mainly in comparing the output of the network to the expected output, to allow the network to "learn" from its errors. This method of learning, known as supervised learning, is not the only possible way to train a neural network, but it is the most commonly used when the number of output categories is known *a priori*. In this case, bearing in mind that the number of evaluations to be used by users were limited to 6, this approach seemed to be the most appropriate.

The range of application for ANNs is very extensive. They are intensively used to solve problems regarding financial prediction [10] industrial process control [11], pattern recognition [12] and much more. As for GAs, one of the main advantages of ANNs is their ease of implementation, furthermore they have the ability to process large amounts of data in parallel.

[13] used a recurrent neural network approach to address the problem of composing music that was good enough to fool a human listener into believing that it was the product of a human composer.

4   Practical Use of the Two Methodologies – GAs and ANNs

4.1   The Genetic Algorithm Used for This Project

A way to control the initial population of riffs, and also give precise rules on the legality of the chromosomes, has been implemented. To try to have an initial population that is not completely random and completely unrelated to the musical tastes of the user, this project makes use of a seeding technique.

The seeding process usually consists of using blocks of information that have already been evaluated and standardised according to specific parameters, to try and create a good initial population. In this case, however, several parameters are created and controlled (e.g. density of the notes with respect to rests, maximum duration of notes, etc.) to replace the traditional seeding, to try to "guide the randomness" in the first generation.

4.2   Riff Creation

4.2.1   Encoding Chromosomes

Rhythm and pitch, are two distinct traits of a melody. We normally listen to them together and when we compose we tend to consider them as one single entity. But they can be seen as two independent components. During this project we first created the rhythmic part of riffs, adding the pitch to each note only after the rhythmic structure was created.

To encode the chromosomes in order for the GA to handle them, the first step is to understand the type of information that should be contained in the chromosome. In this case, the rhythm part of a riff can be represented in a binary way, using the symbol 1 for the beginning of an event (note or rest), and the symbol 0 to indicate the continuation of the event in time. Rhythm is composed of blocks of a given duration which determine the length of a note or of a rest.

Theoretically, a computer could play notes at a speed that would be physically impossible for a human and so, to give the experiment more realism, it was decided to implement 1/16th as the minimum and 4/4th as the maximum duration of a note or rest. The duration of each riff is two measures with a metric in 4/4, then 16/16 per measure, namely 32/16 to represent the two measures. To define the melody a number was assigned to each note. Zero was used to indicate a rest, the numbers other than zero to define notes. The number representing a note or rest, is repeated for the duration of the event indicated by the rhythmic structure as shown in the examples below.

An example of the rhythmic part of the chromosome, considering, for the sake of convenience, just one measure, 16/16 as shown in Fig. 1.

1	0	0	0	1	0	1	1	1	1	1	0	0	1	0	0
1/4				1/8		1/16	1/16	1/16	1/16	3/16			3/16		

Fig. 1. Rhythm representation.

Therefore, the rhythmic structure, expressed in musical notation is as shown in Fig. 2.

Fig. 2. Equivalent rhythm in standard notation.

The corresponding melodic structure could be, with a range of one octave is as shown in Fig. 3.

2	2	2	2	5	5	6	6	0	0	1	1	1	3	3	3
1/4				1/8		1/16	1/16	1/16	1/16	3/16			3/16		

Fig. 3. Melody representation.

Superimposing this on the rhythmic structure would originate the following phrase results in the notation shown in Fig. 4.

Fig. 4. Riff in standard notation.

4.2.2   Evaluating the Fitness Value of a Solution

To allow for a precise rhythmic placement of the riff and facilitate its evaluation, a background drum track was played during the listening, and the riff (which by its nature has to sound good when repeated) was played twice in succession.

The evaluation parameters are summarized in Table 1.

Table 1. Riff evaluation table.

Value	Meaning
0	The proposed riff has no rhythmic or melodic meaning, should be discarded
1	The proposed riff has some rhythmic OR melodic meaning in some of its parts, still not good but it can survive
2	The proposed riff has both some rhythmic AND melodic meaning in some of its parts, it can survive
3	The proposed riff is nice, has some meaning in most or all of its parts. It can be an inspiring riff after some adjustment. It can survive
4	The proposed riff is good. With some minor adjustment it could be played as it is. It can survive
5	The proposed riff is very good. No need for adjustment, it can be played as it is

Selection. After being evaluated, all the riffs with valuation not equal to 0 are considered for the selection process for the next generation. There are various types of selection. In this project, a fitness based selection, also known as roulette wheel selection, was used.

Crossover and Mutations. In practical terms the chromosome, although composed of 64 genes, is as if it were composed of 32. In fact, at each crossover, there is the need to verify whether the rhythm is consistent with the distribution of the notes of the melody or vice versa. Considering rhythm and melody as two separate entities of 32 genes each, makes it easier to perform such verification.

The software includes various parameters for the mating procedure and the generation of new populations. In fact, it is possible to have 2 or 3 parents that generate 1 or 2 offspring. If no crossover occurs and if the mating is required to create one descendant, the first parent selected for that single mating is cloned for the next generation, regardless of the number of parents. If 2 descendants are generated, the first two parents are cloned, regardless of whether 2 or 3 were selected for mating.

Seeding. Seeding was obtained by using some parameters set by the user at the beginning of the entire process.

These parameters are:

- tonal or dodecaphony (twelve-tone) selection; if tonal is selected then only 8 or 14 notes are used (depending on the range), these notes are in C-major (or A-minor). When dodecaphony is selected then all the 12 or 24 (on a 2 octave range) notes of the chromatic scale are used;
- one or two octaves range; this allows the selected tonal/dodecaphony mode to range over one octave (from C3 to C4) or over 2 octaves (C3 to B4);
- acephalous start; this simply allows a riff to start with a rest instead of a note;
- note on the last 1/16; this control was created when the first experiments were being carried out. Especially with a high tempo, a 1/16 note in the last position of the riff proved to be annoying. So in the event that there is a 1 in the rhythmic part on the last 1/16, it can be set to 0 (rest) in the melodic part;

- notes density; the probability of a note instead of a rest. This is set at 90% by default, a proportion that is just about right, considering tonal mode;
- maximum/minimum notes/rest duration; set by default at 1/8 and 2/4 to avoid extreme durations.

It should be noted that most of these parameters (except the note range, dodecaphony/tonal mode and note on the last 1/16) would only influence the first population and that there would be a slow decay of these limitations, as expected with a traditional approach to seeding.

4.3 The Artificial Neural Network

Recent studies [14] show that the pleasure we get from music is directly related to the expectations that it can create and the meeting (or even surpassing) of these expectations. More precisely, there are three main parameters, managed by the brain, involved in feeling that pleasure: pattern recognition (an ability that is acquired through time and exposure to a certain kind of music), prediction and emotions.

Artificial neural networks have been used extensively for pattern recognition and to predict the likelihood of a given output given a set of inputs, so they were a "natural" choice for this project. The ANN architecture used for this project was the multilayer feed-forward, which is widely used in classification problems and pattern recognition.

The number of input neurons was set at 64, that is, for each 1/16th of the riff, both rhythmic melodic, there is an input. The number of hidden neurons was calculated by considering the average performance of the network using a k-fold validation (with $k = 10$). The advantage of this kind of validation is that by using different groups of individuals in the training and testing phases, the risk of overfitting is lower and thus the network should maintain a good generalisation ability.

A sigmoid was used as activation function, and a resilient backpropagation algorithm for the supervised learning. The error threshold to stop the training of the network is 0.02 (or 2%). This value was chosen after some preliminary tests carried out with larger and smaller values. Values greater than 0.02 led to fluctuations in performance during validation, smaller values led to convergence problems, as well as placing the system at risk of excessive overfitting.

Having decided in advance the minimum value of the error allowed, made it possible, at a later stage, to speed up the training procedure. There is also a threshold of 2000 epochs for training the network. This is a sufficiently high threshold as it has been noted that convergence occurred in a matter of hundred epochs.

4.3.1 Interpretation of Classification

When assessing the results, as early as the preliminary testing phase, the problem that occurred immediately concerned interpretation of the output.

In fact, mapping the discrete input (normalised) on a continuous output, did not produce the expected result. To compute the classification error, to map a continuous function on a discrete one, a technique of "belonging to the nearest class" was used between adjacent classes.

The conversion between continuous and discrete values is shown in Table 2.

Table 2. Nearest class classification.

Actual network output	Converted to
0.0–0.09999	0.0
0.1–0.29999	0.2
0.3–0.49999	0.4
0.5–0.69999	0.6
0.7–0.89999	0.8
0.9–1.0	1.0

4.3.2   Training the Artificial Neural Network

For the training part, four independent populations of riffs, evolved by the same subject, have been considered, 3 at a time for the whole training and k-fold validation part, and one for testing, all on a rotational basis.

As can be seen in Figs. 5 and 6, which show the expected values and those obtained after a test (both series normalised), there was a certain tendency of the practical results to follow the trend of the theoretical ones. As can be noted, the main problem lies in the distinction between adjacent classes, i.e. the network tends to have the worst performance when trying to classify, for example, riffs in class 0.2 and 0.4 rather than 0.2 and 0.8. The outliers that are far from the expected value are, in fact, very few compared to the overall population. The charts provide data on just one of the many cycles of training/testing, but the trend was very similar during all preliminary experiments.

The idea of initial classification was then revisited. The decision was made to keep the 6 parameters for the genetic algorithm, in order to allow the user to express more degrees of opinion and to maintain the highest concentration. What is more, evaluating riffs in a binary manner would lead to the population converging very rapidly because many more riffs would be suppressed, and consequently a lot more effort would be required by the user to obtain a significant population.

With regard to the neural network however, according to the table of evaluation parameters it is possible to see that there is a fairly clear break between classes 2 and 3. In the first case we have riffs that begin to make sense rhythmically and melodically, in fragments of medium size. In the second case the riffs, though requiring some changes (one or two notes not exactly in time or outside the melodic context etc.), are still able to provide inspiration to a musician.

The riffs were then grouped with respect to the evaluation received from the subject, in the following way: those assessed with grade 0, 1 and 2 were classified as 0, those assessed with 3, 4 and 5 were classified as 1. At this point, in order to perform a comparison, the output of the network also had to be converted to binary, simply considering as 0 all those values smaller than 0.5, and as 1 all those between 0.5 and 1.

It is possible to see the change within data classification here below, the same results showed in the charts above are now represented in a binary way.

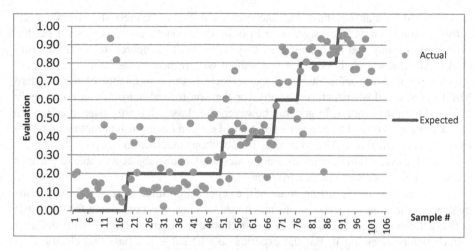

Fig. 5. One example of training/validation results.

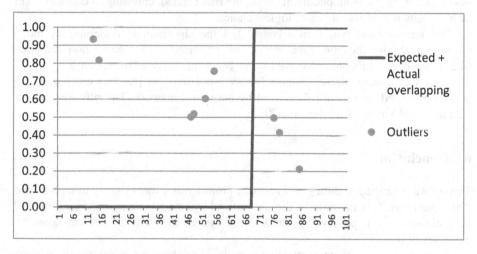

Fig. 6. The same example, binary representation.

5   Results

During the development phase of the genetic algorithm, the software was used by 3 different subjects, two with formal musical education, and one without.

Each user was asked to take particular care in evaluating the first generations. They were asked to follow the guidelines in order to generate the right amount of evolutionary pressure while avoiding depletion of the genetic diversity of the population, by eliminating solutions that could include some rhythmic or melodic fragments that were catchy.

During the evolution process, in fact, subjects with musical training showed a tendency to give higher evaluations on average. We are not able to explain this, but one reason could be that they have the unconscious ability to "correct the errors" of the software, for example, they were able to draw their conclusions just from a rhythm even if the melody had no meaning, or they were able to synchronize, with the drum track, a riff that sounded good, but was shifted with respect to the beat.

One problem encountered by all the subjects is the low quality of the standard MIDI sounds of Java which, especially for the non-trained subject, can cause early fatigue during the process. In general, however, the classes that are easier to assign are the extreme ones (0 and 5) as even a non trained ear can distinguish complete nonsense from a catchy riff that can be played as it is, without modifications.

Once the evaluation parameters were understood, each subject was able to perform each evaluation, without encountering problems.

On completion of the testing phase of the genetic algorithm, a set of riff populations evolved by the same subject, with formal music training, was considered for the neural network training phase. The subject could choose to listen to the riff with different sounds before assessing it. For the experiments, the subject, a bass and electric bass player, listened to the riffs using the MIDI electric bass sound, thus considering them as bass riffs. Given the monophonic nature of the riffs created, choosing to consider them as bass parts is perhaps the most logical choice.

The same subject was then asked to test the algorithm in dodecaphony mode (without modifying the other parameters). This produced another population of unique riffs. Some of the riffs obtained, even if not beautiful, at least "made sense".

After the training phase, to have further proof that the results were sound, the subject evaluated new tonal riffs created by the neural network. The riffs were evaluated as "good" most of the times (>70%).

6 Conclusions

The software developed during this research project was a means to try to answer two main questions. Is it possible to use an artificial system to compose original music? And moreover, is it possible for an artificial system to learn our musical tastes by examples only?

Through the use of an interactive genetic algorithm and a structurally simple artificial neural network, an attempt to answer these questions was made. The results of the experiments lead to more questions than answers.

It was, in fact, possible to create original musical phrases (in a reasonable time), starting from an initial population of melodies created in a controlled manner and then allowed to evolve. Controlling the parameters of creation of the first population, although contributing to limiting the solution space for the genetic algorithm, still made it possible to achieve a good number of solutions that meet the aesthetic taste of the subjects that actually evolved the population.

But can this aesthetic taste be imprinted in a dynamic structure such as an artificial neural network? In this case the results were conflicting. On the one hand, with populations of tonal riffs evolved by the same person, there has been an ability of the network to distinguish between good and bad riffs which can hardly be due to chance, having far exceeded the level of reliability of a coin toss, even if it failed to express a gradient of evaluations and had to fall back on a binary evaluation.

On the other hand, the very nature of ANNs makes it impossible to fully understand the mechanism behind their behaviour, thus preventing a definitive answer.

Tested with the dodecaphonic riffs evolved by the same subject and with a population of tonal riffs evolved by another subject, the network did not perform as well as before. With dodecaphony, this could be due to the fact that the population contained few positive examples, and those present were borderline, and because the network was not flexible enough to generalize these few positive examples.

But what about the tonal riffs? Was it mere coincidence or was it due to the fact that the network "absorbed" a kind of fingerprint which identifies individual taste, and so was not able to perform with a different population evolved by someone with different tastes? With the data currently available there cannot be a definite answer. To be more certain and have more opportunity to explore the tools used in this project, it might be appropriate to repeat the evolutionary processes of the musical phrases using a greater number of subjects, in order to be more sure of the actual performance of the tools themselves. One solution could be to make the software available as a web application so that data can be gathered from a wide variety of users.

Furthermore, an approach that could lead to improving the results and making them more consistent, would be to analyse the importance of the rhythmic component, with respect to the melodic component, within a musical phrase, to discover if it is possible to create intelligent structures that are able to measure the two aspects separately and summarise them in a correct evaluation.

7 Future Work

As future development of the above findings, a comparison among various techniques of symbolic music classification and creation will be carried out, using different features from the ones used in the past and, if possible, find out if there are extra features which have not been considered yet. Another important step would be finding out how rhythm and melody influence our perception of music. Would perhaps a rhythmic structure be enough for our brain to consider a riff as a good riff? This is just one of the questions which need to be answered to gain new knowledge about how to develop new systems.

The ultimate goal of future work will be in fact to find new methods (or combination of existing methods) that could perform better than current ones in terms of precision and speed.

References

1. Miranda, E., Anders, T.: A computational model for rule-based microtonal music theories and composition. Perspect. New Music. **48**(2), 47–77 (2010)
2. Korman, M.J.: Melodic Composition with Genetic Algorithms (2004)

3. Gudwin, R., Manzolli, J., Moroni, A., von Zuben, F.: An evolutionary approach to algorithmic composition. Organ. Sound **4**(2), 121–125 (1999)
4. Özcan, E., Erçal, T.: A genetic algorithm for generating improvised music. In: Monmarché, N., Talbi, E.-G., Collet, P., Schoenauer, M., Lutton, E. (eds.) EA 2007. LNCS, vol. 4926, pp. 266–277. Springer, Heidelberg (2008). https://doi.org/10.1007/978-3-540-79305-2_23
5. Matić, D.: A genetic algorithm for composing music. Yugosl. J. Oper. Res. **20**, 157–177 (2010)
6. Wells, D., ElAarag, H.: Novel approach for automated music composition using memetic algorithms. In: 48th Annual ACM Southeast Conference, Kennesaw, GA, pp. 155–159 (2011)
7. Olseng, O.: An Application of Evolutionary Algorithms to Music: - Co-Evolving Melodies and Harmonization (2016)
8. Horowitz, D.: Generating rhythms with genetic algorithms. In: Proceedings of the 1994 International Computer Music Conference, ICMA, San Francisco (1994)
9. Biles, J.A.: GenJam: a genetic algorithm for generating jazz solos. In Proceedings of the 1994 International Computer Music Conference, ICMA, San Francisco (1994)
10. Kutsurelis, J.E.: Forecasting financial markets using neural networks: An analysis of methods and accuracy. Master thesis, Naval Postgraduate School (1998)
11. Petre, E., Selisteanu, D., Sendrescu, D.: Neural network based adaptive control of a fermentation bioprocess for lactic acid production. In: Watada, J., Phillips-Wren, G., Jain, L. C., Howlett, R.J. (eds.) Intelligent Decision Technologies, vol. 10, pp. 201–212. Springer, Heidelberg (2011). https://doi.org/10.1007/978-3-642-22194-1_21
12. Basu, J.K., Bhattacharyya, D., Kim, T.H.: Use of artificial neural network in pattern recognition. Int. J. Softw. Eng. Its Appl. **4**(2), 23–34 (2010)
13. Agarwala, N., Inoue, Y., Sly, A.: Music Composition Using Recurrent Neural Networks. Paper, Stanford University (2016)
14. Salimpoor, V.N., van den Bosch, I., Kovacevic, N., McIntosh, A.R., Dagher, A., Zatorre, R. J.: Interactions Between the Nucleus Accumbens and Auditory Cortices Predict Music Reward (2013)

Evolutionary Art with an EEG Fitness Function

Ingrid Němečková, Carl James-Reynolds[✉], and Edward Currie

Middlesex University, London, UK
C.James-Reynolds@mdx.ac.uk

Abstract. This project involved the use of an interactive Genetic Algorithm (iGA) with an electroencephalogram (EEG)-based fitness function to create paintings in the style of Piet Mondrian, a Dutch painter who used geometric elements in his later paintings. Primary data for the prototype was gathered by analysis of twenty-seven existing Mondrian paintings. An EEG gaming headset was used to read EEG signals, which were transmitted by Bluetooth to an Arduino running an iGA. These values were used as the iGA fitness function. The data was sent to a PC running Processing to display the artwork. The resultant displayed artwork evolves to favour higher attention and meditation levels, which are considered to represent greater mindfulness. The process ends when the observer identifies a piece of art they would like to keep. However, convergence of the algorithm is difficult to test as many parameters can affect the process. A number of issues arising from the research are discussed and further work is proposed.

Keywords: interactive Genetic Algorithm · Generative art · EEG

1 Background

1.1 Context

Mondrian was a Dutch painter and theoretician who is viewed by many as one of the greatest artists and pioneers of the 20th century abstract art movement. His work inspired fashion designers such as Lola Prusac, who worked for Hermes in Paris and Yves Saint Laurent, who introduced The Mondrian Collection in 1965. He also inspired the serialist composer Pierre Boulez and the development of an esoteric programming language "Piet" in which programs resemble abstract art." [1].

At the start of World War One Mondrian became acquainted with M.H. J. Schoenmaekers, a theosophical philosopher whose work on the symbolical meaning of lines and the mathematical construction of the universe had a decisive influence on Mondrian's vision of painting. It is this that seems to have inspired Mondrian to start using just the three primary colours; he "wrote in 1915 in 'The New Image of the World' that red, yellow and blue are the only true colours, because all others can be derived from these three" [2]. Mondrian and Theo van Doesburg, an artist and architect, founded the journal De Stijl [3] in 1917, in which Mondrian published his concepts of art and colour. De Stijl, ("the style"), also known as Neoplasticism was a

© Springer Nature Switzerland AG 2019
M. Bramer and M. Petridis (Eds.): SGAI-AI 2019, LNAI 11927, pp. 241–252, 2019.
https://doi.org/10.1007/978-3-030-34885-4_19

movement among Dutch artists, architects, and designers that presented an ideal of total abstraction as a model for harmony and order across the arts [4]. The movement had a far-reaching effect on the development of both abstract art and modern architecture and design.

In 1919 Mondrian moved back to Paris, where he began creating the iconic abstract paintings for which he is most famous. He began using only the primary colours red, yellow and blue, together with the non-colours white, black and grey [2]. Mondrian wrote to his friend Van Doesburg: "I am in search of the perfect harmony of rhythm... that's really difficult." [2] He became obsessed with perfect harmony and determined to reflect it in his paintings. Initially, Mondrian's use of primary colours was experimental. He mixed them with white and black to experiment with different shades of the primary colours and sometimes gave his painting a grey or brown over-shade. He then moved away from the shades of grey and brown and also decided that all lines in his paintings should be equally black. At first the lines were thin, tending to fade at the edges. [1] On 4 December, Mondrian wrote to his friend Van Doesburg that he had finished "a thing" that pleased him more than all previous works. This was possibly an early version of Composition A. [2] he adopted the use of a "rhythmic" pattern of squares in his paintings. During the period 1920–1939, he created his most iconic paintings, at first exhibiting them without any frames. Later, he edged them with thin white wooden strips and later moved on to building white shadow boxes.

1.2   Interactive Art Projects

Edmonds states that "Art becomes interactive when audience participation is an integral part of the artwork." [5] It should draw the audience into becoming part of the project, by active participation or passive exploration. New technology, mainly microprocessor based, has empowered the rise of new interactive art.

According to Tempel "Generative art is created by a system that operates autonomously, or semi- autonomously, rather than directly by the artist, it is a sub-category of temporary art. Generative art systems are usually computer programs." [6]. One of the early pioneers was the artist Harold Cohen who is the creator of AARON [7], a computer program written in the LISP programming language, designed to produce art autonomously. Cohen improved his program throughout his life and paintings created by the program were not only valued by the public, but also by art critics. Cohen traveled the world with AARON, exhibiting his art at numerous prestigious museums and galleries.

Since Harold Cohen, the generative art movement has produced acknowledged artists such as Sonia Landy Sheridan, who founded the first generative systems department at the Art Institute of Chicago in 1970 [8] and Lillian Schwartz, who set about demonstrating that Da Vinci himself was in all probability the model for the Mona Lisa by using computer software in 1984 [9]. Due to the increasing popularity of generative art, new computer programs were developed over the years. One such is Processing [10], which has become popular recently and is based on Java. Generative art has flourished since the start of the 21st century. Artists in this area have created a strong on-line community of open-source websites where ideas, code and results are shared. Low cost micro-controller platforms such as Arduino [11] are frequently used for digital installations and other physical computing projects, which has also contributed to this phenomenon.

1.3   Related Work

Mondrian-style work has been explored by a number of computer artists. "ARTMOVEMENT", created by Dominic Fee [12], was a "web-based educational resource, with interactive elements, designed to assist in the education and appreciation of fine art." This allows users to interactively create their own versions of abstract art by Mondrian, Albers, Malevich, Martin, Rothko, Riley, Kline and Pollock. The artwork is modified by mouse manipulation and the system was created using Processing. The system allows the user to move away from Mondrian's chosen colours and elements; for example the canvas can be changed to a single colour and lines can be colours other than black.

Shen and Gedeon [13] explored similarities in Mondrian's paintings and focused on the repetitiveness of the lines, which were split into 8 different sections. They created one ultimate rule in their software: "Each line in a Mondrian-like graph, must have one of its ends being nodal or online, another end being terminal, nodal or online." They applied an Interactive Bacterial Evolution Algorithm where the first painting created was the parent generation, which went through evolution by each chromosome being assigned a value by the fitness function, which represented its quality. The chromosome absorbs good gene pieces from another one to replace its own. This results in the next generation, which was evaluated by a human. The researchers were however not interested in how the human liked the generated Mondrian graph, but the evaluation was specific to shape, colour, none or both. Depending on the answer of the human a new graph was generated. The conclusion of this research was that "Mondrian paintings are more than random compositions of lines and rectangles by revealing the fact that even minor modifications lead to less subjective satisfaction of audiences."

1.4   Genetic Algorithms

"Genetic algorithms (GA) were invented by John Holland in the 1960s and were developed by Holland and his students and colleagues at the University of Michigan in the 1960s and the 1970s." [14] They adopt a heuristic approach in applying the principles of evolutionary biology to the solution of complex problems for which there is no usable exact algorithm [15] and are a subset of evolutionary computations in the field of artificial intelligence. Evolutionary computations use techniques that mimic known evolutionary processes such as selection, reproduction, mutation and crossover, as described by Charles Darwin in his book "On the Origin of Species by Means of Natural Selection, or the Preservation of Favoured Races in the Struggle for Life" [16] Individuals in a population of candidate solutions undergo an evaluation of their fitness to survive. The natural process of selection will preserve the individuals with the best genetic characteristics to survive in their environment, which then become the next generation of candidate solutions. An individual can be represented as a binary string of ones and zeros or a matrix. The development of the population then proceeds by repeating the above mentioned operations [17].

The terminology used for GAs is derived from genetics. Individuals are referred to as genotypes, genomes, chromosomes which are structures representing their characteristics. These characteristics can be presented as binary values. Chromosomes in nature consist of deoxyribonucleic acid (DNA) forming strings of DNA. A chromosome is divided into genes, the order of which is important. Each gene encodes an individual trait such as eye colour, hair colour or height; these individual traits are called alleles. In a GA these traits can be modelled in binary to represent a candidate solution [14] (see Fig. 1).

Fig. 1. Binary representation of chromosome.

The principle of the GA process is the repeated creation of new populations of individual solutions to the problem. As the population evolves, solutions improve. Typically, the first generation of individuals is created randomly, although it may be seeded to ensure a wide range of differences in the initial parents. In each successive generation, a fitness function value is calculated for each individual, which expresses the quality of the solution represented by that individual. According to this quality, individuals are selected who are then modified (by mutation and crossover) to produce a new population. This process is continuously repeated so that the overall quality of the solutions is improved. The algorithm is usually stopped after a certain time or number of generations, or if a sufficient quality of solution is achieved [18].

1.5   Fitness Function

To create a new population from the previous population it is necessary to define the criteria for selecting successful individuals (parents). In nature, individuals compete with each other in their natural environment, and the more successful individuals have a greater probability of surviving to produce more offspring than the less successful. In an artificial environment it is necessary to create similar competition for survival, to simulate the natural process and the fitness function plays a key role in this [18]. Its function is to evaluate each individual against the expected solution and individuals with scores closest to the expected solution are preferred in the production of the next generation.

1.6   Roulette Wheel Selection

This has been described as "a genetic operator used in genetic algorithms for selecting potentially useful solutions for recombination." [19] Individuals of the population are assigned sectors of the simulated 'wheel', the size of each sector being directly proportional to the fitness value of the individual [14]. Insertion of the ball into the roulette wheel and spinning the wheel until the ball settles in one of the sectors is then simulated and the corresponding individual is selected for breeding. Several balls can be inserted at the same time, but no more than the number of individuals to be selected from [18] In this case all parents can be selected in one roulette spin. "Once a pair of parents is selected, they cross over to form two offspring." [14] If the same parent is chosen twice, another choice is made until the two parents differ.

1.7 Mutation and Crossover

Mutation serves to create genetic diversity in the population genome. It is a genetic operator that changes one or more gene values in the chromosome of an individual. A simple example of a mutation is changing number 0 to 1 or vice versa [18]. This operator is used based on a given probability value of the mutation occurrence, which may be set by the user [20]. The probability of mutation occurrence should be set with caution, as too high will result in degradation of the GA and too low may result in the GA converging on local maxima in the solution space.

Crossover is a reproduction operator that simulates the random exchange of information contained in parents when creating a new child. During a crossover a combination of genetic information from two parents occurs. It may be single point crossover, or multi point crossover. The crossover points are typically randomly selected [20].

2   Methodology

An initial prototype was developed based on the work described in [21] who published his code on GitHub. This raised issues including the distribution of colours, the generation of appropriate random data and the distinction between squares and rectangles in the initial analysis of ten Mondrian paintings using Google's Vision API. [22]. The code was then written from scratch to address these issues.

A total number of 27 Mondrian paintings were chosen for analysis:

- Composition A, 1920
- Composition B, 1920
- Composition with Yellow, Red, Black, Blue and Gray, 1920
- Composition with Yellow, Blue, Black, Re and Gray, 1921
- Composition with Large Blue Plane, Red, Black, Yellow and Gray, 1921
- Tableau I, with Black, Red, Yellow, Blue, and Light Blue, 1921
- Composition with Red, Yellow, Black, Blue and Gray, 1921
- Tableau II, with Red, Black, Yellow, Blue and Light Blue, 1921
- Composition with Red, Blue, Yellow, Black and Gray, 1992
- Composition with Blue, Yellow, Red, Black and Gray, 1992
- Composition with Blue, Red, Yellow and Black, 1922
- Composition with Blue, Yellow, Black and Red, 1992
- Tableau 2, with Yellow, Black, Blue, Red and Gray, 1992
- Tableau with Yellow, Black, Blue and Red and Gray, 1923
- Tableau No II. With Black and Gray, 1925
- Composition with Red, Yellow and Blue, 1927

- Composition with Black, Red and Gray, 1927
- Composition: No. III with Red, Yellow and Blue, 1927
- Composition I: with Black, Yellow and Blue, 1927
- Large composition with Red, Blue and Yellow, 1928
- Composition No III. With Red, Blue, Yellow and Black, 1929
- Composition No I. with Red, 1931
- Composition with Blue and Yellow, 1932
- Composition with Black and White, with Double Lines, 1934
- Composition with Double Lines and Blue, 1935
- Composition A with Double Lines and Yellow, 1935
- Composition White, Red and Yellow: A, 1936

2.1 Analysis of Mondrian's Paintings

Colour Analysis					
	RGB Colours				FINAL
Yellow	241,199,21	246,209,22	253,216,13	252,216,14	251,237,68	249,215,28
Red	220,67,45	229,83,51	218,56,42	204,72,49	199,38,48	214,63,47
Blue	27,74,115	31,48,75	27,64,115	18,71,131	75,121,174	36,76,122
Gray	240,240,243	228,228,228	229,231,237	224,224,224	238,238,237	232,232,234

Fig. 2. Analysis of colour in Mondrian painting.

Piet Mondrian chose to limit his paintings to the use of the three primary colours red, blue and yellow together with black, white and grey. Mondrian referred to this genre as 'Neo-Plasticism'. Because the artist was so specific in the colours he used it was important to represent those colours as accurately as possible. It was decided to use the Google Vision API for the analysis. The image analysis was able to identify the colours and represent them in RGB format. The pictures of paintings were taken from Piet Mondrian: Life and Work [2], scanned and analysed. In order to use the Google vision API it was important to choose paintings of predominantly one colour in order to analyse the RGB content for each of the colours. From the selection of paintings 5 were chosen for each colour to analyse and the results are shown in Fig. 2.

2.2 Physical Construction

Processing [10] was used to create the display software. It is open source, has built in graphics libraries and works well with the Arduino Platform [11]. Arduino uses Atmel processors and has its own compiler with many libraries available. Arduino was used to run the iGA and also to create the random variables for the initial population; the code for this was an adaptation of the code used by James-Reynolds and Currie [23]. It was decided that the complexity of the paintings, including the number of columns and rows and the number of colours would be decided by the iGA, but the precise details of where the colours would be distributed would be random. The fitness function used EEG data from a NeuroSky Brainwave Starter Kit [24]. The code allows EEG signals for attention, meditation or mindfulness (a combination of both signals) to be used.

Using EEG signals as the basis for the fitness function enables the evaluation to take place in a subconscious way. The interaction is not about users performing an conscious action, but instead a more subtle interaction that can be clearly demonstrated.

The integration of the iGA and the EEG was based on previous work [23]. A gaming headset [24] was used to capture and transmit the EEG readings via Bluetooth. A Bluesmirf receiver using an RN-41 module [25] TX pin was connected as shown in Figs. 3 and 4 to the RX pin on the Arduino. The data from the headset was parsed and attention and meditation values extracted from the data stream. One Arduino managed this process and passed the data over an I2C connection to a second Arduino running the iGA code.

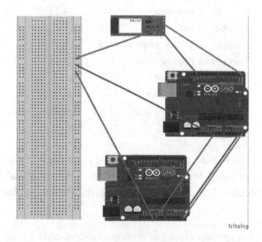

Fig. 3. Schematic of Arduino boards and Bluetooth.

Fig. 4. The equipment: Arduino boards and BlueSmirf.

The code firstly generates 8 parameters for each of 4 parent individuals. The selection of future parents in each generation is generated by the roulette approach based on the EEG-based fitness function.

Random numbers in Arduino are generated using randomSeed() which initialises the pseudo-random generator. To ensure that a different starting point in the pseudo-random sequence was obtained each time, the command analogRead() on an unconnected pin was used as an argument to randomSeed() The mutation rate for the iGA was set at 3%.

Table 1 shows the visual analysis of the paintings that provided data for setting the limitations of the solution space.

Table 1. Findings from analysis of paintings.

Second painting analysis		
Item	Number	Average
Number of rows	3–9	4,85
Number of columns	2–7	4,11
Number of red objects	0–3	1
Number of yellow objects	0–4	1,18
Number of blue objects	0–4	1,11
Number of black objects	0–4	1
Number of grey objects	0–13	4,25
Number of white objects	0–17	2,88

During this analysis it was discovered that the numbers of coloured objects in Mondrian paintings appeared within certain limits. The mean value for each represented colour was calculated and used as starting values for a colors[] array.

Table 2. Serial monitor output of Arduino random code - Final Version.

Arduino serial monitor - output 3	
Columns: 4 Rows: 9 Cells: 36 Gray: 9 White: 6 Yellow: 4 Blue: 9 Black: 1 Red: 4	Columns: 3 Rows: 6 Cells: 18 Gray: 6 White: 4 Yellow: 3 Blue: 2 Black: 2 Red: 1
Columns: 4 Rows: 3 Cells: 12 Gray: 4 White: 3 Yellow: 4 Blue: 1 Black: 0 Red: 0	Columns: 4 Rows: 8 Cells: 32 Gray: 9 White: 7 Yellow: 5 Blue: 4 Black: 1 Red: 2
Columns: 4 Rows: 9 Cells: 36 Gray: 12 White: 5 Yellow: 4 Blue: 6 Black: 3 Red: 2	Columns: 3 Rows: 5 Cells: 15 Gray: 4 White: 3 Yellow: 3 Blue: 1 Black: 1 Red: 1
Columns: 2 Rows: 5 Cells: 10 Gray: 4 White: 3 Yellow: 1 Blue: 2 Black: 0 Red: 0	Columns: 6 Rows: 5 Cells: 30 Gray: 9 White: 6 Yellow: 6 Blue: 2 Black: 3 Red: 0

(continued)

Table 2. (*continued*)

Arduino serial monitor - output 3	
Columns: 2 Rows: 5 Cells: 10 Gray: 4 White: 3 Yellow: 1 Blue: 2 Black: 0 Red: 0	Columns: 6 Rows: 5 Cells: 30 Gray: 9 White: 6 Yellow: 6 Blue: 2 Black: 3 Red: 0
Columns: 3 Rows: 5 Cells: 15 Gray: 6 White: 5 Yellow: 2 Blue: 1 Black: 0 Red: 0	Columns: 2 Rows: 6 Cells: 12 Gray: 4 White: 3 Yellow: 1 Blue: 1 Black: 1 Red: 0
Values of Columns: 3 Rows: 6 Cells: 18 Gray: 7 White: 4 Yellow: 1 Blue: 2 Black: 0 Red: 2	Columns: 6 Rows: 8 Cells: 48 Gray: 10 White: 7 Yellow: 9 Blue: 9 Black: 2 Red: 5

Table 2 shows examples of the initially generated parents. The Arduino was passing 8 values to Processing; 6 for colours, 1 for number of rows and 1 for number of columns. The distances between the lines were generated randomly and not decided by the algorithm.

3 Testing

Testing was performed with volunteers. The volunteers varied in gender and nationality, but because they were all students, the age range was limited; they were typically around 20 years of age. Each volunteer sat in front of a laptop and was given a brief explanation of the process. They were then instructed to sit back, relax and just look at the paintings. A new painting was generated every 5 s for a period of 2 min, so that in total 36 paintings were generated and presented to each volunteer.

The pattern of changes in the complexity of the paintings seemed to depend upon the individual volunteer; for some, complex paintings evolved into simpler ones and vice versa for other volunteers.

The original aim of testing was to see if the generated paintings would become more or less complex. However, this became hard to differentiate as there was not a consistent direction in the paintings' development, and no 'final' state where the subject's ideal painting had emerged. Furthermore, different subjects had different preferences. There were no sudden changes from complex to simple paintings or vice versa - the transitions seemed to be smooth and gradual. However, there was a slight distinction between different volunteers on how much the paintings simplified. Generally, initial populations contained more complex images and tended to stay complex (as in Fig. 5) or simplify (as in Fig. 6) depending on the user. With some users the images did not evolve towards simplicity, although those that did seemed to stay in this area of the solution space.

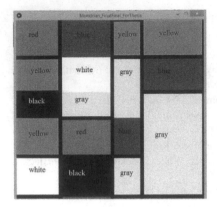
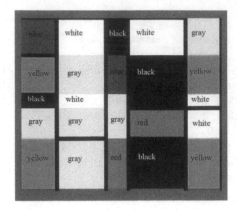

Fig. 5. More complex paintings produced by subjects.

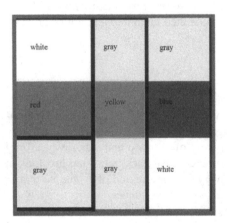
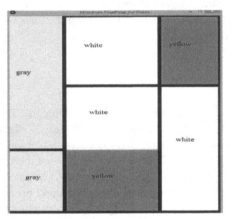

Fig. 6. Simpler paintings produced by subjects.

4   Discussion

Whilst we can see a general pattern of convergence, the results are difficult to quantify. The validity of judging a piece of art by a subconscious response as opposed to a conscious one can also be questioned. Some pieces of art need to be lived with before a deeper appreciation grows and many pieces of art are created not to induce a calm, mindful state of mind but to provoke and challenge. It is unfortunate that we cannot ask Mondrian these questions as we appear to be exploring the concept of "harmony of rhythm" by directly looking at the effect of art on brain activity. Although convergence was observed, the test environment itself may have been a distraction as could the novelty of the approach and it is possible that a test subject may try to consciously effect choices. A better strategy would be the use of a Virtual Environment with less distractions in which the images could be more three dimensional, allowing for more realism in the texture of the canvas and its hanging in a space. Whilst more sophisticated EEG devices might have provided better data for these experiments, a gaming headset was used as this does not pose the ethical considerations that this would entail, due to the potential for intrusive monitoring of likes and dislikes.

Planned future work includes exploration of the differences between using a conscious and subconscious response. Removing some of the random elements of the image presentation and making all parameters controlled by the iGA would make it possible to explore some art theory and see if, for example, golden section values emerged. In this work the solution space was confined to values that were derived from the analysis of Mondrian's paintings but it would be possible to employ a less constrained solution space.

5   Conclusion

This paper has presented an innovative approach to art generation using EEG waves as a fitness function. While the project has not produced easily quantifiable results, it has nevertheless raised interesting new questions about how we can interact with art through software.

While the current research has limitations, it has enabled the exploration of new approaches to generative art through the application of evolutionary systems and has brought some insights in this area and pointers to future work. The developed platform is viable for some of this future research.

References

1. Blotkamp, C.: Mondrian: The Art of Destruction. Reaktion Books (2001). ISBN: 9781861891006
2. De Jong, C.: Piet Mondrian: Life and Work. Abrams (2015). ISBN: 9781419714085. Knuth
3. Bris-Marino, P.: La influencia de la teosofía sobre la obra neoplástica de Mondrian. Arte, Individuo y Sociedad **26** (2014). https://doi.org/10.5209/rev_ARIS.2014.v26.n3.42960
4. Foundation, The Art Story: De Stijl (2019). https://www.theartstory.org/movement-de-stijl.htm. Accessed 12 Nov 2018
5. Edmonds, E.: Interactive Art (n.d.). https://pdfs.semanticscholar.org/e245/971a.pdf. Accessed 15 Nov 2018
6. Tempel, M.: Generative art for all. J. Innov. Entrep. **6** (2017). https://doi.org/10.1186/s13731-017-0072-1
7. Cohen, H.: 1988-How to Draw Three People in a Botanical Garden 10 (n.d.)
8. Sheridan, S.L.: Mind/senses/hand: the generative systems program at the art institute of Chicago 1970-1980. Leonardo **23**, 175 (1990). https://doi.org/10.2307/1578602
9. Schwartz, L.F.: Art Analysis - 1984 THE HIDDEN MONALISA (1984). http://lillian.com/art-analysis/. Accessed 20 Nov 2018
10. Reas, C., Fry, B.: Processing: A Programming Handbook for Visual Designers and Artists. The MIT Press, Cambridge (2015). ISBN: 9780262321853
11. Arduino Platform. https://www.arduino.cc/. Accessed 20 June 2019
12. Fee, D.: Supplementing Fine Art Education with Digital Interactivity 49 (n.d.)

13. Shen, J.Y., Gedeon, T.: Cyber-Genetic Neo-Plasticism – an AI program creating Mondrian-like paintings by using interactive bacterial evolution algorithm (2007). http://cs.anu.edu.au/escience/project/06S2/report/JianShen_report.pdf
14. Melanie, M.: An Introduction to Genetic Algorithms 162 (n.d.)
15. Banzhaf, W., et al.: Genetic Programming Arduino (2019). Arduino. https://www.arduino.cc/. Accessed 02 Dec 2018
16. Darwin, C.: On The Origin of Species by Means of Natural Selection, or Preservation of Favoured Races in the Struggle for Life, p. 1859. John Murray, London (1809–1882)
17. Hudson, D.L., Cohen, M.E.: Neural Networks and Artificial Intelligence for Biomedical Engineering. IEEE Press Series in Biomedical Engineering. Institute of Electrical and Electronics Engineers, New York (2000)
18. Haupt, R.L., Haupt, S.E.: Practical Genetic Algorithms, 2nd edn. Wiley, Hoboken (2004)
19. Thierens, D., Goldberg, D.: Convergence models of genetic algorithm selection schemes. In: Davidor, Y., Schwefel, H.-P., Männer, R. (eds.) PPSN 1994. LNCS, vol. 866, pp. 119–129. Springer, Heidelberg (1994). https://doi.org/10.1007/3-540-58484-6_256
20. Srinivas, M., Patnaik, L.M.: Adaptive probabilities of crossover and mutation in genetic algorithms. IEEE Trans. Syst. Man Cybern. **24**(4), 656–667 (1994)
21. WillPhelps1.   https://gist.github.com/WillPhelps1/4da7f9b2eb718340bedf885b63c9f729. Accessed 02 July 2019
22. Google Cloud: Vision API (2018). https://cloud.google.com/vision/. Accessed 27 December 2018
23. James-Reynolds, C., Currie, E.: EEuGene: employing electroencephalograph signals in the rating strategy of a hardware-based interactive genetic algorithm. In: Bramer, M., Petridis, M. (eds.) Research and Development in Intelligent Systems XXXIII, pp. 343–353. Springer, Cham (2016). https://doi.org/10.1007/978-3-319-47175-4_25
24. NeuroSky: NeuroSky Brainwave Starter Kit (2018). https://store.neurosky.com/pages/mindwave. Accessed 01 Feb 2019
25. Microchip RN-41. https://www.microchip.com/wwwproducts/en/RN41. Accessed 02 July 2019

A Multi-objective Design of In-Building Distributed Antenna System Using Evolutionary Algorithms

Khawla AlShanqiti[1,2(✉)], Kin Poon[1], Siddhartha Shakya[1],
Andrei Sleptchenko[2], and Anis Ouali[1]

[1] Emirates ICT Innovation Center (EBTIC),
Khalifa University, Abu Dhabi, UAE
{khawla.alshanqiti,kin.poon,sid.shakya,
anis.ouali}@ku.ac.ae
[2] Department of Industrial and Systems Engineering,
Khalifa University, Abu Dhabi, UAE
andrei.sleptchenko@ku.ac.ae

Abstract. The increasing data traffic inside buildings requires maintaining good cellular network coverage for indoor mobile users. Passive In-building Distributed Antenna System (IB-DAS) is one of the most efficient methods to provide an indoor solution that meets the signal strength requirements. It is a network of spatially distributed antennas in a building connected to telephone rooms which are then connected to a Base Transmission Station (BTS). These connections are established through passive coaxial cables and splitters. The design of IB-DAS is considered to be challenging due to the power-sharing property resulting in two contradicting objectives: minimizing the power usage at the BTS (long-term cost) and minimizing the design components cost (short-term cost). Different attempts have been made in the literature to solve this problem. Some of them are either lacking the consideration of all necessary aspects or facing scalability issues. Additionally, most of these attempts translate the IB-DAS design into a mono-objective problem, which leads to a challenging task of determining a correct combined objective function with justified weighting factors associated with each objective. Moreover, these approaches do not produce multiple design choices which may not be satisfactory in practical scenarios. In this paper, we propose a multi-objective algorithm for designing IB-DAS. The experimental results show the success of this algorithm to achieve our industrial partner's requirement of providing different design options that cannot be achieved using mono-objective approaches.

Keywords: Distributed Antenna System · Multi-objective evolutionary algorithm · Non-dominated Sorting Genetic Algorithm · Crowding distance · Normalization

© Springer Nature Switzerland AG 2019
M. Bramer and M. Petridis (Eds.): SGAI-AI 2019, LNAI 11927, pp. 253–266, 2019.
https://doi.org/10.1007/978-3-030-34885-4_20

1 Introduction

Next generation cellular networks are rapidly improving, pushing the mobile data traffic to a new level [1]. By 2021, the mobile data traffic per month will increase to 49 billion gigabytes globally, where more than 70% of it is being consumed indoor [2]. Accordingly, the need for preserving a good cellular network coverage is increasing, both for outdoor and indoor environments. Outdoor cellular coverage solutions had been successfully provided for wide areas in the past. However, the complexity of indoor environments' layouts makes it very difficult for the wireless signal to pass through buildings without suffering from attenuation [3], such as wall penetration and multipath effect. Sometimes signal coming from outside can be completely blocked by buildings. As a result, a dedicated indoor system that provides the required signal strength for the indoor mobile users is needed. In-Building Distributed Antenna System (IB-DAS) is known as one of the most efficient networks to achieve this purpose [1].

An IB-DAS is a network that supplies cellular signal within a large building. It generates, or receives the signal from outside, and distributes it within the building. It contains several spatially separated reduced power antennas at each floor of the building. These antennas are fed by a signal source. The signal source could be an off-air, via an antenna installed on the roof floor or a Base Transmission Station (BTS) that provides the distributed power and cellular signal.

There are two main types of IB-DAS: passive and active. In the passive IB-DAS, the base station provides the amplified signal that is distributed to the antennas through passive components that do not require any electrical power. In fact, antennas on each floor are connected to a telephone room through different types of components such as cables, splitters and tappers. Splitters split the power evenly, where tappers split the power in a way that each output has a different attenuation. Cables can be co-axial and/or fiber optics based on the types of IB-DAS. Telephone rooms are then connected to the BTS through the previously mentioned components.

In contrast, an active IB-DAS sends the Radio Frequency (RF) signal to a digital converter that converts it to an optical signal and sends it through fiber optic cables to remote radio units (RRUs). These units convert it back to RF analog signal. Then the units amplify the signal and send it through coaxial cables to the distributed antennas.

The choice of using the IB-DAS type depends on their application. A passive IB-DAS is less expensive than the active system as it uses fewer number of components. In addition, it does not require a conversion unit and can serve different carriers and frequencies. However, due to the signal degradation caused by the coaxial cables, it is not recommended for large buildings and shopping malls, where active IB-DAS is recommended. In this paper, our focus is on passive IB-DAS. Passive IB-DAS can be challenging to implement in comparison to other wireless networks due to their use of a single power source which is shared by the entire network [4]. Also, the requirement to optimize conflicting objectives during design poses a further challenge. For example, minimizing the power deviation between the required and supplied power of antennas may lead to higher overall component cost.

IB-DAS design can be evaluated using different performance metrics, including their coverage and capacity. It is important to come up with good designs that satisfy these two contradictory metrics while minimizing the cost, which is not trivial [1]. As shown in Fig. 1, the entire passive IB-DAS problem can be split logically into 3 independent optimization sub-problems [5, 6].

1. **Antennas location optimization:** Determines the locations of antennas on each floor considering its layout to achieve the required cellular coverage.
2. **Intra-floor connection optimization (Horizontal Design):** Determines the optimal connections between the antennas and the telephone room through splitters and coaxial cables, with the given locations of antennas on each floor.
3. **Inter-floor connection optimization (Vertical Design):** Finds the optimal connections between telephone rooms and BTS through splitters and coaxial cables, with the given required power demand for each telephone room.

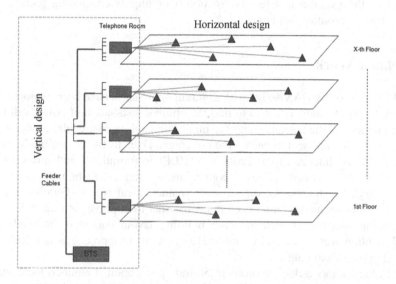

Fig. 1. Vertical and horizontal designs of passive IB-DAS elements.

In our case, the locations of antennas and the horizontal design are determined by the planners. Therefore, the focus is on the vertical design. A method is presented to obtain a tree structure that connects the telephone rooms of all of the floors to the BTS using cables, different types of splitters and tappers. Particularly, we present an enhancement to the design approach found in [5] that is based on a weighted sum single-objective Genetic Algorithm. Due to the requirement of our industrial partner to provide multiple designs, and also to improve on [5] by dealing with the contradicting objectives explicitly, we propose to use a multi-objective evolutionary algorithm, called Non-dominated Sorting Genetic Algorithm II (NSGA II) [7]. NSGA II is one of the popular Multi-objective optimization algorithms that has been successfully used to solve many real-world optimization problems [4, 8]. This approach removes the need for creating the correct combined objective function that requires a justified determination of the exact weighting values associated with each objective. It further fulfills our partner's request to come up with multiple solutions that are naturally provided by a Pareto-set in NSGA-II. The two objectives to optimize are: (i) minimizing the base station required power and (ii) minimizing the cost of the equipment. Minimizing the power demand of BTS will minimize the risk of interference with the outside signals, as well as achieve consistent savings over the long-term by using less power. Minimizing the cost of equipment relates to deployment cost to build the network with minimal cables, splitters and tappers and lower the short-term cost. The results show that NSGA II was capable of achieving these objectives, and simultaneously generating results that could not be obtained by the combined-objectives GA approach in [5].

The rest of this paper is divided into the following six sections: Sect. 2 describes the related work and discusses its limitations. Section 3 provides the problem formulation. Section 4 explains implemented NSGA II and its requirements, while Sect. 5 summarizes the experimental results. Section 6 highlights concluding remarks with possible future recommendations.

2   Related Work

Several attempts of IB-DAS design with different approaches have been explored in the literature. In [1], the authors aimed to find the optimal installation of power splitters in order to connect all the antennas with the minimum cabling cost while satisfying each antenna power requirement to ensure the coverage. Their focus was on the horizontal design. A Mixed Integer Linear Program (MILP) is formulated and three types of constraints were identified: topology constraints, splitter installation constraints and antenna power constraints. An off-the-shelf mathematical solver (Gurobi) has been applied to optimize the design for each floor. In order to improve the time efficiency, a preprocessing was used to integrate the building layout data into the model. The optimal solution was successfully found. However, their approach is not scalable to handle large-sized buildings.

In [4], the authors tackle the problem of finding the optimal number, locations and transmitted power of antennas for each floor. Their problem involved power optimization. They formulated a multi-objective optimization to minimize the deployment cost, the power loss outside the building, and simultaneously, to maximize the capacity and the indoor coverage. Two methods were used to handle these contradicting objectives and the results were compared. The first method was a weighted sum Genetic algorithm (GA) [9], which was achieved by converting the problem to a mono-optimization problem through multiplying each individual objective function by a certain coefficient. The second method was based on the Non-dominated Sorting GA II (NSGA II). They found that NSGA II outperformed weighted sum GA for the power optimization. However, their research only focused on the location of antennas but not the connectivity of IB-DAS design as described in this paper.

A particle swarm optimization (PSO) [10] based approach was described in [6], where both the vertical and the horizontal designs were tackled. Two heuristic algorithms of generating horizontal design were applied. A PSO was applied for the vertical design. It was achieved by using the Prufer code [11] to derive a tree structure of the splitter connectivity. Their work, however, does not address some required cost factors in practical scenarios such as the power deviation of the required and supplied power for the antennas.

Another study to find the optimal antennas' locations and power was demonstrated in [12]. The output power of each antenna was determined to achieve the required coverage and avoid interference. A multi-objective optimization problem was formulated to minimize the deployment cost and power leakage, and simultaneously maximizing wireless coverage. A Simulated Annealing algorithm was proposed and its results were studied. The usefulness of the method was demonstrated, however, similar to [4], it is a limited case of IB-DAS design that is not tackling the horizontal nor the vertical designs.

In [13], the authors aimed to minimize either the total or the largest power deviation among all antennas, where an exact pseudo and full-polynomial time approximation schemes for both objectives were developed. It optimized the tree structure of the nodes connections. However, it does not consider the minimization of the equipment cost, which is also required in a practical scenario.

The authors in [5] created a software application that automates the vertical design. The objective was to minimize the cost in terms of: the total power demand required at the base station, the cost of splitters and tappers, the cost of cables and the power deviation. Similar to the previous mono-optimization approach, all the costs are combined together in a single objective as a weighted sum of all the objectives. The inputs to their software are the number of floors in the building, the base station's location, BTS power supply and the power required on each floor. They applied GA [9] along with a greedy logic to decide on the splitters and tappers locations, types and connections and demonstrated that the solution is scalable for a large number of floors. Our work extends on [5] and applies a multi-objective algorithm to handle the problem.

3   Problem Formulation

As in [5], we use V to denote the IB-DAS vertical design. It is defined by the following four parameters:

$$V = \{F, R, B, S\} \tag{1}$$

where:
 F represents the number of floors in the building,
 R_i is the power requirement on each floor i,
 $B = \{B_L, B_P\}$, defines the base station location and supplied power respectively.

The previous three parameters are the inputs of the design. However, the fourth parameter S is a set of decision variables that determines the full IB-DAS design. Namely, S is the set of configurations for the splitters/tappers and can be further defined as:

$$S = \{S_L, S_T, S_C\} \tag{2}$$

where:

S_L denotes the floor location of each splitter/tapper,

S_T denotes the types of each splitter/tapper,

$S_C = \{S_i, S_j\}$ are the list of connections for all splitters/tappers, where S_i is the source splitter, and S_j is a child splitter or a telephone room on a floor.

The cost of the vertical IB-DAS design consists of the following costs:

$E(V)$ = Total equipment cost,

$P(V)$ = The BTS power demand cost.

The total equipment cost $E(V)$ consists of cabling cost, splitters/tappers cost and the power deviation cost $N(V, i)$ of each antenna.

The equipment cost $E(V)$ can be further calculated as:

$$E(V) = \sum_{(s1,s2)\in S_c} C_c \times C_L(s1, s2) + \sum_{t\in S_t} \sum_{l\in S_L} C_s(t) \times cmp(l, t) + \sum_{i\in F} N(V, i) \tag{3}$$

where:

C_c is the cable unit cost per meter, $C_L(s1, s2)$ is the cabling length, i.e. the distance between s_1 and s_2 in meter, $C_s(t)$Cost of a splitter/tapper of type t, $cmp(l, t)$ is a binary function that determines whether a component of type t is placed at location l, $N(V,i)$ is the power deviation at each floor i, calculated by the difference between the supplied and the required power of a telephone room at floor i.

The BTS power demand cost is calculated as:

$$P(V) = \max_{i\in F}(R_i + L_i) \tag{4}$$

where:

L_i is the signal loss on the connectivity route from the BTS to floor i.

L_i is calculated as:

$$L_i = \sum_{(s1,s2)\in S_c} OnRte(s1, s2, i) \times C_L(s1, s2) \times L_c + \sum_{(s1,s2)\in S_c} OnRte(s1, s2, i) \times cLoss(s1, s2) \tag{5}$$

where:

L_c denotes the signal loss in dBm of one meter of cable, $OnRte(s1, s2, i)$ is a binary function that indicates whether the route to floor i goes through the link $(s1, s2)$, $cLoss(s1, s2)$ is a binary function that represents the signal loss caused by the equipment at location s1 on the link $(s1, s2)$.

4   Optimization Model

In this section, a tree structure to represent an IB-DAS design is described. It also provides the devised NSGA II algorithm that uses this solution representation and evolves a Pareto set of designs.

4.1   A Solution Representation for IB-DAS

Given the total number of floors in the building F, the location of the base station and supplied power B and the power requirement R of each floor, the IB-DAS vertical design V of splitters and tappers configuration S is determined [5]. A solution $x = \{x_1, x_2, ..., x_n\}$ is represented as a string of integers where each integer represents a node in the tree. This node could be a leaf node or a parent node depending on its connections in the tree. The value of each integer corresponds to the parent node of this node, where -1 indicates that the parent node is the base station (BTS), (i.e. this node is directly connected to the BTS). Accordingly, tracing the connections from each node should eventually lead to -1. Figure 2 shows an example of a possible solution structure for 8 floors building. Nodes 1 to 8 are leaf nodes representing the floors. Other positive integer nodes (9, 10, 11 and 12) are parent nodes. -1 represents the root node which is the BTS. The possible connections are constrained by the given set of splitter types (i.e. 2-way, 3-way, 4-way and 6-way). Each type is determined by the number of its output ports. As can be seen in Fig. 2, two of 3-way splitters and three of 2-way splitters are used in this example. Generating this tree structure will determine the type of splitters/tappers and their connections. However, their locations still need to be determined. This is achieved by using greedy logics that test all the possibilities of floor location (i.e. 1st floor to 8th floor in this case) and select the one that minimizes the cabling cost.

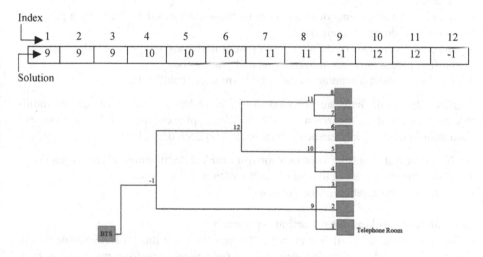

Fig. 2. An output of the vertical design: integer string and its tree representation.

4.2   NSGA II Approach to Solving the Problem

As mentioned earlier, NSGA II is one of the popular Multi-objective optimization algorithms, proposed as an extension to Genetic Algorithms to explicitly handle multiple objectives. The following is the pseudocode of the derived NSGA II (calculation details are provided in the next subsections):

1. Generate an initial parent population P_t ($t = 0$ initially) randomly, that consists of N solutions.
2. Apply a non-dominated sorting [7] to determine the non-dominated set (front rank: F_n) that each solution belongs to.
3. Calculate the crowding distance value (C_d) [7] to every solution for each front, according to the objectives of the problem.
4. Evaluate solutions according to F_n and C_d.
5. Build a breeding pool by selecting N solutions from P_t.
6. Perform crossover and mutation operators on the breeding pool to generate an offspring population Q_t of size N.
7. Create a combined population $R_t = P_t \cup Q_t$ of size $2N$.
8. Re-calculate F_n and C_d for the combined population R_t, and sort R_t accordingly.
9. Select the top distinct N solutions (best ones) to create the new population P_{t+1}.
10. Go back to step 2, and repeat the steps until the maximum number of generations is reached.

Similar to [5], the customized crossover and mutation operators had to be implemented in order to maintain the tree structure, where a one-point crossover and 5 different mutation operators were designed. They involved:

a. *Swap* – where parents of two randomly chosen nodes are swapped.
b. *Move1* – where parent of a randomly chosen node is replaced by a parent of another randomly chosen node.
c. *Move2* – where parents of two randomly chosen nodes are replaced by a parent of another randomly chosen node.
d. *Merge* – where two randomly chosen parent nodes are merged, i.e., all children of the first parent node are moved to second parent node.
e. *Random* – inject a random solution with small probability P_r.

More details of these are provided in [5]. Here however we focus on the multi-objective aspect of the algorithm. To successfully implement the NSGA II and achieve good solutions, three key elements need to be considered carefully:

A. Non-dominated sorting approach for front rank determination of each solution.
B. Crowding distance calculation of each solution.
C. Diversity preservation in the population.

Element A: Non-dominated Sorting Approach
A fast-non-dominated sorting approach [7] was applied for this IB-DAS problem. The objective is to find the non-domination level (non-dominated front rank: F_n) of each solution and sort the solutions accordingly. This will order the solutions from best to worst, where a lower front rank indicates a better solution. This is an important step before the selection process of the algorithm. In addition, the design options that are provided to the decision-maker/planner at the end of the algorithm are the elements of the first non-dominated set of the last generation.

Two important parameters are required to find the non-domination level of each solution. The first one is the domination count N_P, which represents the number of solutions dominating solution P. The second counter is S_P, which indicates the number of solutions dominated by solution P and they are listed in Q_P list. Solution (a) is considered to be dominating solution (b) if and only if, it was not worse than (b) for all objectives, and it is strictly better in at least one objective. According to this definition, N_P and S_P counters are calculated for all of the solutions. Any solution that has a domination count (N_P) equals to zero, will belong to the first non-dominated set. For each solution P in the first non-dominated, Q_P list will be re-visited, and its domination count will be decreased by 1. In addition, if the domination count of any solution becomes zero, it will belong to the second non-domination level. This process continues until all of the solutions are classified in their correct non-dominated fronts.

Element B: Crowding Distance Calculation

It is clear that a solution with a lower front rank is better and preferred to be selected. However, within the same non-dominated set, a solution in a less crowded region is preferred. This is to maintain the diversity to make sure the solution space is explored properly. In order to determine this, crowding distance value (C_d) is calculated as follows, where a higher C_d value indicated a preferred solution.

1. Select the elements of the first non-dominated set (first front).
2. Set all their initial C_{d0} values to zero.
3. For the first objective:
   a. Sort the solutions according to the objective value from worst to best.
   b. Set the boundaries C_d values to infinity, so that they are always selected.
   c. Set t to 1.
   d. For all other points (non-boundaries), use the following equation to calculate its C_d of this iteration:

$$C_{dt} = C_{dt-1} + \frac{Ob(previous\ solution) - Ob(next\ solution)}{Ob(\text{Max}) - Ob(\text{Min})} \tag{6}$$

   where:

   Ob is the objective value of a given solution

   e. Update t by 1.
   f. Repeat steps (a) to (e) for all other objectives.
4. Repeat for all other front sets.

Element C: Diversity Preservation

Due to the convergence of solutions to the Pareto-optimal set, it is desired to use some techniques to ensure that an evolutionary algorithm is maintaining a good spread of solutions in that set. These techniques are applied in steps 5 and 9 of the NSGA II pseudocode. We perform a random permutation of solutions in step 5 to create the breeding pool rather than using normal GA solution operators such as tournament or truncation selection. Since selection pressure is again applied in step 9 with a version of truncation solution [9], by simply applying permutation in 5 would maintain the number of unique solutions for longer. In step 9, the selection process commences again for the combined old and new population and since the combined population is already sorted the solutions are selected from top to bottom as per truncation selection strategy. However, before adding the solutions in the next population, they are compared to all of the already selected ones. A certain solution will be added to the new population if it was distinct from all of the previously added solutions. This will further maintain the diversity in the population.

5 Experimental Results

Experiments were performed with four different floor configurations: 12 floors, 25 floors, 48 floors and 60 floors. They were also designed to test different aspects of implemented algorithms, and divided into three parts:

1. Pareto-optimal front representation.
2. Comparison of NSGA II vs. GA.
3. Run time analysis of NSGA II.

5.1 Pareto-Optimal Front Representation

First, experiments were conducted to find the best parameters settings for NSGA II. The parameters and probabilities were set empirically, by performing multiple experiments and choosing the ones that provide best solution. Using this approach, the population size for NSGA II was set to $c \times l$, where l is the length of the solution string and c is a parameter that was set to 6. The solution length l is calculated as $l = (F \times 2) - 1$, which defines the maximum number of possible nodes in the tree with F floors. The maximum generation was set to $b \times l$ and b was fixed to 3. The crossover probability, pc, was set to 0.6 and the mutation probability, pm, was also set to 0.6. The probability to inject occasional random solution, pr, was set to 0.001.

A plot of the solution set provided by our multi-objective model, for 48 floors building is shown in Fig. 3. It represents the set of Pareto-optimal front solutions of the final generation. The typical behavior of the set of solutions in the figure verifies that the fronts calculation was achieved correctly. In addition, this graph gives a visual representation of the possible costs in relations to both objectives, making it simpler for the decision-makers to choose a unique solution that suits their requirement.

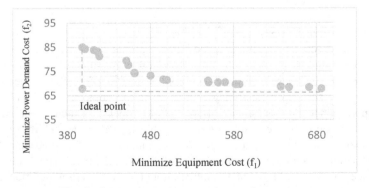

Fig. 3. Power demand cost against equipment cost.

To illustrate the presentation of multiple designs in Pareto front further, Fig. 4 shows a visual representation of the design generated by NSGA II. 12 floors configuration is selected due to the space constraint. Three designs from the Pareto-optimal front set are shown to illustrate the transition and the variations in the design. The three selected points are the extreme corner points (Fig. 4a and c), and the nearest point to the ideal point (Fig. 4b). The equipment costs are 98.4, 68.9 and 57.5 for Fig. 4a, b and c respectively and they are "decreasing". However, the power demand costs are 31.6, 32.7 and 38.7 for Fig. 4a, b and c respectively and they are "increasing". Depending on the preference of decision makers/planners, if they want to obtain the cheapest power demand cost, they can choose Fig. 4a design. However, if they need the lowest equipment cost, they can choose Fig. 4c design, which clearly uses a smaller number of splitters and less cables. The variety in the design options is exactly the desired purpose of using a multi-objective evolutionary algorithm. It is a perfect fit for our application where the requirement was to produce multiple designs with different extremes.

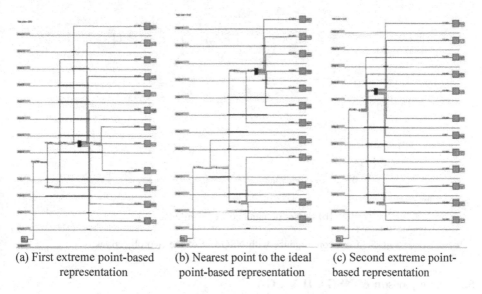

| (a) First extreme point-based representation | (b) Nearest point to the ideal point-based representation | (c) Second extreme point-based representation |

Fig. 4. Vertical design options of IB-DAS.

Table 1. Individual cost comparison of the two approaches.

Floors	Avg GA		NSGA II	
	F_1	F_2	F_1	F_2
12	56.0394	40.9683	59.5	34.7
25	109.74	42.6517	128.7	42.3
48	292.944	85.6917	401.7	84.3
60	650.017	126.433	790.2	124.3

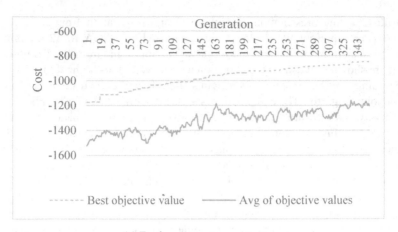

(a) Equipment cost convergence

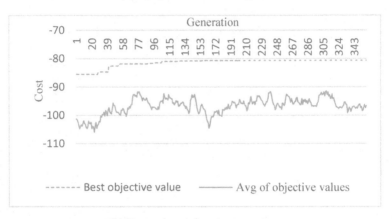

(b) Power demand cost convergence

Fig. 5. Cost convergence with NSGA II of the two objectives.

5.2 Comparison of NSGA II Vs. GA

The results were also compared against weighted sum GA approach results described in [5] for the different floors configurations. Since NSGA II provides multiple solutions in a Pareto set, a certain point should be selected for the comparison with GA. In our case, the *ideal* point [14, 15] was found and plotted in Fig. 3. An ideal point is a point with the minimum value of the Pareto front at each objective. The distance of all of Pareto front solutions to the ideal point was calculated. After that, the nearest point to the ideal was selected for the comparison. Table 1 shows the average GA solutions against NSGA II selected solutions for the different floors' configurations. F_1 and F_2 represent the first and the second objectives, which are the equipment cost and the power demand cost respectively. It can be seen that NSGA II was consistently able to save demand power with the solution closer to the ideal point. It is important to note that the selected solution is not the extreme solution for any of the objectives but simply one of the solutions within Pareto-set. However, analysis of the extreme solution in Pareto-set shows that NSGAII can come up with solutions that cannot be generated by GA, such as those which maximize one objective in the expense of another, while GA would always find a middle ground.

5.3   Run Time Analysis of NSGA II

Typical run time behaviors of NSGA II are shown in Fig. 5a and b. Each one shows how the objective evolves as generation progresses. For each objective, the best objective values found (in dashed line) against the average value of that objective in the population are plotted for each generation. This is achieved for a typical evolution to reach the near-optimal solutions for a 60-floor building. To show the objective value increasing over time, the cost has been multiplied by -1. It can be noticed that both maximum and average values increase as generation progresses. Furthermore, the diversity in the population is also maintained as the average objective line stays further away from the best solutions line. This helps in keeping the new solution found in better fronts.

6   Conclusion and Future Work

In this paper, an optimization model using NSGA II to solve the IB-DAS design problem was presented. The formulation of the problem was described, and the steps of the algorithm were explained. Results comparison with a previous GA-based approach [5] was also provided. It was demonstrated that the conversion from a single-objective approach to a multi-objective approach provides a set of options among the different trade-off solutions to the decision-maker which is beneficial. In fact, this was the motivation for this work inspired by the real-world requirement of our partners. Moreover, for the different configurations of the floors, it was found that NSGA II optimized consistently the desired objective of power demand cost. Results show that NSGA II was capable of solving the problem and providing multiple design options. The proposed algorithm is scalable and can accommodate high rise buildings. It can potentially be extended to solve the horizontal design problem. Finally, other advanced multi-objective evolutionary algorithms such as MOGA will be further investigated, to see if better results can be obtained.

References

1. Chen, L., Yuan, D., Song, H., Zhang, J.: Mathematical modeling for optimal deployment of in-building Distributed Antenna Systems. In: 1st IEEE International Conference on Communications in China (ICCC) (2012). https://doi.org/10.1109/iccchina.2012.6356992
2. Cisco Vision: 5G - Thriving Indoors Whitepaper. https://www.cisco.com/c/dam/en/us/solutions/collateral/service-provider/ultra-services-platform/5g-ran-indoor.pdf. Accessed 29 June 2019

3. Yang, C., Shao, H.: WiFi-based indoor positioning. IEEE Commun. Mag. **53**(3), 150–157 (2015). https://doi.org/10.1109/mcom.2015.7060497
4. Atawia, R., Ashour, M., El Shabrawy, T., Hammad, H.: Indoor distributed antenna system planning with optimized antenna power using genetic algorithm. In: 78th IEEE Conference on Vehicular Technology, Las Vegas (2013). https://doi.org/10.1109/vtcfall.2013.6692238
5. Shakya, S., Poon, K., Ouali, A.: A GA based network optimization tool for passive in-building distributed antenna systems. In: Proceedings of the Genetic and Evolutionary Computation Conference, GECCO (2018). https://doi.org/10.1145/3205455.3205640
6. Atia, D.Y., Ruta, D., Poon, K., Ouali, A., Isakovic, F.: Cost effective, scalable design of indoor distributed antenna systems based on particle swarm optimization and prufer strings. In: IEEE Congress on Evolutionary Computation (CEC), Vancouver, pp. 4159–4166 (2016). https://doi.org/10.1109/cec.2016.7744318
7. Deb, K., Pratap, A., Agarwal, S., Meyarivan, T.: A fast and elitist multi-objective genetic algorithm: NSGA-II. IEEE Trans. Evol. Comput. **6**(2), 182–197 (2002). https://doi.org/10.1109/4235.996017
8. Kannan, S., Baskar, S., McCalley, J.D., Murugan, P.: Application of NSGA-II algorithm to generation expansion planning. IEEE Trans. Power Syst. **24**(1), 454–461 (2009). https://doi.org/10.1109/TPWRS.2008.2004737
9. Goldberg, D.: Genetic Algorithms in Search Optimization and Machine Learning. Addison-Wesley, Reading (1989)
10. Zhou, L.P., Li, B.R., Wang, F.C.: Particle swarm optimization model of distributed network planning. J. Netw. **8**(10), 2263–2269 (2013). https://doi.org/10.4304/jnw.8.10.2263-2268
11. Julstrom, B.A.: Quick decoding and encoding of prufer strings: exercises in data structures. Department of Computer Science, St. Cloud State University (2005). http://citeseer.ist.psu.edu/326681.html
12. Atawia, R., Ashour, M., El Shabrawy, T., Hammad, H.: Optimized transmitted antenna power indoor planning using distributed antenna systems. In: Proceedings of 9th Wireless Communications Mobile Computing Conference, pp. 993–1000 (2013). https://doi.org/10.1109/iwcmc.2013.6583692
13. Adjiashvili, D., Bosio, S., Li, Y., Yuan, D.: Exact and approximation algorithms for optimal equipment selection in deploying in-building distributed antenna systems. IEEE Trans. Mob. Comput. **14**(4), 702–713 (2014). 10.1109/tmc.2014.2331976
14. Miettinen, K.M.: Nonlinear Multiobjective Optimization. International Series in Operation Research and Management Science. Kluwer Academic Publisher, New York (1998)
15. Blasco, X., Herrero, J.M., Sanchis, J., Martínez, M.: New graphical visualization of n-dimensional Pareto front for decision-making in multi-objective optimization. Inf. Sci. **178**(20), 3908–3924 (2008). https://doi.org/10.1016/j.ins.2008.06.010

Machine Learning for Time Series Data

Investigation of Machine Learning Techniques in Forecasting of Blood Pressure Time Series Data

Shamsul Masum, John P. Chiverton$^{(\boxtimes)}$, Ying Liu, and Branislav Vuksanovic

University of Portsmouth, Portsmouth, UK
shamsul.masum@myport.ac.uk, john.chiverton@port.ac.uk

Abstract. The aim of this paper is to investigate different machine learning based forecasting techniques for forecasting of blood pressure and heart rate. Forecasting of blood pressure could potentially help a clinician to take preventative steps even before dangerous medical situations occur. This paper examines forecasting blood pressure 30 min in advance. Univariate and multivariate forecast models are considered. Different forecast strategies are also considered. To compare different forecast strategies, LSTM and BI-LSTM machine learning algorithms were included. Then univariate and multivariate LSTM, BI-LSTM and CNN machine learning algorithms were compared using the two best forecasting strategies. Comparative analysis between forecasting strategies suggest that MIMO and DIRMO forecast strategies provide the best accuracy in forecasting physiological time series data. Results also appear to show that multivariate forecast models for blood pressure and heart rate are more reliable compared to blood pressure alone. Comparative analysis between MIMO and DIRMO forecasting strategies appear to show that DIRMO is more reliable for both univariate and multivariate cases. Results also appear to show that the forecast model that uses BI-LSTM with the DIRMO strategy is the best overall.

Keywords: Time series forecasting · Univariate data · Multivariate data · Forecast strategies · LSTM · BI-LSTM · CNN · Blood pressure · Heart rate

1 Introduction

Long-term time series forecasting of physiological data could potentially help health care professionals to predict and perhaps even prevent needing to treat patients based on their diagnosis. Forecasting physiological data 30 min in advance could potentially help a health care professional in this way. For instance, for general decision making or possibly intervening dangerous clinical events such as hypotensive events [22]. However, physiological times series analysis has been mostly conducted on event prediction thus limited to short-term and single-step prediction [5,17,36,39]. Most of these works directly map

© Springer Nature Switzerland AG 2019
M. Bramer and M. Petridis (Eds.): SGAI-AI 2019, LNAI 11927, pp. 269–282, 2019.
https://doi.org/10.1007/978-3-030-34885-4_21

input physiological signals to output values. Moreover, they are unable to model the underlying temporal dependencies in time series, such as those present in physiological data dynamics. These works have difficulty in modelling contextual information and sequential measurements simultaneously. This results in a decay in accuracy over time and requires frequent re-calibration. There is a very limited number of works that actually perform forecasting on continuous values of physiological data. In contrast to this, continuous monitoring is often a crucial part of clinical decision making. Examples could potentially include glucose monitoring [32] and EEG monitoring in the ICU [43].

Forecasting across multi-step and for a long-term horizon is very challenging [3,7,29]. Also, the literature that forecasts physiological time series data does not usually consider different forecast strategies [8,23,24]. This can be an important consideration [29,30]. Taieb et al. described different forecast strategies and showed that forecast strategies play a vital role in long-term forecasting scenario [42]. Comparison of different forecast strategies can help to show which strategy is best for the forecast model. This is therefore a consideration here, particularly for the case of physiological time series data.

Forecasting with univariate and multivariate time series data has been a great consideration for researchers in forecasting for many years. Preez and Witt compared univariate and multivariate time series data in forecasting international tourism demand and found forecasting based on univariate time series data outperforms multivariate data [10]. Aboagye-Sarfo et al. found multivariate time series data outperformed univariate time series data in forecasting emergency department demand [2].

However, such comparisons are lacking when considering physiological data. Billis and Bamidis forecast artificial univariate blood pressure time series data [8] thus missing the multivariate comparison. Li et al. forecast blood pressure (BP) with multivariate data [24] but did not compare the results with the univariate case. Li et al. considered a number of different machine learning techniques, combined with a Contextual Layer. This enabled relative constants, such as BMI to be included at a different point in learning process. Lee and Mark performed forecasting of 30 min continuous mean arterial blood pressure (MAP) values. They used multivariate physiological time series [23]. Their work included age and medication information as well. However they did not compare against univariate physiological time series performance or forecast strategy. In more recent work, Su et al. [41] predicted Systolic BP and Diastolic BP sequences using a multi-layer BI-LSTM network. They used a univariate BP dataset extracted from 84 and 12 healthy people. It would be of interest to compare univariate and multivariate approaches in time series forecasting of blood pressure. Forecast strategy is also another important consideration. It is therefore of interest to explore whether an additional vital sign such as Heart Rate (HR) could improve the forecast accuracy of the response variable or perhaps only the past data of the response variable is good enough in forecasting.

There are quite a wide range of machine learning algorithms. This includes Naive Bayes [25], Support Vector Machines [34], Support Vector Regression [40],

Gradient Boosted Regression Tree [11], Factorisation Machine [35] and Multi-layer Perceptrons. They can be applied to time series forecasting of blood pressure but they are not specifically designed to deal with temporal data. On the other hand, it was also discovered that machine learning based sequential techniques are well suited for such problems [4,13,20]. Examples include Gaussian Processes (GP)s, Hidden Markov Models (HMM)s, Conditional Random Fields (CRF)s. Unfortunately they are unable to handle long-term dependencies. A bit more recent development has been Long-Short-Term-Memory (LSTM) and Bidirectional- LSTMs (BI-LSTM). These are based on Recurrent Neural Networks (RNN)s. They have gained attention for time series forecasting in different fields. This has included traffic speed prediction [27], solar power forecasting [12], electric load forecasting [30] and natural language processing [44]. LSTMs and BI-LSTMs have also been applied to medical time series data. Lipton et al. used LSTM networks to assign diagnostic information learned using multivariate time series of clinical measurements [26]. Nguyen et al. used both LSTMs and BI-LSTMs to predict mortality outcomes of patients in Intensive Care Units (ICU)s by modelling physiological time-series data [33]. Zhu et al. considered supervised BI-LSTM RNNs to predict ICU mortality [45].

Convolutional Neural Networks (CNN)s have been used for time series forecasting. Applications have included ECG classification [19], structural health monitoring [1] and motor-fault detection [15]. These techniques were found to be effective in capturing long term dependencies and the nonlinear dynamics especially in comparison to classical machine learning algorithms. However, typically, they are used to perform classification rather than actual forecasting of physiological data. Time series can also be used in combination with e.g regression to forecast future values of the physiological state of a patient. However, to the best of the authors' knowledge relatively few works actually consider this.

In contrast, time series forecasting of physiological data for both BP and HR is considered 30 min in advance. This paper compares different forecast strategies in order to identify the best strategy. Following this, to compare univariate and multivariate approaches, forecast models with LSTM, BI-LSTM and CNN algorithms are compared. The two best performing forecast strategies, Multiple Input Multiple Output (MIMO) and DIRMO are also included. These forecast models are used to forecast blood pressure 30 min in advance for both univariate (i.e. BP) and multivariate (i.e. BP and HR) cases.

2 Forecasting Strategies

Taieb et al. [42] compared five forecast strategies: recursive strategy, Direct strategy, DirRec strategy, MIMO strategy and DIRMO strategy. They applied their work to neural network based time series modelling consisting of cash machine withdrawals. The same set of strategies are also considered here but with application to physiological time series forecasting. The details of each strategy and their differences can be seen in e.g. [42]. Among these strategies, MIMO strategy produces multiple outputs from a single-step forecast. All the other strategies need to be performed in multiple steps to forecast multiple outputs.

3   Machine Learning Algorithms

Three machine learning algorithms are considered here.

Long-Short-Term-Memory (LSTM) was introduced by Hochreiter and Schmidhuber [14] in 1997. LSTMs are able to learn long-term dependencies better than the simpler Recurrent Neural Network (RNN) architecture. In theory, an RNN appears to pass some potentially useful properties for long-term forecasting. Perhaps it is even capable of handling long-term dependencies [16]. In practice, however, these characteristics do not hold as shown by Bengio et al. [6]. The motivation behind developing the LSTM was to remove the vanishing gradient issues that occur with RNNs when processing long-term dependencies. The standard RNN consists of a chain of repeating modules of the neural network, where each module consists of a single hyperbolic tangent layer structure. This can be compared with the LSTM module structure. It is relatively more complex where each module consists of four layers rather than a single layer as for an RNN module. LSTM modules or memory blocks consist of an input gate, a forget gate, an output gate and the cell state. All these layers interact in a particular way, see e.g. [30] for more details. Information that will be added or removed to the cell state is controlled by three gates. Different combinations of these gates can be used for the memory cells to deal with data with a longer horizon.

Bidirectional Long-Short-Term-Memory (BI-LSTM) shares some similarities in terms of the mechanisms as a bidirectional RNN [38] where the data sequence is fed in both forward and backward directions using two separate hidden layers. These are then connected to an output layer. The typical unrolled architecture of a bidirectional LSTM consists of a forward LSTM layer and a backward LSTM layer. The forward layer output sequence is calculated using inputs in a forward sequence from time $t - n$ to time $t - 1$. The backward layer output sequence is calculated using the reversed sequence from time $t - 1$ to $t - n$. Outputs of both layers are calculated by using the standard LSTM equations [30]. An output vector Y_n is generated from forward and backward LSTM layers using $Y_n = \sigma(h_n, h_n)$ where, n is the time step, σ is a function used to combine the outputs of forward and backward LSTM layer. It can be a concatenating function, a summation function, an average function or a multiplication function. Concatenate is considered here for the model.

Convolutional Neural Networks are feed-forward artificial neural networks consisting of alternating convolutional and sub-sampling layers, comparable with simple and complex cells in the human visual cortex. CNNs can be considered to mimic the human visual system and have achieved state-of-the-art performance with recognising patterns, structures and other functions such as tracking [21]. CNNs were primarily developed for 2D signals but recently 1D CNNs have been used for applications such as ECG classification [19], structural health monitoring [1] and motor-fault detection [15]. 1D CNNs have a very simple structure and can be trained with a limited amount of data compared to 2D CNNs.

CNNs are a very good candidate in time series forecasting because of the filter feature extraction and composition ability. CNNs are also easier to train in comparison to RNNs because CNNs use convolution operations as opposed to recursion. The sliding window approach used with RNNs could also be used to train CNNs for time series forecasting.

4 Methodology

Time series forecast analyses on physiological data sets (BP and HR) are performed with 10 forecast models by combining two machine learning algorithms each with five forecast strategies. This has been considered to find the best forecast strategy in physiological time series forecasting. Following this, time series forecasting on physiological data sets are performed to find the best approach between univariate and multivariate data. Here, 12 forecast models are considered by combining three machine learning algorithms, two forecast strategies each implemented for both the univariate and multivariate cases. Forecast performance of all models in forecasting blood pressure are compared.

4.1 Data Set

The MIMIC II database is a freely accessible critical care database which consists of various vital sign information. Patients' data were collected from a variety of ICUs in Beth Israel Deaconess Medical Center in Boston, Massachusetts [37]. Advantages of using the MIMIC II database is that all data are anonymized and open to researchers. For this paper, minute by minute MAP and heart rate time series data of 30 patients have been extracted. Experimental data sets were selected from the hypotension group of an ICD-9 code. The MAP is a measure of blood pressure [28] which is calculated from systolic and diastolic pressure following the Eq. 1.

$$MAP = [2(DP) + SP]/3 \tag{1}$$

During the data selection procedure here, it was ensured that there were no missing values in the selected time series. Moreover, length of the time series data of each data set are variable. The time series were scaled to values between -1 and 1, this is because LSTM and BI-LSTM algorithms require data to be within the scale of the activation function of the network [31].

Supervised learning is very common in practical machine learning. In supervised learning, a machine learning algorithm is used to learn the mapping function between the input variables (X) and output variables (Y). The aim is to teach the model well during the training process so that for a new input data (X), the model can predict the output variables (Y) for that data. To undertake supervised learning, a time series data set needs to be processed to a form that can be used in a supervised training process. Extracted time series data has been used to create samples for the prediction models. Each sample consisted of two-time intervals; observation window (X) and target window (Y) achieved through the sliding window method, see e.g. [9] for more details. The observation window is also known as the input and its size in the sample depends on the user-defined sequence (for this work 30 min observation window is considered). The target window is known as the output and its size in the sample depends on the forecast strategies. For example, a forecast model with a MIMO forecast strategy to predict a 30 min window will require a 30 min target window (Y). This process was applied to all 30 patients' time series data.

Both blood pressure and heart rate are considered for the univariate case. The univariate time series data sets are converted to supervised data sets consisting of samples. The samples include an observation window (X) of 30 min of BP or HR for all strategies. However, the target window (Y) varies following different strategies. For example, the MIMO strategy requires 30 min of BP or HR as a target window whereas recursive strategy only requires 1 min of BP or HR as the target window.

The source of the multivariate data are blood pressure and heart rate time series data which are used to forecast future blood pressure. The multivariate time series data set is converted to supervised data set consist of samples. The samples consist of an observation window of 60 min which includes 30 min of BP and HR each. The 60 min of observations (X) is consistent for all strategies. However, the target window (Y) varies depending on the strategy and the response variable. For example, if BP is the response variable and MIMO is the forecast strategy then the target window requires 30 min of BP values.

4.2 Forecast Model Formulation

First, the forecast models were built to investigate the scope of forecasting strategies in forecasting physiological time series data. LSTM and BI-LSTM algorithm are used here in conjunction with the aforementioned time series forecasting strategies to build the forecast models. This gives a total of 10 forecast models to compare the forecast strategies performance on univariate physiological time series data (HR and BP). Then following the outcome of different forecast strategies, 12 forecast models were built to investigate the scope of univariate and multivariate approaches in forecasting physiological time series data. LSTMs, BI-LSTMs and CNNs are used here in conjunction with the best two forecast strategies (MIMO and DIRMO).

The forecast models with LSTM and BI-LSTM RNNs are designed here with a network structure consisting of 1 hidden layer with 10 LSTM units, then an output layer with a hyperbolic tangent activation and target window (Y) as output values which varies following the forecasting strategy. LSTM is stateful in the designed network and the network was fitted with 5 epochs. The forecast model with the CNN algorithm was designed with a network structure consisting of one convolutional hidden layer followed by a max pooling layer. The filter maps are then flattened before being interpreted by a dense layer and outputting a prediction. The output layer consisting of a tanh activation and output values equal to the target window (Y). The batch size of the networks was set to 1. The target window was varied according to the number of time steps over which a forecast was required depending on the forecasting strategy. The number of neurons in the output layer also differs depending on the forecasting strategy.

Iterative, Direct and DirRec strategies predict one step ahead at a time so one neuron is required at the output layer of the model. Whereas, MIMO and DIRMO models predict multiple points so more than one neuron is required at the output layer of the model. More specifically in MIMO, the number of neurons in the output layer is equal to the number of predictions needed in each regression. For DIRMO, the number of neurons in the output layer are calculated by dividing the number of prediction points by the number of models. The network also uses the Root Mean Squared Error (RMSE) as a loss function and the ADAM algorithm [18] as an optimiser. The parameters of the developed forecast models were not tuned and random parameters were set. This is because the experiments in this paper were not performed for a specific medical problem. Rather the main aim of the experiments was to compare the univariate and multivariate approaches along with forecast strategies and machine learning algorithms. However, parameter tuning is essential when physiological time series forecasting is applied to specific medical applications.

All models were developed using the Python ecosystem [31]. To perform forecasting using the models, each data set were split into train and test. The aim is to forecast 30 min in advance and rest of the samples were used to train the models. Samples consisting of the last 30 min of data of the data set were used for test. The test data were used for performance characterisation. In Direct, DirRec and DIRMO strategies the training data are used multiple times as these strategies require multiple models to forecast the required target window (Y). In the testing phase, the predict function of the model is called to make predictions on given input values (X). The forecasting process varies following different strategies. The Recursive and DirRec strategies use past predicted data to feed back into the model during the multi-step forecast. MIMO, DIRMO and DirectH strategies are not recursive strategies so the predicted data do not feedback to the model. The predicted value is then re-scaled to get the actual predicted output. To measure the performance of the models, the RMSE is calculated here. Using

$$\bar{e} = \sqrt{\frac{1}{m} \sum_{i=1}^{m} (y_i - \widehat{y}_i)^2}$$ where, y_i are actual values, $\widehat{y}_i$ are forecast values and m

is the number of target output data. The standard deviation of the RMSE was also calculated.

4.3   Results

The aim of all the developed models is to forecast physiological data (HR and BP) 30 min in advance. In comparing the forecast strategies, average RMSE and the RMSE standard deviation of patients following all models are shown in Fig. 1. Average RMSE and the RMSE standard deviation of patients following all models are shown in Fig. 2 in comparing the univariate and multivariate approaches. To compare DIRMO and MIMO based strategies in detail, average RMSE and the RMSE standard deviation of patients of univariate and multivariate approaches are also plotted in Fig. 3.

Comparison of Forecast Strategies. To compare forecast strategies, the performance of the 10 different forecast models was assessed by forecasting HR and BP. Average RMSE and the RMSE standard deviation of patients following forecast models combining LSTM and BI-LSTM algorithm along with all aforementioned strategies are shown in Fig. 1 in comparing the forecast strategies. It can be observed that the MIMO and DIRMO forecast strategies appear to exhibit lower RMSE forecast performance. Traditional strategies like Recursive, Direct and DirRec forecast performance were poor compared to MIMO and DIRMO strategy in forecasting both Blood Pressure and Heart Rate. Following the outcome, MIMO and DIRMO forecast strategies were considered in this paper to develop forecast models for different other comparison scenarios.

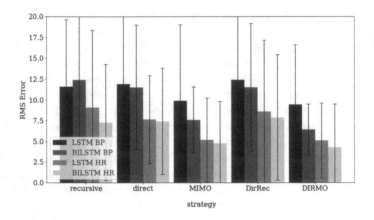

Fig. 1. Performance of forecast models with different forecast strategies in forecasting Blood Pressure (BP) and Heart Rate (HR) 30 min in advance.

Comparison of Forecasting with Univariate and Multivariate Data. Twelve forecast models have been tested combining 3 machine learning algorithms and 2 forecast strategies, covering both univariate and multivariate techniques. Average RMSE and the RMSE standard deviation from all patients are taken into consideration and are shown in Fig. 2. Careful observation of the average RMSE and the RMSE standard deviation of all patients appears to show that the multivariate approach outperforms the univariate approach in all forecast scenario. So overall it appears that multivariate techniques can provide better performance in forecasting blood pressure 30 min in advance compared to univariate techniques.

The comparison shown in Fig. 2 includes the results for the DIRMO and MIMO forecasting strategies. The results are shown differently in Fig. 3 to enable easier comparison between these two strategies. These show that DIRMO forecasting strategy provides lower RMSE and less standard deviation in comparison to MIMO forecasting in all scenarios. Thus, it can be tentatively concluded that DIRMO forecasting performs better than MIMO based forecasting in forecasting blood pressure 30 min in advance.

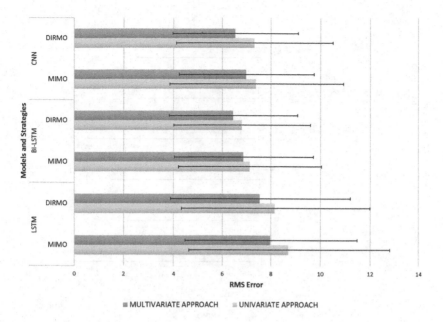

Fig. 2. Comparison of univariate and multivariate cases considering the average RMSE and standard deviation of all patients

Best Forecasting Model can be considered given these empirical results seen here. It is observable in Fig. 2 that the forecast model with the BI-LSTM algorithm outperforms the CNN and LSTM algorithms. From Fig. 2 it is also observable that the forecasting model with the BI-LSTM algorithm along with a DIRMO strategy and multivariate configurations performs best. Moreover, in Figs. 2 and 3 it appears that the forecast model with the BI-LSTM algorithm outperforms the models with the CNN and LSTM algorithms. This is true for both the univariate and multivariate approaches. Overall, it can therefore be tentatively concluded that BI-LSTM forecasting using DIRMO strategy is the best model. Furthermore the multivariate case seems to enhance the results even further.

So far only a single forecast horizon has been considered for all forecast models. This has involved forecasting of physiological data which was 30 min. However, a further range of forecast horizons were also considered. Forecast horizon up to 2 h with intervals of 10 min were also considered for forecasting BP with the multivariate data. The forecasting error across this range is shown in Fig. 4 for the best forecast model (BI-LSTM algorithm, DIRMO strategy, multivariate data). It is observable that, as the forecast horizon increases, the RMSE increases. Furthermore, from 60 to 120 min the RMSE increases linearly.

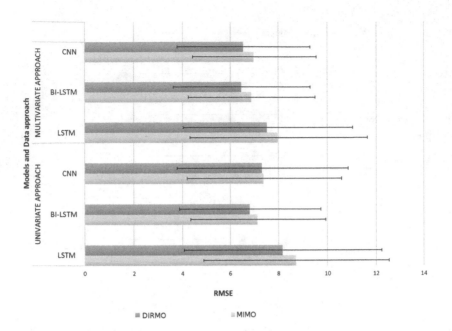

Fig. 3. Comparison of DIRMO and MIMO forecasting strategies considering using RMSE and standard deviation of all patients.

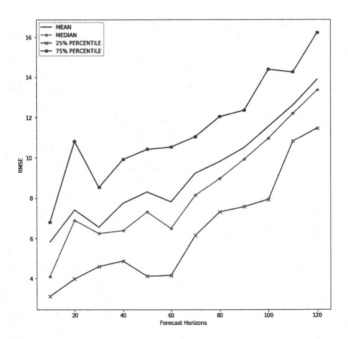

Fig. 4. RMSE of forecasting of blood pressure for different forecast horizons using BI-LSTM with DIRMO strategy with multivariate data.

5   Discussion

Analysis of different forecast strategies can help in the selection of the best forecast strategy. This is important when building a forecast model for a particular application such as for forecasting of physiological data. The results appear to suggest the best performing strategy is DIRMO. This appears to be in agreement with the work of Taieb et al. [42]. There, various different types of MIMO and DIRMO were compared along with DIR, REC and DIRREC forecasting strategies. There DIRMO was also found to outperform MIMO but not in all cases: only when no input selection had taken place which is also the case here. Multivariate forecasting with machine learning algorithms and forecast strategies in forecasting of blood pressure might also have another potential advantage. The inter-relationship between blood pressure and heart rate can also be considered. The dependency between the time series on each other is implicitly modelled here for the multivariate approaches. This has resulted in improved forecast accuracy in forecasting blood pressure. Lee and Mark in [23] also made use of HR and BP. They also included a number of different manually derived measures derived from either BP, HR or a combination of both. However they did not provide any comparison with forecasting for the univariate case. Their investigation also only considered a single forecast strategy and machine learning model. The multivariate approach presented here, which uses the BI-LSTM algorithm and DIRMO forecast strategy has proved to be the best model in forecasting blood pressure 30 min in advance. Such modelling might be a useful technique which could potentially help health care professionals in planning, decision making and predicting the event.

The multivariate approach provides insight into the dynamic relationships of the used variables but in such cases, more variables, data points and data sets are required. Data points of all variables need to be measured at the same time period and this is the subject of ongoing work.

6   Conclusions

The results shown here appear to demonstrate that multivariate time series modelling is more reliable in forecasting blood pressure 30 min in advance. The multivariate approach along with a BI-LSTM algorithm and DIRMO strategy provide more accurate forecasting performance. This is in comparison to the univariate approaches and the other machine learning algorithms and forecast strategies. It is also observed that the BI-LSTM algorithm with a DIRMO strategy provides the smallest standard deviation which makes this combination favourable for forecasting blood pressure. Overall, the comparison of forecast strategies and data approaches contributes to improving the current techniques in the applied forecasting and machine learning literature.

References

1. Abdeljaber, O., Avci, O., Kiranyaz, S., Gabbouj, M., Inman, D.J.: Real-time vibration-based structural damage detection using one-dimensional convolutional neural networks. J. Sound Vib. **388**, 154–170 (2017)
2. Aboagye-Sarfo, P., Mai, Q., Sanfilippo, F.M., Preen, D.B., Stewart, L.M., Fatovich, D.M.: A comparison of multivariate and univariate time series approaches to modelling and forecasting emergency department demand in western australia. J. Biomed. Inform. **57**, 62–73 (2015)
3. Ahmed, N.K., Atiya, A.F., Gayar, N.E., El-Shishiny, H.: An empirical comparison of machine learning models for time series forecasting. Econ. Rev. **29**(5–6), 594–621 (2010)
4. Baccouche, M., Mamalet, F., Wolf, C., Garcia, C., Baskurt, A.: Sequential deep learning for human action recognition. In: Salah, A.A., Lepri, B. (eds.) HBU 2011. LNCS, vol. 7065, pp. 29–39. Springer, Heidelberg (2011). https://doi.org/10.1007/978-3-642-25446-8_4
5. Bassale, J.: Hypotension prediction arterial blood pressure variability. Technical report (2001)
6. Bengio, Y., Simard, P., Frasconi, P., et al.: Learning long-term dependencies with gradient descent is difficult. IEEE Trans. Neural Netw. **5**(2), 157–166 (1994)
7. Berardi, V.L., Zhang, G.P.: An empirical investigation of bias and variance in time series forecasting: modeling considerations and error evaluation. IEEE Trans. Neural Netw. **14**(3), 668–679 (2003)
8. Billis, A., Bamidis, P.D.: Employing time-series forecasting to historical medical data: an application towards early prognosis within elderly health monitoring environments. In: AI-AM/NetMed ECAI, pp. 31–35 (2014)
9. Dietterich, T.G.: Machine learning for sequential data: a review. In: Caelli, T., Amin, A., Duin, R.P.W., de Ridder, D., Kamel, M. (eds.) SSPR/SPR 2002. LNCS, vol. 2396, pp. 15–30. Springer, Heidelberg (2002). https://doi.org/10.1007/3-540-70659-3_2
10. Du Preez, J., Witt, S.F.: Univariate versus multivariate time series forecasting: an application to international tourism demand. Int. J. Forecast. **19**(3), 435–451 (2003)
11. Friedman, J.H.: Greedy function approximation: a gradient boosting machine. Ann. Stat., 1189–1232 (2001)
12. Gensler, A., Henze, J., Sick, B., Raabe, N.: Deep learning for solar power forecasting an approach using autoencoder and LSTM neural networks. In: IEEE International Conference on Systems, Man, and Cybernetics (SMC), pp. 002858–002865 (2016)
13. Hill, T., O'Connor, M., Remus, W.: Neural network models for time series forecasts. Manag. Sci. **42**(7), 1082–1092 (1996)
14. Hochreiter, S., Schmidhuber, J.: Long short-term memory. Neural Comput. **9**(8), 1735–1780 (1997)
15. Ince, T., Kiranyaz, S., Eren, L., Askar, M., Gabbouj, M.: Real-time motor fault detection by 1-D convolutional neural networks. IEEE Trans. Ind. Electron. **63**(11), 7067–7075 (2016)
16. Jain, L.C., Medsker, L.R.: Recurrent Neural Networks: Design and Applications. CRC Press, Boca Raton (2000)
17. Janghorbani, A., Arasteh, A., Moradi, M.H.: Prediction of acute hypotension episodes using logistic regression model and support vector machine: a comparative study. In: 19th Iranian Conference on Electrical Engineering, pp. 1–4. IEEE (2011)

18. Kingma, D.P., Ba, J.: Adam: a method for stochastic optimization. In: 3rd International Conference on Learning Representations (2015)
19. Kiranyaz, S., Ince, T., Gabbouj, M.: Real-time patient-specific ECG classification by 1-D convolutional neural networks. IEEE Trans. Biomed. Eng. **63**(3), 664–675 (2016)
20. Lafferty, J., McCallum, A., Pereira, F.C.: Conditional random fields: Probabilistic models for segmenting and labeling sequence data (2001)
21. LeCun, Y., Bengio, Y., Hinton, G.: Deep learning. Nature **521**(7553), 436 (2015)
22. Lee, J., Mark, R.: A hypotensive episode predictor for intensive care based on heart rate and blood pressure time series. In: Computing in Cardiology, pp. 81–84. IEEE (2010)
23. Lee, J., Mark, R.G.: An investigation of patterns in hemodynamic data indicative of impending hypotension in intensive care. Biomed. Eng. Online **9**(1), 62 (2010)
24. Li, X., Wu, S., Wang, L.: Blood pressure prediction via recurrent models with contextual layer. In: 26th International Conference on the World Wide Web, pp. 685–693 (2017)
25. Lipton, Z.C., Berkowitz, J., Elkan, C.: A critical review of recurrent neural networks for sequence learning. arXiv preprint: arXiv:1506.00019 (2015)
26. Lipton, Z.C., Kale, D.C., Elkan, C., Wetzel, R.C.: Learning to diagnose with LSTM recurrent neural networks. In: 4th International Conference on Learning Representations (2016)
27. Ma, X., Tao, Z., Wang, Y., Yu, H., Wang, Y.: Long short-term memory neural network for traffic speed prediction using remote microwave sensor data. Transp. Res. Part C Emerg. Technol. **54**, 187–197 (2015)
28. Mann, D.L., Zipes, D.P., Libby, P., Bonow, R.O.: Braunwald's Heart Disease E-Book: A Textbook of Cardiovascular Medicine. Elsevier Health Sciences, Philadelphia (2014)
29. Masum, S., Liu, Y., Chiverton, J.: Comparative analysis of the outcomes of differing time series forecasting strategies. In: 13th International Conference on Natural Computation, Fuzzy Systems and Knowledge Discovery, pp. 1964–1968. IEEE (2017)
30. Masum, S., Liu, Y., Chiverton, J.: Multi-step time series forecasting of electric load using machine learning models. In: Rutkowski, L., Scherer, R., Korytkowski, M., Pedrycz, W., Tadeusiewicz, R., Zurada, J.M. (eds.) ICAISC 2018, Part I. LNCS (LNAI), vol. 10841, pp. 148–159. Springer, Cham (2018). https://doi.org/10.1007/978-3-319-91253-0_15
31. McKinney, W.: Python for Data Analysis: Data Wrangling with Pandas, NumPy, and IPython. O'Reilly Media, Inc., Sebastopol (2012)
32. McLachlan, K., Jenkins, A., O'Neal, D.: The role of continuous glucose monitoring in clinical decision-making in diabetes in pregnancy. Aust. N. Z. J. Obstet. Gynaecol. **47**(3), 186–190 (2007)
33. Nguyen, P., Tran, T., Venkatesh, S.: Deep learning to attend to risk in ICU. In: 2nd International Workshop on Knowledge Discovery in Healthcare Data Co-located 26th International Joint Conference on Artificial Intelligence, pp. 25–29 (2017)
34. Ongenae, F., et al.: Time series classification for the prediction of dialysis in critically ill patients using echo statenetworks. Eng. Appl. Artif. Intell. **26**(3), 984–996 (2013)
35. Rendle, S.: Factorization machines. In: IEEE International Conference on Data Mining, pp. 995–1000 (2010)

36. Rocha, T., Paredes, S., De Carvalho, P., Henriques, J.: Prediction of acute hypotensive episodes by means of neural network multi-models. Comput. Biol. Med. **41**(10), 881–890 (2011)
37. Saeed, M., Lieu, C., Raber, G., Mark, R.G.: MIMIC II: a massive temporal ICU patient database to support research in intelligent patient monitoring. In: Computers in Cardiology, pp. 641–644. IEEE (2002)
38. Schuster, M., Paliwal, K.K.: Bidirectional recurrent neural networks. IEEE Trans. Signal Process. **45**(11), 2673–2681 (1997)
39. Sideris, C., Kalantarian, H., Nemati, E., Sarrafzadeh, M.: Building continuous arterial blood pressure prediction models using recurrent networks. In: IEEE International Conference on Smart Computing, pp. 1–5 (2016)
40. Smola, A.J., Schölkopf, B.: A tutorial on support vector regression. Stat. Comput. **14**(3), 199–222 (2004)
41. Su, P., Ding, X.R., Zhang, Y.T., Liu, J., Miao, F., Zhao, N.: Long-term blood pressure prediction with deep recurrent neural networks. In: IEEE EMBS International Conference on Biomedical & Health Informatics (BHI), pp. 323–328 (2018)
42. Taieb, S.B., Bontempi, G., Atiya, A.F., Sorjamaa, A.: A review and comparison of strategies for multi-step ahead time series forecasting based on the NN5 forecasting competition. Expert Syst. Appl. **39**(8), 7067–7083 (2012)
43. Vespa, P.M., Nenov, V., Nuwer, M.R.: Continuous EEG monitoring in the intensive care unit: early findings and clinical efficacy. J. Clin. Neurophysiol. **16**(1), 1–13 (1999)
44. Zhou, P., et al.: Attention-based bidirectional long short-term memory networks for relation classification. In: 54th Annual Meeting of the Association for Computational Linguistics. Short Papers, vol. 2, pp. 207–212 (2016)
45. Zhu, Y., Fan, X., Wu, J., Liu, X., Shi, J., Wang, C.: Predicting ICU mortality by supervised bidirectional LSTM networks. In: 27th International Joint Conference on Artificial Intelligence (IJCAI 2018) (2018)

Stock Index Forecasting Using Time Series Decomposition-Based and Machine Learning Models

Dhanya Jothimani[✉] and Ayşe Başar

Data Science Lab, Ryerson University, Toronto, Canada
dhanya@ryerson.ca

Abstract. Forecasting of financial time series is challenging due to its non-linear and non-stationary characteristics. Due to limitations of traditional time series models, it is difficult to forecast financial time series such as stock price and stock index. Hence, we used ensemble of time series decomposition-based models (such as Discrete Wavelet Transform, Empirical Mode Decomposition and Variational Mode Decomposition) and machine learning models (such as Artificial Neural Network and Support Vector Regression) for forecasting the close price of 25 major stock indices for a period of 10 years ranging from January 1, 2009 to December 31, 2018. Decomposition models are used to disaggregate the time series into various subseries and machine learning models are used for forecasting each subseries. The forecasted subseries are then aggregated to obtain the final forecast. The performance of the models was evaluated using Root Mean Square Error and was validated statistically using Wilcoxon Signed Rank Test. We found that the performance of ensemble models better than traditional machine learning models.

Keywords: Financial time series · Forecasting · Non-classicial decomposition models · Stock indices

1 Introduction

Forecasting of financial time series, especially, stock price is considered to be one of the difficult tasks. This could be attributed to complex dynamics of the stock market. Several factors including socio-political events and investors' behaviour contribute to the complexity of the stock market. It is hard to predict the direction of movement of stock prices accurately, and this ultimately affects the trading decisions. Therefore, prediction of stock prices has become a popular research topic for analysts and academicians from several domains including Finance, Mathematics and Computer Science.

This research is supported in part by the following grants: NSERC CRDPJ-499983-16; OCE VIP II 26280; and TMX.

M. Bramer and M. Petridis (Eds.): SGAI-AI 2019, LNAI 11927, pp. 283–292, 2019.
https://doi.org/10.1007/978-3-030-34885-4_22

Various researchers have used various statistical and computationally intelligent models to capture and predict the stock price dynamics accurately but they are not without their own limitations [1,2]. Statistical models like AutoRegressive Moving Average (ARMA) and AutoRegressive Integrated Moving Average (ARIMA) work on the assumption that data is linear and stationary. Computationally intelligent models such as Artificial Neural Network (ANN) and Support Vector Regression (SVR) suffer from the limitations of getting stuck in local optima and are sensitive to parameters. This led to the concept of *Ensemble Models*.

Ensemble models work on the principle that use of multiple predictors over any of base predictors could improve the prediction accuracy [20]. These models can be categorized into two types, namely, pre-processing and post-processing. In pre-processing, the data is deconstructed into various components, where each component can be forecasted using same predictor or multiple predictors. Decomposition of time series can be classified here. In post-processing, selection of predictors is based on data characteristics. For instance, ARIMA and ANN are used for modelling linear and non linear data, respectively [23].

Classical decomposition model yields three components, namely, trend, seasonal and random. It has been widely used for time series analysis but it suffers from few limitations. It does not handle non-linear data quite well and it ignores random component while aggregating the forecasts of the components, thus, leading to loss of information [23]. These weaknesses led to use of few signal processing techniques like Discrete Wavelet Transform (DWT) and Empirical Mode Decomposition (EMD), Complete Ensemble Empirical Mode Decomposition with Adaptive Noise (CEEMDAN) and Variational Mode Decomposition (VMD) for decomposing time series in time-frequency domain and time domain, respectively [12,15,18]. These techniques are classified under non-classical decomposition technique. More details on the types of ensemble forecasting models can be found in Jothimani and Yadav [13].

Our study presents six ensemble forecasting models, namely, DWT-ANN, DWT-SVR, EMD-ANN, EMD-SVR, VMD-ANN and VMD-SVR models to forecast 1-step ahead close price for 25 major stock indices. In first stage, non-classical decomposition models (i.e., DWT, EMD and VMD) are used to decompose time-series into various components. In second stage, ANN and SVR are used to forecast each component. The forecasted components are then aggregated to obtain the final forecast.

The contributions of this study are two-fold. First, it demonstrates the use of ensemble model of non-classical decomposition models and machine learning algorithms for stock index forecasting. Second, it highlights the application of VMD as a data preprocessing technique and the improvement in prediction accuracy over DWT and EMD.

The organization of the paper is as follows: Non-classical decomposition models (i.e., DWT, EMD and VMD) are summarised in Sect. 2. Data and Methodology adopted in this paper are discussed in Sect. 3. Performance analysis of the models is provided in Sect. 4 followed by threats to validity in Sect. 5. Section 6 concludes the paper.

2   Non-classical Decomposition Models

2.1   Discrete Wavelet Transform

Wavelet analysis helps to analyse localized variations of signal within a time series. Both the dominant modes of variability and their variations in time by decomposing a time series into time-scale (or time-frequency) space.

Discrete Wavelet Transform (DWT) decomposes the signal in both time and frequency domain simultaneously. On the other hand, Fourier Transform decomposes the signal only in frequency domain; information related to occurrence of frequency is not captured and it eliminates the time resolution [21].

Any function $y(t)$ can be decomposed by a sequence of projections onto wavelet basis:

$$s_{J,k} = \int y(t)\Phi_{J,k}(t)dt \qquad (1)$$

$$d_{j,k} = \int y(t)\Psi_{j,k}(t)dt \qquad (2)$$

where J represents the number of multiresolution; Φ is the father wavelet and Ψ is the mother wavelet.

Among the other types of wavelets such as Haar, Daubechies, Morlet and Mexican Hat, Haar wavelets are advantageous for time series analysis since they are capable of capturing fluctuations between adjacent observations [15, 16, 19, 21].

One of the limitations of DWT is the requirement of length of the dataset to be dyadic (i.e., power of 2). Also, the output generated by DWT is highly dependent on origin of the signal being analyzed. A small shift in origin affects the outputs generated and this problem is called Circular shift. Due to circular shift, it is difficult to align the transformed signals with time. To overcome the above two limitations, a modification of DWT called Maximal Overlap Discrete Wavelet Transform (MODWT) is used. MODWT is shift invariant and is not limited by the dyadic length constraint, hence the signals are easier to interpret for time series analysis. DWT and MODWT are used interchangeably this point forward.

Practical applications of wavelets in Finance and Economics can be found in Genşay et al. [8], Ortega and Khashanah [21] and Lahmiri [15].

2.2   Empirical Mode Decomposition

Empirical Mode Decomposition (EMD) was proposed by Huang et al. [9]. Using Huang-Hilbert Transform, it decomposes a series into a set of adaptive basis function called Intrinsic Mode Function (IMF). It does not need any prior information related to level of decomposition, hence it is adaptive. The steps for decomposing the original time series $F(t)$ are detailed in Huang et al. [9] and [10].

Though EMD is adaptive, it suffers from limitation of mode mixing problem. Mode mixing is defined as either presence of signals of widely different scales in a single IMF or presence of signal of a similar scale in different IMF components [24, 26]. Mode mixing is caused by signal intermittency, which could affect the physical meaning of IMF.

2.3 Variational Mode Decomposition

Variational Mode Decomposition (VMD), is developed by Dragomiretskiy and Zosso [7], is an adaptive quasi-orthogonal decomposition model to decompose multi-component signal to a set of finite band-limited intrinsic mode functions (IMFs). The IMFs generated are called modes and are different from those obtained using EMD. The important steps of VMD are:

1. The modes are updated using Wiener filtering in the Fourier domain.
2. The center frequencies are updated using the center of gravity approach
3. The Lagrange multiplier is updated as dual ascent to ensure exact reconstruction of signals.

Since VMD uses Wiener filtering, it is robust to noise in the signal. Unlike EMD, it is non-recursive in nature. Review of non-classical decomposition models can be found in Jothimani et al. [11,12].

3 Ensemble Forecasting Framework

3.1 Data

We used weekly closing price of 25 major stock indices covering a period of 10 years from January 1, 2009 to December 31, 2018 for analysis. The indices considered are: S&P 500, TSX Composite index, Nifty, Russell 2000 index, SSE composite index, Merval, Jakarta Composite Index, OMX Stockholm 30 index, PSE composite index, Ireland Stock Exchange Overall index, TA 125 index, Ibovespa Brasil Sao Paulo Stock Exchange index, IBEX 35, DAX index, Amsterdam Exchange index, Hang Sang index, Nikkei 225, IPC Mexico, ASX 200, CAC 40, S&P/CLX IPSA, BEL 20, TAIEX, KOSPI composite index and NZX 50 index. We downloaded the data from Yahoo! Finance.

3.2 Methodology

Phase I: Non-classical Decomposition of Close Price of Stock Indices.
We used EMD, VMD and DWT to decompose the original series. For instance, both EMD and VMD yielded a total of six relatively stationary IMFs and a residual component for Nifty (refer Fig. 1). We limited the number of components to 8 in case of DWT (as it is not adaptive like EMD and VMD). We can observe a difference in frequency can be observed. High frequencies of IMF_1 to IMF_4 show the randomness present in the data. IMF_5 to IMF_6 represent the periodic component in the data. IMF_7 depicts the trend component of the financial series (refer Fig. 1).

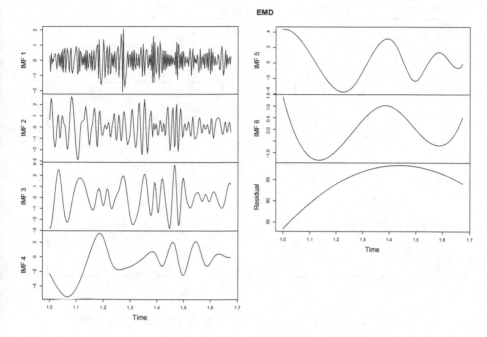

Fig. 1. Decomposition of close price of Nifty Using Non-Classical Decomposition Model

Phase II: Prediction of Subseries Using Machine Learning Models. In this phase, we determined appropriate model parameters for machine learning models (i.e., ANN and SVR) to forecast each component independently.

(a) **Determination of Lag Parameter:** We checked the stationarity for all components using Augmented Dickey-Fuller (ADF) test [4,5]. In case of a non-stationary series, we obtained the first difference, second difference and we repeated the process till either the sub-series becomes stationary or when maximum of number of iterations is reached.

We used Auto Correlation Function (ACF) and Partial Auto Correlation Function (PACF) to identify the lag parameters, which are used as input parameters for both SVR and ANN models. Figure 2 shows the ACF and PACF plot for subseries IMF_3 obtained using EMD. Since IMF_3 of Nifty cuts off at lag 4, the series is dependent on its past four values and can be expressed mathematically as: $IMF_3(t) = f[IMF_3(t - 1), IMF_3(t - 2), IMF_3(t - 3), IMF_3(t - 4)]$. Similarly, we determined the lag values for other IMFs and residual component.

(b) **Prediction:** Once the lag parameters are determined, we used ANN and SVR to obtain 1-step ahead forecasts for respective (DWT, EMD, VMD)-based ANN and (DWT, EMD, VMD)-based SVR models. Since both ANN and SVR are supervised machine learning algorithms, we used first 70% and rest 30% of data for training and testing the model, respectively. We used two cross-validation procedures, namely, out-of-sample and blocked k-fold

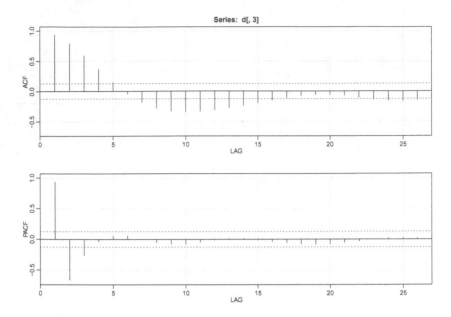

Fig. 2. ACF and PACF plot for IMF_3 of Nifty Obtained Using EMD

cross-validation procedures, to avoid overfitting of the model and to assess the generalizability of the models.

We normalised the data between $[0,1]$, $[-1,1]$ and using z-scores. This data preprocessing step helps to reduce the probability of overfitting and the probability of the predictive models getting trapped in local minima. Further, it speeds up the training process [3,25]. The performance of the model preprocessed using z score was found to be better than the remaining models.

– **ANN Model:** We determined the number of input neurons based on the lag parameter and the number of hidden neurons based on best performances of the model. The input data format of IMF_4 of EMD-ANN model based on ACF and PACF is as follows: $IMF_4(t) = f[IMF_4(t - 4), IMF_4(t - 3), IMF_4(t - 2), IMF_4(t - 1)$.

  We used Resilient Propagation algorithm [22] for training the model because of its superior performance over the widely used backpropagation algorithm. In addition, it quickens the training process and does not require specification of parameters (momentum and learning rate) during training process [18].

– **SVR Model:** We used the past values of IMFs and residual components as the input parameters for SVR. We implemented Grid search to minimize the parameter sensitiveness (C and ϵ) of SVR [17]. In grid search, values of C and ϵ are increased exponentially (for instance, $C = 2^{-5}, 2^{-3}, 2^{-1}, ..., 2^{15}$) to determine their best values. This helps to reduce the mean square error of the model.

We removed the transformation applied on the sub-series such as first difference, second difference and normalization before obtaining the final forecasts.

(c) **Obtaining Final Forecasts:** We obtained the final forecasts of each model by adding up the forecasts of their respective subseries. The final forecasts of the respective models can be obtained using the following equation: $F'(t + 1) = IMF'_1(t+1) + IMF'_2(t+1) + ... + IMF'_N(t+1) + R'_N(t+1)$, where, $F'(t + 1)$ is the 1-step ahead forecast of original series $F(t)$, $IMF'_1(t + 1)$, ... , $IMF'_N(t+1)$ are the 1-step ahead forecasts of subseries, and $R'_N(t+ 1)$ is the 1-step ahead forecasts of residual component.

4   Results and Discussion

We forecasted the close price of 25 major stock indices using six ensemble models, namely, DWT-ANN, DWT-SVR, EMD-ANN, EMD-SVR, VMD-ANN, VMD-SVR. We used Root Mean Square Error (RMSE) to evaluate the performance of the ensemble models. In addition, to evaluate and validate the results statistically, we used Wilcoxon Signed Rank Test (WSRT). It is a non-parametric and distribution-free technique. It helps to compare and analyze the predictive capability of two models [6]. Null hypothesis of WSRT states that there is no difference in forecasting accuracy of two models. It compares the sign and ranks of the forecasted values [14].

4.1   Performance Comparison of Ensemble Models with Standalone Models

We carried out two-tailed WSRT on RMSE values to compare the performance of standalone models with the ensemble models (Refer Table 1). Since the z statistics is beyond $(-1.96, 1.96)$, the null hypothesis of no difference in forecasting accuracy of two models is not accepted. The results are significant at 99% confidence level $(\alpha = 0.01)$. The superior and under performance of ensemble models over traditional models is shown by "+" and "−" signs, respectively and "=" represents that there is no difference in the performances of both ensemble and traditional models.

4.2   Comparison of Performance Among Decomposition-Based ANN Models and SVR Models

Table 2 presents the performances of SVR and ANN in the ensemble models. The statistics show SVR (DWT-SVR, EMD-SVR and VMD-SVR) has performed better than ANN (DWT-ANN, EMD-ANN and VMD-ANN) in all three ensemble models. Better performance of SVR could be attributed to few factors such as tuning of smaller number of parameters (C, ϵ) as compared to neural networks (size of the network, learning parameters and training could affect the prediction performance), structural minimization principle aids in better generalization of SVR models, and unlike ANN, it does not get stuck in local minima.

Table 1. WSRT Results of ensemble models and standalone models

	z	WSRT
ANN-based models		
DWT	−2.157	-
EMD	−4.670	-
VMD	−5.524	-
SVR-based models		
DWT	−5.654	-
EMD	−3.320	-
VMD	−2.568	-
+ : DWT-ANN > ANN, EMD-ANN > ANN, VMD-ANN > ANN		
+ : DWT-SVR > SVR, EMD-SVR > SVR, VMD-SVR > SVR		
= : DWT-ANN = ANN, EMD-ANN = ANN, VMD-ANN = ANN		
= : DWT-SVR = SVR, EMD-SVR = SVR, VMD-SVR = SVR		
− : DWT-ANN < ANN, EMD-ANN < ANN, VMD-ANN < ANN		
− : DWT-SVR < SVR, EMD-SVR < SVR, VMD-SVR < SVR		

Table 2. WSRT Results of ensemble-based ANN Vs ensemble-based SVR Models

Models	z	WSRT
ANN vs. SVR	−3.802	-
DWT-ANN vs. DWT-SVR	−4.320	-
EMD-ANN vs. EMD-SVR	−3.970	-
VMD-ANN vs. VMD-SVR	−5.670	-
+ : ANN > SVR, DWT-ANN > DWT-SVR, EMD-ANN > EMD-SVR, VMD-ANN > VMD-SVR		
= : ANN = SVR, DWT-ANN = DWT-SVR, EMD-ANN = EMD-SVR, VMD-ANN = VMD-SVR		
− : ANN < SVR, DWT-ANN < DWT-SVR, EMD-ANN < EMD-SVR, VMD-ANN < VMD-SVR		

5   Threats to Validity

The study suffers from following threats to validity:

1. Although we analysed the dataset for a period of ten years from 2009 to 2018, it does not cover the period of global financial crisis.
2. In general, a stock index is a weighted average of prices various stocks selected based on free-floating market capitalization. So, in terms of data characteristics, stock market index is not volatile compared to prices of stock. Hence, the results are not generalizable for forecasting of prices of stocks.

6   Conclusions

We used ensemble of time-series based decomposition and machine learning models such as DWT-ANN, DWT-SVR, EMD-ANN, EMD-SVR, VMD-ANN and

VMD-SVR for forecasting financial time series. We evaluated the effectiveness of these models using 25 major stock indices. Also, we compared the performance of the models using RMSE and validated the results using non-parametric Wilcoxon Signed Rank Test.

The concluding remarks are summarized below:

- Ensemble forecasting models outperformed both ANN and SVR models (without decomposition).
- Among the ensemble-based ANN models, VMD-ANN outperformed both EMD-ANN and DWT-ANN models. Similarly, the performance of VMD-SVR model was found to be superior among other ensemble-based SVR models.
- VMD-SVR outperformed other ensemble models. It can be concluded that VMD enhanced the performance of SVR model as the subseries generated using VMD were free from mode mixing problem.

Stock indices covered in this study are from three markets, namely, developed, emerging and frontier markets. Stock index forecasting models are helpful to institutional investors to construct portfolio from these indices, thus, helping in stock market integration.

We plan to evaluate the performance of the models on intraday data and also evaluate the effectiveness using different trading strategies. Also, we plan to test the effectiveness of boosting and bagging algorithms in ensemble models and use deep learning approaches for forecasting the subseries.

References

1. Atsalakis, G., Valavanis, K.: Surveying stock market forecasting techniques - Part II: soft computing methods. Expert Syst. Appl. **36**(3, Part 2), 5932–5941 (2009)
2. Atsalakis, G., Valavanis, K.: Surveying stock market forecasting techniques - Part I: conventional methods. In: Zopounidis, C. (ed.) Computation Optimization in Economics and Finance Research Compendium, pp. 49–104. Nova Science Publishers, Inc., New York (2013)
3. Crone, S.F., Guajardo, J., Weber, R.: A study on the ability of support vector regression and neural networks to forecast basic time series patterns. In: Bramer, M. (ed.) IFIP AI 2006. IFIP AICT, vol. 217, pp. 149–158. Springer, Boston (2006). https://doi.org/10.1007/978-0-387-34747-9_16
4. Dickey, D.A., Fuller, W.A.: Distribution of the estimators for autoregressive time series with a unit root. J. Am. Stat. Assoc. **74**(366), 427–431 (1979)
5. Dickey, D.A., Fuller, W.A.: Likelihood ratio statistics for autoregressive time series with a unit root. Econometrica **49**(4), 1057–1072 (1981)
6. Diebold, F.X., Mariano, R.S.: Comparing predictive accuracy. J. Bus. Econ. Stat. **13**, 253–265 (1995)
7. Dragomiretskiy, K., Zosso, D.: Variational mode decomposition. IEEE Trans. Signal Process. **62**(3), 531–544 (2014). https://doi.org/10.1109/TSP.2013.2288675
8. Gençay, R., Selçuk, F., Whitcher, B.: Discrete wavelet transforms. In: Whitcher, R.G.S. (ed.) An Introduction to Wavelets and Other Filtering Methods in Finance and Economics, pp. 96–160. Academic Press, San Diego (2002)

9. Huang, N., et al.: The empirical mode decomposition and the Hilbert spectrum for nonlinear and non-stationary time series analysis. Proc. R. Soc. Lond. A Math. Phys. Eng. Sci. **454**(1971), 903–995 (1998)

10. Huang, N.E., Wu, M.L., Qu, W., Long, S.R., Shen, S.S.P.: Applications of Hilbert Huang transform to non-stationary financial time series analysis. Appl. Stoch. Model. Bus. Ind. **19**(3), 245–268 (2003)

11. Jothimani, D., Shankar, R., Yadav, S.S.: Discrete wavelet transform-based prediction of stock index: a study on National Stock Exchange fifty index. J. Financ. Manag. Anal. **28**(2), 35–49 (2015)

12. Jothimani, D., Shankar, R., Yadav, S.S.: A comparative study of ensemble-based forecasting models for stock index prediction. In: MWAIS 2016 Proceedings, p. 5 (2016). http://aisel.aisnet.org/mwais2016/5

13. Jothimani, D., Yadav, S.S.: Stock trading decisions using ensemble-based forecasting models: a study of the Indian stock market. J. Bank. Financ. Technol., June 2019. https://doi.org/10.1007/s42786-019-00009-7

14. Kao, L.J., Chiu, C.C., Lu, C.J., Chang, C.H.: A hybrid approach by integrating wavelet-based feature extraction with MARS and SVR for stock index forecasting. Decis. Support Syst. **54**(3), 1228–1244 (2013)

15. Lahmiri, S.: Wavelet low- and high-frequency components as features for predicting stock prices with backpropagation neural networks. J. King Saud Univ. Comput. Inf. Sci. **26**(2), 218–227 (2014)

16. Li, T., Li, Q., Zhu, S., Ogihara, M.: A survey on wavelet applications in data mining. SIGKDD Explor. Newsl. **4**(2), 49–68 (2002). https://doi.org/10.1145/772862.772870

17. Lin, C., Hsu, C., Chang, C.: A practical guide to support vector classification. Technical report, Department of Computer Science and Information Engineering, National Taiwan University, Taipei (2003)

18. Liu, H., Chen, C., Tian, H., Li, Y.: A hybrid model for wind speed prediction using empirical mode decomposition and artificial neural networks. Renew. Energy **48**, 545–556 (2012)

19. Murtagh, F., Starck, J., Renaud, O.: On neuro-wavelet modeling. Decis. Support Syst. **37**(4), 475–484 (2004). Data mining for financial decision making

20. Opitz, D., Maclin, R.: Popular ensemble methods: an empirical study. J. Artif. Intell. Res. **11**, 169–198 (1999)

21. Ortega, L., Khashanah, K.: A neuro-wavelet model for the short-term forecasting of high-frequency time series of stock returns. J. Forecast. **33**(2), 134–146 (2014)

22. Riedmiller, M., Braun, H.: A direct adaptive method for faster backpropagation learning: the RPROP algorithm. In: IEEE International Conference on Neural Networks, vol. 1, pp. 586–591 (1993)

23. Theodosiou, M.: Forecasting monthly and quarterly time series using STL decomposition. Int. J. Forecast. **27**(4), 1178–1195 (2011)

24. Torres, M.E., Colominas, M.A., Schlotthauer, G., Flandrin, P.: A complete ensemble empirical mode decomposition with adaptive noise. In: 2011 IEEE International Conference on Acoustics, Speech and Signal Processing (ICASSP), pp. 4144–4147, May 2011

25. Wu, G., Lo, S.: Effects of data normalization and inherent-factor on decision of optimal coagulant dosage in water treatment by artificial neural network. Expert Syst. Appl. **37**(7), 4974–4983 (2010)

26. Wu, Z., Huang, N.E.: Ensemble empirical mode decomposition: a noise-assisted data analysis method. Adv. Adapt. Data Anal. **1**(1), 1–41 (2009)

Effective Sub-Sequence-Based Dynamic Time Warping

Mohammed Alshehri[1,2], Frans Coenen[1(✉)], and Keith Dures[1(✉)]

[1] Department of Computer Science, University of Liverpool, Liverpool, UK
{M.A.Alshehri,Coenen,K.Dures}@liverpool.ac.uk
[2] Department of Computer Science, King Khalid University, Abha, Saudi Arabia

Abstract. k Nearest Neighbour classification techniques, where $k = 1$, coupled with Dynamic Time Warping (DTW) are the most effective and most frequently used approaches for time series classification. However, because of the quadratic complexity of DTW, research efforts have been directed at methods and techniques to make the DTW process more efficient. This paper presents a new approach to efficient DTW, the Sub-Sequence-Based DTW approach. Two variations are considered, fixed length sub-sequence segmentation and fixed number sub-sequence segmentation. The reported experiments indicate that the technique improvs efficiency, compared to standard DTW, without adversely affecting effectiveness.

Keywords: Time series analysis · Dynamic Time Warping · k-Nearest neighbor classification · Splitting method

1 Introduction

Over recent years there has been a significant increase in the amount of data that commercial enterprises and institutions collect. This has largely been as a consequence of technical advances. The data collected takes many forms; one such form is temporal data, specifically time series data [10]. In the field of data mining, much research, development and empirical experimentation have been conducted in the usage of time series data [15]. Time series data typically comprises a collection of values recorded chronologically, such as electrocardiogram (ECG) data [8], daily stocks prices [5] or daily temperatures [4]. However, the points do not have to be chronologically ordered; they can be ordered in some other way, for example, the outline of an object in an image [16]. In time series analysis, determination of the similarity between time series is a challenge [15]. One of the most frequently used similarity measurement techniques is Dynamic Time Warping (DTW).

DTW is founded on the idea of identifying an optimal alignment between two time series which may be of different lengths [12,14]. Unlike Euclidean distance similarity measurement, DTW matches time series sequences by "warping" them in a nonlinear fashion (hence the name). DTW was first proposed in the context

© Springer Nature Switzerland AG 2019
M. Bramer and M. Petridis (Eds.): SGAI-AI 2019, LNAI 11927, pp. 293–305, 2019.
https://doi.org/10.1007/978-3-030-34885-4_23

of speech recognition for the comparison of speech patterns [11]. Subsequently, it has been used for many other applications, for example, music analysis [6].

One of the main disadvantages of DTW is its quadratic complexity. DTW operates using a "distance matrix" measuring x^2, where x is the length of the two time series being compared (assuming they are of the same length). The time complexity of the DTW algorithm is therefore $O(x^2)$. This quadratic complexity therefore renders DTW to be impractical with respect to many application domains. The idea presented in this paper is to segment the time series into s sub-sequences of roughly equal size. The time complexity of the DTW then reduces to $O(\frac{x^2}{s})$; still quadratic but substantially less than $O(x^2)$. The first question to be answered is then how to define s; either as a fixed parameter or in terms of a predefined sub-sequence length. The second question is how to define s without any loss of functionality (consequent classification accuracy).

The rest of this paper is organised as follows. Section 2 presents a brief description of DTW. Section 3 considers some relevant previous work in the domain of DTW; the following Sect. 4, presents the proposed mechanism, Sub-Sequence-Based DTW. The time complexity is discussed in Sect. 5. Section 6 presents the evaluation strategy with an overview of the evaluation Datasets. Finally, Sect. 7 presents the main findings of the paper. A symbol table is given in Table 1 lists the symbols used throughout the paper.

Table 1. Symbol table

Symbol	Description
p or q	A point in a time series described by a single value
S	A time series such that $S = [p_1, p_2, \ldots]$ or $S = [q_1, q_2, \ldots]$
x or y	Length of a given time series
M	A distance matrix measuring $x \times y$
$m_{i,j}$	The distance value at location i, j in M
WP	A warping path $[w_1, w_2, \ldots]$ where $w_i \in M$
wd	A warping distance derived from WP
U	A time series sub-sequence after segmentation. $U \subset S$
ℓ	Length of time series sub-sequence after segmentation, $\ell < x$ and $\ell < y$
$\mathcal{P}$	percentage (%) of the actual length of individual time series
s	A number of sub-sequences into which a given time series is split
C	A set of class labels $C = \{c_1, c_2, \ldots\}$
D	A collection of time series $\{S_1, S_2, \ldots, S_r\}$
r	The number of time series in D
z	The runtime (secs.) to process a single point p in the context of DTW

2   Background

The DTW process can best be described by considering two time series $S_1 = [p_1, p_2, \ldots, p_x]$ and $S_2 = [q_1, q_2, \ldots, q_y]$, where x and y are the lengths of the two series respectively and $x, y \in \mathbb{N}$. The first step is to construct a "distance matrix" M of size $x \times y$ where the value held at each cell $m_{i,j} \in M$ is the distance from point $p_i \in S_1$ to point $q_j \in S_2$. This distance is normally calculated in terms of Euclidean distance:

$$m_{i,j} = \sqrt{(p_i - q_j)^2} \tag{1}$$

An alternative might be absolute value distance calculation.

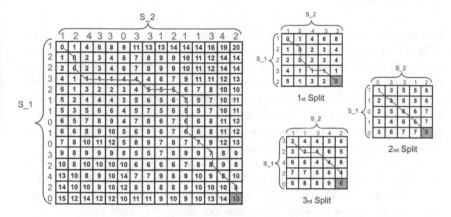

Fig. 1. Distance Matrix and Warping Path (line passes through cells) for the example time series S_1 and S_2 generated using standard DTW.

Fig. 2. Distance Matrices and Warping Paths (lines passes through cells) for the example time series S_1 and S_2 generated using sub-sequence splitting method.

The distance matrix M is used to determine a minimum warping distance wd, which is then used as a similarity measure. A wd is a function of the minimum warping path, WP, from cell $m_{0,0}$ to cell $m_{x,y}$. A minimum warping path is thus a sequence of cell locations, $WP = [w_1, w_2, \ldots]$ in the matrix M, that minimises the warping distance. Given two time series $s_1 = [p_1, p_2, \ldots, p_x]$ of length $x \in \mathbb{N}$ and $s_2 = [q_1, q_2, \ldots, q_y]$ of length $y \in \mathbb{N}$, and using "Big O" notation, the complexity of DTW can be expressed as: $O(x \times y)$, or if $x = y$ $O(x^2)$. Thus DTW becomes computationally expensive when x and/or y are large [14].

From the foregoing, it can be seen that the operation of DTW is such that it meets the following conditions [13]:

1. **Monotonic Condition**: The path will stay the same or increase. Both i and j indexes never decrease.

2. **Continuity Condition**: The path continues one step at a time. Both i and j can only increase by 1 on each step along the path.
3. **Boundary Condition**: The path starts at the bottom left $m_{(0,0)}$ and ends at the top right $m_{(x,y)}$.

The basic DTW process is illustrated in Fig. 1. The figure shows the distance matrix M given two time series assuming two time series, $S_1 = [1, 2, 2, 3, 2, 1, 1, 0, 1, 0, 3, 2, 4, 2, 0]$ and $S_2 = [1, 2, 4, 3, 3, 0, 3, 3, 1, 2, 1, 1, 3, 4, 2]$. The minimum warping path is shown by the line passes through cells. The final warping distance arrived at is highlighted using a dark box in the corner.

3   Previous Work

This section details some related work that has been conducted to speed up DTW. These techniques are directed at limiting the number of distance matrix values to be calculated in the matrix M or at minimising the number of comparisons need to be considered. In other words by placing constraints on the matrix area to be considered when calculating a minimum warping distance. This is a different approach to that considered in this paper. To the best knowledge of the authors, the idea of sub-sequence splitting presented in this paper has not been previously reported in the literature.

An example of the approach where constraints have been placed on the matrix calculation found be found in Silva et al. [12]. Silva et al. proposed a method to speed up DTW known as PrunedDTW. The fundamental idea was to place upper bounds on the calculation process. The distances along the prime diagonal, from $m_{0,0}$ to $m_{x,y}$, are first calculated using the squared Euclidean distance. These are considered to be "upper bounds". Then for each point in the diagonal the distances along each row are calculated moving away from the diagonal, in row and column order, until a distance greater than the current upper bound is reached, further cells are "pruned" from the distance matrix. The result will be a pruned DTW which holds the minimum warping distance.

In the context of limiting the number of DTW comparisons with respect to time series classification where a new time series to be classified is compared to a bank of time series, Rakthanmanon et al. [9] reported on four different techniques for achieving this. The first promulgated the idea of early abandonment, stopping the warping path calculation if the wd value so far is equal to or larger than the best so far; otherwise, the new value is the best so far. The second considered the idea of reordering the time series in the "bank" so that the time series that are likely to be the most similar to the new time series are tested first so that the early abandonment process will result in less calculation than if the time series were not ordered in this way. One way of ordering time series is according to Euclidean distance similarity (much cheaper than DTW calculation). The third considered pruning time series that were unlikely to be a close match. One way of doing this is by using the lower bounding technique proposed in [7], the so called the LB_{Keogh} technique. This operates by superimposing a band, defined by a predefined offset value referred to as the lower bound, over each time series in the bank and calculating the complement of the overlap with the new time series. Where the calculated value exceeds a given threshold the associated time series is discounted. The fourth idea was directed at using a "cascading lower bound" where different lower bounds are considered to identify the bound most suitable for the dataset in question. Further work on lower bounding can be found in [3,17].

4   Sub-Sequence-Based DTW

In this section, the proposed Sub-Sequence-Based DTW mechanism is presented. The fundamental idea of the proposed process is to divide (segment) the input time series (sequences) into sub-sequences. Then apply DTW to correlated sub-sequence pairs. Thus, given two time series S_1 and S_2, these would be divided into s sub-sequences so that we have $S_1 = [U_{1_1}, U_{1_2}, \ldots U_{1_s}]$ and $S_1 = [U_{2_1}, U_{2_2}, \ldots U_{2_s}]$. DTW is then applied to each sub-sequence paring U_{1_i}, U_{2_j} where $i = j$. The final minimum warping distance arrived at will then be the accumulated warping distance for each sub-sequence of s applications of DTW. Thus, returning to the example given in Fig. 1, and assuming $s = 3$, there will be three subsequences in each time series of length $\ell = 5$, $S_1 = [U_{1_1}, U_{1_2}, U_{1_3}] = [[1, 2, 2, 3, 2], [1, 1, 0, 1, 0], [3, 2, 4, 2, 0]]$ and $S_1 = [U_{2_1}, U_{2_2}, U_{2_3}] = [[1, 2, 4, 3, 3], [0, 3, 3, 1, 2], [1, 1, 3, 4, 2]]$. Three distance matrices will result as shown in Figure 2.

There are two mechanisms whereby s can be defined:

1. **Fixed Number**: The simplest is to specify s as a predefined parameter in which case the length of the individual time series sub-sequences, ℓ, will vary according to the input data; $\ell = \frac{x}{s}$. This may not be desirable.
2. **Fixed Length**: The alternative is to pre-specify the length of the desired time series sub-sequences, ℓ, in which case s will vary according to the input data, $s = \frac{x}{\ell}$. This may also not be desirable.

However, rigid implementation of s might not result in the best segmentation. Good points at which to cut the time series is where they meet, or at least at points where the distance between corresponding pairs of points is at a minimum. Thus a degree of *fuzziness* should be included to derive the best segmentation. This is defined by specifying a *tail*, t, measured backwards from ℓ, within which the cut should be applied; thus the cut will fall between $\ell - t$ and ℓ measured from the start of the time series on the first iteration and from the end of the previous segment on further iterations. The split point will be selected according to the minimum distance associated with the points from $\ell - t$ to ℓ. This is illustrated in Fig. 3 which shows a "distance list" generated with respect to the two example time series given in Fig. 1, and assumes $\ell = 10$ and $t = 3$; hence the selected split point is at index 9 (assuming the start of the sequence is index 1)

Having selected the split point there are three options as also illustrated in Fig. 3: (i) include the split point value as the last value in the previous segment

(Option A), (ii) include the split point value at the start of the following segment (Option B) or (iii) include the split point value in both the previous and following segments (Option C).

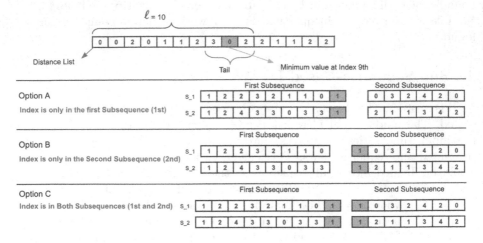

Fig. 3. Segmentation example given two time series S_1 and S_2, and Options A, B or C.

5 Time Complexity

The time complexity of the proposed mechanism is considered in this section. In time series classification, the complexity of the comparison between two time series, S_1 and S_2, when using Standard DTW, is given by $O(x \times y)$ where x and y are the lengths of S_1 and S_2 respectively. For the classification application under consideration, all the time series are of the same length, as in the case of the evaluation presented in the following section, this simplifies to:

$$DTW_{complexityStand} = O\left(x^2 \times z\right) \tag{2}$$

where z is a constant describing the time complexity associated with a single cell $m_{i,j}$ in the distance matrix M. The time complexity when using the proposed mechanism, Sub-Sequence-Based DTW, with fixed length segments ($DTW_{complexitySplit_{len}}$) and fixed number segments ($DTW_{complexitySplit_{num}}$) is then:

$$DTW_{complexitySplit_{len}} = O\left(\frac{x^2}{\frac{x}{\ell}} \times z\right) \tag{3}$$

$$DTW_{complexitySplit_{num}} = O\left(\frac{x^2}{s} \times z\right) \tag{4}$$

The most commonly used time series classification mechanism is k Nearest Neighbour (kNN) classification [1,14] where a previously unseen time series is compared with a "data bank" of time series whose class label is known and the label for the new time series derived from the k most similar time series in the bank. The most commonly used value for k in time series analysis, using DTW, is $k = 1$, this we have 1NN. If we have a data repository with r examples the time complexity to classify a single record using 1NN is given by:

$$O\left(r \times DTW_{complexity}\right) \tag{5}$$

If there are t new time series to be classified ($t > 1$) the complexity is given by:

$$O\left(r \times DTW_{complexity} \times t\right) \tag{6}$$

In the case of cross-validation, as presented in the following section, the complexity becomes:

$$O\left(r \times DTW_{complexity} \times t \times numFolds\right) \tag{7}$$

When using ten cross validation the data set D is split into tenths, in which case $r = \frac{9 \times |D|}{10}$, $t = \frac{|D|}{10}$ and the number of fold will equal 10:

$$O\left(\frac{9 \times |D|}{10} \times DTW_{complexity} \times \frac{|D|}{10} \times 10\right) \tag{8}$$

Which simplifies to:

$$O\left(\frac{9 \times |D|^2}{100} \times DTW_{complexity}\right) \tag{9}$$

6   Evaluation

In this section, the evaluation of the proposed Sub-Sequence-Based DTW mechanism is presented. This mechanism was used in connection with the 1NN classification and the ten selected datasets from the UEA-UCR Time Series Classification repository [2]. Further detail concerning the selected data sets is given in Subsect. 6.1. The objectives of the evaluation were:

1. To compare the operation of fixed length and fixed number Sub-Sequence-Based DTW.
2. To determine the most suitable value for t, the sub-sequence tail.
3. To analyse the runtime of the proposed Sub-Sequence-Based DTW mechanism.
4. To evaluate the classification effectiveness of the proposed approach in comparison with Standard DTW (using accuracy and F1-score as the evaluation metrics).

Each is considered with respect to the results obtained in Subsect. 6.2 below. For each set of experiments Ten Cross Validation (TCV) was adopted. A desktop computer with a 3.5 GHz Intel Core i5 processor and 16 GB, 2400 MHz, DDR4 of primary memory was used throughout.

6.1   Data Sets

In this subsection, a brief overview of the evaluation datasets is presented. Some statistics concerning the ten datasets are given in Table 2. Column five represents the overall size of each dataset calculated using $x \times r$, where x is the length (number of points) of an individual time series and r is the number of time series (records) in each dataset D; the significance is that this is a good measure of the overall size of a time series data set. The nature of the data (time series) collected for each dataset is represented by its type (column seven). Motion indicates that the time series represents body movements, Spectro means that the time series comprises spectrograph data, Sensor that the time series data were collected using sensors (such as an electric power signal sensor), Simulation means that time series data was collected using some form of simulation and image means image segmentation translated into a time series form.

Table 2. Time series datasets used for evaluation purposes.

ID No.	Dataset	Length (x)	Num. records (r)	Size x_r	Num. Classes	Type
1	GunPoint	150	200	30000	2	Motion
2	OliveOil	570	60	34200	4	Spectro
3	Trace	275	200	55000	4	Sensor
4	ToeSegment2	343	166	56938	2	Motion
5	Car	577	120	69240	4	Sensor
6	Lightning2	637	121	77077	2	Sensor
7	ShapeletSim	500	200	100000	2	Simulated
8	DiatomSizeRed	345	322	36000	4	Image
9	Adiac	176	781	137456	37	Image
10	HouseTwenty	2000	159	318000	2	Image

6.2   Evaluation Results

To compare the operation of fixed length Sub-Sequence-Based DTW with fixed number Sub-Sequence-Based DTW, two sets of experiments were conducted. The first considered the parameters ℓ and s required by the two mechanisms using Option A and $t = 0$. A range of values for ℓ was considered from 10 to 50 increasing in steps of 10, $\ell = \{10, 20, 30, 40, 50\}$. For the parameter s this was defined in terms of a percentage of the overall length of the overall input time series length from 5% to 25%, $\{5\%, 10\%, 15\%, 20\%, 25\%\}$, which translated to $s = \{20.00, 10.00, 6.67, 5.00, 4.00\}$. Note that wherever an exact segmentation of a time series could not be achieved a "short" segment was included at the end of the segment collection. A summary of the results obtained is presented in Table 3, best F1 scores with respect to the proposed mechanism are highlighted in bold font. From the table it can be seen that best classification results were obtained

Table 3. Average results of TCV classification accuracy (Acc) and F1 Scores (F1), and run times (sec), obtained over 10 evaluation datasets using a range of ℓ and s values, and Option A and $t = 0$, compared with standard DTW; best results with respect to the proposed Sub-sequence Based DTW mechanism highlighted in bold font.

Fixed Length ℓ	Avg Acc	Avg F1	Avg Run-Time (sec)
Standard	88.15	0.87	115.46
10	85.02	0.86	16.76
20	86.36	0.87	15.90
30	86.98	0.88	16.11
40	**87.78**	**0.88**	**17.15**
50	87.39	0.88	17.91

Fixed Number s	Avg Acc	Avg F1	Avg Run-Time (sec)
Standard	88.15	0.87	115.46
5%	87.96	0.87	18.79
10%	88.59	0.88	21.90
15%	88.25	0.88	24.94
20%	**89.24**	**0.89**	**31.16**
25%	89.16	0.89	35.04

Table 4. Fixed length $\ell = 40$: Accuracy, F1-score and runtime results (Option $= A$ and $t = 0$).

Dataset	Acc (SD)	F1 (SD)	Runtime (Secs)
Gun point	99.47 (0.01)	0.99 (0.02)	5.76
Olive oil	90.95 (0.12)	0.09 (0.14)	1.61
Trace	97.50 (0.03)	98 (0.04)	5.98
ToeSegmentation2	89.13 (0.05)	0.89 (0.06)	6.69
Car	83.33 (0.09)	0.82 (0.10)	4.40
Lighting2	81.54 (0.09)	0.80 (0.11)	5.00
Shapelet sim	89.97 (0.06)	0.90 (0.06)	11.48
DiatomSize reduction	100 (0.00)	1.00 (0.00)	20.50
Adiac	64.42 (0.04)	0.61 (0.04)	94.55
House twenty	93.71 (0.04)	0.94 (0.05)	18.86

Table 5. Fixed number $s = 20\%$: Accuracy, F1-score and runtime results (Option $= A$ and $t = 0$).

Dataset	Acc (SD)	F1 (SD)	Runtime (Secs)
Gun point	95.50 (0.04)	0.96 (0.05)	6.39
Olive oil	89.52 (0.15)	0.89 (0.16)	2.46
Trace	97.00 (0.04)	97 (0.04)	6.96
ToeSegmentation2	89.17 (0.05)	0.88 (0.07)	8.38
Car	82.50 (0.07)	0.82 (0.8)	7.70
Lighting2	90.32 (0.08)	0.90 (0.9)	9.66
Shapelet sim	88.89 (0.07)	0.89 (0.07)	18.46
DiatomSize reduction	99.68 (0.01)	0.99 (0.01)	27.05
Adiac	65.45 (0.03)	0.62 (0.04)	96.29
House twenty	94.38 (0.05)	0.95 (0.05)	128.07

using $\ell = 40$ and $s = 20\%$ ($s = 5$). Note also that the recorded runtimes for the proposed mechanism were significantly less than that required by "standard" DTW. More detailed results concerning $\ell = 40$ and $s = 20\%$ settings are given in Tables 4 and 5; where the numbers in parentheses are the standard deviation in each case.

The second set of experiments used $\ell = 40$ and $s = 20\%$, a range of values for t, $\{2, 3, 4, 5, 6, 7, 8, 9, 10\}$ and considered all three options A, B and C (see Subsect. 4). The results are presented in Tables 6 and 7 (standard deviations are given in parentheses). The results clearly indicate that, regardless of whether

Table 6. Average results of TCV classification accuracy (Acc) and F1 Scores (F1), obtained over 10 evaluation datasets using a range of values for t, all three options and the fixed length variation with $\ell = 40$; best result in bold font.

t	Option					
	A		B		C	
	Acc (SD)	F1 (SD)	Acc (SD)	F1 (SD)	Acc (SD)	F1 (SD)
2	88.63	0.89	89.74	0.89	**90.03**	**0.90**
3	89.19	0.89	89.35	0.89	89.48	0.89
4	89.69	0.89	89.26	0.89	89.17	0.89
5	89.36	0.89	88.58	0.88	88.43	0.88
6	88.97	0.88	89.21	0.89	87.68	0.88
7	88.58	0.88	88.83	0.88	88.26	0.88
8	88.67	0.88	88.84	0.88	88.19	0.88
9	89.22	0.89	88.15	0.88	88.22	0.88
10	88.53	0.88	88.02	0.87	88.14	0.88

Table 7. Average results of TCV classification accuracy (Acc) and F1 Scores (F1), obtained over 10 evaluation datasets using a range of values for t, all three options and the fixed number variation with $s = 20\%$; best result in bold font.

t	Option					
	A		B		C	
	Acc (SD)	F1 (SD)	Acc (SD)	F1 (SD)	Acc (SD)	F1 (SD)
2	89.18	0.89	88.88	0.88	**89.27**	**0.89**
3	89.22	0.89	87.81	0.88	88.71	0.88
4	88.59	0.88	88.64	0.88	88.18	0.88
5	89.01	0.89	88.75	0.88	88.79	0.88
6	88.77	0.88	88.69	0.88	88.83	0.88
7	89.12	0.89	88.65	0.88	88.84	0.88
8	89.19	0.89	88.75	0.88	88.86	0.88
9	88.51	0.88	89.00	0.89	89.20	0.89
10	89.01	0.88	88.64	0.88	88.84	0.88

the fixed length or fixed number variation of the proposed mechanism is used, best results are obtained when $t = 2$ and Option $= C$.

Considering the recorded runtimes, from the tables it is clear that the proposed Sub-Sequence-Based DTW is faster than standard DTW without loss of effectiveness, in fact with a slight improvement in effectiveness in terms of the F1 measure. This is emphasised by the graph presented in Fig. 4 which shows the recorded runtimes using the best performing parameters with respect to each variation $ell = 40$ and $s = 20\%$, and $t = 2$ and Option $= C$, and the recorded runtime using standard DTW. In the figure, the x-axis records the identification number of the relevant dataset (see Table 2) and the y-axis the runtime in seconds.

Overall there is also little to choose between the two variations of the proposed Sub-sequence Based DTW mechanism, although an argument could be made in favour of the fixed length variation. A more detailed breakdown of the results obtained using this variation with $\ell = 40$, $t = 2$ and Option $= C$ is therefore given in Table 8.

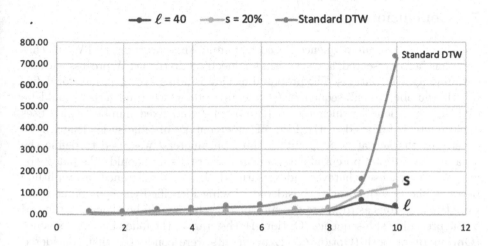

Fig. 4. Run time results (seconds) using best performing parameters for Sub-Sequence-Based DTW compared to Standard DTW.

Table 8. Fixed Length: Accuracy, F1-Score and Runtime Results ($\ell = 40$, Option $= C$ and $t = 2$), compared to standard DTW.

Dataset	Fixed length			Standard DTW		
	Acc (SD)	F1 (SD)	Runtime (Secs)	Acc (SD)	F1 (SD)	Runtime (Secs)
GunPoint	99.00 (0.02)	0.99 (0.02)	3.11	93.97 (0.04)	0.94 (0.05)	8.11
OliveOil	90.12 (0.10)	0.89 (0.12)	1.43	89.52 (0.15)	0.88 (0.16)	8.06
Trace	96.50 (0.04)	97.00 (0.04)	4.94	99.00 (0.03)	99.00 (0.03)	18.41
ToeSegmentation2	92.26 (0.03)	0.92 (0.04)	5.85	89.07 (0.09)	0.88 (0.10)	23.81
Car	82.50 (0.10)	0.81 (0.11)	4.86	80.83 (0.07)	0.80 (0.9)	32.45
Lighting2	87.40 (0.08)	0.87 (0.9)	6.10	87.74 (0.09)	0.87 (0.8)	37.69
ShapeletSim	93.00 (0.04)	0.93 (0.04)	12.79	82.37 (0.09)	0.81 (0.011)	64.02
DiatomSizeReduction	100 (0.00)	1.00 (0.00)	19.54	99.36 (0.01)	0.99 (0.01)	77.91
Adiac	64.98 (0.03)	0.62 (0.04)	55.64	64.63 (0.03)	0.62 (0.04)	156.81
HouseTwenty	91.17 (0.07)	0.91 (0.07)	32.68	95.00 (0.03)	0.95 (0.05)	727.47
Average	**90.03**	**0.90**	**14.99**	**88.15**	**0.87**	**115.47**

7   Conclusion

In this paper the Sub-Sequence-Based Dynamic Time Warping (DTW) mechanism has been presented, a mechanism for speeding up the DTW process without entailing approximations. The proposed mechanism has two variations for defining the number of sub-sequences (segments) into which time series should be divided, fixed length which uses a parameter ℓ and fixed number which uses a parameter s (defined in the form of a percentage of time series length). To determine the actual "split point" a third parameter t was used to define the area at the end of a potential sub-sequence where a split should take place, the idea was to choose whatever index featured the least difference in amplitude between the two time series considered. Having identified the split point there were three options as to where the split index value should be allocated: the end of the preceding sub-sequence (Option A), the start of the following sub-sequence (Option B) or both (Option C). Experiments were conducted that considered these different parameter settings, variations and options by considering a 1NN classification scenario. It was found that best results were obtained when $\ell = 40$, $s = 20\%$, $t = 2$ and using Option C. There was little to choose between the two variations, fixed length or fixed number, however, an argument could be made in favour of the fixed length variation. Whatever the case, both variations outperformed standard DTW in terms of run time by a considerable margin, with no detriment to the recorded accuracy.

References

1. Bagnall, A., Lines, J.: An experimental evaluation of nearest neighbour time series classification. arXiv preprint (2014). arXiv:1406.4757
2. Bagnall, A., Lines, J., Bostrom, A., Large, J., Keogh, E.: The great time series classification bake off: a review and experimental evaluation of recent algorithmic advances. Data Min. Knowl. Disc. **31**(3), 606–660 (2017)
3. Bringmann, K., Künnemann, M.: Quadratic conditional lower bounds for string problems and dynamic time warping. In: 2015 IEEE 56th Annual Symposium on Foundations of Computer Science, pp. 79–97. IEEE (2015)
4. Byakatonda, J., Parida, B., Kenabatho, P.K., Moalafhi, D.: Analysis of rainfall and temperature time series to detect long-term climatic trends and variability over semi-arid botswana. J. Earth Syst. Sci. **127**(2), 25 (2018)
5. Chen, M.Y., Chen, B.T.: A hybrid fuzzy time series model based on granular computing for stock price forecasting. Inf. Sci. **294**, 227–241 (2015)
6. Deng, J.J., Leung, C.H.: Dynamic time warping for music retrieval using time series modeling of musical emotions. IEEE Trans. Affect. Comput. **6**(2), 137–151 (2015)
7. Keogh, E., Ratanamahatana, C.A.: Exact indexing of dynamic time warping. Knowl. Inf. Syst. **7**(3), 358–386 (2005)
8. Phinyomark, A., Scheme, E.: An investigation of temporally inspired time domain features for electromyographic pattern recognition. In: 2018 40th Annual International Conference of the IEEE Engineering in Medicine and Biology Society (EMBC), pp. 5236–5240. IEEE (2018)

9. Rakthanmanon, T., et al.: Searching and mining trillions of time series subsequences under dynamic time warping. In: Proceedings of the 18th ACM SIGKDD international conference on Knowledge discovery and data mining. pp. 262–270. ACM (2012)

10. Roberts, D.R., et al.: Cross-validation strategies for data with temporal, spatial, hierarchical, or phylogenetic structure. Ecography **40**(8), 913–929 (2017)

11. Sakoe, H., Chiba, S.: Dynamic programming algorithm optimization for spoken word recognition. IEEE Trans. Acoustics, Speech, and Signal Process. **26**(1), 43–49 (1978)

12. Silva, D.F., Batista, G.E.: Speeding up all-pairwise dynamic time warping matrix calculation. In: Proceedings of the 2016 SIAM International Conference on Data Mining, pp. 837–845. SIAM (2016)

13. Silva, D.F., Giusti, R., Keogh, E., Batista, G.E.: Speeding up similarity search under dynamic time warping by pruning unpromising alignments. Data Min. Knowl. Disc. **32**, 1–29 (2018)

14. Tan, C.W., Herrmann, M., Forestier, G., Webb, G.I., Petitjean, F.: Efficient search of the best warping window for dynamic time warping. In: Proceedings of the 2018 SIAM International Conference on Data Mining, pp. 225–233. SIAM (2018)

15. Wang, X., Mueen, A., Ding, H., Trajcevski, G., Scheuermann, P., Keogh, E.: Experimental comparison of representation methods and distance measures for time series data. Data Min. Knowl. Disc. **26**(2), 275–309 (2013)

16. Wegner Maus, V., Câmara, G., Appel, M., Pebesma, E.: dtwsat: time-weighted dynamic time warping for satellite image time series analysis in R. J. Stat. Softw. **88**(5), 1–31 (2019)

17. Zhou, M., Wong, M.H.: Boundary-based lower-bound functions for dynamic time warping and their indexing. Inf. Sci. **181**(19), 4175–4196 (2011)

Applications of Machine Learning

Developing a Catalogue of Explainability Methods to Support Expert and Non-expert Users

Kyle Martin[1]([envelope]) [ID], Anne Liret[2] [ID], Nirmalie Wiratunga[1] [ID], Gilbert Owusu[3], and Mathias Kern[3]

[1] Robert Gordon University, Aberdeen, Scotland
{k.martin,n.wiratunga}@rgu.ac.uk
[2] BT France, Paris, France
anne.liret@bt.com
[3] British Telecommunications, London, UK
{gilbert.owusu,mathias.kern}@bt.com

Abstract. Organisations face growing legal requirements and ethical responsibilities to ensure that decisions made by their intelligent systems are explainable. However, provisioning of an explanation is often application dependent, causing an extended design phase and delayed deployment. In this paper we present an explainability framework formed of a catalogue of explanation methods, allowing integration to a range of projects within a telecommunications organisation. These methods are split into low-level explanations, high-level explanations and co-created explanations. We motivate and evaluate this framework using the specific case-study of explaining the conclusions of field engineering experts to non-technical planning staff. Feedback from an iterative co-creation process and a qualitative evaluation is indicative that this is a valuable development tool for use in future company projects.

Keywords: Machine learning · Similarity modeling · Explainability · Information retrieval

1 Introduction

Growing social and ethical responsibilities are being faced by organisations to ensure that decisions made by their intelligent systems are explainable. These responsibilities are supported by European legislation which dictates 'an individual's right to an explanation' and ensures that organisations are held accountable for the decisions made by these systems [4]. Furthermore, there is a need at an operational level for users to better understand the systems they are using to achieve superior working performance, nurture trust and ultimately increase productivity [11,15]. In a real-world case, the quality and benefits of explanation depend on how timely and comprehensively they are produced.

© Springer Nature Switzerland AG 2019
M. Bramer and M. Petridis (Eds.): SGAI-AI 2019, LNAI 11927, pp. 309–324, 2019.
https://doi.org/10.1007/978-3-030-34885-4_24

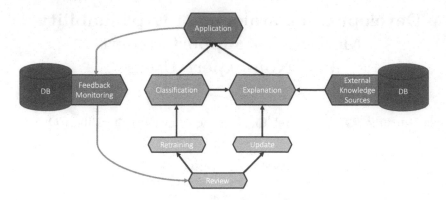

Fig. 1. A flow diagram of the developed system, displaying its linked components.

However, explanations are typically crafted to respond to specific user needs and specific applications [1,2,11]. This practice is both time-consuming and inefficient. We believe that there are overlaps between the requirements of an explanation for different applications. In particular, we believe that responding to user needs can be effectively achieved by co-creating and co-maintaining explanations between the developer and the user. We are therefore motivated to create a general purpose explanation framework which can interface with a broad variety of projects across an organisation to reduce the cost of provisioning an explanation for individual applications.

We present a framework formed of three components; a classification engine, an explainability engine and a feedback loop to ensure iterative refinement (see Fig. 1). The classification engine is completely modular, and can be switched with other learned models as necessary. The explanation engine operates upon the classification engine's output (as well as some external knowledge bases), incorporating a catalogue of explainability techniques to provide transparency around system decision-making and improve user understanding of the source data. Three progressive levels of explanation content have been developed: low-level explanations which provide key insights on the data; high-level explanations which generate relevant sentence summaries; and co-created explanations, where user needs are combined with extra knowledge (either from external source of information or from user detailed feedback). The purpose of this approach is to target an increasing quality of explainability support.

We demonstrate the capabilities of this explanation framework with the real-world use case of improving the transfer of information between telecommunication field engineers and desk-based planning agents. In this use case, the treatment of complex orders (such as fibre access installation) requires decomposition into a chain of tasks, together described as an 'order journey'. Each individual task can involve various external dependencies (e.g. traffic management, hoist, digging) and be subject to hazards or delays. Throughout the journey, planning agents must decide the next action to progress the order on the basis of notes reported by technical engineers. However, understanding these notes can be challenging for non-experts in telecommunication engineering. Therefore, to support planning agents we have developed a recommender system to identify the most appropriate scenario for a given query note. This recommender acted as the classification engine to test our framework, and allowed the opportunity to co-create various explanation methods with a real user base. Though we have adopted a specific use case for this model, one can imagine that the explanation engine could be integrated with any classifier model in future.

The contributions of this paper are as follows. Firstly, we (1) outline the development of a modular explainability framework and detail several of its sample modules. We (2) implement a live version of this catalogue to answer the real-world problem of supporting desk-based planning agents. Lastly, we (3) perform a qualitative evaluation to understand user opinion on the quality of provided explanations.

The paper is structured in the following manner. In Sect. 2 we provide some details on related work. In Sect. 3 we motivate the need for our framework through the use case of improving the transfer of information between technical field engineers and desk-based agents. In Sect. 4 we provide details about our explainability framework and give examples for each of the categories of low-level, high-level and co-created explanations. In Sect. 5 we detail the user interface of the web service application and provide images of example usage. In Sect. 6 we provide details of a qualitative evaluation on explanation quality. Lastly, in Sect. 7 we offer some conclusions.

2   Related Work

At an individual level, a user's need for an explanation is often characterised by a discrepancy between the formal objectives of the learned model and its practical application [9]. In practice this can occur when the expectations of a system's user group do not match up with one another, or are not aligned with the system's output. A common cause for this is when individuals' capabilities and expertise are not considered [18]. Understanding the relationship between the needs of a technical expert and the needs of a non-technical user is of fundamental importance for the success of a deployed industrial application [16]. It is often the misalignment of objectives between these two parties, or the inability to effectively transfer information between them, that leads to costly errors. In domains such as field service provisioning for telecommunication organisations where the technical experts heavily rely upon their non-technical counterparts for administrative and logistical purposes, it is vital that a clear and understandable flow of information is maintained between the two groups.

In [14] the authors suggest that users of an intelligent application can be divided into three groups (novice users, domain experts and AI experts), each with distinct explanation needs. While AI experts are usually satisfied by global explanations describing how the learned model operates, novice and non-AI knowledgeable domain experts are more likely to require local explanations contextualised by specific input-output examples. However, there remains a wide gap between these latter groups in regards to their contextual domain knowledge. This motivated us to develop a catalogue of explanations with progressing levels of contextualisation and user involvement, allowing users to utilise the most suitable combination of explanation mechanisms to meet their needs.

Importantly, the framework should be accessible and easily navigated via a clear structure. The authors in [19] propose five goals that an explainable system should be able to achieve: it should be (1) transparent; (2) able to justify its decisions; (3) support the user in their ability to conceptualise necessary features; and (4) ensure that the approach adopted by the system is relevant to the problem. These aspects should (5) support the user in their ability to learn both about the system and the problem domain [19]. Aligning explanation mechanisms with their goal clarifies what information is being provisioned, directing the user towards explanation that best meets their needs.

3   Use-Case - Explaining Engineering Notes to Desk-Based Agents

The personnel within complex services provisioning for telecommunication organisations can be broadly divided into two categories; the specialist-skilled workforce who fulfill the required technical work (such as field engineers) and those who support them in their capacity to do so (such as planning agents). In regards to this former category, we highlight the telecommunications field engineering force whom develop expertise in network equipment installation and repair. Field engineers are allocated tasks to ensure continuous service delivery. In this domain, a task typically represents a time-sensitive activity on a piece of equipment (such as maintenance, installation or decommissioning) or interacting with and responding to customer inquiries (both home and business). As part of work force auditing, field engineers record information about the tasks they have completed in text documents called "notes". These notes form a knowledge-base of experiential content and are comprised of rich, heterogeneous information.

From the other perspective, one of the responsibilities of planning agents is to incorporate knowledge sourced from task update notes to identify and regulate suitable task intervention or assistance. We describe this process as anticipating the next 'scenario' for a given task. Though these agents develop aptitude in understanding some aspects of telecommunication engineering, they are not experts nor do they benefit from the experience or training that technical experts receive. The result is an increased likelihood of human-error and decreased efficiency when they interpret engineer notes to anticipate the appropriate scenario, particularly in cases where the notes are complex.

A recommender system offers means to support the desk-based agents in their work and pave the way for potential automation of this task in future. However, such a system would need to prove its trustworthiness for real-world application through transparent and explainable decision-making. The goal of the system is therefore to identify the appropriate scenario for a desk-based agent given an engineering note and explain why that scenario was selected.

3.1   The Dataset

We extracted 46 days worth of engineering note data, spread between the months of May, August, September and October. In total, we extracted approximately 6,800 task notes over 33 unique scenario types (classes). We then removed any class which contained less than 5 examples. It also became clear that a certain scenario, "No New Action Required" (NNR), was fully reliant on external information and not on the contents of the note. This was because the NNR class was only relevant if a scenario had already been organised for a given task. Based upon feedback gained from co-creation with the user group, we decided to remove this class until the external data source was available. The resulting dataset contained 5,343 notes spread between 29 classes. There was notable class imbalance, with the rarest class containing only 20 notes while the most populated class contained 1,200.

3.2   Evaluation of Classification Engine

We performed an exploratory evaluation to understand the effectiveness of different representation learners and classifiers on the above dataset by creating a classification task where notes were classified according to one of 29 scenarios. The dataset was divided into distinct training and test sets using 5-fold cross-validation. We considered both a distributional (term-frequency/inverse-document-frequency) and a distributed (Document-2-Vector) method of learning representations. We also considered three classification methods - k-Nearest Neighbour (kNN), Logistic Regression (LR) and a Multi-Layer Perceptron (MLP). We used accuracy in a classification task as a proxy measurement for representation goodness.

Term frequency-inverse document frequency (tf-idf) is a statistical measure to develop representations for documents in a corpus based upon the terms they contain. The value for each term is calculated by dividing the frequency of its usage within a document over the number of documents which contain the term within the corpus and controlled by a normalising factor [17]. Therefore, each feature of a document vector is a value which represents an individual word from the corpus vocabulary and so vectors can be very sparse. Document-2-Vector (Doc2Vec) [8] is an extension of the Word2Vec algorithm [12]. In Word2Vec, the representation for each word is learned by training a small neural network on word co-occurence. The neural network learns a representation for each word such that words with similar context will have a similar representation. The result is a representation of each word which is indicative of how it relates to every other word in the vocabulary (which gives an idea of what concepts the word belongs to). In its simplest form (and the one we use in this work) Doc2Vec is merely an average of the word embeddings to give a representation for a document.

Linear regression is a statistical approach where the classifier learns a predictor function to model the relationship between a document and each of its features. When this function is averaged across a large set of documents it tends to generalise well to unseen examples. We can then apply this function to get a label for query documents. K-NN classifies a query document based upon a (potentially weighted) vote of the k most similar examples from a set of documents. The value k is an integer to threshold the number of neighbours to consider during the voting process. Weighted variations of k-NN ensure that the most similar documents will have more weight during voting. An MLP is a neural network trained by providing a large number of labelled examples to learn a set of weights and biases which approximate the relationship between each document and its label. Once sufficient accuracy is achieved through training, these weights and biases can be applied to a query document to establish the probability of the document belonging to each label which was provided during training. We take the label with the maximum probability as our classification.

The hyperparameters for both representation learners and all three classifiers were optimised using a gridsearch. In the case of tf-idf, this meant data was pre-processed by removing stop words and stemming words to their root form. We then considered the 300 most common unigrams (n-gram range of 1) to build a representation. Finally, this output was normalised using cosine normalisation. For Doc2Vec, a window size of 10 was used to identify semantically related words and generated a representation of 300 features. In regards to our classifiers; for kNN this meant we used the 5 nearest neighbours and the voting mechanism was weighted by distance and for LR, we used L2 penalties with no class weighting and a maximum of 100 iterations. Lastly, our MLP classifier was formed of a single layer containing 100 neurons. This was trained for 200 epochs using ReLU activations and a categorical cross-entropy loss function supported by the Adam optimizer [7].

Table 1. Classifier performance on tf-idf and Doc2Vec representations with/without NNR class.

Representation	Classifier	Accuracy (%)	
		w/NNR	w/out NNR
TF-IDF	kNN	50.88	**99.10**
	LR	54.60	76.08
	MLP	54.30	98.25
Doc2Vec	kNN	27.70	16.24
	LR	22.80	23.64
	MLP	28.10	28.06

3.3   Results and Discussion

The results of the experimentation can be seen in Table 1. Tf-idf offered superior performance on this problem when compared to Doc2Vec, both when including the NNR class and when not. This is for two reasons. Firstly, Doc2Vec (like other neural network based approaches) commonly requires a large training set to function very effectively. Pre-training of a Doc2Vec model is also not valid here, due to the high usage of unique technical vocabulary in the notes. This also informs the second reason for the better classification performance achieved by representations learned via tf-idf. The likely scenario for a given note is highly reliant on the technical vocabulary which is used to describe the work performed as part of the task. In light of this we also tried a simple rule-based token-matching approach, but its performance did not match either of the above methods. This suggests that the additional information that tf-idf offers about term rarity (in the form of its idf portion) is important.

Removing the NNR class offers a much improved performance for the classifiers using representations gained from tf-idf. As above, this is likely due to the focused technical vocabulary of the notes, a mixture of which would be used throughout the NNR class. This is misleading, as the vocabulary used within a note is irrelevant to whether it should be classified NNR or not. Hence the decision to remove the NNR class from our dataset. That said, it is interesting to note that (with the exception of kNN) removing the NNR class did not overly affect the classification accuracy gained from the Doc2Vec representations. We take this as further support that a much larger volume of text would be needed to ensure that Doc2Vec could function effectively on this problem. This is supported by the improved performance of kNN on Doc2Vec representations when the NNR class was present. Direct similarity comparisons are more likely to suffer than approaches that perform further feature engineering, when the learned representations are non-optimal.

As a result of this evaluation, we elected to use representations learned from tf-idf and classified according to kNN as the classification engine for our use case.

3.4 Co-creation of Explanation Methods

The use case also offered a platform for co-creation to identify what the users considered important aspects of explanation. Meetings with the end user group or their managerial representatives occurred weekly throughout development of the framework. There were two important findings that were identified throughout these meetings. Firstly, the desired explanations were to be counterfactual, supporting findings in [13]. Co-creation participants were particularly interested to understand why a certain scenario was recommended before another, and what made a given note unique among similar notes. Secondly, and most surprisingly, was that participants believed explanation should highlight information important to human decision-making even if it was not relevant to the system's classification process. It was agreed among most of the contributing participants that this was important to establish trust in the system. Though initially this caused debate about the remit of the framework, we ultimately established the scope of our explanation; since the framework should be generalisable to every level of expertise within the business, if additional information was required to make sense of the classification or source data, then this should be offered. This meant that it was relevant to consider the provision of supporting information for example.

4   The Explanation Engine

In this paper we present a framework of explainability mechanisms that support a classification engine by explaining its output. The idea is that combining different mechanisms will ensure generalisablility of the framework. We divide mechanisms into three categories:

- **Low-level explanations methods** allow the user to visualise key information that provide insight to system decision-making and support interpretation.
- **High-level explanation methods** augment one or more low-level explanations with contextual information to enable more comprehensive explanation.
- **Co-created explanation methods** rely on user interaction to better emulate the subjectivity of personal recommendations.

We provide an example of a module from each category below. Furthermore, as inspired by [19], we highlight each goal that a specific module is designed to achieve.

Though the use case we have selected for discussion in this paper is confined to the use of textual data, the goal of the framework is to be data agnostic. The idea is that this will provide a resource for developers within the telecommunication organisation to easily and quickly integrate with their projects. Effective cataloguing (i.e. allowing searching by explanation type, the explanation goal it supports and data type) is key to provisioning a maintainable and accessible framework.

4.1   Low-Level Explanations

Low-level explanation methods describe key information directly extracted from the data itself or generated as part of the decision-making process. In the literature these are described as analytic explanations [14].

Confidence Measures. We can establish the confidence of our predictions with the traditional method of using similarity as a proxy [2]. If similarity is sufficiently high, we can be confident that our classification is correct. We base our confidence on the similarity of the nearest neighbour from a given label (which is the method that we have used in deployment). Confidence measures can be seen as a form of justifying the decision which has been made by the system.

Word Scoring and Overlap. Inspired by work in [11], where the authors found that it was important for users to understand the differences between a query and its neighbours, we designed this module to promote understanding of the impact that note vocabulary has on system decision-making. The overlap component identifies key terms which appear both in the query and within the neighbour set of a particular label. This enables the user to quickly visualise key similarities or differences between the notes and inform about complementary terms from similar notes in the corpus. The word scoring module then measures the activation of terms to highlight the influence of each term's local similarity on selection of a given neighbour note.

This method can be extended to cover phrases or distributed approaches [1]. Word scoring and identification of overlapping terms is a method of improving the user's ability to understand the underlying concepts of system decision-making and improve interpretability of the process.

4.2 High-Level Explanations

While low-level explanations identify key information about the query or recommendation, they are potentially inaccessible to non-expert users. In these scenarios, it would be helpful to give the information context by incorporating relevant background knowledge. High-level explanations cover verbal and visual explanations [14], which are generated by building on insights from low-level (analytic) explanations. In this work, we use the example of generating summaries to contextualise similarities and differences between notes based on the output of the 'word overlap and scoring' component.

Summarisation of Similarities/Differences. We consider a method of extractive summarisation to create a verbal explanation of similarities and differences between a query note and its neighbour set. First introduced in [10] as a means to create abstracts for journal papers, extractive summarisation is reliant upon the identification, extraction and combination of content representative sentences to summarise a document. It is applicable in domains where documents share unique technical vocabulary, such as law reports [6] or research papers with similar focus [3]. Our method of summarisation builds upon those mentioned. Given a query and a neighbour note (or set thereof), we are interested in summarising the similarities or differences. This means we are generating a summary from a list of overlapping and non-overlapping terms, as opposed to generating a summary from a full document. Essentially, we are augmenting the technical vocabulary which is highlighted by the low-level 'word overlap and scoring' mechanism and giving context to that information with free text.

From the notes, we generate a case-base of sentences which will act as summaries. Each note is divided into multiple sentences by slicing at natural end points (such as the end of a sentence, or beginning of a new topic). We transform these sentences in the same way as our full dataset, which in the case of the above problem means that their word contents have been stemmed, stop words removed and transformed using tf-idf. When the classification model is queried, we identify overlapping (or non-overlapping) words between the query and its return set. We transform this list with our representation learner to create a vector which is used to query our summarisation case-base and find the most similar sentence to act as a summary of similarities (or differences). This process is demonstrated in

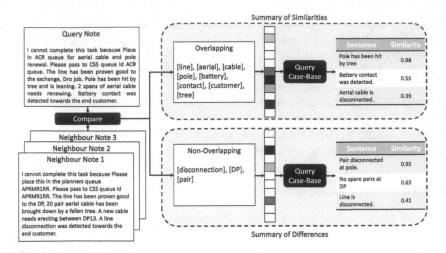

Fig. 2. Summarisation of similarities/differences between a query note and a set of neighbours.

Fig. 2. Words can be weighted using their idf score to emphasise rare terms and we can integrate aspects of query expansion from information retrieval research and augment queries with further information using local context.

This summarisation method produces a sentence in the engineers own words. This is useful for two reasons. Firstly, when engineers use the system it can be reassuring and trust building for them to see the difference clearly in their own words. Secondly, in the instances where non-experts are using the system, the summary of similarities and differences can expose them to language that engineers use in a controlled environment and supported by the other low-level explanation methods. This can improve learning about the original source data. However, autonomously evaluating the quality of explanations gained in this manner is difficult. Though we can empirically measure whether the retrieved sentence is sufficiently similar to (or different from) the query, it is difficult to identify whether the retrieved sentence is a meaningful summary without qualitative examination. As such, as part of our future work we are investigating methods of autonomous explanation quality measurement.

4.3   Co-creation of Explanations

Co-created explanation methods offer a means to ensure that explanations are always relevant to user needs. As with many other specialist areas, the field of telecommunication engineering is dynamic and any model or vocabulary learned is unlikely to remain stable for any significant length of time. This problem is often described as concept drift [20]. There must be some concept of updating both classification and explanation engines to correspond to the evolving needs of the user and the organisation as a whole. We explore this further in our example module below.

Provision of Supporting Information. As is often the case when non-expert users are exposed to a technical vocabulary they are unfamiliar with, desk-based agents are forced to use the context of a given term (or phrase) to infer its meaning if they do not understand it. This can pose an issue in instances where the meaning is incorrectly inferred, or when its importance to the next scenario is misunderstood. Thus there is a need to provision supporting information that can assist a desk-based agent's understanding of the query task. In our target use-case, this takes the form of highlighting terms that present potential hazards for a task.

Hazard terms are identified from the notes by consulting an external knowledge base which we have extracted from 2 documents summarising UK and EU government health and safety guidelines for telecommunication and underground work. If a term (or phrase) is identified as a hazard, we can highlight it within the application. Hazards can be scored by severity, meaning that we can differentiate the danger by presenting a simple LOW, MEDIUM, HIGH score. Maintaining the knowledge base and ensuring it meets the needs of the organisation is then a co-operative exercise between the developer and the user. It is the developer's responsibility to ensure that the original knowledge base is up to date (e.g. by keeping up with the latest health and safety regulation) to lessen the data collection burden on users. Users are expected to add missing hazard terms to the knowledge base as they appear through daily use, such that they are known for future. Conversely, if users feel that a term should not be identified as a hazard, we can prevent the term from being highlighted as a hazard for that user group in future. In such a way the knowledge base is personalised to the needs of specific user groups. An example of where this is relevant is in the case of 'optical fibre cabling'. Optical fibre cabling is highlighted as a hazard in both guideline documents due to the potential for permanent eye damage if suitable protection is not worn when installing a main line. In practice this is only relevant to one engineering worktype (underground), whereas others (such as consumer delivery) are routinely installing home optical fibre cabling, which has significantly reduced risk.

5   The Application

We have deployed a prototype of the described framework applied to our use case and accessible on the company intranet as a web application (see Fig. 3). When a query is entered, the application uses the classification engine to make recommendation from the known 29 scenario labels and guide task intervention. For example, in Fig. 3 the system has recommended the scenario NDT (No Dial Tone), which will be translated into the followup action 'further equipment tests'. In response to a recommendation, users may feedback on whether it is 'good' or 'bad' and optionally enter feedback text and a corrected label. The user can access an ordered list of other potential scenarios by selecting 'Recommending Other Scenarios (ordered per confidence score)'.

The application uses the explainability framework to explain the ordered list of recommendations. We compare the query to each label by aggregating the

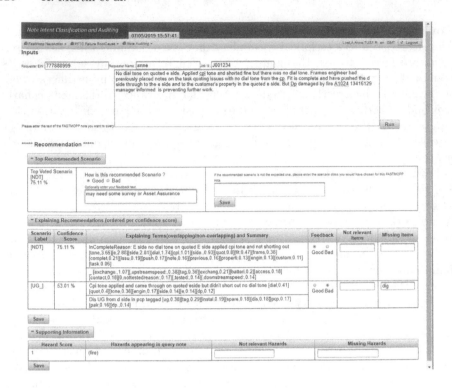

Fig. 3. Example of the system in action.

explanations for each note within the kNN neighbourhood that possesses that label. The confidence of the recommendation of each scenario is based upon the similarity of the nearest neighbour with that label, while direct note comparisons (e.g. the word scoring and overlap) are aggregated using a distance-weighted average. The focus of this explanation is therefore linked to identifying the most suitable scenario to be recommended. This allows the system to demonstrate the similarities and differences between a query and each label by displaying the identified overlapping and non-overlapping terms ordered by their score. A sentence summary (generated by the method defined in Sect. 4.2) then contextualises this information. There is also a mechanism for the user to feedback on the explanation to improve further query note explanation mechanisms. Finally, supporting information is highlighted for the label and each query.

6   Evaluation of Explanation Framework

Evaluating the quality of explanations is traditionally difficult due to their inherent subjectivity. The needs of different user groups can be very different, which is reflected in their expectations of what an explanation should offer. With this in mind, we evaluate the quality of explanations using qualitative feedback from telecommunication field engineers. Technical experts were selected to identify whether explanations emulated their decision process, as was requested during co-creation. We retrieved qualitative feedback on explanation quality from individual engineer comments verbally communicated during a beta test of the software. In total we observed 23 interactions between users and the system. All users provided a simple positive/negative score on whether the provided explanation was useful, and 17 also provided qualitative feedback. An example of feedback (and the explanation case it refers to) can be seen in Table 2.

In this paper we measure the effectiveness of our explanation by applying the model suggested in [5]. The model divides evaluation of an explainable systems into five different headings: user satisfaction (e.g. the clarity and utility of the explanation); mental model (e.g. the ability to understand individual decisions and identify strengths and weaknesses of the model); task performance (e.g. whether user ability to complete the task is improved by using the system); trust assessment (e.g. whether the system is trustable); and correctability (e.g. the user can rectify incorrect decisions). We examine each of these aspects in turn. As the model is live as a prototype, we cannot measure its impact on task performance, but we plan to do so in future.

6.1   Results and Discussion

User satisfaction with the system seems reasonably high. Of the 23 interactions with the system, 15 (65%) users left positive feedback regarding the explanation quality. Word matching and scoring was the most popular explanation mechanism, with almost every observed engineer discussing the selected words (both formally as recorded comments and informally with the researcher). Though summaries were observed, they were not discussed in the same level of detail. This is indicative that domain experts require less contextualisation from an explanation to understand it, likely because they can infer their own context. In future work, it will be interesting to compare the explanation needs of engineers (technical experts) against planning agents (non-experts) to identify different usage of the growing framework.

One disadvantage of this was that although engineers understood that the model was reliant on task note vocabulary, there was a tendency to misunderstand the learned model as simple token matching. As such, engineers often criticised the lack of keywords identified for certain notes, even when they had little or no impact on model decisions. In one example, an engineer stated that 'leaning' and 'tree' should be highlighted as key words, even though the word leaning is too generic to be represented by the vocabulary. This is indicative that engineers were able to understand some aspects of system decision-making (e.g. that it was vocabulary-based), but unable to mentally model the entire system. In future work, we aim to improve this.

In almost all cases (7 of 8 or 87.5%) where negative feedback was provided, the explanation was associated with an incorrect classification. This suggests that when a user discovers an error in the system decision-making, they are also likely to find a fault in its explanation of that decision. Our model offers a

Table 2. Example of qualitative feedback on explanation quality from field engineers.

Query		Drop Wire already up at front of property but landlord wants the customer drop wire moved to the wall of the flat which is above the flat roof and to drill out where the socket is required is out to the flat roof
Recommended Scenario (Action)		Out of Time (Re-allocate engineer)
Keywords	Overlap	[flat, 3.33] [roof, 2.76] [wire, 1.43] [drop, 1.18] [abov, 0.7]
	Non-Overlap	[one, 0.29] [insid, 0.29] [coil, 0.28] [side., 0.27] [build, 0.27]
Summary	Similarities	Drop wire is already up at front of property
	Differences	I have fitted the socket inside and left a coil of cable
Feedback		Roof is rightly highlighted. Fair explanation since engineer faced additional steps on the customer site (drill out)

means for users to submit corrections, which was well received by testers. Of the 23 interactions with the system, 15 (65%) made use of the feedback system to highlight missing or non-relevant words and phrases. Several users commented that they felt more comfortable with the system due to this feedback component. This suggests that correctability of an explanation is an important consideration when users are deciding whether to trust the system.

7   Conclusions

We have described the development of a framework to promote explainability of machine learning methods within a telecommunication organisation. We have motivated and explored the application of this framework to the specific use case of explaining technical engineer notes to non-technical planning personnel. An evaluation of this framework indicates that it meets the criteria for user satisfaction, trust assessment and correctability, but improvements are needed to facilitate mental modelling. In future work, we aim to address this and improve framework coverage of different explanations. In addition, we plan to extend the framework to incorporate explanations which acknowledge sequential and co-occurring scenarios, as these are necessary concepts for full automation. We also aim to apply this framework to further use cases, enabling us to better understand the explanation needs of users from different work types and experience levels.

References

1. Arras, L., Horn, F., Montavon, G., Müller, K.R., Samek, W.: "What is relevant in a text document?": an interpretable machine learning approach. PLoS ONE **12**(8), 1–23 (2017). https://doi.org/10.1371/journal.pone.0181142
2. Cheetham, W.: Case-based reasoning with confidence. In: Blanzieri, E., Portinale, L. (eds.) EWCBR 2000. LNCS, vol. 1898, pp. 15–25. Springer, Heidelberg (2000). https://doi.org/10.1007/3-540-44527-7_3
3. Collins, E., Augenstein, I., Riedel, S.: A supervised approach to extractive summarisation of scientific papers. arXiv preprint arXiv:1706.03946 (2017)
4. European Parliament and Council: Regulation (EU) 2016/679 of the European parliament and of the council of 27 April 2016 on the protection of natural persons with regard to the processing of personal data and on the free movement of such data, and repealing directive 95/46/EC (general data protection regulation)
5. Gunning, D.: Explainable artificial intelligence (XAI). Defense Advanced Research Projects Agency (DARPA), and Web (2017)
6. Hachey, B., Grover, C.: Extractive summarisation of legal texts. Artif. Intell. Law **14**(4), 305–345 (2006)
7. Kingma, D.P., Ba, J.: Adam: a method for stochastic optimization. arXiv preprint arXiv:1412.6980 (2014)
8. Le, Q., Mikolov, T.: Distributed representations of sentences and documents. In: Proceedings of the 31st International Conference on International Conference on Machine Learning, ICML 2014, vol. 32, pp. II-1188–II-1196. JMLR.org (2014)
9. Lipton, Z.C.: The mythos of model interpretability. arXiv preprint arXiv:1606.03490 (2016)
10. Luhn, H.P.: The automatic creation of literature abstracts. IBM J. Res. Dev. **2**(2), 159–165 (1958)
11. Massie, S., Craw, S., Wiratunga, W.: Visualisation of case-base reasoning for explanation. In: Proceedings of the ECCBR 2004 Workshops, pp. 135–144 (2004)
12. Mikolov, T., Chen, K., Corrado, G., Dean, J.: Efficient estimation of word representations in vector space. CoRR abs/1301.3781 (2013)
13. Miller, T.: Explanation in artificial intelligence: insights from the social sciences. Artif. Intell. **26**, 1–38 (2018)
14. Mohseni, S., Zarei, N., Ragan, E.D.: A survey of evaluation methods and measures for interpretable machine learning. arXiv preprint arXiv:1811.11839 (2018)
15. Muhammad, K., Lawlor, A., Smyth, B.: On the pros and cons of explanation-based ranking. In: Aha, D.W., Lieber, J. (eds.) ICCBR 2017. LNCS (LNAI), vol. 10339, pp. 227–241. Springer, Cham (2017). https://doi.org/10.1007/978-3-319-61030-6_16
16. Nordin, I.: Expert and non-expert knowledge in medical practice. Med. Health Care Philos. **3**(3), 295–302 (2000). https://doi.org/10.1023/A:1026446214010
17. Ramos, J.: Using tf-idf to determine word relevance in document queries. In: Proceedings of the First Instructional Conference on Machine Learning, pp. 133–142 (2003)

18. Ras, G., van Gerven, M., Haselager, P.: Explanation methods in deep learning: users, values, concerns and challenges. In: Escalante, H.J., et al. (eds.) Explainable and Interpretable Models in Computer Vision and Machine Learning. TSSCML, pp. 19–36. Springer, Cham (2018). https://doi.org/10.1007/978-3-319-98131-4_2
19. Sørmo, F., Cassens, J., Aamodt, A.: Explanation in case-based reasoning - perspectives and goals. Artif. Intell. Rev. **24**(2), 109–143 (2005)
20. Tsymbal, A.: The problem of concept drift: definitions and related work. Computer Science Department, Trinity College Dublin, **106**(2), p. 58 (2004)

A Generic Model for End State Prediction of Business Processes Towards Target Compliance

Naveed Khan[1]([✉]), Zulfiqar Ali[1], Aftab Ali[1], Sally McClean[1], Darryl Charles[1],
Paul Taylor[2], and Detlef Nauck[2]

[1] School of Computing, Ulster University, Newtownabbey, UK
{n.khan,z.ali,a.ali,si.mcclean,dk.charles}@ulster.ac.uk
[2] Applied Research, BT, Ipswich, UK
{paul.n.taylor,detlef.nauck}@bt.com

Abstract. The prime concern for a business organization is to supply quality services to the customers without any delay or interruption so to establish a good reputation among the customer's and competitors. On-time delivery of a customers order not only builds trust in the business organization but is also cost effective. Therefore, there is a need is to monitor complex business processes though automated systems which should be capable during execution to predict delay in processes so as to provide a better customer experience. This online problem has led us to develop an automated solution using machine learning algorithms so as to predict possible delay in business processes. The core characteristic of the proposed system is the extraction of generic process event log, graphical and sequence features, using the log generated by the process as it executes up to a given point in time where a prediction need to be made (referred to here as cut-off time); in an executing process this would generally be current time. These generic features are then used with Support Vector Machines, Logistic Regression, Naive Bayes and Decision trees to predict the data into on-time or delayed processes. The experimental results are presented based on real business processes evaluated using various metric performance measures such as accuracy, precision, sensitivity, specificity, F-measure and AUC for prediction as to whether the order will complete on-time when it has already been executing for a given period.

Keywords: Business processes · Automated system · Process prediction · End state prediction

1 Introduction

Over the last few decades, there has been a significant ongoing interest in research into Business Process Management (BPM) with the aim of predicting future process states [2]. Here a process is a series of tasks or steps, terminated by

© Springer Nature Switzerland AG 2019
M. Bramer and M. Petridis (Eds.): SGAI-AI 2019, LNAI 11927, pp. 325–335, 2019.
https://doi.org/10.1007/978-3-030-34885-4_25

an event and taken in order to achieve a particular end. Such prediction can help to gain operational excellence, and boost productivity, customer satisfaction and cost effectiveness [1]. The monitoring of a complex and dynamic business process is essential for analysis and identification when process instances do not perform as required. The timely prediction of such behaviours from online data can facilitate intervention and avert an undesired state of a process from occurring [1].

Moreover, the existence of such inefficiencies in business processes can greatly affect performance, ultimately increasing cost and having a negative impact on customer satisfaction [7]. Therefore, predictive process monitoring can utilize data generated during process execution so as to continuously monitor process performance [8]. Continuous monitoring of a business process can facilitate pre-emptive actions to attain the desired process outcome.

In this paper, machine learning techniques have been investigated for online process analysis to extract useful and discriminating information from raw data. Such information can be used to discover patterns that characterize an outcome as very likely and subsequently perform online prediction on incomplete process instances when this pattern has been observed. Therefore, the focus is to develop a system that will extract generic features from new processes for early prediction of a timely outcome, i.e. situations where the order can be delivered on-time, as opposed to delayed or cancelled. These techniques will help to uncover deeper insight into patterns which are difficult to execute manually or through visualization. Such analysis will enable domain experts to address these inefficiencies and help to streamline the process. The novelty here resides in the development of online strategies for predicting outcomes based on heterogeneous process data where we train and test by mapping the (online) processes onto the percentage of time until target has been reached. The generic feature selection approach, which is based on a portfolio of process, event log, graphical and sequence features, is also novel.

The remainder of this paper is organised as follows: in Sect. 2 the end state prediction framework is discussed. In Sect. 3, Feature extraction and dataset description is discussed with results and discussions presented in Sect. 4. Finally, Conclusions and Future Work are presented in Sect. 5.

2   A Framework of End State Prediction of Business Process Data

In many enterprises, early predictions of business processes are very helpful and can make the business more cost effective. Although analysis of such processes is quite complex and challenging, the capability of perceiving the likely conclusion of an ongoing process in advance would help business managers to react in time and help to avoid any delays or undesirable situations. In this paper, we consider an example of timely and early prediction of BT consumer processes, where the data contains the information for landline telephone and/or broadband orders. The aim is to develop a system that will extract generic features from processes for early online prediction that either the order will be delayed/cancelled or delivered on-time. Moreover, it is very difficult for the human mind to classify a multidimensional feature vector [6] and hence automated pattern recognition becomes essential and provides help in analyzing and understanding of complex data. Also, if the extracted features are generic in nature, then the system developed using such features can also be used for a new problem without making significant changes in our approach.

3   Dataset Description

In our experiments, a BT consumer dataset is used for analysis and evaluation. The complete dataset consists of 505,632 instances; however, in current experiments, we have only extracted instances of consumers, who have ordered landline telephone and/or broadband. These instances are used with the labels Y and N, where Y represents on-time delivered orders and N represents delayed/cancelled orders. Initially, a total of 15,523 on-time delivered processes and 1,585 processes delayed processes were extracted. Pre-processing and feature extraction are the most crucial steps in prediction [3] and are used to extract useful information for prediction into timely or delayed process instances.

3.1   Pre-processing

In the pre-processing step, we have processed the raw data of consumers, which are new orders for land line telephone and/or broadband. From the total of 15,523 on-time delivered processes, only 725 processes were used in our experiments to extract useful information since for the remainder of the processes either the tasks are recorded as zero duration or Target date and time (T_{dt}) were missing. Here Target date represents a target by which the process should, be completed. Similarity, for delayed processes, a total of 5830 processes were extracted, out of which 1,585 processes were used in our experiments because for the remaining processes either the task durations are 0 or Target date and time (T_{dt}) were missing, as before. The extracted features from successful on-time processes and unsuccessful delayed processes are then used to predict on-time and delayed/cancelled orders.

In our framework as shown in Fig. 1, initially the features are extracted from a process by taking cut-off time 25%, 50%, 75%, 85%, 95% and 100% from the starting date and time (S_{dt}) of the process until Target date and time (T_{dt}). Here (T_{dt}) is an initial target for the process completion date and time. The cut-off time means the percentage of time that point in target time which we regard as current so that we can make predictions using data only relating to the history up to that point in time and then compare them with the actual compliance, or otherwise. Cut-off time here is calculated as a percentage of the target.

Hence, if a process completes according to the estimated Commitment date and time it will be considered to be an on-time delivery, otherwise it will be considered to be a delayed process. For instance, consider, an example process initiated at a particular instance of date and time (e.g. Start date and time - 11/05/2018 10:35:00) with an initial estimate to complete this process by Commitment date and time (30/07/2018 23:59:59). In order to predict the process at different cut-off time ratios, we calculated the cut-off time using Eq. 1.

$$Cut - off\ Time = (T_{dt} - S_{dt}) * Th\% \qquad (1)$$

The T_{dt} is the Target date and time, S_{dt} is the process starting date and time and $Th\%$ is the 25%, 50%, 75%, 85%, 95% and 100% is the process cut-off time. As shown in Fig. 1, the cut-off time was explored for different ratios of 25% (dotted lines), 50% (dashed lines) and 75% (dashed line) and 100% (dotted line) of the time difference between start date and time and the corresponding target date and time.

3.2   Feature Extraction

The feature extraction step is first used offline to compute the likely most discriminating features from the data since success of prediction is strongly dependent on the extraction of highly relevant features form the raw data [4]. Moreover, if the extracted features are generic in nature, then the system developed using such features can also be used in a new domain without applying significant changes. Here, the process of feature extraction is elaborated by considering the randomly selected order as an example process from the raw data for ease of understanding. For such processes a number of generic features are typically available, such as process, event log, graphical and sequence features. Thus, for example, process features are known at the start of the process and do not change with time while event log features are revealed as the process executes the different tasks which it comprises. Graphical and sequence features, on the other hand, relate to the currently available event tree, which will be incomplete if the process is still ongoing. Here graphical features are a measure of how complex the event tree is e.g. how many nodes are repeated or how wide the tree is, while sequence features relate to the order of events within the process tree and whether there are common patterns or motifs which might indicate success or failure, in this case a timely outcome, or otherwise.

Moreover, the node features, on the other hand are all types of graphical feature which quantify the complexity of the log graph traversed to date. For example, the repetition of tasks can be a crucial indicator for the prediction of orders, as the repetition of some tasks may cause a delay in process completion.

A complete process with all associated tasks is shown in Fig. 1. Different measures are computed from the raw data to form the feature vector. The general form of seven-dimensional feature vector F used for prediction is given in Eq. 2.

$$F = [aT \quad uT \quad rT \quad nRT \quad perT \quad t_{Time} \quad r_{Time}] \qquad (2)$$

where

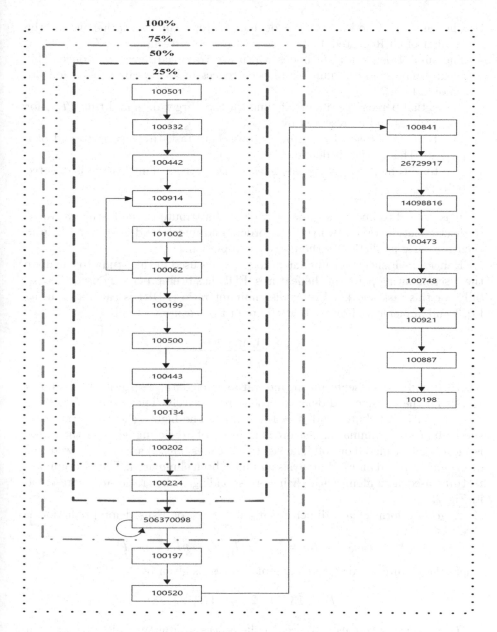

Fig. 1. Task execution of a process for different cut-off percentages.

1. The number of all traversed nodes including repetition are Appeared Tasks. This feature is denoted by aT.
2. All nodes having a degree exactly equal to 1, in fact, these are Unique Tasks which appear only once and are denoted by uT.

3. The number of nodes having a degree greater than 1. In other words, the number of all Repeated Tasks. This feature is represented by rT.
4. The sum of degrees of all nodes which are traversed more than once. This feature represents the number of occurrences of all repeated tasks and are denoted by nRT.
5. The actual percentage of cut-off time till the Target date and time (T_{dt}) for each process and represented by $perT$.
6. The total time taken by a process to execute tasks from start to end of a process. This feature is denoted by (t_{Time}).
7. The total time taken by repeated tasks in a process. This feature is denoted by (r_{Time}).

It is critical to know the capability of each attribute in the feature vector F to discriminate between two types of orders and understand how it can help in accurate early prediction of the process completion.

Hence, the Fisher discriminant ratio (FDR) is used in this study to calculate the discriminating power of the features. FDR has been previously used successfully for this task e.g. [2]. Fisher discriminant ratio (FDR) is calculated using Eq. 3 and implemented for each attribute of the feature vector F.

$$FDR_f = \frac{(\mu_Y - \mu_N)^2}{\sigma_Y^2 + \sigma_N^2} \tag{3}$$

where μ and σ represents mean and variance of data, respectively, Y and N stands for the on-time and delayed orders, respectively. The variable f signifies the number of attributes and $f = 1, 2, 3, ..., n$. The higher the ratio, the more successful the discriminating feature is in terms of predicting whether the target is successfully achieved or not. The last two features (t_{Time}) and (r_{Time}) were less discriminant based on FDR analysis and have been eliminated. The discriminant features used here along with their corresponding Fisher ratio are represented in Fig. 2.

A generic form of a 5-dimensional feature vector F used for prediction is given as:

$$Feature\ Vector = [aT \quad uT \quad rT \quad nRT \quad perT]$$

where the feature vector for an example process is given by:

$$F = [13 \quad 9 \quad 2 \quad 4 \quad 45.35\%]$$

These features were used to predict the process compliance with the target at different cut-off time ratios to predict whether the process will complete on-time or will be delayed. For simplicity, we diagrammatically represented an example of 50% cut-off time for a process as shown in Fig. 3, where 15 tasks appeared before the cut-off time, of which 9 were unique tasks and 3 tasks were repeated 6 times and 50% is the actual percentage of cut-off time until the Target date and time (T_{dt}).

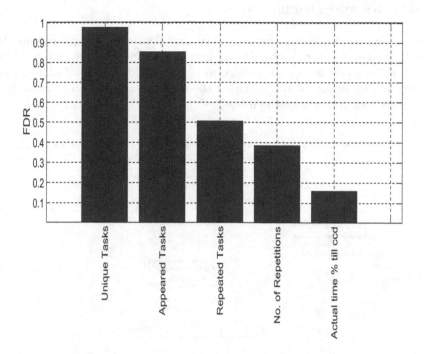

Fig. 2. Discriminant features using fisher ratio

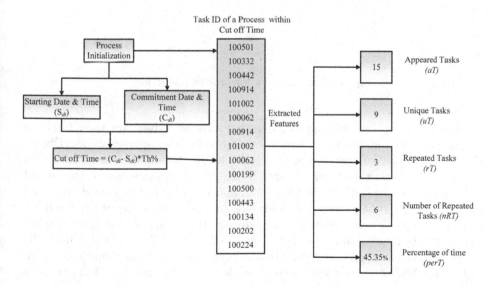

Fig. 3. Feature Extraction Framework of an Incomplete Process at 50% cut-off time with $Th = 0.5$

4   Results and Discussion

We have implemented various machine learning algorithm using the computed multi-dimensional feature vector for prediction of process compliance with target. Our experiments have been performed using 10-fold cross validation to evaluate the predictive model and partition the original sample into a training set and a testing set to evaluate the model.

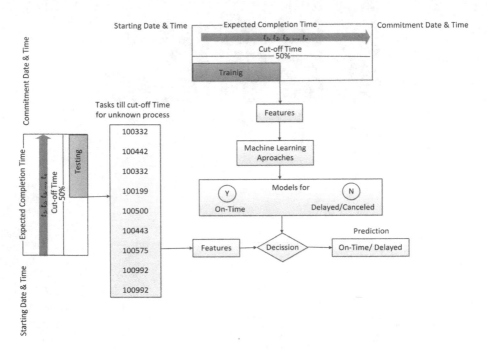

Fig. 4. Block diagram for process prediction

The advantage of this approach is that process values are used for both training and testing, and each observation is used for testing exactly once. During the testing phase, an unknown process is fed to the system, the relevant features are extracted, and the system records if the process finishes before the cut-off time ratio (i.e. 25%, 50%, 75%, 85%, 95%, and 100%) it will be considered as an on-time delivery otherwise we predict it as a delayed process. In our approach, we consider the processes start time (time since initialization of that process) with different cut-off time ratio (i.e. 25%, 50%, 75%, 85%, 95% and 100%) until the initial estimation of process completion (Commitment date and time) as shown in Fig. 4. The features are extracted from the raw data and these features were used to train the model. Different machine learning algorithms such as Support Vector Machines (SVM) [9], Logistic Regression [5], Naive Bayes [11] and J48 [10], are used to predict the outcome of the process.

Table 1. Prediction results of different machine learning algorithms for different metric measures

Algorithm	25% cut-off time					
	Accuracy %	Precision %	Sensitivity %	Specificity %	F-measure %	AUC
Logistic Regression	73.66	90.73	76.07	61.85	82.76	0.73
J48	74.61	88.86	77.92	61.93	82.94	0.70
SVM	74.73	89.19	77.78	62.61	83.10	0.73
Naive Bayes	62.75	60.39	81.33	42.85	69.31	0.71
Algorithm	50% cut-off time					
	Accuracy %	Precision %	Sensitivity %	Specificity %	F-measure %	AUC
Logistic Regression	75.10	92.22	77.03	65.33	83.85	0.74
J48	75.07	84.95	80.59	59.36	82.71	0.68
SVM	75.07	90.45	77.70	63.32	83.59	0.74
Naive Bayes	55.72	44.14	85.95	38.67	58.33	0.72
Algorithm	75% cut-off time					
	Accuracy %	Precision %	Sensitivity %	Specificity %	F-measure %	AUC
Logistic Regression	74.60	91.30	76.07	61.85	82.75	0.77
J48	73.32	87.39	77.60	56.79	82.20	0.69
SVM	75.14	90.45	77.82	62.67	83.66	0.76
Naive Bayes	64.16	57.02	87.91	44.14	69.18	0.75
Algorithm	85% cut-off time					
	Accuracy %	Precision %	Sensitivity %	Specificity %	F-measure %	AUC
Logistic Regression	75.41	90	78.35	62.75	83.77	0.78
J48	74.38	87.83	78.43	59.09	82.87	0.72
SVM	75.71	89.45	78.93	62.85	83.86	0.78
Naive Bayes	65.54	58.46	88.90	45.31	70.54	0.76
Algorithm	95% cut-off time					
	Accuracy %	Precision %	Sensitivity %	Specificity %	F-measure %	AUC
Logistic Regression	77	90.18	79.95	65.39	84.76	0.78
J48	75.74	87.74	79.96	61.03	83.67	0.76
SVM	77.21	89.45	80.53	64.97	84.76	0.78
Naive Bayes	66.81	63.96	85.54	45.72	73.19	0.75
Algorithm	100% cut-off time					
	Accuracy %	Precision %	Sensitivity %	Specificity %	F-measure %	AUC
Logistic Regression	77.20	90.45	80	65.80	84.90	0.78
J48	79.16	86.39	84.56	64.96	85.47	0.82
SVM	77.12	89.36	80.51	64.56	84.71	0.77
Naive Bayes	67.53	67.29	83.74	46.06	74.62	0.73

During the testing phase, an unknown process is fed to the system, the relevant features are extracted, if the processes finishes before the cut-off time ratio (i.e. 25%, 50%, 75%, 85%, 95%, and 100%) it will be considered as an on-time delivery, and if not then the decision is made by the predictive model that the process is delayed as shown in Fig. 4.

Different performance measures such as accuracy, precision, sensitivity, specificity, F-measure and AUC are used to evaluate the performance of the chosen machine learning algorithms. In business processes, accuracy is not considered to be the best measure for performance evaluation of prediction algorithms due to the fact that accuracy is sensitive towards class imbalance [7], which is a characteristic of our current problem. Therefore, true positive (the proportion of correctly classified instances) and false positive (proportion of incorrectly classified instances) rates are more important from a cost-benefit perspective and due to their being agnostic towards data skewness. The results of our experiments are evaluated using various performance measures such as accuracy precision, sensitivity, specificity, F-measure and AUC as presented in Table 1. The F-measure is regarded as the best performance metric for imbalanced data and AUC is used to determine which of the used models have predicted the classes best.

As presented in Table 1, in the case of a 25% cut-off time, it is observed that the support vector machine (SVM) and logistic regression perform slightly better than the other algorithms in terms of accuracy (74.73% and 73.66%), precision (89.19% and 90.73), sensitivity (77.78%, 76.07%), F-measure (83.10% and 82.76%) and the AUC is the same (0.73%).

Similarly, in the case of a 50% cut-off time, the logistic regression algorithm achieved 75.10% accuracy, 92.22% precision, 77.03% sensitivity, 83.85% F-measure and 0.74% AUC. On the other hand, SVM and J48 are close competitors of logistic regression with the same accuracy 75.07%, precision (90.45% and 84.95%), sensitivity (77.70 and 77.03), F-measure (83.59% and 82.71%) and AUC (0.74% and 0.68%).

As the cut-off time increases (i.e. to 75%, 85% and 95%), SVM and logistic regression perform better than the other algorithms as presented in Table 1. However, in the case of 100% cut-off time, the J48 algorithm performs better than other algorithms and achieved 79.16% accuracy, 86.39% precision, 84.56% sensitivity, 85.47% F-measure and 0.82% AUC. If we rank the algorithms based on the average of all performance parameters, then logistic regression and SVM have a very close contest as is evident from Table 1. AUC is the most important evaluation metric used for checking prediction model performance where a high AUC value represents more accurate prediction made by the model as presented in Table 1.

In case of 25%, 50%, 75%, 85% and 95% cut-off time logistic regression compared to SVM either achieved slightly high or same AUC value of 0.73%, 0.74%, 0.77%, 0.78% and 0.78%. However, in case of 100% cut-off time, J48 achieved AUC value of 0.82%. Also, the result shows that as we increase the cut-off time, prediction is improved, as expected, particularly towards the end of the process.

5   Conclusion

The monitoring of a business processes to avoid delay in the delivery of a customers order is a crucial element for better customer experience and to avoid financial loss for the company. The proposed system tries to provide a solution to this problem, where the real issue is to provide a means of monitoring the progress of an order in real time and assess whether we can infer a likely breach of target compliance and predict delay at an early stage. Finding the optimal time for intervention and mediating against the evolving situation is a trade-off between having confidence in our prediction and intervening in a timely manner. Our current predictions achieve reasonable success where performance is seen to increase as the process evolves towards the target, and more process data is exposed. By using generic features for prediction, we hope in further work to explore different feature selection and classification options as well as diverse problem domains.

Acknowledgement. This research is supported by the BTIIC (BT Ireland Innovation Centre) project, funded by BT and Invest Northern Ireland.

References

1. Aalst, W.: Business process management: a comprehensive survey. ISRN Softw. Eng. **2013**, 1–37 (2013)
2. Al-Nasheri, A., et al.: An investigation of multidimensional voice program parameters in three different databases for voice pathology detection and classification. J. Voice **31**(1), 113–e9 (2017)
3. Alasadi, S.A., Bhaya, W.S.: Review of data preprocessing techniques in data mining. J. Eng. Appl. Sci. **12**(16), 4102–4107 (2017)
4. Aparna, U., Paul, S.: Feature selection and extraction in data mining. In: 2016 Online International Conference on Green Engineering and Technologies (IC-GET), pp. 1–3. IEEE (2016)
5. Menard, S.: Applied Logistic Regression Analysis, vol. 106. Sage, Thousand Oaks (2002)
6. Mesallam, T.A., et al.: Development of the Arabic voice pathology database and its evaluation by using speech features and machine learning algorithms. J. Healthc. Eng. **2017**, 1–13 (2017)
7. Taylor, P.N., Kiss, S.: Rule-mining and clustering in business process analysis. In: Bramer, M., Petridis, M. (eds.) SGAI 2018. LNCS (LNAI), vol. 11311, pp. 237–249. Springer, Cham (2018). https://doi.org/10.1007/978-3-030-04191-5_22
8. Von Rosing, M., Von Scheel, H., Scheer, A.W.: The Complete Business Process Handbook: Body of Knowledge from Process Modeling to BPM, vol. 1. Morgan Kaufmann, Boston (2014)
9. Wang, L.: Support Vector Machines: Theory and Applications, vol. 177. Springer, Heidelberg (2005). https://doi.org/10.1007/b95439
10. Witten, I.H., Frank, E., Hall, M.A., Pal, C.J.: Data Mining: Practical Machine Learning Tools and Techniques. Morgan Kaufmann, San Francisco (2016)
11. Zhang, H.: The optimality of naive bayes. Am. Assoc. Artif. Intell. **1**(2), 3 (2004)

An Investigation of the Accuracy of Real Time Speech Emotion Recognition

Jeevan Singh Deusi[✉] and Elena Irena Popa

School of Computing and Mathematical Sciences,
University of Greenwich, London, UK
jeevan.deusi@ntlworld.com, e.i.popa@greenwich.ac.uk

Abstract. This paper presents an investigation of speech emotion systems and how the accuracy can be further improved by exploring machine learning algorithms and hybrid solutions. The accuracy of machine learning algorithms and speech noise reduction techniques are investigated on an embedded system. Research suggests improvements could be made to the feature selection from speech signals and pattern recognition algorithms for emotion recognition. The system deployed to perform the experiments is EmotionPi, using the Raspberry Pi 3 B+. Pattern recognition is investigated by using K-Nearest Neighbour (K-NN), Support Vector Machine (SVM), Random Forest Classifier (RFC), Multi-Layer Perception (MLP) and Convolutional Neural Networks (CNN) algorithms. Experiments are conducted to determine the accuracy of the speech emotion system using the speech database and our own recorded dataset. We propose a hybrid solution which has proven to increase the accuracy of the emotion recognition results. Results obtained from testing, show the system needs to be trained using real cases rather than using speech databases (as it is more accurate in detecting the user's emotion).

Keywords: Embedded system · Ensemble methods · Non-linear algorithms · Machine learning · Support Vector Machine · K-Nearest Neighbour · Random Forests · Convolutional Neural Networks · Multi-Layer Perception · Neural networks · Speech emotion recognition

1 Introduction

Humans express emotions in several ways: heart rate, perspiration, facial expressions, body language, voice tone, crying and laughing [1]. These emotions are automatically expressed and recognised by humans. Speech emotion recognition is the identification of emotion from speech, such as happy, sad, neutral and anger.

Schuller [1] questions "Alexa, Cortana, Siri, and many other dialogue systems have hit the consumer home on a larger scale than ever. Nevertheless, do any of them truly notice our emotions and react to them like a human conversational partner would?"

Speech emotion systems have a wide range of applications ranging from education [2], robotics [3], law, healthcare, government agencies, public services, society issues and interviews [4]. Speech emotion recognition is beneficial for society in the

© Springer Nature Switzerland AG 2019
M. Bramer and M. Petridis (Eds.): SGAI-AI 2019, LNAI 11927, pp. 336–349, 2019.
https://doi.org/10.1007/978-3-030-34885-4_26

"new digital world" [5]. For example, in an educational environment, they can be used to manage and reduce stress or aid in lack of emotion [2].

Likewise, the development and the demand on robots has increased (as of 2014), therefore more attention needs to be carried out on the design of vocal emotion for AI robots [3]. Ivanovic et al. [3] suggests to upgrade robots, it is necessary for robots "to be not only emotionally rich in vocal expression, but also capable of performing vocal emotion recognition."

An embedded device is a bridge for speech emotion recognition with robotics (as it can control robotic hardware, such as Servos & motors). Emotion detection with robotics can be employed on a stand-alone embedded device or on cloud connected smart devices. Cloud connected smart devices are suitable for critical applications (e.g. aircraft/vehicle, patients or occupant safety in the smart home) where a more powerful machine is required for real time execution [6]. A cloud connected smart device system requires a powerful machine, reliable connectivity, security and additional software for each device.

The Raspberry Pi (a stand-alone embedded device) was chosen for this project as a simpler solution, as it is portable; can efficiently perform signal processing and can measure analogue signals [5]. The Raspberry Pi can be programmed in a variety of languages such as Python, bash, Java and MATLAB. The Raspberry Pi 3 B+ is ideal for speaker and microphone connectivity.

Speech emotion recognition requires three high level components: a dataset; feature extraction techniques to extract the audio features; feature normalisation; a pattern recognition algorithm (machine learning algorithm or classifier) to train and predict specific emotions. Real time speech emotion systems require a voice detector and a pre-processing component. The pre-processing component removes the noise and normalises the audio in the speech file. A voice detector detects the presence of the user's voice.

Dimitrieva and Nikitin [7] suggests, improvements could still be made to the feature selection and pre-processing for speech emotion systems. The authors also suggest it is interesting to investigate the combination of classifiers (such as SVM, deep learning - neural networks and HMM) as it could improve the accuracy and performance [7]. A hybrid or a combination of the algorithms may need to be employed for a speech emotion system [3]. Wu, Huang, and Zhang [8], suggest improvements could be made by investigating robustness of deep learning models. However, Kerkeni et al. [2] comments, "no classifier has been considered as most suitable for emotion classification".

Furthermore, real time speech emotion recognition requires recorded datasets. Speech captured by microphones adds other problems, such as noise and room reverberation [6]. Hence, the recordings have been played-back from the speech emotion database, in order to investigate the accuracy of the speech noise reduction techniques.

2 Proposed System

2.1 Hardware and Programming Language

Python 3.5 was chosen for the programming language, as it included a vast array of machine learning frameworks; feature extraction libraries and is ideal for the Raspberry Pi 3 B+. Bash (command line interface) was utilised for noise reduction, as it included a larger variety of speech noise reduction libraries, compared to Python. Figure 1 shows how the hardware is connected to the Raspberry Pi.

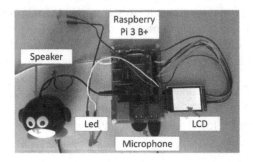

Fig. 1. Raspberry Pi, USB Microphone, AUX speaker & other hardware for viewing data.

2.2 Voice Detector

The voice detector chosen is a hotword detector, which detects the presence of a keyword (such as Snowboy). The library used is Snowboy. The library also includes a VAD to record the voice, after a hotword is detected. Initially a VAD was utilised for the voice detector however, when testing the library, the VAD can mistake noise as a human voice. Hotword detection has been found to be more reliable compared to a VAD for voice detection.

2.3 Pre-processing

The system removes the noise from the audio file and normalises the sound in the audio file (using the SoX library in bash). The noise reduction library removes any static noise from the microphone (as the microphone can record static noise from the speaker). Audio normalisation regulates the volume in the audio file to be consistent for emotion recognition at different distances. Before the features are extracted, any silent sections of the audio file are removed.

2.4 Feature Extraction

Dimitrieva and Nikitin [7] highlights "feature extraction is the most important and complicated step". In order to effectively recognise emotion from speech, relevant features are extracted. The two types of feature extraction techniques are global and local features. Global features (calculated statistics) are more 'superior' compared to local features (continuous data) in terms of accuracy and time for classification [9].

Research suggests the most suitable types are TEO and spectral features. Teager Energy Operator (TEO) can detect stressed emotions [10]. TEO reflects the interaction between the frequency components and can be used to classify "loud, angry, Lombard, clear and neutral" emotions [9]. Spectral features (such as MFCCs, MEDC, Spectral Energy and LPC) have higher accuracy compared to energy and pitch (88.67% for MFCC + MEDC vs 33.33% for energy + pitch) [11].

Evidently, the system extracts 222 statistical/global features (which are min, max, median, mean, interquartile-range (IQR) and standard deviation) from the audio file, in order to achieve high overall accuracy. The features extracted from the system are ZCR, Energy, Entropy of Energy, Spectral Centroid, Spectral Spread, Spectral Entropy, Spectral Flux, Spectral Rolloff, MFCCs, Chroma Vector, Chroma Deviation (from the pyAduioAnalysis library). Other, TEO A, TEO B, LPC features were extracted from other libraries, through windowing and framing of the audio signal.

2.5 Feature Normalisation

Before pattern recognition is carried out, the data is normalised using sckit-learn's StandardScaler. Ayadi et al. [9] highlights, it is necessary to normalise the data or it may be "ill conditioned". sckit-learn's StandardScaler uses a Z-score normalisation, where z is the Z-score, μ is the mean, X is the feature and σ is the standard deviation (1).

$$Z = \frac{X - \mu}{\sigma} \tag{1}$$

2.6 Pattern Recognition Algorithms

Modern algorithms have been selected for machine learning: Support Vector Machine (SVM), K-Nearest Neighbour (KNN), Random Forest Classifier (RFC), Multi-Layer Perception (MLP) and Convolutional Neural networks (CNN). All of the classifiers selected are non-linear classifiers, as in real life most feature vectors are not linear [12]. Most non-linear algorithms achieve high accuracies (above 75%).

SVM is a common algorithm and has achieved 88.8% using the Berlin dataset [13]; 80.1% from using own dataset [14] and 78.2% using own dataset [15]. K-NN has achieved 81% using the Berlin dataset [7] and 75.6% using own dataset [14]. Neural networks is a modern algorithm and has achieved 88.4% using own dataset [15].

Hybrid classifiers have been selected, since they usually have higher accuracies compared to single classifier systems (at a cost of complexity). RFC has also been selected, as it achieves high accuracies with a hybrid of other algorithms. For example, [16] achieved an accuracy of 84.68% for Convolutional Neural Networks + Random Forest (CNN-RF) and just 81.43% for CNN using the Berlin dataset. In some cases, a single classifier can outperform weaker algorithms. For example, Dimitrieva and Nikitin [7] achieved 81% for K-NN, 76% for PCA + LDA and 81% for PCA + LDA + SFFS (using the Berlin dataset). In this case, K-NN outperformed a combination of weaker algorithms. Therefore, the best algorithms (which have achieved the best accuracies) have been selected for the proposed system.

Multi-Layer Perception (MLP) Models Architecture. Three models have been devised to investigate and choose the best MLP model for the system (see Table 1). All the MLP models use three Dense layers. The input layer size is the same from feature extraction (222 neurons), the next layer has 40 neurons, and the output layer is 8 neurons for various emotions (see Fig. 2). The models have been trained for 1000 epochs with a batch size of around 34 for neural network training.

Table 1. MLP models configuration.

Name	Model configuration	Library
NN1	The model uses the Adam optimiser for the solver function of the neural network. Adam optimiser is probably the most popular solver function [17]. The activation function is relu (rectifier), which is a common activation function used for neural networks [17]	Keras
NN2	The model uses the rmsprop optimiser for the solver function of the neural network. Rmsprop optimiser prevents overfitting of the model. Thereby, will probably improve accuracy and is also quite popular. The activation function is sigmoid, which is a less commonly used activation function	Keras
MLP	Same configuration as NN1	Scikit-learn

Convolutional Neural Networks (CNN) Model Architecture. The CNN model devised uses 6 layers and is one dimensional (as the input data is one dimensional). The activation function used is sigmoid and the solver function is SGD. The input layer (convolutional layer) has 222 neurons and accepts a 2D array. Followed by a max pooling layer (which extracts the max value). A batch normalisation layer was included, to improve the overall accuracy. Followed by a flatten layer (which flattens the data to a 1D array) and a hidden dense layer of 1000 neurons. The output layer has eight neurons (number of classifier objects, i.e. eight possible emotions), for the output. For more information see Fig. 3. The model has been trained for 1000 epochs with a batch size of 34.

The CNN model has been used for the speech databases experiments but removed from the real time speech emotion system due to performance issues whilst training the model.

Other Non-linear Algorithms Architecture. The other non-linear algorithms used for the system utilise the Scikit-learn library (see Table 2).

Hybrid Classifier Algorithms. The hybrid classifier algorithms vote on solutions from CNN, NN1, NN2, MLP and SVM algorithms (KNN has not been included as the accuracy is lower compared to the other algorithms). CNN algorithm has been removed; it is provided in the results section. Similarly, the ensemble probability algorithm has been disregarded due to an error with the SVM algorithm when using probability (found out for Sect. 3.2 Real time speech emotion case-based study).

The ensemble classifier and the ensemble probability algorithms have been proposed for this system. Ensemble classifier uses the results from the algorithms to calculate the most common result (or the most common detected emotion). Ensemble probability uses the mean of the probability results, then calculates the index of the max value (to obtain the most common emotion).

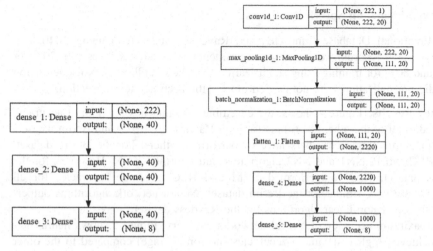

Fig. 2. MLP model architecture for Keras and Scikit-learn libraries.

Fig. 3. CNN model architecture for Keras

Table 2. Other non-linear algorithms configuration.

Algorithm name	How the algorithm is configured?
Support Vector Machine (SVM)	SVM is configured with a linear kernel
K-Nearest Neighbour (KNN)	KNN is configured with 1 neighbour and 1 job
Random Forest Classifier (RFC)	RFC is configured with 1000 estimators and a random sate of 42. 1000 estimators are chosen in order to maximise accuracy against performance

3 Experiments

3.1 The Dataset

To evaluate the accuracy of the algorithm, two datasets were used: The Berlin Emotional Database (Emo-DB) and the Ravdess dataset. Many of the Emo-DB files have been acted (speeches are acted by professionals and are often exaggerated) [9, 18], however it is commonly used amongst researchers. The dataset consists of 7 emotions: neutral, anger, boredom, disgust, anxiety/fear and sadness.

The Ravdess dataset was chosen as it uses induced emotions [19]. The Ravdess dataset is recorded from professional actors; validated from 247 raters and overall correctness is 60% [19]. Ravdess dataset contains eight emotions: surprised, disgust, fearful, angry, sad, happy, calm and neutral. Ravdess emotional database was utilised for real life experiments, as it is an English dataset.

3.2   Experiments on Speech Databases

Berlin Emotional Database (Emo-DB) and Ravdess dataset (containing 1440, and respectively 535 records) were used for experiments and the dataset was split 20% for testing and 80% for training using scikit-learn's StratifiedShuffleSplit. Noise reduction and audio normalisation were not carried out for the accuracy results section.

Accuracy Results. Figure 4 shows, the ensemble classifier has the highest accuracy, compared to all of the other algorithms for both Ravdess (67.19%) and Berlin datasets (83.27%). Some single classifiers have outperformed others. For the Berlin dataset, SVM, RFC, MLP, NN1 and NN2 algorithms outperformed KNN. However, for the Ravdess dataset, KNN outperformed SVM and RFC. Average accuracies for all algorithms are very similar for the Berlin dataset. Neural network algorithms outperformed the other non-linear algorithms for the Ravdess dataset.

The maximum accuracy of Neural networks can vary. Figure 5 shows neural networks achieved higher maximum accuracies (not on average) compared to the other non-linear algorithms (such as SVM, RFC and KNN) for the Berlin dataset. NN1 maximum accuracy was 86.92%, whereas the minimum was 74.77%; CNN maximum accuracy was 82.24% and the minimum accuracy was 73.83%. Hence, the maximum accuracy of Hybrid classifier algorithms varies, as they include neural network algorithms. The maximum accuracy for the Ensemble classifier was 87.85% and the minimum was 80.37%. The maximum accuracy for Ensemble probability was 85.98% and the minimum was 80.37%.

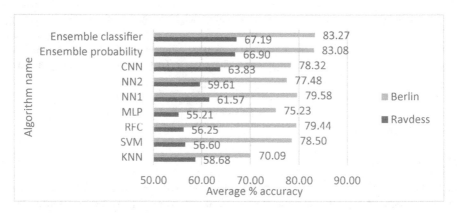

Fig. 4. Average accuracy of algorithms for the Berlin and Ravdess datasets.

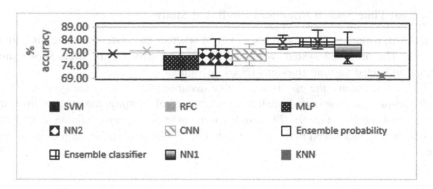

Fig. 5. Boxplot of the variance in accuracy for each of the models for the Berlin dataset.

Speech Noise Reduction Techniques. Speech noise reduction techniques were tested on two different libraries: SoX and RNNoise. For this experiment, SoX was utilised for audio normalisation and for audio noise removal. Whereas, RNNoise was only utilised for noise removal. The Berlin dataset was recorded, by playing back the audio files from the dataset in a quiet room (using the sounddevice library). The speaker was placed approximately 20 cm away from the microphone.

The highest accuracy (72.43%) for the ensemble classifier algorithm was achieved without using audio noise reduction or audio normalisation. Whereas Sox noise reduction achieved 68.69% accuracy (see Fig. 6). Sox noise reduction yielded the highest accuracy for the noise reduction (68.69% vs 66.36% for RNN noise using the ensemble classifier algorithm). Audio normalisation also reduced the accuracy. The ensemble classifier achieved an accuracy of 66.36% for RNNoise vs. RNNoise + Sox normalisation, which achieved 58.88%.

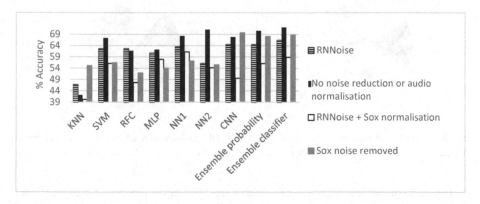

Fig. 6. Average accuracy of algorithm against speech noise reduction techniques from recording the Berlin dataset.

3.3   Real Time Speech Emotion Case-Based Study

An essential aspect of this research was to test whether the system accuracy is high in real life. The proposed system was used for this experiment; the users spoke short phrases and acted various emotions (N = 3 people).

The results assume the user is at a similar distance when testing the system. A total of 32 samples were assessed against the accuracy of training the system from the speech database (see Fig. 9). 27 samples were assessed against training the system from the user's data stored in the system (see Fig. 10). A total of 59 samples have been used.

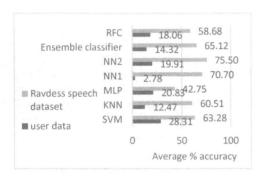

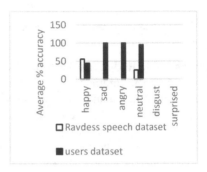

Fig. 7. Average accuracy of algorithms from training the system using users' data vs speech dataset.

Fig. 8. Average accuracy of emotions for the ensemble classifier from training the system using the speech database vs users' data.

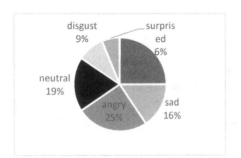

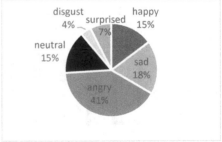

Fig. 9. Distribution of emotions tested when trained from the speech database (N = 32).

Fig. 10. Distribution of emotions tested when trained from the users' data (N = 27).

Figure 7 shows the accuracy of training the system on the user's data is higher compared to training the system on the speech database. The results show the best algorithms are NN1 and NN2; followed by the ensemble classifier.

Some of the emotions, such as Anger were not getting detected initially (see Fig. 8). Hence after training the system for a user's dataset, the recognition of these emotions improved. Accuracy of disgust and surprised are very low, as not enough samples have been recorded for these emotions. Further research is desired into induced emotions on a larger sample size.

4 Evaluation

4.1 Results Evaluation

The accuracy results show a big difference in the results between the acted and induced data sets, similar to what Rong et al. [20] noticed. The Berlin database is acted, whereas the Ravdess dataset is induced. The accuracies for the Berlin dataset are higher compared to the Ravdess dataset.

The accuracy results show that overall NN1 has achieved the highest accuracy compared to the other MLP models, NN1 slightly outperformed NN2 and MLP. Keras library outperformed scikit-learn library for the three MLP models.

Moreover, the accuracy of neural network models varied, when compared to the other non-linear models (however neural network algorithms achieved higher maximum accuracies compared to non-linear models). It is essential to use other non-linear models in the hybrid solution, where the accuracy does not vary, in order to maximise accuracy (e.g. SVM and RFC). No single classifier is best for speech emotion recognition. The hybrid solution (ensemble classifier) has the highest accuracies for both Ravdess and Berlin datasets.

The Berlin dataset was used for the recorded results, as it is louder compared to the Ravdess dataset (the Ravdess dataset was re-recorded, however the audio files were too quiet). The highest accuracy was achieved without using noise reduction or audio normalisation, which contradicts the need to remove any static noise from the microphone, however it is still essential to normalise the sound, if the voice is at different distances.

For the real-life case study, results show the system needs to be trained from the user's data. The most obvious variable that can affect the accuracy is the microphone. Lower accuracy was obtained from training the system from the speech database compared to the users' data.

4.2 Performance on the Raspberry Pi 3 B+

Hotword detection, performed very well compared to a VAD for the Raspberry Pi. Hotword detection was perceived to be faster than a VAD (due to the processing constraints of real time voice on an embedded system). The Raspberry Pi 3 B+ did not require a cloud service, as only 222 global features are utilised. Possibly an Arduino or a smartphone may require a cloud service. The Raspberry Pi 3 B+ took about 24 s to detect an emotion (while also running the user interface and the communication).

Neural network algorithms took longer for training compared to other non-linear algorithms (such as RFC, SVM and KNN) when tested on the Raspberry Pi. CNN performed the worst out of all the algorithms for the Ravdess dataset, as it took approximately 8 h to train. While, the other algorithms finished within approximately 1 h.

Therefore, CNN has been removed for the real time system, as it can be time-consuming to train the users data. All the algorithms perform very well on the Raspberry Pi 3 B+ for predicting data. Extra swap memory was added (3 GB) to increase the memory of the system.

Table 3. Comparison with other speech emotion systems for the Berlin dataset.

Accuracy	Classification	Feature set	Reference
Average 83.27% Max 87.85%	*Ensemble Classifier (shown in Sect. 2.6)*	*222 features (shown in Sect. 2.4)*	*Proposed system*
80%	CNN-LSTM	MFCC	Basu and Chakraborty [21]
81%	PCA + LDA + SFFS	381 features: Pitch, ZCR, MFC, LPC Formants, Speaking Rate, Jitter and Shimmer	Dimitrieva and Nikitin [7]
~88.88%	SVM	120 features – Fourier parameters	Wang et al. [13]
86.6%	Deep Belief Network (DBN) to combine the features and a SVM classifier	Fundamental frequency, power, Wavelet Packet Cepstral Coefficients (WPCC) and weighted WPCC	Wu, Huang, and Zhang [8]

Table 4. Comparison with other speech emotion systems for the Ravdess dataset.

Accuracy	Classification	Feature set	Reference
Average 67.19%	*Ensemble Classifier (shown in Sect. 2.6)*	*222 features (shown in Sect. 2.4)*	*Proposed system*
64.29%	Binary emotion classifier with fusion (MTFS/MTFL model)	65 Low level descriptors to generate 1170 acoustic features: energy, spectral, MFCC and voicing-related features	Zhang et al. [22]
83.15%	Regularized multi-task SVM	Visual features (user's face) and 1170 acoustic features: energy, spectral, MFCC and voicing-related features	Zhang et al. [23]

4.3   Comparison with Other Speech Emotion Systems

Originality of the Hybrid Method. The hybrid solution incorporates a varied range of algorithms (CNN, NN1, NN2, MLP and SVM shown in Sect. 2.6) and feature types (shown in Sect. 2.4); these are currently not present in other researchers' solutions which we researched.

The Proposed Hybrid Solution Performance. The comparison with other systems is shown in Table 3 for the Berlin dataset and in Table 4 for the Ravdess dataset.

The average accuracy of the hybrid solution outperformed most of the existing hybrid solutions. For example, Dimitrieva and Nikitin [7]; Basu and Chakraborty [21]; Zhang et al. [22]. The maximum accuracy of the system was slightly higher compared to Wu, Huang, and Zhang [8] implementation; yet similar to what Wang et al. [13] achieved. However, the average accuracy was lower compared to Wang et al. [13]; Wu, Huang, and Zhang [8]; Zhang et al. [23].

Wavelets and Fourier Parameters are feature types. Wang et al. [13] (utilised Fourier Parameters); Wu, Huang, and Zhang [8] (utilised a DBN + SVM classifier and Fundamental frequency, power, Wavelet Packet Cepstral Coefficients (WPCC) and weighted WPCC features), achieved a higher accuracy compared to the average. However, Python does not have a suitable library to implement Fourier Parameters, and does not have a wide support for WPCCs compared to MATLAB.

Only speech is investigated in this study for emotion detection, which is captured from the microphone rather than the user's face [6]. Zhang et al. [23] attained a higher accuracy by utilising visual features (user's face) and acoustic features (audio features).

5   Conclusions and Future Work

Based on the experiments we carried out, the pattern recognition algorithm which performed best is the hybrid approach (83.27% for the Berlin dataset and 67.19% for the Ravdess dataset) as the accuracy outperforms the single classifiers proposed and is similar to the results other researchers achieved.

Some classifiers (e.g. CNN) may need to be removed for training, due to the performance constraints on an embedded system. However, in real life it is necessary to utilise user data for training. Speech emotion systems have not been employed in real life, due to challenges with accuracy.

The overall accuracy could be further improved by investigating features such as Fourier Parameters (FP) and WPCC. Gaussian Mixture Models (GMM), Hidden Markov Model (HMM) and Deep Belief Network (DBN) models could be investigated for hybrid classifiers with other algorithms, to see if it improves the accuracy.

For the real time emotion system, it is essential to investigate noise robustness in noisy environments. Future work could also investigate VADs, which are robust to noise. It would be interesting to investigate the accuracy of detecting emotion from different distances or to further experiment with noise reduction techniques.

References

1. Schuller, B.W.: Speech emotion recognition: two decades in a nutshell, benchmarks, and ongoing trends. Commun. ACM **61**, 90–99 (2018). https://doi.org/10.1145/3129340
2. Kerkeni, L., Serrestou, Y., Mbarki, M., Raoof, K., Mahjoub, M.A.: A review on speech emotion recognition: case of pedagogical interaction in classroom. In: 2017 International Conference on Advanced Technologies for Signal and Image Processing (ATSIP), pp. 1–7 (2017)
3. Ivanovic, M., et al.: Emotional intelligence and agents: survey and possible applications. In: Proceedings of the 4th International Conference on Web Intelligence, Mining and Semantics (WIMS 2014), Thessaloniki, Greece, pp. 52:1–52:7. ACM (2014)
4. Lugović, S., Dunđer, I., Horvat, M.: Techniques and applications of emotion recognition in speech. In: 2016 39th International Convention on Information and Communication Technology, Electronics and Microelectronics (MIPRO), pp. 1278–1283 (2016)
5. Mishra, A., Patil, D., Karkhanis, N., Gaikar, V., Wani, K.: Real time emotion detection from speech using Raspberry Pi 3. In: 2017 International Conference on Wireless Communications, Signal Processing and Networking (WiSPNET), pp. 2300–2303 (2017)
6. Ahmed, M.Y., Chen, Z., Fass, E., Stankovic, J.: Real time distant speech emotion recognition in indoor environments. In: Proceedings of the 14th EAI International Conference on Mobile and Ubiquitous Systems: Computing, Networking and Services, pp. 215–224 (2017). https://doi.org/10.1145/3144457.3144503
7. Dimitrieva, E., Nikitin, K.: Design of automatic speech emotion recognition system. In: Proceedngs of the International Workshop on Applications in Information Technology (2015)
8. Wu, A., Huang, Y., Zhang, G.: Feature fusion methods for robust speech emotion recognition based on deep belief networks. In: Proceedings of the Fifth International Conference on Network, Communication and Computing, pp. 6–10. ACM (2016)
9. Ayadi, M.E., Kamel, M.S., Karray, F.: Survey on speech emotion recognition: features, classification schemes, and databases. Pattern Recogn. **44**, 572–587 (2011). https://doi.org/10.1016/j.patcog.2010.09.020
10. Bandela, S.R., Kumar, T.K.: Emotion recognition of stressed speech using teager energy and linear prediction features. In: 2018 IEEE 18th International Conference on Advanced Learning Technologies (ICALT), pp. 422–425 (2018)
11. Pan, Y., Shen, P., Shen, L.: Speech emotion recognition using support vector machine. Int. J. Smart Home **6**, 101–108 (2012)
12. Basu, S., Chakraborty, J., Bag, A., Aftabuddin, M.: A review on emotion recognition using speech. In: 2017 International Conference on Inventive Communication and Computational Technologies (ICICCT), pp. 109–114 (2017)
13. Wang, K., An, N., Li, B.N., Zhang, Y., Li, L.: Speech emotion recognition using Fourier parameters. IEEE Trans. Affect. Comput. **6**, 69–75 (2015). https://doi.org/10.1109/TAFFC.2015.2392101
14. Majkowski, A., Kolodziej, M., Rak, R.J., Korczyacuteηski, R.: Classification of emotions from speech signal. In: Signal Processing: Algorithms, Architectures, Arrangements, and Applications (SPA), pp. 276–281. IEEE (2016)
15. Rajisha, T.M., Sunija, A.P., Riyas, K.S.: Performance analysis of malayalam language speech emotion recognition system using ANN/SVM. Procedia Technol. **24**, 1097–1104 (2016). https://doi.org/10.1016/j.protcy.2016.05.242

16. Zheng, L., Li, Q., Ban, H., Liu, S.: Speech emotion recognition based on convolution neural network combined with random forest. In: 2018 Chinese Control And Decision Conference (CCDC), pp. 4143–4147 (2018)
17. Gulli, A., Pal, S.: Deep Learning with Keras. Packt Publishing Ltd., Birmingham (2017)
18. Anagnostopoulos, C.-N., Iliou, T.: Towards emotion recognition from speech: definition, problems and the materials of research. In: Studies in Computational Intelligence, pp. 127–143 (2010)
19. Livingstone, S.R., Russo, F.A.: The Ryerson Audio-Visual Database of Emotional Speech and Song (RAVDESS): a dynamic, multimodal set of facial and vocal expressions in North American English (2018). https://doi.org/10.1371/journal.pone.0196391
20. Rong, J., Chen, Y.P., Chowdhury, M., Li, G.: Acoustic features extraction for emotion recognition. In: 6th IEEE/ACIS International Conference on Computer and Information Science (ICIS 2007), pp. 419–424 (2007)
21. Basu, S., Chakraborty, J., Aftabuddin, M.: Emotion recognition from speech using convolutional neural network with recurrent neural network architecture. In: 2017 2nd International Conference on Communication and Electronics Systems (ICCES), pp. 333–336 (2017)
22. Zhang, B., Provost, E.M., Essl, G.: Cross-corpus acoustic emotion recognition from singing and speaking: A multi-task learning approach. In: 2016 IEEE International Conference on Acoustics, Speech and Signal Processing (ICASSP), pp. 5805–5809 (2016)
23. Zhang, B., Essl, G., Provost, E.M.: Recognizing emotion from singing and speaking using shared models. In: 2015 International Conference on Affective Computing and Intelligent Interaction (ACII), pp. 139–145 (2015)

Contributing Features-Based Schemes
for Software Defect Prediction

Aftab Ali[1(✉)], Mamun Abu-Tair[1], Joost Noppen[2], Sally McClean[1],
Zhiwei Lin[1], and Ian McChesney[1]

[1] School of Computing, Ulster University, Newtownabbey, UK
{a.ali,m.abu-tair,si.mcclean,z.lin,
ir.mcchesney}@ulster.ac.uk
[2] Applied Research, BT, Ipswich, UK
johannes.noppen@bt.com

Abstract. Automated defect prediction of large and complex software systems is a challenging task. However, by utilising correlated quality metrics, a defect prediction model can be devised to automatically predict the defects in a software system. The robustness and accuracy of a prediction model is highly dependent on the selection of contributing and non-contributing features. Hence, in this regard, the contribution of this paper is twofold, first it separates those features which are contributing towards the development of a defect in a software component from those which are non-contributing features. Secondly, a logistic regression and Ensemble Bagged Trees-based prediction model are applied on the contributing features for accurately predicting a defect in a software component. The proposed models are compared with the most recent scheme in the literature in terms of accuracy and area under the curve (AUC). It is evident from the results and analysis that the performance of the proposed prediction models outperforms the schemes in the literature.

Keywords: Machine learning · Intelligent information retrieval · Prediction models

1 Introduction

According to a study at Cambridge University, the cost of software defects has increased to $312 billion per annum globally [1]. The reason behind the cost increase is that developers spent most of their time on finding and fixing defects. The developer's ultimate goal is to release defect free software to the end user. Unfortunately, software defects are inevitable; for example the US Department of Defence is spending over four billion dollars for software failures per year [2].

Techniques of software testing are mostly used to reduce defects and ensure high quality systems [3–5]. However, such testing requires some tedious and exhaustive test cases to be executed, and this makes the process quite expensive, especially since the defect removal effectiveness of traditional testing activities can be very low [6]. According to NIST [7] and [8], finding defects early in the development process greatly lowers the average cost of defects. Moreover, inadequate software testing is causing

© Springer Nature Switzerland AG 2019
M. Bramer and M. Petridis (Eds.): SGAI-AI 2019, LNAI 11927, pp. 350–361, 2019.
https://doi.org/10.1007/978-3-030-34885-4_27

$3.3 billion to U.S. software developers and users in the financial services sector. According to a study software defects cost U.S. industry $60 billion a year [9]. This supports our case that accurate and automatic software defect prediction should be an important part of the software development process.

In [10], the authors used an approach similar to our work for finding contributing features for defect prediction using logistic regression and considering object-oriented metrics. The authors performed experiments on the open source web and e-mail suite Mozilla version 1.7. The authors examined a total of eight performance metrics (i.e. LCOM (Lack of Cohesion on Methods), DIT (Depth of Inheritance Tree), RFC (Response For a Class), WMC (Weighted Methods per Class), NOC (Number Of Children), CBO (Coupling Between Object classes), LCOMN (Lack of Cohesion on Methods allowing Negative value), and LOC (Lines Of Code)), where only one metric is found to be non-contributing. In another paper, Malhotra [11] reviewed such approaches and found that logistic regression performed poorly, in terms of prediction, when compared with machine learning approaches. However, logistic regression provides good explainability by identifying which features are important in predicting bugs and quantifying this.

Our current approach therefore combines this explanatory capability of logistic regression with the diversity provided by a tree-based approach to improve prediction performance. In this paper, we propose contributing features-based logistic regression (CFLR) and Ensemble Bagged Trees-based (EBT) models to predict software defects. The proposed approaches first find those attributes (features) which are contributing or significant in terms of defect prediction by using logistic regression. Once those features are identified in the next step, CFLR and EBT prediction models are applied to the selected attributes to predict those instances which contains defects. The proposed schemes have a number of differences from [10]. The current approach examines eight datasets from different projects with different features for defect prediction. Once the most appropriate features are selected by using the CFLR scheme, then these features are passed on to the EBT algorithm for defect prediction and analysis

The rest of the paper is organised as follows: Sect. 2 presents defect prediction related work while Sect. 3 elaborates the proposed contributing features-based logistic regression scheme. Experimental setup, results and discussions are covered in Sects. 4 and 5.

2   Related Work

Many machine learning algorithms have been used in the literature to solve the software defect prediction problem. A systematic review of Machine Learning based schemes for software defect predictions is presented in [11]. A random forest-based defect prediction scheme is presented in [12], where the authors compare different schemes in terms of accuracy. An artificial immune system is used in [13], to predict software defects in five NASA defect prediction datasets.

Osman et al. [14] studied the impact of feature selection on predicting bugs in software systems. More specifically, they considered the impact of two different feature selection methods: correlation-based feature selection (CFS) and wrapper feature selection methods. The paper considers five different bug prediction models: Linear Regression, Random Forest, K-Nearest Neighbour, Multilayer Perceptron, and Support Vector Machine. The results show that by using a proper feature selection method, the accuracy of the bug prediction models could be increased by 33%.

In [15], the authors proposed semi-supervised deep fuzzy C-mean (DFCM) clustering for software fault prediction. The proposed solution is compared with four different bug prediction models including Class Mass Normalization (CMN) methods, Low-Density Separation (LDS), Support Vector Machine (SVM) and Expectation-Maximization (EM-SEM). The paper shows that the proposed method outperforms the four selected bug prediction models in term of probability of detection using both AUC and F-Measures.

Arasteh [16] proposed a fault prediction method based on combining Neural Network and the Naïve Bayes algorithms. The author compares the proposed approach with three different bug prediction models including Support Vector Machine (SVM), Artificial Neural Network (ANN) and Naïve Bayes.

In this paper we proposed a logistic regression-based contributing feature selection process using P-values. While utilising the advantage of logistic regression simplicity and expandability, it is also used for prediction of bugs. Moreover, to add some more diversity, the ensemble bagged trees are used alongside the logistic regression contributing feature selection process.

3 Contributing Features-Based Logistic Regression

Pre-processing of data to extract useful information (also referred as feature extraction) is one of the most crucial steps in classification and prediction tasks [17]. The accuracy of classification and prediction is strongly dependent on the extraction of relevant features from the raw data [18]. For the feature selection process we use logistic regression as given in the following equation.

$$\log\left(\frac{\pi}{1-\pi}\right) = a + b_1 x_1 + \ldots + b_n x_n$$

Where $\frac{\pi}{1-\pi}$ is the log odds; a_1, b_1, ... b_n are the constants which we estimate (learn) from the repository data; and $x_1, \ldots x_n$ are the features which we extract from the repository data e.g. loc, cyclomatic complexity etc.

Logistic regression is used for predictive analysis of data to identify the relationship between a dependent binary variable and one or more independent variables by estimating the probabilities using a logistic function [19]. The reason for choosing logistic regression is that it is quite extensible and explainable [20, 21], and it is fairly simple in terms of implementation. In logistic regression for every feature the P-value is calculated, and the features are then ranked based on the P-value. A P-value less than 0.05 indicates that a particular feature is significant. The greater the P-value the more the feature's significance decreases, while the lower the P-value the more its significance increases.

3.1   A Case Study of Contributing Feature Selection

In our experiments, we used eight different datasets [22] for results and analysis. However, as a case study, only one dataset (i.e. CM1) is selected to explain and dry run the feature selection process. Below the process of contributing and non-contributing feature selection is explained with reference to the CM1 dataset.

Table 1. Description of data attributes for CM1.

S. no	Attribute	Description	S. no	Attribute	Description
1.	loc	line count of code	2.	v(g)	cyclomatic complexity
3.	ev(g)	essential complexity	4.	iv(g)	design complexity
5.	n	Halstead total operators + operands	6.	v	Halstead "volume"
7.	I	numeric % Halstead "program length"	8.	d	Numeric % Halstead "difficulty"
9.	I	Halstead "intelligence"	10.	e	Halstead "effort"
11.	b	Halstead	12.	t	Halstead's time estimator
13.	lOCode	Halstead's line count	14.	lOComment	Halstead's count of lines of comments
15.	lOBlank	Halstead's count of blank lines	16.	locCodeAndComment	
17	uniq_Op	unique operators	18.	uniq_Opnd	unique operands
19.	total_Op	total operators	20.	total_Opnd	total operands
21.	branchCount	% of the flow graph	22.	defects	(false, true) module has/has not one or more reported defects

The dataset (CM1) used in the case study is a NASA spacecraft instrument written in C language. The dataset consists of a total of 498 instances, where 49 records are for the modules which contains bugs, while the rest are normal records without bugs. The data is extracted by using McCabe [23] and Halstead [24] metric extractors from the source code. A short description of the features in the dataset is given in Table 1. These features were defined to characterize code features that are associated with software quality. The McCabe and Halstead measures are calculated based on modules (functions), where a module is the smallest unit of functionality.

Similarly, for contributing feature selection, we applied a 0.08 threshold to find contributing features in the data. Contributing features are those features, which have comparatively high potential to participate in the prediction process. Table 2 shows the selected contributing features along with the corresponding P-value. In the original dataset we have 22 features as presented in Table 1, while after selecting the contributing features we have only 7 features as presented in Table 2.

Table 2. Selected features by applying the threshold.

Attribute	P-Value
v(g)	0.0784
iv(g)	0.0334
total_Op	0.0189
uniq_Opnd	0.0080
i	0.0033
uniq_Op	0.0016
lOComment	0.0001

4   The Prediction Models

Once the contributing features are selected (using LR), then first (step 1) a logistic regression-based prediction model is applied to predict buggy and non-buggy modules in the input dataset. A simple diagrammatic representation of the proposed contributing features-based logistic regression (CFLR) model is presented in Fig. 1, where $X_1 \ldots X_n$ are the input attributes while $W_1 \ldots W_n$ are the corresponding weights for each attribute.

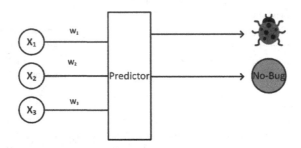

Fig. 1. Logistic regression-based classifier

By using a tree-based approach, Step 2, we can incorporate diversity into the logistic regression parameterisation, thus allowing us to recognise and model different types of bugs with potentially different significant features and models. Ensemble Bagged Trees-based (EBT) scheme is applied on the selected contributing features (i.e. the features are first selected by using logistic regression and then the EBT scheme is applied on those features. The EBT model is a combination of several decision tree classifiers to produce better predictive performance than a single decision tree classifier. The basic principle is to create several subsets from training data chosen randomly with replacement, where, each collection of subset data is used to train the corresponding decision trees and end up with an ensemble of different models. The average of all the predictions from different trees is used resulting in a more robust model compared to a single decision tree.

In Fig. 2, a generic EBT model is given, where the training data is divided in to multiple subsets (i.e. $Data_1...Data_M$), and the leaners (i.e. M different trees) are trained with the different subtests of the data.

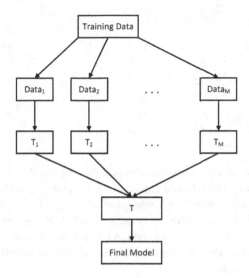

Fig. 2. A generic EBT model

5 Experiments and Analysis

The performance of logistic regression and EBT models are evaluated using 10-fold cross validation to evaluate the predictive model and partition the original dataset into a training set to train the model and a testing set to evaluate the model. In 10-fold cross-validation, the data is divided into 10 equally sized segments, called folds, where one-fold is kept for validation, while the other 9 folds are utilized for training the model. The trained model is then applied to predict the target variable in the testing data. This process is repeated 10 times, with the performance of each model in predicting the set being bold. The performance is measured by calculating metrics such as accuracy, receiver operating characteristic (ROC), and area under curve (AUC). The advantage of this approach is that the input dataset is used for both training and testing, and each observation is used for testing exactly once.

5.1 Results and Discussions

The ROC is a measure of predictor performance. The concern here is the area under the ROC curve which is AUC. In our experiments we achieved significantly higher values of accuracy and AUC compared to previous work, which indicates that the predictor does a good job in discriminating between the modules containing bugs and the ones without a bug which comprise our target variable.

Table 3. Accuracy and AUC comparison

Dataset	Before feature selection			After feature selection		
	No. of attributes	Accuracy (%)	AUC (%)	No. of attributes	Accuracy (%)	AUC (%)
CM1	22	86.9	57	07	90.4	80
JM1	22	81.4	71	17	82.04	71.4
AR1	30	86.7	51.2	14	87.6	67.3
KC1	22	85.6	79.5	14	86.5	80.4
KC2	22	83.12	82.2	06	85.5	83.3
PC1	22	92.43	80.9	07	93.5	81.9
PC3	38	89.6	82	12	89.6	80
PC4	38	91.56	91.6	10	91.69	92.1

Moreover, we performed the experiments on the original dataset (i.e. containing all attributes), as well as on the selected contributing features dataset (i.e. containing only reduced set of attributes). We found that generally the selected contributing feature analysis performed better in terms of accuracy and AUC as presented in Table 3. However, in many cases the accuracy and AUC are not improved significantly, but achieving slightly better accuracy and AUC with a reduced number of attributes is a good performance indication.

5.2 Comparative Analysis

The proposed contributing features-based logistic regression (CFLR) and Ensemble Bagged Trees-based (EBT) schemes are compared with Huda et al. [3] and Arar et al. [4] in terms of accuracy and AUC as can be seen in Table 4. In [3] the authors present SVM and ANN filters and wrappers for significant attribute selection to predict software defects. Similarly, the scheme in [4] uses ANN and Artificial Bee Colony (ABC) algorithms with a cost-sensitive function to deal with the imbalanced data for defect prediction.

Table 4. Comparative analysis.

Dataset	Logistic regression (selected features)		Ensemble bagged trees		Huda et al. scheme [3]		Arar et al. Scheme [4]	
	Accuracy (%)	AUC (%)	Accuracy (%)	AUC (%)	Accuracy (%)	AUC (%)	Accuracy (%)	AUC (%)
CM1	90.4	80	90.8	73	82.94	56.8	68	77
JM1	82.04	71.4	82.3	73	81.23	70.1	61	71
AR1	87.6	69.0	91	79	55.9	52.7	NA	NA
KC1	86.5	81	87.3	82	86.1	69.1	69	80
KC2	85.5	84	79	84	84.7	68.8	79	85
PC1	93.5	82	94	81	93.99	68.1	65	82
PC3	89.6	80	90.4	80	88.05	68.8	NA	NA
PC4	91.69	92.1	91.8	94	91.05	64.2	NA	NA

The two important parameters True Positives (TP) and False Positive (FP) should be considered for a cost-effective bug prediction process [25]. Here FP represent an instance that does not contains any bug but has been identified as a bug by the predictor, whereas TP shows the total number of accurately classified instances. Now, consider the results in Table 4, Logistic Regression has very high AUC results when compared to the schemes in [3] and [4]. This clearly demonstrates that the proposed solution has precisely predicted the bugs in all eight datasets when compared to the schemes in [3] and [4]. This can be further elaborated as, for example, where a bug affects only one in a thousand instances, a completely poor prediction model will always report "negative" (i.e. will not be able to predict that bug) but will still be 99.9% accurate. Unlike accuracy, AUC is insensitive to class imbalance; a poor prediction model would have an AUC of 0.5, which is like not having a prediction at all.

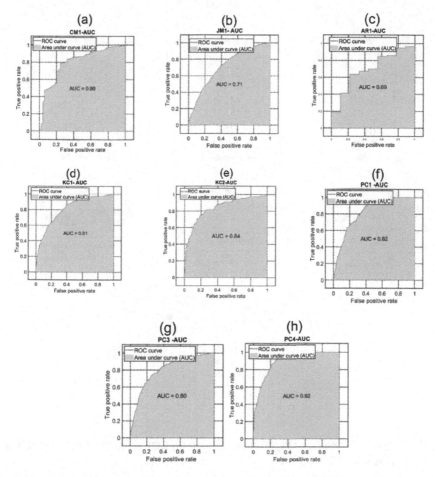

Fig. 3. ROC and AUC for (a) CM1, (b) JM1, (c) AR1, (d) KC1, (e) KC2, (f) PC1, (g) PC3, and (h) PC4 datasets using CFLR scheme.

Here, the CFLR and EBT schemes perform better for most of the datasets, while they perform equally well in few cases. In the case of the CM1 dataset, it is evident that the CFLR and EBT approaches achieve 90.4% and 90.8% accuracy while maintaining 80% and 73% of AUC, while the schemes in [3] and [4] have 82.94% and 68% accuracies, and 56.8% and 77% AUC, respectively.

For the AR1 dataset, the CFLR and EBT schemes reach 87.6% and 91% accuracy, while attaining 69% and 79% AUC, while the scheme in [3] makes essentially almost no prediction at all with 55.9% accuracy and 52.7% AUC, barely exceed the 50% default.

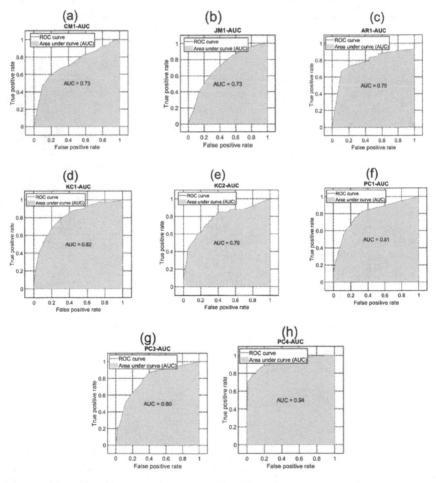

Fig. 4. ROC and AUC for (a) CM1, (b) JM1, (c) AR1, (d) KC1, (e) KC2, (f) PC1, (g) PC3, and (h) PC4 datasets using EBT scheme.

Similarly, for PC1 dataset, our CFLR and EBT schemes have 93.5% and 94% accuracy with 82% and 81% AUC, the scheme in [3] has almost equal accuracy (i.e. 93.99%) but with a lower AUC (i.e. 68.1%); this decreased AUC is a sign of lower TP. However, the scheme in [4] had 82% AUC but with a lower accuracy (i.e. 65%), this lower accuracy being due to the lower True Negative (TN).

This lower TP and TN can also be observed in the case of the KC1 and KC2 datasets, where the CFLR scheme accuracies are 86.5% and 85.5% with 81% and 84% AUC, respectively. Similarly, the EBT scheme achieves 87.3% and 79% accuracy, and 84% and 82% of AUC. However, in comparison [3] has 86.1% accuracy but with 69.1% AUC for KC1, and 84.7% accuracy with 68.8% AUC for KC2. On the other hand, [4] has 69% accuracy with 80% AUC for KC1 and 79% accuracy and 85% AUC for KC2.

In case of PC3 and PC4 the CFLR scheme has 89.6% and 91.69% accuracy and 80% and 92.1% AUC, respectively. While the EBT scheme has achieved 90.4% and 91.8% accuracy, and 80% and 94% AUC. However, [3] has almost the same accuracy (i.e. 88.05% and 91.05%) but with a lower AUC (i.e. 68.8% and 64.2%), which shows that in case of PC3 and PC4 again its performance is degraded by lower TP. A comparison of the all eight datasets in terms of AUC can be seen in Fig. 3 for CFLR and Fig. 4 for EBT.

JM1 is the only case where the accuracy and AUC of the CFLR (i.e. 82.04% and 71.4%) and EBT (i.e. 82.3% and 73%) schemes are almost equal (i.e. 81.23% and 70.1%) to [3]. But again [4] is suffering with low TN resulting in a very low accuracy.

6 Conclusion

Due to the rework cost arising from late discovery of defects, there is a need for more accurate and efficient automated software defect prediction. There are numerous software quality metrics available in the literature which can inform defect prediction. These include traditional code metrics such as McCabe's complexity measures and Hallstead's Software Science (as already noted in the CM1 dataset), object oriented metrics of which the Chidamber and Kemerer suite [26] is the most widely cited, and process metrics such as code churn and code deltas. A challenge for the practitioner is to know which metrics are most valuable in improving the accuracy and efficiency of defect prediction and how they should be used.

In this paper, we first identify and select the most significant metrics using a logistic regression-based scheme. Once the most significant metrics are selected, we then applied the two prediction schemes (i.e. CFLR and EBT) on the selected metrics for accurate prediction of defects. The performances of the proposed schemes are compared with other schemes on eight different datasets, and it is evident from the results that the proposed schemes perform better in terms of accuracy and AUC.

For the software engineer, the role and application of such defect prediction is varied. First, since defect prediction will operate in the context of a software organization with specific process and project challenges to address, then an overall structured approach to its application is necessary. The Goal-Question-Metric approach is an established framework for identifying important dependent and independent product and process features whose values are necessary to achieve some overall software engineering management goal [26]. For example, organization goals might require post-hoc project analysis for the purpose of process improvement, or in-process defect monitoring and prediction for agile process control. There is also the distinction between defect data arising from operational use of a system and/or defect data arising during software verification and validation activities.

The availability of independent variables in a given project will depend on factors such as the integrated development environment in use (e.g. Eclipse, Microsoft Visual Studio), the availability of code analyzers for the programming languages used, the capability of tools used for collection and export of project issues (e.g. Jira, Bugzilla) and the process data available through the project's code repository and version history.

In this context, the selection of a data mining approach will likely be iterative. The conduct of a pilot data collection exercise is a first step, to explore the fit between (a) best practice in defect prediction, (b) the available data and (c) the organization's overall process objectives. It is also the case that defect prediction modelling would complement rather than replace the quality assurance expertise within a software team.

Acknowledgement. This research is supported by the BTIIC (BT Ireland Innovation Centre) project, funded by BT and Invest Northern Ireland.

References

1. Brady, F.: Cambridge University Study States Software Bugs Cost Economy $312 Billion Per Year. Cambridge University (2013)
2. Dick, S., et al.: Data mining in software metrics databases. Fuzzy Sets Syst. **145**(1), 81–110 (2004)
3. Huda, S., et al.: A framework for software defect prediction and metric selection. IEEE Access **6**, 2844–2858 (2018)
4. Arar, Ö.F., Ayan, K.: Software defect prediction using cost-sensitive neural network. Appl. Soft Comput. **33**, 263–277 (2015)
5. Kassab, M., DeFranco, J.F., Laplante, P.A.: Software testing: the state of the practice. IEEE Softw. **34**(5), 46–52 (2017)
6. Ebert, C., Jones, C.: Embedded software: facts, figures, and future. Computer **42**(4), 42–52 (2009)
7. Planning, S.: The economic impacts of inadequate infrastructure for software testing. National Institute of Standards and Technology (2002)
8. Eckardt, J.R, Davis, T.L, Stern, R.A, Wong, C.S, Marymee, R.K, Bedjanian, A.L.: The Path to Software Cost Control. Defense Acquisition, Technology and Logistics, pp. 23–27 (2014)
9. Tassey, G.: The economic impacts of inadequate infrastructure for software testing. National Institute of Standards and Technology, 2002. Forschungsbericht (Zitiert auf Seite 2) (1996)
10. Gyimothy, T., Ferenc, R., Siket, I.: Empirical validation of object-oriented metrics on open source software for fault prediction. IEEE Trans. Softw. Eng. **31**(10), 897–910 (2005)
11. Malhotra, R.: A systematic review of machine learning techniques for software fault prediction. Appl. Soft Comput. **27**, 504–518 (2015)
12. Guo, L., et al.: Robust prediction of fault-proneness by random forests. In: 15th International Symposium on Software Reliability Engineering (2004)

13. Catal, C., Diri, B.: Investigating the effect of dataset size, metrics sets, and feature selection techniques on software fault prediction problem. Inf. Sci. **179**(8), 1040–1058 (2009)
14. Osman, H., Ghafari, M., Nierstrasz, O.: Automatic feature selection by regularization to improve bug prediction accuracy. In: 2017 IEEE Workshop on Machine Learning Techniques for Software Quality Evaluation (MaLTeSQuE) (2017)
15. Arshad, A., et al.: Semi-supervised deep fuzzy c-mean clustering for software fault prediction. IEEE Access **6**, 25675–25685 (2018)
16. Arasteh, B.: Software fault-prediction using combination of neural network and Naive Bayes algorithm (2018)
17. Pendharkar, P.C.: A data envelopment analysis-based approach for data preprocessing. IEEE Trans. Knowl. Data Eng. **17**(10), 1379–1388 (2005)
18. Aparna, U.R., Paul, S.: Feature selection and extraction in data mining. In: 2016 Online International Conference on Green Engineering and Technologies (IC-GET) (2016)
19. Le Cessie, S., Van Houwelingen, J.C.: Ridge estimators in logistic regression. Appl. Stat. **41**, 191–201 (1992)
20. Catal, C.: Software fault prediction: a literature review and current trends. Expert Syst. Appl. **38**(4), 4626–4636 (2011)
21. Sunil, J.M., Kumar, L., Bhanu Murthy, N.L.: Bayesian Logistic Regression for software defect prediction (2018)
22. Sayyad Shirabad, J., Menzies, T.J.: The PROMISE Repository of Software Engineering Databases. School of Information Technology and Engineering, University of Ottawa, Canada (2005)
23. McCabe, T.J.: A complexity measure. IEEE Trans. Softw. Eng. **SE-2**(4), 308–320 (1976)
24. Halstead, M.H.: Elements of Software Science, p. 128. Elsevier Science Inc., New York (1977)
25. Taylor, P.: Autonomic Business Processes. University of York (2015)
26. Chidamber, S.R., Kemerer, C.F.: A metrics suite for object oriented design. IEEE Trans. Softw. Eng. **20**(6), 476–493 (1994)

Induction Motor Inter-turn Short Circuit Fault Detection Using Efficient Feature Extraction for Machine Learning Based Fault Detectors

Muhammad Mubashir Hussain[1], Tariq Jadoon[1],
and Mian M. Awais[2(✉)]

[1] Department of Electrical Engineering,
Syed Babar Ali School of Science and Engineering,
Lahore University of Management Sciences, Lahore, Punjab, Pakistan
[2] Department of Computer Science,
Syed Babar Ali School of Science and Engineering,
Lahore University of Management Sciences, Lahore, Punjab, Pakistan
awais@lums.edu.pk

Abstract. Inter-turn short circuit of the stator is one of the most common faults of an induction motor that degrades its performance and ultimately causes it to break down. To avoid unexpected breakdown, causing an industrial process to halt, it is desirable to continuously monitor the motor's operation using an automated system that can differentiate normal from faulty operation. However, such automated systems usually require large datasets containing enough examples of normal and faulty characteristics of the motor to be able to detect abnormal behavior. The aim of this paper is to present some ways to extract such information or features from the available sensor signals data like motor currents, voltages and vibration, to enable a machine learning based fault detection system to discern normal operation from faulty operation with minimal training data.

Keywords: Induction motors (IM) · Stator inter-turn short circuit (ITSC) fault · Features · Machine Learning (ML)

1 Introduction

Induction motors are the workhorse of the industrialized world and are highly reliable. However, due to operation outside normal permissible limits, they may get damaged and halt the entire industrial process. Major faults are of the following two types:

1. Electric: this includes, stator inter-turn short circuit (ITSC) and broken rotor bars.
2. Mechanical: Eccentricity and bearing faults.

In this paper, the focus is on detecting the ITSC fault that is one of the most common faults of an induction motor. The second emphasis is on the automatic detection of the fault and remedial action with a safe shut down of the industrial process utilizing the motor. The main advantage of such a system is cost saving in the form of the need to perform maintenance when required, instead of periodic maintenance without the need to purchase and store inventories of spare parts.

© Springer Nature Switzerland AG 2019
M. Bramer and M. Petridis (Eds.): SGAI-AI 2019, LNAI 11927, pp. 362–378, 2019.
https://doi.org/10.1007/978-3-030-34885-4_28

Although such an automated system offers numerous advantages, however, building such a system is a challenge since it must be trained using known examples of the normal and faulty operation of the motor. In other words, it must be provided with data for both normal and faulty operation, extracted from motor signals such as currents, voltages and vibrations. However, since induction motors (IMs) are highly reliable, usually, only normal operation data is available.

This paper utilizes the GOTIX dataset [1] that provides separate datasets for different faults of the IM, including the ITSC fault. It provides, three-phase voltages, three-phase currents, horizontal and vertical vibration readings using accelerometers and tachometer (RPM) signal from an IM. The dataset:

- is skewed, i.e., includes more examples for faulty than normal operation.
- has some missing samples.
- has some data readings with two current sensors connected in reverse.

Thus, dataset pruning was done to select examples with no errors. However, this further aggravated the skewness of the dataset. To alleviate this issue, an attempt has been made to extract features that help in distinguishing normal from faulty operation data using the Diagnostic Feature Designer App of MATLAB[1], in addition to generic functions.

The balance of the paper is as follows: in Sect. 2, a literature survey is provided to highlight similar techniques. Section 3 describes how features are extracted from the GOTIX Vibration dataset using the Diagnostic Feature Designer App. Section 4 provides steps for generating same features from the GOTIX Electric dataset. Section 5 covers extraction of features from envelope spectrums of the vibration signals and Sect. 6 covers feature extraction from the average spectrum versus order plots. Finally, Sect. 7 concludes the paper.

2 Literature Survey

All existing Machine Learning (ML) based ITSC fault detectors for IMs have these common processing stages: (1) Feature extraction, (2) Feature selection, and (3) ML based classification model selection. For example, in [2] a data-driven, multiple features extraction and selection method using an ensemble of multiple classifiers is proposed for on-line ITSC fault detection of IMs under varying operating conditions. Features are extracted using FFT, Perceptual Linear Prediction (PLP) and 'db4' Wavelet Packet Transform. The Fisher's Ratio is used as a feature selection method, where a higher value of the ratio indicates a better feature. The ML models considered are Naïve Bayes, Neural Network, SVM and Extreme Learning Machine whose outputs are combined through majority voting to implement the ensemble operation. An ML based fault diagnosis method is proposed in [3] for IMs. Faults are detected by monitoring stator currents and vibration signals of the motors. Matching Pursuit (MP) and Discrete Wavelet Transform (DWT), are used for feature extraction. Also,

---

[1] Mathworks Inc. www.mathworks.com.

Support Vector Machine (SVM), K-nearest neighbors (KNN), and Ensemble, with 17 different classifiers available in MATLAB's Classification Learner App are used to check the suitability of different classifiers for IM fault diagnosis. It is noted that Fine Gaussian SVM, Fine KNN, Weighted KNN, Bagged Tree and Subspace KNN achieved 100% classification accuracy.

Some other techniques such as Fuzzy Logic [4] and Neuro-Fuzzy [5] are also used for detecting the ITSC faults. Another Feature Selection method is described in [6].

Although some Feature extraction and selection methods and classification models for detecting ITSC fault of IM have been described but it is noted that they are separately implemented and evaluated using different tools. However, in this paper an easy and convenient procedure is described for performing feature extraction, feature selection, and evaluation of multiple potential ITSC fault classification models using only MATLAB's Diagnostic Feature Designer and Classification Learner Apps. Despite performing an exhaustive literature search, no other application of the proposed procedure was found to implement an ITSC fault classifier.

3   Features Extracted from the GOTIX Vibration Dataset

The GOTIX Vibration Dataset includes vibration signals from the vertical and horizontal accelerometers placed on the IM shaft and RPM signals from tachometer. Features given in Table 1 are extracted from the two vibration signals using MATLAB's Diagnostic Feature Designer App. Parameters for the two power spectrum estimation methods used are given in Table 2.

Table 1. Features extracted using the Diagnostic Feature Designer App.

Time domain signal features	
Basic Statistics	Mean, RMS, Standard Deviation & Shape Factor
Higher Order Statistics	Kurtosis & Skewness
Impulsive Metrics	Peak Value, Crest Factor, Impulse Factor & Clearance Factor
Signal Processing Metrics	Signal-to-Noise Ratio, Total Harmonic Distortion & SINAD
Spectral features extracted from both parametric & non-parametric power spectrum estimations	
Spectral Peaks	Peak Amplitude & frequency
Band Power	–

Table 2. Parameters for power spectrum estimation methods.

Non-parametric - Welch's method		Parametric - Autoregressive model	
Window type	Hamming	Model order	4
Window size	Auto	Approach	Forward-backward
Overlap percent	50%	Windowing method	No windowing

The App plots histograms for all the extracted features. An example of the generated histograms is shown in Fig. 1. Bars corresponding to fault and non-fault examples are well separated for features that are best able to discern the two classes (fault/non-fault), e.g., Skewness (top-right). The features are also available in tabular form as given in Table 3.

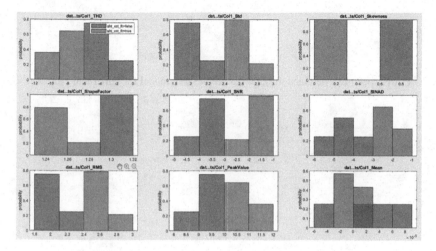

Fig. 1. Histogram for some extracted features.

Table 3. Feature table for GOTIX Vibration dataset.

	data_H_stats/Col1_ClearanceFactor	data_H_stats/Col1_CrestFactor	data_H_stats/Col1_ImpulseFactor	data_H_stats/Col1_Kurtosis	data_H_stats/Col1_Mean	data_H_stats/Col1_PeakValue	data
1	6.0873	4.0827	5.1457	3.1226	1.0902e-05	11.1594	
2	6.2090	4.1537	5.2444	3.0919	-7.6879e-06	11.1831	
3	6.1330	4.1053	5.1763	3.0775	-1.6641e-05	10.9154	
4	6.1288	4.1355	5.1899	3.0297	1.2507e-05	11.2570	
15	7.0372	4.4743	5.8447	3.9901	-5.8664e-05	9.4987	
16	7.4151	4.6993	6.1502	3.9870	4.9957e-05	9.6993	
17	7.2922	4.6167	6.0465	3.9980	6.2113e-05	9.4214	
18	7.0803	4.4726	5.8528	3.7714	3.5708e-06	8.7375	

Power spectrums obtained using the Autoregressive model and Welch's method are shown in Figs. 2, 3, 4 and 5. The Autoregressive model generates spectrums that ably differentiate fault from non-fault, through separate groups of plots for fault/non-fault examples. Similarly, frequency peaks and their values for faulty/non-faulty examples are discernable to some extent in the spectrums obtained through Welch's method.

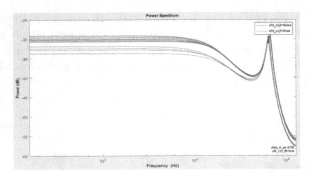

Fig. 2. Power spectrums obtained through Autoregressive model for horizontal vibration signal.

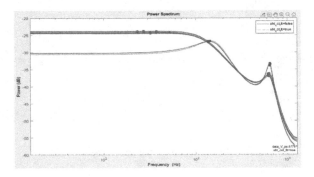

Fig. 3. Power spectrums obtained through Autoregressive model for vertical vibration signal.

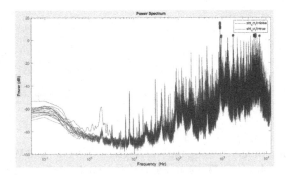

Fig. 4. Power spectrums obtained through Welch's method for horizontal vibration signal.

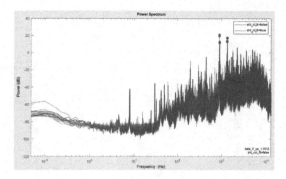

Fig. 5. Power spectrums obtained through Welch's method for vertical vibration signal.

In Fig. 6, all extracted features are graded according to the T-test ranking algorithm. It is found that the 'peak frequency' property of the power spectrum obtained through Welch's method for vertical vibration signal is the best feature for discerning faulty examples from non-faulty examples. The lowest ranking feature is the 'peak frequency' property of the power spectrum obtained through autoregressive method for horizontal vibration signal.

Fig. 6. Features sorted according to T-test ranking algorithm.

Most relevant features are assumed to be those that have a high value of the T-test rank and their histograms depict evident separation between bars for fault and non-fault examples. These features are manually selected from the list of sorted features. MATLAB provides the option to easily export the sorted and selected features to the Classification Learner App for testing different machine learning classification models for discerning faulty from non-faulty examples. When the feature table is exported to the Classification Learner App, the predictor features and the response variable are automatically identified as shown in Fig. 7. Using the default 5-fold cross validation, the App then provides options to train different type of models and shows a 2D scatter plot depicting the classification results for any two features along with a summary of the features table as shown in Fig. 8. Training performance metrics of each trained model along with the option to compare their classification accuracies, ROC and Confusion Matrices, are available.

Fig. 7. Classification Learner App with some of the selected features.

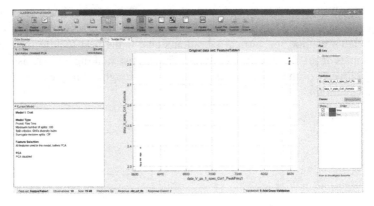

Fig. 8. Classification Learner interface for training models and displaying classification results.

The Classification Learner App gives the option to train 'All quick to train', 'All linear' and 'All' models. Classification accuracies for all available models trained using the 34 features returned by the Diagnostic Feature Designer are given in Table 4. Accuracy of 100% suggests possible overfitting, requiring Principal Component Analysis (PCA) operation on the 34 features. After PCA, only 17 features remain that explain 95% variance. All the models are checked again with the 17 PCA features and the changes in accuracies noted as shown in Table 4. The Confusion Matrix and ROC curve are same for all the models that achieve 100% accuracy and are depicted in Figs. 9 and 10.

Considering that Fine Tree is the simplest and quick to train classifier, it is selected as one of the possible models to implement an ITSC fault classifier. Linear SVM is also selected as the second choice. As advised by the App, for a new table T, containing the reduced features, the two exported models can be used as "yfit = LinSVM.predictFcn(T)" and "yfit = FineTree.predictFcn(T)".

Table 4. Classification accuracies for models available in the Classification Learner App.

Model	Accuracy (%)	Model	Accuracy (%)	Model	Accuracy (%)	Model	Accuracy (%)
Results without PCA							
Quick to train models							
Fine Tree	100	Fine KNN	100	Coarse KNN	77.8	–	–
Medium Tree	100	Weighted KNN	100	Cosine KNN	77.8	–	–
Coarse Tree	100	Medium KNN	77.8	Cubic KNN	77.8	–	–
Linear models							
Linear SVM	100	Linear Discriminant	100	–	–	–	–
Other models							
Coarse Gaussian SVM	100	Gaussian Naïve Bayes	100	Logistic Regression	100	Ensemble – Boosted Trees	77.8
Quadratic SVM	100	Ensemble – Bagged Trees	100	Kernel Naïve Bayes	88.9	Quadratic Discriminant	failed
Medium Gaussian SVM	100	Ensemble – Subspace KNN	100	Fine Gaussian SVM	88.9	–	–
Cubic SVM	100	Ensemble – Subspace Discriminant	100	Ensemble – RUSBoosted Trees	77.8	–	–
Changes after PCA							
Coarse Gaussian SVM	100 to 77.8	Medium Gaussian SVM	100 to 77.8	Kernel Naïve Bayes	88.9 to 100	Fine Gaussian SVM	88.9 to 100
Quadratic Discriminant	Failed to 100	–	–	–	–	–	–

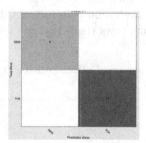

Fig. 9. Confusion Matrix for all models with 100% accuracy.

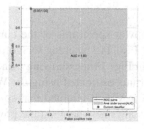

Fig. 10. RoC for all models with 100% accuracy.

4   Features Extracted from the GOTIX Electric Dataset

The GOTIX Electric Dataset includes three-phase current signals IU, IV & IW and voltage signals VU, VV & VW from the IM. The features given in Table 1 were extracted for this dataset using the Diagnostic Feature Designer App. The different options given in Table 5 for both parametric and non-parametric spectrum estimation methods available in the Diagnostic Feature Designer App were explored and it was found that they resulted in very minor, hardly distinguishable changes in the estimated spectrums.

Table 5. Options for spectrum estimation methods for GOTIX Electric dataset.

Non-parametric Welch's method	
Window types	Hamming, Hann, Kaiser (Beta = 0.5) & Rectangular
Window size	Auto
Overlap percent	10%, 50% & 90%
Parametric Autoregressive	
Model order	4
Approach	Forward-backward, Burg's Lattice-based, Geometric Lattice, Least squares & Yule-Walker
Windowing method	No windowing, Post windowing, Pre- and Post- windowing, Pre- windowing

Some of the features extracted from the dataset discern the faulty examples from non-faulty examples in a much better way than others just like in case of the vibration dataset. Numerical values for some extracted features are given in Table 6. As is evident, the values in last four rows (non-fault feature values) are remarkably different from the values in the remaining rows (fault feature values).

Table 6. Feature table depicting numerical values for some extracted features from current IU.

	data_IU_stats/Col1_ClearanceFactor	data_IU_stats/Col1_CrestFactor	data_IU_stats/Col1_ImpulseFactor	data_IU_stats/Col1_Kurtosis	data_IU_stats/Col1_Mean	data_IU_stats/Col1_PeakValue	d
1	4.6623	3.5212	4.1159	1.9864	7.3476e-04	292.9520	
2	4.4874	3.3913	3.9622	1.9737	0.0046	281.9120	
3	4.9250	3.7232	4.3488	1.9680	-0.0036	309.5790	
4	5.0156	3.7915	4.4284	1.9722	0.0059	316.5300	
15	20.7383	6.5158	10.8181	4.5946	0.2572	352.0318	
16	22.9968	7.2203	11.9992	4.6257	0.2461	392.9086	
17	20.4630	6.4457	10.6850	4.5366	0.2460	348.6813	
18	21.3111	6.6966	11.1298	4.6365	0.2502	366.4993	

Results of estimating the power spectrums of the current signal IU using Autoregressive algorithm is given in Fig. 11, whereas for voltage signal VU it is given in Fig. 12. The spectrums for IU in Fig. 11 are showing peaks but no significant peaks are visible in Fig. 12. Power spectrums estimated using the Welch's method. are shown in Fig. 13 for IU and in Fig. 14 for VU. It is noted that spectral peaks for faulty signals and those for non-faulty signals are discernable in the power spectrums obtained using the Welch's method.

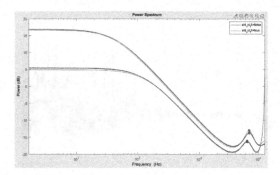

Fig. 11. Power spectrums for current IU estimated using Autoregressive algorithm.

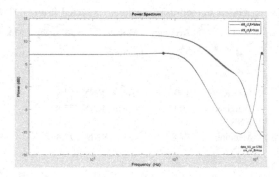

Fig. 12. Power spectrums for voltage VU estimated using Autoregressive algorithm.

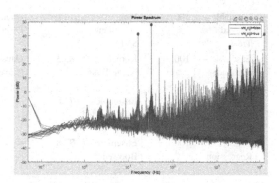

Fig. 13. Power spectrums for current IU estimated using Welch's method.

In case of the GOTIX Electric dataset, 97 features are exported to the Classification Learner App. Classification accuracies for the different models without and with use of PCA are given in Table 7. After PCA only 17 features remain that explain 95% data variance. Ultimately, for sake of simplicity and ease of implementation, among the models with 100% accuracy, Fine Tree and Linear SVM are selected as possible models for implementing an ITSC fault classifier that uses the GOTIX Electric dataset.

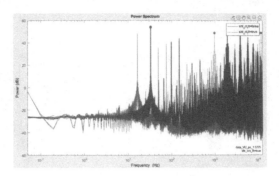

Fig. 14. Power spectrums for voltage VU estimated using Welch's method.

Table 7. Accuracies for models trained using features extracted from GOTIX Electric dataset.

Model	Accuracy (%)	Model	Accuracy (%)	Model	Accuracy (%)	Model	Accuracy
Results without PCA							
Quick to train models							
Fine Tree	100	Fine KNN	100	Coarse KNN	77.8	–	–
Medium Tree	100	Weighted KNN	100	Cosine KNN	77.8	–	–
Coarse Tree	100	Medium KNN	77.8	Cubic KNN	77.8	–	–
Linear models							
Linear SVM	100	Linear Discriminant	Failed	–	–	–	–
Other models							
Coarse Gaussian SVM	100	Ensemble – Bagged Trees	100	Fine Gaussian SVM	100	Quadratic Discriminant	Failed
Quadratic SVM	100	Ensemble – Subspace KNN	100	Kernel Naïve Bayes	83.3	Gaussian Naïve Bayes	Failed
Medium Gaussian SVM	100	Ensemble – Subspace Discriminant	100	Ensemble – RUSBoosted Trees	77.8	–	–
Cubic SVM	100	Logistic Regression	100	Ensemble – Boosted Trees	77.8	–	–
Changes after PCA							
Linear Discriminant	Failed to 100	Coarse Gaussian SVM	100 to 77.8	Medium Gaussian SVM	100 to 77.8	Gaussian Naïve Bayes	failed to 100
	failed to 100	Quadratic Discriminant	Failed to 100	–	–	–	–

Other features were also extracted from the dataset using the relevant MATLAB functions. Feature values for one example of faulty and another of non-faulty data and their comparisons are given in Table 8. These features extracted from the whole dataset can then be ultimately used for fault classification by a ML system.

Table 8. Some more features extracted from GOTIX Electric dataset.

	IU	IV	IW	VU	VV	VW	Remarks
Last value of cumulative sum							Good feature
No Flt.	5.1e+05	5.2e+05	5.1e+05	5e+05	5.2e+05	5.2e+05	
Flt.	1504.8	482.41	−4005.9	405.09	4433	−3842.4	
Cumulative maximum							Voltage values not useful
No Flt.	356.5	359.69	360.53	495.68	495.91	497.37	
Flt.	292.95	344.01	277.16	496.5	493.16	495.35	
Cumulative minimum							Voltage values not useful
No Flt.	−216	−214.37	−209.53	−495.09	−494.14	−496.8	
Flt.	−243.79	−233.98	−228	−494.49	−496.93	−498.39	
Energy							Good feature
No Flt.	5.8e+09	6.3e+09	5.9e+09	8.4e+10	8.4e+10	8.4e+10	
Flt.	1.4e+10	1.4e+10	1.2e+10	1.7e+11	1.7e+11	1.7e+11	
Mean absolute deviation							Good feature
No Flt.	31.909	33.077	31.961	136.56	136.43	136.71	
Flt.	71.176	69.842	65.886	271.06	271.02	271.63	
Mean frequency							Good feature
No Flt.	6400	6400	6400	6400	6400	6400	
Flt.	632.34	525.87	663.34	2151.1	2151	2151.3	
Median							Good feature
No Flt.	0.5	0.5	0.5	0.5	0.5	0.5	
Flt.	−1.3629	0.23882	3.5759	6.8432	5.3235	3.3349	
Median absolute deviation							Good feature
No Flt.	0.026629	0.027542	0.027448	0.0003878	5.48e−05	0.0018922	
Flt.	69.78	69.463	65.088	284.29	284.14	284.8	
Margin Factor							Useful for current only
No Flt.	0.34747	0.32627	0.35018	0.026533	0.026591	0.026564	
Flt.	0.057826	0.070523	0.063848	0.0067576	0.0067139	0.0067138	
Peak 2 Peak							Voltage values not useful
No Flt.	572.5	574.07	570.07	990.78	990.05	994.17	
Flt.	536.74	577.99	505.16	991	990.09	993.74	
Root Sum of Square							Good feature
No Flt.	76185	79134	76810	2.9e+05	2.9e+05	2.9e+05	
Flt.	1.2e+05	1.2e+05	1.1e+05	4.1e+05	4.1e+05	4.1e+05	
Spectral Entropy							Good feature
No Flt.	0.52054	0.50864	0.56539	0.66168	0.66161	0.66164	

(continued)

Table 8. (*continued*)

	IU	IV	IW	VU	VV	VW	Remarks
Flt.	0.40859	0.39519	0.40364	0.60066	0.6006	0.60057	
Variance							Good
No Flt.	2834	3057.7	2880.7	40920	40846	41009	feature
Flt.	6921.5	6677.9	5946.1	80690	80659	81020	
Spurious free dynamic range							Good
No Flt.	0	0	9.6433e−16	0	0	1.9287e−15	feature
Flt.	17.453	18.093	17.156	1.1928	1.218	1.2066	
Largest spurious frequency							Good
No Flt.	12784	12784	12784	11820	11820	11820	feature
Flt.	97.913	97.913	97.913	1960.8	1960.8	1960.8	
Power of largest spurious frequency							Good
No Flt.	30.625	31.086	30.25	37.849	37.833	37.857	feature
Flt.	20.41	19.713	20.079	42.811	42.8	42.825	
99% occupied bandwidth							Good
No Flt.	12767	12767	12767	12767	12767	12767	feature
Flt.	11732	11732	11732	10032	10032	10032	
Lower bounds of the 99% occupied bandwidth							Good
No Flt.	16.269	16.269	16.269	16.269	16.269	16.269	feature
Flt.	32.631	32.631	32.631	32.631	32.631	32.631	
Upper bounds of the 99% occupied bandwidth							Good
No Flt.	12784	12784	12784	12784	12784	12784	feature
Flt.	11765	11765	11765	10065	10065	10065	
Occupied bandwidth power							Good
No Flt.	2805.7	3027.2	2851.9	40511	40438	40599	feature
Flt.	6852.3	6611.1	5886.7	79883	79852	80209	

Joint moment of the time-frequency distribution of a signal

Order	1 & 1	1 & 2	1 & 3	1 & 4	2 & 1	2 & 2	2 & 3	2 & 4
IU								
No Flt.	256046	3.1e+9	3.9e+13	4.8e+17	1.4e+7	1.6e+11	2.1e+15	2.6e+19
Flt.	23722	1.8e+8	1.6e+12	1.7e+16	1.3e+6	9.4e+9	8.5e+13	8.3e+17
IV								
No Flt.	256057	3.1e+9	3.9e+13	4.9e+17	1.4e+7	1.7e+11	2.1e+15	2.6e+19
Flt.	19762	1.5e+8	1.3e+12	1.3e+16	1.1e+6	7.8e+9	7.0e+13	6.8e+17
IW								
No Flt.	256042	3.0e+9	3.7e+13	4.6e+17	1.4e+7	1.6e+11	2.0e+15	2.4e+19
Flt.	24853	2.0e+8	1.9e+12	1.9e+16	1.3e+6	1.1e+10	1.0e+14	1.0e+18
VU								
No Flt.	255953	2.8e+9	3.3e+13	4.0e+17	1.4e+7	1.5e+11	1.8e+15	2.1e+19
Flt.	83810	3.7e+8	2.1e+12	1.5e+16	4.5e+6	2.0e+10	1.1e+14	8.0e+17
VV								
No Flt.	255947	2.8e+9	3.3e+13	4.0e+17	1.4e+7	1.5e+11	1.8e+15	2.2e+19

(*continued*)

Table 8. (*continued*)

Joint moment of the time-frequency distribution of a signal

Order	1 & 1	1 & 2	1 & 3	1 & 4	2 & 1	2 & 2	2 & 3	2 & 4
Flt.	83796	3.7e+8	2.2e+12	1.5e+16	4.5e+6	2.0e+10	1.1e+14	8.1e+17
VW								
No fault	255951	2.8e+9	3.3e+13	4.0e+17	1.4e+7	1.5e+11	1.8e+15	2.1e+19
Fault	83812	3.7e+8	2.2e+12	1.5e+16	4.5e+6	2.0e+10	1.1e+14	8.0e+17

Order	3–1	3–2	3–3	3–4	4–1	4–2	4–3	4–4
IU								
No fault	8.15e+8	9.87e+12	1.23e+17	1.54e+21	5.2e+10	6.3e+14	7.84e+18	9.85e+22
Fault	7.55e+7	5.64e+11	5.1e+15	4.95e+19	4.82e+9	3.61e+13	3.25e+17	3.16e+21
IV								
No fault	8.14e+8	9.95e+12	1.24e+17	1.57e+21	5.2e+10	6.35e+14	7.94e+18	10.0e+22
Fault	6.29e+7	4.64e+11	4.18e+15	4.04e+19	4.02e+9	2.96e+13	2.67e+17	2.58e+21
IW								
No fault	8.15e+8	9.57e+12	1.17e+17	1.45e+21	5.2e+10	6.11e+14	7.47e+18	9.28e+22
Fault	7.90e+7	6.37e+11	6.0e+15	5.99e+19	5.04e+9	4.06e+13	3.83e+17	3.81e+21
VU								
No fault	8.14e+8	9.01e+12	1.06e+17	1.27e+21	5.2e+10	5.75e+14	6.78e+18	8.12e+22
Fault	2.67e+8	1.18e+12	6.81e+15	4.79e+19	1.7e+10	7.5e+13	4.35e+17	3.06e+21
VV								
No fault	8.14e+8	9.0e+12	1.06e+17	1.27e+21	5.2e+10	5.75e+14	6.78e+18	8.13e+22
Fault	2.67e+8	1.18e+12	6.84e+15	4.82e+19	1.7e+10	7.51e+13	4.37e+17	3.08e+21
VW								
No fault	8.1e+8	9.0e+12	1.1e+17	1.3e+21	5.2e+10	5.7e+14	6.8e+18	8.1e+22
Fault	2.7e+8	1.2e+12	6.8e+15	4.8e+19	1.7e+10	7.5e+13	4.4e+17	3.1e+21

Joint Moment is computed for 1. Mean, 2. Variance, 3. Skewness and 4. Kurtosis, in the order: [1 1; 1 2; 1 3; 1 4; 2 1; 2 2; 2 3; 2 4; 3 1; 3 2; 3 3; 3 4; 4 1; 4 2; 4 3; 4 4]. As is evident, values for non-fault/fault cases are markedly different.

5   Features from the Envelope Spectrums of the Vibration Signals

It was noted that spectrums obtained from the envelopes of the horizontal and vertical vibration signals could provide valuable features. Example spectrums are plotted in Fig. 15 for non-fault and fault signals. As is evident, the number, locations and amplitudes of the spectral peaks are different for non-fault and fault signals.

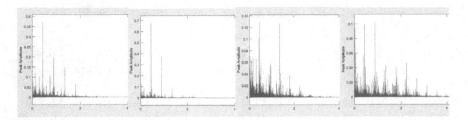

Fig. 15. Plots of envelope spectra (L-R) No fault + fault – Horizontal vibration and No fault + fault - vertical vibration.

Since there are numerous spectral peaks, only the peaks with amplitudes greater than 0.1 are considered. Their locations and amplitudes as given in Table 9 are used as features to discern non-fault from fault signals.

Table 9. Features extracted from envelop spectra.

Non fault		Fault	
Peak locations (kHz)	Peak amplitudes	Peak locations (kHz)	Peak amplitudes
0.469	0.118	0.093	0.126
0.939	0.104	1.396	0.677
1.408	0.373	1.397	0.142
2.346	0.109	2.793	0.378
2.816	0.195		
4.224	0.147		

6   Features from the Average Spectrum Versus Order for Vibration Signals

When the average spectrum is plotted against order for both non-fault and fault, horizontal vibration signals, the plots shown in Figs. 16 and 17 are obtained. For generating these plots, the RPM data is obtained from GOTIX dataset. The order and amplitude values for three largest spectral peaks are used as features as given in Table 10.

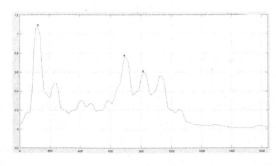

Fig. 16. Avg. spectrum vs Order plot for horizontal vibration non-fault signal.

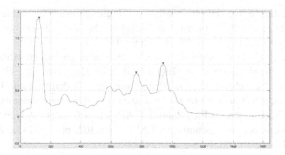

Fig. 17. Avg. spectrum vs Order plot for horizontal vibration fault signal.

Table 10. Features extracted from Avg. spectrum vs Order plots.

Non- fault		Fault	
Peak orders	Peak amplitudes	Peak orders	Peak amplitudes
122.0	1.076	122.5	1.864
691.4	0.761	938.95	0.995
813.4	0.597	762.05	0.819

7   Conclusion

In this paper different feature extraction methods including the Diagnostic Feature Designer App and generic functions of MATLAB were explored for getting appropriate features from multiple signals obtained from the sensors mounted on an IM. The generated features were used for efficient and easy detection of the ITSC fault by multiple ML models. It was also described how these features extracted from the Gotix dataset that is a skewed dataset, helped in discerning faulty from non-faulty examples. MATLAB's Classification Learner App was employed to train multiple ML models using the extracted features with and without PCA and accuracies were compared. It was shown how most models achieved 100% accuracies despite the original dataset being skewed. Thus, it was claimed that by selecting appropriate features, a smaller and skewed dataset didn't offer challenges to a ML system for discerning normal from ITSC affected IM operation.

References

1. Gotix Dataset. http://www.gipsa-lab.grenoble-inp.fr/projet/gotix/experimental_bench.html
2. Xu, Z., et al: Data-driven inter-turn short circuit fault detection in induction machines. IEEE Access **5**, 25055–25068. IEEE (2017). https://doi.org/10.1109/ACCESS.2017.2764474
3. Zawad Ali, M., Shabbir, Md., Liang, X., Zhang, Y., Hu, T.: Machine learning-based fault diagnosis for single- and multi-faults in induction motors using measured stator currents and vibration signals. IEEE Trans. Ind. Appl. **55**(3), 2378–2391 (2019). https://doi.org/10.1109/tia.2019.2895797

4. Benbouzid, M.E.H., Nejjari, H.: A simple fuzzy logic approach for induction motors stator condition monitoring. In: IEEE International Electric Machines and Drives Conference 2001. IEEE (2001). https://doi.org/10.1109/iemdc.2001.939380
5. Dash, R., Subudhi, B.: Stator inter-turn fault detection of an induction motor using neuro-fuzzy techniques. Arch. Control. Sci. **20(LVI)**(3), 363–376 (2010). De Gruyter
6. Likitjarernkul, T., Sengchaui, K., Duangsoithong, R., Chalermyanont, K., Prasertsit, A.: Correlation feature selection analysis for fault diagnosis of induction motors. In: Sulaiman, H. A., Othman, M.A., Othman, M.F.I., Rahim, Y.A., Pee, N.C. (eds.) Advanced Computer and Communication Engineering Technology. LNEE, vol. 362, pp. 1219–1228. Springer, Cham (2016). https://doi.org/10.1007/978-3-319-24584-3_104

Hybrid Feature Selection Method for Improving File Fragment Classification

Alia Algurashi and Wenjia Wang[✉]

University of East Anglia, Norwich, UK
{a.algurashi,wenjia.wang}@uea.ac.uk

Abstract. Identifying types of file fragments in isolation from their context is an essential task in digital forensic analysis and can be done with several methods. One common approach is to extract various types of features from file fragments as inputs for classification algorithms. However, this approach suffers from dimensionality curse as the number of the extracted features is too high, which causes the learning and classification to be both inefficient and inaccurate. This paper proposes a hybrid method to address this issue by using filters and wrappers to significantly reduce the number of features and also improve the accuracy of file type classification. First, it uses and combines three appropriate filters to filter out a large number of irrelevant and/or less important features, and then some wrappers to reduce the number of features further to the most salient ones. Our method was tested on some benchmark datasets - GovDocs, and the experimental results indicated that our method was able to not only reduce the number of features from 66,313 to 11–32, but also improve the accuracy of the classification, compared with other methods that used all the features.

Keywords: File fragment classification · Feature selection · Filters · Wrappers · Hybrid method · Forensics

1 Introduction

Digital forensics analysts frequently need to recover deleted or damaged files, analyse memory dumps, detect malicious files, or extract evidence from a collection of file fragments. However, they often only have file fragments to work with that do not contain any characteristics (e.g. header information), to identify their type. In this case they have to analyse the binary contents of the file to classify file fragments.

Digital files are represented as a sequence of bytes, with each byte containing 8 bits with a value between 0–255. A content-based approach aims to extract a pattern for each file type from its binary contents. The majority of previous studies that have produced acceptable results adopted a combination of machine learning techniques, N-gram, and other statistical measures. However N-gram analysis is an expensive process from a computational perspective, especially

© Springer Nature Switzerland AG 2019
M. Bramer and M. Petridis (Eds.): SGAI-AI 2019, LNAI 11927, pp. 379–391, 2019.
https://doi.org/10.1007/978-3-030-34885-4_29

when N is greater than 1. Therefore, it is necessary to reduce the complexity in file fragment classification.

In machine learning, selecting the most relevant features could assist in eliminating unnecessary complexity that consumes large amounts of time and space. In addition, the feature selection process would help to improve classification result. There are two main strategies for feature selection; filters and wrappers. Filters work fast and independently, but they are usually less accurate and different filers produce different results. In contrast, wrappers can produce more accurate results but are usually very slow, especially when the number of features is high. Both filters and wrappers have been used as a feature selection method in file type classification problem but they were used separately. This paper, however, proposes a hybrid approach that combines both filters and wrappers in sequence to harness their strengths and avoid their weaknesses. Our hybrid method can effectively reduce the number of features from hundreds of thousands down to less than 100 and even below 30. Our experiments results show that when a small number (e.g. 30) of the selected features is used, learning is much faster and the classifiers can be more accurate.

The rest of the paper is structured as follows. Section 2 gives an overview of related work. Section 3 describes the methodology of our proposed framework. Section 4 presents the experimental design and results. In Sect. 5 we conclude the paper and suggest future research.

2   Related Work

Many studies have been conducted in content-based file type classification within the last few decades; most of them were for forensics purposes.

McDaniel and Heydari [1] introduced the idea of creating a file type fingerprint. They believe that each file type has its unique fingerprint, that contain typical features that are type-specific. These researchers developed three algorithms called Byte Frequency Analysis (BFA), Byte Frequency Cross-Correlation (BFC) and File Header/Trailer (FHT), which attempted to address the file type classification problem. The first two methods achieved variable accuracies from as low as 27.50% to 45.83%. The third algorithm demonstrated high accuracy (96%) but it was mostly because the file types are already explicitly included in the file headers. Therefore, it was not surprising FHT performed well. Their study, although not very accurate, still had a considerable influence on the studies as many used Byte Frequency Distribution (BFD). Other researchers have combined BFD with statistical analysis and improved the detection rate of files. For example, Li et al. [2] followed their approach and introduced file prints that utilised N-gram analysis of block contents. They produced three different models: single centroid (one model for each file type), multi centroid (multi models for each file type) and an exemplary file model. With these, they ran several tests using the n-byte of a file and the whole file. They achieved almost 100% success when they only used the first 20 bytes. However, their finding was again not surprising because the file signature information is usually located in the first few bytes, which indicate what type the file is; therefore, there is no need to use any classification method. In reality, such information is not often available, so this method has a limited use in practice.

Karresand and Shahmehri [3] introduced the Oscar method. They used a centroid byte frequency similar to Li et al's work. However, in their case, the centroid is represented by two features: the mean and standard deviation of the byte value frequency distribution. Their approach has been optimised for JPEG files, where specific markers are explicitly used to improve the accuracy. Their method can recognise JPEG fragments with an accuracy of 99.2%, but this exceptional result is limited only to JPEG fragment types, which contain special file structure information that is not available in other file types. They later improved their Oscar method with a new metric [3], the Rate of Change (RoC). The RoC measures the difference between two consecutive byte values. In this way, the byte order is taken into consideration.

Since 2006, the classification of file fragments has moved away from threshold based metrics and tended toward supervised and unsupervised machine learning methods [4]. Supervised algorithms include support-vector machines (SVM), artificial neural network (ANN), decision tree (DT), genetic programming (GP), and linear discriminant analysis (LDA).

Li et al. [5] used SVM for file classification. Their method also relied on the use of file header bytes to identify the files. They reported accuracy levels that rang between 61% and 100%. However, their method suffers the same problem as the method [2]; hence, its application is very limited.

Fitzgerald et al. [6] considered 9000 fragments of 512 bytes that had been segmented from 24 file types taken from the GovDoc dataset. They also used SVM to classify these fragments, based on uni-gram and bi-gram features. They reported an overall accuracy of 47.5% for all file types, but only 21.8% for compressed files. This difference could be explained by the fact that classifying high entropy files is a challenging task.

Beebe et al. [4] developed Sceadan by combining uni-gram (BFD) and bi-gram, like Fitzgerald et al. as an input to SVM classifier. Additionally, they used 11 statistical measurements as fragment features. Their experiments included 38 different file types, which produced 10,000 fragments of 512 bytes and achieved a detection rate of 73.4%.

As can be seen, almost all the major researches extracted a large number of various types of features and used them for training classifiers and their classification results varied for file types and classifiers. Moreover, one common issue with these works is that they did not pay much attention to reduce the large numbers of the features they generated and their methods may have been overwhelmed by the very high dimensionality of the data and hence their classification performances were compromised.

3   Proposed Hybrid Feature Selection Method

In this research we proposed a hybrid method to select the most salient features to improve the efficiency and accuracy of file fragment classification.

Figure 1 shows the framework of the proposed method, which has five components: 1. Data collection/extraction, 2. File fragmentation, 3. Feature extraction, 4. Feature selection with two hybrid levels of filters and wrappers, and 5. Classification. Each component will be described in detail as follows.

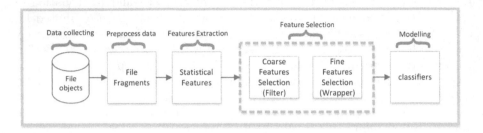

Fig. 1. The functional framework of the proposed hybrid method for file type classification.

3.1   Data Collection/Extraction

This component collects or extracts files and/or file fragments from data storages or disks. The assumption is that when a data disk is corrupted or partially damaged or some files were have been deleted, the files on these types of data storage media can not be opened and viewed correctly in normal ways, but some parts of the files may be extracted out as binary data; (although their types often cannot be recognised). These unknown files (as a whole or in parts) will be then put together to form a file dataset ready for the next step.

3.2   File Fragmentation

The file fragmentation component basically chunks each file in a file dataset into fragments of a specified size. The size of the fragments is measured by the number of bytes and can affect the classification performance. In general, the smaller a fragment is, the less structural information it contains and the harder it is to be recognised [7]. In this study, we chose a size of 512 bytes because it is the worst possible case in the fragmentation problem. The segmentation process is followed by the random selection of fragments from each type of file without replacement, which excludes the first and last two bytes of each file that could include metadata.

3.3   Feature Extraction

The feature extraction component extracts various features from the file fragments. This investigation considered statistical measures and six separate feature vectors for each file fragment, which are described in detail below:

1. BFD (Byte Frequency Distribution): sometimes called a uni-gram. Any file is an object that consists of a sequence of bytes. A byte contains 8 bits; hence a byte can be represented as a numerical value ranging from 0x00 - 0xFF. The BFD extraction in our study counted the occurrence of each byte value in the fragment, producing a vector of 256 features in each instance.
2. A bi-gram vector can be extracted for each instance. A bi-gram is similar to a uni-gram, but it takes the sequence of each two consecutive bytes into consideration. Hence, a word two bytes in length is represented as a numerical value ranging from 0x0000—0xFFFF. To find the bi-gram vector, we counted the occurrences of each word value (two bytes) in each instance, resulting in a 65,536 dimensional vector.
3. ROC (Rate of Change): The difference between two consecutive byte values is the rate of change (ROC). In this way, the byte order is taken into consideration.
4. Low ASCII frequency is the frequency of bytes values ranging between 0x00 - 0x1F in the fragment.
5. Medium ASCII frequency is the frequency of bytes values ranging between 0x20 - 0x7F in the fragment.
6. High ASCII frequency is the frequency of bytes values ranging between 0x80 - 0xFF in the fragment.

In addition to these vectors, 8 separate statistical features were calculated for each file fragment. These features are described here:

1. Entropy: In Information Theory, entropy measures the randomness of data; the more random a set of bytes, the higher the entropy. For this research, we used Shannon's classic formula to find the entropy of uni-gram byte values.
2. Fragment mean is defined as the average of all byte values. In a file fragment, the mean of fragment byte value x_i is calculated by dividing the sum of all byte values with the fragment size n_i.
3. Mean absolute deviation is the statistical measure of dispersion at byte level.
4. Hamming weight: Total number of set bits divided by the total number of bits in the block.
5. Standard Kurtosis: This measures whether data is heavily or lightly tailed when compared with data which has a normal distribution. Determines the extent of peaks in the byte values.

$$K_i = \frac{1}{n_i - 1} \frac{\sum_{j=1}^{n_i} (x_{ij} - x_i)^4}{s_i^4}$$

6. Standard skewness: The standardized skewness is a measurement of asymmetry of the byte value distribution graph when related to the mean.

$$G_i = \frac{1}{n_i - 1} \frac{\sum_{j=1}^{n_i} (x_{ij} - x_i)^3}{s_i^3}$$

7. Average contiguity: Average difference between the values of each two consecutive bytes if calculated by:

$$C_i = \frac{1}{n_i - 1} \frac{\sum_{j=1}^{n_i} (x_{ij} - x_i)^4}{(\sum_{j=1}^{n_i} (x_{ij} - x_i)^2)^2}$$

8. Maximum byte streak: The length of the longest streak of repeating bytes in the block.

So in total, 66,313 features can be extracted for each file fragment and this is very high in terms of dimensionality and should be reduced.

3.4   Features Selection

The feature selection component employs filters and wrappers to build a hybrid coarse-to-fine procedure for selecting the most relevant features. In theory, the best subset of features can be found by employing an exhaustive search and evaluation function but this method has an exponential computing complexity (2^n, n = number of features) and is unrealistic when the number of features is large.

Therefore, we devised a two-stage hybrid feature selection method that used filters and then wrappers in sequence. The filtering stage employs three filters to rank features based on their relevancy with simpler computations. A part of our dataset was used to rank the features first and then classifiers were built and tested using the different part of the dataset.

The ranked features from these three filters are then assessed with 5 types of classifier to find out which filter performed consistently better. Then from the feature ranking produced by the performed filter, we selected the top 1000 relevant features as candidates for the refining stage. As can been seen, using a filter method, we significantly reduced the number of irrelevant features, which helps reducing the running time of the learning algorithm used in the wrappers. To determine which filters should be used in this study as our coarse feature selection method, we designed and carried out some initial experiments. We evaluated three different and commonly used filters.

For simplicity, only 512 features were involved in this initial experiment. The ranked features were divided into subsets to include a different number of features in each subset. This number varied from the 5 most relevant features to the entire set of the features. Two different step sizes were used for searching: initially 5 for the first 45 features, and then 20 for the remainder. This process produced 33 subsets of features from each of the 3 filters.

The next step is to apply various wrappers for a fine selection from the coarse selected features. A wrapper basically employs a learning algorithm to learn from the data and then assesses the accuracy of classifiers it generated with all the possible subsets of the features presented in the data. If a classifier is more accurate, then the features it used are considered as more relevant and hence selected. However, as a wrapper replies on the learning algorithm it uses to learn from the data, its accuracy in selecting features then varies from a learning algorithm to another. This makes a wrapper model-dependent. In order to produce a more consistent and accurate result in feature selection, we used a number of wrappers with different learning algorithms. Their outputs are then assessed with other learning algorithms to determine which subsets of the features are more important for training classifiers.

3.5   Classification

The classification component uses the selected features to train classifiers to test the effectiveness of the selected features in terms of their classification accuracy. In this step, Random-Forest (RF) models were trained for each file type using the fine-selected features for the file type. The choice of Random-Forest as the base learning algorithm is based on the result of the initial experiments detailed in the following section.

4   Experiments and Results

4.1   Data and Feature Extraction

In this experiment, we collected five data sets. The first dataset contains 800 text files, and 200 files for each of 4 other file types: PDF, JPEG, SWF and LOG. The second set includes 800 PDF files and 200 files from each of other 4 types. We continued this process for the remaining file types: JPEG, SWF, and LOG. Using the methods described earlier, 66, 313 features were extracted from these file fragments.

4.2   Experiments for Selecting Appropriate Filters and Classifiers

We evaluated three commonly used filters: InfoGainAttributeEval, Correlation-AttributeEval and GainRatioAttributeEval. The best-first searching algorithm was used to rank the relevant features from the most to the least relevant. We then used the five learning algorithms: Decision Trees (DT), k-Nearest Neighbors (kNN), Support Vector Machine (SVM), Naive-Bayes (NB) and Random-Forest (RF) for assessing how they perform with the subsets of the features selected by the three filters and then deciding which one should be used as the base learner.

Figures 2, 3 and 4 show the accuracy achieved by the 165 classifiers that used the 33 subsets of features using the InfoGainAttributeEval, GainRatioAttributeEval and CorrelationAttributeEval filters. The five classifiers achieved their best accuracy levels at different points; for example in Fig. 2, the KNN classifier achieved its highest accuracy level when using just 5 features, whereas RF needed 45 features to achieve its best rate of classification.

Figures 2, 3 and 4 show the accuracies of 5 classifiers when using different features selected by three filters: InfoGainAttributeEval, CorrelationAttributeEval and GainRatioAttributeEval, respectively. Figure 5 presents the average

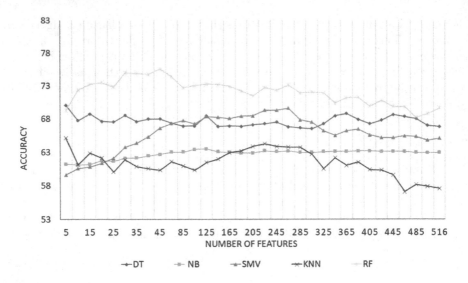

Fig. 2. InfoGainAttributeEval.

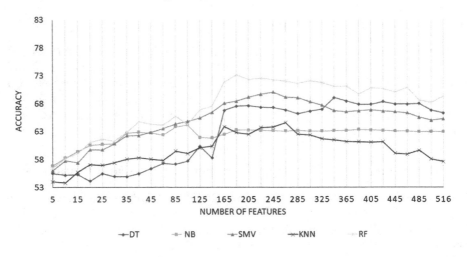

Fig. 3. GainRatioAttributeEval.

accuracy of different classifiers using the features selected from three filters. These graphs indicate that the classifiers generally performed better when using features ranked by the InfoGainAttributeEval filter.

4.3 Implementing Hybrid Feature Selection Method

Coarse Selection with the Chosen Filter: Based on the initial experiments we decided to use the InfoGainAttributeEval filter to rank our 66,313 features for the five different data sets. After all the features had been ranked, it was clear

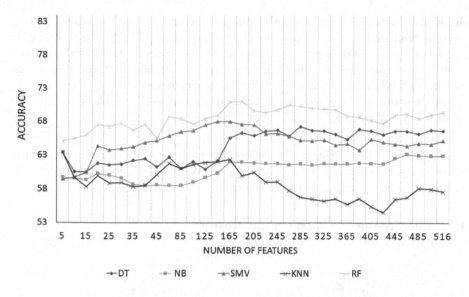

Fig. 4. CorrelationAttributeEval.

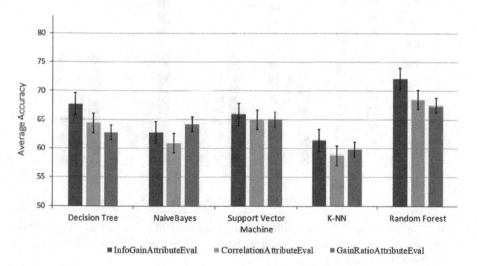

Fig. 5. The comparison of classifiers generated with the features selected by three different filters.

that most of the features showed no or very little relevance to the classification targets, and the top 1000 features appeared to be more relevant than all the others, so they were selected for the second stage of feature selection.

Fine Selection with the Chosen Wrappers: Two wrappers: Classifier-SubsetEval and WrapperSubsetEval, were considered because of their relative simplicity over others, and the latter one was eventually used to select the best features from the features chosen by the coarse filters. The forward evaluation and selection approach is employed in the chosen wrapper to estimate the salience of the coarse-filter selected 1000 features. The RF method was chosen as a base classifier based on the results of our initial experiments.

In this step, we selected the best 5 feature subsets for each of the five file classes: TXT, PDF, LOG, JPEG, and SWF.

Generation of Classifiers: Five different classifiers were trained using the five feature subsets produced in the previous step. We used a 10-fold cross-validation to evaluate the accuracy of the classifiers.

4.4   File Fragment Classification Results

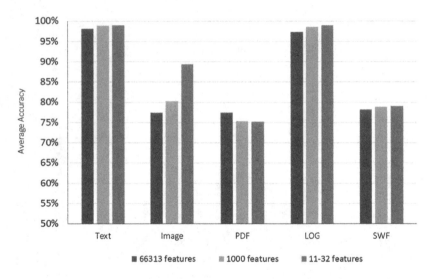

Fig. 6. The accuracies of file classifiers using fragments of size - 512 bytes and three different levels of features: all the features, 1000 features from the coarse-filter and the subsets from the wrappers.

Figure 6 shows the mean classification accuracies of our test results for the classifiers that were trained with the coarse-selected 1,000 features, the variable numbers of the fine-selected features, and with all the 66,313 features as a baseline for comparison. Table 1 provides the actual number of features identified by our method and the classification accuracy for each file type.

In general, our results indicate that the learning algorithms worked better and similar with a much smaller number of the selected features. In just one file type, PDF, the accuracy was slightly decreased. Our results are explained below.

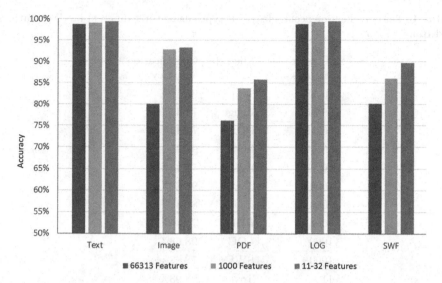

Fig. 7. The classification accuracies of file types with a larger file fragment size - 4096 bytes using three different levels of features and Random Forest.

For TXT files, we achieved a 98.10% mean accuracy with the full set of the features. This was increased marginally to 98.88% when using 1,000 selected features. Then more significant result is that when our classifiers used as few as only 11 fine-selected features, the accuracy was even increased slightly to 98.98%. That means that our hybrid method was effective in getting rid of a great deal majority of irrelevant features and accurate in picking up very few truly useful features. The same patterns were observed in most of other types of file classification.

For JPEG files, we also saw a strong improvement in classification accuracy. At first, we achieved 77.43% accuracy with all the features, which rose to 80.33% with 1,000 selected features. Finally, when the best 17 selected features were used, our method achieved 89.38% - the highest accuracy.

With LOG files, our method achieved 97.38% of accuracy at first, which was increased to 98.63% with 1,000 features; and to 99.00% when only 15 features selected by our hybrid method, which again demonstrated the ability of our method.

Considering SWF files, we obtained an accuracy of 78.18% with all 66,313 features, 78.88% with the 1,000 selected features, and 79.10% with only the 30 best features.

Lastly, we saw a slight drop in accuracy for PDF file fragments. With the full set of features, we achieved an accuracy of 77.43%. This was decreased to 75.35% with 1,000 selected features and decreased again to 75.25% when using the selected 32 features. But considering that the number of features was reduced from 66,313 to only 32, about 99.96% of the features were removed, a decrease

Table 1. The classification accuracies of file types using three different levels of features and Random Forest.

Number of features	File type	Classification accuracy
66,313	Text	98.10%
66,313	Image	77.43%
66,313	PDF	77.43%
66,313	LOG	97.35%
66,313	SWF	78.18%
1000	Text	98.88%
1000	Image	80.33%
1000	PDF	75.35%
1000	LOG	98.63%
1000	SWF	78.88%
11	Text	98.98%
17	Image	89.38%
32	PDF	75.25%
15	LOG	99%
30	SWF	79.10%

of only 2% in accuracy should be still viewed as a very good result because the time and space saved in training.

For 66,313 number of features, our method takes approximately 8760 s to train models. Our results show that if we filter our number of features down to between 11–32, then the average training time linearly decreases to approximately 70 s.

In addition, we investigated whether the size of the file fragments for each file type would affect the overall classification accuracy. We repeated all the above procedures and experiments with a larger size - 4096 bytes. Figure 7 shows the classification accuracies for each file type. It is clear that increasing the size of the file fragment to 4096 bytes improved the classification accuracy. This improvement was particularly noticeable for PDF files, the accuracy rose from 75.25% to 85.75% by using the same 26 features. This improved result likely reflects the fact that PDF files are container files and thus are easier to classify in larger chunks.

5   Conclusion

In conclusion, our results demonstrated that using our hybrid feature selection method - a two stage coarse-to-fine selection procedure, can not only reduce the dimensionality of the dataset significantly and but also improve the accuracy of file classification effectively in all but one cases. Particularly our method was able to achieve a very high accuracy of 99% for LOG files, which will be most useful in the fields of security and digital forensics.

Based on our results, we recommend using the InfoGainAttributeEval filter to rank the relevant features of each file, as this helped the classifiers to perform better. Furthermore, we suggest that using a forward selection approach with WrapperSubsetEval saves time.

Although we had a lower accuracy for PDF files, our research indicated that increasing the file fragment sizes from 512 to 4096 bytes is capable of also increasing the accuracy. This is due to the particular characteristics of PDF files.

In the future, we will carry out more in-depth analysis of the minimum number of selected features, expand our investigations to include more file types.

References

1. McDaniel, M., Heydari, M.H.: Content based file type detection algorithms. In: Proceedings of the 36th Annual Hawaii International Conference on System Sciences, 10-pp. IEEE (2003)
2. Li, W.-J., Wang, K., Stolfo, S.J., Herzog, B.: Fileprints: identifying file types by n-gram analysis. In: Information Assurance Workshop, IAW 2005. Proceedings from the Sixth Annual IEEE SMC, pp. 64–71. IEEE (2005)
3. Karresand, M., Shahmehri, N.: Oscar — file type identification of binary data in disk clusters and RAM pages. In: Fischer-Hübner, S., Rannenberg, K., Yngström, L., Lindskog, S. (eds.) SEC 2006. IIFIP, vol. 201, pp. 413–424. Springer, Boston (2006). https://doi.org/10.1007/0-387-33406-8_35
4. Beebe, N.L., Maddox, L.A., Liu, L., Sun, M.: Sceadan: using concatenated n-gram vectors for improved file and data type classification. IEEE Trans. Inf. Forensics Secur. 8(9), 1519–1530 (2013)
5. Li, B., Wang, Q., Luo, J.: Forensic analysis of document fragment based on SVM. In: International Conference on Intelligent Information Hiding and Multimedia Signal Processing, IIH-MSP 2006, pp. 236–239. IEEE (2006)
6. Fitzgerald, S., Mathews, G., Morris, C., Zhulyn, O.: Using NLP techniques for file fragment classification. Digit. Investig. 9, S44–S49 (2012)
7. Garfinkel, S., Farrell, P., Roussev, V., Dinolt, G.: Bringing science to digital forensics with standardized forensic corpora. Digit. Investig. 6, S2–S11 (2009)

Optimization of Silicon Tandem Solar Cells Using Artificial Neural Networks

Jatin Kumar Chaudhary[1]([✉])[iD], Jiaqing Liu[2], Jukka-Pekka Skön[3],
Yen Wie Chen[2], Rajeev Kumar Kanth[3], and Jukka Heikkonen[1]

[1] University of Turku, Turku, Finland
jatinkchaudhary@gmail.com
[2] Ritsumeikan University, Kyoto, Japan
[3] Savonia University of Applied Sciences, Kuopio, Finland

Abstract. The demand for photovoltaic cells has been increasing exponentially in the past few years because of its potential for generating clean electricity. Yet, due to low efficiency, this technology has not demonstrated complete reliability and poses tremendous amount of constraints even after the possibility of substantial power outputs. The concept of multi-junction solar cell has provided partial solution to this problem. Since the multi-junction solar cell was developed, its optimization has posed a great challenge for the entire community. The present study has been conducted on Si tandem cell, which is a two-junction three-layered solar cell. Silicon (Si) tandem cell was one of the initial developments in the domain of multi-junction solar cells and is most commercially fabricated photovoltaic cell. In this paper, the optimization challenge of multi-junction solar cells has been attempted with the use of Artificial Neural Network (ANN) technique. Artificial Neural Network was trained by using Bayesian Regularization algorithm, and used. Input parameters were taken as spectral power density, temperature and thickness of the layers of cells. Voltage of the cell was kept as a biasing input, and the output parameter was taken to be current density. I-V characteristics were plotted which was further used to calculate the open-circuit voltage (Voc), Fill Factor of the cell (FF), short circuit current density (Jsc) and Maximum Power Point (MPP). The output generated by the trained model of ANN has been compared with the values generated by more than a million iteration of the solar cell model. The implementation of this algorithm on any model of the multi-junction solar cell can lead to the development of highly efficient solar cells. Thus, with due consideration of physical constraints of the environment where it is to be installed; maximum amount efficiency can be achieved.

Keywords: Artificial Neural Network · Multijunction photovoltaic cell · Optimization

1 Introduction

The development of the photovoltaic cell is one of the most significant steps that mankind has taken towards research and practice on clean energy. The invention is a distinctive step towards the reduction in carbon emissions being rendered by

© Springer Nature Switzerland AG 2019
M. Bramer and M. Petridis (Eds.): SGAI-AI 2019, LNAI 11927, pp. 392–403, 2019.
https://doi.org/10.1007/978-3-030-34885-4_30

continually pronounced increments in carbon-based fossil fuel consumption by the post-modern economies. Apart from its potential to render zero carbon emissions, solar cell technology has also gained significant attention because of the economic benefits it posits [1]. At present, research has culminated in successful development and fabrication of the third-generation photovoltaic cells which are multi-junction thin-film solar cells. Yet, it is argued that the potential of this invention remains largely untapped. Also, motivation for growth in the invention, as well as further development of this field remains equivalent to what it was decades ago [2].

The efficiency of a solar cell, i.e., its energy conversion ratio, because of weakly optimized and modestly efficient cells has emerged as a significant challenge during the development of this technology. Furthermore, the economic output and adoption of the multi-junction solar cell remains significantly less than its theoretically calculated potential [3]. While it can be said that the efficiency of solar cells has been increased through the implementation of modern fabrication techniques. There is a need to examine methods for further optimization of parameters to improve the outcomes and hence, bring out the best possible efficiency ratio in a particular solar cell. One such method with high potential to address this problem is the integration of Artificial Neural Networks (ANN) in the field of solar cells.

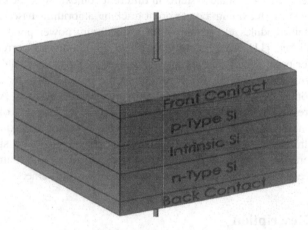

Fig. 1. Si tandem cells used for the development of datasets which has been used to train the ANN.

ANN has been successfully applied in prior studies of different parameters of solar cells, especially for tracking maximum power point prediction - an extreme measure of efficiency [4]. State-of-art research in the field is currently focused on training multiple neural networks by different techniques to predict the most suited neural network model for a given solar cell [4]. The research community is rigorously working towards the development of an ANN which can optimize a multi-junction photovoltaic technology.

This study focuses on developing an ANN model by training data taken by multiple iterations of a silicon tandem cell, which, as per our knowledge, is one of the most commercially fabricated multi-junction solar cells [5]. After training the ANN model by different training algorithms, Bayesian Regularization algorithm was found to give the best result with the least error, and the resultant output has been presented in this paper. The values extracted from the neural network model have been used to report the parameters of optimized model and further, to get the IV curves. There has been a thorough comparison between the optimized values attained by iterations on SCAPS (Solar Cell Capacitance Simulator) and the optimized values achieved from the ANN. Figure 1 shows the structure of the Si tandem cells on which the study has been done. This study can be taken further for utilization in various geographical regions, post - consideration of spectral power density and temperature of the location. Hence, a cell may be modelled according to different instalment sites to get the most efficient and optimized output for a particular instalment site.

2   Previous Works

A considerable amount of research has been conducted to optimize several performance parameters of photovoltaic systems in different contexts with the efficient use of an ANN. For instance, maximum power point tracking algorithms based on ANN may force photovoltaic modules to operate at their maximum power points for all environmental conditions [11]. Further, an ANN-based algorithm may correctly track the maximum power point even under abrupt changes in solar irradiance and improve the dynamic performance across the DC capacitor in the power converter that serves as interphase to connect photovoltaic power plants into the AC grid [7]. A summary of critical studies related to the use of ANN in optimizing the performance of photovoltaic systems in chronological order is presented in Table 1. However, the existing literature suggests that almost all of the experiments have been conducted with single-junction solar cells. Therefore, there is a research gap on optimizing performances of multi-junction solar cells, and the present study aims to address the same.

3   Dataset Description

SCAPS is a one-dimensional solar cell simulation program developed at the Department of Electronics and Information Systems (ELIS), University of Gent, Belgium [5]. The photovoltaic cell in Fig. 1 was iterated by simulations for various spectral densities, temperature and thickness of the three layers and hence, the I-V characteristics along with J_{SC}, V_{OC}, and FF of the cell were noted. In total, 5143 iterations were run and 61,716 values were calculated that were used to train the neural network model for generating the dataset for the Neural Network model hence developed. Further, this dataset was split into Training (70%), Testing (10%) and Validation (20%) so as to get maximum output from the modelled ANN. The dataset was generated by varying all the input parameters and calculating the current density values with voltage as a biasing unit.

Table 1. Summary of important studies.

Author(s) (year)	Study objective	Study findings
Kalogirou [9]	Use of artificial intelligence methods like neural networks and genetic algorithms in optimizing a solar-energy system	A system is modelled using a TRNSYS computer program where weather conditions are embedded to the input data used to train the model. Such methods pioneered the optimization of complicated solar-energy systems
Karatepe, Boztepe and Colak [10]	An application of artificial neural networks to photovoltaic module modelling	The dependence on environmental factors of the circuit parameters involves a set of nonlinear relationships that are difficult to express by analytical equations. However, a neural network may overcome the difficulty
Bae, Jeon, Kim, Kim, Kim, Han and May [6]	Techniques for optimizing processes in cascaded solar cell fabrication following neural networks and genetic programming modelling	The five variables, namely, texturing time, amount of nitrogen, DI water, diffusion time, and temperature are key to the recipe for solar cell fabrication. Repeated applications of particle swarm optimization yielded process conditions with smaller variations, and, greater consistency in recipe generation
Rai, Kaushika, Singh and Agarwal [12]	An artificial neural network based maximum power point tracking controller to predict maximum power voltage and maximum power current under varied atmospheric and load conditions	A model for the energy generation by a photovoltaic array has been developed to capture the effect of solar irradiance, atmospheric temperature, wind speed and variability of the load in the circuit. Its maximum power point tracking performance excels over the conventional PID controller and avoids the tuning of controller parameters
Subiyanto, Mohamed and Hannan [13]	A method for maximum power point tracking of a photovoltaic module by using the Hopfield neural network optimized fuzzy logic controller	Simulation and experimental results show that the method proposed in the study is more robust and accurate compared to the conventional methods. Further, this method successfully tracks the global maximum power point of a photovoltaic energy harvesting system

(*continued*)

Table 1. (*continued*)

Author(s) (year)	Study objective	Study findings
Chen, Gooi and Wang [8]	Use of fuzzy and neural networks to forecast solar radiation accurately at different weather conditions	The mean absolute percentage error produced by this technique is much smaller compared to that of the other methods when used in grid-connected photovoltaic systems
Yuan, Xiang and He [14]	A mutative-scale parallel chaos optimization algorithm using crossover and merging operation to optimize photovoltaic system performance	This technique outperforms other meta-heuristic algorithms commonly deployed for extracting different parameters of solar cell models, such as double diode, single diode, and photovoltaic module, among others

4   The Architecture of an Artificial Neural Network

MATLAB® (2019a) was used to perform ANN modelling. The Neural Network Toolbox of MATLAB has been used for the fitting of the curve and creation of a successful model of the network [15].

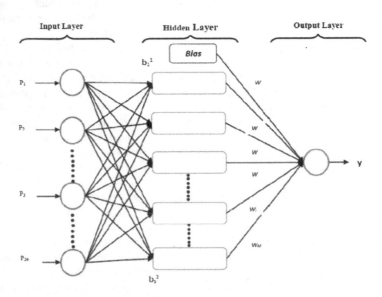

Fig. 2. Basic architecture of an Artificial Neural Network.

Multilayer Perceptron (MLP) Feed Forward Fully Connected Neural Network has been modelled for optimization of parameters. In MLP networks, there is an input layer, an output layer, and hidden layers. The hidden layers are associated with the weights which are calculated during the training of the model. Figure 2, shows the basic architecture of an ANN. Multilayer Perceptron network was trained with five inputs parameters (Spectral Power Density, Temperature, the thickness of three layers of the cell), one biasing parameter (Voltage), one hidden layer with 40 neurons and one output parameter (Current Density). In this study, series and shunt resistances have been taken as zero, i.e. ideal condition of a solar cell has been considered.

The Tansig function (Hyperbolic tangent sigmoid transfer function) has been used as the activation function for the neural network. This hyperbolic tangent transfer function is related to a bipolar sigmoid which has an output in ranging from {−1 to +1}. Tansig function is given by the following equation:

$$n = \frac{2}{1 + e^{-2n}} \tag{1}$$

The Purelin function has been used in the network as the transfer function of the output layer, which as a linear transfer function denoted by:

$$\Psi(n) = n \tag{2}$$

ANN is trained to minimize error between the target to be achieved and the input parameters. Further, to get the desired ANN i.e. with least error and best fir parameter, the error is minimized by adjusting the weights and biases which has been computed in the previous cycle of training. By dynamic updating of weights and biases, a reliable network i.e. least error is obtained. The ANN with minimum error is hence used to predict data for inputs. Objective function of the training algorithm of Neural Network is given by:

$$E = \frac{1}{n} \sum_{i=0}^{n} |y_i - x_i|^2 \tag{3}$$

where, E = Error of the Neural Network,

$$x = \text{Input data} = [x_1, x_2, x_3, \ldots, x_n]$$

$$y = \text{Target datasets} = [y_1, y_2, y_3, \ldots, y_n]$$

It can be easily noticed that this is the equation for the Mean Squared Error and hence, the minimization of this equation is the objective as that implies minimization of the error incorporated during the training process. The extensive use of regularization techniques is to ensure the freedom from the overfitting of data.

In particular, the Bayesian Regularization algorithm enhances the performance of ANN and makes it more reliable by minimizing the error. This is achieved by an algorithm which penalizes the sum of the squared errors and revises reassignment the weights dynamically according to the magnitude of the error that had occurred. This modified objective function of the basic ANN is considered to be a Bayesian Function and the parameters i.e. the biases and the weights are taken to be a random variable. The updated objective function is:

$$F = \beta E_D + \alpha E_w \qquad (4)$$

where, E_w = Sum of squares of the Network weight
E_D = Sum of squared errors
α, β = Objective function parameter or weight coefficient.

The error incorporated in the network depends on the variation of the weight coefficients which gets dynamically updated in an ANN. If $\alpha << \beta$, then the training algorithm will derive smaller error, whereas when $\alpha >> \beta$, training will tend to reduce weight size, at an expense of network error but would produce a smoother network response [16, 17].

The weight of the Bayesian Regularization algorithm is updated by the back-propagation technique which uses the following equation:

$$w_x = w_x - \alpha \left[\frac{\partial E}{\partial \omega} \right] \qquad (5)$$

Where, w_x = Weight assigned to the parameter
α = Learning rate
$\left[\frac{\partial E}{\partial \omega} \right]$ = Derivative of error w.r.t. weight

The weights after the training of the ANN contain meaningful information, i.e. they convey the relationship between the input and the target, whereas before training the weights are just random values without any implacable meaning.

5   Results and Discussions

The network was modelled and trained as per previously discussed process. Multilayer Perceptron (MLP) Feed Forward Fully Connected Neural Network with one hidden layer consisting of 40 neurons was trained with Bayesian Regularization Algorithm on MATLAB (2019a) software on a system with memory of 16 GB. After training, the network outcomes were reported as per the information presented in Table 2.

Table 2. The Neural network training parameters and results.

Training Samples	3600
Validation Samples	1028
Testing Samples	514
Mean Square Error for Training	0.00313071
Mean Square Error for Test Samples	0.00377475
Regression Values for Training Samples	0.9998
Regression values for Test Samples	0.99978
Time Taken	30 s

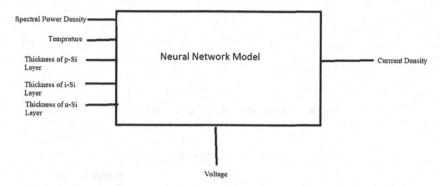

Fig. 3. Architecture of the modeled neural network with five input, one biasing and one output parameter.

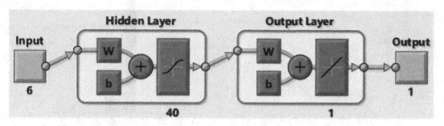

Fig. 4. The neural networks with 40 hidden neurons and an output layer with the Tansig and the Purelin function, respectively.

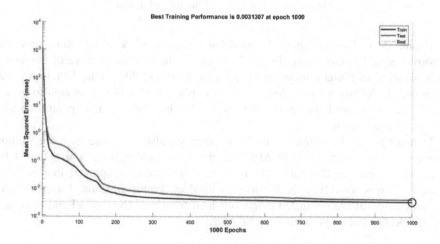

Fig. 5. Performance graph for neural network trained.

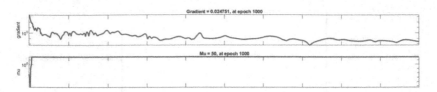

Fig. 6. Training state of neural network model.

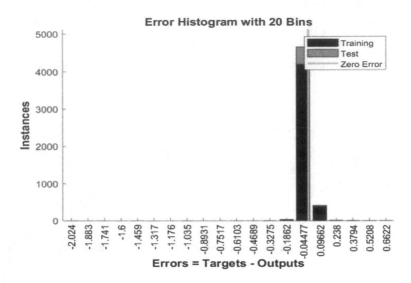

Fig. 7. Error histogram of the trained model.

Figures 3, 4, 5 and 6 show the modeled neural network architecture, structure, performance and training state. Figure 7 represents the regression curve of the model where it can be seen that a linear line passes through almost 90% of the data. Hence, the regression model has a value close to 1 and implies to be efficient enough to give a reliable data This also indicates that the relationship between the input parameters and the target values are relatable.

In order to get the optimized model through simulations, more than one million iterations were performed in SCAPS and the points for optimization obtained by simulation were noted. After the training of the ANN, points of optimization produced by the ANN was noted from the fit curve obtained by 'Plotfit' function. Table 3, shows the comparison of the optimized points obtained from the ANN model and computational experimentation performed on SCAPS.

It can be noted that the points obtained by both the experiments has very less quantitative difference. Analyzing both the methods of obtaining optimization points, we come to an inference that the ANN takes only 30 s to be trained to produce a result whereas SCAPS takes a relatively longer time and more computational expense.

Table 3. Points of optimization obtained from the trained model.

	SCAPS	ANN
Spectral Power Density (W m-2)	767.17	861.6
Temperature (K)	354.37	349.3
Thickness of p-layer (μm)	9.9678	9.45
Thickness of i-layer (μm)	1.897	1.61
Thickness of n-layer (μm)	6.4557	8.5

Using both the output points, a simulation of the Si tandem solar cell was performed on SCAPS and Fig. 8, shows the IV characteristic of the cell. It can be observed that the curves are optimized and which is also proven by various parameters on which efficiency is directly dependent. Table 4, shows the data obtained from the IV characteristics of the optimized cell from both the techniques.

Table 4. The efficiency measures of the photovoltaic cell whose parameters were calculated by SCAPS and ANN.

	Optimization points obtained from SCAPS	Optimization points obtained by ANN
Open Circuit Voltage (Voc) (V)	0.7804	0.794719
Short Circuit Current Density (mA cm-2)	11.318835	11.37040531
Fill Factor (%)	57.00	58.8717
Maximum voltage point (V_{MPP})	0.543262	0.567910

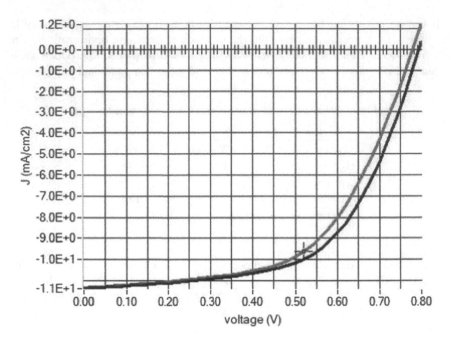

Fig. 8. IV characteristic of the optimized solar cell as from the output of SCAPS and neural network model. (Left (Grey) = output from SCAPS and Right (Black) = output from ANN).

6 Conclusion

This study was based on the significant need for the optimization of a multi-junction solar cell. In this research, modeling was done on the data obtained for a Si tandem cell using Artificial Neural Network. A network with 40 hidden neurons was developed on MATLAB which was trained using Bayesian Regularization algorithm through 61,716 values obtained by iterations done on the cell. This trained network was used to predict values of the input parameters to generate the most optimum model of the solar cell. This model was compared with optimization values obtained by SCAPS. These values were tested on the Si tandem cells and the obtained I-V characteristic proved that the algorithm worked well. It also implicates the efficient capability of predicting highly optimized multi-junction solar cells.

References

1. Roessner, J.D.: Government-industry relationships in technology commercialization: the case of photovoltaics. Sol. Cells **5**(2), 101–134 (1982)
2. Third Generation Photovoltaics (2012)
3. Gul, M., Kotak, Y., Muneer, T.: Review on recent trend of solar photovoltaic technology. Energy Explor. Exploit. **34**(4), 485–526 (2016)

4. Ramaprabha, R., Gothandaraman, V., Kanimozhi, K., Divya, R., Mathur, B.L.: Maximum power point tracking using GA-optimized artificial neural network for solar PV system. In: 2011 1st International Conference on Electrical Energy Systems, pp. 264–268. IEEE, January 2011

5. Burgelman, M., Nollet, P., Degrave, S.: Modelling polycrystalline semiconductor solar cells. Thin Solid Films **361**, 527–532 (2000)

6. Bae, H., et al.: Optimization of silicon solar cell fabrication based on neural network and genetic programming modeling. Soft. Comput. **14**(2), 161–169 (2010)

7. Carrasco, M., Mancilla-David, F., Fulginei, F.R., Laudani, A., Salvini, A.: A neural networks-based maximum power point tracker with improved dynamics for variable dc-link grid-connected photovoltaic power plants. Int. J. Appl. Electro Magn. Mech. **43**(1–2), 127–135 (2013)

8. Chen, S.X., Gooi, H.B., Wang, M.Q.: Solar radiation forecast based on fuzzy logic and neural networks. Renew. Energy **60**, 195–201 (2013)

9. Kalogirou, S.A.: Optimization of solar systems using artificial neural-networks and genetic algorithms. Appl. Energy **77**(4), 383–405 (2004)

10. Karatepe, E., Boztepe, M., Colak, M.: Neural network based solar cell model. Energy Convers. Manag. **47**(9–10), 1159–1178 (2006)

11. Kulaksiz, A.A., Akkaya, R.: Training data optimization for ANNs using genetic algorithms to enhance MPPT efficiency of a stand-alone PV system. Turk. J. Electr. Eng. Comput. Sci. **20**(2), 241–254 (2012)

12. Rai, A.K., Kaushika, N.D., Singh, B., Agarwal, N.: Simulation model of ANN based maximum power point tracking controller for solar PV system. Sol. Energy Mater. Sol. Cells **95**(2), 773–778 (2011)

13. Subiyanto, S., Mohamed, A., Hannan, M.A.: Intelligent maximum power point tracking for PV system using hopfield neural network optimized fuzzy logic controller. Energy Build. **51**, 29–38 (2012)

14. Yuan, X., Xiang, Y., He, Y.: Parameter extraction of solar cell models using mutative-scale parallel chaos optimization algorithm. Sol. Energy **108**, 238–251 (2014)

15. MATLAB and Neural Network Toolbox Release: The Math-Works, Inc., Natick, Massachusetts, United States (2018b)

16. San, O., Maulik, R.: Neural network closures for nonlinear model order reduction. Adv. Comput. Math. (2018). https://doi.org/10.1007/s10444-018-9590-z

17. Dan Foresee, F., Hagan, M.T.: Gauss-Newton approximation to Bayesian learning. In: Proceedings of International Conference on Neural Networks (ICNN 1997) (n.d.). https://doi.org/10.1109/icnn.1997.614194

Stochastic Local Search Based Feature Selection for Intrusion Detection

Dalila Boughaci[✉]

LRIA-FEI- USTHB, Algiers, Algeria
dalila_info@yahoo.fr, dboughaci@usthb.dz

Abstract. Intrusion detection is the ability to mitigate attacks and block new threats. In this paper, we deal with intrusion detection as a pattern classification problem where a connection is defined as a set of attributes. The latter forms a pattern that should be assigned to one of existing classes. The problem is to identify the given connection as a normal event or attack. We propose a stochastic local search method for feature selection where the aim is to select the set of significant attributes to be used in the classification task. The proposed approach is validated on the well-known NLS-KDD dataset and compared with some existing techniques. The results are interesting and show the efficiency of the proposed approach for intrusion detection.

Keywords: Intrusion detection · Feature selection · Stochastic local search · Classification · NLS-KDD

1 Introduction

Intrusion detection is an important issue in computer security. Intrusion detection is the ability to monitor computer system or network where the aim is to detect malicious activities or policy/rules violations. Intrusion detections models can be divided into two main categories: anomaly detection and misuse detection [4, 14].

The anomaly detection model is based on users' profiles also called user's behavior. It permits to describe the usual profile of a given user in the hope to detect this user's anomalous and its unusual activities. Several methods have been used to describe users' profiles. Among these methods, we mention: the statistical methods where the user's behavior is computed from attributes taken randomly and sampled at regular intervals [2, 28]. For instance, these attributes can be the number of connections, the number of erroneous passwords, etc. The neural networks [12] and expert systems [21] are the most popular methods to compute the user's profile.

The misuse detection model also called signatures based model. The latter defines a set of anomalous behavior to analyze data susceptible to be attacks. Various methods have been proposed to detect attacks or intrusions. Among them, we find: the expert systems [19], agents-based detection intrusion [8], the Data mining approaches [9, 10, 20, 27], the clustering technique [23], Fuzzy logic [1, 6, 18], naïve Bayes [3] and the Bayesian network [22, 26].

In this work, we focus on Intrusion detection as a pattern classification problem where the aim is to identify the given connection as a normal event or attack.

M. Bramer and M. Petridis (Eds.): SGAI-AI 2019, LNAI 11927, pp. 404–417, 2019.
https://doi.org/10.1007/978-3-030-34885-4_31

A connection is defined as a set of attributes. We propose a stochastic local search based feature selection method as a preprocessing step before starting the classification task. The aim is to search for a set of significant attributes to be used in the classification task. This method is combined with some classifiers to show its efficiency. We consider both the naïve Bayes and Bayesian network in the classification step. The overall method is validated on the well-known NLS-KDD dataset [31] which is a well-known oriented intrusion detection dataset, and compared with some existing techniques. More precisely, we handle 20% of the NLS-KDD dataset. The dataset includes 22 different attack types which can be classified into four main categories namely Denial of Service (DoS), Remote to User (R2L), User to Root (U2R) and Probing. The results are interesting and show the efficiency of the proposed approach for the intrusion detection.

The rest of the paper is organized as follows: Sect. 2 gives a background on the main concepts used in this study. Section 3 presents our proposed approach for intrusion detection. Section 4 gives some numerical results. Finally Sect. 5 concludes and gives some perspectives.

2 Background

The aim of this section is to give a background about classification, feature selection and stochastic local search which are the main concepts used in our study.

2.1 Classification

Classification is an important means of data mining. It is the process of classifying data into classes. The classification task permits one to find the best described computer model from a dataset with the correct class variable. It is a supervised learning technique that creates a model based on training dataset and uses this model to classify new data [24, 25, 29]. The training dataset is a set of instances having the form $\{x_i; y_i\}$ $(i = 1 \dots m)$. For the intrusion detection, the xi are called input connections. Each input vector has a number of attributes. The y_i are the response variables also called labels. In binary classification, the input vectors are paired with corresponding labels to find the correct class variable. $y_i \in \{1; 0\}$, {normal, attack}.

The classification problem is to predict whether a given connection or a given testing data belongs to one of the existing classes.

2.2 Feature Selection

Feature selection is a pre-processing step that may be launched before the classification task. The aim is to select a set of significant attributes to build a model for the data classification. Feature selection permits to remove the redundant attributes deemed irrelevant to the data classification task [7, 11, 15].

Various methods have been proposed to handle the feature selection. These methods can be divided into two main categories: the wrapper methods and the filtering methods [11, 15].

- The filtering methods are based on heuristics. They eliminate and filter out the undesirable attributes before launching the classification task. The best-first search and the ranking filter information gain are two examples of filtering methods.
- The wrapper methods are based generally on machine learning algorithm for searching the best subset of attributes. The machine learning algorithm selects the best attributes with high classification accuracy.

2.3   Stochastic Local Search

The stochastic local search (SLS) is a local search meta-heuristic which has been already studied for several optimization problem such as satisfiability and optimal winner determination problem (WDP) in combinatorial auctions [5, 17]. SLS starts with an initial solution generated randomly. Then, it performs a certain number of local steps that combines diversification and intensification strategies to locate good solutions in the search space. In the diversification step, we select a random neighbor solution. In the intensification step, we select the best neighbor solution according to the accuracy measure. To avoid local optima and explore effectively the search space, the intensification step is applied with a fixed probability $wp > 0$ while the diversification step is applied with a probability $1 - wp$. The wp is a probability fixed empirically.

SLS is an iterative process that should be repeated until a certain number of iterations or a criterion is reached. In this work, we use SLS as a feature selection method. The objective is then to find the optimal subsets of features by finding optimal combinations of features from the dataset. The selected potential features can improve the classification rate.

3   Proposed Approach

The role of the feature selection is to search for a significant set of attributes to be used with the classifier to build model for the data classification task.

In the following, we propose to use SLS based method to search for the best solution which is a vector of attributes maximizing the classification rate (the accuracy rate).

3.1   Proposed Architecture for Intrusion Detection

First, we give the overall architecture of our proposed system for intrusion detection. As shown in Fig. 1, the proposed architecture is divided into two main parts: Part 1 and Part 2.

1. In Part 1, we select a subset of attributes by using the SLS feature selection method. The aim is to select the optimal attribute combination maximizing the classification accuracy and minimizing the number of the selected attributes.
2. In Part 2, we do the classification task. We build models. We work only on the set of selected attributes. The latter are sent to the classifier for data classification. We study two classifiers in this step which are: the naïve Bayes and the Bayesian network.

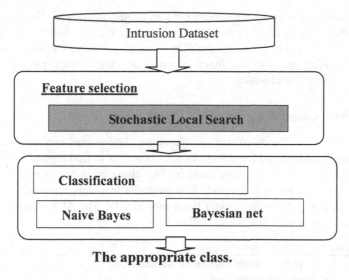

Fig. 1. Proposed architecture.

3.2 Solution Representation

We use a binary vector to represent the set of the attributes present in the dataset, with the length of the vector equal to n, where n is the number of attributes. If an attributes is selected, the value 1 is assigned to it, a value 0 is assigned to it otherwise.

For example, Fig. 2 gives an example of vector for a data with eight attributes where the first, the second, the fifth and the eighth variables are selected.

Fig. 2. Solution representation.

3.3 SLS for Feature Selection

We propose a stochastic local search based method for feature selection. The method starts with an initial solution considering all attributes of the dataset. Then we generate a set of neighbors' solutions by applying both intensification and diversification strategies. The intensification step consists in searching for best neighbor solution according to the accuracy rate. The neighbor solution x' of a current solution x is obtained by modifying one bit.

For instance, let us consider the current solution x = 00001111 of eight attributes, then the set of possible neighbor solutions can be represented as:

{**1**0001111, 0**1** 001111, 00**1**01111, 000**1**1111, 00000111, 0000**1**011, 00001**1**01, 0000111**0**}.

The intensification consists in selecting the best neighbor solution among the set of the possible solution having the best accuracy value.

In the diversification step, we select a random neighbor solution. The intensification step is applied with a fixed probability $wp > 0$ and the diversification step with a probability $(1 - wp)$. The wp is a probability fixed empirically. The solution quality is measured by using an objective function which is the accuracy rate. The latter is computed by using the classifier.

3.4   SLS with Classifier for Intrusion Detection

The proposed SLS is combined with classification. The overall method starts with an initial solution considering all the features and then tries to find a good solution in the whole neighborhood in an iterative manner. The classifier is built for each candidate solution constructed by SLS method. The overall method is repeated for a certain number of iterations (*max_iterations*) fixed empirically. The SLS method combined with classification is sketched in Algorithm 1.

Algorithm 1. SLS with classification

Data: n the number of attributes, *max_iterations*, *wp*.
         f is the objective function
Result: A set of selected attributes xbest, Best accuracy.

1: Start with all features.
2 : Apply classifier on the current data
3 : Evaluate the quality of x noted $f(x)$ by using accuracy rate.
4: **For** (i = 1 to *max_iterations*) **do**
5 : r ← random number between 0 and 1.
6 : **if** (r < wp) **then**
7 : //*Step 1
8 : Generate the neighborhood solutions of x;
9 : *xnewi* = the best neighbor solution
10 : **else**
11 : //*Step 2
12 : I ← first random position in the current solution.
13 : J ← second random position in the current solution
14 : *xnewi* = new solution where all positions between I and J are flipped.
15 : Apply the classifier on the current data
16 : **endif**
17 : **if** (*f(xnewi)* < *f(x))* **then**
18 : *x=xnewi*
19 : **endIf**
20 : **endfor**

3.5   The Considered Classifiers

In the classification step, we consider two classifiers in this study. The naive Bayes classifier is based on the Bayesian theorem with independence assumptions between the attributes of the instances. To predict the class of a given instance, the naive Bayes classifier analyses the relationship between each attribute and the class for each instance [26]. Also, we consider the Bayesian network which is a probabilistic graphical model that represents a set of random attributes and their conditional dependencies via a directed acyclic graph [13].

4   Experiments

In this section, we give the results of the empirical studies. The purpose of these experiments is to evaluate the performance of our method for intrusion detection. The codes are written in java programming language. We used the Weka Library package for the classifiers [30]. Weka is a collection of machine learning algorithms for Data Mining tasks; it was developed at the University of Waikato in New Zealand in Java.

4.1   The Considered Datasets

The considered data is a set of connections defined by their attribute values called instances. The NLS-KDD dataset contains 41 attributes labeled as normal or attack. These 41 attributes are grouped into 4 categories: basic attributes, content attributes, time-based traffic attributes, and host-based traffic attributes.

Table 1 shows the sample size of the considered dataset. Also it presents the attacks types in the 20% NLS-KDD dataset. Table 2 gives the list of the 41 attributes of the considered dataset.

Table 1. Attack types and sample size of the 20% NLS-KDD.

Class	Number of samples	
Normal	13449	
Attack	Attack type	**Number of samples**
	DOS	9234
	U2R	11
	R2L	209
	Probing	2289
	TOTAL	11743
TOTAL	**25192**	

Table 2. List of the 41 attributes of the dataset.

A1–A10	A11–A20	A21–A30	A31 –A41
A1: Duration (Continuous),	A11: Num-failed-logins (Continuous)	A21 Is-host-login (Discrete)	A31 Srv-diff-host-rate (Continuous)
A2: Protocol-type (Discrete),	A12 Logged-in (Discrete) A13 Num-compromised (Continuous)	A22 Is-guest-login (Discrete)	A32 Dst-host-count (Continuous)
A3: Service (Discrete),	A14 Root-shell (Continuous)	A23 Count (Continuous)	A33 Dst-host-srv-count (Continuous)
A4: Flag (Discrete),	A15 Su-attempted (Continuous)	A24 Srv-count (Continuous)	A34 Dst-host-same-srv-rate (Continuous)
A5: Src-bytes (Continuous),	A16 Num-root (Continuous) A17 Num-file-creations (Continuous)	A25 Serror-rate (Continuous)	A35 Dst-host-diff-srv-rate (Continuous)
A6: Dst-bytes (Continuous),	A18 Num-shells (Continuous)	A26 Srv-serror-rate	A36 Dst-host-same-src-portrate
A7: Land (Discrete),	A19 Num-access-files (Continuous)	(Continuous)	(Continuous)
A8: Wrong-fragment (Continuous),	A20 Num-outbound-cmds (Continuous)	A27 Rerror-rate (Continuous)	A37 Dst-host-srv-diff-hostrate (Continuous)
A9: Urgent (Continuous),		A28 Srv-rerror-rate (Continuous)	A38 Dst-host-serror-rate (Continuous)
A10: Hot (Continuous),		A29 Same-srv-rate (Continuous)	A39 Dst-host-srv-serror-rate (Continuous)
		A30 Diff-srv-rate (Continuous)	A40 Dst-host-rerror-rate (Continuous) A41 Dst-host-srv-rerror-rate (Continuous)

The NSL-KDD dataset mainly contains four types of attacks.

- Denial of Service (DoS) Attack: When an attacker succeeds in rendering computing and memory resources too busy, or deny access to a machine to legitimate users, are called DoS attack.
- Remote to Local attack (R2L): In R2L attack, an attacker wants to gain local access as a user of a particular machine without any account. To do this, an attacker sends a packet to a remote machine on a network and exploits vulnerability.
- User to root attack (U2R): Using this type of attack, the attacker can access the normal user account on the system and gain root access to the system and exploit certain vulnerabilities.
- Probe: In this kind of attack, by scanning the computers network, the attacker can gather all the necessary information on the target system where to find known vulnerabilities.

4.2 Evaluation Measures

To evaluate the models, the dataset needs to be split into training and testing sets. In our case, we used the 5-fold cross-validation technique where the dataset is randomly split into a five equal sized subsamples (folds). As shown in Fig. 3, the splitting is repeated for five iterations. In the first iteration, the first fold is used as a testing dataset and the rest of folds are used as a training dataset. With the same manner, in the second iteration we used the second fold to test model and the rest to train model, and so on until each fold of the five folds have been used as a testing dataset. We note that the models are constructed on the training data by using the considered machine learning algorithms and validated on the testing data.

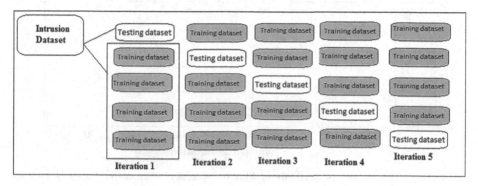

Fig. 3. 5-fold cross validation technique.

The classifier is evaluated on the training data to get a model. Then, the obtained model is applied on the test data to find the appropriate class.

To evaluate models, there are various measures. We used the following performance indicators given as:

- True Positives (TP): is the number of positive examples, labeled as such.
- False Positives (FP): is the number of negative examples, labeled as positive.
- True Negatives (TN): is the number of negative examples, labeled as such.
- False Negatives (FN): is the number of positive examples, labeled as negative.

We considered the following measures [24]:

- Sensitivity (True positive rate or Recall) = TP/TP+FN
- Specificity (True negative rate) = TN/TN+FP
- False negative rate = FN/FN+TP = 1 − Sensitivity
- False positive rate = FP/FP+TN = 1 − Specificity
- Precision = TP/TP+FP.
- Accuracy = (TP+TN)/(TP+TN+FP+FN)

4.3   Parameters Tuning and Impacts

In this section, we give the numerical results found by the proposed method. The adjustment of SLS parameters are fixed by an experimental study. The probability wp is fixed to 0.65 and the maximum number of iterations is fixed to 150.

We carried several experiments to measure the impact of parameters on the classification rate obtained by each method. Figure 4 (respectively Fig. 5) shows the impact of the number of iterations on solution quality of the SLS method with the naïve Bayes (respectively with the Bayesian network). From the figures, we can see that the solution quality is improved when the number of iterations is increased. However, after a certain number of iterations the solution quality remains the same with no improvement.

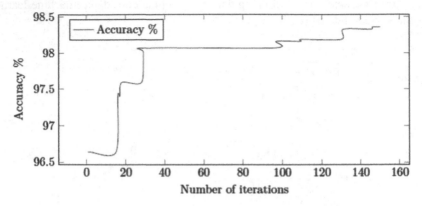

Fig. 4. Impact of number of iterations of SLS on accuracy when Naïve Bayes is used as classifier.

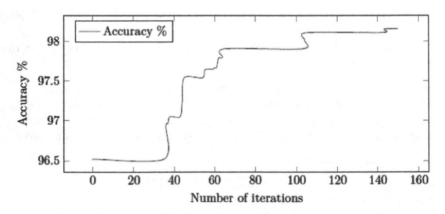

Fig. 5. Impact of number of iterations of SLS on the accuracy when Bayesian network is used as classifier.

From Figs. 6 and 7, we see the impact of the number of iterations on the number of selected attributes. When the number of iterations grows the quality of solutions is improved. The number of selected attributes is decreased but it can be increased when a new improved solution with a high accuracy is found.

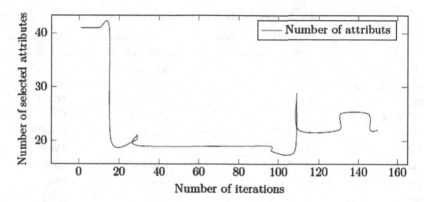

Fig. 6. Impact of number of iterations of SLS on the number of selected attributes when Naïve Bayes is used as classifier.

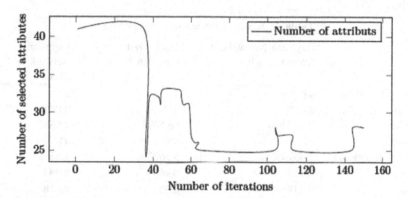

Fig. 7. Impact of number of iterations of SLS on the number of selected attributes when Bayesian network is used as classifier.

4.4   Numerical Results

This section summarizes the results obtained with the proposed methods. To evaluate the performance of the proposed approaches, we used several measures. We give the results found by the classifier (naive Bayes and Bayesian network) when executed alone without feature selection. Also we give the results when we executed the two classifiers with a discretized preprocessing step and when executed with the proposed SLS feature selection.

Tables 3 and 4 compare the three approaches in term of the number of selected attributes, the number of correctly Classified Instances, the number of Incorrectly Classified Instances, TP Rate, FP Rate, Precision, and Recall points of view. We give also the List of the selected attributes by the proposed method SLS. The best results are in bold font.

We note that the discretization is the process of quantizing continuous attributes by grouping those values into a number of discrete intervals.

Table 3. Results obtained with Naive Bayes.

	Naive Bayes without feature selection	Discretized Naive Bayes	Naive Bayes with SLS
Number of attributes	41	41	**28**
Correctly Classified Instances	22596 89.69%	24315 96.51%	**24727 98.15%**
Incorrectly Classified Instances	2596 10.3049%	877 3.4813%	**465 1.845%**
TP Rate	0,897	0,965	**0,982**
FP Rate	0,105	0,039	**0,020**
Precision	0,897	0,966	**0,982**
Recall	0,897	0,965	**0,982**
List of selected attributes by SLS	A3 A5 A6 A8 A9 A10 A11 A13 A14 A15 A16 A17 A18 A19 A20 A21 A26 A31 A32 A33 A34 A35 A36 A37 A38 A39 A40 A41		

Table 4. Results obtained with Bayes NET

	Bayesian Net without feature selection	Discretized Bayesian Network	Bayesian Network with SLS
Number of attributes	41	41	**22**
Correctly Classified Instances	24321 96.5426%	24345 96.6378%	**24778 98.35%**
Incorrectly Classified Instances	871 3.4574%	847 3.3622%	**414 1.65%**
TP Rate	0,965	0,966	**0,984**
FP Rate	0,038	0,037	**0,018**
Precision	0,966	0,967	**0,984**
Recall	0,965	0,966	**0,984**
List of selected attributes by SLS	**A3 A 5 A 6 A7 A8 A10 A11 A 13 A16 A17 A23 A24 A32 A33 A34 A35 A36 A37 A38 A39 A40 A41**		

From the numerical results given in both Tables 3 and 4, we can see that the discretization process improves the overall performance of classification. Also, our proposed method SLS for feature selection greatly improves the performance of classification. Further the Bayesian network combined with SLS succeeds in finding good results with a good quality solution and with a reduced number of attributes. We find a solution with only 22 significant attributes with an accuracy of **98.35%**, and a FP rate equals to 1.8% (0.018). This is due to the SLS feature selection that explores the search space efficiently for locating good solutions.

4.5 Further Comparison

Table 5 compares the proposed approach SLS and two well-known feature selection methods: CFS [16] and Information gain. Information gain is a technique used to evaluate the rank of attributes based on the concept of entropy. In the correlation based feature selection (CFS) which is a filter algorithm, the attributes are evaluated based on the hypothesis that good attributes are those highly correlated with the class [11, 15]. The comparison depicted in Table 5 shows that the proposed SLS approach succeeds in finding good results compared to both CFS and Information gain methods.

Table 5. Comparative study.

Feature selection method	Naïve Bayes	Bayesian Net
SLS	98.15%	**98.35%**
CFS	88.31%	96.19%
Information gain	89.59%	96.56%

We found a solution with an accuracy of **98.35%** when using SLS with Bayesian net. This confirms the effectiveness of our proposed method for intrusion detection.

5 Conclusion

In this paper, we were interested in intrusion detection field. We tackled this problem as a classification problem where a feature selection based method was proposed to enhance the performance. The proposed stochastic local search was combined with the naïve Bayes and Bayesian network and classifiers and valuated on NLS-KDD dataset. The numerical results are very encouraging and demonstrate the benefits of the proposed approach for the intrusion detection. As future work, we plan to evaluate our approach on others datasets.

References

1. Abadeh, M.S., Habibi, J., Lucas, C.: Intrusion detection using a fuzzy genetics-based learning algorithm. J. Netw. Comput. Appl. **30**(1), 414–428 (2007)
2. Aha, D.W., Kibler, D., Albert, M.K.: Instance-based learning algorithms. Mach. Learn. **6**(1), 37–66 (1991)
3. Ben Amor, N., Benferhat, S., Elouedi, Z.: Naive Bayes vs decision trees in intrusion detection systems. In: Proceedings of the 2004 ACM Symposium on Applied Computing, pp. 420–424 (2004)
4. Anderson, D., Frivold, T., Valdes, A.: Next-generation intrusion detection expert system (NIDES): A summary. SRI International, Computer Science Laboratory (1995)
5. Boughaci, D.: Metaheuristic approaches for the winner determination problem in combinatorial auction. In: Yang, X.S. (ed.) Artificial Intelligence, Evolutionary Computing and Metaheuristics. SCI, vol. 427, pp. 775–791. Springer, Heidelberg (2013). https://doi.org/10.1007/978-3-642-29694-9_29

6. Boughaci, D., Kadi, M.D.E., Kada, M.: Fuzzy particle swarm optimization for intrusion detection. In: Huang, T., Zeng, Z., Li, C., Leung, C.S. (eds.) ICONIP 2012, Part V. LNCS, vol. 7667, pp. 541–548. Springer, Heidelberg (2012). https://doi.org/10.1007/978-3-642-34500-5_64

7. Boughaci, D., Alkhawaldeh, A.A.: Three local search-based methods for feature selection in credit scoring. Vietnam J. Comput. Sci. **5**(2), 107–121 (2018)

8. Boughaci, D., Ider, K., Yahiaoui, S.: Design and implementation of a misused intrusion detection system using autonomous and mobile agents. In: EATIS 2007, p. 12 (2007)

9. Breiman, L., Friedman, J., Olshen, R., Stone, C.: Classification and Regression Trees. Wadsworth, Belmont (1984)

10. Breiman, L.: Bagging predictors. Mach. Learn. **24**(2), 123–140 (1996)

11. Caruana, R., Freitag, D.: Greedy attribute selection. In: Proceedings of the Eleventh International Conference on Machine Learning (ICML 1994), New Brunswick, New Jersey, pp. 28–36. Morgan Kauffmann, San Francisco (1994)

12. Debar, H., Becker, M., Siboni, D.: A neural network component for an intrusion detection system. In: Proceedings of the 1992 IEEE Computer Society Symposium on Research in Security and Privacy, pp. 240–250 (1992)

13. Freund, Y., Schapire, R.E.: A decision-theoretic generalization of on-line learning and an application to boosting. J. Comput. Syst. Sci. **55**, 119 (1997)

14. Friedman, N., Geiger, D., Goldszmidt, M.: Bayesian network classifiers. Mach. Learn. **29**, 131–163 (1997)

15. Kiennert, C., Ismail, Z., Debar, H., Leneutre, J.: A survey on game-theoretic approaches for intrusion detection and response optimization. ACM Comput. Surv. **51**(5), 90:1–90:31 (2019)

16. Hall, M.: Correlation-based feature selection for machine learning. In: Methodology, vol. 21i195-i20, pp. 1–5, April 1999

17. Hoos, H.H., Stutzle, T.: Stochastic Local Search: Foundations and Applications. Morgan Kaufmann Publishers, San Francisco (2004)

18. Ishibuchi, H., Murata, T.: Techniques and applications of genetic algorithms-based methods for designing compact fuzzy classification systems. Fuzzy Theory Syst. Tech. Appl. **3**(40), 1081–1109 (1999)

19. Lee, S.C., Heinbuch, D.V.: Training a neural-network based intrusion detector to recognize novel attacks. IEEE Trans. Syst. Man Cybern. Part A Syst. Hum. **31**(4), 294–299 (2001)

20. Lee, W., Stolfo, S.J.: Data mining approaches for intrusion detection. Defense Technical Information Center (2000)

21. Lunt, T.F., Jagannathan, R.: A prototype real-time intrusion-detection expert system. In: Proceedings of the 1988 IEEE Symposium on Security and Privacy, pp. 59–66 (1988)

22. Mehdi, M., Zair, S., Anou, A., Bensebti, M.: A Bayesian networks in intrusion detection systems. J. Comput. Sci. **3**(5), 259–265 (2007)

23. Portnoy, L., Eskin, E., Stolfo, S.: Intrusion detection with unlabeled data using clustering. In: Proceedings of ACM CSS Workshop on Data Mining Applied to Security (DMSA 2001) (2001)

24. Powers, D.M.W.: Evaluation: from precision, recall and F-measure to ROC, informedness, markedness and correlation. J. Mach. Learn. Technol. **2**(1), 37–63 (2011)

25. Quinlan, J.R.: Simplifying decision trees. Int. J. Man Mach. Stud. **27**, 221–234 (1987)

26. Quinlan, J.R.: C4.5: Programs for Machine Learning. Morgan Kaufmann, San Mateo (1992)

27. Rennie, J., Shih, L., Teevan, J., Karger, D.: Tackling the poor assumptions of Naive Bayes classifiers. In: ICML (2003)

28. Salo, F., Injadat, M., Nassif, A.B., Shami, A., Essex, A.: Data mining techniques in intrusion detection systems: a systematic literature review. IEEE Access **6**, 56046–56058 (2018)

29. Vapnik, V.: Statistical Learning Theory. Wiley, New York (1998)
30. Waikato Environment for Knowledge Analysis (WEKA), Version 3.9. The University of Waikato, Hmilton, New Zealand. http://www.cs.waikato.ac.nz/. Accessed November 2018
31. Data set. http://iscx.ca/NSLKDD/

Knowledge Acquisition

Improving the Adaptation Process
for a New Smart Home User

S. M. Murad Ali$^{(\boxtimes)}$ ⓘ, Juan Carlos Augusto ⓘ, and David Windridge ⓘ

Middlesex University, London, UK
sa2305@live.mdx.ac.uk, {j.augusto,d.windridge}@mdx.ac.uk

Abstract. Artificial Intelligence (AI) has been around for many years and plays a vital role in developing automatic systems that require decision using a data- or model-driven approach. Smart homes are one such system; in them, AI is used to recognize user activities, which is a fundamental task in smart home system design. There are many approaches to this challenge, but data-driven activity recognition approaches are currently perceived the most promising to address the sensor selection uncertainty problem. However, a smart home using a data-driven approach exclusively cannot immediately provide its new occupant with the expected functionality, which has reduced the popularity of the data-driven approach. This paper proposes an approach to develop an integrated personalized system using a user-centric approach comprising survey, simulation, activity recognition and transfer learning. This system will optimize the behaviour of the house using information from the user's experience and provide required services. The proposed approach has been implemented in a smart home and validated with actual users. The validation results indicate that users benefited from smart features as soon as they move into the new home.

Keywords: Smart home · User adaptation · Activity recognition · Transfer learning

1   Introduction

"I'd rather die than be a burden on my daughter"—this sentiment is common among older people [8]. Older people desire to continue living independently. Nevertheless, it is natural for their families to be hesitant and worried, regardless of how well-managed the home may be. The dangers for elderly people who live alone are many, and unpredictable. Smart homes and associated conveniences could help improve their lives and mitigate most concerns [13].

Imagine a scenario in which Bob/Betty is an elderly person who has decided to continue living independently. Despite concerns about safety and proper care, his/her family decides to accommodate Bob/Betty in a new smart home where technology can facilitate their activities of daily living, such as personal hygiene and food preparation. The same home can also provide advanced functionalities such as fall detection, as well as other safety and security services.

© Springer Nature Switzerland AG 2019
M. Bramer and M. Petridis (Eds.): SGAI-AI 2019, LNAI 11927, pp. 421–434, 2019.
https://doi.org/10.1007/978-3-030-34885-4_32

In this scenario, a critical question might be raised: Will the chosen technology be able to provide the expected help to Bob/Betty immediately after he/she moves into this new home? The answer to this question might be "no" due to the reliance of smart homes on a sufficient amount of data to recognize, understand and predict user behaviour and to provide the required services. This data dependency may increase Bob's/Betty's family's concern about his/her independent living, especially when he/she first moves in, causing them to underestimate the long-term capabilities of the smart home.

From the description above, it could be concluded that a data-driven smart home cannot provide for all of a user's needs from day one. Now, two scenarios will be created in which the house attempts to provide automated responses to Bob's/ Betty's needs as soon as he/she starts living there.

Scenario (Morning): The user wakes up, uses the toilet, and then goes to the kitchen make their breakfast, eats breakfast, goes back to bedroom, gets ready, and goes outside. In this scenario, the user expects lights in the bedroom, corridor, toilet, kitchen, shower, and on the table to switch on automatically when required, as well as the kettle and radio in the kitchen. All automated devices will be switched off if the user forgets to switch them off before leaving the house.

Scenario (Evening): The user come back from office, changes their clothes, uses the toilet, then goes to the sitting room, reads the newspaper, goes to the kitchen, makes dinner, eats dinner, and then goes to the bedroom to sleep. The user demands all automated devices turn on when appropriate and switch off after he is asleep.

This research proposes a User-guided Transfer Learning (UTL) approach to develop a system that provides the occupant with an Assisted Living Facility (ALF). This article is structured as follows: Sect. 1 gives background information. Section 2 discusses the findings of related work, Sect. 3 explains the user-guided transfer learning method, and Sect. 4 describes the user-guided transfer learning interface. The process of system validation is explained in Sect. 5 and discussed in Sect. 6, while conclusions are presented in Sect. 7.

2   Related Work

User adaptation in smart homes is always a challenging and long-term process. Human activity recognition is one fundamental task of the adaptation process. There are two main approaches for activity recognition: knowledge-driven [12] and data-driven [10]. Knowledge-driven methods use prior domain knowledge to model current activities and involve knowledge acquisition, formal modelling and knowledge presentation. Logical reasoning tasks such as deduction, induction and abduction are used for activity recognition or prediction in knowledge-driven models. Their design is semantically clear, logically elegant and make it easy for the user to get started, offering a solution to the "cold-start" problem [3]. However, this model is weak in handling uncertainty and temporal information; thus, it is considered a static method.

On the other hand, a data-driven approach mainly concentrates on designing a system that works smoothly without any user interruption. These approaches may not work at times because of the complex and irregular nature of human behaviours [4]. In both data-driven and knowledge-driven approaches, knowledge gained from monitoring user activity is used to improve the system during the development process. Only in very limited cases is the user engaged in the development of the system.

Currently, most research on activity recognition in smart homes focuses on the introduction of new machine learning algorithms [10]. However, machine learning algorithms cannot provide immediate benefit to the smart home user in cases where there is little or no training data. Few scholarly works have focused on the new smart home adaptation process using a data-driven approach. The approach proposed by Chiang and Hsu [5] illustrates a possible new smart home adaptation process. This method accommodates a user in a model of the new smart home in a laboratory environment for data collection. After data collection, a transfer learning approach is used to pass the data to the new smart home. Chiang et al. [6] showed that without target data (no data), the amount of transferred knowledge is insufficient, but it can be increased using a small amount of labelled data.

Data-driven approaches are still a challenging approach to adaptation for new smart homes. Researchers are trying to use transfer learning approaches [7] to diminish the problem. But purely transfer learning-based processes struggle to satisfactorily address the problem. This research aims to tackle the challenge by proposing an approach for development of an integrated system using a user-centric approach [1] comprising survey, simulation, activity recognition and a transfer learning approach.

3   User-Guided Transfer Learning (UTL)

There is a specific gap in data-driven activity recognition whereby the system does not provide the prospective service immediately after installation. Here, we explain the method of data collection and illustrate how the scenario can be decomposed into activities.

In the above scenario in Sect. 1, Bob/Betty is expecting very basic functions from their smart home. It is possible to provide these functions if the home has an idea about their behaviour. Presently, data-driven activity recognition systems predict human behaviour via analysis of the user's dataset of past daily living. As Bob/Betty is a new occupant of the home, the system does not yet have any records about him/her.

At this point, we required a method which familiarizes the house with Bob's /Betty's habits before he/she moves in. We introduced an integrated system using user centric approach that brings four approaches—survey, simulation, activity recognition and transfer learning—together to provide a smart home facility from day one.

Figure 1 shows the architecture of the system. The user is at the heart of this system; every step of the development process is concluded by considering user

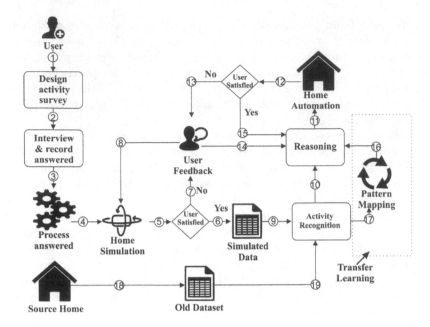

Fig. 1. Conceptual model of the proposed system.

feedback and satisfaction. After simulation, the user is invited to become familiar with the house (Fig. 1, step 5). This process helps the user gain confidence about the new house. After the system is implemented in the house and the user has started living in the house user feedback is collected again (Fig. 1, step 12). The incorporation of feedback from the user at each stage may help in the development of trust in the system.

3.1   Survey

AI implemented automated house should act as a person. It should able to sense the house environment, process the information and react accordingly. Basically the process starts by the data collection.

In order to enrich the data available to the system from the beginning, a questionnaire has been designed for users in which he/she is asked questions (Fig. 1, step 2) about activities of daily living. The questionnaire can be found here: https://doi.org/10.22023/mdx.8789987. The main objective of the questionnaire is to help the system learn about the user's daily activity and behaviours. To simplify the survey process, the activities are divided into two categories, called *simple activity* and *complex activity*. The number and sequence of actions in the simple activity category is the same for any user. As an example, the "wake up" activity is detected by three sensors, bed pressure, bedroom motion and bedroom light. So, the "wake up" activity is similar for all users, but the time at which it occurs is different. On the other hand, the number of actions and their sequence differs for complex activities. As an example, making tea could be different for users because tea can be made in different ways; some people use milk, some do not, and the sequence of actions in the process could also be different.

Table 1. Sample answers from the user for specific activity.

Activity	Location	Object involve	Duration	Time
Eating breakfast	Kitchen or sitting room	Plate, radio, tea, medicine	5–8 min	7:10–7:30 AM
Reading newspaper	Bedroom or sitting room	Sofa, table lamp	15–20 min	7:00–7:30 PM

In the survey process, first, target activities are selected, and afterwards, the user is asked to describe a day in which the target activities take place, including features such as the sequence of activities and start time of each activity. The activity's location is sometimes important, for instance, a particular user may want to read the newspaper in the bedroom instead of the sitting room. The objects used to complete each activity are also important, because this information suggests to the system what sensor(s) will be used to detect the activity. Finally, time is the most valuable parameter used to detect user behaviours. In case the user provides the wrong answered, it will be identified at the end of the process when the automation happened at the wrong time. As we are following the user-centred approach, the problem would be tackled by the user feedback (Fig. 1, step 13). Table 1 gives a clearer picture of what type of answers are sought when users answer the questionnaire. Based on the collected answers, a simulation is designed.

3.2 Simulation

The purpose of the simulation (Fig. 1, step 4) is to giving the user knowledge about the new house and model the user behaviour based on the user's answer and generate the dataset.

UbikSim [14] is used to design the simulation. UbikSim is open source, has a rich library, and is Java-based. These features make it easy to integrate with the rest of the part of the proposed system. Ubik was initially developed to study complex multi-agent systems (MAS); it has since been modified, including the addition of new features for this project. UbikSim is implemented in two phases, namely virtual house design and user behaviour design.

Virtual House Design. The first step is to design a 3D virtual house to look like the real smart house where the user will live. In the design stage, our aim is to provide knowledge about the house, so when the user starts living in the new

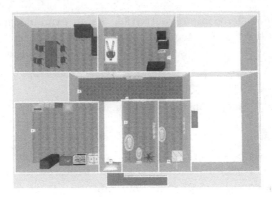

Fig. 2. A virtual design of real Smart Space Lab at Middlesex University.

house, he/she does not feel uncomfortable with any of the appliances, furniture and or other devices that may be integrated with the sensors. Some features of the home may not be available in UbikSim. In such cases, we can use the rich Sweet home library to improve the design. Figure 2 shows the virtual design of the real smart space lab at Middlesex University.

User Behaviour Design. User behaviour design is based on the user's answers. Here, we follow an interactive approach, using an avatar-an interactive object that can move within the virtual smart home and passively or actively interact with the virtual sensors-to represent the behaviour of the real inhabitant. The avatar interacts with virtual sensors and data on these interactions is saved in the server.

In the scenario, Bob/Betty wants to live independently in a smart home. After an interview in which he/she completes the questionnaire, Bob/Betty is invited to interact with the simulation. Thus, Bob becomes familiar with the new house and its facilities before he/she starts living in it. Bob's/Betty's activities are simulated according to their answers. If he/she is satisfied with the activity processes, the next step is initiated; otherwise, the step is repeated.

The simulation model is generated after complete user satisfaction is reached. Finally, the simulation data are generated based on the requirements of the activity recognition tools. Figure 3 shows user daily living activity data generated using a virtual smart home.

3.3   Activity Recognition

To provide the user smart home automation services, we need to detect the habits of the user. Automatically habit detection possible when machine learn and understand the user activity. To detect the user habit we consider LFPUBS [4]. LFPUBS is used as an activity recognition tool, capable of finding the most frequent patterns from a dataset. Like UbikSim, LFPUBS is also open source

idMeasure	idUser	idDevice	oldValue	newValue	time
87245	1	446	1	0	04/06/2019 14:10
87244	1	505	1	0	04/06/2019 14:10
87243	1	35	1	0	04/06/2019 14:10
87241	1	505	0	1	04/06/2019 14:09
87242	1	446	0	1	04/06/2019 14:09
87240	1	35	0	1	04/06/2019 14:09
87239	1	450	1	0	04/06/2019 14:09
87238	1	505	1	0	04/06/2019 14:09
87237	1	35	1	0	04/06/2019 14:09

Fig. 3. Daily living activity data for a user generated by Simulation.

and Java-based. LFPUBS uses its own language, called LLFPUBS, based on Event-Condition-Action (ECA). The output created by its application is also in ECA format. Its architecture has translation, learning and application layers.

Each of these layers plays a vital role in understanding data. The translation layer receives raw data, processes it, and splits it into sequences to create a sensible dataset. The learning layer is the core of LFPUBS, which probes for patterns, creates a frequency set of actions, quantitative time relations and specific conditions. The application layer shows and saves the knowledge discovered by the learning layer.

After detecting user behaviour, a reasoning system needed that acts in real time and provide the automation services based on the acquired knowledge. Although quite well known in the AI community, the actions of the reasoning system will be caught by the learning system. For reasoning, we use Mreasoner [9]. Mreasoner is a reasoning system capable of handling causality in context-aware systems. As LFPUBS and Mreasoner both have different functionality and data format. So, use a translator LFPUBS2M [15] that translate LFPUBS pattern to M rules which we can use for the Mreasoner.

3.4 Transfer Learning

A novel method is proposed to allow the user enjoy the smart home's automation services as soon as he/she starts living there. To provide the user with more accurate smart home automation services, we integrate the transfer learning technique with the proposed method. As discussed above, a simulation is designed and a dataset generated based on each user's answers and the designer's experience. However, no activities were practised in a real house. As a result, the duration of each activity could be different in a real house, which may affect the user's experience as he/she tries to receive the desired services. As an example, the user could say, or the designer assume, that traveling from the bedroom to the kitchen will take 3 s, or making a cup of tea 5 min, but these durations may not apply to the real house. Thus, at this point, we must find a way to improve the system's knowledge about the real house.

With transfer learning, a system can leverage experience from previous tasks to improve the performance of a new task. We propose an interface (Fig. 1, step

17) to analyse the activity recognition patterns developed from the simulated and real datasets. The pattern will be finalize based on user preference; however, any conflict detected will be solved using the method of Oguego et al. [11]. The proposed method assumes that source data have been collected from a house with the same layout as the experimental house.

4   User-Guided Transfer Learning (UTL) Interface

The system has been designed to integrate multiple system—UbikSim, LFPUBS, LFPUBS2M and MReasoner. Each of these systems requires a specific format for its input data and outputs data in its own format. To overcome compatibility problems, we designed the UTL interface (Fig. 4), which automatically converts each system's output to the appropriate format for the next system to use as input.

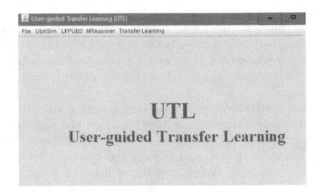

Fig. 4. User-guided Transfer Learning (UTL) interface.

5   Validation

The key objective of the validation process to examine the system designed using the proposed the method to ensure it is capable of providing a user with automation services as soon as he/she starts living in the new smart home.

As we mentioned above, the user is at the heart of our system development process. To simplify the validation process, instead of validating the whole system at once, we can perform validation in three steps: data validation, simulation validation, and automation validation. Every step consists of a loop which allows refinements to the system based on user feedback.   Any intelligent environment (IE) requires the interfacing of hardware, software, networks, and physical space. This type of system also involves different simulations be designed for each user, and the number of iterations required may require a long development time. Thus, in this work, five users participated in the validation process. Validation is carried out at the Smart Spaces lab at Middlesex University (Fig. 5), most

Fig. 5. A map of the lab including sensor hardware.

part of which is set up as a smart home. This area consists of a living room, a bedroom, a kitchen, a toilet, a shower room and a corridor space. 6 Motion, 11 door, 3 object and 6 light sensors are installed. The smart home behaviour is driven by the SEArch architecture [2]. The system uses rule based reasoning [9,11] and performs the user behaviour learning [4].

Data Validation. This step gathers detailed user activity data via face-to-face interviews. Participants are asked pre-designed questions (see Sect. 3.1). In the interview, the user naturally explains how he/she performs morning and evening activities of daily living. The user may perform various types of activities in morning and evening, but we consider only the preselected activities the system can monitor and provide automation to support.

At this step, the simulated home is displayed to the participants so they can become familiar with new home and devices; this is intended to reduce future discomfort with new devices. Users' answers are processed to sequence activity based on the scenarios, to separate data into complex and simple activities, to organise action sequences that are involved with particular activities, and to rename complex activities (Tables 2, 3, 4).

The users are then invited for another interview, shown the summary from the previous interview, and asked for feedback. All users expressed satisfaction with the processed data.

Simulation Validation. This step seeks to ensure the users are satisfied with the simulation. UbikSim is chosen from the UTL interface to design the simulation, and morning and evening scenarios are designed separately. The simulation, in which an avatar performs daily activities as previously described by the user, is played for the user. This step required repetition; users 1 and user 2 accepted the first iteration, users 4 and user 5 the second, and user 3 the third.

After the simulation is accepted by the user, the data is converted to a particular format so that it can be use in LFPUBS as an input. LFPUBS is a learning

Table 2. User's weekday activity sequences

User	Time range	Scenario	Activities and sequences
User1	08:30–09:30 AM	Morning	Wake Up → Use Toilet → Make Tea → Go Outside
	07:00–10:00 PM	Evening	Enter Home → Use Toilet → Relaxing → Make Tea → Sleeping
User2	06:00–07:00 AM	Morning	Wake Up → Use Toilet → Make Tea → Use Shower → Go Outside
	08.00–10.00 PM	Evening	Enter Home → Make Tea→ Relaxing→ Make Tea → Sleeping
User3	08:30–09:00 AM	Morning	Wake Up → Use Toilet → Use Shower → Make Tea → Go Outside
	08:00–10:00 PM	Evening	Enter Home →Make Tea → Sleeping
User4	06:00–07:00 AM	Morning	Wake Up → Use Toilet → Use Shower → Make Tea → Go Outside
	08:00–11:00 PM	Evening	Enter Home → Use Toilet → Make Tea → Sleeping
User5	08:30–09:00 AM	Morning	Wake Up → Use Toilet → Make Tea → Use Shower → Go Outside
	08:00–10:00 PM	Evening	Enter Home → Make Tea → Relaxing → Sleeping

Table 3. Example of simple and complex activities.

Scenario	Simple activity	Complex activity
Morning	Wake up, use toilet, use shower, go outside	Make tea
Evening	Enter home, Use toilet, sleeping	Make tea, relaxing

system that acquires knowledge of user behaviour from the user activity dataset. A sample of such acquired knowledge is shown in Fig. 6. It is a fraction of the activity pattern, where *General Conditions* are calendar information boundaries representing when the action is performed. There *ON* clause defines the event, *IF* defines the necessary condition, and *THEN* defines the action that needs to be carried out. Then, *Action Pattern 1* describes that when Entrance sensor is OFF and Corridor sensor is OFF, and then the Toilet sensor expected to be OFF after 230s. If *THEN* clause mentions an actuator, then triggered otherways it is used for monitoring purposes. This way LFPUBS creates links between two events. As stated in Sect. 3.3, that pattern is not directly executable by Mreasoner. So LFPUBS2M used to translate the dataset to Mreasoner executable format. Figure 7 shows part of the rules that are sequentially executed by the Mreasoner to accomplish the automation task. Here the rules define that the kitchen Light will be turned on when Pattern_0 to Pattern_9 are satisfied.

Table 4. Users' action sequences for particular activities.

User	Activity name	Action involves	New name
User1	Make Tea	KitchenDoor ON → KitchenMotion ON → Kettle ON → Cupboard ON → Fridge ON	Milk Tea
	Relaxing	SittingroomMotion ON → SittingroomLight ON → SittingroomSofa OFF	Relaxing in sitting
User2	Make Tea	KitchenDoor ON → KitchenMotion ON → Kettle ON → Cupboard ON	Red Tea
	Relaxing	SittingroomMotion ON → SittingroomLight ON → SittingroomSofa OFF	Relaxing in sitting
User3	Make Tea	KitchenDoor ON → KitchenMotion ON → Kettle ON → Cupboard ON	Red Tea
	Relaxing	SittingroomMotion ON → SittingroomLight ON → SittingroomSofa OFF	Relaxing in sitting
User4	Make Tea	KitchenDoor ON → KitchenMotion ON → Kettle ON → Cupboard ON → Fridge ON	Milk Tea
	Relaxing	BedroomMotion ON → BedroomLight ON → BedPressure OFF	Relaxing in Bed
User5	Make Tea	KitchenDoor ON → KitchenMotion ON → Kettle ON → Cupboard ON → Fridge ON	Milk Tea
	Relaxing	BedroomMotion ON → BedroomLight ON → BedPressure OFF	Relaxing in Bed

Action Map 0

(General Conditions)

context (DayOfWeek (=,Monday,Tuesday,Wednesday,Thursday,Friday))&
context (TimeOfDay(>,09:24:08)) & context (TimeOfDay(<,00:00:00))

(Action Pattern 0)
ON occurs (start,--,t0) Frequency: 7
IF context ()
THEN do (unordered,((OFF,Entrance (0)) & (OFF,Corridor (0))), t) when --

(Action Pattern 1)
ON occurs (unordered,((OFF,Entrance (0)) & (OFF,Corridor (0))), t0) Frequency: 21
IF context ()
THEN do (simple,(OFF,ToiletMove (0)) , t) when t = t0 + 230.6107692718506 s.

Fig. 6. Sample of LFPUBS generated pattern.

Where each of the patterns satisfied with a certain state of the sensors for example, Pattern_8 will be satisfied if kitchen door open between 13:41:32 to 13:57:41 on Monday to Friday.

```
ssr( ( weekDayBetween(monday-friday ) ) ->actionMap_day_context ) ;
ssr( ( #weekDayBetween(monday-friday ) ) ->#actionMap_day_context );
ssr( ( clockBetween(13:41:59-13:58:41 ) ) -> actionMap_time_context );
ssr( ( #clockBetween(13:41:59-13:58:41 ) ) -> #actionMap_time_context );

ssr( ( KitchenDoor ^ actionMap_time_context ^ Pattern_1 ^ actionMap_day_context )
-> Pattern_0 );
ssr( ( [-][05s.]#BedRoomDoor ^ actionMap_time_context ^ actionMap_day_context )
-> Pattern_1 );
ssr( ( #KitchenDoor ^ actionMap_time_context ^ Pattern_0 ^ actionMap_day_context
) -> Pattern_2 );
ssr( (Pattern_2 ) ->KitchenLight );
```

Fig. 7. Sample of LFPUBS2M translated rules.

Smart Home Automation Validation. The objective of this step is to acti-
vate the devices and provide the user with the promised automation. To accomplish this, each user is invited to visit the lab twice, once in the morning and
once in the evening. The Mreasoner from UTL was chosen to perform the real-
time home automation based the on rules generated (as described in the previous
section). User feedback about the automation services is collected from each user
and used as a basis to modify the rules.

Table 5. Study questions for measuring the acceptance of the system and user
satisfaction.

No	System acceptance and user satisfaction question
1	How useful is it that the smart home provides services from day one?
2	How similar did you find the simulated and real smart home?
3	How close was the simulated behaviour to the answers you provided?
4	How useful was the simulation in adjusting to the real house?
5	How will did the house provide its automation services?
6	What improvements would you make to the system?

After finishing the validation process, we asked the participants six questions
(Table 5) to measure their acceptance of and satisfaction with the new system.
We used a three-point Likert scale to analyse participant' responses (Fig. 8).
Four (80%) of users felt that smart home automation from day one is very useful,
and that the smart home simulation helped the user adapt to their new home.
Users did not find substantial similarity between the simulated and real homes;
however, they suggested that it gave them a basic idea about how the actual
house would be. Users were generally satisfied with house automation time;
Three participants (60%) agreed the automation happen on correct time. Most
users agreed that the actual behaviours were similar to those in the simulation
based on their answers.

All of the resources which gather used and generated in from the validation process, such as questionnaires, users' answered, simulation, simulated data, LFPUBS-produced patterns, LFPUBS2M-generated rules, and the results of house actuation when user exercised the scenarios can be found here at https://doi.org/10.22023/mdx.8789984.

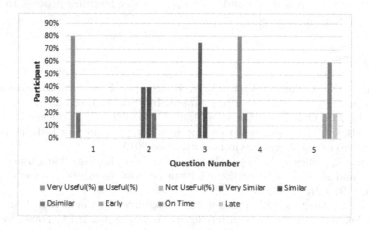

Fig. 8. Users' responses based on questions in Table 5.

6   Discussion

We performed validation considering the two scenarios described in Sect. 1. Our aim was to provide the user with home automation services as soon as he/she starts living in the house. Five users participated in the user-centred validation process. The user-centred nature of the process makes it highly unlikely the user will be unsatisfied with the resulting system. Participants' response results show that a user expect automation functionality as soon as he/she start living in the house. Our design system was able to provide appropriate automation immediately over 60% of on time; user feedback shows our design is useful in helping new users understand the features of their new smart home.

7   Conclusion

Data-driven activity recognition is one of the most active and challenging lines of research in the field of smart home development. The goal in this work was to create a user-centric approach to develop a system that immediately provides smart home automation services to new users, thereby increasing user satisfaction and acceptance of the technology. To that end, this research designed an integrated systems that pre-determines user behaviour patterns using user-provided data. These approach complement of unsupervised existing strategy. These patterns are used to feed a reasoning system that can help provide the functionality that the user requires. The resulting system is user-centric, with every step incorporating user feedback. This minimizes the chance that users will be unsatisfied with the results. We successfully designed and implemented the system and validated it in a real smart home. The system shows promise; participants report that the system is very useful for adapting to their new smart home. Our next step will be validating the transfer learning process to further increase automation accuracy.

References

1. Augusto, J.C., Callaghan, V., Cook, D., Kameas, A., Satoh, I.: Intelligent environments: a manifesto. Hum. Centric Comput. Inf. Sci. **3**(1), 12 (2013)
2. Augusto, J.C., Quinde, M., Gimenez Manuel, J.G., Ali, S.M.M., Oguego, C., James-Reynolds, C.: The search smart environments architecture. In: 15th International Conference on Intelligent Environments, June 2019
3. Azkune, G., Almeida, A., López-de Ipiña, D., Chen, L.: Combining users' activity survey and simulators to evaluate human activity recognition systems. Sensors **15**(4), 8192–8213 (2015)
4. Aztiria, A., Augusto, J.C., Basagoiti, R., Izaguirre, A., Cook, D.J.: Learning frequent behaviors of the users in intelligent environments. IEEE Trans. Syst. Man Cybern. Syst. **43**, 1265–1278 (2013)
5. Chiang, Y.t., Hsu, J.Y.j.: Knowledge transfer in activity recognition using sensor profile. In: 2012 9th International Conference on Ubiquitous Intelligence & Computing and 9th International Conference on Autonomic & Trusted Computing (UIC/ATC), pp. 180–187 (2012)
6. Chiang, Y.T., Lu, C.H., Hsu, J.Y.J.: A feature-based knowledge transfer framework for cross-environment activity recognition toward smart home applications. IEEE Trans. Hum. Mach. Syst. **47**, 310–322 (2017)
7. Cook, D., Feuz, K.D., Krishnan, N.C.: Transfer learning for activity recognition: a survey. Knowl. Inf. Syst. **36**(3), 537–556 (2013)
8. Hanson, M.: I'd rather die than be a burden on my daughter like many older people (2016). https://www.theguardian.com/commentisfree/2016/dec/15/old-people-dementia-deathsocial-care-costs.html. Accessed 15 Dec 2016
9. Ibarra, U.A., Augusto, J.C., Goenaga, A.A.: Temporal reasoning for intuitive specification of context-awareness. In: 2014 International Conference on Intelligent Environments, pp. 234–241, June 2014. https://doi.org/10.1109/IE.2014.44
10. Jakovljevi, M., Njegu, A., Donov, N.: Data-driven human activity recognition in smart environments. In: International Scientific Conference on ICT and E-Business Related Research, pp. 94–99 (2016)
11. Oguego, C., Augusto, J., Muñoz, A., Springett, M.: Using argumentation to manage users' preferences. Future Gener. Comput. Syst. **81**(1), 235–243 (2018)
12. Rawashdeh, M., Zamil, M.G.A., Samarah, S., Hossain, M.S., Muhammad, G.: A knowledge-driven approach for activity recognition in smart homes based on activity profiling. Future Gener. Comput. Syst. (2017)
13. Sadri, F.: Ambient intelligence: a survey. ACM Comput. Surv. **43**(4), 36:1–36:66, October 2011
14. Serrano, E., Botia, J.A., Cadenas, J.M.: Ubik: a multi-agent based simulator for ubiquitous computing applications. J. Phys. Agents **3**(2), 39–43 (2009)
15. Zinkunegi, E.A.: LFPUBS 2 M (2016). https://github.com/estibalitz/lfpubs2m

Short Application Papers

Analysis of Electronic Health Records to Identify the Patient's Treatment Lines: Challenges and Opportunities

Marjan Najafabadipour[1]([⊠]) [iD], Juan Manuel Tuñas[1] [iD],
Alejandro Rodríguez-González[1,2] [iD], and Ernestina Menasalvas[1,2] [iD]

[1] Centro de Tecnología Biomédica, Universidad Politécnica de Madrid,
Madrid, Spain
{m.najafabadipour,alejandro.rg,
ernestina.menasalvas}@upm.es, juan.tunas@ctb.upm.es
[2] ETS de Ingenieros Informáticos, Universidad Politécnica de Madrid,
Madrid, Spain

Abstract. The automatic reconstruction of the patient's treatment lines from their Electronic Health Records (EHRs) is a significant step towards improving the quality and the safety of the healthcare deliveries. With the recent rapid increase in the adaption of EHRs and the rapid development of computational science, we can discover new insights from the information stored in EHRs. However, this is still a challenging task, being unstructured data analysis one of them. In this paper, we focus on the most common challenges for reconstructing the patient's treatment lines, which are the Named Entity Recognition (NER), temporal relation identification and the integration of structured results. We introduce our Natural Language Processing (NLP) framework, which deals with the aforementioned challenges. In addition, we focus on a real use case of patients, suffering from lung cancer to extract patterns associated with the treatment of the disease that can help clinicians to analyze toxicities and patterns depending on the lines of treatments given to the patient.

Keywords: Electronic Health Records · Natural Language Processing · Named Entity Recognition · Temporal relation identification

1 Introduction

Treatments target the symptoms, the disease, the impairments in physical and psychosocial functioning, disabilities, comorbidities, and the trajectory of the disorder [1]. This makes the detection of treatment lines from the clinical texts a fundamental task in the clinical information extraction, where a treatment line is a collection of drugs with their dosage and its starting and ending time points. The detection of treatment lines has several applications in the medical research such as assessing the healthcare quality [2], understanding the patient's treatment course [3] and improving the detection of adverse drug reaction [4].

Towards the digitization of medical data, clinicians chronologically record the details of the patient-clinician encounters in the computerized documents, known as

© Springer Nature Switzerland AG 2019
M. Bramer and M. Petridis (Eds.): SGAI-AI 2019, LNAI 11927, pp. 437–442, 2019.
https://doi.org/10.1007/978-3-030-34885-4_33

"Electronic Health Records (EHRs)" [5]. EHRs are therefore textual (unstructured) clinical documents containing several medical events related to the patient's treatment and the corresponding chronological sequence, which allows the reconstruction of the treatment lines. A typical treatment line can be composed of many EHRs, including tens of thousands of words. This makes the manual analysis of EHRs for identification of such a line a time-consuming and costly task. For this reason, the automatic discovery of treatment lines from clinical texts requires a great attention.

Identification of treatment lines includes several challenges: (1) NER, a paramount step of NLP to extract drug concepts, dosage metrics and time expressions from clinical texts; (2) temporal relation identification, to link treatment concepts to time expressions; and (3) the integration of structured results, to deal with the redundant information and to reconstruct the treatment lines.

Although, several NLP systems have been developed for extraction of information from clinical texts such as Apache cTAKES [6], MEDLEE [7], MetaMap [8], H2A [9], C-liKES [10], to name a few, the problem of the discovery of treatment lines from all the patient's EHRs still remains unsolved.

In this paper, we deal with the challenges associated with NER, temporal relation identification and the integration of structured results for a specific use case related to lung cancer domain. The EHRs of lung cancer patients used in our studies are available in Spanish. The main objective of this research is to contribute to the existing solutions by providing a prototype, indicating that analyzing EHRs enables the reconstruction of the patient's treatment lines. To do so, an NLP framework together with built in modules to extract concepts, detect temporal relations and build treatment lines is being designed.

The rest of paper is organized as follows: Sect. 2 explains the challenges associated with reconstructing the patient's treatment lines from their EHRs. Afterwards, Sect. 3 is dedicated to explaining our framework and its application to lung cancer domain. Finally, Sect. 4 describes the conclusions and future works.

2   Challenge for Reconstructing the Patient's Treatment Lines

Reconstruction of the patient's treatment lines from EHRs entails three main challenges: (1) NER; (2) temporal relation identification; and (3) the integration of structured results. These challenges are discussed in detail in the following Sub-sections.

2.1   Named Entity Recognition Challenges

EHRs contain a vast amount of valuable information written in narrative form, which lacks structure or have a structure depending on the hospital, service or the clinician generating them. Thus, the extraction of information from clinical texts is difficult.

Annotation of treatment events is highly dependent on the dosage metrics. Within clinical texts, recognition of these metrics introduces three main challenges. First of all, although the NER process relies on ontologies such as SNOMED [11] and UMLS [12], these ontologies are limited to completely provide dosage metrics. Secondly, abbreviations are integral part of dosage metrics; it is thus difficult to assign semantics to them. Finally, the dosage metrics can be mentioned as simple as including only one variable or as complex as including several variables, which are very common, and yet are difficult to decode in an exact way.

Another interesting challenge is related to the recognition of time expressions from EHRs due to the limitation of ontologies to provide them, various formats, styles, categories (i.e., relative and absolute) a time expression can be written in, and the difficulty to interpret relative time expressions.

2.2 Temporal Relation Identification Challenges

Clinical texts include complex, diverse and sometimes, non-standard linguistics mechanisms to mention temporal relations. In addition, in some cases, the time point associated to the medical event is not even explicitly mentioned in EHRs. These make the automatic detection of temporal relations a very challenging task.

2.3 The Integration of Structured Results Challenges

The problem of Information redundancy is a fundamental concept associated with EHRs due to the interest of clinicians to "cut and paste" texts from past EHRs for summarizing past information in the newly generated EHRs. This creates another layer of complexity to reconstruct the patient's treatment lines from EHRs as many redundancies and references to the past treatments can appear with the current treatment lines. In addition, it can happen that a treatment line has to be discontinued due to no effect, toxicities or the side effects. This challenge also should be tackled in order to find the lines of treatments of the patients.

3 Solution

The main goal of this research is to be able to reconstruct the patient's treatment lines. As mentioned in Sect. 1, we are working specifically on a use case related to the patients suffering from lung cancer. Therefore, we present our framework to analyze EHRs in order to reconstruct the lung cancer patient's treatment lines (Fig. 1). Our framework is responsible for analyzing EHRs to annotate concepts from clinical texts, identify temporal relations and build the treatment lines.

We will describe in what follows, the annotators used and developed to be able to recognize drug concepts, dosage metrics and time expressions from clinical texts. In NER, the first step is to annotate concepts using standard ontologies. To recognize drug concepts from clinical texts, we use the UMLS annotator of C-liKES [10], which is built upon the Unstructured Information Management Architecture (UIMA) framework. The UMLS annotator can identify noun and noun phrases concepts that have relevant matches in the UMLS ontology. We here focus on recognizing the specific treatments concepts of tyrosine kinase inhibitor, chemotherapy, radiotherapy, immunotherapy, and antiangiogenic for our implementation.

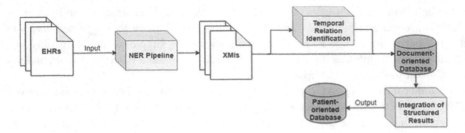

Fig. 1. Architecture of our framework

Apart from the treatment concepts, new annotators should be developed for annotation of dosage metrics and time expressions as they are not provided in the UMLS. To recognize dosage metrics associated with drugs for the aforementioned lung cancer treatments, a rule-based NLP annotator is being developed. In addition, to extract and normalize time variables appeared in the clinical texts, we use a rule-based NLP annotator built over UIMA framework, named Temporal Tagger that is presented in a previous work of the authors [13].

To process EHRs using these annotators, we have implemented them under a single NER pipeline. Once the clinical texts are ingested, the outcomes of annotation process are stored in a set of XML Metadata Interchange (XMI) files.

Then, a temporal relation identification process is implemented using a rule-based approach to link annotated time expressions to treatment concepts in clinical texts. Although once the information in EHRs has been annotated, one could use search engines to retrieve the information. However, our aim here is to extract specific patterns that can be used for reconstruction of treatment lines.

Afterwards, the information stored in XMI files and generated by the temporal relation identification process is stored into a document-based relational database. As this database only provides insights to the information at document level and does not facilitate the integration of information for patients, so we cannot query the treatment lines for patients. Therefore, the integration of structured information is still required for reconstructing the patient's treatment lines.

At this stage, a specific module is developed to integrate the information of document-oriented database and to deal with information redundancy. As each patient can have many EHRs generated for him during his treatment course, several redundant information is included in these clinical documents. Therefore, there is a need for development of a specific post-process module to deal with information redundancy to be able to then reconstruct the lines of treatments. For this purpose, an algorithm with a set of heuristics rules is being developed that is based on the clinician's knowledge and experience for determining what kind of treatments with specific dosage can be pre-scribed for the patients at the same or different time intervals. This algorithm accepts the structured information of document-oriented database and follows the steps dis-cussed below:

- For each treatment type, temporally order the treatment concepts. Then, select the earliest mention of its drug and dosage from EHRs, and start the treatment line X.

- While the end time point of X is not found, include all the mentioned unique drug concepts with their dosage from EHRs in X. The end time point of X is found when:

  - More than N months have been passed without the mention of the last drug concept of X within EHRs or without the mention of a new compatible drug. Note that, the value of N for months is different for each treatment type.
  - A new drug with a specific dosage is mentioned in an EHR that is not compatible with other drugs in X.

Once, the above algorithm is implemented and the lines of treatments are identified for each patient, they will be stored into a patient-oriented database from which query and answering process can be followed for having the detailed information for each line. Figure 2 presents an example of the output stored by our framework in the patient-oriented database for a patient, who has gone through the chemotherapy treatments.

Finally, Fig. 3 depicts the summary of the concepts extracted from EHRs towards generating the patient's treatment lines.

Id	Treatment	Line	Init	Finish	Drugs	Dosage
6695	chemotherapy	1	2017-06-01	2017-08-07	carboplatino	396 ma
6695	chemotherapy	2	2017-11-08	2018-02-22	docetaxel|pemetrexed	75 ma/m2|500 ma/m2

Fig. 2. Example of the output of our framework in the patient-oriented database

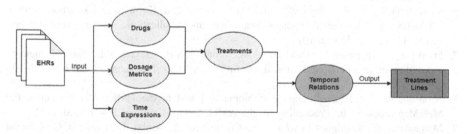

Fig. 3. Concepts extracted From EHRs towards reconstructing the patient's treatment lines

4   Conclusion and Future Work

In this paper, we have analyzed challenges associated with the process of reconstructing the patient's treatment lines from their EHRs. We have focused on the NER, temporal relation identification and the integration of structured information. This work is an ongoing research in which future works will be aimed at the validation and the improvement of the framework. However, the validation of each of the modules in the framework is a difficult and time-consuming task as it requires the manual inspection of the EHRs to check their performance accuracy. In addition, it is significant to note that some of the steps of temporal relation identification and the integration of structured results are not yet completely automatic as they are dependent on the way the clinical texts are written. Thus, future improvements go to automatizing these processes completely.

Acknowledgment. This paper is supported by European Union's Horizon 2020 research and innovation programme under grant agreement No. 727658, project IASIS (Integration and analysis of heterogeneous big data for precision medicine and suggested treatments for different types of patients). MN is also supported by UPM (Universidad Politécnica de Madrid) Programa Propio of PhD grants.

References

1. Ursano, R.J.: Disease and illness: prevention, treatment, caring, and health. Prev. Chronic Dis. **8**(6), A128 (2011)
2. Roth, C.P., Lim, Y.-W., Pevnick, J.M., Asch, S.M., McGlynn, E.A.: The challenge of measuring quality of care from the electronic health record. Am. J. Med. Qual. **24**(5), 385–394 (2009)
3. Ghitza, U.E., Sparenborg, S., Tai, B.: Improving drug abuse treatment delivery through adoption of harmonized electronic health record systems. Subst. Abuse Rehabil. **2**, 125–131 (2011)
4. Liu, M., et al.: Large-scale prediction of adverse drug reactions using chemical, biological, and phenotypic properties of drugs. J. Am. Med. Inform. Assoc. **19**(e1), e28–e35 (2012)
5. Najafabadipour, M., Tuñas, J.M., Rodríguez-González, A., Menasalvas, E.: Lung cancer concept annotation from Spanish clinical narratives. In: Auer, S., Vidal, M.-E. (eds.) DILS 2018. LNCS, vol. 11371, pp. 153–163. Springer, Cham (2019). https://doi.org/10.1007/978-3-030-06016-9_15
6. Savova, G.K., et al.: Mayo clinical Text Analysis and Knowledge Extraction System (cTAKES): architecture, component evaluation and applications. J. Am. Med. Inform. Assoc. **17**(5), 507–513 (2010)
7. Friedman, C., Hripcsak, G., DuMouchel, W., Johnson, S.B., Clayton, P.D.: Natural language processing in an operational clinical information system. Nat. Lang. Eng. **1**(1), 83–108 (1995)
8. Aronson, A.R.: Effective mapping of biomedical text to the UMLS Metathesaurus: the MetaMap program. In: Proceedings of the AMIA Symposium, pp. 17–21 (2001)
9. Menasalvas, E., Rodriguez-Gonzalez, A., Costumero, R., Ambit, H., Gonzalo, C.: Clinical narrative analytics challenges. In: Flores, V., et al. (eds.) IJCRS 2016. LNCS (LNAI), vol. 9920, pp. 23–32. Springer, Cham (2016). https://doi.org/10.1007/978-3-319-47160-0_2
10. Menasalvas Ruiz, E., et al.: Profiling lung cancer patients using electronic health records. J. Med. Syst. **42**(7), 126 (2018)
11. SNOMED International. https://www.snomed.org/. Accessed 13 Jul 2018
12. Unified Medical Language System (UMLS). https://www.nlm.nih.gov/research/umls/. Accessed 4 May 2018
13. Najafabadipour, M., et al.: Recognition of time expressions in Spanish electronic health records. In: 2019 IEEE 32nd International Symposium on Computer-Based Medical Systems (CBMS), pp. 69–74 (2019). https://doi.org/10.1109/CBMS.2019.00025

Characterisation of VBM Algorithms for Processing of Medical MRI Images

Martin Svejda$^{(\boxtimes)}$ and Roger Tait

Birmingham City University, Birmingham, UK
{martin.svejda,roger.tait}@bcu.ac.uk

Abstract. In Voxel-Based Morphometry (VBM), spatial normalisation is a major process which transforms images into a standard space and is often referred to as co-registration. This project is a comparison and observation of differences in the performance, measured as the overlap between images, of two co-registration algorithms used in VBM on human brain Magnetic Resonance Imaging (MRI) data. Here we show differences between genders and algorithms on specific regions of the brain using grey matter segments and unsegmented MRI images. Results show that there are significant differences in the overlap of regions depending on the algorithm which may be considered in addition to current knowledge on the subject. Importantly, we are interested in investigating what these differences mean to published and on-going research as well as observing whether said difference spans all the way to the Parahippocampal Gyrus and other important regions associated with psychological related diseases.

Keywords: VBM · Structural MRI · Temporal lobe · Gender

1 Introduction

According to Shen et al. [1] VBM is an automated method allowing identification of structural anatomical differences in the whole brain without the pre-specification of a Region Of Interests (ROI). While Zhang et al. [2] says that VBM is a more recent and automatic approach that performs "a voxel-wise comparison of the local concentration of grey matter" between subject groups. In general, VBM allows rapid exploratory brain study of large samples and has been applied extensively in schizophrenia and other related research [3,4]. A comparison between two different co-registration algorithms, the *FMRIB Software Library* (FSL) [5] and the *Advanced Normalised Tools* (ANTs) [6], will be looked at in this study. FSL is a comprehensive library of analysis tools for functional, structural and diffusion MRI brain imaging, written mainly by members of the Analysis Group, FMRIB, Oxford. ANTs is an open source software library consisting of state-of-the-art image registration, segmentation and template building tools for quantitative morphometric analysis.

© Springer Nature Switzerland AG 2019
M. Bramer and M. Petridis (Eds.): SGAI-AI 2019, LNAI 11927, pp. 443–448, 2019.
https://doi.org/10.1007/978-3-030-34885-4_34

1.1 Image Registration (Co-registration) Algorithms

At the technical level, Maurer et al. [7] states that co-registration is the determination of a one-to-one mapping between the coordinates in one space and
those in another, such that points in the two spaces that correspond to the same
anatomical location are mapped to each other. According to Tait et al. [8] the use
of optimisation schemes to explore a search space of allowable transform parameters is particularly susceptible to noise which manifests itself as local optima.
Because intensity-based methods exploit voxel intensities without any kind of
scene analysis, they are highly sensitive to image acquisitions conditions. As a
result, miss-alignment can occur during registration due to the lack of details in
the images being registered. Smooth areas of the fixed image, for example, can
be matched incorrectly with smooth areas of the moving image due to a lack of
discriminating features.

In this study we focus on reporting the accuracy of overlap of anatomical
regions after co-registration based on the algorithms introduced. Unlike others
[9,10], we investigate the performance of the algorithms based on both segmented
and non-segmented images. We also make no attempt to quantify differences in
macroscopic and microscopic structures and instead are only interested in gross
morphological change.

2 Methodology

These data have been processed using bias field correction routines to remove
field inhomogeneities. Parcellations, accounting for approximately 120 known
anatomical structures, are also provided as an outline and as filled volume formats. In total there are 18 subjects spread across a range of demographic factors.

To perform this study, 8 IBSR subjects, 4 males and 4 females have been
co-registered into Montreal Neurological Institute (MNI152) template space and
their associated ROI warped using the same transformation. The resulting overlaps reported as DICE [11] coefficients averaged over gender, are shown as the
Y-axis in Fig. 1. To observe the effects that tissue segmentation has we have
co-registered both whole brain images and grey matter segments independently.

In Fig. 1, we present overlaps for ROI number 16, commonly known as *T3p*
in the left temporal lobe. An algorithmic difference is clearly visible in the Whole
Brain graph, where FSL is producing better overlaps compared to ANTs for both
genders. Importantly, the gender difference in overlap shown by FSL alone is
significant at ($p = 0.024$) while for ANTs is not ($p = 0.221$). For the Grey Matter
Segments graph, FSL is only better for males but not for females. Although the
algorithm by image type difference appears to be lost the gender differences in
overlap shown by FSL ($p = 0.037$) and ANTs ($p = 0.391$) remain.

Average DICE coefficient, across genders and algorithms, is shown in Fig. 2
where lighter colours represent good overlap and darker colours represent poor.
The template's left-hand pial surface is shown on the top row while the right hand
surface is shown on the bottom. Unsurprisingly the thicker cortical structures
like the Insula demonstrate the best overlap and are hence clearly visible in dark.

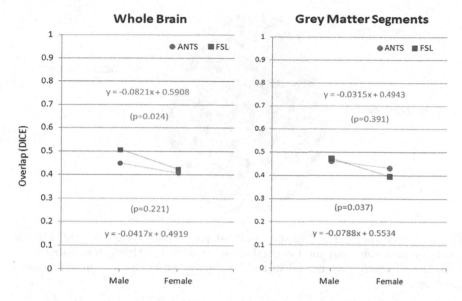

Fig. 1. On the left are ANTs and FSL representing overlaps imposed directly on the template. Right side representing registration based on grey matter segments. Slopes are signifying the difference between algorithms and points representing genders.

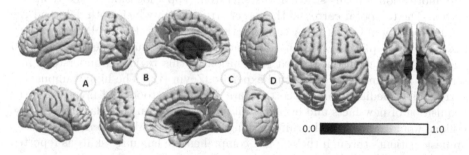

Fig. 2. Dice coefficient averaged over the Whole Brain for both *ANTs* and *FSL*. Higher overlap values can be seen in (A) Insula (B) Medial Frontal Cortex (C) Precuneus regions while reduced overlap can be seen in the (D) Posterior Parietal Cortex.

The area of the Corpus Callosum, showing no overlap, represents central brain structures that did not have associated parcellations or segmentations nor medial surfaces.

Figure 3 shows *Left-T3p* and its proximity to the Parahippocampal Gyrus. T3p's close proximity to an important anatomical structure like the Parahippocampal Gyrus makes it an ideal candidate for an investigation into the effects of co-registration on reporting psychological condition. We focused specifically on Left-T3p in this work because of its location. There are however other regions which have demonstrated significant algorithmic differences which we intend to report upon in future stages of this study.

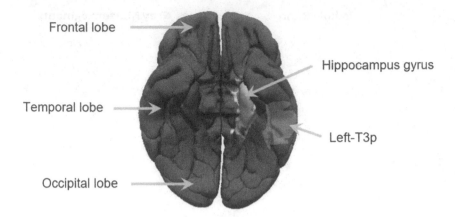

Fig. 3. The location of *left T3p* and the Parahippocampal Gyrus highlighted in relation to Frontal, Temporal and Occipital brain sub-divisions Although repeated on the right, the symmetric nature of T3p and Parahippocampal Gyrus brain structures is not shown.

2.1   Temporal Cortex

Our motivation for this study also stems from T3p's location in the temporal cortex. The temporal cortex is the larger structure in which both T3p and the Parahippocampal Gyrus sit. A sub-structure, the bilateral ventral temporal cortex has been implicated in many tasks involving perceptual expertise for visual stimuli. A specialisation for text recognition in this region is understood and serves as an example of perceptual expertise, Zevin [12]. The hippocampus and surrounding medial temporal cortices are also understood and involved in the acquisition of new facts and events, so it serves to reason that damage to these regions would impair the learning of language. This has been demonstrated by amnesic patients through their loss of comprehensive language skills as reported by Stark et al. [13].

3   Discussion

In conclusion, the results show that there are differences in the overlap between image type and gender depending on the algorithm and as such provides strong evidence to support the hypothesis set at the beginning of this study that algorithmic differences in VBM implementations exists. It must, however, be taken into consideration that the numbers of subjects need to be increased whilst maintaining gender balance in order to substantiate our results. For both algorithms, modulation was carried out by multiplying the transformation Jacobian with warped grey matter segments. A greater number of segmentations and parcellations would also allow us to increase our spatial resolution so that better anatomical location accuracy can be achieved.

To better describe the algorithm by gender by image type relationship analyses of covariance (ANOVA) will be employed to determine the existence of factor by level interactions. We intend to extend this study by investigating the Parahippocampal Gyrus itself as well as its subdivisions and surrounding brain structures. Although the results of this study have highlighted the fact that FSL outperforms ANTs in the Left-T3p, it does not do so consistently over all IBSR parcellations. Crucially, knowing how different algorithms perform over the entire cortical surface is key to informing researchers about the bias they may be introducing into their analyses.

We also intend to investigate the relationship between co-registration algorithm, gender and cortical thickness. Cortical thickness is the distance along a perpendicular vector between the white/grey matter interface and the pial surface. Reporting of cortical thickness is common practice in longitudinal neurological research as normal trajectories are well understood and employed as baselines on which samples are tested against. Unsurprisingly, bias reporting will undoubtedly have a large implication on the quality of research output or any further stages of planned studies using the co-registration algorithms described.

References

1. Shen, S., Sterr, A., Szameitat, A.: A template effect study on voxel-based morphometry in statistic parametric mapping. In: 2005 IEEE Engineering in Medicine and Biology 27th Annual Conference, pp. 3051–3054 (2005). https://doi.org/10.1109/IEMBS.2005.1617118
2. Zhang, J., Buchsbaum, M.S., Chu K., Hazlett, E.A.: Comparison between voxel based morphometry and volumetric analysis in schizophrenia. In: 2008 International Conference on BioMedical Engineering and Informatics, vol. 2, pp. 48–52 (2008). https://doi.org/10.1109/BMEI.2008.208
3. Melonakos, E., Shenton, M., Rathi, Y., Terry, D., Bouix, S., Kubicki, M.: Voxel-based morphometry (VBM) studies in schizophrenia–can white matter changes be reliably detected with VBM? Psychiatry Res. **193**(2), 65–70 (2012). https://doi.org/10.1016/j.pscychresns.2011.01.009
4. McNabb, C.B., et al.: Functional network dysconnectivity as a biomarker of treatment resistance in schizophrenia. Schizophr. Res. **195**, 160–167 (2017). https://doi.org/10.1016/j.schres.2017.10.015
5. Jenkinson, M., Beckmann, C.F., Behrens, T.E.J., Woolrich, M.W., Smith, S.M.: FSL. NeuroImage **62**, 782–790 (2012). https://doi.org/10.1016/j.neuroimage.2011.09.015
6. Avants, B.B., Epstein, C.L., Grossman, M., Gee, J.C.: Symmetric diffeomorphic image registration with cross-correlation: evaluating automated labeling of elderly and neurodegenerative brain. Med. Image Anal. **12**, 26–41 (2008). https://doi.org/10.1016/j.media.2007.06.004
7. Maurer, C.R., Fitzpatrick, J.M., Wang, M.Y., Galloway, R.L., Maciunas, R.J., Allen, G.S.: Registration of head volume images using implantable fiducial markers. IEEE Trans. Med. Imaging **16**, 447–462 (1997). https://doi.org/10.1109/42.611354

8. Tait, R.J., Schaefer, G., Hopgood, A., Nakashima, T.: High performance medical image registration using a distributed blackboard architecture. In: Proceedings of the 2007 IEEE Symposium on Computational Intelligence in Image and Signal Processing, CIISP 2007, pp. 252–257 (2007)
9. Eggert, L.D., Sommer, J., Jansen, A., Kircher, T., Konrad, C.: Accuracy and reliability of automated gray matter segmentation pathways on real and simulated structural magnetic resonance images of the human brain. PloS ONE **7**(9), e45081 (2012). https://doi.org/10.1371/journal.pone.0045081
10. Radua, J., Canales-Rodríguez, E.J., Pomarol-Clotet, E., Salvador, R.: Validity of modulation and optimal settings for advanced voxel-based morphometry. Neuroimage **86**, 81–90 (2014)
11. Dice, L.R.: Measures of the amount of ecologic association between species. Ecology **26**, 297–302 (1945). https://doi.org/10.2307/1932409
12. Zevin, J.: Encyclopedia of Neuroscience, pp. 517–522. Academic Press (2009). https://doi.org/10.1016/B978-008045046-9.01881-7
13. Stark, S.M., Stark, C.E.L.: Neurobiology of language. In: Introduction to Memory, Chap. 67, pp. 841–854 (2016). https://doi.org/10.1016/B978-0-12-407794-2.00067-5
14. Avants, B.B., Tustison, N.J., Song, G., Cook, P.A., Klein, A., Gee, J.C.: A reproducible evaluation of ANTs similarity metric performance in brain image registration. NeuroImage **54**, 2033–2044 (2011). https://doi.org/10.1016/j.neuroimage.2010.09.025
15. IBSR Data Set v2.0. https://www.nitrc.org/frs/shownotes.php?release_id=2316

Analogical News Angles
from Text Similarity

Bjørnar Tessem[(✉)]

Department of Information Science and Media Studies,
University of Bergen, Bergen, Norway
bjornar.tessem@uib.no

Abstract. The paper presents an algorithm providing creativity support to journalists. It suggests analogical transfer of news angles from reports written about different events than the one the journalist is working on. The problem is formulated as a matching problem, where news reports with similar wordings from two events are matched, and unmatched reports from previous cases are selected as candidates for a news angle transfer. The approach is based on document similarity measures for matching and selection of transferable candidates. The algorithm has been tested on a small data set and show that the concept may be viable, but needs more exploration and evaluation in journalistic practice.

Keywords: Computational creativity · Analogical reasoning ·
Document similarity · Journalism

1 Introduction

Artificial intelligence is considered to have great potential in journalism [10], already found in robot journalism [12], content verification [6], and data analysis [8]. One way to go is to support the journalist creativity by providing suggestions for new angles to a new report on an event, e.g., a new news paper article. This is the aim of the News Angler project where we aim to support journalists with such creativity tools [5,11].

The term *news angle* was coined already in the seventies by Altheide [1] who observed that reporters rely on "'angles,' or story lines, which give the specific events new meaning". So, finding a new angle on an event is what the reporter relies on to make the report interesting for a user even though the event already has been described in several reports and in many news media.

One approach to proposing news angles to the journalist is to find and suggest reports from other events that are similar to the current event, but with angles that have not been tried on the current event. This constitutes a form of analogical reasoning where an algorithm identifies unmatched aspects of a base case and transfers them to a new target case, parallel to the *transfer* part of Falkenhainer et al.'s structure mapping engine [4]. This paper describes an

© Springer Nature Switzerland AG 2019
M. Bramer and M. Petridis (Eds.): SGAI-AI 2019, LNAI 11927, pp. 449–455, 2019.
https://doi.org/10.1007/978-3-030-34885-4_35

analogical search algorithm that uses text similarity metrics for news reports and events to identify reports that can provide the journalist with an unused news angle. Even with a simple technique like the use of tf-idf (term frequency - inverse document frequency [9]) we are able to see some promising results.

2   Assumptions

Any news event consists of entities, most often humans, their properties, relations, situations and sub-events that transform the state of some entity [11]. It is the journalist's task to pick a subset of these features from an event and present them in a report, and it is this subset that can be considered the particular angle on the event. Here, these entities, properties, relations, states, and situations are not explicitly known, but are *externalised* in news reports that we use.

Thus, the collection of journalists that have reported from the event is seen as data generating entities. In each report they tell about the event using one or a few angles. Further, in the reports the choice of angle(s) will influence the final wording. The final wording may then be used to compute text based similarities among reports. Finally, events themselves have the collected set of reports and additional information about the entities from other sources (e.g. Wikipedia) as an input to a general event similarity, which may also be computed from text similarity metrics.

3   Finding Unmatched News Reports

An optimization approach is used to identify unmatched reports in an analogical event. Assume that we have a target event τ with n_τ news reports $t_j \in T$ that we want to find a new angle for, as well as an *identified and similar* base event β that has n_β base news reports $b_i \in B$. Also assume that we have a similarity measure $sim(b_i, t_j) \in [0, 1]$ for each pair of reports $b_i \in B$ and $t_j \in T$. See Sect. 4 for realisations of similarity measures.

Now, let A be a binary matrix with entries $a_{ij} = 1$ if there is a *match* between $b_i \in B$ and $t_j \in T$, otherwise 0. A represents the total matching between base and target. The idea is that a matching between reports indicates that they have similar or same angles. There is a couple of domain based heuristic constraints, in addition to maximum similarity among matched reports, that should be fulfilled for a matching to have high quality. First, reports with low similarity should not be matched; second, reports should usually not match more than one other report.

To handle the problem with low similarity we may subtract a constant c_l from all similarity values to ensure that all matched reports have a similarity above the limit c_l. To ensure almost one-to-one matching we introduce a penalty for having more than one match in a row or column. So we need to count the number of 1's in each row (cr_i) and each column (cc_j) of A. The penalty for having more than one 1 in a row or column is c_p. A matching of high quality is then found by maximizing the objective function

$$f(A) = \sum_{i,j} a_{ij}(sim(b_i, t_j) - c_l) - \sum_i max(0, cr_i - 1) \cdot c_p - \sum_j max(0, cc_j - 1) \cdot c_p$$

The matching A can be found in a greedy manner by maintaining a sorted list L of indices (i, j) referring to reports $b_i \in B$ and $t_j \in T$ that may be matched. We include only the pairs with a positive $sim(b_i, t_j) - c_l$ in L, as the others will contribute negatively to the total matching score. For each index pair we also maintain a $gain(i, j) = -sim(b_i, t_j) + c_p \cdot (ind(i) + ind(j))$ where $ind(i) = 1$ if i is found in more than one candidate pair in L, otherwise 0 (similar for $ind(j)$). We repeatedly remove the pair with most gain from L, and update the gain for the remaining pairs. When there are no pairs with positive gains left, L represents an optimal matching A, where a_{ij} is 1 if L contains the pair (i, j), 0 otherwise.

When we have found the solution A, there will be reports about the base event which are unmatched, i.e., there are rows in A where all entries are 0. Each of these unmatched base reports may suggest a new angle. Journalists could be responsible for investigating the candidates, but may need some guidance. The most relevant candidate could for instance be the unmatched report that has the highest similarity to any existing report in the target, i.e., has the highest $rel_\tau(b_i) = max_j \, sim(b_i, t_j)$.

From here, it is possible to rank candidates from all possible base events β_k by combining event similarity with the relevance score for each report. For now, let us assume that we are able to compute the event similarity $sim(\beta_k, \tau)$ for all base events β_k and the target τ (see Sect. 4). Further, assume that we for each β_k have an optimal report matching A^k. All unmatched reports in the events β_k will now be candidates for a transferred angle. To rank all these selected reports, we use the event similarities as well as the relevance-measure $rel_\tau(b_i)$:

$$score_\tau(b_i^k) = sim(\beta_k, \tau) \cdot rel_\tau(b_i^k)$$

4   Similarity Measures

There are many ways of measuring text similarity; this includes the use of standard IR techniques like tf-idf [9], the use of topic modeling [2], word2vec [7], graph2vec [13] (provided we are able to lift the knowledge about the event and its reports into knowledge graphs), and most recently the BERT [3] and XLNet [14] frameworks. The outcome of the analogical search algorithm presented above will depend on the quality of the similarity measures we use, so there is a need to experiment with these.

The tf-idf model of document similarity is a natural starting point and will serve as a base line for further explorations of the general algorithm. So far we have been able to run tests on a small collection of ten events with 20 reports each, with Wikipedia articles (about 20 in each event) about entities occurring in the events as supporting data. To run tf-idf models we have relied on the

Python gensim library for text processing[1]. All texts were lemmatized using gensim algorithms and only verbs, nouns, adjectives, and adverbs were included.

The eleven tf-idf models in use were:

- one for the whole collection of events, where each event's reports and Wikipedia texts were concatenated into one text document. This gave us a document base of 10 large documents, enabling us to get a similarity measure for each pair of events.
- one for each of the ten events, where the document collection was the individual reports and the Wikipedia articles. These models allow us to compute similarities between any report and each of the reports of the event, for example $sim(b_i, t_j)$. Thus, similarity to reports of a particular event is based on the reports of that event itself only.

5   Results

The data for these initial experiments were reports from 10 events collected in March 2019. The events (and two letter codes for later references) are

College scandal (CS) Wealthy Americans getting their children into prestigious schools by paying school officers.

Zuma nepotism (ZN) Previous South African president awards political positions to rich people who supports his family economically.

Barry Bonds case (BB) Disclosure of doping tests that showed that famous baseball player Barry Bonds were doped in parts of his career.

Penelopegate (PG) French president candidate used his position to give family members public positions.

Menendez corruption (MC) Democratic senator accused of accepting gifts from wealthy friend in exchange of favors in political decisions.

Armstrong doping (AD) The doping case against world famous cyclist Lance Armstrong.

Sudan protests (SP) Series of demonstrations against long term Sudanese president Omar al-Bashir.

Russian doping (RD) Systematic government supported doping in Russian sport.

Trudeau scandal (TS) Politician close to Canadian prime minister Justin Trudeau illegally influenced the justice system on behalf of a Canadian construction company.

Mueller report (MR) The release of the Mueller report about Russian meddling with the 2016 presidential election in USA.

In the experiments, most computed similarities between events were small (less than 0.01). Anyhow, here it is the relative sizes that count, as a ranking is more interesting than the numbers themselves. However, notice that the three doping events have the highest similarities $sim(BB, AD) = 0.079$,

---

[1] https://radimrehurek.com/gensim/.

$sim(\mathrm{BB}, \mathrm{RD}) = 0.103$, and $sim(\mathrm{AD}, \mathrm{RD}) = 0.270$ indicating that wording in the reports on these three cases are very similar, and containing specific doping related words.

The next step was to compute for each event (as a target event) the potential unmatched reports from each of the other events (as base events). We used the matching algorithm, calculated relevance scores $rel_\tau(b_i^k)$ and further a total $score_\tau(b_i^k)$ for all unmatched reports. Results showing the most promising transfer candidate for each target event are found in Table 1. The title of the report with most promising new angle is given for each event, and also a suggestion for a journalistic transfer of the angle.

Table 1. Suggested transfers of angles

Event	Article title for transfer	Journalistic angle
CS	BB: Lawyer jailed for leaking steroids testimony	Has anyone been convicted?
ZN	SP: Sudan protesters move to protect Khartoum	No immediate angle
BB	RD: Russian Olympic team's drug usage could have long term effects on athletes' health	Has Barry Bond's health been influenced by doping?
PG	AD: Cycling bosses slammed over Lance Armstrong	What do powerful people think of Penelopegate?
MC	MR: Barr scours Trump-Russia report to see how much to open	No immediate angle
AD	RD: Russian doping said to run deep	Are there powerful people involved in Armstrong's doping?
SP	ZN: Zuma plea as protests sweep the townships: South Africa's president calls for an end to the violence as he admits that he needs time to end corruption and improve government services	What does al-Bashir say to protesters?
RD	AD: Armstrong's biggest sponsors sever ties	How are sponsors of Russian sport reacting?
TS	ZN: In Gupta Brothers' Rise and Fall, the Tale of a Sullied A.N.C	What does the scandal mean for the reputation of the Liberal Party?
MR	RD: 'My message to the British runners who lost to our drug cheats? Sorry'	Has Mueller a comment to the Democrats about the election meddling

6   Conclusion and Further Work

This paper has described initial work on a tool for providing journalists with information that may suggest a new angle to an event. Here we have presented an algorithm that suggests for a journalist working on a particular event, the transfer of news angles found in reports of a different event, based on document similarity and a form of analogical reasoning. The results so far are not much more than a proof-of-concept, but show some interesting results, even with unsophisticated methods for document similarity.

The suggestions for journalistic angles here are suggestions based on our own perceptions, and we found a plausible one for eight of the ten events. Practicing journalists may think otherwise about what angles are interesting, and the results need to be validated against their opinions, i.e., which report from base events gave the best idea for a new news angle. We need to set up experiments with journalists for this purpose. A second important task is to explore other similarity measures. The algorithm itself will be valid, but may get better results from improved document similarity measures for instance taking into account context sensitivity.

Acknowledgement. The News Angler project is funded by the Norwegian Research Council's IKTPLUSS programme as project 275872.

References

1. Altheide, D.L., Rasmussen, P.K.: Becoming news: a study of two newsrooms. Sociol. Work. Occup. **3**(2), 223–246 (1976)
2. Blei, D.M., Ng, A.Y., Jordan, M.I.: Latent Dirichlet allocation. J. Mach. Learn. Res. **3**, 993–1022 (2003)
3. Devlin, J., Chang, M.W., Lee, K., Toutanova, K.: Bert: pre-training of deep bidirectional transformers for language understanding. arXiv preprint arXiv:1810.04805 (2018)
4. Falkenhainer, B., Forbus, K.D., Gentner, D.: The structure-mapping engine: algorithm and examples. Artif. Intell. **41**(1), 1–63 (1989)
5. Gallofré Ocaña, M., Nyre, L., Opdahl, A.L., Tessem, B., Trattner, C., Veres, C.: Towards a big data platform for news angles. In: Proceedings of the 4th Norwegian Big Data Symposium (NOBIDS 2018), vol. 2316, pp. 17–29. CEUR Workshop Proceedings, November 2018
6. Gravanis, G., Vakali, A., Diamantaras, K., Karadais, P.: Behind the cues: a benchmarking study for fake news detection. Expert. Syst. Appl. **128**, 201–213 (2019)
7. Kusner, M., Sun, Y., Kolkin, N., Weinberger, K.: From word embeddings to document distances. In: Bach, F., Blei, D. (eds.) Proceedings of the 32nd International Conference on Machine Learning. Proceedings of Machine Learning Research, vol. 37, pp. 957–966. PMLR, Lille, France, 07–09 July 2015
8. Lewis, S.C., Westlund, O.: Big data and journalism: epistemology, expertise, economics, and ethics. Digit. J. **3**(3), 447–466 (2015)
9. Manning, C.D., Raghavan, P., Schütze, H.: Introduction to Information Retrieval. Cambridge Univ. Press, New York (2008)

10. Miroshnichenko, A.: AI to bypass creativity. Will robots replace journalists? (the answer is "yes"). Information **9**(7), 183 (2018)
11. Opdahl, A.L., Tessem, B.: Towards ontological support for journalistic angles. In: Reinhartz-Berger, I., Zdravkovic, J., Gulden, J., Schmidt, R. (eds.) BPMDS/EMMSAD -2019. LNBIP, vol. 352, pp. 279–294. Springer, Cham (2019). https://doi.org/10.1007/978-3-030-20618-5_19
12. Simonite, T.: Robot Writing Moves from Journalism to Wall Street (2015). https://www.technologyreview.com/s/533976/robot-journalist-finds-new-work-on-wall-street/
13. Speer, R., Chin, J., Havasi, C.: Conceptnet 5.5: an open multilingual graph of general knowledge. In: Proceedings of the 21st AAAI, San Francisco, USA, 4–9 February, pp. 4444–4451 (2017)
14. Yang, Z., Dai, Z., Yang, Y., Carbonell, J., Salakhutdinov, R., Le, Q.V.: XLNet: Generalized Autoregressive Pretraining for Language Understanding. arXiv:1906.08237 [cs], June 2019. http://arxiv.org/abs/1906.08237

Mindfulness Mirror

C. James-Reynolds[(✉)] and Ed Currie

Middlesex University, London, UK
C.James-Reynolds@mdx.ac.uk

Abstract. This paper explores the use of an interactive Genetic Algorithm for creating a piece of visual art intended to assist in promoting the state of mindfulness. This is determined by a Bluetooth gaming electroencephalography (EEG) headset as the fitness function. The visual display consisted of an infinity mirror with over two hundred Neopixels with fade times and colour of zones controlled by two Arduinos running the software. Whilst we have observed some convergence of solutions, the results and user observations raised some interesting questions about how this strategy might be improved.

Keywords: Interactive genetic algorithm · Mindfulness · Electroencephelograph

1 Introduction

This paper describes the development of a piece of interactive art, driven by an interactive genetic algorithm (iGA) powered by the user's subconscious degree of mindfulness as measured by the nature of their brain activity. The purpose was threefold; to produce an interesting piece of art, to explore the extent to which the genetic algorithm converged on any 'optimum' states and to ascertain whether there could be other applications for this or related systems, for example in a therapeutic context.

2 Genetic Algorithms

Genetic Algorithms (GAs) are a specific type of evolutionary algorithm that provide solutions to search and optimization problems through the use of a biologically inspired approach akin to Darwinian evolutionary theory. They were first popularised by Holland [1] and later developed by Goldberg [2].

Genetic Algorithms operate by the encoding of an individual's relevant characteristics to represent their genetic makeup. The structure is analogous to a biological chromosome and the attributes correspond to individual genes. The algorithm proceeds by creating an initial population of such structures, each of which represents a potential solution.

These individuals are evaluated using a fitness function and assigned a probability of becoming a parent in proportion to their assigned rating. Those individuals whose characteristics are closest to the desired outcome are the most likely to become the parents of the next generation.

M. Bramer and M. Petridis (Eds.): SGAI-AI 2019, LNAI 11927, pp. 456–461, 2019.
https://doi.org/10.1007/978-3-030-34885-4_36

Pairs of parents are selected according to these probabilities and combined to create a population of new individuals. A common algorithm for this combining of parents' genes is crossover, in which each member of the next generation "inherits" variables from each of the two randomly chosen parents. The crossover points are typically randomly selected [3]. Another possible algorithm is co-dominance, in which typically a gene at a given position in the chromosome of the offspring is derived from some kind of averaging of the genes at the corresponding position in each of the parents [4]. This may be applicable where combining the genes of two strong candidate individuals produces a strong offspring.

The strategy adopted in the current work for the choice of parents is the so-called 'roulette wheel' approach [5], whereby each potential parent is assigned a sector of a circle, subtending an angle proportional to that individual's fitness rating [6]. The spinning of the roulette wheel is then simulated, and parents are chosen for breeding according to the ball's position. Alternative selection techniques are discussed in [7].

When the new generation has been created, a small probability of mutation may be introduced whereby the values of some characteristics of some individuals may be changed randomly [3]. The choice of mutation rate is important, because if it is too low, the GA might converge on local, but not optimum, maxima and if it is too high, the GA might not converge at all.

This process repeats, creating successive generations of individuals, and typically ends when an individual is generated that scores higher than some pre-agreed value of the fitness function, or an agreed number of generations have been created.

3   Interactive Genetic Algorithms

An interactive Genetic Algorithm (iGA), as used in our project, proceeds in the same manner as a conventional GA, except that it employs human judgement of the generated individuals as the fitness function. The concept is appropriate where evaluation of individuals is difficult to automate; for example where quality is a matter of aesthetic judgement. Early work on iGAs is described in [8].

The initial population size of an iGA should be large enough to enable effective exploration of the solution space, but not be too large, as this can introduce user fatigue. The deficiencies of smaller population sizes may be compensated for by strategies such as seeding [9] and increasing the mutation rate. The relationship between mutation, crossover and selection are explored in [6]. We adopted a single, randomly chosen crossover point in the current work.

4   Mindfulness

The idea of Mindfulness is derived from Buddhist doctrine, but has been redefined by psychologists in a number of ways. Ryan M. Niemiec presents three different definitions, but favours the following: "Mindfulness is the self-regulation of attention with an attitude of curiosity, openness, and acceptance" [10].

The Mental Health Foundation website [11] defines mindfulness as "…an integrative, mind-body based approach that helps people to manage their thoughts and feelings and mental health. It is becoming widely used in a range of contexts. It is recommended by NICE (National Institute for Health and Care Excellence) as a preventative practice for people with experience of recurrent depression."

Mindfulness is now a recognised strategy for helping people to maintain good mental health. With this in mind, it is interesting that there appears to be no universal definition of the term [12].

A review of the neurophysiology of mindfulness concluded that a "co-presence of elevated alpha and theta may signify a state of relaxed alertness which is conducive to mental health" [13]. We therefore chose to adopt this in our work.

5   Bio Feedback and Human Issues

Bio feedback uses the principle that knowledge about the state of one's body allows the user to learn how to control that state. Informal observations on approximately 1000 people at the New Scientist Live Show [14] and other events indicated that the ability to achieve a state of mindfulness was enhanced by training in a martial art or meditation. In previous work using a simple infinity mirror (without an iGA), indicating meditation state by a change of colour, we found that when subjects became aware of reaching a state of mindfulness, this awareness often then interrupted that state. This also manifested in an experiment with an adapted Scalextric car racing set controlled by a Neurosky MindWave headset [15], whereby achieving the mindful state would cause a car to move. Users would lose focus when the car started moving and it would come to a halt. There are existing apps to assist in developing a mindful state, however, the use of a screen has also been shown to disrupt attention and have an impact on EEG signals [16]. For the infinity mirror project, the user did not have a specific goal to achieve and so in theory, a high degree of mindfulness might be achieved and then maintained if the successive states of the mirror were able to promote this. EEG was used as the rating system, because it allows a reasonable indication of the mindfulness state, without a consciously provided input from the user. The scenario differed from that with the Scalextric cars in that the users did not have a specific goal in mind and therefore no direct feedback to indicate reaching that goal.

It is often claimed that Einstein said that "The definition of insanity is doing the same thing over and over again, but expecting different results". However, this is precisely what we may appear to get with iGAs and users. Issues such as fatigue, distraction and boredom can all play a part in the subconscious user interaction with the iGA system.

6   Construction of the System

The mirror was constructed from a polystyrene 5 mm mirror sheet and a 5 mm clear acrylic sheet with a semi-silvered layer, so that the latter acted as a two-way mirror. A gap of 1 cm between the sheets was used and the mirrors were cased in a wooden frame. A strip of addressable Neopixel LEDs made up the display. The display geometry consisted of three zones; an outer square, an outer circle and an inner circle.

The Neopixel strip was cut and joined underneath the display with wires, enabling the three zones to be formed from one continuous LED strip which was connected to a single control pin on an Arduino via a 57 Ω resistor.

The rating strategy adopted for this work, which had previously been deployed in [17], was to employ subconscious rating of the generated individuals by electroencephalogram (EEG) signals derived from a Neurosky Mindwave EEG headset with one electrode. We employed seeding, whereby the initial population was created by hard-coding with a range of different parameter values. The mutation rate was set to 5%. The code enables the use of a crossover approach where each characteristic value comes from either one parent or the other, or a co-dominance approach where the mean of corresponding characteristic values from each parent is used.

Each of the four individuals in the population was genetically coded by an array of 21 elements, which comprised a transition time and RGB values for two 'extreme' colours for each of the three display zones. These values were passed to a method which 'played' the individual on the display. Playing the individual in this context meant that, for each of the three display zones, the pixel colour would cycle gradually between its two extreme colours, that zone's transition time being the time taken to move from one colour to the other. The play method would carry out this activity for some fixed period of time (set for 20 s for purposes of testing and demonstrating), then the user's EEG mindfulness reading would be taken and used to score that individual. This was repeated for each of the four individuals, after which the iGA used a roulette wheel approach to breed the next generation. The mutation rate could be varied and parents could be combined using co-dominance or splicing as desired.

The headset was used with a Bluesmirf silver module and an Arduino to capture and parse the data. Although some studies have been quite critical of the Mindwave [18], others [19] find it adequate for capturing simple EEG data. We found that the use of a conductive gel and careful placing of the electrode improved accuracy.

Two Arduinos were used; the first (master) captured and parsed EEG readings using an adaption of software provided by Neurosky [15] and the second (slave) contained the iGA and the display algorithms utilising the Adafruit Neopixel display library [20]. These communicated over an I2C connection.

7   Results and Discussion

Some degree of convergence was observed, taking up to 20 min. We ran the iGA with a high mutation rate (5%), as the starting population was small (only four individuals). This enables wider exploration of the solution space, but also poses a problem, as when the system approaches good solutions, they are subject to the same high mutation rate, thus moving them away from the "optimal solutions". The co-dominance approach seems suitable for some variables, but can lead to early averaging of results rather than the best solution if the mutation rate is not sufficiently high.

When running the test on the same subjects on different days we observed convergence, but not necessarily to similar individual solutions. This was anticipated, as we did not expect that there would be one optimal solution for any given user. For the few subjects that were prepared to sit for 30 min, once a high level of mindfulness had been achieved, this state tended to be maintained for a period of time before decreasing then rising again with a different individual solution.

It is difficult to quantify the performance of the iGA. However, some convergence was observed and we were able to make subjective measurements of how the users felt about the results. With iGAs, the endpoint is usually considered to be reached when the output meets the user's criteria. However, it has been observed with the infinity mirror that, whilst a specific state might elicit a high rating for a period of time, after a while the EEG output changes and therefore there is no clear endpoint for the running of the algorithm.

Mindfulness has been recognised by the National Institute for Health and Care Excellence as a strategy for maintaining good mental health, which raises the question as whether the artefact could be deployed in this respect; for example as a training tool for awareness of anxiety and stress. Recent work such as [21] shows that effective strategies are available for analysing human emotion and "tastes". We can see the potential for small bio sensors wirelessly connected, where the data might be processed to give information that can be used for feeding iGAs that modify the environment. This might have significant therapeutic benefits in the future as sensors become smaller, more portable and wearable.

8   Conclusion

This work explores the potential of using sensors, in this case an EEG headset with an iGA to promote mindfulness through the manipulation of a physical piece of art. Whilst there are many limitations arising from the choice of platform and hardware, we did see some convergence, although given the nature of the artefact, this is over a relatively long period of time. The main contributions of this work are in exploring the use of sensors for subconscious user interaction with iGAs in place of the traditional approaches and an initial exploration of how iGAs can run continuously to optimize solutions where the nature of the best solution changes according to the changing whims of the user.

References

1. Holland, J.H.: Adaptation in Natural and Artificial Systems. University of Michigan Press, Ann Arbor (1975)
2. Goldberg, D.E.: Genetic and evolutionary algorithms come of age. Commun. ACM **37**, 113–119 (1994)
3. Srinivas, M., Patnaik, L.M.: Adaptive probabilities of crossover and mutation in genetic algorithms. IEEE Trans. Syst. Man, Cybern. **24**(4), 656–667 (1994)
4. Dahlstedt, P.: Creating and exploring huge parameter spaces: interactive evolution as a tool for sound generation. In: Proceedings of the 2001 International Computer Music Conference, pp. 235–242 (2001)

5. Thierens, D., Goldberg, D.: Convergence models of genetic algorithm selection schemes. In: Davidor, Y., Schwefel, H.-P., Männer, R. (eds.) Parallel Problem Solving from Nature — PPSN III, pp. 119–129. Springer, Berlin (1994). https://doi.org/10.1007/3-540-58484-6_256

6. Melanie, M., n.d. An Introduction to Genetic Algorithms 162

7. Goldberg, D.E., Deb, K.: A comparative analysis of selection schemes used in genetic algorithms. Urbana **51**, 61801–62996 (1991)

8. Todd, S., Latham, W.: Evolutionary Art and Computers. Academic Press, Cambridge (1992)

9. Caetano, M.F., Manzolli, J., Von Zuben, F.J.: Interactive control of evolution applied to sound synthesis. In: FLAIRS Conference, pp. 51–56 (2005)

10. Ryan, M.: Niemiec Psychology today. https://www.psychologytoday.com/gb/blog/what-matters-most/201711/3-definitions-mindfulness-might-surprise-you. Last Accessed 3 Jul 2019

11. Mental Health Foundation. https://www.mentalhealth.org.uk/a-to-z/m/mindfulness

12. Bishop, S.R., n.d. Mindfulness: A Proposed Operational Definition 12. Clinical Psychology: Science and Practice; Autumn, vol. 11(3), Health Module, p. 230 (2004)

13. Lomas, T., Ivtzan, I., Fu, C.H.Y.: A systematic review of the neurophysiology of mindfulness on EEG oscillations. Neurosci. Biobehav. Rev. **57**, 401–410 (2015)

14. New Scientist Live 20–13rd September 2018 ExCel London. https://live.newscientist.com/2018-official-show-guide#/

15. NeuroSky (2018): NeuroSky Brainwave Starter Kit. http://developer.neurosky.com/docs/doku.php?id=mindwave_mobile_and_arduino. Last accessed 1 Jul 2019

16. Cajochen, C., et al.: Evening exposure to a light-emitting diodes (LED)-backlit computer screen affects circadian physiology and cognitive performance. J. Appl. Physiol. **110**, 1432–1438 (2011)

17. James-Reynolds, C., Currie, E.: EEuGene: employing electroencephalograph signals in the rating strategy of a hardware-based interactive genetic algorithm. In: Bramer, M., Petridis, M. (eds.) Research and Development in Intelligent Systems XXXIII, pp. 343–353. Springer International Publishing, Cham (2016). https://doi.org/10.1007/978-3-319-47175-4_25

18. Maskeliunas, R., Damasevicius, R., Martisius, I., Vasiljevas, M.: Consumer grade EEG devices: are they usable for control tasks? PeerJ **4**, e1746 (2016)

19. Chee-Keong Alfred, L., Chong Chia, W.: Analysis of single electrode EEG rhythms using MATLAB to Elicit correlation with cognitive stress. Int. J. Comput. Theor. Eng. **7**, 149–155 (2015)

20. Adafruit Neopixels Library. https://github.com/adafruit/Adafruit_NeoPixel

21. Khosrowabadi, R., Quek, C., Ang, K.K., Wahab, A.: ERNN: a biologically inspired feedforward neural network to discriminate emotion from EEG signal. IEEE Trans. Neural Netw. Learn. Syst. **25**, 609–620 (2014)

Predicting Bid Success with a Case-Based Reasoning Approach: Explainability and Business Acceptance

Mathias Kern and Botond Virginas[(✉)]

BT Applied Research, Adastral Park, Suffolk, UK
{mathias.kern, botond.virginas}@bt.com

Abstract. With an ever growing demand for providing AI solutions within business there is a tendency to expect end to end standardised solutions to problems. These solutions are expected to be accurate and to be seamlessly integrated within existing business processes. However, achieving higher accuracy could be detrimental not only to explainability (if a blackbox solution is provided) but also need to be accepted and used within existing business processes. This paper describes a Case-Based Reasoning (CBR) solution to a real problem within a telecommunications company together with the reasoning behind selecting this particular approach. The solution has been integrated within existing business processes which has been a real challenge besides satisfying all the technical ability criteria.

Keywords: Case-Based Reasoning · Machine learning · Decision trees · Explainable AI · Business user acceptance

1 Background

With the very fast spread of AI solutions both in research and industry there is a tendency to solve machine learning (ML) problems by providing better and better predictive algorithms with higher accuracy and standardising AI processes in businesses providing end to end pipelines. Because of the black box nature of many ML algorithms explainability has been addressed more and more [1–4]. However, besides explainability there is another very important aspect of consuming machine learning in industry which is business user acceptance. The ML solutions, tools and systems need to be embedded within existing business processes and should be accepted by business users. This paper is a reflection on a real solution to a real problem within a telecommunications company (but it could apply to other types of business) where the results of a machine learning algorithm need to be conveyed and accepted by business.

The initial requirement was to provide an analytical tool based on historical observed patterns to predict success chance of open bids. Bidding teams have limited resources and the tool should give them the ability to focus limited resources on more promising bids. The team looked at explainability and user acceptance from a CBR perspective. The nature of the problem directed us to this technique because of its suitability how the human bidding teams base their decisions on their past experiences

© Springer Nature Switzerland AG 2019
M. Bramer and M. Petridis (Eds.): SGAI-AI 2019, LNAI 11927, pp. 462–467, 2019.
https://doi.org/10.1007/978-3-030-34885-4_37

regarding similar bids. This became evident once interviewing the bidding team and they questioned why a set of bids in the past had different outcomes from the predicted ones in earlier trials with other approaches such as decision tree models.

2 Case-Based Reasoning: An Alternative

One way of classifying AI systems is to group them into data driven AI systems and knowledge based AI systems [5]. Knowledge-based AI, which has become applicable in the late seventies, attempts to model human knowledge in computational terms. Knowledge-based AI emphasizes conceptual models, ontologies, common sense knowledge bases, reasoning and problem solving strategies, language processing, and insight learning. Data-driven AI, also commonly known as machine learning, starts in a bottom-up fashion from large amounts of data of human activity, which are processed with statistical machine learning algorithms, such as Deep Learning algorithms, in order to abstract patterns that can then be used to make predictions, complete partial data, or emulate behaviour based on human behaviours in similar conditions in the past.

With the recent boom in AI research the data-driven approaches have been clearly favoured and the successes in Deep Learning is a justification for this preference. Nevertheless several researchers have argued that a stronger knowledge-based influence is needed beyond the current upswing of AI [6].

For this paper's perspective we applied CBR techniques as an alternative to ML data driven approaches, and we have chosen it precisely for the human like nature of the technique and its strength in explainability. As noted by Watson and Marir [7], the explanations provided based upon individual and generalised cases tend to be more satisfactory than explanations generated by chains of rules.

CBR has long been regarded as a technique which can aid explanations in predictive systems and is intuitively preferred by users [8]. Roth-Berghofer [9] presented general questions of CBR Based explainability and examined a number of future research directions

Dissemination of CBR technology begins with the users' conviction that it can be useful for them. After technical validity, user acceptance is a key point in using a product. The user's acceptance of the technology is greatly increased when the tool provides self-generated explanations of its features and/or its conclusions [10]. Moreover, the main aspect of user acceptance is the user interface—therefore it is necessary to put a strong emphasis on the interface's quality and usability.

Bichindaritz et al. [11] describe the synergies between Case-Base Reasoning and other machine learning technologies and among the identified themes explainability and transparency figure prominently. An example is a recent research paper on using Explainable CBR system in the medical domain [12].

3   Case-Based Reasoning Approach

Our approach to predicting the win chances of commercial bids follows the standard Case-Based Reasoning mantra; that is to predict the chances of succeeding with a new bid based on the outcome of similar historic biding processes.

Information about bids, both new open and old closed bids, is stored in a central data store. We select and load common bid characteristics such as the type of bid, the geography, the industry sector, the customer, the key product, the cost of the bid, gross margin, the complexity of the bid, the term length of the contract, the main competitor if known, and so on, to establish how similar, or dissimilar, two bids are. The similarity of two bids is calculated in two steps:

i. Calculate similarity for individual characteristics of the bids as a percentage between 0% and 100%
ii. Calculate overall similarity of the bids, once more as a percentage between 0% and 100%

Having established the similarity measure, we then calculate the prediction for a new bid via a majority vote among the k most similar historic bids. If a majority of those historic cases resulted in a win, we predict another win, otherwise we predict a loss. This is the well-established k Nearest Neighbour (kNN) approach.

But of course two important details of this CBR method have not been addressed yet: what weights to use for the similarity calculations, and how to choose k, i.e. how many neighbours to consider for the majority vote. Recommendations by domain experts about which bid characteristics they considered as important and how many historic bids they would usually look at gave us a good baseline.

We then used a Genetic Algorithm (GA) to optimise the aforementioned weights and the value for k. The fitness of a particular candidate solution considered by the GA, was established by applying the encoded similarity measure plus kNN classifier to a historic data set. Furthermore, the GA recommended that k = 7 was a good choice for the kNN classifier (we allowed the GA to consider values between 1 and 15). Other values for k work well too, e.g. k = 3 or k = 5 lead to a comparable accuracy, but especially k = 1 and k >= 11 result in lower overall accuracies.

Without divulging too much detail due to the commercial sensitivity of the underlying information, we utilised a data set of approximately 4,000 historical bids, and for each bid more than 40 attributes were available. Using this data set, our CBR approach achieved a prediction accuracy of 85% on the set of all closed historic bids, and an accuracy of 79% on the set of closed historic bids that reached at least a certain maturity point (bidding processes that are cancelled early on are easier to predict).

With regard to the technical realisation of our approach, we used Java for the GA parameter optimisation stage, implemented the data manipulation and similarity calculations via procedures in an Oracle database, and shared the results via an Excel-based dashboard, all of which allowed us rapid proto-typing and simple communication and visualisation of the results.

4 User Engagement and Acceptance

Having a prediction algorithm with good accuracy is only the first step to getting it accepted by the user community and embedded into any existing, or new, business process. Figure 1 shows the dashboard used to share the results of the bid success prediction algorithm; the data used in the example is synthetic, and we show only a selection of the data fields available in the real-world application. It allows users to select any open bid, automatically displays the 7 most similar historic bids, it allows users to compare the key characteristics of these bids and visualise how similar the bids are, both for individual data fields and overall.

Feature	Bid in Focus	Most Similar Historic Bids						
Opportunity ID	OPEN BID	SIMILAR CLOSED BID 1	SIMILAR CLOSED BID 2	SIMILAR CLOSED BID 3	SIMILAR CLOSED BID 4	SIMILAR CLOSED BID 5	SIMILAR CLOSED BID 6	SIMILAR CLOSED BID 7
Opportunity Type	Renewal	Renewal	Renewal	Renewal	Renewal	Renewal	Renewal	Renewal
Sales Stage	Open	Closed Won	Closed Won	Closed Won	Closed Lost	Closed Won	Closed Won	Closed Won
Created Date	2015	2016	2018	2017	2017	2015	2018	2017
Close Date		2016	2018	2017	2017	2015	2018	2017
Customer	Customer X	Customer X	Customer X	Customer X	Customer X	Customer X	Customer X	Customer X
Account	Account X	Account X	Account X	Account X	Account X	Account X	Account X	Account X
Contract Value	1,600,000	1,600,000	600,000	900,000	1,100,000	700,000	3,400,000	300,000
Opportunity Owner	Opportunity Owner 1	Opportunity Owner 2	Opportunity Owner 3	Opportunity Owner 2	Opportunity Owner 2	Opportunity Owner 1	Opportunity Owner 1	Opportunity Owner 2
Main Competitor								
Market Unit	Europe	Europe	Europe	Europe	Europe	Europe	Europe	Europe
Has Bid Manager	Y	Y	Y	Y	Y	Y	Y	Y
Bid Manager	Bid Manager 1	Bid Manager 1	Bid Manager 1	Bid Manager 2	Bid Manager 2	Bid Manager 1	Bid Manager 1	Bid Manager 1
Gross Margin %	10	9	12	9	6	15	6	9
Industry Sector	Industry Sector 1	Industry Sector 1	Industry Sector 1	Industry Sector 1	Industry Sector 1	Industry Sector 1	Industry Sector 1	Industry Sector 1
Country	Country A	Country A	Country A	Country A	Country A	Country A	Country A	Country A
Maximum Term	36	36	36	12	36	36	24	36
Lead Product	Product 1	Product 1	Product 1	Product 1	Product 1	Product 1	Product 1	Product 1
Number Products	1	1	1	1	1	1	1	1
Win Likelihood	☺	Win	Win	Win	Loss	Win	Win	Win
		Similarity						
OVERALL		99.2%	96.9%	96.9%	96.9%	95.7%	96.3%	96.3%
Opportunity Type		100.0%	100.0%	100.0%	100.0%	100.0%	100.0%	100.0%
Customer		100.0%	100.0%	100.0%	100.0%	100.0%	100.0%	100.0%
Account		100.0%	100.0%	100.0%	100.0%	100.0%	100.0%	100.0%
Contract Value		98.3%	38.1%	96.5%	71.1%	44.2%	47.5%	19.8%
Opportunity Owner		0.0%	0.0%	0.0%	0.0%	100.0%	100.0%	0.0%
Main Competitor		0.0%	0.0%	0.0%	0.0%	100.0%	100.0%	0.0%
Market Unit		100.0%	100.0%	100.0%	100.0%	100.0%	100.0%	100.0%
Has Bid Manager		100.0%	100.0%	100.0%	100.0%	100.0%	100.0%	100.0%
Bid Manager		100.0%	100.0%	0.0%	0.0%	100.0%	100.0%	100.0%
Gross Margin %		89.7%	84.4%	61.0%	56.5%	68.0%	62.6%	83.1%
Industry Sector		100.0%	100.0%	100.0%	100.0%	100.0%	100.0%	100.0%
Country		100.0%	100.0%	100.0%	100.0%	100.0%	100.0%	100.0%
Maximum Term		100.0%	100.0%	33.3%	100.0%	100.0%	66.7%	100.0%
Lead Product		100.0%	100.0%	100.0%	100.0%	100.0%	100.0%	100.0%
Number Products		100.0%	100.0%	100.0%	100.0%	100.0%	100.0%	100.0%

Fig. 1. Dashboard used to communicate and visualise bid success predictions.

However, further customisation was required, three aspects of which are discussed below:

1. Although the weights for the similarity calculations were optimised and set to values that achieved the best overall accuracy across the historic data set, users asked for weights to be configurable. To show the impact of modified weights on the overall accuracy, we developed a capability to recalculate overall accuracy in the dashboard, giving the user control over the weights but at the same time highlighting any potential downside in reduced accuracy.
2. A second addition to the tool was the incorporation of a what-if analysis. By allowing users of the dashboard to change the values for certain bid characteristics, such as cost, margin or term length, and recalculating the most similar bids on-the-fly, domain experts have the ability to explore how to improve their bid's success chances.

3. Thirdly, the dashboard in Fig. 1 does not simply display a binary win or loss prediction for an open bid, but rather a red-amber-green (RAG) status-based prediction. The ranges behind these statues can be configured, and that allows biding teams to include fewer or more bids in those statuses. The output of the dashboard therefore is not simply a binary likely to win/likely to lose answer, but rather a user-configurable labelling of bids into three categories the boundaries of which can be moved based on external factors.

A further important lesson from our engagement with domain experts is that certain aspects of bids are simply not captured in the available historic and/or live data. This can include soft measures such as the quality of relationships with key contacts, specific local information, e.g. on legislation, domain expert assessment, and so on. Therefore the prediction tool cannot be the only aspect when evaluating a bid, but rather it should form a key part of and input to a wider bid assessment process that combines both quantitative and qualitative elements into an overall picture.

We are currently engaging with a small community of trial users to integrate our prediction application into their existing process, aiming to build and ensure user acceptance. The trial phase continues at this moment in time to collect sufficient data.

One final word on the management of the life cycle of our application. The accuracy of a model needs to be regularly checked, and the model itself might need to be updated when accuracy trends too low. In our case, we regularly update the dashboard and check the accuracy achieved for bids closed over the recent past. If that accuracy falls under a certain threshold, e.g. if we didn't get predictions right often enough for bids completed over the past year, we update the time window used for identifying cases for our library of historical bids, and re-run the optimisation of the predictor.

5   Conclusions

This real case example was inspired by our journey in analysing, designing, implementing and delivering a machine learning solution to a real business problem. We cannot go into too much of the finer detail and the data due to commercial sensitivity, but we wanted to share our approach and learning in a real-world case study.

The first challenge from the research perspective apart from the usual requirements and data understanding was to understand the current business processes around bid management and the way how the bidding decisions are being made. The soft measures as highlighted in the previous section are very hard to capture and we believe that somehow it is being contained in similar historical bids which was one reason that lead us towards Case-Based Reasoning.

Another reason for our choice was a matter of trust from the user's perspective. As discussed in Sect. 1 the initial decision tree highlighted discrepancies between the human success likelihood perception and the machine generated prediction. The CBR solution was greeted with a lot of approval from the user community and they happily engaged in customizing the initial solution as discussed in Sect. 4.

In summary, four key lessons learnt from this project are:

1. Prediction accuracy is important, but so is an effective explanation and communication of the results.
2. Engage early and regularly with your customers and domain experts.
3. Truly understand the existing data and processes.
4. Consider how to best integrate and/or combine a new prediction method with existing approaches.

Future steps include a full industrialisation of the tool that will see a web-based version or the integration of the prediction approach into existing bid management platforms. Additional factors such as local developments, legal constraints and 'soft' human insights will be incorporated into the prediction.

References

1. Baehrens, D., Schroeter, T., Harmeling, S., Kawanabe, M., Hansen, K., Muller, K.-R.: How to explain individual classification decisions. J. Mach. Learn. Res. **11**, 1803–1831 (2010)
2. Bansal, A., Farhadi, A., Parikh, D.: Towards transparent systems: semantic characterization of failure modes. In: European Conference of Computer Vision (ECCV) (2014)
3. Wang, F., Rudin, C.: Falling rule lists. In: Artificial Intelligence and Statistics (AISTATS) (2015)
4. Ribeiro, M.T., Singh, S., Guestrin. C.: Why should I trust you?: explaining the predictions of any classifier. In: Proceedings of the 22nd ACM SIGKDD International Conference on Knowledge Discovery and Data Mining, ACM (2016)
5. Barcelona Declaration for the Proper Development and Use of Artificial Intelligence in Europe. http://www.bdebate.org/sites/default/files/barcelona-declaration_v7-1-eng.pdf. Last accessed 8 Mar 2017
6. Domingos, P.: The Master Algorithm: How the Quest for the Ultimate Learning Machine Will Remake Our World. Basic Books, New York (2015)
7. Watson, I., Marir, F.: Case-base reasoning: a review. The Knowledge Engineering Review, vol. 9, no. 4, pp. 327–354 (1994)
8. Cassens, F., Sormo, J., Aamodt, A.: Explanation in case-based reasoning-perspectives and goals. Artif. Intell. Rev. **24**, 109–143 (2005)
9. Roth-Berghofer, T.: Explanations and Case-Based Reasoning: Foundational Issues. ECCBR (2004)
10. Althoff, K.-D.: Evaluating Case-Based Reasonic Systems: The INRECA case study. University of Kaiserslautern, Habilitationschrift (1997)
11. Bichindaritz, I., Marling, C.R., Montani, S.: Recent themes in Case-Based Reasoning and Knowledge Discovery. Flair Conference (2017)
12. Lamy, J.-B., Sekar, B., Gueznenec, G., Boruaud, J., Seroussi, B.: Explainable artificial intelligence for breast cancer: a visual case-based reasoning approach. Artif. Intell. Med. **94**, 42–53 (2019)

Data Augmentation for Ambulatory EEG Based Cognitive State Taxonomy System with RNN-LSTM

Sumanto Dutta[(⊠)] and Anup Nandy

National Institute of Technology Rourkela, Rourkela, Odisha, India
sumanto.nitrkl@gmail.com, nandy.anup@gmail.com

Abstract. Emotion detection is an important step for recognizing a person's mental state. A physiological signal, Electroencephalogram (EEG) is analyzed to detect human emotion with promising results. The cost of information gathering and lack of number of participants incur a limitation on the size of EEG data set. The deficiency in acquired EEG data set makes it difficult to estimate mental states with deep learning models as it requires a larger size of the training data set. In this paper, we propose a novel data augmentation method to address challenges due to scarcity of EEG data for training deep learning models such as Recurrent Neural Network - Long Short Term Memory (RNN-LSTM). To find the performance of mental state estimator such models are applied before and after proposed data augmentation. Experimental results demonstrate that data augmentation improves the performance of mental state estimator with an accuracy of 98%.

Keywords: Data augmentation · EEG (Electroencephalogram) · Recurrent Neural Network (RNN) · Long Short Term Memory (LSTM)

1 Introduction

In recent years, deep learning techniques achieved great success especially in image processing and speech recognition areas. It is essential to encourage the study on EEG-based mental state detection with deep learning models. Ullah et al. [3] proposed a system based on ensemble of pyramidal one-dimensional convolutional neural network (P-1D-CNN) models. They adopted a refinement approach in order to achieve generalization model as compared to classical CNN model with 61% fewer parameters. Further two data augmentation structures were proposed to achieve better classification results. Zhang, Liu [5] proposed conditional Deep Convolutional Generative Adversarial Networks (cDCGAN) method to create more amount of artificial EEG signals for data augmentation to improve the performance of cDCGAN in BCI field. The results obtained from

Partially Funded by SERB (Science and Engineering Research Board, Government of India) and NVIDIA Corporation.

their experiments demonstrated that data augmentation had higher accuracy than normal EEG data. Zhang et al. [6] discussed a novel data augmentation method where new signals were generated by adding disturbances to amplitudes of EEG signal. The results produced higher accuracies as compared to those without data augmentation. Wang et al. [4] explored the evaluation of sentiment recognition with the help of shallow and deep computing models, with and without data augmentation on two existing EEG data sets. The results illustrated improvement of sentiment recognizer after data augmentation. Bresch et al. [1] detected different sleep phases of a person from single channel EEG signal using recurrent neural networks. The outcomes proved that certain factors such as the size of data set, choice of architecture design for RNN and regularization had an immense impact on the classifier performance. This paper is organized as follows: Sect. 2 deals with the proposed work, Sect. 3 addresses results analysis and discussion. Conclusion and future work is discussed in Sect. 4.

2   Proposed Work

2.1   Data Collection Procedure

External stimuli from different sources are used to generate different mental states such as EOS (Emotion Oriented State), TOS (Thinking Oriented State), MOS (Memory Oriented State) and Simple Regular Oriented State (SROS) as shown in Table 1. The corresponding environments are created using vision based stimuli. The experimental data are collected from sixteen participants based on the proposed protocol approved by IRB, NIT Rourkela. Subjects are mentally and physically fit for this experiment and the written consent is taken from them for our proposed work. The protocol used in this experiment is shown in Figs. 1a and b. It consists of four sessions with a session break of 5–10 min between each session. Each of the sessions has four different walking speeds - slow, natural, fast and running respectively. For each walking speed, video clips are displayed for 15–30 s depending on different mental states. The subjects are asked to walk on different speeds on the treadmill in novel event driven environment. Also they are asked to wear the Emotiv EPOC+ 14 channel headset for collection of ambulatory EEG signals. The interval between different walking speeds are provisioned for certain reasons such as brain relaxation and avoidance of the

Table 1. Proposed methods for the generation of different mental states

Walking speed	EOS	TOS
1.5 km/h, 3 km/h, 5 km/h, 6 km/h	Geneva affective picture database (GAPED)	Logical Puzzles, Crossword
	MOS	SROS
	Remembering any Pattern such as VIBGYOR colours, Shapes, Number etc.	Any kind of stimuli

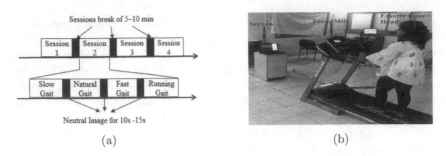

(a)   (b)

Fig. 1. (a) Proposed EEG data collection protocol. (b) Experimental setup.

influence of one walking speed over the other. The protocol lasts for 30 min approximately. The EEG signals corresponding to the different cognitive states are collected and processed further.

2.2 Proposed Methodology

A modern machine learning algorithm is applied to improve the performance of mental state estimator through data augmentation process. The proposed methodology is explained in Fig. 2. The raw ambulatory EEG signal is captured through our proposed event driven environment. The EEG data are preprocessed using bandpass filter to generate a refined signal with reduced levels of noise. The data augmentation process is applied on processed EEG data for each subject. Moreover, the signal collected from each channel is decomposed into its elemental sinusoidal waves with a distinct change in frequency using empirical mode decomposition (EMD) method. These elemental signals from different participants are merged randomly to form a new signal for corresponding channel for new training sample. Each feature is assigned to different class labels such as positive, negative and neutral for each of the mental states. The deep learning model based on RNN-LSTM is applied to learn the pattern. The learned model is fed with unkonwn EEG signals to predict class labels associated with different mental states.

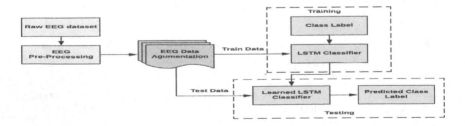

Fig. 2. Proposed methodology

2.3   Data Augmentation Method

Fawzi et al. [2] discussed data augmentation method of increasing variety of samples by changing training data with the goal of refining the accuracy and strength of classifiers. In image processing, two data augmentation methods are used: (1) Geometric Transformations like shift, scale, rotation and reflection. These are not appropriate for expanding and generating new synthetic EEG sample for our dataset. The EEG signal is a continuous signal which varies over period of time. If geometric transformation is performed on EEG signal it destroys the time domain feature of the signal. (2) Noise Addition like Gaussian, Poisson, Salt, Pepper, etc. are not recommended to apply on data augmentation for our dataset. The EEG signal has strong arbitrariness and dynamicity over time. So addition of noise to these signals may change the EEG data locally. Based on these facts, we decompose EEG data of each subject for each channel into its elemental sinusoidal waves with a distinct change in frequency. These elemental signals from different subjects are merged to generate a new signal. The following steps are applied to obtain augmented EEG data using EMD method. (1) Calculate local maxima and minina to get upper (S_{up}) and lower (S_{lo}) envelope of the signal $(S(t))$. For each ith iteration, find mean envelope $M_{x,i}(t)$ $M_{x,i}(t) = \frac{1}{2}[S_{up}(t) + S_{lo}(t)]$. (2) Subtract mean envelope from residual signal where $Df_x(t) = S(t)$ for $i = 1$, $Df_x(t) = Df_x(t) - M_{x,i}(t)$. (3) Subtract the xth IMF (Intrinsic Mode Function) from Res_{x-1}. If $Df_x(t)$ matches then $Res_x(t) = Res_{x-1}(t) - Df_x(t)$. (4) Repeat the above process taking $Res_x(t)$ as new signal and $Df_x(t)$ as IMF till current relative tolerance is less than sift relative tolerance. The proposed RNN-LSTM framework coupled with data augmentation method is illustrated in following Fig. 3.

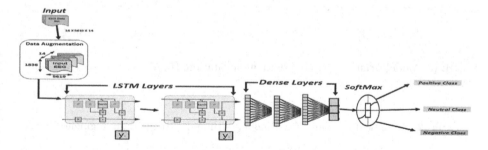

Fig. 3. Architecture diagram of proposed RNN-LSTM framework using data augmentation

3   Result Analysis and Discussion

In our experiment we use Emotiv EPOC+ 14 channel headset to collect ambulatory EEG data from sixteen participants. In order to process EEG data, a system with a NVIDIA's GeForce Titan Xp GPU with 12 GB RAM is used for implementing deep learning algorithm. The EEG data is augmented by empirical mode decomposition after pre-processing step. The size of the new generated dataset is $(M \times N \times K)$, where M denotes total number of samples (in our case M = 1836). N denotes feature points (in our case N = 5619) and K denotes number of channels (in our case K = 14). After augmentation, the data set is divided into 70% of training samples and 30% of testing samples and fed to RNN-LSTM network. This network is trained with different modules (with data augmentation and without data augmentation). The model accuracy for both the modules is shown in Fig. 4a and b respectively. It can be inferred from this analysis that validation accuracy for augmented data is better than non augmented data. A separate analysis on RNN-LSTM model loss with and without data augmentation is depicted in Fig. 5a and b. It can be concluded from this analysis that validation loss for augmented data is better than non augmented data. It can also be noted from Figs. 4a and 5a that training of actual data has many dropouts and the path to reach optimum is not so smooth which shows the sign of underfitting of classifier. The performance of this model is evaluated with standard statistical metrics like precision, recall, f1 score and accuracy. Table 2, shows the results of the model for two different modules. It is visible from Table 2 that our proposed model achieves a better performance on ambulatory EEG data set with data augmentation method.

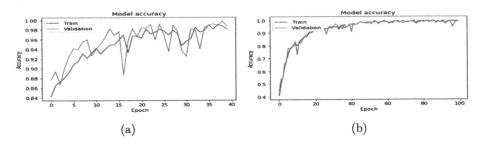

(a)   (b)

Fig. 4. (a) Model Accuracy without data augmentation. (b) Model Accuracy with data augmentation.

Table 2. Statistical measures for a model with and without data augmentation

	Precision	Recall	F1 score	Accuracy
Without data augmentation	0.88	0.84	0.86	0.96
With data augmentation	0.90	0.89	0.89	0.98

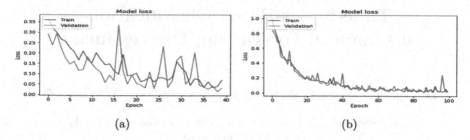

Fig. 5. (a) Model Loss without data augmentation. (b) Model Loss with data augmentation.

4   Conclusion and Future Work

Data augmentation is a process in deep learning models where synthetic data is created for better performance of classifiers. In our case it demonstrates a good performance as compared to without data augmentation. The RNN-LSTM model achieves 98% accuracy with augmented data and the same is reported for other statistical measures as well. Future works involve development of applications to optimize the use of limited bandwidth and to make real time system using deep neural network for unsupervised learning like Restricted Boltzmann Machine or Deep Belief Network.

References

1. Bresch, E., Grossekathofer, U., Garcia-Molina, G.: Recurrent deep neural networks for real-time sleep stage classification from single channel EEG. Front. Comput. Neurosci. **12**, 85 (2018)
2. Fawzi, A., Samulowitz, H., Turaga, D., Frossard, P.: Adaptive data augmentation for image classification. In: 2016 IEEE International Conference on Image Processing (ICIP), pp. 3688–3692. IEEE (2016)
3. Ullah, I., Hussain, M., Aboalsamh, H., et al.: An automated system for epilepsy detection using EEG brain signals based on deep learning approach. Expert Syst. Appl. **107**, 61–71 (2018)
4. Wang, F., Zhong, S., Peng, J., Jiang, J., Liu, Y.: Data augmentation for EEG-based emotion recognition with deep convolutional neural networks. In: Schoeffmann, K., et al. (eds.) MMM 2018, Part II. LNCS, vol. 10705, pp. 82–93. Springer, Cham (2018). https://doi.org/10.1007/978-3-319-73600-6_8
5. Zhang, Q., Liu, Y.: Improving brain computer interface performance by data augmentation with conditional deep convolutional generative adversarial networks. arXiv preprint: arXiv:1806.07108 (2018)
6. Zhang, X.R., Lei, M.Y., Li, Y.: An amplitudes-perturbation data augmentation method in convolutional neural networks for EEG decoding. In: 2018 5th International Conference on Information, Cybernetics, and Computational Social Systems (ICCSS), pp. 231–235. IEEE (2018)

Time-Series-Based Classification
of Financial Forecasting Discrepancies

Ben Peachey Higdon$^{(\boxtimes)}$ [ID], Karim El Mokhtari [ID], and Ayşe Başar [ID]

Data Science Laboratory, Ryerson University, Toronto, Canada
bpeachey@ryerson.ca

Abstract. We aim to classify financial discrepancies between actual and forecasted performance into categories of commentaries that an analyst would write when describing the variation. We propose analyzing time series in order to perform the classification. Two time series classification algorithms – 1-nearest neighbour with dynamic time warping (1-NN DTW) and time series forest – and long short-term memory (LSTM) networks are compared to common machine learning algorithms. We investigate including supporting datasets such as customer sales data and inventory. We apply data augmentation with noise as an alternative to random oversampling. We find that LSTM and 1-NN DTW provide the best results. Including sales data has no effect but inventory data improves the predictive power of all models examined. Data augmentation has a slight improvement for some models over random oversampling.

Keywords: Time series classification · Data augmentation · LSTM · Machine learning

1 Introduction

An important aspect of budgeting for large companies is having reliable forecasts of future performance. Finance managers aim to understand the variance between a financial forecast and actual performance. They generate commentaries to explain the reasons for such variance by collecting information from different aspects of the organisation such as sales, inventory and logistics.

In our previous work [4], we proposed generating these financial commentaries based on variance data from a consumer goods company using recurrent neural networks. The commentaries we used were inconsistently worded which made this a challenge when working with real world data. In this paper we simplify the problem and aim to predict the category of commentary rather than generating the text itself. Additionally, we now consider training on a one year long monthly time series of variance to account for past patterns. We test two vector-based algorithms and compare them to two time series classification algorithms and

Supported by SOSCIP and Mitacs.

M. Bramer and M. Petridis (Eds.): SGAI-AI 2019, LNAI 11927, pp. 474–479, 2019.
https://doi.org/10.1007/978-3-030-34885-4_39

a deep learning approach. We also investigate including auxiliary datasets to improve predictions. We apply data augmentation techniques to the time series and compare this approach against random oversampling.

2   Background

Time series classification algorithms can be grouped into families depending on how the classification is performed. One family of algorithms relies on distance measures to determine the similarity between time series instances. Commonly used is a nearest neighbour classifier with dynamic time warping (DTW) as the distance measure [1]. DTW is an elastic distance measure that allows for some warping on the time axis to find a better match between time series.

One nearest neighbour (1-NN) classification with DTW is found to be a strong baseline when compared to many time series classification algorithms [1].

Other time series classification algorithms first define features of the series such as the mean or standard deviation [10]. A classifier is then trained on the features and not the values of the time series. This approach can be extended to calculate features for specific intervals of the time series. One such algorithm known as time series forest (TSF) trains decision trees on features from randomly selected intervals and the majority vote from all trees is the final output [3]. The calculated features used in TSF are the mean, standard deviation and the slope of the chosen intervals. Interval feature methods such as TSF can provide insight into the location of the most important regions and features of a phase-dependant time series. Bagnall et al. [1] conducted experiments using several algorithms on a large time series repository and found TSF to be one of the stronger algorithms albeit its simplicity.

Recurrent neural networks (RNNs) are a family of deep learning models that excel at processing sequential data. Long short-term memory (LSTM) networks [6] are RNNs that have become popular as they can retain information across long sequences. Lipton et al. [9] used LSTMs to predict diagnoses from multivariate time series of medical observations such as blood pressure. Their LSTMs were able to outperform a strong baseline with hand-engineered features.

Inspired by data augmentation in image classification [8,11] we explore augmenting time series. In image classification tasks, data is augmented by transforming the images in such a way that the label is preserved e.g. rotation, translation. The advantage of augmentation is two-fold – the risk of overfitting is reduced and more training examples are generated [8].

3   Dataset Description

The main dataset that an analyst uses to write a commentary consists of the difference of the forecasted and actual shipments in dollars for every brand and every customer. For us, the targets to predict are the commentary classes. We split the commentaries into five classes (*promotion*, *point of sale*, *phasing*, *other* and *no comment*) based on a list of keywords common to each class. We remove some labels from very few multi-labeled instances according to a class prediction priority. For example, if an instance is labeled as both *promotion* and *phasing*, and *phasing* is higher on the priority list, the label is changed to be only *phasing*.

For every brand, month and customer, we construct a time series of the past 13 months of variance data $V = (v_1, v_2, \ldots, v_{13})$ where v_{13} is the variance corresponding to the month the commentary is generated. We remove any brands that fall within a threshold variance as well as all time series with zero data, as these will be automatically classified as *no comment*.

Additionally, we have been provided with point of sale (POS) and inventory datasets from one of the customers of the consumer goods company. The POS dataset lists total sales in dollars and the number of items sold for each brand. The inventory dataset lists the various inventory measures including the amount of units in stock. With these auxiliary datasets we construct 13 month time series of average unit price and average amount of in-store stock. Including these extra datasets requires us to only use data from the one customer which leaves us with a smaller subset of data. The full data and this one customer subset are imbalanced, with most of the time series having no comment.

4   Methods

We employ two widely used machine learning algorithms as a baseline: support vector machine (SVM) and a random forest (RF). Both SVM [7] and RF [1] have been shown to be well suited towards time series classification and both are thoroughly described in literature. We implement two algorithms, 1-NN DTW and TSF which are well suited to time series classification to compare against the baselines. We choose these two algorithms for their simplicity as a first step towards investigating time series classification algorithms for this application. Interval based time series such as TSF are especially interesting as we foresee some regions of the time series will carry more meaningful information.

We also employ two LSTM-based models, the first of which is a single LSTM followed by a softmax layer to output the classification. The second architecture, a multi-LSTM, depicted in Fig. 1, has an LSTM layer per dataset. The encoded results of each LSTM are concatenated and passed to a softmax layer. This is a more complex model and takes more time to train than a single LSTM but we believe it better represents the different patterns in each dataset.

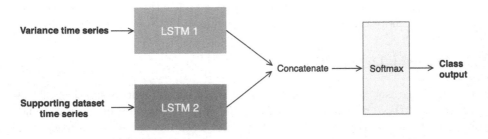

Fig. 1. The multi-LSTM architecture used when including supporting data

When including the supporting datasets, the vector-based classifiers train on the concatenated values of the time series involved. For the LSTM, TSF and 1-NN DTW models the time series can be treated as multidimensional. The multi-LSTM receives the time series separately.

To overcome the class imbalance problem we randomly oversample, copying instances from the smaller classes until the class distribution is balanced [5]. As an alternative to random oversampling we investigate adding Gaussian noise to augment the data [2,11]. Instead of duplicating the smaller classes we augment the time series to achieve a balanced class distribution. We predict that it is not the values of the time series that are most important but the trends of the data. We do not expect that adding a small amount of noise to this data will impact the true class but it will provide us with a more diverse training set than randomly oversampling.

We train the models on seeded resampled train-test sets and average the results across all runs. For every run the time series are z-normalized then oversampling or augmenting are applied to the training set. We use macro-averaged F1 score as the main performance metric. The macro-average of a metric is the average of the metric calculated for each class. If there are no positive predictions for a class the F1 score is treated as zero for that class. We choose this metric because it can reveal the performance on minority classes [5,7].

5   Experiments

In the first experiment we use a one customer subset of the variance data and compare results when including the POS or the inventory dataset. Model parameters are optimized for each combination of supporting data to account for the new information. Training data is randomly oversampled across all runs in this experiment. As seen in Fig. 2 the inclusion of POS data has no benefit whereas the inventory dataset does improve the mean F1 score in all models.

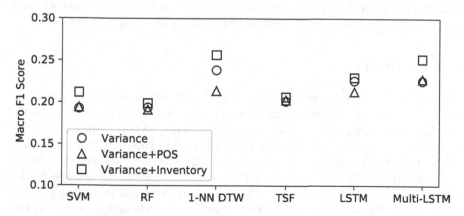

Fig. 2. Mean macro-averaged F1 scores on single customer subset when including supporting POS and inventory data

We use the full variance data in the second experiment to test whether we can improve over randomly oversampling by augmenting the time series with added Gaussian noise with mean of 0 and standard deviation of 0.01. Model parameters are kept constant across all tests. The results are shown in Fig. 3. Augmentation slightly improves over random oversampling with the RF and the LSTM models. The time series classification algorithms are not affected by augmenting likely because they are already capturing the trend of the data.

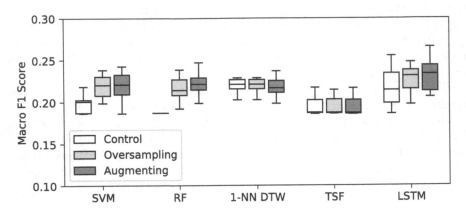

Fig. 3. Macro-averaged F1 scores on full variance data when oversampling and augmenting compared to the control

In both experiments 1-NN DTW and the LSTM outperform the baseline algorithms. Although we expect TSF to do well it does not surpass the baseline. This may have to do with how the random intervals are chosen. Since all intervals are equally likely, the points in the centre of a time series are more likely to be included. However, the edges of our time series have essential information, i.e. current month and previous year. We expect that selecting intervals with the goal of a uniform point distribution would perform better on our data.

6   Conclusion

In this paper we investigate techniques for classifying financial time series into categories of commentaries used in forecasting reports. We examine the effect of including supporting sales and inventory time series. When adding a supporting dataset we see that an LSTM per dataset architecture outperforms a single LSTM. Our results show a positive effect in all models when including inventory data. Although these supporting datasets are difficult to acquire for the consumer goods company we show that inventory data can be valuable to the classification. Finally, we compare data augmentation via added noise and random oversampling as methods to reduce overfitting and show that augmenting has a minor improvement over random oversampling.

Across both the full data and the one customer subset, the 1-NN DTW and LSTM models are seen to be the strongest. Because these two successful models are specialized at capturing patterns from sequences we draw the conclusion that there are temporal features in the data that aid in the classification of the forecasting discrepancies. This validates our approach of analyzing time series for this application.

In future work we will continue to investigate the effect of including supporting datasets. With POS and inventory data from more customers we will have a larger subset of the data to work with and thus more meaningful results. Since 1-NN DTW has proven to be effective we will evaluate further time series classification algorithms.

Acknowledgments. This work is supported by grants from Mitacs and Smart Computing for Innovation (SOSCIP) consortium.

References

1. Bagnall, A., Lines, J., Bostrom, A., Large, J., Keogh, E.: The great time series classification bake off: a review and experimental evaluation of recent algorithmic advances. Data Min. Knowl. Discov. **31**(3), 606–660 (2017)
2. Cortes-Ciriano, I., Bender, A.: Improved chemical structure-activity modeling through data augmentation. J. Chem. Inf. Model. **55**(12), 2682–2692 (2015)
3. Deng, H., Runger, G., Tuv, E., Vladimir, M.: A time series forest for classification and feature extraction. Inf. Sci. **239**, 142–153 (2013)
4. El Mokhtari, K., Maidens, J., Bener, A.: Predicting commentaries on a financial report with recurrent neural networks. In: Meurs, M.-J., Rudzicz, F. (eds.) Canadian AI 2019. LNCS (LNAI), vol. 11489, pp. 531–542. Springer, Cham (2019). https://doi.org/10.1007/978-3-030-18305-9_56
5. He, H., Garcia, E.A.: Learning from imbalanced data. IEEE Trans. Knowl. Data Eng. **21**(9), 1263–1284 (2009)
6. Hochreiter, S., Schmidhuber, J.: Long short-term memory. Neural Comput. **9**(8), 1735–1780 (1997)
7. Köknar-Tezel, S., Latecki, L.J.: Improving SVM classification on imbalanced time series data sets with ghost points. Knowl. Inf. Syst. **28**(1), 1–23 (2011)
8. Krizhevsky, A., Sutskever, I., Hinton, G.E.: ImageNet classification with deep convolutional neural networks. In: Advances in Neural Information Processing Systems, pp. 1097–1105 (2012)
9. Lipton, Z.C., Kale, D.C., Elkan, C., Wetzel, R.: Learning to diagnose with LSTM recurrent neural networks. arXiv preprint: arXiv:1511.03677 (2015)
10. Nanopoulos, A., Alcock, R., Manolopoulos, Y.: Feature-based classification of time-series data. Int. J. Comput. Res. **10**(3), 49–61 (2001)
11. Zur, R.M., Jiang, Y., Pesce, L.L., Drukker, K.: Noise injection for training artificial neural networks: a comparison with weight decay and early stopping. Med. Phys. **36**(10), 4810–4818 (2009)

Predicting Soil pH by Using Nearest Fields

Quoc Hung Ngo[✉], Nhien-An Le-Khac, and Tahar Kechadi

University College Dublin, Dublin 4, Belfield, Ireland
hung.ngo@ucdconnect.ie, {an.lekhac,tahar.kechadi}@ucd.ie

Abstract. In precision agriculture (PA), soil sampling and testing operation is prior to planting any new crop. It is an expensive operation since there are many soil characteristics to take into account. This paper gives an overview of soil characteristics and their relationships with crop yield and soil profiling. We propose an approach for predicting soil pH based on nearest neighbour fields. It implements spatial radius queries and various regression techniques in data mining. We use soil dataset containing about $4,000$ fields profiles to evaluate them and analyse their robustness. A comparative study indicates that LR, SVR, and GBRT techniques achieved high accuracy, with the R_2 values of about 0.718 and MAE values of 0.29. The experimental results showed that the proposed approach is very promising and can contribute significantly to PA.

Keywords: Soil prediction · Regression techniques · Precision agriculture · Data mining

1 Introduction

Precision agriculture can be described as an autonomous process that collects data and presents it to analysis systems to mine it. And the application of data mining to agricultural data becomes highly important, as it is capable of mining huge collections of data to look for new knowledge and, thus, improve the current practices. In this context, soil profile is one of preconditions for making good agronomic decisions. This practical information can be obtained by soil sampling, however, it is costly and very time consuming. In addition, it is often not necessary to conduct soil tests for all fields when the field conditions can be similar to the neighbourhood fields.

In general, the use of data mining techniques allows us to study a large number of soil profiles [11] and monitor soil characteristics and other factors that affect crop yield [7,12]. These data mining techniques have been successfully used to classify soil data [6], to predict soil map [2] and soil salinity [15]. However, to the best of our knowledge, there is no study on predicting soil characteristics for new fields with only their locations and some other features. Prediction of soil features based on nearest fields not only supports to fill omitting values for soil profiling but also reduces cost for soil sampling.

© Springer Nature Switzerland AG 2019
M. Bramer and M. Petridis (Eds.): SGAI-AI 2019, LNAI 11927, pp. 480–486, 2019.
https://doi.org/10.1007/978-3-030-34885-4_40

In this paper, we propose a solution to generate features for new fields without sampling. This is of great help, mainly when some data values were missing during their collection. We also propose a data mining approach to predict soil pH values based on neighbourhood field values. Finally, we test and evaluate our approach experimentally on real data collected from about 4, 000 soil profiles. The next section gives an overview of soil properties and reviews several soil studies that are related to precision agriculture.

2   Related Work

The most important soil characteristics can be divided into three categories: composition, physical and chemical characteristics [9]. In addition, there are several features, which relate to soil fertiliser and biological properties, such as CEC (Cation exchange capacity), SOC (soil organic carbon), and EC (Soil electrical conductivity). In fact, soil profiles mainly include physical and chemical characteristics (such as pH, N, P, K, etc), SOC, or SEC [4,11,12]. These soil characteristics were already represented using the AgriOnto ontology [8]. Many studies can be found in the literature on building soil profiles or datasets, monitoring soil characteristics that affect crop yield. Many of those studies use data mining techniques on soil characteristics to predict crop yield and other measures or objectives.

Wei Shangguan et al. [11] built a China soil dataset of 8, 979 soil profiles for land surface modelling. The data set includes 28 attributes for 8 vertical layers (from 0 to 2.296 m) which were collected from 2, 444 counties, 312 national farms and 44 forest farms. In an other soil study, Singh et al. [12] monitored pH, EC, CEC, and chemical characteristics of soil samples during and after crop harvesting to evaluate the effect of waste water on soil properties, crop yield and the environment.

In Han et al. [6], soil colour characteristics are used to classify 10 soil types. They used soils layers in a depth of $40-80$ cm below the surface. Their classifier is based on RGB signals and principal component analysis (PCA) to classify the data. The experimental findings have been obtained and evaluated on a data set of 50 soil samples per soil type (500 samples in total).

For the prediction of soil characteristics, authors in [4] compared 3 prediction methods for mapping CEC. Their study was carried out on a 74ha field in Australia for a duration of 2 years (1996 sorghum and 1997 wheat). [15] predicted soil salinity in three geographically distinct areas in China. They compared five regression algorithms based on 21 data sets with 189 soil samples to predict soil salinity. In their experiments, random forest (RF) and stochastic gradient treeboost (SGT) achieved the highest accuracy with R^2 score of 0.63. However, the scores of RF and SGT predictions are not stable by time and locations. The most wide range of soil chemical and physical characteristics prediction was conducted by Aitkenhead et al. [1]. They used artificial neural networks (ANN) and the soil color (RGB values) to predict 44 soil parameters including chemical, physical characteristics and soil texture. They also demonstrated that several soil parameters can be predicted accurately (with $R^2 > 0.5$).

In summary, several studies on the use of data mining techniques to predict other soil characteristics of each soil profile or predict other factors related to soil characteristics have been presented in the literature. To the best of our knowledge, there is not any study on predicting new soil profiles without main soil characteristics. Moreover, previous studies on soil profile prediction based on soil characteristics constitute a solid foundation for us to carry on this work.

3   Predicting Soil pH

3.1   Soil Dataset

The soil dataset includes soil sampling of 3, 809 fields, which are extracted from a large raw agriculture dataset of the CONSUS project. The soil datasets were collected from a widely distributed agriculture area of the UK. These fields grow many different plants, but the collected datasets were mainly focus on crops, fruits, vegetables, and grass. Each record in the dataset corresponds to one field, which includes field information, location information (longitude, latitude), chemical features (pH, P, K, Mg), and soil texture (sand, clay, and silt percentage). According to [10], soil pH is the most important attribute. The values of this attitude are between 0 and 14, but, they are mainly from 5 to 8.5 for cultivated fields in our dataset.

3.2   Features Based on Nearest Fields

The number of fields, which have nearest fields within the radius of 250 m, is the highest and most fields have neighbours within the radius of 2, 000 m (3,760 of 3,809 fields, as shown in Table 1). But, there are several fields that only have nearest fields in the radius of 10, 000 m (10 km). There are about 50 fields without neighbours within the radius of 2, 000 m.

Table 1. Validate soil feature by nearest fields

Radius (m)	Fields have neighbours	Number of neighbours	Distance (m)	Average of max-min(pH)
100	25	1.12	78.2	0.03
200	756	1.28	147.42	0.09
300	2, 102	1.67	185.22	0.19
400	2, 945	2.27	210.35	0.31
500	3, 295	3.01	232.57	0.44
750	3, 594	5.07	296.29	0.67
1,000	3, 672	7.11	367.19	0.83
1,500	3, 733	10.65	505.93	1.04
2,000	3, 760	13.66	635.17	1.16

Our approach is based on field's location. For each field in the dataset, we can get the nearest fields that are within a radius of a given field (based on spatial queries). The radius (in meters) is the maximum allowed distance between the given field and the returned list of nearby fields. In our experience, the radius is in the range between $200 - 2,000$ m.

To predict the pH attribute of data object y (or field y), we estimate the average, maximum, and minimum pH values based on the pH values of the returned list of nearby fields of y and the distance $Dist$ between the centre of the list and the location of y.

$$pH_{avg}(y, r_i) = \frac{\sum_{j=1}^{k} pH(x_j)}{k}; Dist(y, r_i) = distance(y, x_{centre});$$

$$pH_{min}(y, r_i) = min(pH(x_j)); pH_{max}(y, r_i) = max(pH(x_j));$$

where k is the number of neighbours in the radius of r_i (e.g. 200 m, 300 m, 400 m, and 500 m), x_j is the neighbour field in this region (j={1..k}), and x_{centre} is the centre of k neighbours for each radius r_i(m).

3.3 Data Mining Techniques for Prediction

There are many data mining techniques used for soil classification and prediction. In our study, we propose to use common data regression techniques to predict soil pH. These techniques include Linear regression (LR), Support Vector regression (SVR) [3], Decision Tree Regression (DTR) [14], Least Absolute Shrinkage and Selection Operator (LASSO) [13], Random Forests (RF) [5], and Gradient Boosting Regression Tree (GBRT) [5]. In our experiments, we use Scikit-learn toolkit (https://scikit-learn.org/) to deploy and evaluate these techniques.

4 Experimental Results

In our experiments, the comparative evaluation of the prediction models is based on the coefficient of determination (R^2) and the mean absolute error (MAE). The best possible coefficient score R^2 is 1.0 and the worst is 0.0. A constant model that always predicts the expected value of y, disregarding the input features, would get a R^2 score of 0.0.

In the first experiment, we apply six regression techniques (LR, SVR, LASSO, DTR, RF, and GBRT) on a part or the whole dataset depending on the evaluated features. For example, when evaluating a group of features related to the radius of 200 m, only 756 fields have neighbour fields, therefore the size of data for evaluating $CropName+Min/Max/Avg200$ features is (756, 4) (Table 2). The obtained results for Soil pH prediction were very low with owned field features (1st row of Table 2). The results improved significantly when adding average pH features. We achieved high results with $CropName+Min/Max/Avg400$ features.

In another experiment, we evaluated the contribution of features to prediction. Only three regression techniques have returned high scores; these are LR,

Table 2. Result of Soil pH regression based on radius-based features *llcn**: Long/Lat/CropName; *r200***: CropName+Min/Max/Avg200

Attr.	LR		SVR		LASSO		DTR		RF		GBRT	
	R^2	MAE	R^2	MAE	R^2	MAE	R^2	MAE	R^2	MAE	R^2	MAE
llcn*	0.084	0.56	0.163	0.52	−0.004	0.61	0.46	0.36	0.162	0.52	0.536	0.35
r200**	0.681	0.33	0.688	0.33	−0.001	0.62	0.47	0.41	0.666	0.35	0.66	0.33
r300	0.695	0.29	0.698	0.29	−0.004	0.6	0.427	0.39	0.66	0.31	0.683	0.29
r400	**0.718**	**0.29**	**0.713**	**0.28**	−0.002	0.63	0.503	0.39	0.68	0.31	**0.703**	**0.29**
r500	0.671	0.31	0.666	0.3	−0.001	0.61	0.411	0.4	0.654	0.32	0.651	0.31
r750	0.633	0.28	0.632	0.27	−0.0	0.62	0.386	0.4	0.645	0.3	0.628	0.28
r1000	0.66	0.31	0.663	0.31	−0.001	0.61	0.452	0.4	0.617	0.32	0.669	0.3
r1500	0.653	0.3	0.647	0.29	−0.001	0.62	0.454	0.36	0.62	0.32	0.656	0.29
r2000	0.623	0.33	0.608	0.32	−0.002	0.62	0.452	0.38	0.596	0.35	0.658	0.32

SVR and GBRT. We have also evaluated the *CropType* feature, which represents a mapping of the crop name to a crop type list (including Crops, Vegetables, Fruits, and Grass) by using lists of concepts and instances from the AgriOnto ontology [8]. Although the *CropName* feature contains over 40 different crop names, it is mapped to the *CropType* feature with four crop types. The results are approximately the same for both experiments (3rd, 4th row of Table 3).

Table 3. R^2 score of Soil pH regression based on individual features

Feature	Size	LR	SVR	GBRT
Long/Lat/CropName	(2945, 3)	0.086	0.17	0.548
Long/Lat/CropName+Avg400	(2,945, 4)	0.717	0.715	0.716
Nb/Dist/Avg400+CropName	(2,945, 4)	0.717	0.714	0.7
Nb/Dist/Avg400+CropType	(2,945, 4)	0.718	0.714	0.696
Nb/Dist/Max/Min/Avg400	(2,945, 5)	0.718	0.709	0.697
+ CropName	(2,945, 6)	0.718	0.708	0.696
+ CropName, CropType	(2,945, 7)	0.718	0.709	0.696

In the next experiments, we extended the number of features to include more radius values. As shown in Table 4, it calculates the average pH value of neighbours in the radius ranging from 200 m to 2,000 m. The same algorithms achieved their highest scores at the radius values 400 m and 500 m.

Table 4. R^2 score of soil pH regression based on combined features

Feature	Size	LR	SVR	GBRT
Long/Lat/CropName	(756, 3)	0.122	0.232	0.545
+ Nb/Dist/Avg200	(756, 6)	0.686	0.667	0.656
+ Nb/Dist/Avg300	(756, 9)	0.699	0.676	0.674
+ Nb/Dist/Avg400	(756, 12)	0.715	0.67	0.684
+ Nb/Dist/Avg500	(756, 15)	0.711	0.638	0.692
+ Nb/Dist/Avg750	(756, 18)	0.709	0.597	0.702
+ Nb/Dist/Avg1000	(756, 21)	0.707	0.58	0.696
+ Nb/Dist/Avg1500	(756, 24)	0.704	0.604	0.703
+ Nb/Dist/Avg2000	(756, 27)	0.702	0.493	0.697

5 Conclusion and Future Work

We presented a short study on soil properties and how to construct soil profiles which can be sued in crop yield management. We proposed an approach to predict soil pH based on the average pH values of the nearest neighbour fields. This can be applied to predict other characteristics of the soil profile if these characteristics were missing. With large soil dataset, our approach based only on neighbour fields has a great potential not only for pH prediction but also to predict other soil features. As a result, we plan to extend our model and perform more experiences to predict other soil characteristics. Moreover, the weather data or crop yield are also highly valuable to add into prediction models.

Acknowledgment. This work is part of CONSUS and is supported by the the SFI Strategic Partnerships Programme (16/SPP/3296) and is co-funded by Origin Enterprises Plc.

References

1. Aitkenhead, M.J., et al.: Prediction of soil characteristics and colour using data from the national soils inventory of Scotland. Geoderma **200**, 99–107 (2013)
2. da Chagas, C.S., et al.: Data mining methods applied to map soil units on tropical hillslopes in Rio de Janeiro, Brazil. Geoderma Reg. **9**, 47–55 (2017)
3. Basak, D., Pal, S., Patranabis, D.C.: Support vector regression. Neural Inf. Process.-Lett. Rev. **11**(10), 203–224 (2007)
4. Bishop, T.F.A., McBratney, A.B.: A comparison of prediction methods for the creation of field-extent soil property maps. Geoderma **103**(1–2), 149–160 (2001)
5. Breiman, L.: Random forests. Machine Learn. **45**(1), 5–32 (2001)
6. Han, P., Dong, D., et al.: A smartphone-based soil color sensor: for soil type classification. Comput. Electron. Agric. **123**, 232–241 (2016)
7. He, J., Li, H., et al.: Soil properties and crop yields after 11 years of no tillage farming in wheat-maize cropping system in north china plain. Soil Tillage Res. **113**(1), 48–54 (2011)

8. Ngo, Q.H., Le-Khac, N.-A., Kechadi, T.: Ontology based approach for precision agriculture. In: Kaenampornpan, M., Malaka, R., Nguyen, D.D., Schwind, N. (eds.) MIWAI 2018. LNCS (LNAI), vol. 11248, pp. 175–186. Springer, Cham (2018). https://doi.org/10.1007/978-3-030-03014-8_15
9. Osman, K.T.: Soils: Principles, Properties and Management. Springer Science & Business Media, Dordrecht (2012). https://doi.org/10.1007/978-94-007-5663-2
10. Pietri, J.A., Brookes, P.: Relationships between soil pH and microbial properties in a UK arable soil. Soil Biol. Biochem. **40**(7), 1856–1861 (2008)
11. Shangguan, W., et al.: A China data set of soil properties for land surface modeling. J. Adv. Model. Earth Syst. **5**(2), 212–224 (2013)
12. Singh, P., et al.: Effects of sewage wastewater irrigation on soil properties, crop yield and environment. Agric. Water Manage. **103**, 100–104 (2012)
13. Tibshirani, R.: Regression shrinkage and selection via the LASSO. J. Royal Stat. Soc.: Ser. B (Methodological) **58**(1), 267–288 (1996)
14. Waheed, T., et al.: Measuring performance in precision agriculture: cart a decision tree approach. Agric. Water Manage. **84**(1–2), 173–185 (2006)
15. Wang, F., et al.: Comparison of machine learning algorithms for soil salinity predictions in three dry land oases located in Xinjiang Uyghur Autonomous Region (XJUAR) of China. Eur. J. Remote Sens. **52**(1), 256–276 (2019)

Information Retrieval for Evidence-Based Policy Making Applied to Lifelong Learning

Jérémie Clos[✉], Rong Qu, and Jason Atkin

Computational Optimisation and Learning Lab,
University of Nottingham, Nottingham, UK
{jeremie.clos,rong.qu,jason.atkin}@nottingham.ac.uk

Abstract. Policy making involves an extensive research phase during which existing policies which are similar to the one under development need to be retrieved and analysed. This phase is time-consuming for the following reasons: (i) there is no unified format for policy documents; (ii) there is no unified repository of policies; and (iii) there is no retrieval system designed for querying any repositories which may exist. This creates an information overload problem for policy makers who need to be aware of other policy documents in order to inform their own. The goal of this work is to introduce a novel application area for studying information retrieval models: the information seeking phase of policy design, applied to life-long learning policy-making. In this paper, we address this problem by developing a common representation for policy documents, informed by domain experts, in order to facilitate their indexing and retrieval by users. This position paper highlights the research questions that we aim to answer in our future work and the dataset that we intend to use to do so. Our main contribution is the creation of a unified dataset of policy interventions which can be used for highly specialised information retrieval tasks, and will be released in order to provide the field with the first unified repository of policy interventions in adult education.

Keywords: Domain-specific search · Information retrieval · Case-based reasoning

1 Introduction

Evidence-based policy making requires the design of policies based on not only ethical and practical goals, but also on evidence in the form of past attempts and their measured results in order to achieve two objectives: to design policies that are the most likely to have the desired effect, and to anticipate side effects that were observed on previous attempts and that might not have been considered.

However, policy making using the context of bounded agency shifts the focus from directly implementing the effects that we want to observe, to instead identifying the barriers and limitations that prevent the desired effects from happening, and implementing changes that diminish the power of such barriers or

M. Bramer and M. Petridis (Eds.): SGAI-AI 2019, LNAI 11927, pp. 487–493, 2019.
https://doi.org/10.1007/978-3-030-34885-4_41

encourage desired behaviour. This complex interplay of social factors makes it difficult to compare policies, since multiple policies with the same final intent (e.g., improving computer literacy in a specific target age range) might use different strategies to arrive at the same desired final result. This creates a particular difficulty for a user attempting to search for policies similar to the one they are trying to design: similarity is not defined with respect to content alone, but with respect to a set of conceptual dimensions which characterise the field of policy making.

In this work, we propose an approach to solving this problem using a high-level representation and a similarity function designed by domain experts for the explicit purpose of storing and retrieving policy documents. We use this approach to point to future research directions, and we discuss the settings of our upcoming evaluation.

2   The Policy Data Model

Our representation scheme was designed in two steps: (1) elicitation of low-level attributes by domain experts in lifelong learning policies, and (2) design of a lower dimensional feature space representing the low-level dimensions while reducing its sparsity. Our objective is to perform the matching phase on the four high-level attributes, while keeping the low-level features for the purpose of presenting information to the user. In this section we first mention the low level features and their elicitation, before moving on to the high level features and how they group low-level features into natural high-level concepts.

2.1   Descriptive Feature Model

A team of domain experts defined 78 attributes to describe the context of a policy. Those attributes represent multiple aspects of a policy, the most important of which are its geographical constraints (e.g. geographical code of the location, rurality/urbanity of the intervention), the socio-economic status of its participants (e.g. social status, social class, employment status), and salient features of the intervention itself (e.g. size and duration of the intervention, funding available). Focusing on those aspects allows the policy searcher to contrast multiple results and manually weigh which attributes might be more relevant to their own policy, which would not be possible if comparing large blobs of text from the source documents.

2.2   Policy Retrieval Model

The numerous descriptive features are then grouped into a higher-level policy model for the purpose of retrieval. A grand total of four features were judged to be sufficient to describe policies in a reasonable and retrievable way: target groups, aims of the intervention, activities performed during the intervention, and location of the intervention. A policy can possess more than one of each attribute (e.g. multiple target groups, or multiple activities).

Target Groups. A target group represents a specific characteristic of the demographics targeted by a potential policy. It can take a specific set of values such as Gender, Ethnicity, Disability status, Age range, or more.

Aims. The aim represents the explicit goal of the intervention described in the document. Such goal is related to a specific barrier between the target groups and the labour market that can be reduced through the activities of the intervention. A policy searcher who is proposing a new policy aiming to provide experience might want to find other approaches in culturally similar locations that aimed to reduce the same barrier in order to contrast with their own proposal.

Activities. The activity focuses on how the aim is achieved, i.e. the activities that were performed during the intervention.

Location. Location represents the geographical boundaries of the intervention described in the document. While the low-level feature model described in the previous section possesses a regional geographical code, the policy model uses a country-based geographical code. The reason for this is that the legal context does not change enough from region to region to justify the differentiation.

3 Query Models for Policy Search

Establishing the form of a query for policy searchers first comes from defining the typical profile of a searcher. We identify two phases in the process of evidence-based policy making, which parallel activities in Ellis' model of information seeking [3,4] and phases of Kuhlthau's information search process model [6].

1. **Exploration** corresponds to the exploration phase in Kuhlthau's information search process, and to the browsing activity in Ellis' model of information seeking. The searcher has a vague idea of their aim, and they seek to explore the policies that have any degree of similarity with that aim, in order to refine their explicit information need;
2. **Exploitation (comparing and contrasting)** is closer to the information collection step of Kuhlthau's information search process: the searcher has refined their information need, and formulates a more precise query. They are essentially filtering policies based on specific contextual constraints (geographical situation, socio-economic status), in order to compare and contrast their major differences. They are interested in high precision results more than recall rate, since they have already formulated the core of their proposed policy. It maps closest to the Differentiating activity in Ellis' model of information seeking: the sources are identified, and the information seeker uses their knowledge to judge their relative relevance.

These information seeking activities lead us to define three approaches for querying the document base: (1) the **free-text query**, suited for the exploratory stage, allows the searcher to match their query to any attribute with no restriction; (2) the **free-text structured query**, i.e. free-text search over attributes, where the query is divided in four different fields and the relevance function is composed of a linear combination of similarities over each field, weighted by a user-defined preference weight in order to let the searcher define the priority of each field; and (3) the **constrained structured query** is a more restricted version of the structured query, where the possible values are restricted to the existing ones in the database and a predefined similarity, designed by domain experts, is used for the retrieval phase. Similarly to the free-text structures queries, the relevance function is computed as a linear combination of the similarities of each attribute, using user-defined weights.

In this section we go over those three activities and the querying models and relevance functions associated to them.

3.1   Free-Text Queries

Free-text querying aims to completely focus on exploratory searches. The relevance function is defined in (1), where f_i refers to attribute i, d_i refers to the field i of the current document, q refers to the query document, and sim refers to a cosine similarity with tf-idf weighting [7], a standard information retrieval baseline. Simply explained, the relevance is the maximum similarity between the entire query and each of the four fields of the documents.

$$rel_{ftq}(d, q) = \max(\text{sim}(d_1, q), \text{sim}(d_2, q), \text{sim}(d_3, q), \text{sim}(d_4, q)) \tag{1}$$

3.2   Free-Text Structured Queries

Free-text structured querying serves as an intermediate step between fully structured and constrained queries and completely unstructured free text queries. It possesses the advantage of free-text query in that it is a high recall approach, but with the extra restriction of forcing the user to decompose their query into multiple fields. It is defined in (2).

$$rel_{fsq}(d, q) = \sum_{i=1}^{|f|} \beta_i \times \text{sim}_{f_i}(d, q) \tag{2}$$

Simply put, the relevance is calculated by a linear combination of similarity between each field f_i of the query q and each field of the corresponding document d, weighted by a preference weight set up by the user β_i.

3.3   Constrained Structured Queries

Constrained structured queries trade the free text fields for a list of choices extracted from existing cases in the database. This lets us use manually designed similarity tables that encode expert knowledge. The relevance score is described in (3), where exp-sim corresponds to the expert-designed similarity. This similarity is passed to a max operator due to the fact that a case might have multiple entries for a given field, and as such the relevance score needs to take the maximum value observed among all those entries.

$$rel_{csq}(d, q) = \sum_{i=1}^{|f|} \beta_i \times \max(\text{exp-sim}_{f_i}(d, q)) \tag{3}$$

The relevance is calculated as a linear combination of those expert-designed similarities for each feature, weighted by a user-defined importance weight β.

4   Evaluation

In this section we discuss the research questions we seek to answer.

RQ1. *Does enforcing structure in the query help match more relevant documents for policy searchers?* This research question can be answered by comparing the relative performance of the free-text structured queries against the free-text queries, given identical query content. An expected result if the structure improves the quality of the search is that the free-text structured queries would outperform complete free-text queries.

RQ2. *Does an expert-designed matching function perform better than a traditional statistical matching function on standard information-seeking tasks for evidence-based policy making?* This research question can be answered by observing the relative performance of the free-text structured queries against the constrained structured queries, given identical queries. An expected result, if the expert-designed matching function is well-suited to the task, is that the constrained structured queries would outperform the free-text alternative which is based on statistical knowledge.

5   The ENLIVEN Dataset

Our evaluation will use a new corpus, the ENLIVEN dataset, composed of 224 cases assembled from previous works in the field of policy making for lifelong learning as part of the ENLIVEN Horizon 2020 European project[1]. They were analysed by a team of domain experts and represented in the proposed high dimensional feature space, before being reduced to the higher conceptual one.

---

[1] https://h2020enliven.org/.

6   Background and Related Works

Structured information retrieval (SIR) focuses on the retrieval of information from structured and semi-structured document bases, such as XML documents [8]. SIR queries can contain structural information, which provide a matching criterion in itself. Case-based reasoning (CBR) is an artificial intelligence methodology that focuses on solving problems by retrieving similar problems with an existing working solution, and adapting them to fit the new problem [2,5].

Structured Information Retrieval. Traditional question answering methods typically retrieve a large number of documents using a bag-of-words model before doing post processing, which creates a computational bottleneck. Structured question answering solves that bottleneck by pre-processing the documents with multiple annotators such as a semantic parser and named entity recogniser [1]. The querying system then not only matches up the query to the answer, but also filters for annotation structures that denote a relevant information need. Similarly in our case, a free-text query would need to be categorised to predict the type of information need that it refers to, and then be matched against the corresponding attribute(s) of the document base.

Case-Based Reasoning. In the context of case-based reasoning (CBR), textual case-based reasoning comes closest to our work. Textual CBR (TCBR) focuses on the application of the CBR methodology on textual case bases [9]. The problem matching is done by comparing text-derived features in order to retrieve a typically textual solution. TCBR differs from information retrieval in goal and context only, and much of the techniques developed for information retrieval systems are used in TCBR systems.

7   Conclusion and Research Directions

In this work we introduced the problem of information retrieval in the perspective of a novel application: the design and development of socio-economic policies. We discussed a policy data model designed by a committee of experts in order to effectively and efficiently retrieve such policies during the information seeking stage of policy design. Finally, we turned our attention to the research questions that we will answer in future works, the corpus that we collected in order to do so, and briefly discussed the background area of our research.

Acknowledgements. This work is funded by European Union H2020-YOUNG-SOCIETY-2015 (Grant agreement no. 693989). We would like to acknowledge and thank the people involved in the collection and categorisation of the ENLIVEN dataset.

References

1. Bilotti, M.W., Ogilvie, P., Callan, J., Nyberg, E.: Structured retrieval for question answering. In: Proceedings of the 30th Annual International ACM SIGIR Conference, pp. 351–358. ACM (2007). https://doi.org/10.1145/1277741.1277802
2. Craw, S.: Case-based reasoning. In: Sammut, C., Webb, G.I. (eds.) Encyclopedia of Machine Learning and Data Mining, pp. 180–188. Springer, Boston (2017). https://doi.org/10.1007/978-1-4899-7687-1_34
3. Ellis, D., Cox, D., Hall, K.: A comparison of the information seeking patterns of researchers in the physical and social sciences. J. Doc. **49**(4), 356–369 (1993). https://doi.org/10.1108/eb026919
4. Ellis, D., Haugan, M.: Modelling the information seeking patterns of engineers and research scientists in an industrial environment. J. Doc. **53**(4), 384–403 (1997). https://doi.org/10.1108/eum0000000007204
5. Kolodner, J.: Case-Based Reasoning. Morgan Kaufmann (2014). https://doi.org/10.1016/c2009-0-27670-7
6. Kuhlthau, C.C.: Seeking Meaning: A Process Approach to Library and Information Services. Libraries Unltd Incorporated, Westport (2004)
7. Salton, G., McGill, M.J.: Introduction to Modern Information Retrieval. McGraw-Hill, New York (1983)
8. Schütze, H., Manning, C.D., Raghavan, P.: Introduction to Information Retrieval, vol. 39. Cambridge University Press, Cambridge (2008)
9. Weber, R.O., Ashley, K.D., Brüninghaus, S.: Textual case-based reasoning. Knowl. Eng. Rev. **20**(3), 255–260 (2005). https://doi.org/10.1017/S0269888906000713

On Selection of Optimal Classifiers

Omesaad Rado$^{(\boxtimes)}$ and Daniel Neagu

Department of Computer Science, University of Bradford,
Bradford BD7 1DP, UK
{o.a.m.rado, d.neagu}@bradford.ac.uk

Abstract. The current advances of computational power and storage allow more models to be created and stored from significant data resources. This progress opens the opportunity to re-cycle and re-use such models in similar exercises. The evaluation of the machine learning algorithms and selection of an appropriate classifier from an existing collection of classifiers are still challenging tasks. In most cases, the decision of selecting the classifier is left to the user. When the selection is not performed accurately, the outcomes can have unexpected performance results. Classification algorithms aim to optimise some of the distinct objectives such as minimising misclassification error, maximising the accuracy, or maximising the model quality. The right choice for each of these objectives is critical to the quality of the classifier selected. This work aims to study the use of a multi-objective method that can be undertaken to find a set of suitable classifiers for a problem at hand. In this study, we applied seven classifiers on mental health data sets for classifier selection in terms of correctness and reliability. The experimental results suggest that this approach is useful in finding the best trade-off among the objectives of selecting a suitable classifier framework.

Keywords: Classification algorithms · Optimization · Pareto set

1 Introduction

The data mining task of classification has been studied for many years. Researchers in the fields of statistics, decision theory, and machine learning (ML) have reported a considerable amount of work on this topic [1, 2]. Significant improvements in classification are achieved, but research remains open for further exploration. One of these areas is the application of model optimisation in classification techniques. The aim of such optimisation problems is looking for maximum or minimum value using a single objective or multi-objective [3] strategy. Model selection is concerned with the development of machine learning models that can provide good results. These models are built and validated to classify existing data. Some models are more effective even on new data and satisfy various quality criteria [4]. A suitable classifier of a dataset in making a decision is highly desirable in various domains such as healthcare [5] and business. The knowledge of the selection model allows an earlier avoiding of those classifiers that may produce unexpected performance results in the last stage of the process of building ML models of high performance.

© Springer Nature Switzerland AG 2019
M. Bramer and M. Petridis (Eds.): SGAI-AI 2019, LNAI 11927, pp. 494–499, 2019.
https://doi.org/10.1007/978-3-030-34885-4_42

There is extensive literature associated with decision making, multi-objective optimisation and machine learning. In recent years many classification algorithms have become available. For example in [6] authors presented an approach called radial boundary intersection for training SVMs on two-class and multiclass data sets. For this multi-objective optimisation framework, Support Vector Machines (SVMs) optimize by maximisation of domain margin. Approaches of minimising the regularisation from the positive class and the negative class are considered as well [7, 8]. Ali et al. presented a study of using multi-criteria decision-making methodology (AMD) for evaluating and ranking classifiers. Thus, end users can choose the top-ranked classifier to build classification models [4]: Czajkowski and Kretowski presented an approach of obtaining a set of non-dominated model trees using the Global Model Tree (GMT) system. Different types of decision trees, including univariate, oblique or mixed; regression and model trees are involved in this study [9]. A review of the methods and application of multi-objective optimisation (MOO) can be found in [10]. Another study proposed an approach using multi-objective optimisation to the evolutionary design of artificial neural networks using the MOEA/DDRA algorithm [5]. Muaafa designed a framework of optimal resource allocation strategies to adequately achieve allocation objectives by using Pareto optimality [11].

The objective of this paper is to apply Pareto-optimality in the optimisation aspects of classification algorithms and investigate the Pareto points of their solution sets. Several issues can be considered simultaneously in this exploration, such as error rate, and the accuracy of the model. However, for clarity and visualisation purposes, the study uses these criteria to minimises the error rate and RSME. These indicated to the correctness and the reliability quality metrics of the classifiers. The definitions of quality metrics of classifiers are found in [4].

The paper is organised as follows: the next section provides some introduction to machine earning and Pareto optimality, then the third section introduces our research methodology, Sect. 4 includes experiments and results, and Sect. 5 presents some conclusions and future work.

2 Research Background

2.1 Machine Learning

Classification algorithms have been used successfully in many domains. Well-known machine learning algorithms are C4.5, k-means, SVMs [11], AdaBoost, k-nearest neighbours (K-NN) [12], classification and regression trees (CARTs), and naïve Bayes. Some classification algorithms are considered as probabilistic classification approach. Probabilistic classification approach aims to estimate the joint probability density function for each class [13, 14].

2.2   Pareto Optimality

Let's consider a vector $f = \{f_1, f_2, \ldots, f_m\}$ in m-dimensional solution space for the section of classifier problem. Dimensions can be evaluation metrics such as the accuracy, the error rate, the cost or the time. Pareto approach works based on the concept of dominance which differentiate the solutions into the dominated and non-dominated solutions [10, 12].

Let us consider m conflicting objectives which need to be minimised simultaneously. A vector $X \in R^m$ and a vector $Y \in R^m$. Which a solution $X = \{x_1, x_2, \ldots, x_m\}$ dominates ($\prec$) solution $Y = \{y_1, y_2, \ldots, y_m\}$ only if:

$$(X \prec Y) \Leftrightarrow \forall i,\, x_i \leq y_i \wedge \exists i\, (x_i < y_i)$$

where, x_i and y_i are objectives and $1 \leq i \leq m$. The Pareto set of S is a set $P \subset S$ of vectors with respect to $\prec$, where, S is a finite set of vectors in R^m. The concept of Pareto set (P) denotes a set of solutions that are non-dominated to each other but are superior to the rest of the solutions in the search space [13].

3   Research Methodology

Machine learning algorithms perform differently on same datasets [3]. To select the best algorithm from candidate algorithms, we need more than a single criterion. In real-world problems, there is no single ideal solution because the objectives can be conflicting [4]. Figure 1 shows seven classification algorithms: Decision trees (J48). Naive Bayes, Random Forests [14], Support Vector Machine (SVM), and Rules Decision Trees (PART) which are tested on mental health. The data is tested using 10-fold cross-validation. The evaluation is performed using accuracy, F-measure, RMSE, and Roc area, as illustrated in Fig. 1.

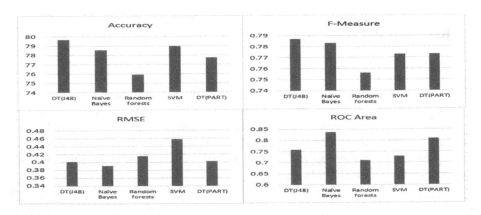

Fig. 1. Assessment of algorithms based on multiple evaluation criteria.

Figure 1 shows that decision trees (j48) provides the best performance in term of accuracy and F-Measure matrices. However, they perform poorly from the perspective of RMSE and ROC Area metrics. Similarly, the performance of the rest of the algorithms for all four criteria on the same data set. shows that no classifier can be chosen based on one single criterion. For example, in medical applications, some measurements may be more relevant than accuracy, especially for discovering accurate information [5] and avoiding false positive or negative for unbalanced data. Consequently, a single criterion of evaluation is not always superior to test a collection of classification algorithms on all problems. The tasks of this methodology of selection suitable classifiers based on Pareto optimality is defined in Algorithm 1 below. We obtained classifiers by applied seven classification algorithms on mental health data sets, namely Decision Trees (J48), Naïve Bayes, Random Forests, SVM, Decision Trees (PART), Bagging and LAD Tree and defining the objectives of the selection process. The goals are the minimisation of Incorrectly Classified and RMSE measures. Next, applying for the performance of the selected evaluation metrics on the considered algorithms on the datasets the principle of Pareto optimality approach is to find a set of Pareto optimal solutions (PS) may give insights into the trade-offs between the objectives [9, 15]. Comparison of the classifiers of PS by applying Paired t-test assists in selecting a suitable classifier [12]. Paired t-test compares two alternative classifiers to test a significant difference in their performance.

Algorithm 1 Selection of classifiers

Inputs: Dataset D
Classifiers $S = \{c_1, c_2, ..., c_m\}$
Output: A selected classifier
    Define $Objectives = \{objective_1, objective_2\}$
    Obtain Performance Results of S
    Identify Pareto set of S, where $P \subseteq S$
    Compare the classifiers in P by Paired t-test
    Return the best classifier c
End

---

4 Experiments and Results

This section provides the description of benchmark data used to experiment our ideas on model selection optimization and discussed the preliminary results.

4.1 The Dataset

The proposed approach validation is performed using real-life dataset from a survey of mental health and frequency of mental health disorders in the tech workplace (2014) [15]. It contains 993 instances with seven attributes. For reducing the dimensionality of the data, importance estimation of a variable category is performed by using the function VarImp in R [16, 17]. The data type of the data is categorical.

4.2   Results

In this section, we visualise the Pareto points for the classifiers on the dataset. Pareto set for the solutions can be visualised in two dimensions as two objectives can be minimised (Incorrectly Classified/error rate and RMSE), or maximised (Accuracy and AUC). Non-dominated classifiers can be illustrated in more than two objectives. However, the visualisation can be done by using a parallel plot as in [5].

We visualise the Pareto set when applied to the classifiers on mental health dataset. Figure 2 shows the results achieved for the seven classification algorithms on mental health dataset. The Pareto approach was made for the multi-objective optimisation problem, which minimised the error rate (incorrectly classified) and the RMSE. The non-dominated solutions that belong to the Pareto front are found as black points. In case of the results for mental health data set, the solution reduced from seven options to two options (Bagging and LAD Tree). However, the decision-maker can choose based on the purpose of the analysis goal in this stage to obtain more accurate results.

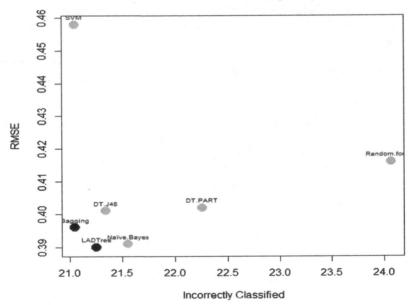

Fig. 2. Pareto points.

Paired t-test can be used to test the difference in the classification performance of two classifiers. The goal is to assess which classifier has a superior classification performance on mental health dataset. The null hypothesis is that the performance of Bagging classifier is the same as the LAD Trees classifier. Based on the obtained results of comparing these two classifiers on mental health dataset at a 5% level of statistical significance, Bagging performs better than LAD Trees.

5   Conclusion and Future Work

This work presents a selection of an appropriate classifier based on Pareto optimality approach. The procedure of determining suitable classifier(s) is validated on seven classification algorithms and real-life data on mental health. Results demonstrate that the proposed method can perform with excellent outcomes. In future, we plan to apply this approach on a big dataset and select different classifiers with selective multi-objective optimization algorithms.

References

1. Kantardzic, M., Data mining: concepts, models, methods, and algorithms (2011)
2. Witten, I.H., Frank, E., Hall, M.A.: Data mining. Data Min. **36**(5), 51–52 (2011)
3. Berrer, H., Paterson, I., Keller, J.: Evaluation of machine-learning algorithm ranking advisors. In: Proceedings {PKDD2000} Work, Data Mining, Decision Support. Meta-Learning {ILP} Forum Practice Problem Present. Prospection Solution, pp. 1–13 (2000)
4. Ali, R., Lee, S., Chung, T.C.: Accurate multi-criteria decision-making methodology for recommending machine learning algorithm. Expert Syst. Appl. **71**, 257–278 (2017)
5. Shenfield, A., Rostami, S.: A multi objective approach to evolving artificial neural networks for coronary heart disease classification. IEEE Conf. Comput. Intell. Bioinforma. Comput. Biol. CIBCB **2015**, 2015 (2015)
6. Datta, S., Das, S.: Multiobjective support vector machines: handling class imbalance with pareto optimality. IEEE Trans. Neural Networks Learn. Syst. **30**(5), 1602–1608 (2018)
7. Burger, S.: Introduction to machine learning with R : rigorous mathematical analysis (2018)
8. Pangilinan, J.M., Janssens, G.K.: Pareto-optimality of oblique decision trees from evolutionary algorithms, vol. 51, pp. 301–311 (2011)
9. Czajkowski, M., Kretowski, M.: A multi-objective evolutionary approach to pareto-optimal model trees. Soft. Comput. **23**(5), 1423–1437 (2019)
10. Gunantara, N.: A review of multi-objective optimization: methods and its applications. Cogent Eng. **5**(1), 1–16 (2018)
11. Muaafa, M.: Multi-Criteria Decision-Making Frameworks for Surveillance and Logistics Applications (2015). https://www.researchgate.net/profile/Mohammed_Muaafa/publication/305754592_Multi-Criteria_Decision-Making_Frameworks_for_Surveillance_and_Logistics_Applications/links/579f34b708ae5d5e1e17ce12/Multi-Criteria-Decision-Making-Frameworks-for-Surveillance-and-Logistics-Applications.pdf. Accessed 23 Oct 2019
12. Moffaert, K.V., Nowe, A.: Multi-objective reinforcement learning using sets of pareto dominating policies. J. Mach. Learn. Res. **15**(1), 3483–3512 (2014)
13. Knowles, J.: Multiobjective Optimization, pp. 193–262, May (2010)
14. Breiman, L.: Random Forests (2001)
15. Mental Health in Tech Survey|Kaggle. https://www.kaggle.com/osmi/mental-health-in-tech-survey. Last accessed 05 Jul 2019
16. Rogers, S., Girolami, M.: A first course in machine learning (2011)
17. Hewson, P.J.: Multivariate statistics with R, pp. 1–189 (2009)

Author Index

Printed in the United States
By Bookmasters